ARNHEM 1944

Other books by Martin Middlebrook

*The First Day on the Somme**
*The Nüremburg Raid**
Convoy
The Sinking of the Prince of Wales *and* Repulse*
(with Patrick Mahoney)
*The Kaiser's Battle**
The Battle of Hamburg
*The Peenemünde Raid**
The Schweinfurt–Regensburg Mission
The Bomber Command War Diaries (with Chris Everitt)
The Falklands War
The Berlin Raids
*The Argentine Fight for the Falklands**
*Your Country Needs You**
*The North Midland Territorials Go To War**
*The Middlebrook Guide to the Somme Battlefields**
(with Mary Middlebrook)
The Bruckshaw Diaries (ed.)
Everlasting Arms (ed.)

*denotes titles in print with Pen & Sword Books Ltd

ARNHEM 1944

The Airborne Battle, 17–26 September

MARTIN MIDDLEBROOK

Pen & Sword
MILITARY

First published by Viking, 1994
Reprinted in this format by
Pen & Sword Military
an imprint of
Pen & Sword Books Ltd
47 Church Street
Barnsley
South Yorkshire S70 2AS

Copyright © Martin Middlebrook, 1994, 2009

ISBN 978 1 84884 075 1

The right of Martin Middlebrook to be identified as
author of this work has been asserted by him in accordance
with the Copyright, Designs and Patents Act 1988

A CIP catalogue record for this book is
available from the British Library

Printed and bound in England
by CPI

Pen & Sword Books Ltd incorporates the imprints of
Pen & Sword Aviation, Pen & Sword Maritime, Pen & Sword Military,
Wharncliffe Local History, Pen & Sword Select,
Pen & Sword Military Classics and Leo Cooper,
Remember When, Seaforth Publishing and Frontline Publishing

For a complete list of Pen & Sword titles please contact
PEN & SWORD BOOKS LIMITED
47 Church Street, Barnsley, South Yorkshire, S70 2AS, England
E-mail: enquiries@pen–and–sword.co.uk
Website: www.pen–and–sword.co.uk

Contents

	List of Photographs	vii
	List of Maps	ix
	Introduction	1
1	The Path to Arnhem	5
2	'First Airborne' and Friends	20
3	The Arnhem Area	49
4	Preparations for Battle	59
5	The Air Armada	75
6	The Morning in Holland	90
7	The Landings	96
8	The Vital Hours	116

Battalion Krafft 117; 1st Parachute Brigade Plan 119; The Reconnaissance Squadron 123; The Divisional Commander 126; The 3rd Parachute Battalion 129; The 1st Parachute Battalion 137; The 2nd Parachute Battalion 142; The Divisional Area 162; The Other Landings 165

9	The Battle in the Town – Monday	167

The 3rd Parachute Battalion 170; The 1st Parachute Battalion 175; C Company and No. 4 Platoon, 2nd Parachute Battalion 184; Reinforcements 186

10	The Battle in the Town – Tuesday	190

The 1st and 3rd Parachute Battalions 195; The 2nd South Staffordshires 200; The 11th Parachute Battalion 206; In the Rear of the Fighting 209

11	Waiting for the Second Lift	217
12	The Second Lift	224
13	The Battle in the Woods	248

The Evening Moves 251; 156 Parachute Battalion – the Dreijenseweg Action 254; The 10th Parachute

Battalion – the Pumping-Station-Area Action 261;
The Third-Lift Glider Landing 269; *The 4th
Parachute Brigade Withdrawals* 272; *Wednesday –
into Oosterbeek* 282

14   The Battle at the Bridge   287
Monday 288; *Tuesday* 300; *Wednesday* 307;
Resistance Fails 317

15   The Formation of the Oosterbeek Perimeter   324
The Eastern Perimeter 324; *The Western
Perimeter* 329; *Wednesday – Lonsdale Force* 331

16   The Battle at Oosterbeek   341
The Thursday Attacks 341; *The Siege – Friday to
Monday* 351; *The Local People* 365; *The Divisional
Units* 372; *The Medical Services* 378

17   The Resupply Flights   386
Tuesday 387; *Wednesday* 391; *Thursday* 393;
The Final Flights 396

18   The Polish Brigade   402
19   The Sacrifice of the Dorsets   418
20   Evacuation   423
21   The Reckoning   436
The Cost 438; *Was It Worth It?* 441
22   The Years That Followed   445

Appendix 1   Order of Battle and Operational Details,
1st British Airborne Division and Attached Units   455
Appendix 2   Order of Battle, Polish Independent
Parachute Brigade Group   461
Appendix 3   Order of Battle, 38 and 46 Groups RAF
and RASC Air Despatch Units   462
Appendix 4   Order of Battle, US Air Units Carrying
British and Polish Parachute Troops on Operation
'Market'   464
Appendix 5   Arnhem Today   465

Acknowledgements   478
Bibliography   486
Index   487

Photographs

1   Waiting for take-off – men of the 1st Parachute Battalion.
2   Horsa glider taking off at Harwell.
3   Albemarle and Horsa taking off at Manston.
4   Flying to Arnhem.
5   Gliders on Landing Zone-Z.
6   C-47s dropping parachutists on Dropping Zone-X.
7   Parachutists landing.
8   Royal Artillery jeep unloading.
9   Men of 1st Battalion near Wolfheze.
10   Arnhem road bridge from the air.
11   SS troops prepare for battle in Arnhem.
12   South Staffords move to Arnhem.
13   Captured South Staffords in Arnhem.
14   Pre-war aerial photograph of Arnhem.
15   SS men in action in Arnhem.
16   Captured men from the Arnhem bridge fighting.
17   Airborne men at Oosterbeek.
18   Stirlings on resupply drop.
19   Mortar team at Oosterbeek.
20   A 75-millimetre gun team.
21   Airborne prisoners on march towards Germany.
22   'Killed in action'.
23   Battle wreckage in Oosterbeek.
24   Survivors who escaped the battle.
25   Maj.-Gens Sosabowski and Thomas.
26   Brig. Hicks, Maj.-Gen. Urquhart and Lt-Gen. Browning on investiture day.
27   Oosterbeek children place flowers on graves.
28   Oosterbeek cemetery today.
29   Memorial at Heelsum.

30 Johannahoeve Farm today.
31 The Arnhem road bridge today.
32 The Arnhem bridge battle area today.
33 St Elizabeth Hospital.
34 Arnhem Museum.
35 Oosterbeek Church.
36 The Hartenstein.
37 Airborne Memorial at Oosterbeek.
38 The Evacuation Memorial.

The author and publishers are grateful to the following for permission to reproduce photographs:

Imperial War Museum – 1, 2, 4–9, 12, 18–20, 24, 26, 27.
Bundesarchiv – 11, 13, 15, 21–3.
Charles Bates – 3.
Col Paddy de Burgh – 10.
KLM Luchtfotographie – 14.
Len Wright – 16.
Mrs Kremer – 17.
The Polish Institute and Sikorski Museum – 25.
Commonwealth War Graves Commission – 28.

Photographs 29–38 were taken by the author.

Maps

Maps by Reginald and Marjorie Piggott from preliminary drawings by Mary Middlebrook

1	The 'Market Garden' Plan	15
2	The Air Armada	84
3	The Landings – First Lift	98
4	1st Parachute Brigade Plan	122
5	1st Parachute Brigade – 2.0 a.m. Monday	151
6	1st Parachute Brigade – into Arnhem	176
7	West Arnhem – Tuesday	192
8	The Second Lift	235
9	4th Parachute Brigade Attacks – Tuesday Morning	253
10	4th Parachute Brigade Withdrawal	278
11	Arnhem Bridge	289
12	The Oosterbeek Perimeter	338
13	Arnhem Today	466–7

Introduction

Arnhem – it was the last major battle lost by the British Army, lost not by the men who fought there but by the overconfidence of generals, faulty planning and the failure of a relieving force given too great a task. If the operation of which Arnhem formed a part had been successful, the outcome of the war and the history of post-war Europe would have been greatly altered. Yet is it worth another book? I had fulfilled all my literary ambitions by researching and writing thirteen full-length books and was ready to retire from that laborious craft when Peter van Gorsel, head of Penguin's Dutch office, asked me to write a book on Arnhem for the fiftieth anniversary in 1994. It was the first time that my publishers had requested a book; all previous subjects had been my choice. I eventually agreed for several reasons. I had not previously researched and written about the British Army in the Second World War and had not previously done any work in Holland; so two fresh fields were opened up to me. I also felt that the fighting in and around Arnhem had still not been described in the detail that it merited.

The preparations have followed my standard procedure. First was the study of prime source documents, not always complete in this case because so few men returned from the battle to write up unit war diaries. But the Airborne Forces Museum at Aldershot has a bulging archive of Arnhem reports built up over the years, and I was most fortunate in being allowed to take home the entire collection for a careful study. Similarly, Dr Adrian Groeneweg and the Airborne Museum at Oosterbeek have also been most diligent in providing help. In addition, I have benefited from the research which several members of the post-war generation in Britain and Holland have carried out; these will be acknowledged in due course but I must mention Jan Hey, a Dutchman who analysed the registers of the Commonwealth War Graves Commission to produce a most useful publication, *Roll of Honour: The Battle of Arnhem, 17–26 September 1944*,[1] which lists the fatal casualties by units. The War Graves Commission registers are freely available for such research, but Jan Hey has added the invaluable information of the original 'field burial' locations before the remains were concentrated into post-war cemeteries.

I then set out to contact as many men as possible who had taken part in the battle – always the most interesting part of my work. A total of 501 men eventually provided their contributions, 156 by personal interview, the remainder by correspondence. Some of the men were regular contributors to Arnhem authors, and their names appear in other books, but hundreds of men have never told their stories, and much new material became available. One man in New Zealand spent eleven days preparing a detailed map and twenty-eight pages of laboriously handwritten notes. Another man who was an officer at Arnhem stressed, with his notes: 'Here rests no hero but the remains of a once young man who was scared out of his wits at the violence and ferocity of dirty little battles in dirty little corners of which the world knew nothing nor ever will.'

A visit to Holland proved most rewarding. I needed to study the ground where the troops landed and on which actions were fought; fortunately, most of the locations are little changed except for the road-bridge area in Arnhem. I was also able to interview some of the Dutch people who were involved in 1944; I will never forget the help and hospitality shown to me by these people. I would normally have travelled to Germany to talk to the German soldiers but did not do so for practical reasons. A new book became available while I was carrying out my research, written by Robert Kershaw, a serving officer of the Parachute Regiment who was attached to the German Army for three years during which he researched and wrote up Operation 'Market Garden' from the German side. There was no way that I could improve on this new work, and I will devote most of my book to fresh material from the British and Dutch sides.[2]

---

[1] Published by the Society of Friends of the Airborne Museum, Oosterbeek, 1986.
[2] Robert Kershaw's book is *It Never Snows in September*, Crowood Press, Marlborough, Wilts, 1990.

The subject of the book is clear – all aspects of the fighting in and around Arnhem but not of the wider Operation 'Market Garden'. The units involved will be the 1st British Airborne Division, the 1st Polish Independent Parachute Brigade Group, and the glider pilot, RAF and USAAF squadrons which carried the airborne men to Holland and, in the case of the RAF, then suffered so grievously in attempting to succour them by dropping supplies. The only ground troops who will be invited to this 'airborne party' will be the 4th Dorsets, who crossed the Rhine towards the end of the battle, and the British and Canadian Royal Engineers, who evacuated the airborne survivors across the river. The geographical area of the battle will be that part of Holland around the communities of Arnhem, Oosterbeek, Wolfheze, Renkum and Driel.

There are no major mysteries or dramatic disclosures about Arnhem – I am not a revisionist historian – and the strategic background will be set in as brief a manner as possible so that I can devote maximum space to a description of the units which went to Arnhem and of the actual fighting. My main intention will be to describe the action in as much detail as possible and with the correct 'balance'. Brave as it was, the oft told story of the holding of the area around the Arnhem road bridge by the 2nd Parachute Battalion and by other troops is too often highlighted to the detriment of other aspects of the battle.

I would like to conclude this Introduction on a personal note. Whatever the success or otherwise of this book, I have been completely absorbed by it and will be well satisfied to see it as my literary swan-song. In some ways it has reminded me of my first book, which was about the opening of the Battle of the Somme.[3] Both that day in July 1916 and those events in September 1944 were disasters that might have been foreseen but had an inevitability which could not be halted. There is a further comparison. The Somme survivors whom I interviewed in the late 1960s were the same age as the airborne men whom I have met more recently. Men at that age, with maturity of mind and with time to spare in their retirement, are ideal contributors. That First World War book

[3] *The First Day on the Somme*, Allen Lane, London, 1971; Penguin, London, 1984.

opened my writing career; I hope that I can close it with a fitting description of what happened in and around Arnhem.

Martin Middlebrook
Boston, England
1994

The Path to Arnhem

The war was exactly five years old in September 1944, almost a year longer than the whole of the First World War. But it seemed to many that the end was in sight, for the signs of German collapse in the first few days of the month had been breathtaking. It had started when Montgomery's plans in Normandy reached fulfilment early in August and the Third US Army under the brilliant Patton broke out and motored deep into the German rear, before swinging round and trapping much of the Seventh German Army in the Falaise Pocket. This was followed by a general Allied advance culminating in a dramatic dash across northern France into Belgium, this time with the British covering the ground fastest. Starting from the Seine, they advanced 200 miles to capture Brussels and Antwerp in just one week. That exhilarating drive ended on 5 September when the Germans were at last able to form a new defence line on the Meuse–Escaut canal to stop the Allies moving on to the liberation of Holland. The British were just able to establish two bridgeheads across the canal before the German defence hardened.

The German losses had been enormous, and it was believed that their defence lines everywhere were paper thin. There was only one problem for the Allies: the fighting units had outrun their supplies. The approaches to the port of Antwerp had not been cleared; recently captured Ostend and Dieppe had only limited cargo capacity, and the Germans had left garrisons at the other Channel ports. Only Cherbourg – 450 miles from the forward British positions and 400 from Patton's in eastern France – was capable of handling appreciable tonnages. A general advance was out of the question until Antwerp could be cleared, and that might allow the Germans to recover unless a decisive move was undertaken at once. Such a move would have to be limited to a narrow frontage because of the supplies position. There was one other factor. There remained in

England an 'airborne army' containing two American and one British airborne divisions, a Polish parachute brigade and an infantry division capable of being lifted by transport aircraft – all fresh and ready for immediate action. But an airborne operation would have to be within the range of the transport aircraft based in England, and there was only one part of occupied Europe that those aircraft could reach from their existing bases – Holland.

Attention can quickly focus upon the 1st British Airborne Division, which was to bear the brunt at Arnhem.[1] This formation contained Britain's earliest airborne units. Parts of the division had fought in North Africa, Sicily and Italy in 1942 and 1943, and the whole division had been standing by in England since early 1944, ready for further action. Its sister division – 6th Airborne – had dropped into Normandy to protect the flank of the British landings; 1st Airborne had been ready to follow in support but had not been required. Since then, no less than fifteen further operations had been planned but then cancelled, usually because ground forces reached the landing area first. Some of these operations would have been carried out in conjunction with American airborne divisions, others would have been solo British efforts.

It was out of the last of these cancelled operations – code-named 'Comet' – that the Battle of Arnhem was born; indeed, the operation which eventually took place was an extension of 'Comet'. The decision to mount 'Comet' was made on 2 September, just as the leading Allied forces were crossing into Belgium from France and before even Brussels was reached. The plan was for the 1st British Airborne Division, with the Polish brigade attached, to drop ahead of the advancing armies and capture the bridges over the rivers and canals flowing across Holland. The 4th Parachute Brigade was to seize the nearest bridge, over the Maas near Grave; the glider-borne 1st Airlanding Brigade, the Poles and divisional headquarters were to land in the centre, around Nijmegen, and capture the

---

[1] General references like this, to 'Arnhem' and to the Battle of Arnhem, include the whole area that would be covered by the battle as it developed; and they particularly include Oosterbeek, where fighting continued for several days after efforts in Arnhem itself had failed. This note is made in deference to the feelings of the men who fought only at Oosterbeek.

bridges over the Waal; and the 1st Parachute Brigade was to drop in the north near Arnhem and capture the crossings over the Rhine.

The initiative behind 'Comet' was that of Field Marshal Montgomery, commander of the British 21st Army Group. Eisenhower, the Supreme Allied Commander, favoured a general move forward by all of his armies. Montgomery, however, was pressing hard for a strong 'single thrust' while the Germans were in such disarray and urged that such a thrust should be northwards and under his command, continuing onwards through Holland over the river crossings captured in Operation 'Comet', outflanking the Siegfried Line, breaking out on to the open country of the North German Plain, which would favour the mobile Allied forces, and pressing on all the way to Berlin – beating the Russians to the German capital and hopefully ending the war before the winter. It was a plan of breathtaking scope. There were two drawbacks: the shortage of supplies already mentioned and the reluctance by Eisenhower to abandon his own plan and give priority to Montgomery at the expense of American commanders, some of whose forces would need to come under Montgomery's control.

Eisenhower gave 'Comet' the go-ahead, but did not yet sanction Montgomery's later plans. Only the British airborne division and the Polish brigade were to be employed; the two American divisions and the airportable division were not included. The reason for this was probably twofold: a smaller force required a shorter planning and preparation period, and there were only sufficient transport aircraft to carry such a force in one lift, factors which enabled the operation to proceed with speed and surprise while the Germans were off balance. It is believed that the start date was initially set for Saturday 9 September, one week later.

The RAF was asked to help by bombing German fighter airfields in Holland and Bomber Command promptly obliged with heavy raids by 675 bombers in daylight on 3 September; only one aircraft was lost. Some urgency might have been added to the planning on 8 September when the German V-2 rocket campaign against London opened from launch sites in Holland. But doubts about the viability of the operation were developing as the week passed. The Allied advance across Belgium ran out of steam; the supply crisis was evident; the German defence on the Dutch frontier was hardening.

Major-General R. E. Urquhart, commander of the 1st British Airborne Division, had received his orders on 6 September and had briefed his brigadiers. Brigadier 'Shan' Hackett, a comparative new-comer to the division, whose 4th Parachute Brigade was to capture the nearest bridge, at Grave, tells of his reaction to the plan:[2]

> The airborne movement was very naïve. It was very good on getting airborne troops to battle, but they were innocents when it came to fighting the Germans when we arrived. They used to make a beautiful airborne plan and then add the fighting-the-Germans bit afterwards. We brigade commanders were at one of the divisional commander's conferences for 'Comet' at Cottesmore airfield where this lovely plan was being presented. The Polish commander, Sosabowski, said in his lovely deep voice, 'But the Germans, General, the Germans!'
>
> Sosabowski and I, and one or two others, knew that, however thin on the ground the Germans were, they could react instantly and violently when you touched something sensitive. Thank goodness 'Comet' was cancelled; it would have been a disaster. But the same attitude persisted with the eventual Arnhem plan.

The period for preparation for 'Comet' ran its full course. All units were briefed; gliders were loaded; parachute-dropping and towing aircraft were ready. But Sosabowski's forceful objections had some result. Urquhart took him by plane to see Lieutenant-General F. M. ('Boy') Browning, who was carrying out the detailed planning of 'Comet' at his headquarters in Hertfordshire. Sosabowski argued that the force to be employed on 'Comet' was not strong enough and that at least two airborne divisions were required. This and possibly other protests, together with the changed ground situation, put an end to 'Comet'. On Friday 8 September the operation was postponed for twenty-four hours, but it was not until 2.0 a.m. on Sunday 10 September, four hours before take-off time, that a message was received at Urquhart's headquarters that 'Comet' was cancelled.

[2] Quotations by participants are from personal interviews or correspondence with the author unless some other source is acknowledged.

Operation 'Comet' was not dead, however; it was about to be transformed into a much larger venture with important changes taking place at both the strategic and the tactical level. The strategy was settled at a meeting later that day, Sunday 10 September, when Eisenhower flew from Normandy to meet Montgomery at Brussels; the ensuing discussion took place in Eisenhower's aircraft because his knee was in plaster following an accident. Montgomery once again urged total commitment to a northern thrust, with Berlin as the eventual objective. Eisenhower was still willing to go along with the airborne plan to seize the Dutch bridges; success in that operation would enable the 400-mile-long Siegfried Line to be outflanked, and operations could then be developed which would hopefully lead to the encirclement of the Ruhr. There were advantages also on the western flank of the proposed operation. A short onward advance from Arnhem to the IJsselmeer (formerly the Zuider Zee) would cut off all German forces in western Holland, and eventually capture the V-2 rocket launch sites, hasten the clearance of Antwerp and overrun Rotterdam to bring two major ports into use and help solve the chronic supply problem. So Montgomery received the go-ahead for an enlarged airborne operation, the original 'Comet' force being supplemented by the two American airborne divisions. Montgomery was also given the support of some American troops on his right flank and an increase in his supplies, but he was not to have absolute priority in supply, and Berlin was not to be his ultimate objective.

So 'Comet' became 'Market Garden'. The reason there were two words in the new code-name was that, instead of the airborne troops being dropped ahead of the still advancing ground force, as in 'Comet', a set-piece ground attack would need to be prepared and set in motion to join up with the air landings. The airborne part in this new combined plan was 'Market', and the ground attack was 'Garden'. The objectives of 'Market' were exactly the same as those of 'Comet' – seizure of the bridges over the waterways in Holland between the existing front and the North German Plain; the main change was in the scale of airborne force to be used. An initial proposal to launch the new operation in a mere five days' time had to be extended, but the start date would be only a week away, on Sunday 17 September.

*

The airborne forces waiting in England came under the First Allied Airborne Army, an organization which had been formed only six weeks earlier to co-ordinate the activities of the various British and American airborne units in England and of the air transport units required to take them into action. Its commander was an American, Lieutenant-General Lewis H. Brereton, who until then had been commander of the US Ninth Air Force; his headquarters were at Sunninghill Park near Ascot. As was normal at that time with 'Allied' formations, an American commander had a British deputy, in this case an army officer with the same rank as the commander – Lieutenant-General F. A. M. Browning; the staff were, again as usual, mixed British and American. Brereton's current directive was to be ready to despatch his airborne units on any operation in support of Montgomery's 21st Army Group, the American sectors on the Continent being now too distant for support by airborne operations. So, when Eisenhower gave Montgomery the go-ahead for 'Market', it was Brereton and his staff who prepared the operation. It would be the first of their many planned operations actually to be launched.

The next level of command was that of 'corps'. The American units came under Lieutenant-General Matthew B. Ridgway's XVIII US Airborne Corps; his main units were the 82nd and 101st Airborne Divisions, which had fought in Normandy but were ready for action again, and the 17th Airborne, which was still assembling and was not yet operational. The British units were under I British Airborne Corps and consisted of the 1st British Airborne Division and the Polish Independent Parachute Brigade Group, both ready for action, the 6th British Airborne Division, just returned from a long spell in Normandy, and an SAS unit. The British corps commander was Lieutenant-General Browning, who thus had two jobs. Both of the two corps organizations were also new, although the British one was really a transformation of the British Airborne Forces HQ, which had been in existence since 1941. Also available was the British 52nd (Lowland) Division, capable of being lifted by aircraft, but this was not officially part of Browning's corps.

The main purpose of the corps organizations was administration and training, and no previous airborne operation had taken place in which a corps headquarters had any operational role. The standard practice was that divisions were dropped independently and came under the command of the relevant ground forces corps headquarters as soon as a link-up was achieved. Three airborne divisions had been dropped in Normandy on D-Day and had performed satisfactorily in that way. But the two corps headquarters under Brereton's command had recently been given a limited operational capability in case circumstances developed in which an operation would require the co-ordinating influence of an airborne corps headquarters on the ground. 'Market' was about to employ three and one-third divisions, dropped at three separate places, and which were hopefully to be relieved within three days by ground forces. On the face of it, these were not the circumstances in which an airborne corps headquarters could be inserted into the operation with any beneficial effect.

But Lieutenant-General Browning – 'Boy' Browning, forty-one years old, handsome and elegant, married to the famous novelist Daphne du Maurier and a qualified glider pilot – was anxious to command troops in action before the war ended. He was a gallant veteran of the First World War, in which he won the DSO and the Croix de Guerre with the Grenadier Guards, but he had not yet had the opportunity to see action in this war. As commander of British Airborne Forces since 1941, his had been the guiding hand in the major build-up of this new arm of the British Army. Now the war might be brought to an end by means of the largest airborne operation of all time, and Browning wanted to be personally involved in it.

As Brereton's deputy and military adviser, Browning had met Montgomery at Brussels immediately after Eisenhower's aircraft took off after the 10 September meeting which inaugurated 'Market', and he brought Montgomery's outline plan back to England; he presented it at Brereton's first planning meeting that evening. Perhaps with Montgomery's blessing or perhaps by persuading Brereton himself, Browning secured agreement that the embryo untried tactical headquarters of his airborne corps should actually take part in the operation, despite the fact that the three divisional drops were to be scattered and despite the fact that the majority of the troops to be used would be American, whose own corps commander, Matthew Ridgway, with his recent battle experience as an airborne divisional commander in Normandy, would have to stand aside to give Browning his chance. In the plan that soon evolved, Browning and his tactical staff would fly in by glider and land on the first day alongside the 82nd US Airborne Division in the middle of the three main dropping areas, near Nijmegen.

The reader may think that this lengthy introduction of 'Boy' Browning and his corps headquarters in the plan for 'Market' is tiresome. But the first contribution to the tragedy of Arnhem had now been made. The signals organization of Browning's tactical headquarters was not complete; many extra men and much signals equipment had to be added during the next few days – much of it from American sources. On landing in Holland, he would be out of touch with two-thirds of his command unless his signals organization worked perfectly. His presence would also mean that, after the ground forces linked up with the air landings, two corps headquarters would be attempting to control operations in the same geographical area. There would be an even more direct effect upon the fortunes of the British troops about to fly to Arnhem. The glider lift of Browning's headquarters would require thirty-eight tug aircraft from the limited air transport force available, and these would be taken from the allotment to the Arnhem lift.

There is no record of any American opposition to Browning's plan, but British officers due to take part in 'Market' ridiculed it. One says: 'Browning's staff came straight from soft living in comfortable houses in England and had never done a single exercise'; and the following is part of a poem written in the last days before 'Market' by an officer due to fly to Arnhem.

> Corps Headquarters is moving to battle
> And they're holding a mammoth display
> Somewhat spoiled by the deafening rattle
> From the throats of the pen-pushers grey.
> ('Oh Doctor! – Quick! – Stretcher this way!')
>
> Corps Headquarters is flying in Gliders
> With Typewriters, Sten Guns and Ink,
> And the sarcasm shown by outsiders
> Would tickle an elephant pink!
> (Does the 'Boy' know the form, do you think?)

And what they Command when they get there
If Command is their ultimate goal
Is a matter it's hard to conjecture
We ourselves and a possible Pole.
(But it's better than drawing the dole!)[3]

Brereton's planning staff worked furiously to enlarge the old 'Comet' plan. The 101st US Airborne Division was allocated the capture of two canal bridges and one small river bridge north of Eindhoven and also to help the ground forces capture that town. The 82nd US Airborne Division came next with the more difficult tasks, first, of securing the Groesbeek heights which threatened the right flank both of their own operations and of the subsequent advance by the ground forces, and then of capturing the major bridges over the rivers Maas and Waal at Grave and Nijmegen, as well as a series of smaller bridges over a canal between the two rivers – seven bridges in all. Finally, the 1st British Airborne Division with the Polish brigade attached was to capture the main road bridge, a railway bridge and a pontoon over the Lower Rhine at Arnhem. It was obvious that the British would have to hold out the longest before being relieved by ground forces, but, with the Polish brigade adding to their strength, they had a greater number of troops. Major-General Urquhart, the British commander at Arnhem, was told after the war that an early version of the plan allocated the 101st US to Arnhem but that his division was then substituted. The main reason for such a change would have been inter-Allied politics; with a basically British plan and with relief at Arnhem dependent upon British ground forces, it was deemed unacceptable that an American division be subjected to the risk of being stranded at the end of the airborne corridor. For those interested in statistics, a total of 33,971 men would go into action by air – 20,190 by parachute, 13,781 by glider – together with 5,230 tons of equipment, 1,927 vehicles and 568 guns.

The ground operation – 'Garden' – would be carried out by General Miles Dempsey's Second British Army. Dempsey selected Lieutenant-General Brian Horrocks's XXX Corps for the task of

---

[3] Written by Captain C. R. Miller, G3 (Air), 1st Parachute Brigade HQ.

breaking through the German forward defences and then pushing up a corridor containing just one road to relieve and join up the airborne landings. Montgomery's order to Dempsey was that this move should be 'rapid and violent, without regard to what is happening on the flanks'.[4] The advance of XXX Corps would be led by the Guards Armoured Division, with the infantry of the 43rd (Wessex) and the 50th (Northumbrian) Divisions following behind. Also in the XXX Corps column would be much extra artillery, to fire into the areas ahead in which the lightly armed airborne divisions would be fighting, plus no less than 2,300 vehicles loaded with bridging material and 9,000 sappers and pioneers to replace or repair any blown bridges. XXX Corps had fortunately captured a bridgehead over the Meuse–Escaut canal at Neerpelt, in Belgium but only three miles south of the Dutch border, which meant one less waterway to cross and also that almost all of the ensuing action would be in Holland. The distance by road from the start line at Neerpelt to the bridge at Arnhem was sixty-four miles, a far deeper airborne penetration than ever before contemplated.

If the combined operations were successful, it was hoped that the British in Arnhem could be reached in three days or less and that a further advance could cut Holland in two by reaching the IJsselmeer on the fifth day. The two American divisions were to be withdrawn immediately to England, but the 1st British Airborne was told that it might be retained to remain in action as ground troops; Rotterdam was hinted at as the next objective for the division, and maps of that area were issued to its units.

A multitude of difficulties were encountered when it came to preparing the air plan, both because there were insufficient aircraft to carry the entire 'Market' force in one lift and because of the difficulty in finding suitable dropping and landing zones. (Parachute troops use a 'dropping zone', gliders a 'landing zone'.) More than three-quarters of the transport aircraft were American, but one of the reasons for creating Brereton's First Allied Airborne Army was to pool air resources. The American aircraft belonged to IX Troop

---

[4] Quoted in Major L. F. Ellis and Lieutenant-General A. E. Warhurst, *Victory in the West*, HMSO, 1968, p. 27.

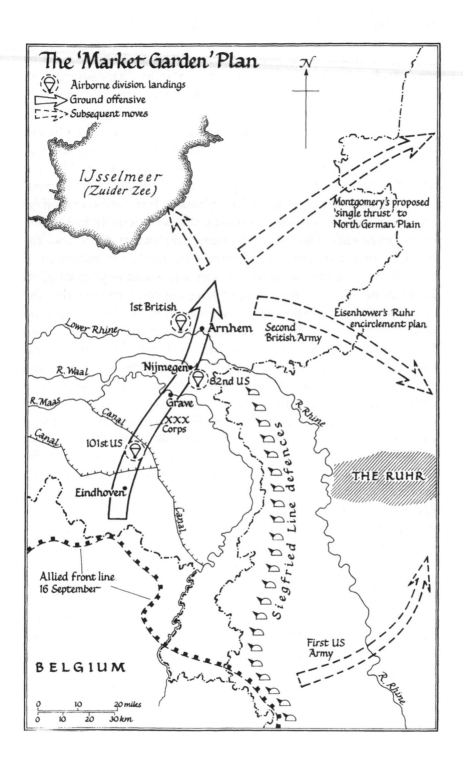

The 'Market Garden' Plan

Airborne division landings
Ground offensive
Subsequent moves

N

IJsselmeer
(Zuider Zee)

Montgomery's proposed
'single thrust' to
North German Plain

1st British

Lower Rhine

Arnhem

Eisenhower's Ruhr
encirclement plan

Second
British Army

R. Waal

Nijmegen

82nd US

R. Maas

Grave

Canal

XXX
Corps

R. Rhine

Canal

101st US

Eindhoven

Canal

Siegfried Line defences

THE RUHR

Allied front line
16 September

First US
Army

BELGIUM

R. Rhine

0   10   20 miles
0   10   20   30 km

Carrier Command under Major-General Paul L. Williams, and he was appointed the air commander for 'Market'. The principle in airborne operations was, and still is, that the military force states its requirements but that the air force involved actually makes the air plan in the light of what it perceives to be possible. The obvious requirement for 'Market' was that as much of the military force as possible be delivered as close to their objectives as possible, and with the greatest degree of surprise. But Williams and his staff quickly found that only half of the airborne force at best could be carried in one lift. The three airborne divisions actually had different requirements. The 101st US, being only twenty miles from the ground-attack start line, would carry only the barest minimum of its artillery, whereas 1st British at Arnhem would require all of its artillery. For the first lift, it might have appeared obvious that the available aircraft be allocated accordingly, but, instead, a decision was taken that two-thirds of the aircraft were allocated to the two US divisions and one-third to the British. It was then decided that the thirty-eight aircraft required to tow the gliders of Browning's corps headquarters should come from the British allocation. The different divisional requirements and the diversion of aircraft from the British allocation for the corps lift had the effect of giving priority 'from bottom to top', with nearly all of 101st US arriving in one lift, nearly all of 82nd US arriving in two lifts, but the British and Poles requiring three lifts. This was a cold-blooded, but probably correct, decision; if the 101st failed, then the other two divisions would be stranded, but it was obviously a grave disadvantage for the British and Poles. The actual allocation of aircraft to divisions for the first lift was: 101st US, 502 aircraft; 82nd US, 530 aircraft; 1st British, 475 aircraft.

There was more trouble to come. Major-General Williams, with Brereton's support, went on to decide that no more than one lift should be flown each day. This was patently disadvantageous to the prospects of the British and Poles at Arnhem; three lifts meant three days! Furthermore, Urquhart found that the dropping and landing zones allocated to his division were too far distant from the Arnhem road bridge. The probable reason for the one-lift-per-day decision was that the American transport units involved were not sufficiently skilled in navigation or formation keeping for the predawn or post-dusk flights that would be required for two flights on an autumn day. Memories of scattered drops by night in Sicily and Normandy were still fresh in the minds of the two American commanders who made that decision. The distant dropping and landing zones decision, however, was made by an RAF officer, Air Vice-Marshal L. N. Hollinghurst, commander of No. 38 Group, the senior RAF officer involved; Brereton and Williams had delegated to Hollinghurst the detailed planning of the Arnhem fly-in. Most of the extensive open area south of the Rhine bridges was 'polderland' consisting of small, low-lying fields intersected by numerous ditches, unsuitable for large-scale glider operations, though possible for parachute dropping. But Hollinghurst was reluctant to use that area because he was anxious about the danger posed to his low-flying transport aircraft by a reported build-up of German flak around the bridges and about the need to fly out over a German airfield north of Arnhem believed to be protected by further flak batteries. Much of the land north of the river was either built up or wooded, but some excellent areas both for parachute dropping and for glider landing existed to the west of Arnhem; unfortunately, they were between five and eight miles from the Arnhem road bridge, Urquhart's main objective.

This was Roy Urquhart's first airborne operation, but he felt that the combination of the lifts spread over three days and the distance from his landing areas to Arnhem would prevent his division from carrying out its task. He asked Brereton and Williams if the Arnhem force could have two lifts on the first day, as had been envisaged for the recent Operation 'Comet'. His request was refused. He then urged that landing zones be found closer to the bridge, at least for a proportion of his division which could act as a *coup-de-main* force. There was some meadowland close by the railway bridge; this was only two and a half miles from the road bridge. There was even room for a few gliders immediately south of the Arnhem road bridge. This time it was his fellow countryman, Air Vice-Marshal Hollinghurst, who declined to change the air plan.

These were further crippling limitations on Urquhart's chances of success. The basic advantages of airborne operations – surprise and the ability to drop astride an objective – were being thrown away. Because of the two main lifts of his division, Urquhart would have to leave half of the limited first day's lift to protect the landing areas, with only a third of his division remaining available to move into Arnhem and seize the bridges. A dropping zone south of the river was allocated to the Polish brigade, which would land by parachute on the third day, but by then, the optimists envisaged, the town of Arnhem would be secure, and the Poles would do no more than move across one of the bridges and take over part of the town perimeter on the north side. The tanks of XXX Corps should arrive by the evening of the third day and motor on towards the IJsselmeer.

Urquhart felt he could do no more and concentrated on his divisional plan, but these decisions by the air planners had already sealed the fate of the division. Urquhart did not know that his fellow British airborne divisional commander, Major-General R. N. ('Windy') Gale, who had taken 6th Airborne to Normandy, was consulted by Browning during the preparation of the Arnhem plan. Gale stated that at least one parachute brigade should be dropped as a *coup-de-main* force adjacent to the road bridge, to hold the bridge until the remainder of the division arrived. Gale said that he would have pressed for that condition 'to the point of resignation'. But the planning process was too far advanced, and Browning did not feel able to intervene on Urquhart's behalf. He asked Gale not to report the conversation to Urquhart for fear of unsettling him on the eve of the operation.[5]

*

[5] Major-General Gale reported this meeting to Major Geoffrey Norton, Curator of the Airborne Forces Museum at Aldershot, in the early 1970s, but only verbally; he stipulated that the information should not be used during the lifetime of any of the personalities involved. Major Norton writes in a letter of 4 March 1992 to Mrs Diana Andrews at the museum but in answer to my query through her: 'The plan would have worked if German opposition was slight. General Windy's gut feelings at the time, based on his respect for the Germans as soldiers and masters of improvisation when the chips were down, was that the German reaction to such a threat to their heartland would be rapid and violent . . . General Gale was unhappy – as the most experienced airborne general – not to have been involved in the planning earlier, when his views might have prevailed, though he was the first to admit that, as it was not his division undertaking the task, he had no right to expect to be asked . . . He felt, even at this late stage, that if enough high level pressure had been exerted, that at least the aircraft to lift the whole division on Day-1 might have

So that was Operation 'Market' – the largest airborne operation of the war and probably of all time, carried out at extreme range from home bases and landing deeper into enemy-held territory than any previous airborne operation. But, essentially, it was a more cautious and methodical plan than that of 'Comet'. The force to be employed was two and a half times larger and was to be landed on a step-by-step basis over a period of up to three days. There were no *coup-de-main* parties landing directly on to objectives. Some say that it was less like an airborne operation seizing its objectives by surprise than an airborne force landing and then manoeuvring like a ground force towards those objectives in the hope that the Germans would not intervene. Both Montgomery and Browning likened the landings to an airborne carpet over which XXX Corps would advance. Browning, despite his keenness for action, was worried about Arnhem; on first hearing the plan from Montgomery he had questioned whether it might not be 'a bridge too far', though he may never have used that particular phrase.

But the optimism of the moment and the benefits if the operation succeeded should never be overlooked. The German Army seemed to have been crushed in Normandy. The Guards Armoured Division which would break through the thin crust, it was hoped, of the German defence on the Dutch frontier was the very same division which had just motored 120 miles from the river Somme to Brussels in three days with both flanks exposed. And a whole series of proposed airborne operations had just been cancelled because ground forces had moved so fast that the airborne operation could not even get started. It did not seem unreasonable that the ground forces would once again leap forward, join up with the airborne men and eventually unleash the mass of armoured and motorized troops available to the Allies on to the open country beyond the rivers, with all the attendant benefits that would produce.

---

been found. If they had, the outcome could have been different.' One of my Polish contributors, Jerzy Dyrda, who as a lieutenant in 1944 was aide-de-camp to Major-General Sosabowski, the commander of the Polish Parachute Brigade, quotes Sosabowski's succinct comment: 'He always told us that an airborne operation is not a purchase by instalments.'

CHAPTER 2

'First Airborne' and Friends

The first British parachute units had been formed in June 1940, after Dunkirk, when Churchill ordered the formation of a parachute force of up to 5,000 men to join with the similarly newly formed Commandos to carry out raids on the coast of German-occupied Europe. But it was not until November 1942 that the airborne force reached divisional strength and the 1st British Airborne Division came into being, eventually settling down with a permanent organization of two parachute brigades and one 'airlanding' brigade, each of three battalions. Major-General Browning was the first divisional commander. Units of the division saw their first major action in November 1942 when the 1st Parachute Brigade carried out drops in Algeria and Tunisia and then fought on in a long and costly ground campaign. This was followed by the invasion of Sicily in July 1943 when the 1st Airlanding Brigade went in by glider on the first night of that operation, and the 1st Parachute Brigade dropped ahead of the ground forces four nights later. Both operations were successful, but casualties were again heavy, many being from causes other than enemy action, such as the premature release of gliders due to a faulty wind forecast, resulting in many men being drowned when gliders came down in the sea, and parachute aircraft being hit by 'friendly' anti-aircraft fire when they flew over the Allied invasion fleet.

The final part of the division's Mediterranean campaign took place when Italy surrendered in September 1943 and some of the airborne units were rushed over by ship to land at Taranto. There was a disaster in Taranto harbour when HMS *Abdiel*, a minelayer, carrying a parachute battalion – the 6th Battalion from the 2nd Parachute Brigade – and part of one of the division's anti-tank batteries, blew up on a mine with heavy loss of life. The division's involvement in Italy was not prolonged and not costly.

A reorganization took place when the 2nd Parachute Brigade was left behind to become an independent brigade, its place being taken by the 4th Parachute Brigade which had been formed in the Middle East. The division which returned to England at the end of 1943 was thus in the form in which it would fight at Arnhem nine months later. There was intense disappointment that the division was not used in Normandy; it stood by for a secondary drop there but was not required and remained in its camps and billets in Lincolnshire, Leicestershire and Rutland.[1]

'Boy' Browning had left the division in April 1943, to continue the airborne build-up, and his successor, Major-General G. F. Hopkinson, was one of the division's last casualties in the Mediterranean when he was killed in Italy. His place was taken by Brigadier Eric Down, an officer described as being 'saturated in airborne experience'; but Down was soon sent to India to form a new airborne division there. Browning was then asked by the War Office if he would accept a new divisional commander from outside Airborne Forces. Browning agreed, but only on condition that he was 'hot from the battle'. The choice thus fell upon Major-General Urquhart – Robert Elliott but always known as Roy – a forty-three-year-old Scot, a former Highland Light Infantryman. Urquhart was indeed fresh from battle, being a product of the Middle East campaigns like so many successful commanders of 1944–5. He took command of 1st Airborne in January 1944.

It has sometimes been said that the choice of Urquhart was an error and that the promotion of a brigadier from within the division would have resulted in the air plan for Arnhem being more vigorously opposed. His was only one of several new faces at the top of the division. The enlargement of Airborne Forces and the recent establishment of the First Allied Airborne Army took away many of the senior staff officers, and most of the replacements came from outside the airborne 'brotherhood'. There was some natural resentment that 'insiders' had not been promoted and also because of the 'new broom' attitude of some of the newcomers. But the new men were all able officers with much recent experience on

---

[1] Appendix 1 shows the divisional order of battle just before Arnhem.

a wider battlefield. Major Philip Tower, the new brigade major to the division's new artillery commander, says: 'We found the airborne boys, with their red berets, etc., hard to convince that other people had done a lot of fighting in the war. General Urquhart found the same and had to take a grip on them. They were a marvellous lot but they overestimated their prowess.' These recent senior arrivals had not volunteered for this airborne duty; they had been appointed by the War Office to their new positions. They did not need to train as parachutists but would go into action by glider. Urquhart actually hated flying.

The main strength of the division was to be found in its two parachute brigades. The men in these units were all of high physical standard and were all volunteers. They were not allowed to come directly into a parachute unit on joining the army as in post-war years but had to apply from other units. Most of the volunteers were infantrymen but suitable volunteers from other arms were also accepted. There was a strong Guards presence in those parachute battalions which were raised in England; former Guards officer Browning ensured that a proportion of senior NCOs in particular came from that source and imposed their high standards of discipline in the parachute battalions.

Once accepted for training, the volunteer then had to complete a parachute course run by the RAF at Ringway (now Manchester Airport). A man could refuse to jump at any time during the training period and return to his old unit, but after completion of his eight training drops – two from balloons and six from aircraft – refusal to jump was a court-martial offence. There were some accidents; British parachute troops did not have a reserve parachute, as had American paratroops, until after the war. Qualified parachutists received extra pay: two shillings a day for other ranks, four shillings (later reduced to two shillings) for officers. The distinctive maroon – not red – beret was introduced in March 1942; 'an inspired move', one man says; 'We were very proud; now the whole world copies us.'

The parachute men were physically tough and aggressive. Their role in war was to seize an objective swiftly and then to hang on at all costs until relieved. Although most of the 1st Airborne Division's units had seen action, it is not correct to say that the whole division was experienced or battle-hardened. Those men who had survived the Mediterranean campaigns certainly were; they were mature, older soldiers, often being pre-war Regulars who had experienced Dunkirk and then joined in the early airborne days. But the casualties of that campaign had been replaced by younger men who had been called up during the war. The casualty lists for Arnhem contain many names of such men, some aged only nineteen years. The same rules applied to officers. The originals had applied from existing units in the quiet years after Dunkirk and had since often been promoted several times in this expanding force. Most officer reinforcements still had to have served in another unit before acceptance, although the very first direct-entry subalterns were just being permitted to join straight from their officer-cadet training units.

The early parachute battalions did not have a parent regiment until August 1942 when the Parachute Regiment officially came into being; they had simply been 'Parachute Battalions' with no guaranteed future. The parachute badge so well known today was not issued until May 1943; until then most men had worn either the badge of their former regiment or that of the Army Air Corps. To many of the pre-war Regulars, this parachute service was probably regarded as no more than temporary duty. (The modern terms 1st Para or 1 PARA, signifying the 1st Battalion of the Parachute Regiment, were not used during the war and are disliked by many wartime men; units were usually referred to simply as the '1st Battalion', '156 Battalion', etc., and that is how they will be described in this book.)

A parachute battalion was a lightly armed, lean unit, its entire being dedicated to swift transport by air and dropping into immediate action. There were three rifle companies instead of the four in a normal infantry battalion. The fittest, keenest soldiers and those with the most initiative were in those rifle platoons – the cream of the division. There was an unusually high proportion of sergeants; the three sections in a platoon were each commanded by a sergeant or a lance-sergeant instead of a normal corporal. There were some heavy weapons in the 3-inch mortar and Vickers machine-gun platoons, but anti-tank weapons at Arnhem were limited to the

Piats and Gammon bombs carried by the rifle platoons. The full war establishment of a battalion was 36 officers and 696 men, but few battalions were up to strength at this time, and most of the transport and administration element did not fly into action but followed up in the 'sea tail'. The parachute battalions flying to Arnhem would do so with an average strength of 548 all ranks. Only seven jeeps and two Bren carriers accompanied the main battalion, those vehicles and their drivers travelling by glider. The average battalion would fly to Arnhem in thirty-four parachute aircraft and eight gliders – seven Horsas and a Hamilcar for the Bren carriers.

The units of the 1st Parachute Brigade were the real veterans, not only of the 1st Airborne Division but of all Britain's airborne forces; the original brigade, as one early officer says, 'was a great thing to be in'. The brigade had suffered heavy casualties in 1943, particularly in Tunisia, with battalions being reduced to strengths of 100 or so men by the end of the campaign. There had been large transfers of replacements from the 2nd Parachute Brigade; many of the lightly wounded later returned, and the remaining gaps were filled by recently trained parachutists. Approximately half of the men in the brigade were now Tunisia veterans; few of the remainder had seen active service. The commander was Brigadier Gerald Lathbury, a former Oxford and Bucks Light Infantry officer who was rich in airborne service. The brigade was now billeted in South Lincolnshire. It would drop in the first lift of the Arnhem operation.

The original members of the 1st Battalion were Britain's very first parachute troops. They were men who had volunteered after Dunkirk for transfer to a force described as being formed 'for parachute training or independent mobile units'. Those volunteers who were accepted became No. 2 Commando, stationed in billets on the outskirts of Manchester and carrying out parachute training at nearby Ringway. Most of this unit became the 11th SAS in November 1940 but was then redesignated 1st Parachute Battalion in September 1941. There had been a Guards troop in the original Commando unit, and T Company of the battalion would continue to have a strong Guards representation. One of my contributors insisted that his rank in 1944 was 'Guardsman' and not the standard 'Private' of a parachute battalion, and another old-timer said that his first loyalty was to the Commandos: 'We were a brotherhood; I'm really a Commando and always will be.'

The 1st Battalion was not pleased when a company of the 2nd Battalion was selected for the Bruneval Raid in February 1942, and a prolonged period without action led to some of the early men requesting returns to their old units. Then came Tunisia, and the desire for action was more than satisfied. A large draft of replacements for the casualties in Tunisia came from the 6th Parachute Battalion which had been formed from the 10th Royal Welch Fusiliers, so in 1944 the battalion had both a Guards and a Welsh character. The battalion was now based at Bourne. There had been two recent changes of command. A new CO arrived who displayed what was thought to be an excessive thirst for discipline and who brought his own – Guards – RSM, who was much resented for 'treating battle-hardened men like children'. There was a mutiny. A parachute exercise was ordered, but 'our rough old crowd' refused to draw parachutes in protest at the new regime. Brigadier Lathbury had the battalion paraded without its officers and listened to the men's grievances. He acted swiftly by posting both the new CO and his RSM and bringing in and promoting young Major David Dobie, a Tunisia veteran who was known and much respected in the 1st Battalion. (The officer who was replaced later had a distinguished career, rising to general officer's rank.)

The 2nd Battalion was formed on 1 October 1941 and, missing the various trials of the 1st Battalion, made smoother progress, its morale being boosted by the success of the company carrying out the Bruneval Raid. Major John Frost, the leader of that raid, became the battalion commander and led it throughout the Mediterranean campaign. Frost was the most experienced battalion commander in the division; one of his officers describes him thus: 'He had a very relaxed style of leadership when out of action, letting the very good company commanders get on with it. But, in action, he was absolutely on the ball and suddenly became five years younger.' Frost was an ex-Cameronian, and the company which went to Bruneval had been mainly Scots. A large draft of reinforcements in Tunisia had come from the 5th Battalion, formerly the 7th Cameron

Highlanders, and others were from the Royal Ulster Rifles; so the 1944 battalion had a strong Scots and Irish character. The battalion was now billeted in and around Grantham.

The 3rd Battalion, formed in October 1941 by Gerald Lathbury, has less of distinction in its description. It never had any regional characteristic, either in its original members or in its later reinforcements. It had performed well in Tunisia, where it had been the first British parachute battalion to drop complete into action when it parachuted on to Bône airfield. The battalion was now located in Spalding, two companies being in a hutted camp on the grammar-school playing field, the remainder in civilian billets. The CO was now Lieutenant-Colonel John Fitch, formerly of the Manchester Regiment, who had served as a company commander with the 2nd Battalion in Sicily and Italy.

The second of Urquhart's parachute brigades was a comparative newcomer to the division. This was the 4th Parachute Brigade, which had been formed as an independent brigade in the Middle East in late 1942 but was transferred to the 1st Airborne Division in exchange for the 2nd Parachute Brigade in 1943. The one and only commander of the brigade was John Hackett, better known as 'Shan', a member of an Irish family but born in Perth, Australia, where his father was a wealthy newspaper proprietor. ('Shan' was a pet name given in childhood. His Irish relatives called him Shaun, but his Liverpool-born nannie changed this to 'Shan', which persisted.) After an academic career at Oxford he joined the army and was commissioned into the 8th (King's Royal Irish) Hussars. Hackett had experienced much action before raising this brigade, being wounded in Syria in 1940 and then wounded and burned when his Stuart tank was hit in Rommel's first desert offensive in May 1942. On recovery, he returned again to the desert but was then brought back to a staff position in Cairo and eventually to raise the 4th Parachute Brigade. Short of stature but brainy, bold, firm and decisive, Hackett had the total loyalty of his men and was looking forward to taking the complete brigade to its first airborne action at Arnhem, but this would not be until the second day's lift.

The senior battalion in the brigade was 156 Battalion. Despite its high numbering, this was a long-serving unit which had been formed – numbered 151 Battalion – as the first parachute battalion to be raised in India in October 1941. Its original members came from no less than twenty-three British regiments and were all pre-war Regulars. When the battalion moved to Egypt to help form 4th Parachute Brigade, it was renumbered 156 to lead enemy intelligence to believe that it was a new unit. The battalion lost many of its members in this period, particularly senior ranks, because they were long overdue for repatriation to England after seven or more years' service in India. The gaps left were filled up with volunteers from various Middle East units, including a party of Life Guards troopers, most of whom became NCOs, and also a party of about twenty Rhodesians. The battalion also received a new commander, Lieutenant-Colonel Sir Richard des Voeux, a Grenadier who had been on Browning's staff in earlier airborne days; a Grenadier RSM was also appointed. The battalion's headwear also changed. Bush hats, which had been worn in India and were popular because they were smart and could easily be folded up inside parachute smocks for a drop, were replaced by maroon berets, which were not liked: 'We had never worn berets and thought red a funny colour for a soldier.' The battalion experienced only two weeks of light action in Italy, but this was useful experience for a unit which, although many of its members were long-service soldiers, had seen no previous action as a unit. On arrival in England it was first billeted in the Uppingham area but was now concentrated around Melton Mowbray, most of the companies occupying hunting lodges.

The 10th Battalion was raised at Kabrit in December 1942 and was almost entirely a product of the Eighth Army. When an infantry brigade consisting of three Royal Sussex battalions was broken up after suffering heavy casualties at El Alamein, the 2nd Royal Sussex was selected as the basis for what became the 10th Parachute Battalion, and 200 of the Sussex men volunteered and were accepted for parachute training. The battalion was made up to full strength by volunteers from the Infantry Base Depot at Geneifa; many were men who had recovered from light wounds received in the desert fighting. The Royal Sussex attempted to keep its link with the battalion by attracting officers of the regiment from as far afield as Tunisia and Malta, and the battalion would continue to have a strong representation from that regiment. The new battalion commander was Lieutenant-Colonel Ken Smyth, from the South Wales Borderers, but his RSM was Royal Sussex; there would be no changes before Arnhem. After serving briefly in Italy the battalion was now billeted in Rutland, partly in the village of Somerby where there was also a Land Army hostel for girls from Nottingham and Leicester, so there were soon several 10th Battalion weddings in those cities.

Hackett's junior battalion, the 11th, had been somewhat of a problem child. By the time this battalion formed at Kabrit in March 1943, many of the most suitable volunteers available for the new parachute brigade had joined the other two battalions. The result was that the 11th was a 'rough, tough' battalion which was not fully trained when the 4th Parachute Brigade left Palestine to join the 1st Airborne Division. One company of the battalion had dropped unopposed on to the island of Cos to secure the local airfield when Italy surrendered, and was later bombed by the Luftwaffe, but this was the battalion's only action before sailing straight to England at the end of 1943 and rejoining its brigade, disappointed that it had missed fighting with the brigade in Italy.

The battalion experienced further difficulties in England. After a spell at various locations in Leicestershire, it finally concentrated and spent many months impatiently waiting at Melton Mowbray. One of the problems was leadership. The first CO was Lieutenant-Colonel Micky Thomas, who had been transferred from 156 Battalion to raise and command the 11th. He was a good officer but 'too much of a gentleman' and not firm enough for this difficult battalion. Trouble blew up one Friday when men who had been used to drawing pay in advance suddenly found that this practice had been stopped, and those in arrears and therefore without walking-out passes made a mass exodus into town. Brigadier Hackett relieved the CO, posting in as his replacement his brigade major, and so the newly promoted Lieutenant-Colonel George Lea (formerly Lancashire Fusiliers) took over and started the task of pulling the battalion into shape. A new second in command also arrived, the rumbustious Major Dickie Lonsdale, whose airborne career seemed to consist of being passed on from one unit to another for unconventional behaviour. The process of recovery proceeded well, but the battalion would be unfortunate at Arnhem in being given a suddenly unexpected and difficult role. (Lieutenant-Colonel Thomas returned to his old regiment – the Wiltshires – and served as a major in the 5th Wiltshires in Normandy. He was killed in a gallant night action near Mont Pincon in July 1944.)

The third brigade of the division was the 1st Airlanding Brigade, made up of three battalions of infantry who flew into action by glider. The role of such units in airborne divisions was to provide a large lift of infantry complete with most of their support weapons and light transport and without the extra training required by parachute troops. Glider units could land almost intact and be ready for instant action; parachute drops were sometimes scattered and required a longer interval for assembly and joining up with vehicles. There were some limitations. Large-scale night landings were almost impossible, and smooth, firm ground was required, whereas parachute troops could land by night and on rougher ground. The Airlanding Brigade's night landing in Sicily had been very costly.

Airlanding battalions were much larger than both the standard infantry battalions and parachute battalions. There were four rifle companies instead of three and four platoons in each company instead of three, giving a total of sixteen rifle platoons compared with only nine in the parachute battalions. Their platoons were slightly smaller, however, in order that each could land complete in a Horsa glider, the standard load of which became twenty-six men, a handcart containing the platoon's ammunition reserve and a small motorcycle. Support Companies were also enlarged. The Bren-carrier platoon was omitted, but the 3-inch mortar, Vickers machine-gun and 6-pounder anti-tank platoons were all doubled in size to provide battalions with more fire-power until relieved by ground forces. The average glider battalion would land at Arnhem with a strength of 773 men – nearly 50 per cent more than a parachute battalion – and would be carried by sixty-two Horsas and a Hamilcar.

The original airlanding battalions had been made up of men from the battalions selected for conversion to the new role, provided they passed a medical examination, one of the most stringent aspects of which was the ear test to ensure the man would not suffer unduly from the rapid change in pressure when a glider dived steeply before landing. Those men found physically unfit for glider operations were replaced by volunteers from other units. Extra payment of one shilling per day was made, half that of the parachute soldier. As with other army units, glider troops could volunteer to go on to parachute training, and many did so, partly for the money, partly for the glamour, but some for fear of another glider operation after the misfortunes in Sicily. Volunteering for glider units ended in 1942, and men with suitable physical qualifications were then compulsorily posted in to keep battalions up to strength. Recent reinforcements had often come from Young Soldiers Battalions in which recruits were held after completing basic infantry training, which resulted in the glider battalions containing the youngest soldiers at Arnhem, some of them only eighteen years of age. All glider troops, whether infantry or other arms, wore the maroon beret which was the mark of all 'airborne' soldiers in those days, not just of parachute soldiers as today. The performance of the glider battalions at Arnhem gives the impression that they may have lacked a little of the aggression in attack of the parachute battalions, but they were steadfast in defence; their character was probably halfway between the doggedness of ordinary British infantry and the dash of parachute troops.

The officers in the battalions mostly came from their respective regiments, with one important exception – the CANLOANS. British infantry divisions preparing for the invasion of Normandy were short of junior officers at the same time as the Canadian Army had a large surplus, usually good NCOs who had completed an officers' training course in Canada and were awaiting vacancies in units of their own army. Under the CANLOAN scheme, 623 infantry officers volunteered to serve in British units, nearly all as platoon commanders. The British troops liked their Canadian officers; they were not as 'regimental' as the British officers. More than twenty Canadian officers fought at Arnhem, nearly all with the Airlanding Brigade, and five of them would be killed.[2]

*

---

[2] Three-quarters of all CANLOAN officers became casualties in 1944–5: 128 killed, 310 wounded and 27 taken prisoner.

The 1st Airlanding Brigade was born in November 1941 out of the 31st Independent Infantry Brigade, which had returned from India in late 1940 and had then been defending Wales against possible invasion. The brigade contained four Regular battalions – the 1st Royal Ulster Rifles, the 2nd South Staffords and the 2nd Oxford and Bucks Light Infantry, which had all been brought back from India, and the 1st Border, which had fought in France in 1940. The Ulster Rifles and the Oxford and Bucks had to leave the brigade when the 6th Airborne Division was formed in 1943; but a new battalion, the 7th King's Own Scottish Borderers, was posted in, and the 1st Airlanding Brigade thus became the three-battalion brigade which flew to Arnhem. All three units had their main base in hutted camps around Woodhall Spa, but they spent much of their time at camps in the South Midlands near the airfields where their tug aircraft and gliders were based, carrying out exercises or preparing for the many operations which were later cancelled. The brigade was due to be the first large force to land at Arnhem and would secure the dropping zones for the parachute troops, although little immediate opposition was anticipated. Most of the brigade would then have to remain outside Arnhem to hold the dropping and landing zones for the second lift before being able to move into the town.

The brigade commander was Brigadier P. H. W. ('Pip') Hicks, who had served with the Royal Warwicks throughout the First World War and again in France in 1940. He had commanded the 1st Airlanding Brigade since early 1942 and led it in the Sicily campaign. He was the oldest of the Arnhem commanders, being six years older than his divisional commander, and would reach his forty-ninth birthday during the battle; he was the only senior Arnhem commander who had served in the First World War.

The 1st Border and the 2nd South Staffords were the only Regular Army battalions to fight at Arnhem. The Border, however, did not contain many pre-war soldiers, having suffered heavily in France in 1940, then losing further members of the rebuilt battalion in the medical tests on becoming 'airborne' and, finally, sustaining the casualties of the glider-release fiasco in Sicily. The battalion now contained a large proportion of reinforcements from the industrial areas of Lancashire and the North-East. The CO was

Lieutenant-Colonel Tommy Haddon, who was destined to have one of the most frustrating experiences of any officer in the Arnhem operation. The South Staffords had been in India on the outbreak of war and so contained more of their original members and native Staffordshire men, though the battalion had also suffered heavily in Sicily. The CO was Lieutenant-Colonel Derek McCardie, a pre-war Territorial officer. By a strange coincidence, the only other Regular South Staffords battalion, the 1st, also had a connection with gliders, being Chindit troops who had flown into Burma in the second Chindit operation earlier in 1944.

The junior battalion in the brigade had a completely different background. The 7th King's Own Scottish Borderers[3] was formed when the Territorial Army was doubled in size after the Munich Crisis in 1938. The 7th (Galloway) KOSBs came into being when the 5th Battalion was enlarged and then split in two, so it was a mixture of pre-war Territorials and Militiamen called up just before the war. Most other battalions formed in this way had fought somewhere in the war by 1944, but not the 7th KOSBs. It had formed part of the Orkney and Shetland Defence Force for a long period and was pleased to be relieved from this boring and remote duty to come south to the pleasant town of Woodhall Spa to become a glider unit and wear the maroon beret. The usual weeding out of men below the necessary medical standard took place, and replacements came in from other KOSB and Scottish units. But the battalion still contained a high proportion of its original members and was the only Scots and only partially Territorial Army battalion to fight at Arnhem. This would be its first and last battle of the war. The CO was Lieutenant-Colonel Robert Payton-Reid, who would be the only battalion commander to return with his unit from the battle.

The parachute and airlanding brigades comprised about two-thirds of the total strength of the 1st Airborne Division. The rest of the division contained most of the supporting elements of a normal

---

[3] The sometimes-used abbreviation 'Kosbies' is not liked by members of the Regiment, being a vulgarity in one of the Indian languages; 'KOSB' is the preferred abbreviation.

infantry division, though in a form and on a scale modified to the airborne role. There were further infantry beyond those units already described. Divisional Headquarters had its Defence Platoon formed of men from the Oxford and Bucks Light Infantry. There was also the 21st Independent Parachute Company, a special unit trained to act as 'pathfinders', dropping just before the rest of the division to mark the dropping and landing zones. When it was formed in 1942, the first members of the company had been disappointed applicants for glider-pilot training supplemented by volunteers from trained parachutists, so each man was a double volunteer and had been carefully selected. A later addition was an intake of about two dozen anti-Nazi German and Austrian refugees from the Pioneer Corps; many changed their names by deedpoll to avoid danger of capture, but the often recorded story that most chose Scottish surnames is exaggerated. The company had seen only limited action in Sicily and Italy and had yet to perform its pathfinding role in action. The company commander was Major B. A. Wilson – 'Boy' to his officer friends, 'Bob' to his men – who, at forty-five years, was the oldest parachutist in the division. Because of his seniority, his friendship with Browning and the independent nature of his company, Wilson was able to take a highly individualistic approach to his unit's activities. It was a large company, with up to sixty men in each platoon, and would be a valuable addition to the division's infantry strength in operations after the landing.

Almost equal in size to the Independent Company, and with an equally well-known and independent commander, was the division's Reconnaissance Squadron. After this unit had failed to find a place in the Sicily operation because of a shortage of gliders, most of the unit's men trained as parachutists; thus only the vehicles and drivers would need to fly in by glider at Arnhem. The fast, tough, manoeuvrable jeep was the squadron's standard vehicle, but it was only armed with a single .303-inch Vickers 'K' machine-gun, and the unarmoured jeep and its occupants would be vulnerable in action. The 6th Airborne Division had Tetrarch light tanks in its Reconnaissance Squadron when it landed in Normandy, but 1st Airborne's had not been similarly equipped. Major Freddie Gough was the squadron's commander, another of the division's 'old men' with the varied service background of Royal Navy midshipman in the First World War and command of a provost section in the Dunkirk campaign. Most of the Reconnaissance Squadron would be given a *coup-de-main* role in the coming operation, being sent ahead of the marching infantry to secure the Arnhem road bridge, but this would prove to be a task for which it was ill suited.

The Royal Artillery had a large presence in the division, with a regiment of light field guns, two anti-tank batteries and a small unit for linking up with ground forces artillery support. Approximately 800 artillerymen would fly to Arnhem in about 170 gliders; many envious eyes in other units were cast on that huge glider allocation. The Commander Royal Artillery (CRA) was Lieutenant-Colonel Robert Loder-Symonds, a 'horse-gunner' and a rising star only recently brought into the division.

The 1st Airlanding Light Regiment was one of the newest units in the division, having been formed in February 1943 with a nucleus from one of the Royal Artillery's élite light batteries of 'pack-gunners' or 'mule-gunners' with much North-West Frontier experience. New guns were provided – the American-made 75-millimetre, with a four-man team, firing a 14.7-pound shell to a range of nearly five and a half miles. This gun did not need to be dismantled to fit into a Horsa glider; indeed, its towing jeep, the gun itself and a trailer of ready-use ammunition could all fit into one glider, so that the gun could be brought into action immediately after landing. The regiment would set off for Arnhem with twenty-four of those guns.

The Light Regiment first saw action in Italy, where it served as mountain artillery in support of several divisions from September 1943 until the end of the year, but it had never operated in the airborne role nor yet with its parent division. When the regiment returned to England in January 1944 to rejoin 1st Airborne, it was billeted in Boston, described by one officer as 'a marvellous place for the troops, with two dance halls, four cinemas, eighty-three pubs, and the girls used to whistle at us; but, being in the Fens, the area was useless when it came to gunnery practice'.

The divisional artillery would normally be responsible for linking up by radio with artillery units of the ground forces and for directing their fire. Three artillery regiments – two mediums and one heavy – were included in the ground-force column specifically to support 1st Airborne. But, because the Light Regiment had no experience of working with such outside artillery, a new unit was created – No. 1 Forward (Airborne) Observation Unit, made up of experienced artillery officers from various sources asked to volunteer, trained as parachutists and forming this unit in June 1944. Such officers, with their signallers, and with jeep drivers and despatch riders at some levels, were attached to every infantry battalion, every brigade, at Divisional Headquarters, at XXX Corps and at each of the three supporting regiments of the ground forces, so that fire support could be given to any unit in 1st Airborne as soon as the ground-force artillery came within range – if all went well.

There were two anti-tank batteries in the division – essential units because the six parachute battalions contained no heavy anti-tank weapons. The 1st and 2nd Airlanding Anti-Tank Batteries were both formed from pre-war Territorial Army units which had their homes in Barrow-in-Furness and Oban respectively. The 2nd Battery had suffered a disaster when HMS *Abdiel* struck a mine in Taranto harbour and many men were drowned. To make up the battery's strength an airborne officer appealed for volunteers to a parade of artillery reinforcements at a camp in North Africa. Gunner George Hurdman describes the result: 'Only one man, a Jew, stepped forward. The officer then walked down the ranks selecting the required fifty of the fittest-looking men and these were sent to the battery. I never regretted it for one moment; it was a fantastic mob to be in.'

The original establishment of each battery was four troops, each of four 6-pounder guns, but there had been a recent reorganization. A larger and more powerful gun, the 17-pounder, had been developed to counter the growing thickness of German tank armour, and it had been found possible to carry one of these guns and its towing vehicle in the new Hamilcar glider. One 6-pounder troop had been converted and three extra troops had been formed for this new gun. This development took place only just before Arnhem; the Germans did not know that the 17-pounder was capable of being glider-borne and would be much surprised by its appearance at Arnhem. Together with the anti-tank platoons of the Airlanding Brigade, a total of fifty-two 6-pounder and sixteen 17-pounder anti-tank guns would set out for Arnhem.

There was a considerable Royal Engineers presence in the division, with more than 500 members of this branch of the army going to Arnhem. The 9th (Airborne) Field Company was one of the oldest units in the Royal Engineers, with an unbroken history going back to 1787. It had become 'airborne' in June 1942 but had suffered a tragic experience in November of that year when the company took part in a glider raid to Norway to attack a heavy-water plant which might have eventually helped to produce a German atom bomb. One of the two Halifax tugs and both of the Horsa gliders crashed, and those of the sappers not killed outright were interrogated under torture – even the badly wounded – and all later executed. The unit had then taken part in the Sicily landing, where the company commander was killed. The 9th Field Company was a glider unit and carried out engineer duties for the whole division. By contrast, the 1st and 4th Parachute Squadrons were wartime-raised units and were integral parts of their respective parachute brigades. Also going to Arnhem was a detachment of 261 (Airborne) Field Park Company, which had also taken part in the Norway raid in 1942. The men of all these units were fully trained infantry and would be useful additions to the division's rifle strength when their specialist roles were completed. The Commander Royal Engineers (CRE) was Lieutenant-Colonel Edmund Myers, an enterprising character known as 'Eddie' since his cadet days because of Eddie Myers, a famous footballer, but now also known as 'Tito' Myers by some of his men because he had recently served with partisans, although in Greece not Yugoslavia.

Most of the transport of the division's RASC (Royal Army Service Corps) would not travel directly to Arnhem but, hopefully, would come up by land later. Three platoons of 250 (Airborne) Light Composite Company would, however, take part in the airborne operation, their main duty being to collect supplies dropped by parachute and distribute the contents to the division's units. A light transport platoon with jeeps and trailers would also come in with a large reserve of ammunition on the second lift. Once again, these men were all trained to fight as infantry.

Most units flew to Arnhem in high spirits and with reasonable confidence, but the Divisional Signals knew that they were likely to be in difficulty when they saw the plan produced for the operation. The maintenance of communications within the division during the critical opening phase of the battle would have to be achieved with equipment which they knew was inadequate for this particular operation. The standard inter-unit radio sets available in 1944 were, in simple layman's terms: the '19' set, a large set with a range of twelve miles in good conditions, but requiring a jeep and a heavy battery charger; the '22' set, a medium-sized set, also carried in a jeep but requiring a smaller battery charger, and with a maximum range of six miles; and the '68' set, a small, man-pack set using replaceable dry batteries and with a range of about three miles. The main communications within the battalions of the division were the 68 sets, which, because they were carried in the kitbag attached to the operator's leg, were immediately available for use after landing. There were also some 22 sets for the divisional command net, but only the artillery had the more powerful 19 sets. So, if an airborne division was dropped within a 'goose-egg'[4] of three miles and radio conditions were good, inter-unit communications should be satisfactory. But if battalions became separated by more than three miles or brigades by more than six miles, or if local conditions such as woods or buildings reduced those ranges – as they would drastically at Arnhem – then radio control would be lost.

When details of the Arnhem plan were received, with parts of the division having to remain at dropping and landing zones outside Arnhem while other units advanced into the town, it was realized that the 'goose-egg' was far too large and that there was no way that infantry units could maintain contact with each other. Major Tony Deane-Drummond, the experienced second-in-command of Divisional Signals, discussed the problem with his CO, Lieutenant-Colonel Tom Stephenson:

We had reluctantly accepted the 68 Sets because the division had laid down, in January 1944, that the maximum diameter

---

[4] 'Goose-egg': so named after the oval circle drawn on planning maps to denote unit locations.

of the divisional 'goose-egg' would be no more than three miles. Most of the previous planned operations had arranged for landings to take place adjacent or near to the objectives, but as soon as we saw the Arnhem plan, we knew that communications would not work until all units were concentrated in Arnhem. We needed more 19 sets; this would have required more jeeps and more gliders, but any changes in allocation would have implications for other units. This could not be contemplated without at least a ten-day sorting-out period, and that was obviously not acceptable. It was all too late; we had to get on with what we had. But the fact that communications would be dodgy was something that the staff should have been aware of when the operation was being planned.

So the 350 or so signalmen who went to Arnhem knew that there would be a preliminary gap in inter-unit communications lasting for at least twenty-four hours, or longer if the division was slow in concentrating. But, as Tony Deane-Drummond concludes: '*Everybody* in the division wanted to get on with the operation after all the cancelled ones. There is no doubt that risks were taken by everybody with eyes wide open. The feeling was that we had to get there before the German Army packed up.'

The remainder of the divisional units can be quickly described. The three medical units attached to brigades were most important elements, because there could be no evacuation of casualties until a link-up with the ground forces was achieved. Nos 16 and 133 Parachute Field Ambulances were attached to the 1st and 4th Parachute Brigades respectively, and 181 Airlanding Field Ambulance would fly in by glider with the Airlanding Brigade. No. 16 Field Ambulance claimed, justifiably, to have been the first 'paramedics'; 133 and 181 both had their original roots in pre-war Croydon Territorial Army units. The 400 RAMC (Royal Army Medical Corps) men would be stretched to the limit at Arnhem in an action that would last longer without outside relief than anyone expected. Seventy men of the REME (Royal Electrical and Mechanical Engineers) would be present, mostly on weapon- and radio-repair duties. The RAOC (Royal Army Ordnance Corps) sent twenty-eight men to identify and sort captured German weapons and equipment and to control the issue of British equipment received on supply drops. Finally, sixty-nine Military Police for traffic control and the guarding of prisoners would be present, together with sixteen Intelligence Corps men fluent in various languages – though none spoke Dutch – with orders to capture as many Gestapo personnel, Dutch collaborators and German documents as possible.

The total war establishment of 1st Airborne was 12,215 men; the total despatched by air to Arnhem is quoted variously between 8,905 and 8,969. Just over half of these had seen action before; the average age was twenty-seven. Nearly all were from the home countries of the United Kingdom, the only known exceptions being the Canadian officers, the Germans and Austrians in the Independent Company, a few Rhodesians in 156 Battalion, two South African officers who could speak Dutch and a French officer who had been attached to 156 Battalion for one of the proposed drops in France and, in the absence of orders returning him to his own forces, volunteered to drop at Arnhem and would die there. Several Dutch personnel and some more Americans would be added in the final stages of preparation. The division was a keen, well-rested force eager for action, although the long wait in England and the many cancellations had created a degree of staleness, so the division was not battle-sharp. It was also going into action for the first time as a complete division, under a new commander with no airborne experience, and with a plan whose implementation would require considerable skill even in favourable conditions.

The glider-pilot units which carried much of 1st Airborne to Arnhem were not part of the division. The Glider Pilot Regiment was, like the Parachute Regiment, part of the Army Air Corps and was available for whichever airborne division was carrying out an operation involving gliders. Glider pilots wore the airborne maroon beret, but there was no regimental badge, only the Army Air Corps 'eagle' badge. The regiment had started to form early in the war with a few army officers holding pre-war pilot's qualifications, but almost the entire regiment was the product of wartime volunteering and training. There was no shortage of applicants, but selection was rigorous, and a high standard was soon achieved, helped along by the usual leavening of Guards NCOs provided by Browning. The glider pilots were trained by the RAF, first on powered aircraft up to solo flight standard and then on gliders. The Horsa and Hamilcar gliders now in use had a crew of two: first pilots, who were at least staff sergeants, and second pilots, who were usually sergeants, had received a shorter training course and wore a smaller 'wings' badge than the first pilots. After an uncertain start, the Glider Pilot Regiment had developed close links with the RAF, and its units were all based on the airfields of RAF transport squadrons.

The standard glider now in use was the Horsa – high wing, tricycle undercarriage, 67 feet long, 88 feet wing-span and with an interior often compared with that of a London underground train carriage. The Horsa had one drawback; it had been designed before the arrival of the airborne jeep and the trailers and various guns the jeep would tow. These could be loaded, carefully and slowly, through the large side door of the glider but, in action, had to be unloaded by removing the high tail and driving down steep ramps. The process was slow and often difficult under operational conditions and extremely hazardous if the landing zone was under fire. One glider pilot says that 'the euphemism of the quick-release bolt was a sore point with us'. The standard American glider, the Waco, had a low undercarriage, and its nose could be lifted up to allow a jeep to drive straight out, but it had a much smaller capacity than the otherwise excellent Horsa.

A much larger British glider, the Hamilcar, had been developed in 1943. It was huge, larger than the four-engined aircraft which towed it. But, once airborne after a long take-off, it was not difficult to fly, though the pilots had to sit one behind the other in the narrow cockpit on top of the high fuselage. The Hamilcar had been developed to carry the light Tetrarch tank which could drive straight out of the up-tilted nose on airborne operations, and this had been done successfully in Normandy. The Tetrarch was not to be used at Arnhem, but the 17-pounder anti-tank gun with its towing vehicle also fitted into the Hamilcar, thus enabling 1st Airborne to take this new gun into action. The selected glider pilots of C Squadron who had been trained to fly the Hamilcar were now based at Tarrant Rushton airfield, where the most powerful aircraft in the transport squadrons – the Halifax – could use the long runway to tow off the huge gliders.

Nearly 90 per cent of the available British glider pilots would be required for Operation 'Market', 1,262 for Arnhem and 76 to take Browning's Corps Headquarters. Because of their long training and the lack of a reserve, glider pilots were usually withdrawn from an operation as quickly as possible; this had been done in Normandy, and only thirty-four glider pilots had been killed there. But they were also well-trained infantry and were given a ground role at Arnhem for what was hoped would be the short interval between landing and the arrival of ground forces. Some were to remain with the infantry and artillery units they carried into action, but were only to be used for defensive action and patrolling; others would form a central reserve under divisional control. The divisional commander would thus have the services of the equivalent of two further battalions of infantry. This fighting capability of the British glider pilot was in contrast to their American counterparts, who were not trained for ground action and actually required infantry to protect them until relieved.

The glider pilots would not be the only addition to Major-General Urquhart's fighting strength, for a Polish brigade – the 1st Polish Independent Parachute Brigade Group – was allocated to Arnhem, albeit not planned to arrive until the third day.[5] This was a unique body, the only Allied parachute unit made up completely of men from one of the occupied countries. Some of the Poles had been waiting for exactly three years to see action, since the brigade's formation in Scotland in September 1941. The unit was an 'independent brigade group', containing infantry, artillery, engineers and support units. The soldiers wore mostly British-type uniforms but with their own parachute beret, steel grey in colour, with their own eagle badge and their rank insignia over the middle of the forehead. The brigade had its own training organization but had not yet reached full strength. It was particularly short of

[5] Appendix 2 gives the order of battle for the Polish brigade.

experienced junior officers, the result of the Russian massacre of approximately 8,000 Polish officers at Katyn and at other as yet undiscovered sites in the spring of 1941. The brigade commander was the legendary Stanislaw Sosabowski, whose service as a soldier went back to his days as a conscript in the Austrian Army in the First World War. Becoming a Regular officer in the Polish Army, he commanded an infantry brigade in the defence of Warsaw until taken prisoner by the Germans on the fall of the city. He managed to slip away, however, eventually reaching Scotland to be given the task of forming the new parachute brigade. Because of the Polish system of promotion – based on service and ability irrespective of the position held – he was now a major-general, equal in theory to Roy Urquhart, under whose command he was to come in the Arnhem operation.

During the first part of its existence, the brigade was responsible only to Polish command and to its own government-in-exile in London. Its men were promised that the brigade's task would be to drop into Poland as soon as conditions were favourable, to join in an uprising of the Polish Home Army and help liberate their country. The brigade's motto was: 'By the Shortest Way'. But this plan had been steadily eroded, to the bitter disappointment of the whole brigade. The change came about through the British realization that a parachute drop around Warsaw would be almost impracticable and also because of the British desire to have the use of the brigade in the campaign following the invasion of France. General Browning, under whose aegis the Poles were being equipped and trained, had initially been on good terms with Sosabowski; he had offered Sosabowski command of a new airborne division in 1942 if he would put his brigade under British command. Sosabowski resisted the offer, stressing the Poles' desire to remain true to their original role. Enormous pressure from the British followed which led to an agreement whereby the brigade was committed to carry out one operation after the invasion and would then be allowed to go to Poland.

So the Polish brigade became part of the First Allied Airborne Army, moving south to the Stamford and Peterborough areas in June 1944, and it was placed under Major-General Urquhart's command on 10 August 1944. Tragically, the Polish Home Army had started the Warsaw Uprising only ten days earlier. This had been preceded by a message from the Home Army to Polish Army Headquarters in London on 25 June: 'We are ready at any time to fight for Warsaw. When the Parachute Brigade joins us, it will have an enormous political and tactical impact.'[6] But the brigade could not answer the call, and it would be left to the hated Russians to halt their advance short of Warsaw, deny the use of airfields for supply aircraft and allow the uprising to fail, even while the Poles were fighting at Arnhem.

The Poles had few friends in high places in the airborne world and were not in happy mood. Despite their shortage of numbers and lack of some equipment, Browning was insisting that the brigade was ready for action, and relations between him and Sosabowski worsened. Training was pushed ahead, and there was a disaster in an exercise when two Dakotas collided over Tinwell, near Stamford, on 8 July, and twenty-six Poles of the 3rd Battalion and the Supply Company, together with eight American airmen, died. The brigade was now firmly under British command and did not even have a representative on the staff of the First Allied Airborne Army, which would decide the Poles' immediate future. Sosabowski's recent outspoken opposition to Operation 'Comet' had further increased the bad feeling with Browning.

It was planned that the Polish brigade would fly in on the third day's lift to Arnhem, most of the brigade parachuting south of the Rhine. The number of Polish troops who would be despatched by air was 1,689. With his enlarged airlanding battalions, the glider pilots able to act as infantry, and then this large Polish reinforcement, Urquhart should eventually have an infantry strength approaching double that of a normal airborne division.

There were even further potential increases in strength. Waiting in England was the 52nd (Lowland) Division, a Scottish Territorial unit which had undergone a long period of training in mountain warfare but was now part of the First Allied Airborne Army, having been additionally trained as 'airportable'. As soon as Deelen airfield, four miles north of Arnhem, was captured, most of this

---

[6] Text provided by the Polish Institute and Sikorski Museum, London.

division was to be flown in and unloaded on the airfield. Two battalions of the division were already in Belgium, ready to come up to Arnhem by road and help unload the Dakotas. The same aircraft would evacuate the Arnhem glider pilots, ready for their next operation, as well as the Arnhem wounded. Also due to be flown to Deelen were two light anti-aircraft batteries and an American aviation engineer battalion which would construct further landing grounds.

There is no need to dwell on these later elements of the plan; they would come to nothing.

As Arnhem was mainly an army operation, written accounts usually make only passing reference to the British and American air units involved, due credit usually being given to the courage shown on the air-supply missions but with little depth of description of the air units or analysis of their operations. It is true that the airmen were not involved in the bloody struggle on the ground, but they delivered the airborne units to Arnhem with great skill, and the proportional casualties of some of the RAF resupply squadrons would equal those of some of the army units. Surviving airmen now join the airborne pilgrimages to Arnhem, where they are treated as full veterans of the 1944 battle.

Two groups of RAF Transport Command were to be heavily involved in the Arnhem operation. No. 38 Group was the oldest, with ten squadrons based on four airfields in the South Midlands and one in Dorset.[7] But the group was equipped with a variety of obsolete bombers, not with properly designed transport aircraft. The main strength was in six squadrons of the large, four-engined Stirling IVs on which the nose guns and mid-upper turret of the bomber version had been removed. There were also two squadrons of Halifax Vs and two of the twin-engined Albermarle with its elegant appearance and tricycle undercarriage – one of the war's forgotten aircraft; but the Albermarles were now in the process of being phased out because of their small load capacity and limited range. All of these aircraft had been used for parachute dropping, although they were far from ideal for that task, having limited fuselage capacity and no seats or windows – and jumps had to be made from floor hatches,

---

[7] Appendix 3 gives the order of battle of the RAF transport squadrons.

which resulted in a slow rate of dropping. But they were adequate for glider towing, and the Stirling was particularly useful in the supply-dropping role because of the large number of positions for parachute containers in its cavernous bomb bay, as well as further containers in the wing root positions, together with panniers carried in the fuselage and pushed out through the floor hatch.

No. 46 Group was a new organization, formed early in 1944 specifically for transport work in connection with the coming invasion. Of the six squadrons in the group in September 1944, two had been converted from Coastal Command Hudsons, two had formerly carried out transport work on Hudsons or Dakotas and two were newly formed; one of these, 437 Squadron, made up from Canadian crews in the group, only came into existence officially at Blakehill Farm near Swindon two days before the Arnhem operation commenced. The group's three airfields were all of the temporary wartime type and were in the same South Midlands area as most of 38 Group.

The great advantage of 46 Group was that it was equipped throughout with the excellent C-47 Dakota. This simple, mass-produced American transport aircraft – the military version of the DC-3 – was ideal as a general transport and for medical evacuation but could operate just as well with airborne forces. It had seats and windows and could carry nineteen fully equipped parachute troops who could jump safely and rapidly from the large side door. It could tow a Horsa glider, and the double roller tracks in the floor of the fuselage enabled nearly two tons of stores to be pushed out in one pass on a supply-dropping mission. Among the Dakota's disadvantages were its limited range and its lack of self-sealing fuel tanks and of any defensive armament; it needed to operate under conditions of complete air superiority. It was only thanks to the Americans that the RAF had any of these superb transport aircraft.

With the exception of the Canadian 437 Squadron, all of 38 and 46 Groups' squadrons belonged to the RAF, though there was a strong representation of individual Commonwealth aircrew members. A few crews had flown operational tours previously with Bomber or Coastal Command. Warrant Officer Bernard Harvey was the flight engineer in a crew which had just completed a tour flying Liberators against U-boats in the Battle of the Atlantic when posted to 299 Squadron at Keevil to fly 'those wretched Stirlings', to be pitched into a repeated round of briefings and cancellations for airborne operations and then to be shot down on the fifth day of Arnhem. But most of the crews were flying their first tours of operations. Pilot Officer Dennis Peel, a Stirling pilot on 295 Squadron, had been at a Bomber Command operational training unit in 1943 when diverted to transport work:

> My crew were pig sick when they heard that we were going to tow gliders, instead of going to Bomber Command; we felt looked down on when people asked what we were doing. It didn't dawn on us until about six months later how lucky we were when we heard how many of the crews we had trained with had been lost in Bomber Command and we realized that glider towing wasn't such a bad deal.

One notable character on 271 Squadron at Down Ampney was Flight Lieutenant Jimmy Edwards, a Dakota pilot already showing signs of his post-war brilliance as a comedian with his antics on trombone or tin whistle. His Dakota was named 'The Pie-Eyed Piper from Barnes' – Barnes being the part of London he came from – with a caricature of Jimmy with his whistle leading a column of RAF 'types'; he is described as 'a veritable bunter of a man, a great boost to morale'.

The squadrons of ex-bomber aircraft in 38 Group were not overworked in the period between D-Day and Arnhem. They practised glider towing regularly and supply dropping sometimes but were unsuitable for general transport work. Their only operational flying at this time was the dropping of supplies, agents or SAS parties to the Resistance, mostly in France. The Dakota squadrons of 46 Group had been carrying out their regular transport and casualty-evacuation flights to France since the invasion; they were only called in for an airborne operation when required, although they had practised all the airborne tasks. The squadrons of both groups would be required to provide a 'maximum effort' for Arnhem.

Working closely with the transport squadrons were the Royal Army Service Corps units – 223, 799 and 800 Air Despatch Companies – based on or near the RAF airfields and responsible for packing, loading and pushing out the baskets of supplies on resupply missions.[8] The men in these companies were not volunteers like RAF aircrew and received no parachute training or flight pay, but they did wear the airborne maroon beret. For the Arnhem operation these regular air-despatch units would be supplemented by men drawn from some of the other RASC companies in the 1st and 6th Airborne Divisions, not from the airborne platoons but from those parts of the companies which did not normally leave England. There would be a considerable RASC effort – and consequent casualty rate – involved in the air-supply flights of the prolonged Arnhem operation.

The Americans were plentifully supplied with good transport aircraft; not only would they provide more than three-quarters of the planes used on 'Market', but those planes were nearly all the versatile C-47 Dakotas. (There were a few C-53 Skytrains, an aircraft similar to the Dakota but with a smaller cargo door, lighter flooring and different propellers.) IX Troop Carrier Command would have no less than 1,175 aircraft available at the opening of 'Market'; they would carry all of the British and Polish parachute troops as well as the entire lifts of their own two airborne divisions. The units allocated to the British and Polish lifts were from the 52nd Troop Carrier Wing based in eastern England.[9] Each airfield contained a troop-carrier group of four squadrons, each squadron having twenty-four aircraft. The British and Poles knew that the Americans would be dropping them on their next operation, and the Americans had carried them on all of the recent training jumps. The American units were fresh and well rested. They were rarely used for general transport work, although there had been a recent flurry of activity carrying fuel to France and Belgium to alleviate the current supply shortage. There had been much criticism of the early American air transport units after some poor performances during the Sicily operation, but the crews about to fly to Arnhem either had been extensively retrained or were the products of an improved training system back home; all would give complete satisfaction to their allies in the coming operation.

[8] The listing of RASC air-despatch units is included in Appendix 3.
[9] Appendix 4 gives details of those USAAF air units involved in the Arnhem operation.

The Americans were happy to be stationed in England, particularly those who had been transferred from the Mediterranean. When the 314th Troop Carrier Group arrived at Saltby, near Grantham, its 62nd Squadron history listed the extensive facilities available but concluded: 'All this we could manage without, for just beyond the gate were girls of fair skin who spoke the same language.' First Lieutenant Bernard Coggins, a navigator in the 315th Group, writes:

> Flying-wise the weather had to be the worst feature. Flying in and out of Burtonwood Air Depot to pick up and deliver freight to all parts of England was, with all of the smog from Liverpool, in many ways worse than actual combat. Getting to fly to all parts of England, Scotland, North Ireland and later to the Continent was very good, as I was a sort of a history buff. Social-wise the language was no barrier; the girls loved dancing, and the fact that our salaries far exceeded that of our English counterparts made life very pleasant.

This description of the American units and flyers ends the 'rollcall' of Allied units which would take part in the Battle of Arnhem.

CHAPTER 3

The Arnhem Area

Arnhem is an attractive residential centre amidst delightful scenery, and with an exceedingly healthy atmosphere.

(Holiday guide, 1930s)

This 'attractive residential centre' is actually a small city, declared to be such as long ago as 1233 when the local ruling nobleman, Count Otto of Zutphen and Gelre, declared that Arnhem was to be the capital of Gelre. It remains the administrative centre of the province now called Gelderland, the largest province in Holland.[1] Several factors led to Arnhem's growth as a modern pre-war community. Its situation on the north bank of the Rhine had always made it a convenient staging point on the route between the great commercial cities of Amsterdam and Cologne without the need to cross any major rivers. That stagecoach route was followed by a railway, then by modern roads, and a new motorway was under construction when the war came. It was only at a comparatively late stage that north–south communications across the river were established. A narrow pontoon bridge, with the middle section removable to allow the prosperous barge traffic to pass, was the only river crossing until a new road bridge was built and opened in 1935.

A second factor leading to the growth of modern Arnhem was its development as a retirement centre in the nineteenth century, particularly for merchants who had prospered in the Dutch colonies. A considerable number of these people had spent their working lives in remote parts of the world and chose this quiet and attractive part of Holland for retirement, bringing with them wealth which in

---

[1] Although technically a city, Arnhem is small enough to be described as a town in general references and will usually be referred to as such in this book.

turn attracted cultural institutions and activities and provided employment for the local workers. Arnhem has frequently been called a Dutch Cheltenham. Not only the merchants from the colonies came; rich businessmen from other parts of Holland soon followed, but retiring administrators mostly settled in The Hague. Although the main retirement phase was over, the effects of it were still present when the war came to Holland in 1940.

Tourism followed the retirement influx. The low rolling hills, heathlands and extensive woods of this part of Gelderland – known as the Veluwe – are like an oasis in the otherwise flat and crowded landscape of Holland; the retirement element of Arnhem society had kept industry out, and the sandy soil was of only limited use for agriculture. A further source of prosperity in the twentieth century was when the Arnhem–Ede–Apeldoorn triangle of towns became the home of the pre-war Dutch Army, with modern barracks in the towns and training areas out on the heathlands. So another comparison with England is with the Aldershot–Farnborough area, though the Dutch Army was only a small one. Arnhem's share of this military presence was the 8th Infantry Regiment and the smaller but highly prestigious Mounted Artillery Regiment – known as the 'Yellow Riders' from the facings on their uniforms; this horse artillery unit was only just starting to become mechanized when the war came in 1940. The Dutch Air Force was also present in the area, building an airfield at Deelen, just north of Arnhem.

In those last days of peace, Arnhem was a prosperous community of 96,000 people, mainly a 'white-collar' city, with much employment in local administration, education and tourism, and with an ever-passing barge traffic on the Rhine. It was a centre of culture, with, as perhaps its most famous cultural establishment (as it still is), the world-renowned Kröller-Müller Museum on the heathland north of Arnhem; this was founded by the wife of a rich Rotterdam shipping owner to house her enormous art collection. The local people had a reputation for being of a quiet, reserved and serious nature. Religious beliefs were mostly Calvinistic, but with sizeable Roman Catholic and Jewish minorities.

Most people refer to 'the Battle of Arnhem', and the town's large road bridge was certainly the main British objective. But only a part of the 1st Airborne Division reached Arnhem, and the period of fighting would be more prolonged in the surrounding area. It cannot be stressed too strongly that other communities were involved, and one – Oosterbeek – for a much longer period than Arnhem itself.

The airborne landings would be west of both Oosterbeek and Arnhem, near the villages of Renkum, Heelsum and Wolfheze. Renkum was a working-class village with a large paper mill and one of the many brickworks on the clay beds alongside the Rhine. Nearby Heelsum was socially 'up' on Renkum and was the home of managers and office workers. Close by was Doorwerth, just a few houses in the late 1930s, but with a castle used as a military museum and as a meeting place for the Dutch branch of the Knights of St John. Wolfheze, further north, and due on the opening day of the battle to be in turn heavily bombed and then the first community to think itself 'liberated', was an example of the way this healthy, low-value land area was utilized by several public and private institutions. Here was built in 1907 the Wolf-heze Asylum, which became the foremost psychiatric establishment in Holland, famed for its modern methods and its spread of elegant buildings and domestic 'lodges' for the patients in an extensive parkland area. A small village with houses for the asylum workers and some shops grew up nearby, soon to be added to by an institute for the blind, a holiday hotel and some holiday homes.

Between these small villages and Arnhem lay Oosterbeek, with a pre-war population of about 10,000, soon to be the scene of fierce fighting and for many years after the war to be the emotional heart of the battle for most of those airborne men who survived. Oosterbeek was a town of two parts: the lower, alongside the river, had been a small farming and market-gardening community on the old stagecoach route; the upper town was more the product of the later merchant retirement and tourism developments, with larger houses, some of them of great elegance, summer-holiday villas and hotels. These latter served the visitors who came for walking, cycling, taking horse-drawn carriage excursions in the woods, swimming in or boating on the Rhine. They also catered for the motorists on the broad modern road from Utrecht which ran right through the upper town. On the northern edge was the railway and, beyond that, in the woods, the main road from Amsterdam and the new motorway under construction. Oosterbeek was thus associated with every one of the east–west communications which had helped develop Arnhem and all of which would be features of the coming battle. But the only bridge across the Rhine at Oosterbeek was a railway bridge, and the only means for civilians to cross the river was a small ferry at nearby Heveadorp. This was often used by Oosterbeek people to cross to the south bank to visit relatives and to buy fruit in the large area of flat, clay land between the Rhine and Waal rivers; known as the Betuwe (meaning 'good soil' in Old Dutch), this was a prosperous fruit-growing area. The nearest village on the Betuwe was Driel, near which the Polish brigade was to drop on the third day of the coming operation.

On 10 May 1940 the Germans invaded Holland without declaration of war. The country had been neutral throughout the First World War and had done nothing to provoke Germany in this new one. There was no serious fighting in Arnhem or Oosterbeek, although the area was in the path of the main German advance. Dutch military engineers blew up the new road bridge at Arnhem, but the main defence line was along some high ground at Rhenen, fifteen miles to the west, where the Dutch Army put up a brave fight but could only hold out for two or three days. Ans Kremer, then a twelve-year-old girl at Oosterbeek, has described the reaction of the local people to the arrival of the Germans:

> The first one I saw was a motorcyclist with a stick grenade tucked into the top of his boot. Everyone was very quiet until a pro-German family started cheering. They were what we call 'NSB-ers' – members of the National Socialist Party; we call them 'Quislings' when talking to British visitors. They were that part of the population which admired Hitler and the Nazis. They had won many seats in Parliament in the 1935 election but lost ground in the 1939 election when people realized what was happening in Germany. Those who remained loyal to the NSB in 1940 were the hard-liners, the opportunists, and they were pleased when the Germans invaded.

So the peace-loving Dutch had to settle down to a long occupation, their Queen and royal family in exile in England. The Germans replaced burgomasters in many places with NSB men, but in both Arnhem and Oosterbeek the existing burgomasters were allowed to remain and, for several years, managed to pursue policies of 'reasonable collaboration' acceptable to both Germans and Dutch. This lasted until July 1944 when the Arnhem burgomaster was dismissed and replaced with a 'real collaborator'. The burgomaster at Oosterbeek remained in office until the town was evacuated after the battle. For most ordinary people, relations with the Germans were strained but not violent. Ans Kremer tells of the long years of 'tension and menace; we children were much restricted and protected by our parents. There were curfews and one never knew what might happen. My parents listened to the BBC, but we were strictly forbidden ever to mention it. We heard of the Gestapo house in Arnhem and knew that terrible things happened there.' German became a compulsory language in secondary schools. German soldiers came to be called 'Moffen', from an Old Dutch swear word for uncouth labourers which goes back to the sixteenth century when Westphalian labourers came to work in Holland. (The original word *Muff* was German – 'a mouldy or musty smell, a grumbler or grouser'.) Girls who went out with Germans were 'Moffenmeiden'; they came from all classes of society and were hated, but there were no known marriages or illegitimate children in Oosterbeek. One section of society suffered tragically. Arnhem contained 1,607 practising Jews in 1940; only 80 were registered in 1944. Most of the others were taken to extermination camps at the end of 1941; a few were hidden by helpers who risked execution if caught.

Both the Germans and the Dutch had need of a new crossing over the Rhine in place of the bridge destroyed in 1940, so a new pontoon was quickly built, again consisting of three sections, while the longer work of rebuilding the road bridge took place. The Germans also resumed work on the unfinished motorway which would provide them with a good link between Germany and the coast. The local people now called it the 'Hazepad' – the 'Hare's Path' or 'Rabbit Run' – 'so that the Germans could run back home when the Allies came'. The Germans used the local barracks to house their own troops, various units moving in and out as the war progressed. So Arnhem saw plenty of German soldiery, but Oosterbeek was comparatively clear until an SS training battalion set up a camp in the woods just north of the town in early September 1944. They called the camp 'Waldfriede' – 'Peace of the Woods' – but this unit's untimely arrival was to prove a major impediment to the airborne men's plans for later in that month.

Oosterbeek may have been spared a heavy occupation, but several houses were forcibly taken over for various periods. Ans Kremer again describes how her family home, No. 8 Stationsweg (now the Strijland Hotel), was requisitioned in 1943:

> There were two families in the house, and the Germans gave us only twenty-four hours' notice. They told us to remove what belongings we could and that what was left would become theirs. Everyone rallied round, and we got nearly everything out. My father deliberately left photographs of Queen Wilhelmina, Princess Juliana and Prince Bernhard as an act of defiance – they would be the first things the Germans saw – also a sign which said, 'East–West, Home Is Best'. We never saw any of those items again. The Germans moved out in June or July 1944 – I think they were sent to the fighting in France – and we were allowed to go back into our home, but they warned us that maybe they would return and that it would be six hours' notice next time. We waited a little and did not go back until August, just in time for the house to be in the front line of the fighting in Oosterbeek when the airborne men came.

The airfield at Deelen became a major Luftwaffe base. A large fighter-control bunker was built in the woods nearby from which the German 3rd Fighter Division controlled a host of successful interceptions of Allied bombers flying over Holland to targets in Germany; it was right on the main approach to the Ruhr. The airfield itself became the headquarters of the Luftwaffe's most prestigious and successful night-fighter unit, Nachtjagdgeschwader 1, but, after repeated bombings and the approach of Allied ground forces, its planes were withdrawn to an airfield in Germany just before Operation 'Market'. Fear of overflying Deelen's flak defences was one of the reasons that persuaded the Allied air planners not to attempt a landing nearer to Arnhem, but much of the flak had recently been removed.

Neither Arnhem nor Oosterbeek suffered any deliberate Allied bombing for most of the war. The steady drone of night raids to Germany was frequently heard passing over the area, and some bombers were shot down; those members of their crews who perished were buried in the local cemeteries – thirty-six at Arnhem, nine at Oosterbeek. This local immunity from bombing ended on an unfortunate day, 22 February 1944, when several formations of B-24 Liberator bombers flying to targets deep in Germany encountered bad weather and were recalled. The formation leaders were free to bomb 'targets of opportunity', but only in Germany – a standard procedure when the main target was cancelled. The various B-24 formations circled, trying to avoid each other, each leader seeking a new target. Unfortunately an unpredicted wind and the frequent changes of course brought them all back over Holland and Enschede, Deventer, Arnhem and Nijmegen were all bombed. Arnhem received the attention of twelve B-24s of the 446th Bomb Group (based at Bungay in Suffolk), which aimed their bombs at the local gasworks. This was hit and badly damaged, and fifty-six Dutch civilians were killed. But, as Pieter van Iddekinge, a local boy in 1944 and later head of the City Archives, says: 'Basically, Arnhem was no more than typical of many other Dutch towns and had suffered little; the war started for us on 17 September 1944.'

The airborne landing at Arnhem would receive little assistance from local Resistance groups. Some of the reasons for this are clear. Holland was a country which did not lend itself readily to Resistance operations. It was small, with none of the rugged, inaccessible terrain that favoured the Resistance in countries such as France and Yugoslavia, and its population contained a higher proportion of Nazi sympathizers, always willing to betray resisters, than any other occupied country. There was another reason: Operation 'Nordpol' or the *Englandspiel*, the 'game with the English', an operation carried out by the Germans from March 1942 until early 1944.

What had happened was that the Germans captured a Dutch agent sent from England and forced him to transmit fake messages. The agent believed that his failure to include routine safety checks in the messages would alert the authorities in Britain to the fact that he was being used by the Germans, but the lack of safety checks was apparently ignored by the SOE (Special Operations Executive) in London. More agents and supplies of weapons followed, all to fall straight into German hands. Sixty-four Dutch agents were eventually captured; nearly all were executed. The RAF lost aircraft and crews at a higher rate than on similar missions to other destinations and eventually refused to carry out the flights. The operation came to an end when the Germans started to receive only bland messages and no more agents or supplies; they realized that their seemingly marvellous run of luck was over and sent a sarcastic message of thanks in clear on April Fool's Day in 1944.

That was the position on the eve of the Arnhem operation. There were no well-armed Resistance groups in Holland, no widespread intelligence network, only a strong distrust by Allied commanders of any remaining Dutch Resistance in case it had also been penetrated. But a new possibility has recently been suggested. It is now believed that the *Englandspiel* may have been a British double bluff, carried out at a time when the Russians were demanding that a 'Second Front' be launched in 1942 or 1943 to relieve pressure on the struggling Soviet Army. Through the sacrifice of more than sixty Dutch agents, some RAF aircraft and crews, and the supplies dropped, and through the inclusion of messages to the Germans that hinted of an Allied landing in Holland during that period, the Germans were persuaded to retain units there which could otherwise have been transferred to Russia, thus helping to prevent a possible Russian collapse before the Second Front could be launched.[2]

---

[2] This recent theory was put forward in Lynette Ramsay Silver's book *The Heroes of Rimau*, Leo Cooper, London, 1991, a description of Australian special operations in the Far East during the war which also suffered heavy losses. Lynette Silver included an appendix on 'The Case of Major Seymour Bingham', the officer handling the Dutch section of SOE in London during most of the *Englandspiel*; he was posted to distant Australia when the 'game' ended, ostensibly in disgrace. The British government will probably never confirm or deny the story. I am not an expert on such matters and can only present this possibility for the reader's interest.

Another betrayal story, one more closely connected with the Arnhem disaster, can be dismissed. Books were written soon after the war which stated that a traitor in the Dutch Resistance, known as 'King Kong' because of his powerful physique, obtained details of the coming operation and gave them to the Germans, who were thus able to station near Arnhem the Panzer units which later defeated the airborne men. That story has been debunked long since. The character called King Kong did warn the Germans that an airborne operation in Holland was possible, but this was at a time when the Germans knew that there were three airborne divisions in England and that Holland was the only German-occupied territory still within reasonable range of the Allied transport aircraft. The Germans' own assessment shows that they believed a landing as far in their rear as Arnhem was unlikely. King Kong's warning was worthless.

Early attempts to form a Resistance in Arnhem met with only modest success. Several small groups of patriots came together during the early years of the German occupation. Contact was made with an agent code-named 'Frank' in Rotterdam, and orders came to collect and pass on news of German troop movements and to stand by for possible future sabotage tasks. One of the Arnhem groups was penetrated by the Germans as early as December 1940, and its leader and several members were executed after being interrogated in the local Gestapo offices. But the Resistance remained active in Arnhem; in particular it had reliable men and women placed in the local telephone exchange and in the provincial electricity supply automatic phone system, which was able to cover a wide area.

There were other ways of defying the Germans. The Boy Scout movement was banned by the Germans, but many continued to operate 'underground' by meeting in the woods around Arnhem without uniforms. Some joined the Red Cross or fire brigade, not only to act as auxiliary helpers in those bodies but also to keep their Boy Scout troops in being and to act as minor intelligence gatherers. It will be shown that some of the Scouts were able to help the airborne men when the battle was fought in their city.

An active Resistance group was formed in Oosterbeek in late

1943, the meetings taking place at a nursing home for old ladies in the town. Intelligence was gathered and illegal newspapers distributed, most of these by Neeltje van Roekel, the group's only female member, who acted as the courier, regularly delivering papers and documents to a meeting point in Utrecht, hiding what she was carrying under her 'pregnancy' dress. One of the group's members, Nico Boven, became head of the whole Gelderland Resistance; but in the early summer of 1944 disaster struck and Boven and most of the men in the group were arrested. Two of them were smuggled out of Arnhem Prison, but Nico Boven and his brother were sent to German concentration camps; only the brother returned after the war. The remainder of the group went into hiding, leaving Oosterbeek without any active Resistance.[3]

The overall situation in the Arnhem area on the eve of Operation 'Market' was thus that there remained a Resistance presence in Arnhem but, because of Allied distrust of the Dutch Resistance generally, no advance warning was given of the operation. There was nevertheless much potential of goodwill and eagerness to help among those people who had suffered the violation of their country and more than four years of occupation. The airborne planners were hoping to harness some of this potential help after their troops landed but, again because of distrust, would make only limited use of it, unlike the Americans in their airborne landings, who made full use of the local Resistance.

[3] I am indebted to interviews with Albert Deuss for information about the Arnhem Resistance; to Wopke Kuik, a Wolf Cub in 1944, for the Boy Scout story; and to Mrs Neeltje Traas van Roekel for details of the Oosterbeek group.

CHAPTER 4

Preparations for Battle

Operation 'Market' was planned, prepared and set in motion in just one week, from Sunday 10 September to the following Sunday. This rapid execution was only possible because so many of the preparations for 'Comet' and the earlier cancelled operations had been made, resulting in nearly all units and equipment being in the right places. In theory, the 1st Airborne Division was based in Lincolnshire, Leicestershire and Rutland, but in practice parts of it were dispersed to such places as the South Midlands, Dorset, Kent and even Belgium, while their commander and most of his staff were living on a golf course just outside London.

The only major units not to have moved were the six parachute battalions, because the American troop-carrier airfields were located close to their regular locations. But the units due to fly by glider had been absent from their normal locations for more than a month, having moved to temporary camps in the vicinity of the airfields on which were based the RAF glider-towing aircraft earmarked for an operation long since cancelled. Such uprooting and departures had been a regular feature of the airborne men's life over the last eight months, off either to an exercise or to one of the many cancelled operations. Many a local young woman's heart had fluttered with anxiety every time the lorry convoys left towns and villages. The 1st Border had spent the last few weeks in billets in the pretty Oxfordshire town of Burford. Corporal Cyril Crickett describes his temporary home:

Our last billets before setting off for Arnhem were pigsties in Burford. Ironically, much earlier in the war, whilst serving with another regiment, I had worked on converting them. There had been an outbreak of swine fever, and pigs could not be kept in them for three years, so they were converted for use by troops. We had many a laugh – not fit for pigs but OK for the lads.

Part of the division was at Manston, on the eastern tip of Kent. This was because the twin-engined Albermarles of 296 and 297 Squadrons could not reach Arnhem with a fully loaded glider from their home airfield at Brize Norton. So fifty-six aircraft from those squadrons, towing Horsa gliders, flew to Manston early in September in preparation for Operation 'Comet'. Waiting there were their glider passengers: two companies of the 2nd South Staffords, the 1st Airlanding Anti-Tank Battery and parts of the Royal Artillery Light Regiment and of 181 Field Ambulance. Manston was one of the RAF's emergency landing airfields with a very long runway and a large dispersal area, but the airfield was still crowded; there were now twelve RAF and Fleet Air Arm squadrons stationed there, mostly fighter squadrons operating against V-1 flying bombs or standing by to escort the air armada to Holland. The RAF messes were under such a strain that an Albermarle and a Horsa had flown back to Brize Norton on 8 September and returned with a load of WAAF waitress reinforcements. The airborne units had a frustrating time when there was a period of very wet weather. The gliders became bogged and had to be moved to firmer ground, and the anti-tank battery abandoned its tents and found accommodation in a nearby village. Major Ian Toler, the commander of the glider-pilot unit at Manston, says:

> It was very frustrating. There was much replanning of our landing zones and loading and unloading of gliders when 'Comet' was cancelled and 'Market' was substituted. We had no secure direct telephone line to Wing Headquarters at Harwell, and I had to keep flying to and fro. I got completely browned off and couldn't have cared less what happened at one stage.

A major part of the division was already over in Belgium. This was the 'sea tail' made up of the division's B Echelon, mostly RASC, REME and other units' heavy transport. A total of 1,100 vehicles and 2,264 men had embarked in American Liberty ships at

London on 14 August, in preparation for one of the cancelled operations, and had been landed on Gold Beach in Normandy three days later. The vehicles carried second-line ammunition and two days' rations for the whole division and much of the airborne men's personal kit. The intention was to travel behind the ground forces and join up with the airborne element of the division, enabling the division to continue in action long after the airborne landing. Also waiting in Belgium were the 'sea tails' of the Polish brigade and the 52nd (Lowland) Division.

After being held at a transit camp in Normandy for over two weeks, during which time it resisted attempts to requisition its transport to help in the ground forces' supply crisis, the large convoy moved forward by stages, first for Operation 'Linnet', then for 'Comet'. Various efforts were made to keep the men entertained. A film show in Normandy – *Dangerous Blondes* – had to be cancelled when rain leaked into the cinema tent and damaged the equipment. A dance in a large garage further into France was disrupted by local French Resistance men ordering out at pistol point all the girls who had consorted with German soldiers during the Occupation. The penultimate waiting place was in the Louvain–Brussels area, where Flanagan and Allen, Florence Desmond and Kay Cavendish appeared in an ENSA concert and where two Polish officers were killed in a road accident; Lieutenant Kazimierz Bogdziewicz and Second Lieutenant Stanislaw Zlotnicki were probably the first deaths of Operation 'Market'. Gunner Harold Lee has described the progress of the sea tail across France and Belgium as 'a leisurely and euphoric journey', but was concerned about lax security when he heard Arnhem being freely mentioned in cafés at Louvain. The 'sea tail' was joined by a few last-minute arrivals from England, then moved up on 15 September to join the huge XXX Corps column of vehicles preparing to move forward behind the ground attack. The 'sea tail' was placed fourteen miles behind the head of the column; Gunner Lee found there 'a carnival atmosphere' in anticipation of the momentous operation about to be launched.

Nearly all of the detailed planning for Arnhem was carried out at Lieutenant-General Browning's Airborne Corps Headquarters, which was located at Moor Park Golf Club in Hertfordshire. Major-General Urquhart and his planning staff had spent most of the last few weeks there, preparing the various operations which had come to nothing, and were now working on this latest plan. The disadvantage of this situation was that the divisional planners were located nearly a hundred miles away from the headquarters of the division's four brigades (including the Poles), and there was a constant shuttling to and fro of brigade commanders and staffs. Sunday 10 September found the brigadiers and their brigade majors – their principal staff officers – at Moor Park, ready, as they thought, to attend the main divisional briefing for 'Comet'. But 'Comet' had just been cancelled, and the visitors could be told no more by Urquhart than that a new operation was pending in which the whole division would fly to Arnhem. It was not until late afternoon of Tuesday the 12th that Urquhart was able to present the Arnhem plan in detail and give out his orders.

That briefing commenced at 5.0 p.m. Present were the four brigadiers with their brigade majors and the commanders of the various arms and services and their staff officers. Major Freddie Gough of the Reconnaissance Squadron was reprimanded when he came in late. Browning was also present, though he need not have been. Perhaps Urquhart had invited him; perhaps Browning wanted to be there, to back Urquhart up and to observe the reactions of the brigadiers. Urquhart went through the details of the plan, with the distant dropping and landing zones, the lifts spread over three days and the faint possibility that elements of German armoured units might be present. Whatever their private thoughts, the brigadiers made no adverse comment or objection in the presence of the two generals, although they all knew the weaknesses of the plan. 'Shan' Hackett says:

> In retrospect, it seems crazy for my brigade to drop on the second day with all surprise gone, but we realized that we had to get into the battle after all those cancellations. You can't go on doing that to troops of quality. They were so good, so fit, so keyed up, so keen to get on, that you had to get into the battle almost at any price. So shortcomings in the plan were readily forgiven as long as we could get in there. Even

Sosabowski was happier this time; it made more sense than 'Comet'. But, really, I think 'Market Garden' was doomed before it started.

Major Philip Tower, brigade major to the Commander Royal Artillery, says: 'Even the most reluctant of us, like the CRA who had seen so much fighting already at Dunkirk and in North Africa, and myself, were sick of all the cancellations and keen to go.'

The visiting officers returned to their own headquarters, where their staff officers started to draft the orders for battalions and other subordinate units. The brigade commanders were ready to give out their orders by Thursday or Friday. General Urquhart was making a tour of his brigades on Thursday and sat in on part of Brigadier Hackett's briefing at Knossington, near Oakham. Captain Nick Hanmer of the 10th Battalion remembers:

Urquhart jokingly said that our brigade, going in on the second day, would probably be just in time to see B Echelon of the Guards Armoured Division going through Arnhem. But after General Urquhart had gone, 'Shan' Hackett said he didn't wish to disagree with the general but, in his opinion, if 50 per cent of us were alive and on our feet within two or three days of this operation commencing, we should consider ourselves fairly lucky. As it turned out, he was exactly correct; thirty-one officers from my battalion flew to Arnhem and fifteen were killed or died of wounds; none returned to British lines.

When Brigadier Lathbury briefed his commanders, Lieutenant-Colonel John Frost remembers 'the great interest in the truly imaginative major use of airborne forces, although there was apprehension over the distance between the dropping zone and the objectives'.

Most units sent their men on forty-eight hours' leave in the middle of the week, and it was Friday or Saturday before commanding officers and company commanders passed on their orders. The companies of the airlanding battalions were initially given the somewhat passive task of guarding various sectors around the landing and dropping zones for the second lift, but the 1st Parachute Brigade was to advance as quickly as possible into Arnhem. The 2nd and 3rd Battalions would set off first, and each designated a 'spearhead company' to lead the way – Major Digby Tatham-Warter's A Company and Major Peter Waddy's B Company respectively. Lieutenant Robin Vlasto was one of Tatham-Warter's platoon commanders; these are his notes written soon after the battle:

> We were pretty pleased with this job, although it did seem rather a complicated method of committing suicide. In the Colonel's own words, 'The Brigadier had promised me this, that the 2nd Battalion will, without any doubt, be put in the best position for taking part in the bloodiest part of any battle we may have – and, believe me, it will be some bloodbath.' No one doubted the veracity of this statement and it was quite clear in everyone's minds exactly which company would be first to dive in.

Lieutenant Eric Vere-Davies remembers that the 1st Battalion officers 'objected without exception to the dropping zone and volunteered *en masse* to jump on or a bit to the south of the objective. This request and the reason for it was passed on to higher command but refused.' Staff Sergeant Alec Waldron of the Intelligence Section of the Glider-Pilot No. 2 Wing was plotting glider landing zones; he realized that most of the polderland south of Arnhem bridge was unsuitable for mass landings but found two medium-sized areas of firmer ground, one just south of the bridge and a second in a loop of river on the north bank between Arnhem and Oosterbeek, where at least one glider battalion could be landed to seize the bridge quickly. He even volunteered to parachute in advance to verify the firmness of the ground.

On Friday 15 September, with only two days to go, the smooth process of preparation at Browning's headquarters was disrupted when his Intelligence Officer attempted to point out the extreme danger of a build-up of German armour in and around Arnhem.

Major Brian Urquhart (no relation to the general) had suffered a severe parachuting accident earlier in the war and was now on Browning's staff, collating all incoming intelligence reports about German strength in the 'Market Garden' area. Such reports came from a variety of sources: prisoners captured in the ground fighting (though Arnhem was well behind the battle front), Dutch Resistance (sketchy and not always trusted), the *Ultra* deciphering of German radio signals (the secrecy of which source had to be protected by limiting the detailed release of its output beyond a limited number of headquarters of which Browning's was not one). In addition to the normal occupation troops expected to be present, it was also known that the survivors of some Panzer units which had suffered heavily in Normandy had passed through Arnhem during the recent headlong German retreat and had halted north of the town. But Brian Urquhart now received information from Montgomery's 21st Army Group in Belgium that two SS Panzer divisions – tentatively identified as the 9th and 10th – were believed to be in the area. Dutch liaison officers at Moor Park were also suggesting that there was more armour in the area than had been originally thought.

None of the reports were precise. Normal intelligence rarely is, and if the reports from 21st Army Group were based on *Ultra* then they would have been deliberately imprecise. It is now known that intelligence officers at SHAEF (Eisenhower's headquarters), at Montgomery's 21st Army Group and at Brereton's First Allied Airborne Army were, to varying degrees, all sure that two Panzer divisions were in the Arnhem area, possibly refitting with new tanks and taking in fresh men. But this huge airborne operation was now in its final stages of preparation, and commanders at all levels either cast doubts on the reports or decided that the operation must go ahead despite the increased risk. In any event, no confirmed reports or official warnings from above reached Moor Park.

Brian Urquhart was convinced that the Arnhem part of 'Market' was in grave danger. He attempted to warn Browning on several occasions but without success. So he asked for oblique aerial photographs to be taken of the wooded areas in which tanks might be sheltering. A Spitfire from a photo-recce squadron obliged, and on the Friday morning prints appeared on his desk showing modern Mark III and Mark IV tanks close to Arnhem. (The two divisions were actually north and east of Arnhem; their nearest elements were ten miles from the Arnhem road bridge and only eight miles from 1st Airborne's landing area.) Urquhart rushed to General Browning with this new evidence, only to be treated once again 'as a nervous child suffering from a nightmare'.[1] Browning then acted decisively, but not in the manner Brian Urquhart expected. Colonel Austin Eagger, Browning's senior medical officer, was told to send Urquhart on sick leave on account of 'nervous strain and exhaustion'. Eagger did so; he was not happy with this but was acting under orders. He comments: 'I supported Brian Urquhart in trying to prevent this [the Arnhem disaster], but we failed.' Brian Urquhart says: 'I always had the impression that he understood better than anyone else on the Airborne Corps staff my own extreme apprehensions about the operation.'[2]

So Brian Urquhart left the scene, 'desolate and miserable'. He admits that he was 'obsessed' about the danger at Arnhem, and an officer friend, Major Tony Hibbert, who would fly to Arnhem, says that Urquhart was 'highly strung but intelligent, and his fear for 1st Airborne's safety were justified'. Brian Urquhart later told Hibbert that he had written a letter to Winston Churchill about the danger of the operation, with instructions that the letter be posted if he did not return; this was while he was still expecting to fly to Holland with Corps Headquarters.

Criticism is usually directed at Browning for ignoring Brian Urquhart's warnings. Yet Browning was faced with an appalling dilemma. He had not received all the intelligence available and he was far from uncaring about the fate of his men; he had threatened to resign over the ill-preparedness of one of the earlier proposed operations. But was a British general to jeopardize this great airborne operation, perhaps the last opportunity of the war, a mainly American operation, for fear of what might happen to British troops? Perhaps Brian Urquhart was wrong. Perhaps the

---

[1] Brian Urquhart, *A Life in Peace and War*, Weidenfeld & Nicolson, London, and Harper & Row, New York, both 1987, p. 73.

[2] These last two quotations are from letters to the author. Colonel (later Brigadier) Eagger refused to amplify his statement or to report conversations with Browning, pleading 'professional confidence' because he treated both Browning and his wife after the war.

German armour, if present, would not react quickly and the bridge at Arnhem could be held until XXX Corps arrived. Morale among the airborne units would certainly suffer if 'Market' was cancelled. Browning decided that it was too late, that the risks must be taken and that the operation must proceed.[3]

Browning's written orders to 1st Airborne, dated 13 September and signed by himself, had contained this paragraph: 'ENEMY INFORMATION The latest Intelligence will be sent to you up to the time of take-off.'[4] But the latest reports were not passed on. General Urquhart may have been told by Browning; his memoirs do not mention this. What is certain is that no official warning of the latest German tank strength reached units, and neither Brereton nor Browning made any attempt to amend the plan to lessen the danger from the Panzers. John Frost says that his battalion would have still been quite happy to carry on with the operation, but could have benefited from a warning by taking more anti-tank weapons and ammunition and possibly leaving such heavy items as mortars behind. There were other alterations that could have been made if warnings of the Panzers had been given.

Meanwhile, various additions were being made to the Arnhem-bound force, all requiring accommodation in the already strained glider and parachute aircraft capacity. Some of these groups and individuals had been earmarked for 'Comet' or even earlier operations, but others were last-minute arrivals.

There were the 'Phantom' and 'Jedburgh' teams. 'Phantom' was a signals detachment of an officer and four men of the GHQ Liaison Regiment with a direct wireless link to the War Office, a standard feature of major operations so that the War Office could receive immediate information on the progress of events. The

---

[3] *Author's note.* I am reminded of an incident in my book *The First Day on the Somme* when, before the opening of the Battle of the Somme in 1916, the commander of an infantry battalion, the 2nd Middlesex, complained vigorously that his patrols had found that the German barbed wire had not been cut by the bombardment and that the attack would be a disaster. But it was too late then; the attack went ahead and was a disaster. The officer concerned was wounded and later committed suicide, blaming himself for not having protested sufficiently.

[4] Copy in Airborne Forces Museum, Browning Barracks, Aldershot, File No. 38.

'Jedburgh' team consisted of an American and a Dutch officer and an American radio operator, and its role was to contact the local Resistance and to harness local volunteer support for labour and guiding duties. Also coming were more Dutchmen – a naval officer to represent the Dutch government-in-exile and a commando officer and ten men who were attached to various airborne units as interpreters. A fourteen-strong public relations team was a later arrival, the first time such a team had accompanied a British airborne operation. A public relations officer, two censors, three film and photographic cameramen and four signallers were all service personnel, but there were two BBC civilian broadcasters and two newspaper journalists whose reports would be pooled on a world-wide basis. A third journalist, Major Tony Cotterill, joined separately.

Two further late additions were signs of hasty improvisation. British airborne forces had no reliable long-range radio equipment, and 1st Airborne needed a good link back to XXX Corps so that the superb British ground-support squadrons of the 2nd Tactical Air Force stationed on the Continent could be brought into the Arnhem battle. This was a vital ingredient, but preparations for it were abysmal. All of the air side of 'Market' was planned in England, and 2nd TAF was only invited at the last minute to send an officer to England to provide liaison. He was unfortunately delayed by bad flying weather and arrived after the final planning conference, too late for serious co-ordination to be arranged. But two American radio teams had been provided for the necessary communications; the teams contained four jeeps, two radio sets, two officers with airborne combat training, eight signalmen and two British drivers. They were scheduled to be carried on the second lift from Manston in four American Waco gliders piloted by British glider pilots.

The last party to be added would meet with a mixture of fiasco and tragedy. In mid-August, the newly formed First Allied Airborne Army became concerned that some of the operations being planned well behind the German lines would have no protection against German night bombers. The RAF had mobile radar stations working with ground troops as a matter of standard procedure; these had operated in North Africa and after the Normandy invasion and could direct night fighters on to German bombers approaching their area. But a distant airborne landing would be beyond the range of such stations, and two mobile units capable of being carried by glider were requested. So Nos 6080 and 6341 Light Warning Units were formed by the RAF and practised loading and unloading their equipment with Horsa gliders. Two units were provided in the hope that at least one would arrive safely. Each contained two fighter control officers and ten or eleven men, mostly radar and radio technicians. Much work has been done by Arnhem researchers on these units in recent years, but some details are still vague. It is probable that they were intended to fly with Browning's Airborne Corps Headquarters glider lift to the Groesbeek area near Nijmegen, from where the Arnhem area, only seventeen miles away, could be covered. The four gliders carrying the units were given 'chalk numbers' from the corps allocation and flew from Harwell, where all the other corps gliders took off. Wing Commander J. L. Brown, a veteran controller from the North African campaign, was put in charge of the whole operation; he would fly in one of the other corps gliders. It will be described later how all this would go wrong and the four gliders would be sent to Arnhem instead, with distressing results. It can be added here that the two units each contained an American controller officer, but these were told that American fighters would not now be involved and that they could withdraw if they wished. One did so, but the second volunteered to stay with the RAF men. That would make a total of thirteen Americans taking part in the Arnhem operation.

When the men of the various divisional units returned from their short leaves, mostly on Thursday the 13th, they found this new operation still 'on' and were immediately involved in the final preparations for it. Most of the troops were briefed on the Saturday. Every soldier was told not only his own unit's part in the coming operation but that of every other part of the division and even an outline of the entire 'Market Garden' plan. The general impression given was that little opposition was to be expected. These are two typical reactions. Gunner Dennis Bowles of the Light Regiment:

They told us the destination and the limited opposition – the old men and the invalids from the Russian Front; Home Guard type opposition was inferred – and that we would probably be relieved after two days. Our Forward Observation party was told that we were going straight to the bridge and there would be a separation from the main unit for twenty-four hours. You tend to hope that it was all true. You realize that it couldn't be as easy as that, but you hoped it was.

Corporal Bob Allen of the 3rd Battalion:

I remember a feeling of shock and disbelief when I heard we were to drop seven miles away from the bridge. I kept my thoughts to myself. The general feeling in my company was that we should drop on the polder immediately south of the objective, rush across the bridge and establish ourselves in the town. We felt that once 1st Para Brigade was there it could hold out indefinitely.

The intelligence report said that the Germans had little equipment, were exhausted and thoroughly disorganized. I took this with a pinch of salt. I knew from experience that 'Brother Bosche' was a sturdy fighter, both in attack and defence. Oh yes, a little German armour was reputed to be refitting in the Arnhem area. But morale was sky high. Most of us were straining at the leash to get into battle.

There was hectic activity at airfields. The transport squadrons had carried out a minimum of operations in the last week and had brought in all their reserve aircraft to ensure maximum availability. There is no record of any glider or parachute party allocated to the first lift failing to leave the ground because of aircraft shortage, although the 1st Airlanding Anti-Tank Battery had to give up two of its gliders to make room for some of the recent additions to the operation. A letter in front of me begs me to mention the hours of hard work put in by RAF and WAAF ground staffs at the airfields, as well as the careful packing of thousands of parachutes at a central packing unit at Credenhill, near Hereford. Gliders carrying vehicles and guns were carefully loaded once again, with the usual attention being devoted to weight distribution. A Horsa was deemed to be perfectly loaded when the glider pilot could pull down the tail and lift up the nose wheel. Also on my desk are copies of two load manifests for gliders at Down Ampney, one carrying a rifle platoon of the 7th KOSBs and the other a jeep and a trailer and six men, also of the KOSBs. Both forms are marked 'COMET' but overprinted 'MARKET'. Each load was almost exactly three tons, and each soldier and his equipment was assumed to weigh 210 pounds (15 stones).

The RASC packed reserve ammunition in containers and took them to the American airfields to be loaded on to the Dakotas. Various items of equipment were issued to every man: a life jacket, two 24-hour ration packs, two hexamine heating blocks, twenty cigarettes, sweets, one candle and a box of matches. There was a pay parade at which private soldiers received ten guilders in newly printed Dutch 'liberation money' and ten German marks; company officers were optimistically given sufficient Dutch money to make a second pay parade one week hence. Some men were offered a new type of armoured vest, but the weight of this caused few to accept. Messenger pigeons were indented for from RAF lofts, and eighty-two birds would actually be taken to Arnhem.

Everyone then had to divide their personal kit into what could be carried and what was to be left behind, hopefully to catch up by land. Lieutenant-Colonel John Frost ordered his batman to load his shotgun and golf clubs into the staff car which would drive down to a port and cross to join the 'sea tail': 'I thought this operation might lead to the end of the war and that 1st Airborne, as the latest arrival, would be retained in Germany for some time, and these items would be useful.' Lieutenant Kenyon-Bell of C Company, 156 Battalion, took the Transjordanian flag which Emir Abdullah had given to the company after a parachute exercise in Transjordan the previous year. Gunner 'Dickie' Bird put more than forty copies of popular sheet music under the driver's seat of his jeep: 'We had been given an indication that we could soon be relaxing in Germany, and surely there would be an available piano in the Reich.' Difficult decisions had to be taken over reading matter; Corporal Jenkins of the 10th Battalion decided to take Vansittart and Sassoon but to leave Rupert Brooke behind. Colour Sergeant Eric Seal of the 1st Battalion, on being told that he would have to go by glider for the first time, loaded a large reserve of tinned food:

As an old foot-slogger I began to like the idea – comfortable seat in a glider, a nice trip across the North Sea to Holland and on landing I would have my own jeep to ride in and plenty of food. I would live the life of Riley. But my glider, on the second lift, was hit by a mortar shell immediately after landing, and the contents all destroyed. I was meant to be a foot-slogger.

Staff Sergeant 'Ginger' Green, PT instructor of the 10th Battalion, packed a deflated football 'in case there was time for a quick game', but he would break his ribs in a heavy parachute landing. Lieutenant Pat Glover, Quartermaster of the same battalion, decided to take his pet chicken tucked into his smock; it had already made several practice jumps and been awarded its parachute wings.

The final moves were made. Some wives living nearby were sent home to parents. Some men returned late from leave, or did not return at all and were marked AWOL ('Absent without Leave'). The overall figure for this is not known but, from various absences recorded, the number could have been about four or five men per battalion, though some absentees heard 'on the grapevine' that the operation was 'on', returned at the last minute and would fly to Arnhem technically under close arrest. A few replacements were available – men with light injuries or young soldiers who had not been included in the original orders – and gaps were made up where possible. One platoon officer says that his absentees were mostly good soldiers; there had been so many cancelled operations that the reasons for absence were more often of a romantic nature than loss of nerve. This was all balanced by a few stowaways. For example, in B Squadron of the Glider Pilot Regiment, the Adjutant, the Quartermaster and a medical orderly, all non-pilots, added themselves as glider passengers at Manston; the Quartermaster, Staff Sergeant James Boyd, would be killed. Lieutenant-Colonel Derek Heathcote-Amory (later a Conservative Cabinet minister) of the GHQ Liaison Regiment obtained two days' leave and persuaded his friend Brigadier Hackett to take him on the operation, being listed as 'Liaison Officer'.

*

There was time for relaxation on the Saturday evening. Troops were supposed to be confined to their camps or billets, but this did not prevent some of them going to a local public house. A church service in a tent at Down Ampney was full to overflowing. Here are a few typical experiences and emotions of that last night. Corporal Alan Sharman of the Independent Company:

> One of the men in my section was skylarking and let off one of our large green smoke flares. It coloured me green all over and I spent most of the rest of the night cleaning myself. I wanted to die clean if I was to die. He made up for it at Arnhem, because I made him dig a trench for me when I had hurt my arm and needed a trench.

Gunner Stan Wrightman of the 1st Airlanding Anti-Tank Battery:

> Bombardier McCullock and I had been to the pub in Tarrant Rushton for a bit of a binge. As we made our way back to camp, singing and rolling, we came across a rubbish dump on which was an old pram which had no wheels. In fun, I said to Jock, 'Hop on and I'll take you home.' I must have dragged him half a mile back to camp; it was quite a laugh at the time. There was just one sad note to the evening. When Jock and I arrived back, he shook hands with me and said what a smashing time he'd had. Then he became upset and said, 'You know, Blackie; I won't come back from this operation.' I told him not to talk so silly and left it at that.

(Bombardier J. J. McCullock was wounded by mortar blast and died at Kate ter Horst's house in Oosterbeek just after the end of the battle.) Signalman 'Taff' Haysom of 1st Parachute Brigade HQ at Syston, near Grantham:

> We walked to the village and saw Olga, the landlady of the Plough Hotel. Over a plate of delicious ham sandwiches we discussed the enigma of an airborne soldier. Here we were, happy and relaxed, but in twenty-four or less hours' time we would be seventy miles behind enemy lines. Someone said,

'Providing we get that far'; this was thought-provoking, and so we returned to camp, got into bed and pretended to sleep.

That night, 223 aircraft of RAF Bomber Command bombed four German fighter airfields and a flak battery in Holland to reduce the danger to the next day's flights to Arnhem and the other landing areas. Two Lancasters were lost, probably when they collided after bombing the flak battery. The fourteen airmen belonging to the crews of Flying Officer Paul Tooley of 90 Squadron and Flight Lieutenant Peter Bickford, a Canadian, of 115 Squadron were all killed, the first British casualties of 'Market Garden'.

CHAPTER 5

The Air Armada

Sunday 17 September dawned a little misty, but with every prospect of a fine day to follow. There was much relief among the various commanders; they need give no thought to cancellation. It would be a day of momentous event, the launching of this huge airborne operation. By coincidence, it was 'Thanksgiving Sunday' for the victory four years earlier of the Battle of Britain. 'Battle of Britain Sunday', as it became known, would be commemorated long after the war, but more than twice as many of the men about to fly to Arnhem would die during the next eight days than the total number of RAF pilots killed in that summer of 1940.

The scale of air operations for 'Market Garden' would be massive. More than 3,500 aircraft would take off from airfields in England to carry the airborne troops to Holland or on some sort of support operation. It is a measure of how Britain's role in the war was now overshadowed by the American effort that less than one-quarter of those aircraft would be British. But concentrating on the 1st British Airborne Division which is the subject of this book, 332 RAF aircraft, 143 American aircraft and 320 gliders would take off with men of the division on this first day's lift. There would be space in these aircraft and gliders for most of Divisional HQ, nearly all of the 1st Parachute Brigade, most of the 1st Airlanding Brigade, the Reconnaissance Squadron, about two-thirds of the artillery and engineers, advance parties of 4th Parachute Brigade units and various support elements – approximately 5,700 men in all.

Eight RAF airfields would be used: Fairford, Harwell, Keevil and Tarrant Rushton in No. 38 Group; Blakehill Farm, Broadwell and Down Ampney in No. 46 Group; and Manston as a forward base for the Albemarles normally based at Brize Norton. Except for twelve Stirlings from Fairford carrying the parachute troops of the Independent Company, the entire RAF effort would be devoted to glider towing. The Stirlings at Fairford, Harwell and Keevil would lift most of the divisional support troops, vehicles and guns, as well as Browning's Corps HQ. The Dakotas of 46 Group mostly carried infantry of the Airlanding Brigade. The Halifaxes at Tarrant Rushton carried 17-pounder anti-tank guns and Bren carriers in Hamilcars and the Reconnaissance Squadron jeeps in Horsas. Away to the east, at Manston in Kent, 296 and 297 Squadrons made the largest contribution in aircraft numbers, despatching twenty-eight Albemarles each; no other RAF squadron managed more than twenty-five aircraft. The large Manston effort was made possible by five Albemarles flying in that morning from a reserve unit. Initially, these were found to be in the way, and their pilots were told that they would probably not be needed and could return whence they had come. Only Flight Sergeant Ralph Trout and his crew accepted this offer, but they later found that the four remaining reserve aircraft were then immediately required; and so, said Trout, 'We missed out on an epic operation.' The Manston glider loads were anti-tank and light artillery, part of the 2nd South Staffords infantry and four Waco gliders carrying the American signalling teams which were brought forward from the second lift to be towed by the four extra Albemarles. It was in the South Staffords' lift that the effects of Lieutenant-General Browning's decision to take his headquarters to Holland were to be seen. An airlanding battalion required fifty-six Horsa gliders, but only twenty-two were available for the South Staffords on this day, while Browning's seemingly unnecessary expedition was flying in thirty-eight Horsas from Harwell. Thirty-four of these would have enabled the remainder of the South Staffords to fly in to Arnhem that day and allow the Airlanding Brigade to arrive complete.

The balance of the first lift to Arnhem is easy to describe. A total of 143 C-47 Dakotas of the American 61st and 314th Troop Carrier Groups at Barkston Heath and Saltby would carry all of the first-lift parachute troops except the Independent Company. The 2nd and 3rd Battalions would fly from Saltby and the 1st Battalion and other elements from Barkston Heath – a total of 2,279 men.[1]

*

[1] There was either a mistake in one part of the divisional orders or a late change in the plan. In the section 'Unit Allotment to Airfields – Parachute Aircraft' the

The late time of the first take-off — about 9.45 a.m. — meant that the army units had spent the night in their camps, with a full night's sleep for those who could sleep and a good breakfast; some of the WAAFs serving breakfast at Manston were seen to be weeping: 'They knew we wouldn't be back for lunch.' Then it was off out to the airfields in hundreds of RASC lorries. Men were split into glider loads or parachute 'sticks' and were driven right up to their glider or parachute aircraft, which were all identified by a 'chalk number' allocated in advance.

The scene on the airfields was of impressive airborne might, not seen in its entirety before because the Normandy take-off had been at night. At the British airfields up to fifty gliders had been marshalled in impeccable formation on the runways; their tug aircraft were just as neatly lined up in echelon at the sides of the runways, ready to move forward one at a time and hitch up on the gliders' tow ropes. And out of the lorries debouched hundreds of heavily armed, fit, keen, young soldiers, ready for what most believed was going to be an operation which would lead to an impressive and important victory, perhaps to the end of the war. It was a beautiful autumn day. Tea and sandwiches were distributed; this would be the last issue of food until the division was reached by ground forces; the forty-eight hours' rations each man carried would have to last until then. The most humorous memory of the operation for Captain Duncan McLean of the 2nd Battalion was of his friend Captain S. C. 'Bombs' Panter in prison camp, 'bemoaning the fact that he left a half-eaten bacon sandwich on the wing of the plane at Saltby; all we ever dreamed about in the bag[2] was food.' Sunday newspapers were delivered. Humorous or rude remarks were chalked on gliders about to make their one-way trips and

airfields were listed as: first lift — Folkingham, Barkston Heath; second lift — Saltby, Cottesmore; third lift — Spanhoe, Cottesmore. These had been the allocations for Operation 'Linnet', the cancelled operation before 'Comet', but they were not correct for Arnhem. Unfortunately Major-General Urquhart included the erroneous table in his memoirs, with the result that many of the 2nd and 3rd Battalion men, to whom one wartime airfield looked like another, believe now that they took off from Folkingham when the reality was Saltby, and similarly the 4th Parachute Brigade HQ, the 10th Battalion and the 4th Parachute Squadron all used Spanhoe instead of Cottesmore on the second day.

[2] 'In the bag': slang for 'in prison camp'.

become scrap by the end of the day. Equipment was checked. At Down Ampney, Major Michael Forman found that most of his company of Scottish Borderers had added extra ammunition to their personal loads; he made his men leave all the surplus behind because of the danger of overloading their gliders. An officer in one small unit had requested to be taken off the operation, and his NCO was ordered to ensure that the officer jumped properly; a firm push out of the doorway of the C-47 in a few hours' time would do the trick. The moment came for men to board their gliders or aircraft; engines were started – the Dakotas with the 'infuriating squeal' of their Pratt & Whitney engines – and then run up and tested at full power, producing a thunderous roar across the airfields.

The first gliders started taking off more than an hour and a half before the main parachute force. This time difference was due to the lengthy assembly procedure of the tug and glider formations and their longer routes. The tug aircraft moved forward slowly until the pilot was advised by his rear gunner that the glider was moving, then full take-off power was applied. The glider became airborne well before the tug. An intercom cable was attached to the tow rope so that the tug crew and the glider pilots could converse throughout the flight. Combinations were soon taking off every thirty-five seconds, waved on their way by crowds of ground personnel, many of the WAAFs again with handkerchiefs to their eyes. There were no serious accidents. One glider at Keevil aborted its take-off and cast off the tow because an ill-balanced load was threatening the glider's safety. A vehicle quickly towed it to the rear of the queue; one man was moved from front to rear of the glider, and a spare Stirling hooked up and took off successfully. Only one of the 359 gliders on the British lift (including the 38 gliders carrying Browning's Corps HQ) failed to leave the ground.

The tugs and gliders from the main group of airfields in the South Midlands had first to fly well to the west before turning over the Bristol Channel and setting course for the North Sea. The reason for this was so that the lengthy taking-off and climbing for height would not result in an elongated stream. To avoid this, the first take-offs flew furthest to the west, 'just as though we were invading Ireland', says Flight Sergeant Jack Howes, a Stirling navigator.

Later take-offs flew progressively shorter distances before turning, so that all would pass their airfield again in a relatively short period and take their places in the gathering streams. Most of the glider force would complete its assembly over Hatfield, passing north of London, but the fifty-six combinations flying from Manston would not join until halfway across the North Sea (see map on page 84). The whole glider force would eventually form up in three parallel streams, one and a half miles apart and nearly 100 miles long.

The assembly of the glider stream did not proceed without mishap. Several tug aircraft experienced engine failure, and their gliders had to cast off and make forced landings. One Halifax towing a Horsa carrying a Reconnaissance Squadron jeep returned to Tarrant Rushton, and the glider changed to a reserve tug, but the new combination also had to turn back because it was so far behind the main formation. Most of the glider failures, however, were due to tow ropes breaking. The main cause of this was the low cloud over Oxfordshire through which many of the combinations had to climb soon after take-off. Towing a glider in cloud was like towing a car on the end of a long rope in dense fog. If tug and glider could maintain a steady course and speed, then all went well; but if the tug had to change course – perhaps to avoid another combination appearing in the cloud – then the tow rope might first slacken, then tighten suddenly, and the glider's weight caused the rope to break. Twenty-two tug aircraft lost their gliders, all Horsas, before reaching the English coast. The Dakotas had the most problems, encountering the worst cloud conditions and, only having two engines, being more sluggish in the tow. There was an added difficulty when the Blakehill Farm formation jostled for position in the stream with the Broadwell aircraft, resulting in many violent changes of course. There were no fatal casualties in the resulting forced glider landings, and any gliders damaged would be repaired or replaced ready for take-off again on the second or third lifts.

Failures of this type were always expected on glider operations, but the infantry of the Airlanding Brigade were particularly unfortunate, the Border and the KOSBs losing fourteen gliders. Among key personnel present in the downed gliders were: Lieutenant-Colonel Tommy Haddon, CO of the 1st Border, and part of his headquarters; Major Robert Cain, a South Staffords company commander; Major Philip Tower, brigade major to the CRA; Major H. P. Maguire and most of the division's intelligence staff; and RSM G. Bayford of the glider-pilot No. 1 Wing. There was some initial rejoicing among glider pilots who did reach Holland when it was learned that RSM Bayford had not arrived. Sergeant Bryan Tomblin says:

> We thought we had got rid of him, but word got round that he had come in on the second lift. Then, when I was in POW camp, I thought we had got rid of him again, but a few days later he turned up and started laying down the law. He was known as 'Tojo' because he was such a fierce disciplinarian, but he had made better soldiers of us.

Major Cain later recorded what happened to his glider; it was a typical incident:[3]

> Five minutes after take-off from Manston, I was standing between the two glider pilots when there was a lurch and I saw the tow rope, coiled like a spring, coming back at us from the tug. It struck us with a crack and we could hear it rumbling along the length of the fuselage. Both the Sergeant-Major and I were swearing as we buckled ourselves in. The glider pilot chose a field and a few seconds later there were the usual shouts of 'Hold it!' and 'Whoa-up!' as we bumped over the rough surface. A rending and snapping followed as we tore through a fence and the glider bumped to a standstill. It was a terrible anticlimax after the tension and high spirits of the morning, and I could hear the lads cursing as they unloaded the handcarts and the lightweight motorcycle. One of the glider pilots went off to telephone Manston, and the other examined the tow rope. The Albemarle's end of the rope was intact; the glider pilot said it must have 'pulled out' from the tug, although he did not know how this could be possible. He said it was 'diabolical'; the same thing had happened to him on D-Day.

[3] From his account kindly provided by the Royal Staffordshire Regiment Museum.

Corporal Cyril Crickett's glider of 1st Border men came down in a field near Hatfield after the Dakota tug's engines had overheated:

This was very much an anticlimax and was most disappointing, but we had a wonderful view of the air armada from the ground. The field in which we landed was carpeted with mushrooms so, whilst awaiting transport, we collected rather a large amount and presented them to the cookhouse at Hatfield aerodrome prior to flying back to Broadwell. We then spent the evening listening to broadcasts of the operation and wondering how things were going at Arnhem.

One incident ended in complete tragedy. The account of Sergeant Wally Simpson, tail gunner in a 299 Squadron Stirling which had taken off from Keevil towing a Horsa glider, describes what happened. The combination was flying westwards from Keevil prior to turning and joining the main stream; the pilot of the Stirling was Flying Officer Geoff Liggins, an Australian:

I was watching the Horsa trailing behind when, suddenly, the glider just seemed to part in the middle; it looked as if the tail portion parted from the front. Horrified, I shouted to the skipper, 'My God, the glider's coming apart.' As the tail section of the glider fell earthwards, its front section was still in tow with the Stirling and falling like a rock to earth. As it fell, the tow rope gave way and fell with the glider still attached to it. Had the tow rope not broken when it did, I shudder to think what might have been. It all happened so quickly. Even if we had been able to release the glider, I still doubt to this day if the release mechanism would have functioned correctly due to the weight and angle of the glider. During this time Geoff was fighting to keep the aircraft flying; he did an excellent job under extreme circumstances.

We left the formation and gradually lost height and turned back to locate the wreckage. Noting the spot, we returned to Keevil and then drove by jeep to the crash location. I described it at the time as being 'like a matchbox that had been stepped on'. The bodies of the men had remained inside. I had no way

of estimating how many dead there were. There were no
survivors.

The glider had contained two glider pilots, and five NCOs and
sixteen sappers of No. 1 Platoon, 9th Airborne Field Company,
Royal Engineers. The other half of the platoon was flying in a
glider just below and watched, with understandable horror, the
wreckage floating downwards. Occupants of gliders were not issued
with parachutes. The tail was empty and fell in a roadway; the
main fuselage fell in a field. The cause of the accident was never
established; various explosive devices were being carried, and it is
possible that one of these went off prematurely.[4]

The take-off and assembly of the 143 American aircraft – 140 C-47
Dakotas and three C-53 Skytrains – carrying 1st Airborne's
parachute troops on this day was a simpler and more incident-free
operation. These aircraft had been marshalled on or close to the
runways, ready to take off in 'vics' of three: seventy-two aircraft at
Saltby, seventy-one at Barkston Heath, an impressive sight and a
tribute to American mass production. The 314th Troop Carrier
Group at Saltby took off first, the leading Dakota leaving the
ground at 11.20 a.m. precisely. The entire unit was airborne in just
under ten minutes, circling slowly to close up its formation before
setting out for the first assembly point over March in
Cambridgeshire. Four more groups of the 52nd Troop Carrier
Wing were also taking off. The 61st Troop Carrier Group at
Barkston Heath was carrying the balance of 1st Airborne's parachute
troops; the other groups at Folkingham, Spanhoe and Cottesmore
were carrying troops of the 82nd US Airborne Division bound for
the Nijmegen area drop. This American part of the Arnhem
operation was carried out with almost total efficiency. The records
of the 52nd Troop Carrier Wing indicate that the entire take-off,
assembly and initial flight were carried out without a hitch and that

---

[4] The crash occurred close to the village of Paulton, near Weston-super-Mare, and
the villagers later erected a memorial on the crash site at which a commemorative
service takes place on the nearest Sunday to 17 September each year. The dead were
all buried in the War Plot of Weston-super-Mare Cemetery.

not one aircraft would be forced to return with engine trouble. The only recorded mishap was the inadvertent release of a parachute container – a 'parapack' to the Americans – over England. The mass of aircraft were flying quite low, no more than 1,500 feet above the ground, and, as with the tug-and-glider formations now converging on the final assembly point on the English coast, were an inspiring sight and a source of much speculation to people on the ground on this sunny Sunday morning.

A 'Eureka' beacon, its position shown on navigation charts for this operation as 'Antigua', marked the Arnhem and Nijmegen forces' departure point on the coast at Aldeburgh. The American air groups fell in behind the British tug and glider force which was leading this northern half of the 'Market' air armada out over the North Sea, but the tugs and gliders of Corps Headquarters would fall in behind the American parachute aircraft. The Manston combinations would join in over the North Sea.

The weather was now almost perfectly clear, the sea below calm. It was ninety-four miles to the landfall on the Dutch coast, about forty minutes' flying time. A chain of naval and RAF rescue ships was positioned along the route; the one halfway across had a radio beacon – 'Tampa' on navigators' charts. The twelve Stirlings carrying the Independent Company had to take a slightly different route, leaving 477 aircraft and 334 gliders of the combined Arnhem and Corps HQ force to set out across the sea. The expression 'the sky was black with aircraft' occurs in many men's accounts. Lieutenant George Guyon of the 1st Battalion observed: 'To port and starboard I could see an immense armada of aircraft, some towing gliders, which stretched as far as could be seen; they floated up and down in unison like an outstretched blanket being gently shaken.' All aircraft were supposed to fly at the same speed, but the four-engined Stirlings and Halifaxes tended to push forward slowly through the stream, although the Dakotas towing the Airlanding Brigade's gliders were always in the lead. Glider pilots, sweating in their large Perspex cockpits, were taking it in turns to fly, usually in the 'high-tow' position above the tug's slipstream. The many hundreds of soldier passengers were so heavily laden with equipment, particularly the parachutists, that movement was difficult.

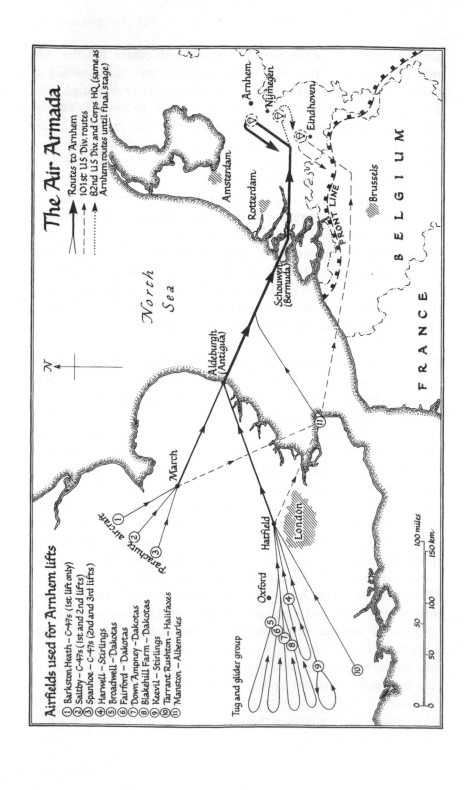

The Air Armada

Airfields used for Arnhem lifts

1. Barkston Heath – C-47s (1st lift only)
2. Saltby – C-47s (1st and 2nd lifts)
3. Spanhoe – C-47s (2nd and 3rd lifts)
4. Harwell – Stirlings
5. Broadwell – Dakotas
6. Fairford – Dakotas
7. Down Ampney – Dakotas
8. Blakehill Farm – Dakotas
9. Keevil – Stirlings
10. Tarrant Rushton – Halifaxes
11. Manston – Albemarles

Routes to Arnhem
101st US Div. routes
82nd US Div and Corps HQ (same as Arnhem routes until final stage)

Parachute aircraft

Tug and glider group

North Sea

Aldeburgh (Antigua)

March

Oxford
Hatfield
London

Schouwen (Bermuda)

Rotterdam
Amsterdam

Arnhem
Nijmegen
Eindhoven

FRONT LINE

Brussels

BELGIUM

FRANCE

N

0   50   100 miles
0   50   100   150 km

They smoked a lot; some slept. Many read paperback books or the Sunday papers bought at the airfields before take-off. Two men of the 3rd Battalion played chess all the way. Some men were frightened, particularly those going into action for the first time or those glider troops who had suffered bad experiences in the Sicily operation when so many gliders came down in the sea. A few men were airsick. Major Alan Bush of the 3rd Battalion says that he was 'the only person to have vomited my way into Europe. I was sick all the way, even though I had flown many times. It wasn't apprehension, because it all went like a practice drop; it was the petrol and oil fumes that did it.'

More gliders fell out of the formation. The tow rope of one broke, and two more had to be released because of engine trouble in the tug aircraft. These three gliders all made safe landings on the sea, and their passengers were quickly picked up by the rescue ships, only one man being injured when the jeep in his glider broke loose. A fourth glider experienced difficulty when its Dakota tug lost power and then surged forward again with the following result, described by one of the glider passengers, Lance-Corporal Stan Livesey of the Scottish Borderers:

The increase in speed whipped the tow rope tight, and that somehow tore a bit out of our port wing near the wing root; the hole extended to the top of the cabin. One of our chaps actually looked out of the hole to report the damage to the glider pilots, and the wind sucked off his red beret. The tug was flying normally now, and we had rejoined the stream, but its engines spluttered once or twice more, and the tug pilot and the glider pilots eventually decided to turn back. We reached the English coast all right, cast off and landed at Martlesham Heath, which was an American base. The amazing thing is that the moment we stopped and opened the door a PX van, with two American girls, was there waiting for us with the coffee and chewing gum – two smashing bits of crumpet they were. Then we were all taken to the officers' mess and fixed up with real ham and eggs.

One interesting experience for part of the Arnhem force was a near encounter with a formation of B-17 Flying Fortresses returning from one of the supporting raids on targets in Holland which had taken place that morning. At first it appeared that the two formations might be on a collision course and the tug aircraft started altering course, even though they, as part of the glider-towing formation, theoretically had the right of way. But the Americans managed to gain height a little and pass safely over the outward-bound formation – 'an awe-inspiring sight', says one glider pilot.

The first fighter escorts appeared, the start of a massive cover that would be provided all the way to Arnhem. A total of 874 fighters – 503 American and 371 RAF, all flying from England – were involved in the escort of the 'Market' formations and in the suppression of any flak guns spotted. The Americans would be the only ones to encounter German fighters in a combat which kept some Focke-Wulf 190s away from one of the other 'Market' formations; the Americans claimed eight of the Germans shot down for the loss of one of their own planes. Not one of the transport aircraft or gliders on any of the 'Market' operations was attacked by a German fighter. But the suppression of flak positions would be more costly to the fighters, with thirteen further American planes and an RAF Tempest being lost.

The head of the formation crossed the Dutch coast at about 12.15 p.m.; the chosen landfall was the lighthouse on Schouwen Island, marked as 'Bermuda' on maps. It was now about 100 miles – forty minutes' flying time – to the Arnhem area. Much of the ground below had been flooded by the Germans to prevent any sea or air landing behind the flank of their front-line positions, which were forty miles to the south, down the coast. Two more gliders dropped out. When one Horsa came down just off the coast, Lieutenant W. G. Beddowe and his KOSB platoon waded ashore to become the first prisoners of war of the Arnhem operation. The occupants of the second glider had a more exciting time. This was a Horsa which was part of the Airborne Corps HQ lift piloted by Captain Wreford Tallentire and carrying an American signals party. The glider's tow rope broke when the Stirling tug flew into a cloud just inland from the Dutch coast. Rather than land in German-held territory, Tallentire was able to glide back to the sea, where he ditched off the island of Walcheren. The nose compartment broke away, but both pilots were able to free themselves and swim back to rejoin the Americans in the main part of the glider, which remained afloat. There now followed the curious experience of a German coastal battery steadily shelling the glider throughout the remaining hours of daylight, but the shells always missing. A British rescue launch, alerted earlier by the Stirling tug, arrived in the evening; this too was shelled but not hit. All aboard the glider were rescued and returned safely to England. Many years later, Captain Tallentire found out why the German shelling had been so inaccurate. The gunners were Russian Armenians pressed into German service. They had deliberately missed the glider and the rescue launch. The Germans executed one of the Armenians after this incident for 'sabotage' and seven more later in the year.[5]

The air armada flew on over Holland, past Breda and Tilburg and on to the last turning-point near 's-Hertogenbosch. There was a little cloud, but this was mostly above the formations, and map reading was easy. Excited Dutch civilians could be seen waving after the flooded area had been crossed. But this was all German-occupied territory, and there was constant danger despite the efforts of the fighters attacking flak batteries; such a mass of low-flying aircraft and gliders in broad daylight would normally have been a flak gunner's dream. It was such a fine day that one of the Horsas carrying South Staffords had been flying with its large side door open; one soldier got up when shells started to burst nearby and slid the thin wooden door shut, to the amusement of his fellows. The side door of each Dakota parachute aircraft had been removed before take-off in case the aircraft was hit by flak and a quick jump had to be made.

Several men in the flimsy gliders were wounded by shell fragments, and there was one fatality. Out in front of the whole formation were three Dakota tugs and Horsa gliders from Broadwell, the tugs flown by senior RAF officers and the gliders by the staff of No. 2 Wing Headquarters. The gliders were all carrying infantrymen of the 1st Border. Several bets had been placed as to who could reach Arnhem first. These leading combinations attracted

[5] Research by P. Pouwels of Elshout, Holland.

several accurate bursts of flak. Padre Chignell, the wing chaplain, was in Staff Sergeant Alec Waldron's glider, kneeling between the two pilots and praying hard. Private Bob Elliott, of the Border, describes what happened in the glider being flown by Lieutenant-Colonel John Place:

> The boys at the back started shouting, 'Cast off! Cast off! The tail's coming off.' The lieutenant who was the glider co-pilot came back and said it was nothing, only minor damage. The two pilots smiled at each other and flew on. But, within five or ten minutes, there was a 'crack' and we were hit again, in the cockpit. The back of the glider-pilot lieutenant's head was all smashed. The blood was running around our feet – what a bloody mess! One or two of them pulled his body on to the floor and just laid him out of the way of the lieutenant-colonel. Tom Watson, our platoon sergeant, was near the front and he was also hit, on the side of the face, but not too badly. He carried on, but was killed four days later.

Private Johnny Peters, another of the Border men, says: 'If I had been frightened before, I was petrified by now, wondering what would happen if Lieutenant-Colonel Place suffered the same fate.'

The death of the lieutenant, Ralph Maltby, had an ironic twist. He had become a glider pilot after serving in the Royal Artillery and was an expert on anti-aircraft fire. Earlier in the war he had flown as a passenger on RAF bomber operations to observe the effects of the German defences and had been decorated with the 'Order of the Patriotic War' by the Russians for some raid which had benefited them. He had often lectured glider pilots on flak, stressing that it was 'nothing to worry about'.

Eight Horsas came down between the landfall on the Dutch coast and their intended landing zone outside Arnhem and at least one from the Corps HQ lift. One was definitely a flak victim, a Horsa with a load of four artillerymen from the Light Regiment with a jeep and trailer. The glider was seen to be hit by flak and to break into two parts; there were no survivors. The occupants of two gliders – a platoon of South Staffords and a gun team from the Light Regiment – which came down north of Tilburg joined up and, together with Dutch helpers and other types of evaders, had many experiences before making contact with Allied forces more than a month later. Two gliders carrying 6-pounder anti-tank guns came down short of their landing zone, but the gunners somehow managed in due course to reach the scene of action with their guns. The parachute aircraft had an almost trouble-free flight, probably because the Allied fighters had pounced on any flak position opening up on the preceding glider formations. Many of the parachute troops who had dropped in Sicily were anxious when flak was encountered in case the American pilots would let them down again, but this time the Americans flew with complete steadiness.

Thanks to Allied air supremacy and the good airmanship of tug and parachute aircraft crews and glider pilots, the first lift of the 1st British Airborne Division had been brought to its destination in good order and without serious loss.

CHAPTER 6

The Morning in Holland

The people of southern Holland had followed the events in France and Belgium over the past few weeks closely. Details broadcast by the BBC of the rapid advance of 200 miles from the Seine to Belgium's frontier with Holland had spread like wildfire, and there had been the visual evidence of a stream of tired and dispirited German soldiers arriving from the south. For a few days early in September it had appeared that the Germans really were beaten and that the longed-for day of liberation was at hand. It was known that British forces had liberated most of Belgium, so it was British troops who were expected to appear. No one thought of an airborne operation; all eyes were on the roads from the south where the British were only seventy miles away. There had been one particular day, 5 September, 'Mad Tuesday', when rumour had flown about that the Dutch border had been crossed in strength and that British forces were streaming into Holland. People were confidently saying that Breda and Dordrecht had already been liberated, but this was the day when the Allied advance ran out of steam, and the Dutch frontier was only reached at one small point.

The rumours persisted for a further day or so. Between Arnhem and Oosterbeek there was a home for retired Catholic priests and lay brothers of the Mill Hill Missionary Society, an Anglo-Dutch order. One of the priests, Father Philip Bruggeman, was keeping a diary:

> *Wednesday, 6 September.* Brothers Philip and Wenceslaus received permission from Father Rector to dig up the bells, so that we can greet the English when they come. Brother Claver, the tailor, will provide the flag. It won't be long now, because the English have advanced as far as Elst. If not today, it will certainly be tomorrow!

Thursday, 7 September. Our wishes have not been fulfilled today; to the contrary, Father Verhoeven, one of the retired priests, just said that all the rumours of the last few days were false. The English were only at Maastricht, nowhere else in The Netherlands.

Friday, 8 September. Last night, at about 11 o'clock, some Germans banged at the door and asked for lodgings. They had come from Northern France with armoured cars but had lost their unit. Fortunately, Father Rector managed to shepherd them into the cobbler's workshop. They left the next morning, giving each of the two lay brothers a bottle of French wine.[1]

A period of uncertainty followed. There was increased air activity. German troops came and went. Fresh flak positions appeared; one battery promptly shot down one of its own side's aircraft. Distant thunderstorms were thought to be gunfire. Many of the schools closed so that children would not be caught away from home if fighting broke out suddenly. Most of the NSB German sympathizers disappeared. Albert Deuss, one of the Arnhem Resistance men, described what happened when an order was received during that time from 'Frank' in Rotterdam to 'keep the railways around Arnhem cut'.

We had received our first plastic explosives from an air drop near Apeldoorn in the middle of the year. We made several attempts to blow up lines after receiving the order, but they all failed. But then one operation was successful and some damage was caused to a railway viaduct over a road just outside Arnhem. There was no serious damage, but the Germans put up posters saying that those involved must give

[1] From the diary kindly provided by Father Bruggeman and translated by Adrian Groeneweg of the Airborne Museum at Oosterbeek. Maastricht, in the extreme south of Holland, had actually been liberated by American troops.

An English nun, Mother Immaculata, was present in the community at that time; because of her advanced age, she was not interned by the Germans. By a coincidence, it was in that week that I started my first term as a student at the Mill Hill Fathers' junior seminary at Freshfield, near Liverpool. That strict establishment did not allow newspapers or radios, so Arnhem was the first major battle of the war that I was not able to follow. It was a surprise and a pleasure to meet the Mill Hill Fathers again at their new home at Oosterbeek.

themselves up to the SD – the Sicherheitsdienst – office in Arnhem by noon on Sunday the 17th, otherwise hostages – the number was not stated – would be taken at random and shot. But it was just before that deadline expired that the bombing raid which preceded the airborne landings took place; the SD never took the hostages and were soon packing up to leave.

Mr Deuss stressed most strongly that the saving of the lives of either the Resistance men or the hostages was 'the only success of the Battle of Arnhem'.

Those bombing raids were an important preparation for the airborne landings later that Sunday morning, the targets attacked being the various barracks known to contain German troops, the airfield at Deelen and all known flak positions. It was not a single, co-ordinated operation. The aircraft involved came from the American Eighth and (it is believed) Ninth Air Forces in England and from the British Second Tactical Air Force now based at forward airfields in France and Belgium. The exact totals attacking the Arnhem area are not known, because unit records for that day contain missions to other targets connected with Operation 'Market'; the bombers probably numbered about 150, together with their fighter escorts. Three aircraft of the 2nd Tactical Air Force were shot down; other losses are not known but were probably light. Deelen airfield and the barracks at Arnhem were obvious targets; the barracks at Ede, ten miles from Arnhem, were included at the request of Brigadier Hackett, whose brigade would be dropping close to Ede on the second lift. The raids all came in mid-morning; local people frequently mentioned that they were at church when the first bombs fell. The barracks at Arnhem were the target of the 2nd Tactical Air Force, which despatched 50 Mosquitoes, 48 Mitchells and 24 Bostons on these and other raids. It is believed that American aircraft of the Eighth and Ninth Air Forces were attacking the other targets.

It was a clear, fine morning, and most of the bombing was accurate. The barracks at Arnhem were well hit and set on fire by Mosquitoes, and the Germans there, from a variety of units, suffered heavy but unknown casualties. Some bombs also fell in the surrounding streets. The nearby Willems Café was hit, but the owner's family in the cellar was unhurt. Closer to Arnhem bridge, the buildings of the Insula Dei Catholic community – a convent, a church and a school – were hit, as too were the nearby prison and the provincial court-house. Much the same thing happened at Ede, where part of an SS Wach battalion (normally concentration-camp guards) and of a marine unit suffered casualties, but where bombs also struck civilian areas. It is known that Dutch casualties at Ede included fifty-nine killed outright, ten dying of injuries later through the bombing and three people shot by the Germans for some reason on that day; these were probably heavier casualties than those suffered by the Germans at Ede. A further thirty-seven civilians died when B-17s bombed a flak battery at Wageningen. The civilian bombing deaths at Arnhem for that morning are not known, being contained in the overall figure of 188 Dutch dead during the entire battle.

The worst tragedy for the Dutch occurred at Wolfheze, where the psychiatric asylum and the village were close by the two landing zones soon to be used by the British gliders. Photographic reconnaissance had shown what appeared to be a flak train equipped with six wagons on which were mounted four-barrelled Vierling 20-millimetre cannons at a railway siding less than half a mile from where the vulnerable gliders would soon be landing. It was also known that German troops were stationed in the asylum buildings. A request was made for these targets at Wolfheze to be bombed, and it is believed that they were allocated to an American B-26 Marauder group of the Ninth Air Force in England. The Americans were unhappy to be given these targets and asked for a written request before they accepted the task; the required letter from Major-General Urquhart duly followed. Cor Janse, a ten-year-old boy at that time, describes what happened:

A lot more people than normal were present. The asylum had taken in extra patients and staff from another asylum in the west of the country, and there were also a lot of people on the run and hiding in the village. There were about 2,000 people, half as many again as usual. There were also extra Germans – from France and Belgium.

There were two bombing runs. The first hit the station area and also left 200 craters north of the station. A second formation came in, and its bombs fell from the centre of the asylum area on into the village. The main building where the Germans were located, the actual hospital building of the asylum, was between the bombing areas and was not hit. About eighty Dutch people were killed, but only a few Germans. The villagers could not understand it. Also no one from the British pilgrimages ever came to Wolfheze and explained why, or to apologize. I lost my whole family and feel very strongly about all this, and about all the fuss made each year at Arnhem and Oosterbeek.

Records show that 46 asylum patients and 44 other civilians died. In another part of the village the home for the blind was hit and burned out; there were no fatilaties, but 'utter chaos' reigned. Books often say that the bombing released the asylum patients from their buildings. This is not correct; the patients were always free to move around inside the grounds. When the Stirlings carrying the Independent Company came over and dropped the 'pathfinder' parachutists, everyone thought that another raid was coming, so both the patients and the village people ran into the woods in all directions. It was those patients who ran towards the west who later stood on the edges of the trees and watched the gliders landing and unloading.

The unhappiest part of this tragedy is that the 'flak train' had been no threat to the landings. There was a wartime branch line from Wolfheze Station to Deelen airfield, and this train had been carrying guns, stores and ammunition back to Germany when the airfield was evacuated earlier in the month, but it had been caught and strafed by Allied fighters while at Wolfheze. The guns were all out of action on the day of the landings, but that could not have been known to the airborne planners. Records show that 46 asylum patients and 44 other civilians died.

The bombings in the Arnhem area made a deep impression on the memories of the local people. Except for a few minutes in February 1944, when an American formation mistakenly dropped its bombs on the edge of Arnhem, no part of the whole area had ever been subjected to bombing or shelling during the war. Now there was the thunder of bombing, first from one direction, then from another, and fighters were swooping down and attacking flak positions and anything else which looked like a valid target. There were no air-raid shelters, and most people huddled in cellars or peered nervously out of windows. Father Bruggeman's diary records:

> The air was full of planes. The English fighters dived down without interruption to seek out targets and to look for any flak positions. A few fighters flew so low along the Amsterdamseweg during lunch that we all dived under the table. We appreciated their activities enormously, but this was rather too much of it. We didn't understand the reason – but not for long!

The air-raid sirens had sounded earlier in the morning in Arnhem, but in the confusion that was soon to follow, the end of the raids was never signalled. As one Dutchman with a sense of humour says: 'We are still waiting for the All Clear.'

CHAPTER 7

The Landings

At 12.40 p.m., exactly on time, six officers and 180 men of the Independent Company started parachuting from the twelve Stirlings which had flown them from Fairford. These planes and their fighter escort had not formed part of the main air armada but had flown by an indirect route, simulating a small bomber force on its way to one of the day's many targets so as not to disclose its destination until the last possible moment. It had been an uncomfortable flight for the parachutists. Few of them had flown in a Stirling before, and fifteen or sixteen men and their equipment had been squeezed into the interior of each aircraft, the men having to sit on the floor of the fuselage. Only one Stirling had been slightly damaged by flak, and there had been no casualties to the occupants. The drop was quickly over, the parachutes soon disappearing behind the trees surrounding the dropping zones from all but immediate eyes. Lance-Corporal Sid Smith, one of the company cooks, says: 'It was a funny feeling coming down on a parachute over enemy territory, in bright sunshine on a Sunday afternoon. I felt a bit of a target.' A few German soldiers were about; two men had bullets pass through their equipment on the way down, and two were injured in heavy landings.

The company had three areas to mark: two glider landing zones, LZ-S and LZ-Z, north and south of the railway line, and one parachute-dropping zone, DZ-X to the west of and alongside of LZ-Z. Each of the company's three platoons had dropped on one of these areas. Part of each platoon immediately 'went defensive' to protect the marking party who set up a 'Eureka' transmitting beacon, laid out the identification letter of the LZ or DZ and a 'T' to denote wind direction in large white panels, and prepared a smoke canister which would also indicate the direction of the wind. The incoming aircraft of the glider force – due twenty minutes after the Independent Company drop – had 'Rebecca' receivers to home in on the 'Eureka' transmissions. These preparations were quickly completed.

The few Germans present quickly surrendered or made themselves scarce. Major 'Boy' Wilson, the company commander, had dropped on LZ-S, close by Reijers-Camp Farm, which was to be his headquarters; his men soon brought in fifteen Germans, mostly horse-transport soldiers based at the farm, caught having their lunch. Lieutenant Hugh Ashmore only saw two Germans when he dropped on LZ-S; they dropped the mess tins from which they were eating and ran off, ignored by the parachutists. Private Alan Dawson says: 'The farmer and his family at Reijers-Camp were delighted to see us. They didn't greet us with champagne and cream buns, but they were obviously pleased. When the gliders did come in, the young German soldiers who were prisoners thought they were dive-bombers and were terrified, running to take shelter among the haystacks.'

The Independent Company had performed its task perfectly, thanks to clear weather, lack of serious opposition and its own skill and training. Leaving only small parties guarding the 'Eureka' beacons, the troops now withdrew to the edges of the open ground from where they were able to watch the fascinating sight of a mass glider landing. There had been no fatal casualties in the unit so far, but one man was killed when the glider carrying the unit's medical supplies was being unloaded later. A loaded rifle, probably with its safety-catch off or loose, went off when it was thrown on to a stretcher, and the bullet went through the neck of the company's medical corporal, Jim Jones. He was buried at the side of a track near Reijers-Camp Farm, in the first of the many little battlefield cemeteries that would be established.[1]

The head of the air armada soon appeared in the distance, flying in from the south-west. The gliders carrying the Airlanding Brigade were due first, all using the northerly of the two landing zones.

---

[1] Reijers-Camp (translation: 'Riders Camp') had formerly been the exercise area for the Dutch Army horse artillery regiment, the 'Yellow Riders', stationed in barracks at Arnhem; it had become a farm when the unit ceased to use it.

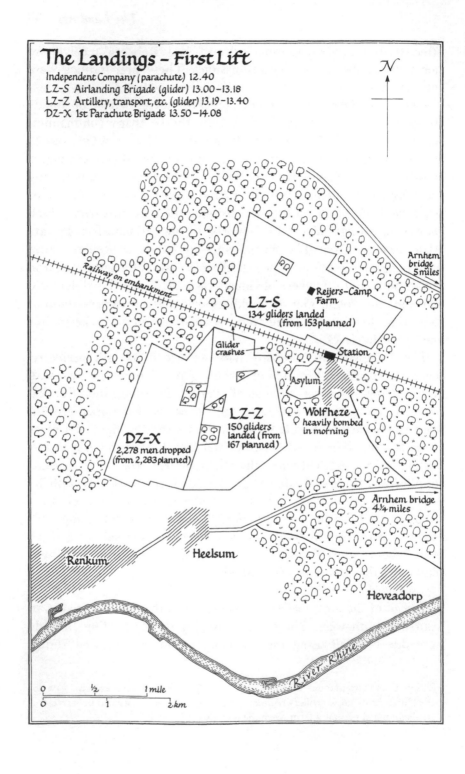

The Landings - First Lift

Independent Company (parachute) 12.40
LZ-S Airlanding Brigade (glider) 13.00–13.18
LZ-Z Artillery, transport, etc. (glider) 13.19–13.40
DZ-X 1st Parachute Brigade 13.50–14.08

N

Railway on embankment

Arnhem bridge 5 miles

Reijers-Camp Farm

LZ-S
134 gliders landed
(from 153 planned)

Glider crashes

Station

Asylum

LZ-Z
150 gliders
landed (from
167 planned)

Wolfheze–
heavily bombed
in morning

DZ-X
2,278 men dropped
(from 2,283 planned)

Arnhem bridge
4¼ miles

Renkum

Heelsum

Heveadorp

River Rhine

0   ½   1 mile
0   1   2 km

After nineteen minutes, LZ-Z, south of the railway, would be brought into use with units arriving in the following order: the 1st Airlanding Anti-Tank Battery in Horsas and Hamilcars, three more Hamilcars carrying Bren carriers, the jeeps of the Reconnaissance Squadron, the vehicles of the 1st Parachute Brigade units and finally the Airlanding Light Regiment and divisional troops. Both landing zones were split up by tree-lined tracks which created a series of smaller sub-areas to which individual units had been allocated. Inevitably there would be some departure from this plan, but conditions were ideal – broad daylight, landing areas free of artificial obstacles, dry and reasonably firm ground and, above all, virtually no opposition – all a far cry from the division's last glider operation to Sicily. Whatever criticism may be levelled at the planners over the distance from the objectives, no better landing zones could have been chosen than those. Forty minutes had been allocated to the glider landing phase, after which the parachute drop would commence.

The glider pilots released their gliders from the tow rope approximately two and a half miles from their intended landing zone. This was the moment when glider pilots could put into effect all their training. Staff Sergeant Trevor Francis of G Squadron had lain awake most of the previous night, going over the theory: 'Cast loose at 3,500 feet. Sink rate at all-up weight of $7\frac{1}{2}$ tons – 400 feet per minute; air speed 83 mph for maximum glide. Time in the air? Go for 2,000 feet at normal glide – therefore five minutes; then the last 1,500 feet medium and full flap – say another one or two minutes.' That was the standard operational approach: a gentle glide after cast-off, then a steeper dive to get through the zone of possible hostile fire, followed by a levelling out just before landing. Staff Sergeant John McGough of C Squadron describes what was probably a typical descent:

Having picked out my particular landing site in a field bounded by woods on two sides and a farm track on the other, I made preparations for the landing. We were at a height of 2,500 feet, and I asked my tug pilot to make one or two slight alterations of course, so that when I cast off I would be in the right area to enable me to land successfully. This he did, and I pressed the red release knob; the tow rope fell away, and the tug flew off, towing it behind. I was now in free flight and flew around for a very short while to plan my final approach and to ensure there was no risk of collision with other gliders. Henry, my co-pilot, must have been concerned, as he said to me, 'For goodness sake, get down; you never know what is going to happen.' I put down half, then full, flap and, as the glider was fully loaded, kept my air speed at about 85 mph and touched down on Dutch soil – not a shot having been fired.

Who was first down? The three pilots from No. 2 Wing HQ who had been vying for that honour believe that Lieutenant-Colonel John Place, with his dead co-pilot aboard, was first, followed by Captain Shuttleworth and Staff Sergeant Waldron, all carrying men of the 1st Border and landing on the western side of LZ-S, north of the railway line. Major Ian Toler, commander of B Squadron, carrying South Staffords, claims to have been the first down on his sector, a mile and a half away on the eastern part of that landing zone. The first pilots to land were supposed to let their gliders run on right to the edge of the landing zone, so that later arrivals had plenty of space in which to land. Staff Sergeant George Milburn of F Squadron describes such a landing:

Being one of the first down on LZ-S, I chose the middle of the landing zone and had an easy landing. It was a good surface; the crop had been harvested, and it was like a field of stubble – probably a hundred-yard run, braking slightly on the last fifty yards. As one of the first in, my job was to get as far forward as possible, so I ran right up to within a few yards of the wood on the western edge of the landing zone. I was conscious of other gliders coming in alongside us. It was just like an exercise and was certainly an unopposed landing. It was so quiet that, after the troops had got out, I stood with the officer in charge of the men in the glider, orientating him and telling him where his RV – rendezvous point – was. He hadn't been able to see out as we came down. Strictly speaking, we should have been down on the ground in a defensive position.

Milburn had landed on the western side of LZ-S where the ground was firm. Major Toler, on the eastern side, found that the ground was soft plough and had the embarrassment of his glider pulling up too quickly, right in the middle of his zone, not at all a textbook landing!

The first gliders all contained infantry platoons, and the occupants were quickly out of the large sliding side door of each Horsa. As soon as it was established that there was no opposition, they hunched up their heavy packs and plodded off to their company rendezvous points on the edges of the landing zones, some hauling handcarts, being watchful on the way for further gliders landing. The rendezvous points of the three airlanding battalions had been chosen with their eventual tasks in mind. The 1st Border went to the railway line running along the south of their landing zone, because they would become responsible for the protection of the landing and dropping zones south of the railway until the second lift had arrived. The KOSBs went to the north, preparatory to moving out to a more distant dropping zone which would be used the following day, and the South Staffords gathered at Reijers-Camp Farm, ready to take over protection of the landing zone on which they had just landed. Major Michael Forman's B Company was the first part of the KOSBs to land, the first members of that battalion to come into action since its formation before the war. He describes his landing:

It was heathery terrain, with ditches. The undercarriage came up through the floor of the glider and everyone was silent and stunned for a moment – everything had stopped moving. The only casualty in my glider was the corporal of my Bren section who got hit by a bullet in his backside. There had been a lot of joking beforehand about the danger of flak, and people were concerned about their backsides, sitting in the glider, and they had said that this chap was most vulnerable because he had a big bum; in fact he was the only casualty in the company.

We got out OK and moved off to the RV – the gliders coming in were whistling past us – terrifying! The battalion RV was by a heap of gravel at the side of a motorway under construction there. It was our company piper, Corporal Ford, who was up on that heap playing 'Blue Bonnets over the Border' for the whole battalion for twenty minutes or so until everyone came in. I found that one of my platoons was missing – I didn't know what had happened to it – and that was annoying because I would be short of a reserve.

It was a typical airlanding-unit experience: just one man wounded, but a complete platoon missing; its glider had come down in England, and the platoon would arrive the next day, though it would not rejoin the company for some time after that. The first impression of Captain James Livingstone, also of the KOSBs, was that 'we had taken off from England, flown across the sea and landed in an area of open ground surrounded by woods. In fact it was just like the country we had just left, round Woodhall Spa in Lincolnshire.'

The glider landing process intensified; they were landing at an average rate of one every nine seconds, and both landing zones became scenes of intense activity. There was hardly any wind into which the gliders could make their final approach, with the result that many pilots overshot slightly. Aerial photographs taken soon afterwards show a large build-up of gliders at the northern end of each landing zone. It was inevitable that there would be some accidents, sometimes with gliders crashing into each other on the ground, but more often as gliders ran on into trees. One photograph shows that six Horsas ran into a small plantation at the north-east end of LZ-Z and were wrecked, and one was in the trees well inside a wood near the Wolfheze Asylum. Another danger was that parts of LZ-Z were unharvested potato fields; gliders frequently dug their nose wheels into the loose soil here and came to an abrupt halt, the tail rising into the air and the nose wheel assembly coming up through the floor of the glider; one Royal Engineer was killed when 'speared' in this way. An artilleryman in another glider, which finished up losing its wheels and skidding along one such patch, remembers 'potatoes flying around the glider like cannon balls'.

Some of the crashes were serious. The pilots of gliders carrying guns or jeeps were in most danger, with the loads behind likely to break their chains and crash into the glider's cockpit. Staff Sergeant Trevor Francis describes a near-disaster:

Just a hundred feet to go; hold the nose up, stall in. Look at those huge furrows! My God! We're down; the tail's coming up, and we're going over. No, kite, you can't! You'll kill us with this load behind. What's happening? My seat's rising; soil is breaking through the nose; my head is touching the cabin roof, and it's going to push me through; it'll break me up. My head is being forced down, and I can hear my neck cracking. Oh, oh!

Stillness. We've stopped, we're safe, but terror hanging above me, those tons of equipment. Will the chains hold? Already I can hear the artillery sergeant cursing as he uses an axe to pound a hole through the side door which is stuck. He's through, and willing hands reach through the cabin door and ease us back off our mound of earth and broken glider. Steve and I stagger out and flop down, physically and emotionally exhausted after three and a half hours of tense flying, plus the nightmare landing.

Up to six glider pilots in Horsas were killed or were so severely injured that they died later. Another lost both legs, and Squadron Sergeant-Major Bill Meadows of the Reconnaissance Squadron fractured his spine when his glider crashed into trees. Sergeant George Barton of the KOSBs describes one of the fatal crashes when his Horsa, loaded with a jeep and a 6-pounder anti-tank gun, crashed into the edge of a wood:

Everything happened in a rush. We were in a dive, then the glider suddenly lifted and the undercarriage caught in the trees. I think the pilot was trying to get over the trees, but everything came to a dead stop. I was flung against the front of the jeep, and my equipment all broke away from me. Fortunately, the jeep was well fastened down, and the gun didn't move either. The glider was nose into the trees with its tail in the air. The driver and I jumped out – about a fourteen-foot drop – and went round to the front to see to the pilots. One was obviously dead, and the other badly wounded around the head and throat from crashing into the Perspex. I gave him some morphia, wrote 'M' for morphia and the time and date on his forehead, and then cleared off. We had been told not to stop for wounded. There was no way we could get the gun out, but I heard later that someone got the jeep out.

The heavier Hamilcars were particularly susceptible to crashes. These gliders had never practised landings in soft soil. They had no nose wheel, and when the wheels sank into the patches of soft soil and stopped abruptly, the nose containing the load went down, the long, light tail came up, and the huge glider was likely to finish up on its back. This was dangerous for the 17-pounder gun crews who were strapped into the towing vehicle and for the Bren carrier drivers, but particularly so for the glider pilots, whose cockpit was situated on top of the glider fuselage, not in the front as in a Horsa. Three of the Hamilcars crashed, two with 17-pounder guns overturning and one hitting the railway embankment and shooting two Bren carriers out of the front; a fourth Hamilcar landed heavily and almost disintegrated. Lance-Sergeant Sid Fitchett was strapped in the driver's seat of the towing vehicle in one of the 17-pounder crashes:

> I can only describe it as a shuddering bump, slight lift in the air and then a crash. We had overturned, and I was left hanging upside-down, my right foot broken and trapped under the brake pedal, my head and face almost covered in what I thought was potato soil, and, to make matters worse, a jerrycan had burst, and petrol was covering me all over. I smelt awful and felt bloody awful. After some time, I felt someone touch me and ask what was wrong. I told him. He tried to release my foot, but I screamed in pain. So he came back with a hand-spike and broke the pedal. He dragged me out and put me on a stretcher on the back of a jeep.

Two glider pilots were trapped in one of the overturned Hamilcars. One was crushed to death, the other badly injured and trapped by the weight of the towing vehicle. Several senior officers, including Colonels Eddie Myers and Graeme Warrack, the division's senior engineer and medical officer respectively, were in attendance, Myers having a 'vivid memory' of the frustration at not having brought a block and tackle for such a situation. It was several hours before the injured pilot was released, but he died later. When Gunner John Winser, who had tried to dig a trench around the injured pilot in an effort to release him, heard that both pilots had died, he was 'very sad because we wanted to congratulate at least one of them on the lovely flight from England'. It is believed that four glider pilots and one artilleryman died in the Hamilcar crashes.

Even after landing safely, those gliders carrying combinations of jeeps and trailers or guns had to be unloaded with extreme care. The standard procedure was for the control wires to the tail to be cut immediately the glider touched down, and then four so-called quick-release bolts securing the tail were carefully unscrewed so that all released at the same time, allowing the tail to drop off and be pulled away. Metal ramps were then laid from the edge of the glider floor to the ground, and the jeep and its trailer or gun were carefully driven down. But if the four bolts were not removed simultaneously, the tail slewed to one side and twisted the whole assembly, or flopped on to the ground if the top bolts released first. If either of these things happened, then the tail had to be removed by a combination of axe, hacksaw, brute force, sweat and bad language. If the glider had dug its nose in, then the even lengthier procedure of removing the vehicles backwards from the sliding side door had to be employed. The average time for unloading gliders with vehicles was about thirty minutes.

It had all gone very well, with only a limited number of accidents – a first-class start to the operation. Of the 320 gliders that had taken off from England, 283 (88.4 per cent) had landed on or close to the landing zones, including the four Wacos with American radio parties which had not been due until the next day. Only a handful of the loads had been lost in accidents, but eleven men – mostly glider pilots – had been killed or would die as a result of landing accidents.

The men of the Independent Company had watched the whole of the landing. Private Alan Dawson found it so orderly that, although impressive, it was almost uneventful. But I remember one glider hitting one of the few trees on the field; the glider struck the tree directly between the two pilots. We rushed over, expecting to see blood and gore, only to hear one of them saying, 'I told you not to put the bloody coffee down there.' Neither pilot was hurt. We watched the gliders being unloaded and the troops moving off to their RVs, but that was all a mystery to us. I was very impressed by how quickly the glider infantry got themselves organized.

Lieutenant Joe Hardy of the Border describes this incident:

On my way to the RV, I came across two very young soldiers who had the idea that everything was so very normal that the obvious thing for them to do was to take off their equipment and brew a cup of tea. I explained, in the way that an ex-sergeant usually explains things – that was, by screaming as loudly as I could – that we were about sixty miles behind the enemy lines, that we were surrounded by German troops, and that this was not really the time for an afternoon tea party. I managed to keep a very straight and very stern face for the few seconds that it took them to get on their way, and as soon as they were out of earshot I allowed myself a good hearty laugh. It was a terrific morale booster to see two kids, who, in a situation of that sort, thought the most important thing was a cup of char.

The parachute aircraft would soon arrive. The commander of each parachute 'stick' and the American aircrew had arranged the timings of the pre-drop preparations before take-off. A preliminary warning was given about twenty minutes before drop time. Each parachutist strapped his kitbag or weapon valise to one leg by a special quick-release fastening, stood up, formed a line, checked the parachute pack of the man in front and then checked his own 'static line' which would pull his parachute open immediately after jumping. A red light came on when there were only five minutes to go, and the stick shuffled forward to close up on the commander who was standing in the doorway waiting for the green light for 'go'.

The first troops should have started dropping at 1.40 p.m. – forty minutes after the first glider landings – but the drop commenced ten minutes late when men started jumping from the leading flight of the 314th Troop Carrier Group, which was led by Lieutenant-Colonel Arthur E. Tappan. Seventy-two C-47 Dakotas of this unit would drop the 2nd Battalion and an RASC platoon from their first 'serial', then the 3rd Battalion and part of 16 Parachute Field Ambulance from the second. The second American formation, seventy-one aircraft of the 61st Troop Carrier Group, made up some of the lost time and would complete its drop by 2.08 p.m., only six minutes late. Its loads would be the 1st Battalion, the 1st Parachute Brigade Headquarters, the 1st Parachute Squadron, RE (Royal Engineers), and parts of Divisional Headquarters and of the Reconnaissance Squadron and of 16 Field Ambulance, together with the Advance Party of the 4th Parachute Brigade, which was due to arrive on the following day.

The dropping zone allocated was DZ-X, an expanse of open ground west of the southern glider landing zone (see map on page 98). It was a large area, up to a mile wide and nearly two miles long. A farm and some small woodlands on the eastern side protruded into the landing zone, but this still left an uncluttered rectangle of ground one and a quarter miles long and half a mile wide. The Dakotas flew in over the village of Renkum and followed the line of a road (the Telefoonweg) which was directly under their heading. Unlike the glider landing, the nearest – southern – part of the dropping zone was used first, with each succeeding flight of nine aircraft dropping their sticks progressively northwards up the zone. The weather remained clear; there was still virtually no opposition; and except for their small delay in arriving, the American airmen performed their role perfectly.

The actual jumping procedure had been practised many times. The nineteen parachutists in each stick had been standing up close together, waiting for the red light to change to green, the senior-ranking man in the stick standing in the doorway, holding on to each side, the second senior rank bringing up the rear of the stick. The American crew chief stood on the far side of the door, ready to help anyone in difficulty, or unhook the static line of anyone who refused to jump. The Dakota had throttled back to fly just above its stalling speed, about 80 to 90 knots, in what was in effect a powered glide, but tail up so that parachutes would not catch on the tail assembly. Height above the ground was only 600 feet at the commencement of the drop; it might be down to 500 feet by the time the last man jumped.

The Dakota's navigator decided the precise moment of the jump, switching the light from red to green and sounding a bell in case the lights failed. It was a moment of great tension. No. 1 in the stick could not see the light. No. 2 could and did two things at once: he smacked No. 1 on the back and pressed a lever releasing the six containers of equipment and reserve ammunition slung underneath the Dakota's wings. Out went No. 1, followed by the rest of the stick moving forward up the aircraft as fast as they could, 'just like a canteen queue – push and shove'. As each man fell away from the aircraft, the static line attached to the interior of the Dakota drew open his parachute and then came free to slap along the side of the aircraft until pulled in by the crew chief after the drop.

Only four men failed to jump. One, an officer's batman in the Reconnaissance Squadron, was lying on the floor of the Dakota, saying that he was sick; the officer came back during the approach, decided it was better to go without him and unhooked his static line. Because the officer did this, it was not classed as a refusal, which would have been subject to disciplinary measures, as would the other three refusals. A fifth man refused to jump on the first run but did so when the Dakota pilot circled back and gave him a second chance.

The average time in the air for each parachutist was a mere fifteen seconds. During this time he had to settle himself under the parachute when it opened, then pull the release on his kitbag or weapon valise and pay it out on the fifteen-foot length of rope so that it hit the ground well before he did and, finally, prepare for his own landing. Corporal John Humphreys of the 1st Parachute Squadron, RE, describes his textbook landing:

> I lowered my kitbag and prepared to land. The last thing that I wanted was a broken limb or back through not paying attention to my landing drill. Head down, shoulders round,

feet together, watch the ground and, up it came in the usual rush, and I made a forward landing and very quickly got out of my parachute harness, took my equipment out of the kitbag, put it on and loaded my Sten gun.

Sapper 'Tam' Hepburn and some friends had eaten a self-cooked meal the previous evening in their billet at Donington:

We had half-cooked over an open coal fire a disgusting combination of grease, soot, cinders and potatoes, washed down with some bottles of Guinness. By the time we were airborne next day, the contents of my innards, compacted with the anxiety of the operational jump, felt like a trampoline going into a spin, but there was nowhere to go for relief, so I just had to endure it. When I was down on the DZ I dropped my parachute and my trousers in almost the same movement and deposited the first Airborne spoor in the Netherlands.

The heavy kitbags which were supposed to be let down on a rope below the parachutist were a frequent cause of trouble. These are typical experiences. Lieutenant George Guyon of the 1st Battalion:

The green light came on, and at this, literally the last moment, my wretched kitbag came adrift, so I clasped it in my arms and stepped out at the despatcher's scream of 'GO!'. The first thing I felt was a violent blow in my face from the kitbag, so I hastily let it go. Looking up, I could see the parachute had opened but realized that my kitbag had gone with my precious reserve of cigarettes, some tea and four mortar bombs.

Private Les True of the 3rd Battalion:

It was my first jump with a kitbag. It had the baseplate of a mortar, plus a lot of other kit; the baseplate alone weighed 45 pounds. I pulled the rope release. It should have been let down through my hands but it didn't; the bag released at the top but not at the ankle; maybe I had not attached it properly.

It just hung down. It all happened very quickly. I hit the ground like a ton of bricks. I may have passed out but when I did come to my senses I could scarcely breathe and I thought I had broken my back.

I looked up and saw hundreds of people in the air and bits and pieces falling all around me. I managed to get a bit of breath back and I think someone took the kitbag off me. I managed to crawl to the edge of the DZ and more or less collapsed there. My back and stomach felt as if I had been kicked by a horse. There were several others there, also hurt on landing.

Many men who had already landed speak of the danger of heavy kitbags hurtling down after coming adrift. There were also the usual crop of injuries sustained by men landing awkwardly or falling into trees at the edge of the dropping zone, but there was only one fatality during the drop. The incident is described by Private Bob Elliott, one of the Border men who had come in by glider and was now sitting on the railway embankment at the northern end of the dropping zone, eating sandwiches and watching the parachute drop:

There was stuff coming down all over the place; as well as the paras, there were containers, cycles, motorcycles, all different-coloured chutes – it was worth seeing. One of the paras came down with a 'Roman candle' – chute not fully opened. We watched him fall, and he hit the ground with a bump about 400 yards away. He was first down in that part; he had left all the others floating down slowly behind him, poor fellow. One or two of our lads thought of going along to have a look, but in the end no one went.

The unfortunate man is believed to have been a private in the 1st Battalion.

The dropping zone was soon a scene of scurrying figures as more than 2,000 men collected their equipment and set off for their rendezvous points. A glider pilot who watched it all says: 'What impressed me was the way they got on with it after landing – no hanging about.' Signalman Bill Jukes was making for the yellow smoke which marked the 2nd Battalion's rendezvous and met his brigade commander 'striding purposefully across my path – we used to call him "Legs" Lathbury – with his batman in tow. He cheerfully called, "Good show, chaps. Give 'em socks", as if we were the school rugger fifteen taking the field. It was the last that most of us ever saw of him.' One man who observed the scene with satisfaction was Major-General Urquhart, whose glider had landed safely in the nearby landing zone and who walked across to watch the parachute drop. Sergeant Michael Lewis, one of the army photographers, quickly went into action taking photographs of Dakotas still arriving and dropping further troops, of the earliest Dutch civilians greeting their 'liberators' and of a Waco glider which had landed on the northern end of the parachute dropping zone, the area given to its pilots when briefed for the second lift.

Each unit had its separate rendezvous on or near the Arnhem side of the dropping zone, each marked by a different-coloured smoke canister. The parachute battalions completed their assembly within an hour of landing. It had been a near-perfect drop. Of the 2,283 parachutists carried, all but four jumped, and only one man had died – a 99.8 per cent success rate. The number of injuries had been reasonable for an operational drop with full equipment. Sapper Arthur Hendy sums it up: 'It was what we called a YMCA drop – just like an exercise, with the YMCA canteen wagon waiting at the end.' Lieutenant Eastwood of the Independent Company, whose platoon had marked the dropping zone, says: 'It was certainly a more successful landing than any of the exercises in which I had done the pathfinding. When the brigade was down, I was able to locate Brigadier Lathbury and obtain his approval to pack up and leave the DZ to rejoin my company.'

The final stages of glider unloading and unit assembly took place. A few Dutch people from the nearby farms were present, and some of the patients from the Wolfheze Asylum who had fled to the woods after the bombing appeared in the trees on the edge of the nearby glider landing zone. Private Fred Hawkesworth of the South Staffords was at his unit's rendezvous at Reijers-Camp Farm when the following charming encounter took place:

Five young Dutch children came running up and stood in a group and sang 'Jingle Bells' to us, but with Dutch words. Then they said, 'Thanks for coming; pleased to see you' – at least that's what their attitude and words seemed to mean. They stood and watched our platoons form up and move off, waving us on our way. I thought it was a nice greeting to start us off with.

The first German prisoners were taken, usually without much of a fight. Lance-Corporal Ken Hope of the Reconnaissance Squadron had been sent to find helpers to remove the jammed tail of his glider:

I tucked the butt of the Bren under the right armpit and strode off towards the woodland fringing the landing zone . . . Four German soldiers approached me, all wearing field service caps, hands clasped above their heads. I assumed that someone had disarmed them, as they had no escort. I could imagine some harassed NCO presented with the problem of prisoners to guard saying, 'Go on; bugger off down there.' They were dismayed, nervous and quite overawed by this sudden turn of events. Their peaceful Sunday afternoon had been rudely shattered. I stared at each one in turn, attempting to give the impression that this situation, for me at any rate, was everyday routine. 'Raus! Raus!' Germans always got a move on when someone bawled this from the cinema screen. They responded, quickening their pace and moving down the path. I felt a trifle sorry for them.

Suddenly, I was aware of two bodies lying to one side of the path below the shading branches of a large tree. They were stretched side by side, an army blanket covering them from view, only the webbing anklets and ammunition boots protruded. Incongruously, I found myself mentally checking whether the boots were shod with the regulation thirteen studs. I paused awhile, experiencing a wave of unpleasant nausea. It was a curious and unexpected reaction, probably induced by my own nervous excitement. Later, I was to see men torn and rent, and remain quite unmoved.

I continued my walk and reached the open heathland. A jeep came roaring and bumping over the turf. It wheeled on to the path, the driver steering towards the heath. The occupants were all Americans wearing their familar olive–drab battle uniforms. They were armed with the much-coveted Garand carbines, and the jeep was decorated with swishing wireless aerials. I wondered whether their glider had joined the wrong formation and should have made a landing with one of the American divisions further south. I never saw them again.

The Germans were unable to make any serious attack against this sudden descent from the sky during that vulnerable hour and a half of the landings, although a few individual efforts took place. Only four men were killed by German fire on or around the landing area, two each from the Border and the South Staffords. This made a total of only seventeen British deaths during that vital landing period: eleven from glider accidents, one parachute death, one firearm accident and four by enemy action.

Those units with journeys to make prepared to set out along the pathways and tracks leading to Arnhem. Most did so in good order, though there were some changes in the minor units attached to the parachute battalions. Each battalion was supposed to have one troop of four 6-pounders from the anti-tank battery that had landed, but in the rush to get off, an extra gun team attached itself to the 2nd Battalion column. Two RASC platoons had arrived, one mainly by parachute to accompany 1st Parachute Brigade Headquarters, which was about to move off towards Arnhem, the other by glider and due to remain with the Airlanding Brigade at the landing area. But the parachute platoon was slow in assembling, and its commander asked the other platoon commander to exchange roles. It was by such hurried decisions that the gun team and the RASC platoon would find themselves at the Arnhem bridge, the survivors all to become prisoners of war, instead of adhering to their original roles, which would have given them a chance of evacuation at the end of the battle. The glider pilots now assumed their ground role. Some were formed into self-contained infantry units – identifiable by the large rucksacks which glider pilots carried instead of the normal infantry webbing equipment – and marched away. Other glider pilots were ordered to stay with the artillery units they had brought from England, to provide local protection parties, and would ride away on jeeps with the gunners. Again, random allocations would lead to life or death, imprisonment or return home.

The Airlanding Brigade units, Divisional Headquarters and part of the Light Regiment did not depart. They were all to remain close by the landing area until the second lift arrived. And so Major-General Urquhart's command, after its spectacularly successful landing, prepared to split into two, never to be reunited. Except for the last few men still trying to release the trapped glider pilots in the overturned Hamilcar or jeeps in crashed Horsas, and some RASC jeeps and trailers collecting ammunition from the containers dropped by the Dakotas, the landing and dropping zones became deserted.

The tug and parachute aircraft were on their way home. The tug aircraft had been given a 'tow-rope-dropping' area, well away from the landing zone and from towns, so that the heavy ropes and metal locking devices would not harm anyone, but some of the tugs were observed releasing the ropes soon after their gliders had cast off, in order to be rid of the cumbersome drag. The returning aircraft suffered no serious incidents. One Stirling of 620 Squadron force-landed in England but so close to its airfield at Fairford that the crew were able to walk the remaining distance. The crews were debriefed but could give little information about the ground operation. Some RAF pilots fulfilled promises to telephone the wives or girlfriends of glider pilots and could mostly report that the gliders had been released in ideal conditions. The Operations Record Book of 620 Squadron recorded that 'a number of war correspondents who were carried in the aircraft gave glowing and not entirely accurate accounts of their experiences'.[2]

Not one of the aircraft on the Arnhem lift had been lost; only seven RAF and five American aircraft had been damaged, only one of the Americans seriously. No casualties among the aircrews were

[2] Public Record Office AIR 27/2134.

reported. It was the end of a first-class air operation which, at least as far as the air forces were concerned, justified the planners' choice of route and landing areas; almost the entire force would be available for the second lift.

The American air units carrying the 82nd and the 101st US Airborne Divisions were not so fortunate. No less than thirty-five C-47s were lost, twenty-seven of them from the 53rd Troop Carrier Wing which was caught by unsuppressed flak batteries, mostly after dropping their loads of parachutists near Eindhoven. Two American generals – Lewis Brereton, the overall commander of 'Market', and Matthew Ridgway, whose Airborne Corps Headquarters had no part to play in the operation – each flew in a B-17 Flying Fortress bomber to observe all three of the divisional drops. Brereton had a close shave from flak near Grave, but Ridgway enjoyed himself by manning one of the nose guns in his Fortress and letting fly at targets on the ground.

CHAPTER 8

The Vital Hours

So far, so good. Approximately two-thirds of the 1st British Airborne Division and its equipment had been lifted from England and landed more than sixty miles behind the German lines, almost without loss and without being immediately engaged by the Germans. But, because of the refusal of the air planners to fly two lifts on this first day, only one brigade of infantry was free to move towards the division's objectives. Before showing how the 1st Parachute Brigade tackled that task, it would be useful to describe how the Airlanding Brigade secured the immediate surroundings of the landing area by capturing the villages of Wolfheze and Heelsum, which were just to the east and south respectively. D Company of the 1st Border had little trouble taking Heelsum, surprising a truck containing German soldiers, killing two and capturing the remainder without itself suffering any casualties. Wolfheze was cleared by two platoons of the South Staffords; there were more Germans in Wolfheze, and the two South Staffords killed that day may have met their deaths in the village. These were the first communities to be 'liberated' in this central part of Holland, and despite the morning's bombing in Wolfheze, a warm welcome was given to the airborne men. Among the many troops in Wolfheze that afternoon were the glider pilots of E Squadron, some of whom were sent into the grounds of the asylum; they found there some opened safes and a crate holding bundles of German, Dutch and French paper money, the contents of a German pay office which its elderly paymaster had only partially burned. Many of the notes finished up stuffed into the pockets of the glider pilots' smocks. One, Sergeant 'Andy' Andrews, returned home after the battle and took the notes to the Bank of Scotland in Dundee, where they were changed into sterling without question 'as if it were a normal daily event'.

The little railway station at Wolfheze became a centre of activity, with many airborne men arriving there from the landing area. One particularly pretty girl – believed at the time to be the daughter of the station master, though this was not so – attracted a lot of attention, including those of 'a ginger-haired war correspondent'. The flak train wrecked in the bombing is frequently mentioned, and a store of twenty-one brand-new 105-millimetre German guns, still in their factory grease, was discovered; they were put out of action by being 'spiked' with hand grenades exploded in the breech by Royal Engineers of No. 1 Platoon, 9th Field Company. The RAMC men of 181 Airlanding Field Ambulance established a Dressing Station and started treating injured and wounded men in some houses on the Duitsekampweg. (This lane was so named because it led to a camp for First World War German internees which had probably been located on LZ-S, where the gliders had just landed.) Brigadier Hicks set up his Airlanding Brigade HQ in a house on the same lane. Also functioning was an office set up by the Divisional Intelligence Section where the first six prisoners of war were being interrogated within an hour of the landing.

Battalion Krafft

The first set-back, small but significant, took place on the road running south-east out of Wolfheze. In the woods alongside the road stood the Hotel Wolfheze. Brigadier Hicks had ordered part of No. 1 Platoon, 9th Field Company, to form a block on this road 'to catch any birds flushed out of Wolfheze' by the South Staffords. But this platoon had lost a third of its strength in the fatal glider crash in England, so the duty was allocated to a section of No. 2 Platoon under the command of a young lieutenant, Roy Timmins. On approaching the hotel, Timmins and his men encountered a strong party of fully armed German combat soldiers; Timmins was killed, and two of his men were so badly wounded that they died the following day.

The Germans who had killed Lieutenant Timmins were from No. 2 Company, SS Panzer Grenadier Depot and Reserve Battalion 16, usually known for short as Battalion Krafft after its commander,

Sturmbannführer (SS Major) Josef Krafft.[1] This unit was not a full-strength battalion, and Krafft's men were not all fully trained. It was the German custom to send partially trained recruits to the occupied countries so that they could complete their training and at the same time act as defence units in those countries. Krafft and his battalion HQ, two recruit companies and various other elements had come to this part of Holland from a location on the coast in early September to strengthen the German presence around Arnhem; a third company was being formed, bringing the unit's total strength on the morning of 17 September to 306. The officers and NCOs were all veteran soldiers, but most of their men were young recruits, although every one was of pure German stock and full of SS zeal. Krafft's war diary refers to the excellent training in 'world philosophy', i.e. Nazism, imparted by the unit's political officer, Obersturmführer Rauli, who would die for his ideals within the next few days. Part of the unit was based in Arnhem, the remainder in Oosterbeek.

On the morning of the airborne landings, the battalion's No. 2 Company had been carrying out a training exercise in the woods between Oosterbeek and Wolfheze and was now at the Hotel Wolfheze; its men had killed Lieutenant Timmins. Krafft himself was in Arnhem, where he had brought the remainder of his unit to readiness after the preliminary air raids. Every German unit had been given instructions on what action to take immediately an airborne landing occurred. When the glider and parachute landings were reported, Krafft realized that his was the nearest unit with a fighting capability to the landing area. He judged that a force as large as that reported landing – estimated at between 3,000 and 4,000 strong (even that was a low estimate) – could only have as its objective something as important as the local Rhine bridges, particularly the road bridge in Arnhem. There were four possible routes that the airborne force could use: the main Amsterdam–Arnhem highway in the north, the railway line, the Utrecht–Arnhem road and the minor road in the south along the bank of the Rhine. Krafft did not have sufficient strength to block all four routes. He decided that the two central ones, the railway line and

---

[1] Krafft's war diary is one of the most detailed German documents surviving from the Arnhem battle, but it needs to be used guardedly because it was written to impress his SS superiors and contains some exaggerations.

1. Members of HQ Company, 1st Parachute Battalion, having tea and sandwiches alongside C-47s of the 61st Troop Carrier Group at Barkston Heath just before taking off for Arnhem.

2. Glider pilots of A Squadron wave off colleagues flying a Horsa on the first lift. The glider was either carrying part of Corps HQ to the landing zone near Nijmegen or an RASC jeep and trailer to Arnhem. Most of the spectators would fly on the second lift.

3. An Albemarle lifts off with a Horsa from Manston.

4. Men of the 1st Battalion's Mortar Platoon give 'thumbs-up' or 'V-signs' for the benefit of one of the official photographers flying in their C-47 on the first lift.

5. Gliders on the north-eastern corner of LZ-Z. Three large Hamilcars (marked with crosses) have landed safely, but five Horsas have run on into the trees and bushes. The trees at the right-hand side of the LZ form part of the grounds of the asylum, and it would have been from there that patients emerged to watch the landing.

6. A 'vic' of three C-47s over DZ-X. The green light has gone on a little later in the left-hand aircraft; it has just released its four supply containers before the stick of parachutists start to jump.

7. Parachutists coming down on DZ-X and among gliders on the edge of LZ-Z.

8. Having been unloaded down the ramps from the rear of their Horsa, Lt-Col Thompson (carrying haversacks), CO of the 1st Airlanding Light Regiment, RA, and his party of signallers and glider pilots prepare to depart. Signalman Desmond Wiggins is trying to make contact with other parts of the unit. (I have always wondered what the complete message chalked on the nearby glider was; Boston – my home town – was the regiment's base before Arnhem.)

9. Men of the 1st Battalion take temporary cover in a bomb crater near Wolfheze before starting their move towards Arnhem on Sunday afternoon.

10. A low-flying Spitfire photographs the ramp of the Arnhem road bridge littered with the vehicles of the 9th SS Panzer Division's reconnaissance unit destroyed in the Monday-morning attack. The angle of the shadows indicates that the photograph was taken that afternoon. Not one of the defenders is to be seen in the open; they are all in buildings which, as yet, show no signs of battle, or in weapons pits. The large building, part of which can be seen in the bottom left-hand corner, is Brigade HQ.

11. Fresh troopers of the 9th SS Panzer Division prepare to go into action on the blocking line near the museum, probably during the Tuesday fighting.

the Utrecht road, were more important because the British would probably take the most direct route to their objective; a marked map found on a British motorcyclist captured in mid-afternoon seemed to confirm that decision. Krafft issued his orders. No. 2 Company at the Hotel Wolfheze was to attack the landing area at once. 'We knew from experience,' the war diary says, 'that the only way to draw the teeth of an airborne landing with an inferior force is to drive right into it.' But the war diary then goes into a flight of fantasy in reporting that No. 2 Company subsequently sent its heavy machine-gun section into action on the glider landing zone north of Wolfheze: 'This created great confusion and wreaked great havoc. The troops from about four gliders were completely wiped out and the gliders shot to pieces.' Nothing of the sort took place.

Krafft's subsequent moves were more effective. He ordered Nos 2 and 4 Companies to form a north–south blocking line just east of Wolfheze, covering the railway line and the Utrecht road lines of possible approach to Arnhem (see map on page 122). He brought up his battalion headquarters and established it at the Hotel Wolfheze, in the centre of the line. Some Dutch 'terrorists' deemed to be interfering with part of these moves were 'suitably dealt with'. By his swift and decisive action, Krafft had his men in position by 3.30 p.m., an hour and an half after the end of the landings and just before the units of the 1st Parachute Brigade set out towards Arnhem. By gathering every possible extra man, the German battalion now numbered 435. The number of men in the British units setting out from the landing area towards Arnhem was about 2,000. Rarely can the disposition of a small force such as Sturmbann-führer Krafft's have had such an effect upon a battle.

1st Parachute Brigade Plan

Brigadier Gerald Lathbury's 1st Parachute Brigade contained the senior and most experienced parachute units in the British Army. The brigade's primary task, in what remained of this day, was to seize the road bridge over the river Rhine in Arnhem.

It is time to introduce the concept of the 'brigade group', a term little known outside military circles. The force about to be sent to

Arnhem contained several further units besides Lathbury's Brigade Headquarters and the three parachute battalions under his command. Also taking part in the coming action would be the 1st Parachute Squadron and part of the 9th Field Company of the Royal Engineers, most of the 1st Airlanding Anti-Tank Battery, 16 Parachute Field Ambulance, No. 3 Platoon of 250 RASC Company and at least two forward artillery observation officers with each battalion and at Brigade HQ together with some glider pilots and various other personnel. The whole force would form four columns, those of the three battalions and of Brigade HQ. That was the 1st Parachute Brigade Group, capable of independent action and embarking now on the task of capturing the Arnhem bridges.

Lathbury had had an initial major decision to make – whether to concentrate his brigade on one single route and attempt to smash through to Arnhem by that one route, or to split it between the various major routes and the many wooded tracks available to him. His choice depended upon whether opposition was likely to be light or heavy; in England he had been told that it would be light, and Lathbury had decided to send his three battalion columns by separate routes. This was an 'advance on a broad front' policy, planned to achieve maximum speed, rather than the whole brigade proceeding by one route in a long column which might become unwieldy. If serious opposition was encountered, however, the single battalion columns might not be strong enough to break through and keep up the momentum of advance which was vital. In the absence of detailed knowledge of where the German defences might be, however, Lathbury hoped that at least part of his brigade might slip through to the road bridge and hold it until relieved by the rest of the division. The main weakness of the plan was that nothing was held back in reserve in case of any serious set-back, although one battalion would not be allowed to set off until he heard that the other two were well started. All of these moves were to be preceded by an attempt by most of the Reconnaissance Squadron to motor, initially by minor tracks, straight through to the road bridge and attempt to seize it as a *coup-de-main* force and hold it until the first of the battalions arrived having covered nearly seven miles on foot, carrying full kit and probably having to fight Germans on the way.

*

This, then, was the detailed plan which Lathbury had made in England:

1 The Reconnaissance Squadron (less one troop retained as divisional reserve) and No. 3 Platoon, 9th Field Company, to drive to the Arnhem road bridge by the northern route (code-named 'Leopard'), remove any demolition charges and hold until relieved.
2 The 2nd Parachute Battalion, with a troop of 6-pounder anti-tank guns and some Royal Engineers, to take the southern, minor road along the north bank of the Rhine (code-named 'Lion' route) to capture the Arnhem road bridge and the railway bridge over the Rhine near Oosterbeek, and to establish one company in a defensive position south of the river in the road-bridge area.
3 The 3rd Parachute Battalion, augmented as the 2nd Battalion but with fewer Royal Engineers, to take the main Heelsum–Arnhem road (code-named 'Tiger' route) into Arnhem and assist the 2nd Battalion to capture and hold the road bridge.
4 The 1st Parachute Battalion, augmented as the 3rd Battalion, to be held back until released by the brigade commander and then to follow the Reconnaissance Squadron on the northern route, turning off later to secure some high ground north of Arnhem.
5 Brigade Headquarters to follow the 2nd Battalion route to a position in Arnhem close to the north end of the road bridge; also in or following this column would be most of the 1st Parachute Squadron, the RASC platoon, the headquarters of 1st Airlanding Anti-Tank Battery, a Military Police field security section, and 16 Parachute Field Ambulance, which was to drop off at St Elizabeth Hospital in Arnhem.

How Brigadier Lathbury and the men of these units would perform in the remaining hours of daylight on that Sunday almost certainly represents the most important part of the Arnhem story. I will attempt to deal with the actions in this period in the detail and with the care which they merit. Nothing less than the ultimate success of Operation 'Market Garden' rested on the ability of the Reconnaissance Squadron and the 1st Parachute Brigade Group to capture and hold the Arnhem road bridge.

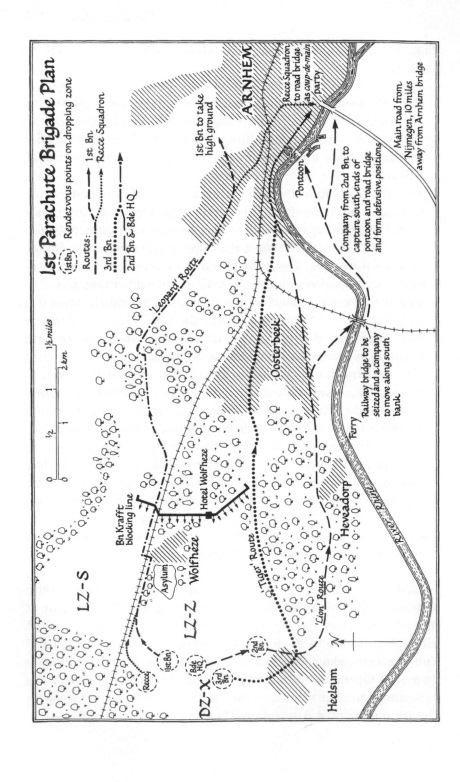

The Reconnaissance Squadron

The first part of Brigadier Lathbury's plan was the despatch of most of the armed jeeps of Major Freddie Gough's Reconnaissance Squadron direct to the Arnhem road bridge. The squadron was a divisional unit allocated to Lathbury's command for this period only; this was not a role for which it had been formed or trained. Gough had wanted to use each of his three troops (each containing eight jeeps) to scout ahead of the three parachute battalions setting out on foot for Arnhem – the unit's normal role. But Lathbury, who had been denied the opportunity to land any of his brigade closer to the bridge as a *coup-de-main* party, intended to use these speedy vehicles as a substitute, and the plan was imposed on Gough. Four jeep loads of sappers from the 9th Field Company were supposed to accompany the column, to disarm any explosive charges found on the bridge, but they never appeared, having been delayed by the slow unloading of gliders and the reorganization process which the company was undergoing after losing the glider that had crashed in England.

The Reconnaissance Squadron had landed in two parts, the jeeps and drivers by glider, most of the troopers by parachute, but a good rendezvous had been made. There were some absences due to one glider casting off over England and two others crashing on landing, but most of these incidents affected A Troop, which was intended to remain behind in divisional reserve. It would be about eight miles from the rendezvous along the intended route to the bridge, less than half an hour's drive. The leading vehicles would be the two jeeps of Lieutenant Peter Bucknall's section from C Troop, so this twenty-three-year-old officer from Birmingham and his nine men should have been the spearhead of the 1st Airborne Division's advance to secure its objective. But the move did not go according to plan. This is the personal account of Trooper Arthur Barlow, normally the wireless operator in Lieutenant Bucknall's jeep:

We had landed by parachute and were at the RV waiting for the jeeps. Lieutenant Bucknall was very impatient; he knew we should be first off. The second jeep arrived first, but not Bucknall's. Most of the others were ready, and Bucknall was very impatient; his language would not be printable; he was furious. So, he took the second jeep, turning the driver out and taking the wheel himself, and telling me to stay behind and wait for No. 1 jeep, which had the wireless. We were at least half an hour late. Bucknall set off, bumping along the track towards Wolfheze, and went out of sight. It was four or five minutes later before the other jeep turned up and we followed, with Lance-Sergeant McGregor in charge. The other sections followed us; they had all assembled properly and they moved off at the proper intervals, within hand-signalling distance of each other, but Lieutenant Bucknall's jeep was five minutes ahead of us and out of sight.

We met no military along the way to Wolfheze, just civilians waving to us from windows or gardens; we didn't stop to speak to anyone. We weren't worried about encountering any resistance; we had been told there would be little opposition. We were hoping that it would be quiet like that all the way through to the bridge. We went over the railway crossing at Wolfheze and turned right, down a track alongside the railway. Then two things happened almost at once. We heard heavy firing from in front, where we assumed the first jeep was, and, at the same time, we were fired on from the top of the railway embankment up the road on the right.

Reg Hasler was driving and immediately stopped the jeep, which had taken a direct burst of machine-gun fire across the radiator. Jimmy Pierce, Tom McGregor and myself ran to the road verge on the right-hand side of the jeep. Dicky Minns, Hasler and 'Taffy' Thomas were to the left of the jeep and partly beneath it. Heavy machine-gun fire continued. Minns, being more exposed, had his hip shattered and other wounds, and lay in the road bleeding profusely, calling for help. Thomas was hit in the foot, while Hasler was hit in both legs and unable to move. On our side of the road, McGregor was to my left, about four or five feet away. He raised himself up on his hands to have a look around and died immediately, falling flat on his face without making a sound, killed by a burst of machine-gun fire in the face and chest. I could have reached out and touched him, and did so later, shaking his shoulder and saying, 'Come on, Mac.'

*

Arthur Barlow and the other survivors continued to exchange fire with the Germans; one shot hit the cocking handle of his Sten gun and another hit him in the thigh. After about half an hour, someone waved a piece of white cloth, and the Germans came and gathered up their prisoners. A German NCO, speaking in perfect English, promised that the severely wounded Minns would be looked after, and the other prisoners were taken away.

Lieutenant Bucknall and the three other occupants of the leading jeep were all dead. The jeep was found by the British the next day at a place where the track ran through a wooded rise; their bodies had been hit in their backs by bullets and were scorched by a flame-thrower in the front. Either the jeep had been travelling so fast that it was past the leading German troops before being fired upon, or the Germans had decided to wait until a second jeep was in sight before firing and exposing their positions. It is not known at what stage the flame-thrower was used.

The remainder of C Troop, under Captain John Hay, could only see what had happened to the second jeep. Hay ordered that the next section should dismount from their jeeps and attempt to move forward on foot – a standard tactic often practised – but the Germans were too strong for such a small force, and it was driven back with two men mortally wounded. So the Reconnaissance Squadron's effort was completely halted less than half a mile after leaving the safety of Wolfheze. Seven men were dead or would die later; four were in German hands.[2]

---

[2] When the dead were recovered the next day and buried near the dressing station which had been set up at Wolfheze, the flame-thrower-burned body of Trooper Ted Gorringe was wrongly identified as that of Trooper Arthur Barlow because of the earlier changing of places in the leading jeeps. When it became known that Barlow was a prisoner of war, that body was classified as 'An unknown British soldier'. It was not until 1987 that Arthur Barlow, with the help of Jan Hey, a Dutch expert, was able to convince the Commonwealth War Graves Commission that it was Trooper Gorringe's grave, and a new headstone was erected over it. Six of the graves are still together in the Arnhem Oosterbeek War Cemetery, in Plot 16, Row B.

The Germans did not come back for the badly wounded Trooper Minns, who had been hit by one bullet in the pit of the stomach which came out through his hip and a second which entered his side and came out through his leg. Minns lay out there all afternoon, evening and night. He tried to crawl to Wolfheze but only managed a few yards before becoming unconscious. He was found and recovered

The Reconnaissance Squadron had been very unlucky. It had encountered the northern end of the Battalion Krafft blocking line which had only just been established. If the jeeps had set off on time, they might have been through before the Germans set up their defence line. If they had taken a more northerly route from Wolfheze, they would easily have outflanked the line. As it was, the squadron had been denied the chance to carry out its proper role of scouting ahead of the parachute battalions and had failed, with tragic loss, in the role imposed upon it. The first attempt to reach the Arnhem bridge had failed almost before it started. Battalion Krafft's war diary recorded the encounter with brevity and exaggeration: 'The enemy has reconnoitred on No. 4 Company front and is attacking with two-company strength. Our advance defences beat him off and took prisoners.' No attempt was made to send either of the Reconnaissance Squadron's remaining two troops, at least thirteen of whose jeeps were available, to the bridge.

The Divisional Commander

All three of Brigadier Lathbury's parachute battalions were already on the move before the Reconnaissance Squadron action. At 3.0 p.m. Lathbury ordered the 2nd and 3rd Battalions to move off by their respective routes (see map on page 122); both battalions did so, their leading companies out in front, moving tactically, then the marching men of the other companies and the jeeps of the battalion and of the various attached units making a long column behind.

Brigadier Lathbury should now have heard that the Reconnaissance Squadron had started its move, but the liaison officer from that unit who should have reported failed to appear, and the only message received indicated that the squadron 'had lost most of its transport' – presumably either through their gliders having failed to

---

next morning by men of his own unit, but was wounded again during the siege at Oosterbeek, was in hospital for two years after the war and crippled for thirty-five years until the Parachute Regiment Association arranged admittance to the Military Hospital at Woolwich for a replacement hip: 'I jokingly asked the surgeon if he could add two and a half inches to my leg, and he did so. It was marvellous; I threw away my built-up boot and caliper.'

arrive or through being trapped in crashed gliders. In fact, twenty-eight of the squadron's thirty-one jeeps had survived the flight and the landing; it was their delay in assembly that was the cause of their slow start.[3] The brigade commander now made every effort to hurry his battalions forward even faster. The 1st Battalion, held as a possible reserve, was released and ordered to move off as quickly as possible along the northern route chosen for it. Lathbury sent wireless messages to the 2nd and 3rd Battalions, telling them of the supposed Reconnaissance Squadron failure and suggesting that each battalion mount a company on all available jeeps and rush them through to the Arnhem road bridge, advice that was ignored by both battalion commanders. Lathbury then dashed off with his Intelligence Officer, Captain Willie Taylor, by jeep to visit his battalions. He soon caught up with the 2nd Battalion and urged them to even greater speed before setting off for the 3rd Battalion. The Brigade HQ column, commanded by Major Tony Hibbert, was now also on the move, following close behind the 2nd Battalion. The approximate timetable of this sequence of events was thus:

2.10 p.m.	Parachute drop complete
2.45 p.m.	All parachute battalions at RVs and on brigade wireless net
3.0 p.m.	2nd and 3rd Battalions set off
3.0 p.m.	Reconnaissance Squadron fails to set off
3.20 p.m.	Reconnaissance Squadron 'has lost its transport' report circulates
3.30 p.m.	1st Battalion ordered to move; Brigadier Lathbury leaves his HQ
3.35 p.m.	Reconnaissance Squadron finally leaves its RV
3.45 p.m.	1st Parachute Brigade HQ and other units set off
3.45 p.m.	Reconnaissance Squadron halted by German opposition

Brigadier Lathbury was not the only commander to be thrust into

---

[3] The story of the Reconnaissance Squadron losing most of its transport found its way into official reports and persisted in post-war books until 1978 when John Fairley's *Remember Arnhem*, Peaton Press, Bearsden, Glasgow, was published, a well-researched account of the Reconnaissance Squadron at Arnhem.

movement by the Reconnaissance Squadron's misfortune. Major-General Urquhart, the divisional commander, was visiting the Airlanding Brigade HQ when he heard news of a set-back, probably news of the actual action not far away on the other side of Wolfheze, not the false report about the Reconnaissance Squadron's jeeps. Urquhart was spurred into action. He wanted to arrange with Major Gough, the Reconnaissance Squadron commander, a fresh attempt by the squadron's jeeps to reach the bridge. He attempted to contact Gough on the wireless set of his jeep, but the Reconnaissance Squadron had been placed under command of the 1st Parachute Brigade for this day, and its headquarters set was on the brigade net, not the divisional one; so Gough could not be reached, even though he was then only three-quarters of a mile away on the other side of Wolfheze. Urquhart left orders at both the Airlanding Brigade HQ and his own headquarters that Gough was to be found and was to come to Urquhart.

Roy Urquhart then made a bad mistake, if an understandable one. He was commanding his first divisional battle and was as aware as anyone else of the need for speed. The thought of Divisional Headquarters and himself playing a static role for nearly twenty-four hour~ until the arrival of the second lift must have been intensely frustrating. He took his jeep, with its driver and wireless operator, invited Lieutenant-Colonel Robert Loder-Symonds, the divisional artillery commander, to accompany him and went off to look for Brigadier Lathbury so as to urge more speed on Lathbury's battalions, even though such a journey, at about 5.0 p.m. now, entailed a drive into comparatively insecure territory and he was travelling without an escort.

Urquhart encountered no danger, however. Following the southern route, he met Lathbury's Brigade HQ column and the rear of the 2nd Battalion, but not Lathbury, who had by now moved on to the 3rd Battalion. Tony Hibbert, the Brigade Major, has the vivid memory of Urquhart shouting out as he raced away: 'Hibbert, for God's sake get your brigade moving or the bloody Germans will get to the bridge before us.' At some stage Loder-Symonds became separated from Urquhart and was able to make his way back to the security of his headquarters. But Urquhart, his driver and his wireless operator continued their journey, making now for the 3rd Battalion on Lathbury's heels.

We will leave both Lathbury and Urquhart making for the 3rd Battalion; both would arrive safely. The unfortunate Major Gough, meanwhile, had received Urquhart's order to meet him while in the middle of the Reconnaissance Squadron's little fight by the railway line and had set out to find Urquhart, travelling in two jeeps loaded with men of his unit. Gough tried to contact Lathbury by wireless but could not reach him, possibly the first example of the sandy soil and wooded nature of this area limiting the range of the division's wireless sets. Gough then drove around, looking for his divisional commander, visiting the Airlanding Brigade and Divisional HQs in turn, then going on to the southern route where Urquhart had last been reported. He failed to find Urquhart here, but decided to continue on that route, towards his unit's original objective, the Arnhem bridge, a decision that would take him away from his unit for the remainder of the battle.

This long and seemingly over-detailed description of the events of the afternoon – a minor clash and the movements of senior officers – is, however, of great importance. They resulted in the only attempt to reach the Arnhem bridge by vehicle being stopped in its tracks, and the Reconnaissance Squadron's commander being sent on a wild goose chase and leaving the bulk of his unit to return tamely to the divisional area, not to be employed again that day in any useful role, and losing its commander for the remainder of the battle. Meanwhile, both the divisional commander and the 1st Parachute Brigade's commander had left their headquarters – in the case of the divisional commander, 'charging around like a wet hen', as one senior officer says. The good news of the afternoon was that all of the units of the 1st Parachute Brigade were well on their way towards Arnhem and had so far met hardly any opposition. It is to their fortunes that we must now turn.

The 3rd Parachute Battalion

It will be convenient if the progress of each of the units on the three routes is followed separately right through to nightfall. We will start with Lieutenant-Colonel John Fitch's 3rd Battalion, which was now moving along the main road from Heelsum leading to the centre of Arnhem. (This road was the Utrechtsestraatweg in 1944 but is now called the Utrechtseweg; it will be more convenient to follow the later usage in this book.) The whole of the 3rd Battalion was present, also three 6-pounder anti-tank guns of C Troop of the 1st Airlanding Anti-Tank Battery, half of an RE troop, an RAMC section, some artillery observation officers and a few Dutch commandos. Unlike the 1st and 2nd Battalions, the 3rd had no subsidiary tasks; it was to become the main force at the northern end of the Arnhem road bridge. The battalion was led by Major Peter Waddy's B Company. Two men from the leading platoon, Lieutenant Jimmy Cleminson's No. 5, were out in front acting as scouts on either side of the road. Sections marched in file on alternate sides of the road, and there was a fifty-yard interval between platoons. Behind the leading company came the remainder of the battalion column, with hundreds of marching soldiers interspersed with approximately twenty jeeps, the anti-tank guns and two Bren carriers. The column was more than a mile long.

The battalion made steady progress for nearly two hours. The airborne men were surprised that, unlike in England, the pre-war road signs were still in place. For most of this period the route along the main road was through woodland, and the troops could keep well to the side, ready to drop into cover if fired upon. But when more houses were encountered, their wire fences along the roadside and between each house – all about four feet high – limited any deployment off the road; this would be a major problem during all of the remainder of the way to Arnhem. Dutch civilians came out to greet the soldiers; the leading company had to brush this welcome aside to keep moving, and it was the rear of the column which received most of the attention. There was almost no opposition, but Corporal Bob Allen, in A Company at the rear of the column, describes the effect of one of the scattered, occasional German efforts to delay the column.

I was walking through trees near the edge of a road; Lance-Corporal Bamsey was a few feet away to my right. We sensed enemy ahead and both paused – me behind one tree, Bamsey at the side of another. A shot rang out from the right. Bamsey collapsed like a puppet whose strings had been cut. I located the source of the shot, then dashed across and pulled Bamsey behind a tree. He had been shot through the throat, and the bullet had broken his neck.

Lance-Corporal W. E. Bamsey, a Welshman from Port Talbot, was almost certainly the 3rd Battalion's first fatal casualty.

Then, suddenly, there was violent action at the front of the column, but not of the type which the troops had been expecting. From a side road to the left appeared a German Army car, a Citroën, which entered the main road behind the scouts of the leading platoon, who were just past the junction. The car started to turn in the Arnhem direction. Lieutenant Cleminson says:

> It appeared without warning, and the front men of each of my leading sections, who were just behind the junction, opened fire with Stens and rifles and riddled its exposed flank. It was all over in a flash. I saw a body leaning out of the door but pressed on, leaving it to someone else to sort out. I didn't know it was a general until after the war. Of course, it put all my platoon on a high.

The senior officer killed was General Friedrich Kussin, the town commandant of Arnhem. He had earlier come out from Arnhem along this road to visit the headquarters of Battalion Krafft at the Hotel Wolfheze, which was only 800 yards away up that side road. After briefing Krafft on the various German moves being made elsewhere and giving the men at Krafft's headquarters a pep talk, Kussin set off on his return journey, refusing to take the advice of Krafft's men that the main road might now be dangerous. So Kussin paid the price, as did his driver and his batman/interpreter. Hundreds of British soldiers during the next two days would pass the scene of his death and remember the sight of the bullet-riddled car and the dead general tumbled out of the door.

Lieutenant Cleminson's platoon moved on, but only for a few hundred yards more before there was another burst of action, this time of a more serious nature. The leading troops were approaching a crossroads when there suddenly appeared from a side turning ahead a German armoured vehicle, described variously as an armoured car or as a self-propelled gun; it was actually either a self-propelled anti-aircraft or anti-tank gun, both of which Battalion Krafft were using. German infantry were in support on either side of the road. The British platoon had a Piat anti-tank weapon in the left-hand leading section, but this was spotted by the Germans and knocked out by machine-gun fire before it could be used. The platoon had no other weapon capable of harming the vehicle and promptly scattered to take cover in the houses and gardens alongside the road. This movement exposed the jeep towing a 6-pounder anti-tank gun a little further down the column, the gun, in the towing position, naturally facing away from the enemy. Before its crew could turn the gun round, it too was fired upon, and two men were hit; Gunner George Robson, stitched across the chest by machine-gun bullets, was killed, and the other man was wounded and later taken away on the German vehicle as a prisoner.[4] The jeep was knocked out, but the gun was recovered by another jeep.

Lieutenant Cleminson describes what happened next:

> I realized that nobody had got their Gammon bombs prepared to chuck at armoured vehicles, as the sticks of plastic explosive were still firmly wedged in our back pockets. I got up into a house and found myself behind the German vehicle. I was joined by Peter Waddy. I shot a German soldier in the garden below me with my Sten and wondered what I could do to get rid of our armoured visitor. Peter suggested firing his Very light – which had singularly little effect – but, fortunately, as a result of the small-arms fire and after they had collected about half a dozen prisoners, the vehicle pulled back down the road with our prisoners and their own wounded and supporting infantry.
>
> The platoon did not seem to be too shaken by the experience but had quickly learned that advancing straight down a main road against armour with no anti-tank weapons was no way to get to the bridge.

---

[4] Gunner Robson's date of death is shown in the Commonwealth War Graves Commission's records as 26 September 1944, one of many incorrect dates caused by the confused nature of the Arnhem fighting. He has no known grave.

Major Waddy normally had a stutter, but it was noticed that whenever the situation became serious he was able to talk clearly.

Either the same German vehicle or a similar one later came out of another side turning alongside Battalion Rear HQ, which was further down the column, only a few yards from Major Alan Bush, the battalion second in command:

> I was behind a tree, and he put the burst of fire meant for me into the base of the tree; he was in danger of cutting the tree down. A man from our Intelligence Section was near me. I told him to throw a grenade, but he froze, stationary as a startled rabbit. I have to admit that I couldn't throw my grenade; I had forgotten to prime it. I ran back, zigzagging, for fifty yards and hid in the undergrowth. The intelligence man was taken prisoner.

The Germans disengaged. At least one more man besides the anti-tank gunner was killed – Corporal Ben Cope, nineteen years old and only recently married – and several more were wounded or prisoners. The duration of the action had been about ten minutes, but Cleminson says: 'It seemed like ages.' The time was now about 5.15 p.m., and the head of the column had nearly reached the halfway mark to the bridge: three miles gone, three and a half to go. B Company sorted itself out and resumed its advance. The encounter had been with No. 9 Company, Battalion Krafft's mobile reserve.

It was obvious that the 3rd Battalion's presence and intentions were known to the Germans and that further opposition along the Utrechtseweg could be anticipated. Lieutenant-Colonel Fitch, urged on by Brigadier Lathbury, who was now present, decided to detach the second company in his column, C Company, and send it off along a nearby side turning on the left – the Bredelaan – in an attempt to outflank any opposition ahead and find a clearer way to Arnhem. The C Company commander was Major 'Pongo' Lewis, so named by naval friends when he had been stationed at Gibraltar before the war. He was called forward by Fitch, given his orders and returned to brief his three platoon commanders. Lieutenant

Len Wright's No. 9 Platoon was to take the lead. Len Wright describes his attempts to brief his men:

> I had my O-Group[5] standing by; that was routine. But, before I could start to brief them, I heard the high-pitched voice of the brigade commander saying, 'Where's the leading platoon commander?' I jumped to my feet, saluted – believe it or not – and said, 'Here, sir.' He asked me what I was doing, and I replied, 'Briefing my O-Group, sir.' He snorted, very sharply, 'They don't need briefing; just tell them that's the bloody way. Get moving!' So I did.

C Company disappeared up the side road.

It was now early evening. The troops at the rear of the column had been surprised when their divisional commander appeared in his solitary jeep. Urquhart moved up the column until he met Brigadier Lathbury, and the two conferred at a point not far from the shot-up German staff car. It was at about this time, approximately 6.30 p.m., that there was further serious action. So far, Major Mervyn Dennison's A Company, the battalion's rearguard, had experienced little more than occasional pot shots and seemingly interminable stops as the column jerked its way forward. The company was now level with a hotel off to the left called the Bilderberg (a smaller building then than now, recently used for pregnant German women bombed out from their homes in the Ruhr). It was from the wooded area around the Bilderberg that A Company was suddenly struck by prolonged machine-gun fire, followed by accurate mortaring. A Company went to ground and started returning fire, although the men could see little to fire at. Lieutenant Tony Baxter, commander of No. 3 Platoon, tells what happened next:

> I had two or three men hit by the first fire. Lathbury and Urquhart were both in the platoon position, taking cover behind a tree. Lathbury knew me and said, 'Baxter, collect up your platoon and clear that wood.' I called out to the three

---

[5] The formal briefing at which an officer passed his orders for the next stage of an operation.

section commanders, telling one to take the right, one the left, and the third to come with me. We just spread out and rushed into the trees.

I was taking a shot at a German I could see, with a rifle I had taken from a man who had been hit. I was looking through the sight, with my left thumb around the barrel, aiming at the German who was about forty yards away, just his helmet showing round a tree. But he shot first; the bullet hit my thumb on the rifle barrel. It cut the bone, and my thumb was hanging loose.

We probably shot three or four Germans and we pushed the others back, but we didn't clear them out completely. Mervyn Dennison told us to withdraw, and we had an O-Group at the edge of the wood. But the Germans we had pushed back returned and started firing their mortars again, and one of the bombs fell among our O-Group. Two or three of the sergeants were killed. I was wounded again – shrapnel in the head and splinters everywhere – and was knocked out cold.

Major Dennison and most of his company spent approximately two hours fighting in those trees, both sides suffering casualties; A Company's numbered eighteen, including three of its five officers wounded, two sergeants killed and a corporal blinded. Twelve prisoners were brought back when the company rejoined the battalion later that evening.

This was the last attempt by Battalion Krafft to halt the British advance. Krafft felt that he was now in danger of becoming surrounded and withdrew his unit to the north-east. He started this move at 9.30 p.m., at about the same time as A Company rejoined the main body of the battalion. Krafft's war diary claimed to have inflicted casualties on the British 'ten to fifteen times as heavy' as his own, although the diary does not specify the German casualties. The claim by Krafft that his unit had kept the 'mass of the enemy' from capturing Arnhem, given his superiors time to bring up their forces and 'thereby initiating the first steps to annihilating the British 1st Airborne Division, England's finest troops', is, however, partially valid.

*

Meanwhile, the rest of the battalion, amounting to little more than one company after the departure of C Company up the side road, but with one major-general and one brigadier present, had come to a halt. Lieutenant Cleminson's platoon, still leading, had reached the grounds of an elegant old hotel marked on maps as 'Hartenstein'. It was getting dark, and the soldiers gingerly entered the building through some cellar windows, there to find what was probably the main course of a standard German cold lunch laid out. They were in the staff mess of no less an organization than Germany's Army Group B, approximately the equivalent of Montgomery's 21st Army Group. The German commander, Field Marshal Model, had been living nearby but he and his staff had all departed on seeing the airborne landing. Cleminson and some of his men, standing at the table, tucked into the food, with firing going on outside, until Major Waddy soon appeared and drove Cleminson and his men out.

No further advance took place. B Company encountered Germans in the parkland at the rear of the Hartenstein, but it was dark, and the strength of the opposition there was not known. There seemed to be a reluctance to press on along the main road directly ahead, through the built-up part of Oosterbeek, although there was no evidence of any strong German presence there. Major Bush and his batman were sent up the side road which C Company had earlier taken, and Bush would later report that he found nothing but some dead Germans. Brigadier Lathbury and Lieutenant-Colonel Fitch had already decided to stay put for the next few hours. It was a decision that has been criticized many times. There should have been no question of fatigue; airborne troops in the first twenty-four hours of action should still have been quite fresh. There were some wounded and prisoners to care for, and not all of A Company had come in yet from its clash to the rear. Lathbury was in touch with his Brigade Headquarters, which was already at the bridge; Major Hibbert had told him that the southern route – only half a mile to the south – had been clear a short time earlier. Hibbert suggested that the 3rd Battalion should come down to that route, but, he says, 'Brigadier Lathbury did not agree.'

There was widespread dismay at the decision to halt. Private Fred Morton says: 'We were being held up by twopenny-ha'penny opposition.' Major Bush says: 'That was the start of the great cock-up.' He is convinced that the main reason for the decision was the presence of the divisional commander:

> I felt very sorry for Colonel Fitch. Urquhart needed to get back to Division, and Lathbury wanted to get forward to the bridge. If we had not had those two with us, Fitch would probably have followed C Company around that route to the north, but he could hardly move without the approval of both the divisional and brigade commanders – a hopeless situation.

Battalion HQ, with the two senior officers, moved into one of the stylish residences on the Utrechtseweg – number 269 on the north side. Outside, the men of the battalion dug slit trenches to make an all-round perimeter.

The 1st Parachute Battalion

It was thought that sufficient forces had been allocated to capture and hold the Arnhem road bridge, so Lieutenant-Colonel David Dobie's 1st Battalion had been given a different objective from the remainder of the brigade. Due north of Arnhem was some open high ground through which ran the main road north to Apeldoorn. It was a road down which German reinforcements might be expected to come and up which the ground forces of XXX Corps would need to move to continue their advance northwards, if and when they arrived. It was to capture this high ground that the 1st Battalion was despatched, to take it and hold it for twenty-four hours until relieved by the 4th Parachute Brigade from the second lift. To reach that area, Dobie had chosen a route which first ran from Wolfheze Station along the track earlier taken by the Reconnaissance Squadron, and then he would strike north, along another track past Johannahoeve Farm, to hit the main Ede–Arnhem road – the Amsterdamseweg, code-named 'Leopard' – until reaching the outskirts of Arnhem, where he would branch off to the left to reach the high ground.

David Dobie was known to dislike the task allocated to his

battalion; his Intelligence Officer, Lieutenant 'Tsapy' Britneff, says:

> He was full of frustration because we had to take the northern route from which enemy reaction would be the first to materialize. Then we had to hang around for over an hour for Brigade's permission to move off. We left the RV and took to the railway line, ambling along like a crocodile. Then, to Dobie's consternation, Major Gough pitched up; his Reconnaissance Squadron should have been at the bridge by now. He told us that enemy troops with tanks were deployed ahead of us. This was the first inkling that things were bad.

The 1st Battalion diary also mentions tanks, although the Reconnaissance Squadron had been beaten back by light infantry weapons, not by armour. The tank report may have come from the South Staffords, who were holding the nearby landing zone and may have heard engine noises.

Dobie had the discretion to alter his route if he wished, as long as he kept moving towards his ultimate objective. He decided to give up the track by the railway line and turn due north at Wolfheze, along a road running direct to the Amsterdamseweg. Dobie's decision to leave his original route has often been criticized, but the diversion was only of half a mile, all along good straight roads, and if he could avoid opposition his battalion would reach its destination intact. It should not be forgotten that an airborne unit's task was to seize and hold its objective, possibly for a long period, and any loss sustained in reaching that objective prejudiced its main role. It is a pity that no one on the spot ordered a couple of the now unemployed Reconnaissance Squadron jeeps to scout out his proposed new route. Criticism of Dobie over his change of direction does not seem valid.

The battalion turned and moved off up the Wolfhezerweg. Initially, this ran across the open ground of the glider landing zone, then, after about 900 yards, the road entered a wooded area. There were Germans in those woods, and the leading company, R Company, commanded by the veteran Major 'Tim' Timothy, who already had an MC and Bar and would receive a second Bar for this action, was soon involved in that difficult fighting in wooded country that was to become a feature of much of the battle. R Company was able to advance through the wood on the left of the road and eventually reached the junction with the Amsterdamseweg, but the Germans had armoured vehicles on that road, and the company could make no further headway. The fighting continued until darkness fell.

Here are some descriptions of that confused period. First, Private John Hall, a Bren gunner in Lieutenant Michael Kilmartin's No. 1 Platoon:

> Our platoon commander led us through the wooded area until we came to a road. We were about to cross when suddenly machine-gun fire opened up; one man fell to the road, his body moving with the impact of the bullets. We returned the fire and after a short while silenced the Germans and continued on our way. Small skirmishes occurred every so often. During one of these encounters a German soldier emerged from the trees, and one of our NCOs went to bring him in; as he did so, other Germans under cover shot him. From then on we said, 'No prisoners' (we had nowhere to put them anyway).
>
> Our platoon commander seemed to keep us to the wooded areas as much as possible, and we made good progress. It only seemed as if a few minutes had gone by when the sound of rumbling could be heard, and we were told to dig in. Out came our entrenching tools, and we dug into the sandy soil to get our bodies below ground level but still have a good firing position. The sound of those tanks was now quite near, and all of a sudden hell seemed to break out – shells bursting, bullets flying and trees cracking with the impact. In the flashes of gunfire we saw the silhouettes of armoured vehicles. We returned the fire. This was the one time I said a prayer – and I do believe it carried me through what was to follow.

Lieutenant George Guyon was the commander of the Mortar Platoon, which was supporting the attack:

> The wood came to an end about a hundred yards short of the

enemy, and the open space beyond was obviously lethal. I had the mortar set up in a clearing, but our wireless, which had worked well up to now, packed up, and I had to string men from the OP [Observation Post] to the mortar. This took time, and the company had some casualties before I could get the first bomb on the ground. My fire controller could see little of the ground ahead due to its broken nature, but he very efficiently searched it with groups of rapid fire which made the enemy withdraw hurriedly, leaving a truck behind. We left this alone, as it was getting dark by now and it might well have been booby-trapped, and we continued the advance after reorganizing. Our casualties were one dead and three or four wounded.

Major Timothy summed it all up as follows:

We kept losing people, a few here and a few there, and by the end of this phase I was down to twenty or thirty men. What happens in close country is that people have a go at this and that and you never see them again. It was a bash-bash-bash sort of business. The missing men weren't all killed or wounded. The idea is that you meet up again somewhere, but it didn't often happen.

Major Ronnie Stark's S Company had also become involved in the fighting, but most of it had managed to disengage when Lieutenant-Colonel Dobie, realizing that the opposition was heavy, swung the remainder of the battalion away along a track through the woods on the right, hoping to reach the Amsterdamseweg by that way. Good progress was made until a report came back that five German tanks and about fifteen half-tracks loaded with infantry were on the main road ahead and further German infantry were digging in near the junction between the track and the main road. Sergeant Frank Manser of No. 7 Platoon, S Company – 'Panzer' Manser to his friends – was probably the bearer of this bad news:

My section had been lead section for some time. Colonel Dobie was up with Company HQ. He knew me well and, when we were resting at the top of a rise and he was unsure of which way to go, he said, 'Manser, go up there and see if we can get that way.' I went up a track, all on my own, about 500 yards, and came to a gate. I looked over it, and there were the Germans at the far end of a field, the nearest about 300 yards away. There were lots of vehicles, armoured cars, etc., and lots of troops moving about – a company at least, possibly more, obviously getting themselves into defence positions. We could have got that way easily, but they had beaten us to it.

The German troops who had earlier fought R Company in the woods were probably from Kampfgruppe Weber, a hastily formed battle group made up of men from the Luftwaffe signals unit at Deelen airfield, but these later arrivals were the first elements to come into action of the two SS Panzer divisions detected by Allied intelligence in the Arnhem area. They were from Kampfgruppe Von Allworden, a three-company-strong mixed unit, mainly of men and vehicles from the 9th SS Panzer Division supplemented by some naval personnel.[6]

Further attempts to bypass the opposition through the woods proved unsuccessful. It was obvious that any attempt to move along that axis of the main road was impossible for this lightly armed battalion. One company was still in the woods more than a mile in the rear; the high ground at Arnhem was still more than three miles distant. It was getting dark. Dobie had sent his second in command, Major John Bune, back by jeep to find out what was happening to R Company. He returned to report that the company had disengaged but its return was being slowed down by the need to care for the wounded. Dobie sent all available jeeps back to evacuate the wounded so that what was left of R Company could hurry its return. It was at about this time that a remarkably clear wireless message came through from the Arnhem bridge. Lieutenant-Colonel Frost, of the 2nd Battalion, reported that his force had arrived at the bridge and that he needed reinforcements, there being no sign of the 3rd Battalion at the bridge. David Dobie

---

[6] These and other German unit identifications are from Robert J. Kershaw, *It Never Snows in September*, Crowood Press, Marlborough, Wilts, 1990.

now made an important decision, described by Major Chris Perrin-Brown, commander of T Company, who was walking alongside Dobie when the signal was received:

> I don't think David Dobie replied to the message. He just called an O-Group. He was of the opinion that we were in such a muck in the woods that we would never fight our way through. He said, 'I'm not going on to the north of Arnhem; we'll try to get down to help Johnnie at the bridge.' I was instructed to lead off.

Guides were left for R Company, who would catch up during the night, but Major Bune and the jeeps carrying R Company's wounded never rejoined. Major Bune was ambushed and killed some time during the night, although the jeep convoy and the wounded are believed to have reached the safety of the main divisional area.

The 1st Battalion moved off again, south-eastwards now. T Company, in the lead, kept meeting a few Germans, and there were frequent delays and more casualties, including one of the platoon commanders, Lieutenant John McFadden, who was wounded and would die in captivity nearly three weeks later. Behind came the rest of the battalion. Lieutenant Britneff says: 'All transport – Bren carriers, anti-tank guns, jeeps and trailers – were manhandled, with no engines started, so as not to alert the Germans. It was extremely heavy going through the woods.' The force made occasional stops, but there would be no overnight break or sleep. The battalion had suffered more than 100 casualties, including Major Bune and eleven men killed. There were many missing, most of whom became prisoners. Lieutenant-Colonel Dobie and his men had made almost exactly the same amount of progress as the 3rd Battalion. They were no more than halfway to Arnhem and had given up the attempt to reach their original objective.

The 2nd Parachute Battalion

Lieutenant-Colonel John Frost's 2nd Battalion had set off on the southern route at the same time as the 3rd Battalion on the central route. The southern route – code-named 'Lion' – ran through the woods from Heelsum and then along the oldest of the east–west roads which ran through this area to Arnhem, close to the Rhine all the way and passing along the lower and older part of Oosterbeek town (see map on page 122). Flying in with a strength of only 481 men, the battalion was more than 100 lower in numbers than either the 1st or 3rd Battalions. Attached to the battalion column were half of B Troop, 1st Parachute Squadron, and part of No. 2 Platoon, 9th Field Company (all Royal Engineers), four 6-pounder anti-tank guns of the 1st Airlanding Anti-Tank Battery, with a fifth gun joining later, also Major Bill Arnold, the battery commander, and most of his headquarters.

The battalion had been entrusted with a variety of important objectives, probably because of John Frost's reputation as 'a thruster'. It was to seize the road and railway bridges – with the road bridge as an absolute priority – and then establish a defensive perimeter on the south bank around the road bridge, ready to greet the ground troops of XXX Corps when they arrived, hopefully within forty-eight hours. A force was also to be detached, if possible, to capture the German Army headquarters in Arnhem. The infuriating aspect of the plan to capture the river crossings was that any basic airborne plan would have dropped or landed at least a small force in the open country on the south side of each crossing. But the Arnhem air planners had refused to do this, so the 2nd Battalion had to reach objectives up to seven miles away, with the certainty of a progressive loss of surprise.

Major Digby Tatham-Warter's A Company, the battalion advance guard, was in action almost immediately, even before the rear of the column was on the move. A small convoy of German vehicles, described variously as 'a column of lorries and a staff car' and 'two lorries and three cars', was heard approaching. Lieutenant Andrew McDermont's No. 3 Platoon, in the lead, took up ambush positions and either killed or took prisoner all of the thirty or so Germans in the vehicles. This was almost certainly the reconnaissance troop of Battalion Krafft's No. 2 Company, which was recorded by the battalion war diary as being 'wiped out'. The battalion then had a trek of almost three miles through the woods. The platoons of A Company took it in turn to lead, and fast progress was made.

Signalman Bill Jukes describes one of the few encounters along this route:

> It was difficult to believe that I was back in the war again. The degree of difficulty I was experiencing must have been nothing compared with that of a German soldier who came cycling towards us down a side road. He must have been out for his afternoon spin and didn't even know we had landed. When he saw us, he probably thought his last hour had come. His machine began to wobble until he eventually fell off. We took him prisoner and loaded him and his bike with all our gear, and took him along with us.

Another man tells of two Germans out walking with Dutch girlfriends also surprised on this Sunday afternoon; the Germans were taken prisoner, while the girls ran off.

Brigadier Lathbury appeared and talked briefly with John Frost, before departing again. It was at about this time that a plan was made to shuttle the platoons of A Company forward in turn by jeeps, to speed up the advance, but nothing came of this plan because the leading troops came under fire just as the end of the wooded area was reached. Lieutenant Robin Vlasto describes what happened; the 'Jack' he mentions was Lieutenant J. H. Grayburn, a fellow platoon commander:[7]

> We come to a T-junction, and Jack seems rather lost but goes left. Just as Digby, Mac and myself approach it, some Jerries concealed in woods ahead opened fire, and we get down sharpish! There is a good deal of rifle fire, and some mortar bombs fall fairly close, but it doesn't seem to be very determined resistance. Jack goes in under a smokescreen, and Mac moves round the left, and enemy shift off fairly quickly – quite as per the training pamphlet, and Digby is as pleased as punch.

Digby Tatham-Warter describes how his earlier service with the

---

[7] From Vlasto's account written soon after the battle, while a prisoner of war.

Oxford and Bucks Light Infantry helped his company communicate with each other in such an action:

> I must explain that, over the years of training, I had never acquired much confidence in the small wirelesses used at platoon and company level, and I had trained my company in the use of bugle calls for signalling orders and intentions in advance-guard actions. The calls were much the same as those used in Sir John Moore's Light Division in the Peninsular Wars. I had found this method extremely successful in training exercises, and it gave me great satisfaction to see it working perfectly under enemy fire. Each platoon and Company HQ had two buglers trained to sound the simple calls we used.
>
> While Jack Grayburn was working round to the right of the enemy machine-gun, I was joined by Colonel Frost. He had been hard on the heels of my company and now came forward, impatient at the delay, to see the situation himself. But we did not have to wait long for Grayburn's bugle call signalling that he was back on the axis road, and I sounded the call to resume the advance.

The battalion passed within a quarter of a mile of the Heveadorp ferry across the Rhine. Divisional Intelligence knew of the ferry, noting that it was capable of carrying eight jeeps on each crossing, but no thought had been given to securing it for later use or to passing a small jeep-mounted force to the southern bank in order to move quickly to the other ends of the bridges – another example of planning based on over-optimism.

It was about 6.0 p.m. when the battalion reached Oosterbeek. It was here that the warmest reception was received from the joyful Dutch civilians. This was a more built-up place than the area through which the 1st and 3rd Battalions were moving at this time. Captain Tony Frank has two vivid memories of the march through this area:

> One was the incredible number of orange flowers or handkerchiefs that suddenly appeared like magic. The Dutch were very much in family groups, in staid clothing, out on this

fine Sunday afternoon. The second memory was of the problem of trying to stop them slowing our men down by pressing cakes, milk, etc., on them. It was an atmosphere of great jubilation at the start of the move, mainly in the country area near Heveadorp and in Oosterbeek, but it petered out when the first hold-up and sporadic firing started. There weren't so many Dutch out then, but a few stout ones stayed on and watched the fun.

Private Sidney Elliott remembers: 'The Dutch population rushed out of their houses, cheered us, shook hands, gave us drinks, apples and marigolds – and some of us were lucky enough to receive the odd kiss. How could this be war? It was a question that would be answered very soon.'

Soon, orders were passed along the column forbidding men to take any of the alcoholic drinks offered. Julie Beelaerts van Blokland, a young lady living in the Hemelse Berg Hall which was near the lower road in Oosterbeek, remembers:

We saw a lot of activity across the field, and the whole family went out. I remember noticing that a lot of the soldiers seemed small, with their squat helmets and laden with equipment. It is a memory I shall never forget, all those men and the jeeps, etc. We were very curious at the strange uniforms, equipment and vehicles. It was all new to us. We were out there a long time; it went on and on and on. We never did see the tail of the column before we went back home.

The Dutch people kept saying that all the Germans had gone to Arnhem, but there were still a few about, and the column was attacked twice more. There was some sniping near Oosterbeek Laag (Lower Oosterbeek) Station, but A Company soon stifled this. In the second incident, the Mortar Platoon, well down the column, was hit by a burst of fire at almost point-blank range from behind a hedge, and at least three men were wounded, one of them, Private George 'Brum' Davies, dying of his wounds the next day.

Major Victor Dover's C Company and some sappers of the 9th

Field Company left the column in Oosterbeek and moved on to the meadowland between the road and the river, preparatory to making their attempt to capture the large railway bridge which ran out from a long embankment to cross the river. Six flak positions plotted from air photographs were found to be deserted, perhaps abandoned after being strafed that morning. The same fire had also killed some cows; a Royal Engineer vividly remembers 'seven dead black-and-white cows; every year when I go back there are always black-and-white cows in that same field'. Major Dover had given Lieutenant Peter Barry's No. 9 Platoon the task of capturing the bridge, with No. 8 Platoon as the supporting force putting down smoke-bombs with its 2-inch mortar. Peter Barry has provided this excellent account:

> While we were waiting behind a bank, I saw a man run out from the other side of the bridge to the centre and saw him bend down and do something. He was dressed in black, with a German Army cap on. We were about 500 yards away. I gave a fire order to the Bren, but the German ran off without being hit. He had obviously done what he was going to do and escaped. Then the company commander came up and said I was to take a section forward and capture the north end – our end – of the bridge. So I took a section of nine men forward with me, leaving the other two sections to give cover.
>
> It was wide-open country. We reached the north end of the bridge and climbed up the embankment. We had got there without any trouble, and I told the men that we might as well carry on and capture the whole bridge. I looked back to see if they would follow me. Only one man said no, shaking his head as though I was a bloody fool, and I don't blame him; but he came. We threw a smoke grenade; unfortunately the wind was in the wrong direction, but it gave us some cover. It was quite a long bridge. We ran across, as fast as we could, through the smoke. We were running on the metal plates, and our hobnailed boots made a hell of a clatter. We got about fifty yards and then needed a pause; we had a lot of equipment on and soon got short of breath. So I told them to get down. We were just above the water by then.

The centre span of the bridge exploded then, while we lay there, and the metal plates right in front of me heaved up into the air. It was lucky that we had stopped when we did, otherwise we would have all been killed; no one was injured by the explosion. Then I felt something hit my leg; I looked back and asked if anyone was shooting. They all said, 'No'; it was a German bullet. Next I felt a searing shot through my upper right arm, and it seemed to become disconnected; it went round and round in circles; the bone had been completely severed. There were only a few shots, but whoever was firing certainly picked me out as a leader and hit me.

Barry withdrew his men from the bridge, losing one man killed when the German rifleman opened fire again. Peter Barry was very bitter over the failure to land closer to the bridge:

If we had only landed there, we could have gone in and got it easily; that bridge was there for the taking. Never mind about flak positions. Right there, on those fields between the railway bridge and Oosterbeek, was the place to land. But they landed us at the wrong place, and we carried the can. It was a perfectly sound bridge; you could have got tanks – anything – across. Instead, they had three hours' warning and were able to blow it.

The Germans at the bridge were from a mobile troop of Battalion Krafft guarding the southern ends of the Rhine ferries and bridges. Lieutenant-Colonel Frost and much of the battalion had seen the failure from the road just over half a mile away. The blowing of the bridge ruined Frost's plan to pass a company across to the south side of the river and capture the southern end of the road bridge in Arnhem. C Company was ordered to withdraw and accompany the battalion into Arnhem, where it would be given the local German headquarters as its next objective.

The 2nd Battalion now had to pass under a railway bridge near Oosterbeek Laag Station in order to make its final approach to Arnhem. It was a narrow underpass with a high embankment at either side. Lieutenant Vlasto's platoon was first under the bridge, going well, when from around the next bend ahead a German armoured car suddenly appeared and opened fire both with its 20-millimetre gun and with a machine-gun. The two men on either side of Vlasto were hit, one killed and the other with his hand shattered. The platoon immediately dropped into cover off the road while the company commander arranged for the leading 6-pounder to be unhitched and engage the armoured car; but the Germans realized what was happening, and the armoured car withdrew. Vlasto moved on again, skirting behind some houses before returning to the road, but the company came under machine-gun fire once again, this time from what was obviously a German position on some high ground called Den Brink, 500 yards off to the left.

The weight of this fire, which dominated the only road available, now forced Lieutenant-Colonel Frost to detach part of his force to overcome it. He called forward Major Doug Crawley of B Company, pointed out the position and briskly ordered him to 'deal with it'. It was still light, the time approximately 7.0 p.m. Crawley gave out his orders. Lieutenant Peter Cane's No. 6 Platoon was to attack up the deep railway cutting, a move which might bring the platoon right up to the German position unobserved. The level of opposition was not known, but all briefings had indicated only weak German forces. Speed was of the essence if the battalion was to be allowed to move on.

Peter Cane led his platoon straight up the railway cutting, not putting scouts or a section out in front as in the textbook. The Germans had put a machine-gun post near a railwaymen's hut on a bend ahead, to protect this approach, and this opened fire, hitting many of the platoon at once. Lieutenant Cane and one of his corporals were killed. Among those wounded were two twins, Privates Claude and Tom Gronert, described as 'nice Cornish boys', who had remained together since the day they had joined the army (their regimental numbers were consecutive). Onlookers believed that one twin was hit and wounded; his brother went across to help and was also hit, and then both were hit again and killed. Major Crawley worried, long afterwards, that he should not have given Lieutenant Cane, his most experienced platoon commander, this task; a newer officer might have proceeded more cautiously. One of Peter Cane's brother officers describes him as 'having a great sense of humour and was a great singer; he knew all the words of "My Brother Sylvest"'; but another says: 'He was always, under the surface, rather sad, as though he had a presentiment that he would not survive the war.'

B Company would be embroiled on the lower slopes of Den Brink for the next four hours. The Germans were not driven off but they were kept occupied until it became too dark for them to threaten the road below. It was not until midnight that the company was able to disengage and resume its progress.

Following hard on the heels of the 2nd Battalion was the headquarters of the 1st Parachute Brigade, under the command of the Brigade Major, Tony Hibbert; there were also the Brigade Defence Platoon, a large part of Major Douglas Murray's 1st Parachute Squadron, RE, being employed as an additional protection party, some Military Police and Intelligence Corps men and the 'Jedburgh' team of an American and a Dutch officer, but without their American sergeant, who had become separated. This force had also been joined by Captain Bill Gell's RASC platoon, mostly on foot but with two jeeps and four trailers loaded with valuable ammunition and bound for the bridge; this was not the platoon's original role, but Gell had accepted it at the landing area when the platoon allocated to it had failed to assemble on time. Three more jeeps turned up later, two containing Major Freddie Gough and his Reconnaissance Squadron men who had given up looking for the divisional commander, and one carrying Major Dennis Munford with his driver and two signallers; Munford was the commander of the Light Regiment battery due to support the 1st Parachute Brigade, and his post would be at Brigade Headquarters.

So Major Hibbert found himself in charge of a 'large and cumbersome column' following the 2nd Battalion. One Royal Engineer said that he had expected a 'walk-run progress', but it became a 'stop-start movement'. A halt of nearly an hour in Oosterbeek had been forced upon this column when the Den Brink action broke out. Part of the 1st Parachute Squadron had been ordered to move off to the left of the road and dig in as a flank

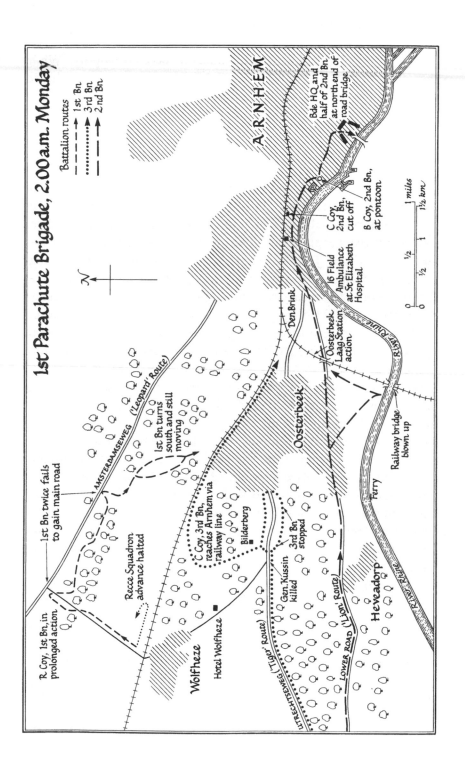

1st Parachute Brigade, 2.00 a.m. Monday

Battalion routes
→ 1st Bn
····→ 3rd Bn
- - → 2nd Bn

ARNHEM

Bde HQ and half of 2nd Bn. at north end of road bridge

C Coy, 2nd Bn, cut off

B Coy, 2nd Bn, at pontoon

16 Field Ambulance at St Elizabeth Hospital

Den Brink

Oosterbeek Laag Station action

River Rhine

Railway bridge blown up

Ferry

Oosterbeek

River Rhine

Heveadorp

LOWER ROAD ('Lion' Route)

3rd Bn stopped

Gen. Kussin killed

Bilderberg

UTRECHTSEWEG ('Tiger' Route)

C Coy, 3rd Bn, reaches Arnhem via railway line

Hotel Wolfheze

Wolfheze

Recce Squadron advance halted

1st Bn turns south and still moving

AMSTERDAMSEWEG ('Leopard' Route)

1st Bn. twice fails to gain main road

R Coy, 1st Bn, in prolonged action

N

0   ½   1 miles
0   ½   1   1½ km

guard to the column in case the hold-up became lengthy. While they dug their slit trenches, an English lady's voice was heard enquiring for 'anyone from Lancashire', and a sapper from that county was produced to talk to her. But the hold-up was soon over, and the column moved off again, following John Frost's men into Arnhem.

The leading men of the 2nd Battalion crossed the town boundary of Arnhem, which was about 500 yards on from the Oosterbeek Laag railway bridge, at about 7.30 p.m. It was not quite dark. There were not many people about. The road bridge was about two miles away. Lieutenant Jack Grayburn's No. 2 Platoon was leading; Lieutenant-Colonel Frost was well up with the leading company. A few individual Germans were met and dealt with; any organized resistance was avoided by taking to back gardens or by slipping up a side street and getting on to another route. Frost once led most of the battalion into a garden and then in through the back door of a house and out of the front door into another street, with the old lady owner 'playing hell with him in her own language'. The area of the pontoon was soon reached; its middle section was still moored on the northern bank as expected. So, dealing with the only two guards there and leaving just a small party behind to wait for C Company to come up from Den Brink, the rest of the battalion pushed on. At one place a group of anti-tank gunners and glider pilots were temporarily halted and were scolded by a man from a bedroom window for talking and waking up his children; he thought they were Germans, but he quickly apologized and brought his whole family to the window to shake the British soldiers by the hand.

Lieutenant Grayburn's platoon reached the bridge at about 8.0 p.m. There was no opposition on the final approach, and the whole of A Company was soon concentrated underneath the ramp carrying the roadway on to the bridge, out of sight of any Germans on the bridge itself. Robin Vlasto later wrote: 'Things were organized amid the most awful row. There was a complete absence of any enemy and the general air of peace was quite incredible. The CO arrived and seemed extremely happy, making cracks about everyone's nerves being jumpy.' Major Tatham-Warter deployed his platoons. Nos 1 and 3 Platoons were placed in buildings either side of the bridge foot to provide the beginnings of a firm holding force for the northern end of the bridge. Lieutenant Grayburn's platoon mounted the steps up the solid embankment further into the town and took up positions either side of the road there, but his men did nothing to stop the occasional German vehicle that passed. A Company was the only rifle company present. There was no sign of the Reconnaissance Squadron, which should have been here hours earlier, nor of the 3rd Battalion, whose entire strength was expected at any time. John Frost chose for his headquarters a large private house, the upper rooms of which provided a good view of the area. Headquarters and Support Companies went into buildings close by, and the vehicles and anti-tank guns moved into the sheltered yard of a large office building also nearby; the anti-tank guns would be moved to action positions later.

The Dutch owners, with varying degrees of willingness, gave up their homes and either departed or took to their cellars while their houses were prepared for defence. Constant Vogel was a twenty-nine-year-old single man, the assistant registrar at Arnhem's law courts, who was living at a large boarding house which was nearly taken over:

A British officer came to the door and spoke to the owner, Mr Kneist, asking if he could put weapons in the building. Mr Kneist pointed out that there were a lot of old people in the building and that he was sorry, but he would rather not have the weapons. So the officer set up this machine-gun on the pavement, pointing towards the bridge. I went into the cellar and, from the window by the pavement, could see the machine-gun and three or four soldiers. I was enormously pleased that something was being done for our liberation − it would have been like coming from hell to heaven. We were full of hope.

From a demonstration by Mr Vogel on his carpet of how the soldiers were sitting, the machine-gun was probably a Vickers.

So Lieutenant-Colonel Frost and part of his battalion had reached their objective and were able to take up defensive positions without hindrance. He and his men had been lucky in being allocated a comparatively undefended route, but much credit is due to Frost and the battalion for pushing on skilfully and swiftly. Particular credit is due to Major Tatham-Warter and A Company, who had led the column throughout at a cost of only one man killed and a handful of wounded. I asked John Frost to describe Tatham-Warter; his answer: 'A Prince Rupert of a man; he would have been a great cavalry commander on the King's side in the war with the Roundheads.' The tall, slender major would be prominent in the coming days, carrying a furled umbrella so that his men could always recognize him. Tatham-Warter himself writes: 'I suppose that, for me, the best moment of all was when I stood on the embankment to the bridge watching my platoons move into position to cover the approaches from the north and the bridge itself.' John Frost says that the best time in the whole battle for him was 'to see that big bridge still intact and our soldiers getting on to it – not blown in their faces like the railway bridge'.

The Brigade Headquarters group also made good progress through Arnhem and arrived at the bridge about forty minutes after the 2nd Battalion men but they suffered some casualties on the way. Sapper Bill Madden was killed on the Utrechtseweg. Further on, the Germans were covering a square near the pontoon area and were firing across it from a distance. Men were split up into small groups to dash across, and several were hit. The driver of one of the RASC jeeps was wounded, but Corporal Doug Beardmore went back, under fire, and drove the jeep clear with its two trailers loaded with ammunition. One man who might have been hit coming across that square was Corporal Arthur Maybury of the divisional Intelligence Section.

Wilhelmina Schouten, a language teacher at a domestic science school on the Rijnkade, was at the school's evening meal when British soldiers suddenly started passing the building. This is an extract from her diary:[8]

Someone opened the front door and, within a moment, the

_____
[8] Kindly translated by Adrian Groeneweg.

ground floor and the basement were full of soldiers. They were tired. The floors and stairs were full of them, but they made very little noise. The fruit which I had brought from the Betuwe that afternoon vanished in no time, and my pupils were pleased to be able to converse with them in English. Tea was made and passed around. They had brought everything and, hoping and fighting, had come all the way from Renkum and Doorwerth. Their next task was to occupy the bridge after a few moments of rest. Quietly and without fuss, they told their stories ... There were several wounded among them. One Irishman had lost two fingers on the way; he did not want to stay behind because, he said, he could still fire with one hand. Another man had been shot in the eye and the thigh. Yet another had been shot in his stomach; he was the worst of all.

Later, after a doctor had called but explained that the Germans were using all the ambulances, Miss Schouten and a male colleague nursed Corporal Maybury, the man with the stomach wound: 'Around midnight the situation changed, but for the worse. "I think he can still hear us," Jan Mielekamp said. "Do you know the Lord's Prayer in English?" And I prayed: "Our Father, who art in heaven, etc." He opened his eyes for a moment; he recognized something. But, before I reached "Amen", he was no longer there.' (Corporal Maybury's body was buried, rolled in a piece of cardboard, in the school garden next morning. Later in the battle, Dr Zwolle, the doctor who had attended Maybury, and Jan Mielekamp, who had nursed him, were in a group of five Dutch men caught by the Germans and shot for alleged looting and 'terrorism'. Arthur Maybury's mother visited Miss Schouten after the war. Maybury was a professional photographer and author who had written travel books before the war and parachute stories during the war.)

The Brigade Headquarters group made contact with the 2nd Battalion and came into the bridge area at about 8.45 p.m. without any further trouble; they outnumbered the 2nd Battalion men already there. Major Hibbert and Lieutenant-Colonel Frost agreed that Brigade Headquarters should be set up in a large office building near Frost's headquarters. This building, originally a hospital, was at that time the headquarters of the Provincial Roads and Waterways Department. Because the strength of the 2nd Battalion was so depleted, with two companies still absent, Hibbert stripped as many men from Brigade Headquarters as possible and sent them, with the various other units that had just come in, to positions in several buildings so that the area under British control could be extended as far as possible. There was still no serious interference by the Germans.

The speed of the airborne men's advance had taken the German command by surprise. There were plenty of German troops in the area, and most of these were in the process of moving to counter both the Arnhem landing and the American one near Nijmegen, but no extra force had yet been allocated to protect the bridge. Only its permanent guard, twenty or so elderly or very young soldiers from a local flak unit, were present, and they were either in a pillbox a quarter of the way across the bridge or asleep in some huts behind the pillbox. They did not seem to be aware of the British arrival.

    The first effort by the 2nd Battalion to gain a foothold on the bridge itself was given to just a rifle section. Lance-Sergeant Bill Fulton of No. 3 Platoon was in a group of men under the bridge ramp when an officer unseen by him in the darkness asked for any NCOs present. Fulton identified himself and was told to take his section and 'capture this end of the bridge':

> I told him I only had seven men, but he said he would send more up to join me as soon as more arrived. I led off first, up those steps on the west side of the bridge. When I reached the top I heard voices – definitely German. I told the section to be quiet and I peeped over. There was a truck with troops in the back, facing south, only fifteen yards or so away. An officer or an NCO was talking to the men in the back. I thought that the element of surprise would be gone if we burst in, so I decided to wait. It was only two or three minutes before the one doing the talking got into the cab, and the truck moved off.

We started to walk along the right-hand side of the bridge. It was very dark, but you could see outlines. I caught a few of the enemy hiding in corners of what looked like small huts and passed them back to the last man in the section and told him to take them down the steps as prisoners. You could hear firing in other parts of the town, but there was no firing on the bridge itself. Then, in the gloom, I saw a rifle starting to point at me. I swung round to the right and started firing my tommy-gun. I know I hit him because he fired his rifle as he was falling forward and I caught the bullet in the top of my left leg. I told the section behind me to report back and say that the bridge was well manned and would need more troops. I managed to crawl behind an iron girder, and eventually a couple of medics came for me.

Bill Fulton spent the next two years in various hospitals.

A stronger attempt was then made. Major Tatham-Warter describes the plan he made with Lieutenant Jack Grayburn, whose platoon would make the attack:

When it was completely dark he would move across the bridge in single files on either side, keeping close to the iron sides of the bridge for camouflage. The rest of the company would provide covering fire if necessary, as well as continuing to watch the northern approaches for the counter-attack we were sure would eventually come. Everything depended on stealth and surprise, and Jack had his men black their faces and bind their boots with strips of material (curtains, I think), and made sure that there was no rattling equipment or weapons.

When the time came the platoon crept up the side of the embankment and began silently to cross the bridge. They had gone a very short distance when a machine-gun opened up on them at point-blank range. The effect was shattering, and they had no choice but to get back as quickly as possible to the cover of the embankment. They suffered heavy casualties; Grayburn was himself hit in the shoulder. The fire had come from a pillbox on the bridge itself near the north end. We had, of course, seen it and checked it out in daylight and we had never thought that the Germans would risk or be able to place a gun in it after dark. The pillbox was almost alongside our forward defences in the houses by the bridge, and the machine-gunner must have been a good soldier and certainly a brave man.

Eight men had been wounded. Signalman Bill Jukes witnessed one after-effect: 'A lone figure came running down the ramp shouting, "Stretcher-bearer, stretcher-bearer!" Colonel Frost stepped out on to the road and said to him, "Stop that noise." The man came to a halt in front of him and said in a perfectly moderate voice, "Excuse me, sir, but I'm fucking well wounded."'

It took almost an hour, until about 10.0 p.m., to prepare the next effort. A 6-pounder anti-tank gun, commanded by Sergeant Ernie Shelswell, was skilfully backed by a jeep two-thirds of the way up a path on the side of the approach road embankment and then, with the aid of two glider pilots, manhandled to the top and placed in position facing the bridge. At the same time, a flame-thrower team was sent to the house nearest the pillbox, where a gap was made in the wall by firing a Piat round into it. When all was ready, the 6-pounder fired four or five rounds of sabot shot – shells with a tungsten-tipped core – at the pillbox. The flame-thrower, operated by Sapper 'Ginger' Wilkinson, then flamed across the gap, but he missed the pillbox, and the flame fell on the first of the huts. It was a petrol and ammunition store. There was a large explosion, and the paintwork on the bridge caught fire; there was soon a large blaze that would burn all night.

It was some time later that a small convoy of German lorries hesitatingly came on to the bridge from the south. The ammunition aboard the lorries exploded, adding to the inferno, and the oc-cupants were either killed by the shooting, burned in the lorries or taken prisoner. One brave German NCO ran up to the British positions, climbed on to a wall and opened fire with a pistol in each hand, wounding one paratrooper before being shot and killed. Another small convoy, ambushed earlier when it approached from the Arnhem side, belonged to a unit which had recently been firing V-2 rockets against England, an activity which the seventeen men taken prisoner wisely did not disclose to their captors.

*

There were a number of comings and goings during the night. The reader will remember that one company of the 3rd Battalion had left the centre route on which the remainder of the battalion was now halted. Moving independently, Major Lewis's C Company found a clear route (see map on page 151), and after numerous incidents part of the company arrived to supplement the bridge force. Various German vehicles had been encountered in the first stage of the journey and several Germans killed, but one of the company's sergeants was shot in the throat and died. Good progress was also made when Arnhem was reached; an armoured car was destroyed with a Gammon bomb, and a large group of German soldiers were deceived when the company formed threes and pretended to be a German unit marching by in the dark. On approaching the bridge, Major Lewis went forward and reported to the 2nd Battalion. Unfortunately, while his company was attempting to come into the perimeter, two of the platoons became mixed up with a German force which was planning an attack from the town centre. There was a violent clash in which one of the platoon commanders and a sergeant were killed and approximately one and a half platoons were taken prisoner. So, of the hundred or so men who had so nearly reached the bridge, only about forty-five came in safely.

Major Doug Crawley's B Company of the 2nd Battalion had been delayed by the Den Brink action but had disengaged and made its way through the darkness of the Arnhem streets to its original objective, the pontoon bridge area. Aerial photographs had shown that the pontoon sections were all in place when this operation was planned, but the centre section had been removed the previous day and was now moored alongside the northern bank section. Lieutenant-Colonel Frost knew that, but he had still directed B Company to the pontoon area in the hope that some means of crossing the river could be improvised. After Lieutenant Grayburn's attack across the road bridge had failed, Frost ordered Major Douglas Murray, commander of the 1st Parachute Squadron, to take some of his sappers, together with Lieutenant Pat Barnett's Brigade HQ Defence Platoon, to go back along the river bank and try to find some boats or move some of the heavy barges there. The intention was to pass B Company and the Defence Platoon to the south side of the river from where they could attack the German bridge defences from the rear and thus enable the entire bridge to be captured. But no boats were found, and the plan had to be abandoned. Captain Frances Hoyer-Millar of B Company says that 'There were all sorts of wild ideas going through everyone's heads.' Most of the men around the pontoon were able to come into the main bridge perimeter the next day with some difficulty, except for No. 4 Platoon, B Company's rearguard, which got cut off. The experiences of that platoon will be described later.

The only other arrival at the bridge during the night was most of No. 2 Platoon, 9th Field Company, RE, adding another thirty or so men to the force at the bridge. The oft recorded story that a captured German lorry commandereed by the RASC and loaded with ammunition drove through to the bridge that night is, however, believed to be incorrect. The lorry reached the outskirts of Arnhem but no further; the 'ammunition taken to the bridge by the RASC' was in the four jeep trailers brought in earlier by Captain Gell's platoon.

Still stranded in Arnhem town was the 2nd Battalion's C Company. After the Germans had blown up the railway bridge near Oosterbeek, the company set out for its second objective, the local German headquarters in Arnhem, which was in a building near the railway station, two miles further on. Initial progress was good. Soon after the company passed the large building of St Elizabeth Hospital a party of German soldiers was seen getting off a bus. Lieutenant David Russell describes what happened:

After a quick whispered briefing by Major Dover, my platoon opened fire with small arms. This resulted in much scuffling, moaning and groaning, shouting – every sign of a party caught by surprise. A number of survivors dived into the shelter of a vehicle against the hospital. The Piat fired on them – more groaning, and the survivors ran off into the hospital entrance. Another Piat was fired which resulted in more cries – 'Nicht schiessen!' and so on. We told them to come to us, and about nine came over. I had learned German at Sherborne; I hadn't been able to get to Germany to complete my linguistic studies, but that would soon be rectified. The Germans said they had come by bus from the centre of Arnhem. They were probably local troops who had no idea where our troops were. They said they had suffered badly from our fire. We then shot up a white vehicle, but this turned out to be a Dutch ambulance with a British medical officer, Captain Tobin, who was very annoyed.

The company then entered a part of Arnhem where the houses came right up to the pavement and where there was nowhere to deploy when they came under fire, as they soon did. The leading troops had to fall back, leaving two men dead, and the whole company sought shelter in a small hotel on the north side of Utrechtseweg, about 600 yards from the German headquarters and a mile from the bridge. The further experiences of C Company will also be described later.

One unit deliberately stayed in the town. The 16th Parachute Field Ambulance had travelled straight to its planned destination, St Elizabeth Hospital, without any difficulty and was functioning inside the hospital by 10.0 p.m. Some casualties from the 2nd Battalion were already there receiving treatment. Two operating theatres were taken over, and Dutch doctors and nurses volunteered to assist the British surgical teams.

Two jeeps actually left the bridge that night. After his arrival there, Major Dennis Munford, the battery commander from the Light Regiment who was with Brigade HQ, found that his signallers could not make contact with their battery either with the 22 set or with the 68 set. Munford checked with Majors Gough and Hibbert and found that none of their sets could make contact with the divisional area either. They all knew that, without communications, there could be no support from the battery of 75-millimetre guns which would move forward to Oosterbeek in the morning. Munford decided that he and one of his officers, Captain Tony Harrison, would go back to the divisional area to check the sets on their jeeps and collect fresh batteries. This the two jeeps did, being driven at top speed along the Utrechtseweg and surprising the Germans who were not expecting any approach from the direction of the bridge. Reaching their destination, Munford left a report on the situation at the bridge – the first news to reach Divisional HQ – had the two sets renetted and their batteries checked, and then set out back to the bridge. Munford's jeep made it, but the second jeep was hit, and Captain Harrison was shot in the stomach and seriously wounded. Dennis Munford's skilful jeep driver who made this round journey of about fourteen miles in the dark through German-occupied areas was Lance-Bombardier Bill Crook. Ironically, while the two officers had been away, Bombardier J. L. Hall, one of the artillery signallers who had been left behind at the bridge, had moved to a different building and, experimenting with different aerial positions, had made contact with his battery on a 68 set.

This ends the description of the attempt by the 1st Parachute Brigade Group to reach and secure its objectives during those first hours when it had the most advantage of surprise. The actions of this period have deliberately been described in the fullest detail because what happened on that Sunday afternoon, evening and night set the scene for the remainder of the battle. It had mostly been a period of disappointment. All of the 1st Battalion and most of the 3rd were stuck well short of their intended destinations; only about 750 men out of more than 2,000 in the brigade group had reached – but had not captured – the bridge. Casualties had not been heavy; forty men were dead (including the seven from the Reconnaissance Squadron), about a hundred were wounded, and possibly about a similar number had been captured by the Germans. In addition, both the brigade commander and the divisional commander had become separated from their respective headquarters.

The Divisional Area

The Germans had made no major attack on the troops of the 1st Airlanding Brigade and the divisional units around Wolfheze and the landing areas. They had used whatever local troops were available to block the British move towards Arnhem, recognizing that the river crossings were the main objectives. Two of the airlanding battalions had moved from the landing zone on which their gliders had come down, but the 2nd South Staffords remained near Wolfhcze, reporting a 'quiet night'. The 1st Border had moved a short distance south to deploy three companies around the landing areas south of the railway line. B Company had gone even further south, to the village of Renkum, where it was now in position around a brickworks by the river, overlooking the main road from the west and the local ferry over the Rhine, by both of which routes the Germans might bring in reinforcements. This company was in an exposed position and would be attacked during the night.

The movements of the other airlanding battalion, the 7th King's Own Scottish Borderers, are a good illustration of the weakness of the landing plan. At a time when every effort should have been directed eastwards, towards Arnhem, the KOSB companies had all moved nearly three miles in the opposite direction. The reason for this was the need to protect a new dropping zone that would be needed for the second day's lift, because two of the three open spaces near Wolfheze were now blocked by the first-lift gliders. The KOSB companies encountered no opposition as they made their separate ways along wooded tracks. No. 5 Platoon, in B Company, apprehended a 'buxom blonde dressed in a smart flannel suit' who emerged from the bushes with her German boyfriend. She turned out to be a member of the Luftwaffe called Irene Reimann. She was passed back to Wolfheze, where she became an object of great curiosity to the airborne men, who described her variously as 'quite pretty, but sulky', 'no great beauty, pug-nosed and surly' and 'crying steadily'. Brigadier Hicks gave her a cup of tea, but she wouldn't drink it until he tasted it first, in case it was poisoned.

The only action experienced by the KOSBs was on the main road, the Amsterdamseweg, at a place called Planken Wambuis, where there was a small café at the roadside.[9] Here, No. 1 Platoon of A Company, commanded by one of the battalion's Canadian officers, Lieutenant L. Kane, was positioned to stop any German traffic moving along the road. Private William Anderson, a Bren gunner, describes one of the subsequent encounters:

---

[9] Planken Wambuis is Old Dutch for 'wooden jacket'; it had been a place where timber was cut to make coffins.

Shortly after we had taken up position at a bend in the road, we heard a car. It was a pick-up type truck and it passed, *and nobody fired a shot*. I don't know why. The platoon commander shouted many things at us – 'When I say fire – ACT!' A little while later, an ambulance, followed by a smaller truck, came round the corner, and we all let loose. Both vehicles ran off the road. When we went down to them and opened the ambulance, we found it was full of fully armed Germans; a few were wounded. The other truck was riddled with bullets; when two of our lads opened the doors, the men inside fell out dripping with blood.

The 'Germans' were members of the 9th SS Wach Battalion coming out from Ede with orders to attack the airborne landing. Many of the men in this unit were Dutch SS volunteers, men who were either Nazi sympathizers or of mixed Dutch–German blood, or those who had joined the SS to avoid deportation to Germany as forced workers. Holland had a higher proportion of SS volunteers than any other occupied country. The company reported heavy casualties of twenty-five dead and sixty wounded, mostly in this action with Lieutenant Kane's platoon.

The remainder of the King's Own Scottish Borderers spent the night quietly in their exposed positions, the most westerly, B Company, being nearly ten miles from the men at Arnhem bridge. This battalion was the only one to have no fatal casualties on that first day.

The divisional units in and around Wolfheze also passed a mostly quiet night. Divisional HQ spent the night in four gliders on the landing zone. Also there was the team of war correspondents. Their signallers managed to contact England on a 76 set – something the Divisional Signals had not yet achieved – and the reports of Stanley Maxted and Alan Wood were relayed to London, where they formed the basis for the first radio broadcasts and press reports of the successful landing.

So ended the first day and night for the 1st British Airborne Division. Fatal casualties for the period numbered ninety: twenty-one in the glider crash in England, sixteen in other incidents in the air or on landing and most of the remainder in the attempts by the 1st Parachute Brigade to reach Arnhem.

The Other Landings

Just twelve miles south of the Arnhem bridge, but beyond the wide river Waal and Nijmegen city, a large part of the 82nd US Airborne Division and the Advanced Headquarters of the 1st British Airborne Corps had landed. Lieutenant-General Browning's Corps HQ had flown from Harwell in thirty-eight gliders – thirty-two Horsas and six American-built Wacos, the latter carrying American signals parties. Three of the Horsas had failed to arrive, one force-landing in England, one in the sea and one in German-occupied Holland. Approximately 200 men and twenty or more jeeps of Corps Headquarters were landed safely; two glider pilots injured were the only landing casualties. The only protection force for Browning's headquarters were the sixty-eight uninjured glider pilots. Before leaving England, the glider pilots of No. 20 Flight, B Squadron, which flew in the Arnhem lift, had been ordered to move from the Arnhem area to Corps HQ by any means possible to supplement the protection force there. Needless to say, this optimistic plan never came to fruition.

The corps landing had taken place in a remote area, and there were no German combat troops present; but a few strays were taken prisoner – an unusual event for a corps headquarters. But there was one tragically fatal casualty after the landing. Lieutenant Fuller Gee of the Royal Signals was sent off on one of the little airborne motorcycles to lay a land-line to the nearby Americans, but ran over a German mine which blew off both of his legs. His colleagues did what they could to succour him, but he died that night. One of the American signals officers attached to Corps HQ, Lieutenant Nick Carter, who was seconded from the 101st US Airborne, took over the task and completed the link. It would not be long before there was a physical junction with the nearby Americans, and Browning and his headquarters were never in serious danger. His signals organization, however, would always be under strain, and hence his influence in the coming battle would be limited. His signallers managed to make contact with the Corps Rear HQ in England that night, but contact with 1st British Airborne, only twelve miles away, was limited to two short periods totalling less than ninety minutes.

The two American airborne divisions had both landed relatively safely. The 82nd successfully captured the important bridges over the river Maas at Grave and over a nearby canal, but the division was not yet able to move to the vital Nijmegen bridge, the last one on the road to Arnhem. Further south, the 101st had captured all but one of its bridge objectives, but unfortunately the Germans managed to demolish a small canal bridge at Son, north of Eindhoven, and the later replacement of this by a Bailey bridge would impose a delay on the advance of the relieving ground forces of XXX Corps. XXX Corps itself, starting its advance at 2.35 p.m., had failed to complete its breakthrough of the German front-line defences. It had advanced no more than eight of the sixty-four miles to Arnhem, and had stopped for the night – a disappointing rate of progress which did not augur well for the future.

CHAPTER 9

The Battle in the Town –
Monday

(*Author's note*. It is my intention to continue the description of each main element of the battle through to its conclusion. Chapters 9 and 10 will thus follow the continuing fortunes of those parts of the 1st Parachute Brigade which were still trying to reach the Arnhem bridge area throughout the whole of Monday and on Tuesday morning, even though the second lift would arrive and the force already at the bridge would be fighting off German attacks during this period.)

Both the 1st and 3rd Battalions were on the move before dawn; indeed, the 1st Battalion had never halted properly during the night. The battalion was moving south-eastwards, hoping to reach the lower road into Arnhem. It entered Oosterbeek from the north, where its progress down the Stationsweg was observed by the Kremer family; daughter Ans gives this description:

> When I woke up it was still dark and all the others had gone. I could hear noises in the street and was very frightened. I found the others at one of the windows, watching those soldiers passing down the street – dark shapes, quietly, in Indian file. Mother asked who they were; Father said they must be English, because they were so quiet. One of them lit a cigarette, and someone immediately knocked it out of his hand. There was some whispering, and then they moved on. In my memory, it went on for hours, but I know that it could not have been so long.
> We had our breakfast then, but all of a sudden we heard

them come back again, one behind the other in single file and again not talking. We went to the door and watched them, no one saying anything; we didn't; they didn't. All of a sudden, Mother said, 'I can't stand it any more', and went into the street and asked, in English, 'Are you English?' The man said, 'Yes', and then laughed and said, 'The Germans aren't awake yet, so we are going to stop and have breakfast.' I remember hanging on to my mother and saying, 'What did he say? What did he say?' That was my first example of British humour.

Both battalions made good early progress, the German opposition which had delayed them the previous day seeming to have disappeared.

The Germans were working to a longer-term plan than the *ad hoc* one implemented by Battalion Krafft and the forward patrols of 9th SS Panzer on the previous afternoon and evening. The landings had caught the German command by surprise; its units on the coast which had seen the air armada pass over had not thought to inform the inland units! But the Germans were usually quick to react and, on this occasion, had the extreme good fortune to have two fortuitous presences immediately on hand to organize and implement a response. The key commander in the overall decision-making was Field Marshal Walther Model, who, as commander of Army Group B, was responsible for half of Germany's entire Western Front. It was only his accidental presence at Oosterbeek at the time of the airborne landing that gave him such an on-the-spot opportunity to direct operations, which would normally have been the province of a more junior officer. The second accidental presence was that of II SS Panzer Korps, whose units had been detected by Allied intelligence in the Arnhem area. Model immediately took the corps directly under his personal command and arranged with its commander, SS General Wilhelm Bittrich, the strategy to be employed against the airborne landings. The Germans were extremely fortunate to have in Model a decisive and able commander of such seniority, together with the two Panzer divisions in Bittrich's corps which were free to turn at once on the airborne troops. The British were most unfortunate in being denied the period of enemy command confusion which normally followed an airborne landing.

The two German divisions were the 9th (Hohenstaufen) and 10th (Frundsberg), which had fought many a battle together in Russia and in Normandy. Both divisions were reorganizing around Arnhem after being extricated from the fighting in France. The 9th was in the process of handing over some of its equipment to the 10th, which was in better shape, and parts of the 9th had already departed for complete refitting in Germany. But the available vehicles and weapons would be shared between the two divisions in the coming battle, and both would be supplemented by local units and reinforcements.

Model ordered Bittrich to deploy his two divisions in a direct and simple way. Obersturmbannführer Walther Harzer's 9th SS Panzer was to concentrate on the British landing, preventing any further British force reaching the bridge and eliminating the troops already there. Standartenführer Heinz Harmel's 10th SS Panzer was to cross the Rhine, move south to Nijmegen and protect the important road bridge there from capture by the airborne troops landing nearby, at the same time preventing any relief reaching the British airborne landing from the south. The implementation of these moves had commenced the previous afternoon. Elements of the 9th SS Panzer Division had already been in action against the British 1st and 3rd Battalions, and that part of the division which had gone to Germany was recalled and would eventually return with new tanks. The most important part of the division's deployment was the formation of a new blocking line west of Arnhem to bar the way to further British units attempting to reach the bridge. This task was entrusted to the division's artillery commander, another example of German flexibility. So Obersturmbannführer Ludwig Spindler – starting with only 120 men of his own artillery regiment acting as infantry, but quickly gathering in several other units – was establishing a line running southwards towards the Rhine and would eventually cover every approach to Arnhem from the west. At the same time Spindler started to form a second blocking line, just over half a mile from the road bridge in Arnhem. Two German women operators in the Arnhem central telephone exchange had stayed at their posts all night, advising on the progress of the British units and helping this line to be placed in the best position. General Bittrich later decorated them with the Iron Cross.

The progress of the 10th SS Panzer Division towards Nijmegen and the formation of Division Tettau, a new organization operating against the western side of the British landings, can be left till later. It will be the 9th SS Panzer Division's Kampfgruppe Spindler which dominates this and the following chapter and the renewed British attempts to reach the bridge at Arnhem.

The 3rd Parachute Battalion

Lieutenant-Colonel Fitch's battalion – less C Company, which had found its way to the bridge by a separate way the previous evening – left its overnight position just west of Oosterbeek at about 4.30 a.m. The direct way ahead was believed to be blocked, but patrols had found that the side roads to the south appeared to be clear. Fitch conferred with Brigadier Lathbury and Major-General Urquhart, who were still present, and decided to abandon the main road and cut south through Oosterbeek to reach the lower road into Arnhem. B Company led, as on the previous day, and good initial progress was made because of the darkness and the absence of opposition. The whole of Oosterbeek was transversed; the bridge under the railway at Oosterbeek Laag Station was safely negotiated; and a further mile was made through the outskirts of Arnhem until the leading platoon reached a building on the edge of the river known as the Rhine Pavilion.[1] A valuable two and a half miles of progress had been made. If the 3rd Battalion had not stopped overnight but had pushed on by this route, it might already have been at the bridge. But that is hindsight; Lieutenant-Colonel Fitch, encumbered by the unwanted presence of two senior officers, did not survive the battle to defend his decisions.

All was not well further back down the column, however. The Germans had sent out a number of snipers, who had climbed trees in the wooded area between Oosterbeek and Arnhem and roped themselves to the trees. As it became light, they started to fire on the centre and rear of the long column. Several of the snipers were shot out of the trees, to hang dangling from their ropes or crash to

---

[1] This 'pavilion' is now part of the dining room of the modern Rijnhotel.

the ground. But the sniper fire and some bursts of machine-gun fire near the railway bridge led to the column being frustratingly held up by what one experienced soldier calls 'minor opposition', and gaps appeared in the column. At one point, when the leading men of HQ Company took cover from fire, they found that the last man of the leading part of the battalion had passed out of sight round a bend in the road. When they resumed their march they took a different route to the one taken by the front of the column. In this way, the battalion's mortars, Vickers machine-guns, transport, A Company and three of the four anti-tank guns all became detached. When the leading element paused at the Rhine Pavilion to take stock, Fitch found that he only had with him B Company, a few Royal Engineers, one anti-tank gun and, as Major Bush, the second in command, says, 'one major-general who needed to get back and one brigadier who wanted to go forward'.

This splitting of the battalion led to the men out in front – Lieutenant Cleminson's No. 5 Platoon – being ordered to halt to wait for the remainder of the battalion to catch up. Cleminson's view is that substantial further progress could have been made if the battalion had been up in strength behind him at that point: 'The Germans were certainly not in major strength yet, and I had only had one serious casualty in my leading section so far that morning.' The bridge was only one mile beyond that furthest point reached; the time was only about 7.0 a.m. Cleminson's platoon was pulled back to take cover with the remainder of B Company in some large houses between the Utrechtseweg and the river. But the separated part of the battalion did not appear; it eventually met up with the 1st Battalion, which was also moving into Arnhem at that time.

It was now full daylight. After seeing Cleminson's platoon retire and observing the British hesitation, the Germans sent forward one of their tanks and possibly a self-propelled gun. They did not know exactly where the airborne men had taken cover. They did not fire into the houses but opened fire with distant and unseen weapons as soon as anyone moved into the open; the pathway on the river bank was similarly dominated by German positions in a factory on the south bank. These conditions kept the 3rd Battalion men pinned down in those houses for the next six hours. German infantry did not become closely involved, and the armoured vehicles were deterred with Gammon bombs, which damaged or disabled them and certainly kept them at a distance. Few casualties were suffered in the houses; it was just a long stalemate. Radio contact was made with the 1st Battalion, which had reached a point about a thousand yards behind the 3rd, and through this link the separated part of the battalion was contacted and told to get through with as much of the reserve ammunition in the Bren carriers as possible so that the attempt to reach the bridge could be resumed.

This appeal had some effect. A Bren carrier loaded with ammunition and a group of men variously reported as numbering between twenty and forty arrived at about 2.30 p.m. The Bren carrier was driven by Lieutenant Leo Heaps, a Canadian officer attached to the 1st Battalion, and the infantry were led by Lieutenant Burwash, an officer from the 3rd Battalion's HQ Company. Burwash could give little news of the remainder of the battalion, although it was known that Major Dennison of A Company had been badly wounded. It was at this time that Major Peter Waddy was killed when he went out into the open to unload the ammunition from the Bren carrier. Major Bush was watching:

> Peter Waddy had no need to go out, but he was very impetuous; he would have a go at anything. 'It's all experience,' he would say with his boyish appearance. I saw him killed. There was just a blinding flash and the muck being blown about from this one mortar bomb, and there he was, prostrate. There was not a mark on him – killed outright by blast.

So perished the gallant Peter Waddy, whose company had led the 3rd Battalion's advance all the way from the dropping zone twenty-four hours earlier. With him died his young company sergeant-major, twenty-three-year-old Reg Allen, who had just been awarded an American decoration for his bravery in Tunisia. They were probably the only fatal casualties of the long stalemate.

It was soon after this that parties of Germans were seen to the west of the houses, threatening to surround the battalion's position. Again, Alan Bush describes this:

One patrol was only twenty yards away. I could see every bit of their equipment. I remember one had a big fat arse and I thought, 'What a target!' They were being very casual. Three of our men were ready to open fire, but I ordered them not to. RSM Lord was there and he nodded approval; you can't start a battle with the divisional commander and the brigadier in the same house.

An officer who had much closer contact with the Germans at this time was Lieutenant Ted Shaw, the anti-tank troop commander who had accompanied the only 6-pounder which had reached this area. This gun, commanded by Sergeant Gus Garnsworthy, had earlier engaged a German light gun south of the river, but had then been put out of action by mortaring. Lieutenant Shaw was in one of the houses:

I was sitting at the foot of the stairs, opposite the door to the street, when a shot whistled past my ear. It was Sergeant Garnsworthy firing a single shot from his Sten, past me and out of the window to the right where he had seen a German infantry section passing. A Bren opened up then, firing from further up the street on the left, and that forced two Germans to come into our house – only six or seven feet from where I was sitting. I fired at them with my Sten; one fell into the house; one fell outside. The one inside was wounded – hit in the stomach. I made him as comfortable as I could in a chair, but I couldn't do much because there was firing at the rear of the house, and it was obvious that we had to get out. We tried the back way. It was quite a drop to the ground, so I got a long table, put it out of the window and slid down it. But I came under rifle fire and had to come back into the house through a door that I found. I eventually got away by dashing down the street with the lads.

Some important decisions were now made. Lieutenant-Colonel Fitch decided that his men must move out of the houses where they had been pinned down throughout the day and, with the recent reinforcement and replenishment of ammunition, seek a new way to the bridge, by a route further away from the river. At about the same time, Brigadier Lathbury suggested to Major-General Urquhart that they should break out and find a way back to safety. The time was about 4.0 p.m., and the entire group started to leave through the back gardens of the houses, their quick escape being hampered by the need to climb over various walls which the bulky Urquhart found particularly difficult to negotiate. The river was in the rear of those gardens, so there was only one way to go, northwards, into the streets of smaller houses which were situated on the north side of the Utrechtseweg and west of St Elizabeth Hospital.

Urquhart, Lathbury and Lathbury's Intelligence Officer, Captain Willie Taylor, became separated from the main group and set off alone down one of the streets, going in the wrong direction, eastwards towards German-held ground. Lieutenant Cleminson saw that the three officers were heading the wrong way and tried to warn them. Cleminson felt that he and one of his sections should follow and protect the senior officers but, Cleminson says, 'The men had more sense and stayed put.' There were thus four officers running wildly through short stretches of street, every intersection of which was under German fire. It was at one of these that Brigadier Lathbury was hit in the leg, with a second bullet chipping his spine. The three others dragged him into a nearby house. Urquhart shot a German through the window at nearly point-blank range with his revolver. Lathbury could not be moved and urged the others to leave him. Urquhart, Taylor and Cleminson then dashed out into the back garden, down a short path between the backs of houses, and sought shelter in another house, where a brave couple, Mr and Mrs Anton Derksen, let them in and ushered them upstairs to their attic and safety. Urquhart was keen to move again, but Cleminson and Taylor persuaded him that this would be too dangerous; the issue was resolved when a German self-propelled gun clattered up and established itself outside the front of the house, and German infantry could be seen in the surrounding streets. The three officers would have to remain where they were for more than twelve hours.

The 3rd Battalion was now free of the encumbrance of the senior officers which had hindered the battalion for twenty-four hours but the attempt by Lieutenant-Colonel Fitch to get his battalion moving forward again failed. German fire still dominated the streets, and Fitch's force had to take shelter again, being split up in two groups of houses in those streets to the west of the hospital. About 140 men would still be available to fight again the next day. Fifteen men had been killed in the day's actions; between forty and fifty had been wounded; some of these casualties would have been suffered by the separated parts of the battalion which had become involved in fighting elsewhere.

The 1st Parachute Battalion

It has already been described how Lieutenant-Colonel David Dobie's battalion had kept moving for most of the night, disengaging from the German opposition encountered on the northern route and striking south-east in an attempt to find a better way into Arnhem. Not all of the battalion was with the main body; R Company had suffered heavily fighting in the woods, and few of its members had yet rejoined. On reaching Oosterbeek, Dobie decided to try the main Utrechtseweg towards Arnhem. He had heard that the 2nd Battalion had been successful in reaching the bridge by the lower Oosterbeek road, but he obviously wanted to save time by trying this more direct route and, having heard nothing from the 3rd Battalion, presumed that it had passed along this route safely. Major Ronnie Stark's S Company was leading the battalion column, with Lieutenant Bob Feltham's No. 7 Platoon out in front. The leading troops left the built-up area of Oosterbeek and came to an area of allotments prior to passing under the railway line ahead. German troops were manning the embankment. The leading two men passed under the railway only to find themselves covered by German weapons and forced to surrender. The remainder of the section scrambled back, and the Germans opened fire on the rest of the platoon, killing three men and wounding Lieutenant Feltham in the arm. The platoon went to ground and returned the fire but was then mortared and suffered further casualties, Lieutenant Feltham being wounded a second time.

The section deployed on the right of the road was commanded

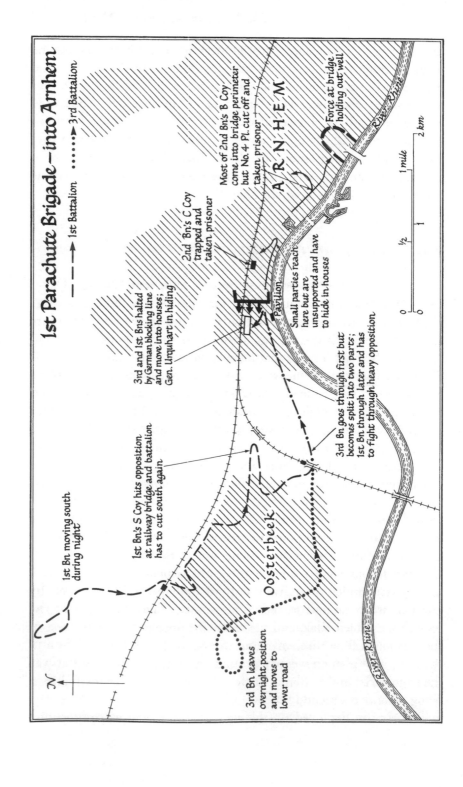

1st Parachute Brigade—into Arnhem

— — — 1st Battalion ········· 3rd Battalion

N

Oosterbeek

ARNHEM

River Rhine

River Rhine

1st Bn moving south during night

3rd Bn leaves overnight position and moves to lower road

1st Bn's S Coy hits opposition at railway bridge and battalion has to cut south again

3rd and 1st Bns halted by German blocking line and move into houses; Gen. Urquhart in hiding

2nd Bn's C Coy trapped and taken prisoner

Pavilion

3rd Bn goes through first but becomes split into two parts; 1st Bn through later and has to fight through heavy opposition

Small parties reach here but are unsupported and have to hide in houses

Most of 2nd Bn's B Coy come into bridge perimeter but No. 4 Pl. cut off and taken prisoner

Force at bridge holding out well

0   ½   1

0   1   2 km

½ mile   1 mile

by Sergeant Frank Manser, and he describes what happened to his men:

> We were advancing, with some large trees between ourselves and the roadway. I passed one of the trees and came upon a German strongpoint, probably put up the day before. It was made of sandbags, and there were four Germans with one machine-gun. It was so unexpected that I still had my tommy-gun slung over my shoulder. They were as surprised as I was; I was only three yards from them. I just said, 'You are my prisoners', even as I was still unslinging the tommy-gun. One of them said 'Englander?', but whoever was behind the gun opened fire down the road towards Lieutenant Feltham; that's when he was wounded in the arm.
>
> I jumped back behind the tree, went back about twenty yards, and called for my section, 'Section forward!' Colonel Dobie came up as well, and I told him what was happening. The section came up, and I got the Bren group organized and started firing at them. The rest of the platoon came across from the other side of the road to me, and the Germans seemed to be reinforced as well. We tried to make a charge, but they were too strong for us. We had one or two wounded in the section, but no one killed.

It had been a typical platoon action, with two men taken prisoner, seven killed, others wounded, and no progress made. Major Stark was in the process of ordering his other two platoons to make a flanking attack when Dobie intervened. He considered the railway embankment too strong an obstacle. A parachute battalion's task was to reach its objective in as intact a manner as possible and then fight its main battle defending that objective until relieved by ground forces. Dobie wanted to reach the Arnhem bridge without fighting any more major engagements on the way. He would side-step again to the south and attempt the lower road route, the last option available to him. The time was still only 5.30 a.m.

The battalion successfully took a side road and moved down to the lower road, troubled only by a sniper who was dealt with, and came

to the railway bridge at Oosterbeek Laag Station. On the approach
to that bridge, some of the detached elements of the 3rd Battalion
were met, and David Dobie was delighted to take them under his
charge. All of his own mortars and some of his Vickers machine-
guns and attached anti-tank guns were still way back with R
Company.

The Germans were also covering this road under the railway
embankment, not by manning the embankment itself but with
recently installed strongpoints in houses alongside the road about
700 yards ahead, together with some armoured vehicles on the high
ground at Den Brink to the north of the road, and infantry
positions in a wool factory and a brickworks to the south, between
the road and the river. The head of the battalion came under fire
soon after it passed under the railway. The time was about 8.0 a.m.,
fully daylight, and there was no longer any place to side-step and
find an easier way; the 1st Battalion had no alternative but to fight
its way through now. The largest set-piece engagement of the day
was about to take place. Major Chris Perrin-Brown's T Company
would carry it out; artillery, anti-tank guns and other heavy weapons
(some belonging to the 3rd Battalion) would also be involved.

Two of T Company's platoon commanders, Lieutenant Jack
Hellingoe of No. 11 Platoon and Lieutenant Eric Vere-Davies of
No. 10 Platoon, have provided excellent descriptions of their parts
in the battle. Hellingoe's starts by telling how his platoon, in the
lead, came under fire; 'Chris' is his company commander:

> When it happened, we just burst in through the doors of the
> nearest house and went upstairs, right into the loft. The
> Germans were spraying the houses; bullets were coming
> through the roofs and windows, whizzing around the rooms
> inside and hitting the walls behind us. They were really
> brassing those two houses up.
>
> Private Terrett, the Bren gunner, bashed some slates off
> with the Bren and put the gun down on the rafters pointing
> through the hole. We could see straight away where the firing
> was coming from, from the houses and gardens up on the
> higher ground, only 150 to 200 yards away. You could easily
> see the Germans moving about there. Most of the fighting in

Arnhem was at very short ranges. I told Terrett to get firing and I think he got a couple of mags off at least before the Germans got on to him and a burst hit him. It took the foresight off the gun, took the whole of his cheek and eye away, and we both fell back through the rafters, crashing down into the bedroom below. I wasn't hit, but Terrett wasn't moving at all. Someone slapped a dressing on him, and he was dragged away. I thought he was dead, but I found out many years after the war that he was still alive – a great surprise. He had lost an eye, but they made a good job of his face.

Chris decided that we should move out to the back of the houses and go through the gardens, which should have been sheltered from the fire from higher up on the left. We had terrible trouble getting through those gardens because of the fences between each garden – netting, stakes, sometimes concrete panels. As soon as we got started, the Germans who were on the right opened fire on us; we didn't know where from. We could only make very slow progress – about 400 yards in about an hour. It was terrible; there were blokes crawling over cesspits, and bullets were coming through the concrete panels which we thought would protect us – they turned out to be hollow. We had a number of casualties. I couldn't see who they were, but you could hear shouts for medics and men saying, 'I'm hit', the usual thing soldiers say when hit. The whole of T Company was involved in that move, and I think we got quite badly mauled.

Eric Vere-Davies tells how Lieutenant-Colonel Dobie personally briefed him for his attack:

He said he was giving the orders personally because it was most important to the battalion that we took the area of the chimneys ahead on the hill and up the road in front of us from where we were being held up, and he knew that I could and *would* do it.

I had got about twelve men left and went straight in with them. We passed our company commander and his second in command lying together by the side of the road in a ditch and looking a bit out of it with the Colonel running the show, and charged straight up the road to the high ground with the buildings at the top. It was a good fast advance under sniper and machine-gun fire, and we all got to the top – no casualties. Once we had taken the factory area, we placed a Bren gun in position to fire into the houses from whence the trouble came, and the gunner engaged the target area by firing into the house windows. He was stopped soon after with a bullet in his face. The house was still occupied by some screaming Dutch people – what a row! A young girl ran from one house doorway to another and was shot through the upper leg. My medics attended to her, but we had to hold the mother off; she went berserk. Food and drink were offered to us by civilians as the battle raged! I had eight or nine men left with me. I decided to try to advance further as the factory was now cleared. The civilians disappeared, sensibly going to their cellars.

We went after a machine-gun nest with a Bren and a rifleman. Old soldiers say that you never see the one that hits you. I did – it was a tracer. I was on one knee and, as I positioned the Bren gunner on to his target, I *saw* the tracer bullet coming over in a flat arc from our right flank. The bullet went through the top of both my legs, severing the sciatic nerve in my right leg on the way. A second bullet then went through my small pack and wounded me in the neck. I believe the same sniper must have got Jack Hellingoe before our chaps got him.

Jack Hellingoe describes his platoon's attack; 'Waho Mahomed!' was the battle-cry that the 1st Parachute Brigade had used in North Africa:

I was called back to an O-Group, with senior officers there. Chris was there and an artillery colonel who, I found out later, was 'Sheriff' Thompson – I knew the name, but not the man – but I don't remember seeing David Dobie there. They were all spread around the garden, keeping their heads down. I was the only platoon commander there. They told me they wanted me to take my platoon and do a sweep through a factory area, a collection of brick buildings with scrub-covered heaps of old stone among them. 'Clear the factory'; that was my order. The artillery colonel said that he would be supporting my attack with his guns. I sent a runner back for the section sergeants and I gave my orders to them in front of all the other officers.

We started off about forty strong; Chris had sent some extra across at the last minute. We came under fire, and some of us were hit, including myself, in the right foot, but I was able to carry on, dragging my foot. We were firing as we went through those scrubby hillocks of stone, shouting, 'Mahomed. Mahomed. Waho Mahomed' to keep our spirits up. My batman, Private Baker, lost his leg there, and I was hit again, in the left ankle. I think most of our casualties were caused by just one German who stayed behind when the others ran, and he was firing single shots at us from close range, but we couldn't see him. We lost our momentum then, and I don't really know what happened after that.

Both Hellingoe and Vere-Davies were out of the battle with their wounds and later became prisoners of war.

T Company continued to attack along that road. There were no subalterns left, so Major Perrin-Brown and his second in command, Captain Jimmy Ritchey, each took an experienced platoon sergeant, divided the available strength of the company into two parts and carried on. It took until nearly 4.0 p.m. to cover the next half-mile, to the junction of the lower road and the Utrechtseweg, coming then to the area where the 3rd Battalion had been in action earlier in the day. German resistance was not strong, but every house had to be checked, and snipers and frequent bursts of long-range machine-gun fire down the roads and across the open spaces caused steady casualties; T Company had only twenty-two men at the end. Corporal Donald Collins of the Royal Signals was with Battalion HQ immediately behind the leading troops and remembers 'bullets flying about everywhere, yet, to my amazement, I saw at different intervals Dutch ladies cleaning the inside of their front windows. I presume that their curiosity overcame their caution, and they were doing this as an excuse to see what was going on.'

Lieutenant-Colonel Dobie decided that his battalion could go no further. A plan to put S Company, still in reasonable shape, into jeeps and push them through to the bridge had to be abandoned because the jeeps could not be produced. The remnants of the battalion moved into the area of houses near St Elizabeth Hospital, close to where the 3rd Battalion had also come to rest. Two soldiers record their experiences in the last hours of the day. Private Douglas Charlton:

> Our numbers were dwindling fast when we got to the hospital. We were ordered out of the hospital grounds by men in white coats because our presence was bringing a lot of fire on the hospital. There were bodies of our 3rd Battalion lying everywhere. Officers and NCOs were running in and out of houses trying to chivvy men along; some had stayed behind to comfort dead or dying comrades.
>
> Someone made tea, and we ate from our ration packs; we also ate bottled pears from the cellar of the house we had occupied. Then I was detailed to go with a sergeant and four men back along our route to look for stragglers. I had been on the move without sleep for more than forty hours and was none too pleased. It was dark now, and we found medics patching up the wounded along the way as well as many reluctant heroes hiding in the houses; these were directed to our new position or they joined us. We were making our way back when the sergeant stopped at the window of a house and listened to the sound of voices inside. He entered; there were shouts and shots; the voices were German. He staggered out of the door and shouted for me to get going and then he collapsed; I never saw him again. The rest of us ran like hell in all directions.

And Private James Shelbourne:

> Eventually the advance came to a frustrating halt below a high boundary wall of St Elizabeth Hospital, and I took a breather in the kitchen of a house there. A group of the lads were standing among the pots and pans, trying to calm down an

incoherent sergeant-major who had evidently received a massive shock to his nervous system. To stay could be unnerving. In the garden of that same house I was startled to find an upturned German helmet filled to the brim with bright red arterial blood. Did this obscene sight trigger off the sergeant-major's breakdown? Perhaps not, but it certainly gave me a turn.

Starting from much further back than the 3rd Battalion, the 1st Battalion had fought its way to come alongside its sister battalion. Twenty-three of its men were killed on this day, the highest single-day battalion loss in the 1st Parachute Brigade for the whole battle. The bridge was only just over a mile away, and the commanders of both battalions were determined to renew their efforts on the morrow, but their strengths were much diminished, while the German defence was steadily hardening.

Two small parties of men managed to get even further forward. Lieutenant John Dickson of the 3rd Battalion had independently led a dash from the Rhine Pavilion along the narrow piece of ground between the lower road and the river; only he reached the end of the open stretch and came to the area of the small harbour near the pontoon bridge (see map on page 176). Here he met two more 3rd Battalion men who had reached this point by other means, and, after finding their way further forward blocked, they all took shelter in a house. Also reaching that area was Major Tony Deane-Drummond of the Divisional Signals. He had come forward from Divisional HQ to inform the units fighting their way into Arnhem of a change in radio frequency for that day. Having done this, Deane-Drummond then took control of a group of leaderless men and forced his way forward to that same little harbour area, eventually taking shelter with the three men remaining with him in a building. So these two groups, numbering just seven men, each party unaware of the other's existence, were the tip of that Monday's advance. German troops entered both buildings; Dickson's party took refuge in the roof, Deane-Drummond's in the basement, and both managed to escape capture for the time being. They were just 800 yards from the nearest part of the bridge perimeter.

C Company and No. 4 Platoon, 2nd Parachute Battalion

Before the action just described came to a halt just west of St Elizabeth Hospital, there had been two groups from the 2nd Battalion who had been hoping to rejoin their battalion at the road bridge during the day just passed. On the Sunday evening Major Victor Dover's C Company had been forced to take shelter in a building on the Utrechtsestraat (the continuation of the Utrechtseweg), only a quarter of a mile beyond the place reached by the recent 1st and 3rd Battalion attacks. Much deeper into Arnhem was Lieutenant Hugh Levien's No. 4 Platoon, which had been cut off from B Company and become stranded a mile short of the bridge. These two parties represented nearly half of the 2nd Battalion's rifle-company strength and were badly needed at the bridge.

C Company had spent the night keeping watch in turns and suffering just one casualty when a man was shot through the head. Radio contact was made with the bridge at 'stand-to' next morning, and fresh orders were received. The company was to abandon its original mission to capture the local German HQ, disengage by withdrawing a little to the west, then cut south to reach the lower road and attempt to come to the bridge by that route. At 7.0 a.m. the company left by the back of the building and attempted to move through the back gardens of the houses on the north side of the Utrechtsestraat. Lieutenant David Russell's No. 7 Platoon was leading:

> The gardens were very tricky, with high walls and many little yards; progress was desperately slow with enemy fire all around us. We eventually emerged into a small garden where fire was falling from the 20-millimetre gun which had been firing on the building we had left and also from a Schmeisser; the Germans were obviously following our route. Victor Dover told me to push on. We had to crawl along through rose beds, our equipment catching in everything; my Sten became clogged with dirt. We reached the point where I decided to cross the road. Cannon fire had set the house we had just left

ablaze, and the road was covered by a machine-gun firing on fixed lines. No. 1 Section ahead of me rose as one man and made a dash for it. I crawled on for a few more yards, gave the signal to Sergeant Campbell behind me to go, and got across the road, luckily unscathed.

No one else followed; only Russell and seven men had got across. This little party went south and met Lieutenant Cleminson's platoon fighting at the head of the 3rd Battalion on the lower road. The remainder of the company did not follow; they tried to move further down the road but were soon pinned down. Major Dover ordered a last stand to be made, but the opposition was too strong, and a white flag was eventually offered. As far as is known, the whole of the remainder of the company – three officers and about a hundred men – became prisoners, the first of several large-scale hauls of men to fall into German hands. They had only been about 400 yards from the leading troops of the 3rd Battalion but had become trapped in the area where the Germans were setting up their inner blocking line.

Lieutenant Levien and most of No. 4 Platoon had been stranded while acting as rearguard when B Company came into the bridge perimeter from its overnight position near the pontoon. They were seen by the Germans in the growing light of that Monday morning and fired upon. Sergeant Frank Kemp was the first man to be hit, in the scrotum and losing a testicle; he calmly reported to Levien that he had 'dropped a bollock', and the Germans allowed his evacuation in a Red Cross jeep. Another man was hit and left in the safety of a private house. A small group under Sergeant Bertie Carrier managed to dash through to the bridge (where two of them were later killed), but the remainder of the platoon was split up and forced into side streets. Lieutenant Levien's party of eleven men were guided by a gallant Dutchman, Jan Brouwer, into a house in the Bakkerstraat where another brave Dutch person, Miss Mieke Engelsman, took them in; her elderly parents were sent to another house. Levien was able to speak on the telephone with his company commander at the bridge, but the house was surrounded by Germans. After holding out for twenty-four hours and using up nearly all their ammunition, this party also surrendered.

Reinforcements

It was obvious that the remnants of the 1st Parachute Brigade Group in the streets of western Arnhem were no longer strong enough to push through to the bridge alone. But help was on the way. Although the divisional commander was absent from his headquarters, someone had been making far-reaching decisions, and two fresh battalions were arriving in the area.

When Major-General Urquhart set out on his travels the previous afternoon, Divisional Headquarters had been left in the care of his Chief of Staff, Lieutenant-Colonel Charles Mackenzie. By Monday morning Mackenzie knew that only part of the 2nd Battalion and some other troops had reached the Arnhem road bridge and that the 1st and 3rd Battalions were well short of their objective and encountering strong opposition. This information probably came from the divisional artillery, whose communications were working well. Mackenzie felt that the vital push into Arnhem needed reinforcing, but the only troops available were the two and a half battalions of the Airlanding Brigade which were now in position protecting the landing areas for the second lift expected later that morning. Mackenzie did not have the authority to move any of these troops.

Before leaving England, Major-General Urquhart had told Mackenzie how command of the division should pass if he became a casualty. His replacement should be the experienced Brigadier Lathbury, a choice to which no one would have objected. In the unlikely event of Lathbury also becoming a casualty, it would be Brigadier Hicks of the Airlanding Brigade and, in the extreme event of Hicks also being out of action, then Brigadier Hackett of the 4th Parachute Brigade. Mackenzie had no problem with the succession at this time. Urquhart and Lathbury were both out of contact; Hicks was only a short distance away; Hackett was in England waiting to board a plane with his men. Mackenzie set out by jeep to fetch Hicks to take command of the division and to suggest that more men should be sent into Arnhem.

Hicks was soon found – the time was now probably between 7.0 and 8.0 a.m. – and Mackenzie put his proposals to him. It is not known how much reluctance there was on the part of Hicks to leave his brigade and also to detach troops from it, but it was not until 9.15 a.m. that Hicks arrived at Divisional HQ. Because the Airlanding Brigade was such a large unit it had a deputy brigade commander, Colonel Hilaro Barlow, and he took over the brigade. The question of whether more troops should be sent to Arnhem had obviously already been discussed, because, within only fifteen minutes, Lieutenant-Colonel Derek McCardie of the 2nd South Staffords was ordered to gather in that part of his battalion that had landed the previous day, about 60 per cent of its strength, and take it into Arnhem. Control of the battalion was to pass to the 1st Parachute Brigade, an almost empty gesture because that brigade had no effective command, though it was hoped that Brigadier Lathbury could be found in Arnhem.

The despatch of this unit was a risk. The task of the Airlanding Brigade battalions was to protect the landing areas until the safe arrival of the second lift. The removal of the South Staffords left the area north of Wolfheze relatively unprotected against any serious German attack from that direction; its defence was handed over to a troop of the Reconnaissance Squadron and fifty glider pilots.

The morning passed, and what scanty information was received indicated that the 1st and 3rd Battalions were still having a tough time making progress in Arnhem. By 2.0 p.m. Brigadier Hicks had made a further decision about reinforcing those efforts. He confirmed that, as soon as the second lift arrived – expected in mid-morning, but delayed for four hours – the remainder of the South Staffords should go straight to Arnhem *and also the 11th Battalion from the 4th Parachute Brigade.* This last was a bold move. Here was one brigadier taking away, without any consultation, a battalion from a second brigadier the moment it arrived. Hicks judged that the existing attempt to reach the bridge was more important than the 4th Parachute Brigade's plan prepared in England days earlier, to skirt around Arnhem and take up position to the north of the town. (It is regretted that this is one occasion where the treatment of the battle by describing each major element through to its conclusion results in an event such as the 11th Battalion's detachment from its parent brigade and its subsequent actions being described before the main story of the second lift's arrival. The manner in which Brigadier Hackett reacted to this will be described in a later chapter.)

The 2nd South Staffords, about 420 strong, were brought in from their positions around Wolfheze and at 10.30 a.m. set off towards Arnhem. They were strafed by German fighters soon after leaving Wolfheze, and some men were wounded. All went well after that until they came to the area where the main road into Arnhem ran through the railway embankment just east of Oosterbeek, the position where the 1st Battalion had been fired upon earlier that morning and been forced south to the lower Oosterbeek railway bridge. The South Staffords had exactly the same experience and, like the 1st Battalion, had to side-step to the lower road. They were fired upon by snipers in Oosterbeek and encountered more serious fire in Arnhem but, by changing their route several times, eventually reached the area near St Elizabeth Hospital, where they met what was left of the 1st Battalion. It had taken seven hours to cover five and a half miles; two men had been killed and several wounded.

The next to arrive was Lieutenant-Colonel George Lea's 11th Battalion, fresh from its parachute drop that afternoon. This unit had left its rendezvous quickly and made a swifter passage, even though there had been a delay of more than two hours near the Hartenstein, to which Divisional HQ had now moved, possibly while Brigadiers Hicks and Hackett argued about the battalion's employment. Major David Gilchrist, commander of A Company, found it 'a nice, quiet afternoon walk to Oosterbeek, with no interference and no sounds of battle, followed by sitting on our backsides for several hours on a grassy bank near the Hartenstein. We were all perfectly happy at that stage.' The battalion was then led skilfully into Arnhem by some Dutch guides, finally coming up to the St Elizabeth Hospital area, but experiencing some fire in Arnhem and suffering at least three men killed. The last of the reinforcements to arrive were the men of the second-lift element of the South Staffords, who were delayed by the difficulty in following the changing path of the first part of the battalion. The men of this group were the last of so many men who passed under the railway bridge at Oosterbeek Laag Station to fight in Arnhem. They arrived in the rear of the 11th Battalion.

The time was about midnight. There were now two fresh battalions, at nearly full strength, together with the weary but still effective remains of the 1st and 3rd Battalions. They were all in the same area and available for a co-ordinated attack to be made for the first time. But there was no overall commander, despite, ironically, there being a wounded brigadier and a healthy divisional commander in hiding only a few hundred yards away. No senior officer had been sent from Divisional HQ to control the vital operations in this area. The scene was now set for the last real chance of getting a sizeable force of troops through to the bridge.

CHAPTER 10

The Battle in the Town – Tuesday

Lieutenant-Colonel Dobie's 1st Battalion HQ became the focus for the coming action, and he took the initiative in co-ordinating the main attempt. The period started with orders, counter-orders and some confusion which must have severely tried Dobie's patience. At 8.0 p.m. on Monday Lieutenant-Colonel McCardie of the South Staffords had come to Dobie and expressed himself willing to comply with the wishes of this officer who seemed to represent the authority of the 1st Parachute Brigade. A plan was made for a two-battalion attack to take place at 9.0 p.m.: the Staffords, about 600 strong, though still split into two parts, to attack on the upper road past St Elizabeth Hospital; the 1st Battalion, now that its R Company had come up, to attack again along the river-bank road. The 3rd Battalion, though close by, was not in contact, and the 11th Battalion had not yet arrived. But, while this move was being prepared, Divisional HQ received a false report that the force at the bridge had fallen, and Brigadier Hicks ordered that any attack being prepared be postponed. Later, at 1.0 a.m. (on Tuesday the 19th), orders came that the whole force should withdraw to Oosterbeek. It took an hour and a half for the false report about the surrender at the bridge to be corrected, and Dobie was ordered to resume his attack. He called Derek McCardie in again, and Lieutenant-Colonel George Lea, whose 11th Battalion had now arrived, also attended. Lieutenant 'Tsapy' Britneff, Dobie's Intelligence Officer, describes that meeting:

> The scene was, I suppose, dramatic – a darkened, bullet-shattered house with Col McCardie and others sitting and standing round a table lit by a single candle; a wireless set

whistling in the background. Dobie and McCardie determined, come what may, to reach the 2nd Battalion at the bridge before dawn. Dobie gave his orders sitting at the head of the dining-room table. 'We must help Johnnie Frost', was the theme. The plan was that the 1st Battalion would take the embankment road. The South Staffords would advance parallel to us along the main road; the 11th Para Battalion would follow on behind. Starting time around 0400 hours. We *had* to reach the bridge *before dawn*, because to be caught on the embankment was death.

Unknown to David Dobie, another effort had preceded his on that embankment by the Rhine. As he and his depleted battalion, having come down from their overnight position, moved forward along the river bank, they met part of Lieutenant-Colonel Fitch's 3rd Battalion which had made an earlier, independent attempt to push along by the same route. Fitch's men had advanced successfully in the dark for about half a mile until heavily fired upon by the German positions at the end of the open area and sustaining about a dozen casualties, including one of the few remaining officers and RSM Lord, both injured. John Fitch could see that there was no way through and, in the process of pulling back his men, met the 1st Battalion coming forward, still in the dark, along the open ground. Major Alan Bush of the 3rd Battalion tells of this conversation between David Dobie and Captain Richard Dorrien-Smith, a 3rd Battalion officer who had once served in the same company as Dobie:

Dobie: Good morning!
Dorrien-Smith: Where the hell do you think you're going?
Dobie: I'm going up here.
Dorrien-Smith: I wouldn't do that if I were you. It's full of mortars and machine-guns.
Dobie: How do you know?
Dorrien-Smith: Because I've bloody well been there.
Dobie: Well, come and show us.
Dorrien-Smith: Not bloody likely.

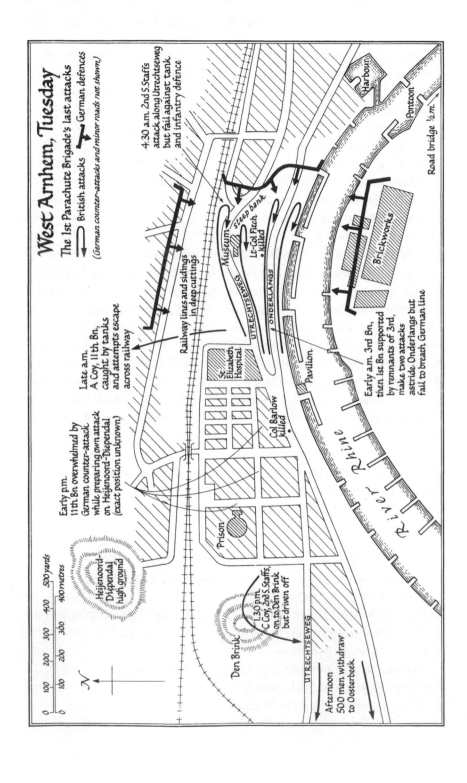

West Arnhem, Tuesday

The 1st Parachute Brigade's last attacks

↑ British attacks   ↱ German defences

(German counter-attacks and minor roads not shown)

4.30 a.m. 2nd S.Staffs attack along Utrechtseweg but fail against tank and infantry defence

Harbour

Pontoon

Road bridge ½ m.

Brickworks

Late a.m.
A Coy, 11th Bn,
caught by tanks
and attempts escape
across railway

Railway lines and sidings in deep cuttings

Museum

steep bank

Lt-Col Fitch killed

ONDERLANGS

UTRECHTSEWEG

Pavilion

Early a.m. 3rd Bn,
then 1st Bn, supported
by remnants of 3rd,
make two attacks
astride Onderlangs but
fail to breach German line

Early p.m.
11th Bn overwhelmed by
German counter-attack
while preparing own attack
on Heijenoord–Diependal
(exact position unknown)

St. Elizabeth Hospital

Col Barlow killed

Prison

River Rhine

Heijenoord–
Diependal
high ground

N

0   100   200   300   400   500 yards

0   100   200   300   400   500 metres

Den Brink

1.30 p.m.
C Coy, 2nd S.Staffs,
mn. to Den Brink
but driven off

UTRECHTSEWEG

Afternoon
500 men withdraw
to Oosterbeek

Lieutenant Britneff observed that Dobie was 'quite infuriated' at the news that the way ahead might be blocked, but he decided to press on. John Fitch decided to lead his weary men forward yet again; Alan Bush says: 'Now that we had got rid of the divisional commander and the brigade commander, Fitch was determined to do everything he could to support David Dobie and help get through to the bridge.' So the fifty men who were now the only effective members of the 3rd Battalion moved on to the slope to the left of the river bank in an attempt to find cover among some bushes from which to give supporting fire to the 1st Battalion attack. (It should be mentioned that among the 3rd Battalion men in this and recent actions was a group of Royal Engineers from C Troop, 1st Parachute Squadron, who had loyally remained with the 3rd Battalion since leaving the landing area.)

A short distance to the north, Derek McCardie's South Staffords started their move forward about half an hour later, astride the main road (the Utrechtseweg, later becoming the Utrechtsestraat) which ran uphill in front of the dominant building of St Elizabeth Hospital. But this road steadily diverged from the river bank, so that the attacking forces gradually separated, and the co-ordination agreed at Dobie's conference did not last long. Both units made good initial progress – and then it started to get light.

The Germans had pulled back the defence line which had held the 1st and 3rd Battalions on the previous evening and had now located it in and around the buildings at the far end of an open space between 700 and 900 yards beyond the starting-point of these new British attacks. But they had also placed forces on either side of that open space, not directly on the edges of it but set well back in cover so that they could not be engaged by the light British weapons but could fire their own heavy weapons into the flanks of the British attacks. These flanking defences were on an embankment on the far side of the railway cutting to the north and in the brickworks on the south of the river. The different levels of the ground meant that the fire from neither German flanking force would hit their own men opposite. Fire from the south bank would finish up hitting the steep embankment; loose shots from beyond the railway would pass over the heads of the

Germans on the south bank. This was a very important point, because the attacking airborne men would be fired on from both flanks as well as having to face the weapons and tanks at the far end of the open space. The Germans had no less than five 'battle groups' manning these defences, one on either flank and three in the main defence line ahead. All were from the 9th SS Panzer Division.

The savage encounter between these German troops and the airborne men advancing here in the growing light would prove to be the turning-point of the Battle of Arnhem. The Germans were well supplied with armour, heavy weapons and ammunition, were comparatively fresh and could remain in the protection of their trenches, house positions or armoured vehicles. Many of the airborne men were very tired and short of ammunition; they were only armed with light weapons. They would need to get to very close quarters to be able to fight on equal terms, and that the coming daylight would not permit. Nor would the airborne men be able to manoeuvre; the railway and the river barriers ruled out any flanking move. There was no effective artillery support, no friendly armour, no fighter bombers. Fighting in the open spaces of Tunisia, Sicily and Italy and exercises in England had not prepared them for anything like the urban conditions here in Arnhem. The results of the optimism over the lack of German opposition and the decision to drop the division so far from its objectives were about to become apparent.

There was one happy result of the withdrawal of the Germans to their new postions; Major-General Urquhart and his two companions were released from their hiding place. An anti-tank officer, Lieutenant Eric Clapham, drove Urquhart and Captain Taylor back to Divisional HQ; Lieutenant Cleminson rejoined the 3rd Battalion.[1] The wounded Brigadier Lathbury was not rescued and had to remain in hiding in another house.

---

[1] When Major-General Urquhart needed a new aide-de-camp in the summer of 1945, he remembered the young officer who had shared his overnight hiding place and chose Cleminson, despite the memory of his irritation during that night at Cleminson's large moustache.

The 1st and 3rd Parachute Battalions

The 1st Battalion attack moved on, Major Perrin-Brown's T Company on the grassy bank on the left of the riverside road (the Onderlangs) and Major Stark's S Company on the esplanade alongside the river itself, though neither company mustered more than a platoon's worth of men. They were spotted in the growing light. I am reluctant to use journalistic phrases like 'a hail of fire', but that is what struck them, mainly from armoured vehicles and infantry weapons located in and around the buildings only 150 yards away on the upper road which the South Staffords had not yet reached. The Germans were even throwing down grenades on the men on the left-hand side of the attack. The airborne men charged. Some outlying German positions in the open space were cleared, by bayonet and grenades mostly, and those Germans in them who were not killed were hustled away as prisoners. When the end of the open area was nearly reached, 800 yards from the starting-point, the German defences ahead opened up. There was a pause at one stage, while David Dobie called for a count of the remaining strength; it was only thirty-nine men including himself. Major Timothy's R Company, just six men, were out in front now. Dobie was up with them, trying to find positions in which to take cover. He was wounded in the head, but not seriously. There was no way through and no immediate shelter. He ordered his men to move to the left and get into some houses there. Major Perrin-Brown and seven men reached one house; Dobie, Major Timothy and five men went into another. Major Stark's group was further back, having taken shelter in some captured German trenches. The attack was finished. The time was about 6.30 a.m.; it had lasted two hours.

These are some 'snapshot' descriptions of that final action by the 1st Battalion. Private Bryan Willoughby:

Every now and again someone was hit, further depleting our numbers as we kept moving in battle formation. Stopping to give help to those hit was unfortunately out of the question. A little further on we were joined by another company. Here we were stopped abruptly by a very determined Spandau machine-gun. I heard an order given by an officer from the newly joined company – 'Take that gun out!' There was a pause; nothing happened; then a rush accompanied by shouts of 'Waho Mahomed!' followed by complete silence. No more machine-gun. I was glad not to be involved in that. However, I got my turn very shortly after this incident – not in any way sought after, I must add. We were being annoyed by fire coming over an embankment between houses on our left. Two of us were sent up to see to it. To complicate the situation, a gun on the right, over the river, kept thudding shells into the embankment. At the top we could see the Germans across a square filing into the houses, so we were able to take some pot shots at them.

On coming down from the embankment, I was sent as Company Runner to tell the remaining platoons to close up for another push forward. There weren't many men left. Just a handful with one officer moved out into the open ground to move finally on to the bridge. We didn't get far. The last thing I remember was firing at anything that moved at a house straight ahead and then seeing the company commander, Major Timothy, giving the 'Close on me' signal outside one of the houses far away on our left. I didn't quite make it, however. I ran into a shower of hand grenades coming from the upstairs windows of the houses in the row and was taken prisoner.

Sergeant Frank Manser:

After about an hour and a half I reached nearly to the houses at the end of the open area. I was fired on there, but for the first time I could see where the fire was coming from. They were about ten yards away in a sandbagged position, possibly a section position with several different weapons. I could see their helmets. I was completely on my own and in completely open ground. I fired back. I had a Colt .45 and the tommy-gun, but I ran out of ammunition, and that is when they hit me. I had lain down with my arms covering my head. I felt them shoot off the haversack on my back, then I was wounded in the left arm and under the heart – two separate shots.

I think the Germans retired from that position, because I was able to get up about ten minutes later and go back to the river side. I was sitting there, nursing my arm and with the pain under my heart, when along came Major Stark waving a revolver. 'Come along, Manser; we've got to get to the bridge.' But I was too far gone. He went on, but I don't think anyone got much further than that.

Private James Shelbourne was in a group which probably advanced further than any other:

Many men fell in the early phase of that attack, at least one of them, a young, recently married officer, cremated by his own phosphorus grenades.[2] I saw German machine-gunners blasted out of their sandbagged emplacements with hand grenades, endured a lively strafing from a brick factory across the river, and engaged a few shadowy targets among the trees of the escarpment immediately to our left.

But opposition diminished to occasional sniper fire after we drew level with the museum high above us. In effect we had breached the enemy line and were now well forward of the South Staffords, who were stalled on the upper road between St Elizabeth Hospital and the museum. Eventually our advance was blocked by the entrance channel to a dock several acres in extent. We could only wheel left, up the escarpment and into a row of houses.

Private John Hall:

There were now only a few of us left, and one of the few NCOs left gave the order – 'EVERY MAN FOR HIMSELF!' My intention then was to get to the river bank, using what cover I could. I planned to make my way along the river and try to swim across. I threw the Bren gun into some bushes; pack and ammunition pouches followed. This left me in my smock, which would give me some camouflage, I

---

[2] I have been asked not to identify the young officer who burned to death.

thought. I made it to the river bank, how I don't know, as we were still being fired upon. Using what cover I could from the shrubs I managed to make some headway, but then I came across a para who was shot in the foot. He asked if I could help him. I removed his boot – a bloody mess, I thought – then I gave him a morphine injection. As I started to bandage him up, I suddenly heard a voice. Looking up, I saw a German SS, a light machine-gun pointing at me. I honestly thought I was going to die there and then; we sometimes did not take prisoners, so I did not expect them to either. Perhaps he thought I was a medical orderly and spared me. I didn't ask.

It took a further hour, until 7.30 a.m., for the Germans to force those who had taken shelter in the houses to surrender. There was no defence to a tank firing shells at point-blank range into a house, all the exits of which were covered by machine-guns. Of the 140 men who carried out the attack, nine had been killed, including an officer and two sergeants; hardly any returned to safety that day, though a few evaded capture or escaped later. The rest were all wounded and taken to St Elizabeth Hospital or were taken away as prisoners under SS escort.

The attempt by the even weaker 3rd Battalion to support the attack had been unsuccessful. Its men had deployed into the bushy bank between the two roads but had been seen by the Germans, who systematically quartered the area with machine-guns and mortars; this soon prevented both forward movement and the setting up of the supporting fire positions for the 1st Battalion which was John Fitch's primary intention. Alan Bush describes how the move was finally halted and forced back:

The Colonel called an O-Group with myself, the Adjutant – Charles Seccombe – and the IO. We were about 250 yards from the pavilion. The Colonel was sitting with his back to the German mortar fire, which was coming down steadily, foot by foot, along the bushes. I could see it coming and said we must get out of there. He told me to get the men back; most of them were behind us; the Colonel was as far forward as anybody. I moved back and found about thirty of our men and told them to run straight back to the pavilion. One or two were badly injured in the arms or shoulders, and I told these to go straight up the slope to St Elizabeth Hospital. I don't know whether they made it; with any luck they should have done. I expected to see the Colonel and the other officers in the pavilion soon after, but they didn't arrive.

Private George Marsh, one of the battalion signallers, tells what happened to the Adjutant:

We hadn't gone more than 200 yards in the attack when Captain Seccombe stopped me and said, 'Get the BBC on your set and see if there is any news of Second Army's progress towards us.' I said, 'Sorry, sir, I am on battalion net and can only call on the hour, every hour, to conserve batteries.' He said, 'I am giving you an order; do it now.' While I was getting the BBC, Captain Seccombe walked about thirty yards away. I had the earphones on but could still hear a large explosion behind me. A mortar bomb had fallen and blown his legs off. I was sickened by the sight but ran over the road on which the 20-millimetre gun was firing and found some medics, who brought a stretcher. It was here that one of my friends lost his arm to a 20-millimetre shell.

(Captain Seccombe – described by his friend Alan Bush as 'known as Good-time Charlie; he liked his beer and was always laughing' – later had the remains of both legs amputated at the hip by the Germans. His girlfriend, a war widow, remained loyal and married him after the war.)

The Intelligence Officer, Lieutenant Vedeniapine, came back, badly wounded with mortar splinters in his back and chest and reported that Lieutenant-Colonel Fitch had been killed by the same mortar bomb that had wounded him. Major Bush went forward again to make sure that Fitch was not still alive and to fetch back any survivors, but he was cut off by the now advancing Germans and forced to hide. Thus ended the last battle of the 3rd Battalion as a formed unit.

The 2nd South Staffordshires

The main attack on the upper road, by Lieutenant-Colonel Derek McCardie's battalion along the Utrechtseweg in front of St Elizabeth Hospital, started half an hour late, at 4.30 a.m. D Company led off, followed by B and A Companies; with Battalion HQ there were about 340 men. C Company was in reserve, and many of the support weapons were also in the rear because they could not be deployed in the darkness and in the urban surroundings in which the battalion would fight its one and only major battle at Arnhem. These were all glider-borne troops, but Lieutenant David Russell and four of his men who had escaped when the 2nd Battalion's C Company had been taken prisoner the previous day voluntarily joined in the attack, hoping it would enable them to rejoin their own battalion at the bridge. Immediately in the rear, however, was a complete parachute battalion, the 11th, ready to support the Staffords' attack.

It was an eerie advance in the dark along that wide main road in front of the well-lit hospital with its large Red Cross flag. Accounts nearly all mention a wrecked tram with a dead German killed the previous day stretched out on the roadway alongside it. David Russell says that 'As we moved over to the south side of the road, we could see big fires near the road bridge, an awesome sight with a church tower silhouetted against the flames and the greying sky.' No one could be quite sure where the Germans were, and the Staffords started nervously forward, taking cover where they could, behind garden walls, bushes, corners of buildings, lamp-posts, trees. Long bursts of machine-gun fire kept swishing along the road from ahead and across it from the side streets and passages on the left. It was a standard German tactic in the dark to fire such bursts at irregular intervals; they had plenty of ammunition. Sergeant Norman Howes says: 'It was totally unlike any other action. We had spent months and months practising battalion attacks on a 400- to 600-yards front, and the battalion finished up attacking up a street no more than fifty yards wide.' There were some Germans in the houses, even though this was not yet the main German line, and the advance was several times held up by opposition. Within half an hour, the leading company lost 40 per cent of its strength in casualties in advancing about 300 yards to just past the hospital. Its commander, Major John Phillp, was shot through the stomach, and two other officers were killed, one of them, Captain 'Oscar' Wyss, described as last seen leading his men 'waving his walking stick and shouting, "Come on, lads!", as if it was only an exercise on Salisbury Plain'.

B Company, meanwhile, had also become involved in the fighting. It would be led by Captain Reggie Foote until Major Robert Cain, whose glider had force-landed in England on the first day, came up later in the morning. The battalion account becomes confused at this point, and it is unclear how far B Company progressed, but it was certainly not much further than the museum, an advance of about 650 yards from where the battalion started and well short of the point reached by the 1st Battalion fighting at the bottom of the steep slope which fell away from the museum area to the river.[3] The reason for the lack of further progress was that tanks were among the houses 150 yards ahead. Derek McCardie sent the third of his companies forward to consolidate the original gain and to provide a firm base for a possible future advance if the opposition ahead could be outflanked. This was Major T. B. Lane's full-strength A Company. Its men moved up, past the hospital and past the dead of the earlier attack, and took cover with Company HQ and one platoon in the museum itself and the other three platoons in and around houses on the other side of the road.

Here the battalion's attack stuck. It was now light. Mortar fire fell among the men who were in the open near the museum; German tanks came forward, almost to point-blank range when the supply of Piat bombs was exhausted, and started firing into the museum and the houses where most of A Company was sheltering. There was a stalemate, any attempts by the Staffords to show themselves at windows or to move in the open drawing instant fire. The Germans brought up self-propelled guns and infantry ready for a counter-attack. Major Cain, who managed to join his company

[3] All South Stafford reports and accounts erroneously refer to the museum as 'the monastery'. It was built as a gentlemen's private club, but this went bankrupt in 1903 and the building became the Arnhem Municipal Museum in 1918 and remains so to this day.

in and around a hollow in the slope outside the museum, later wrote an account of this period:[4]

We found ourselves being attacked by tanks; this was between 9 and 10 in the morning. Our mortars were trying to engage the Germans who were far too close to them. The mortar officer was removing the secondary charges in order to reduce the range of the bombs, and they were shooting straight up in the air. Some tanks came in from the low road, between the river and the bulk of the town. They were firing with 88-mm guns up into the dell which we occupied. We had no anti-tank guns because we couldn't get them up the road, mainly because the pelting fire was so heavy. We had, therefore, to use Piats to cope with the tanks.

We held them for two or three hours. Lieutenant Georges Dupenois was in action with his Piat and Jock Buchanan and I were drawing the fire and trying to get ammunition for Georges, which we did. When a tank appeared, we got four Brens firing on it with tracers. That shut the tank up, because the commander couldn't stand up in the turret. As soon as we let off a Piat at it, we'd move back, and then the German shells would explode below us. We were firing at 100 to 150 yards' range. Dupenois fired about ten to twenty rounds. Once, instead of hitting a tank, he hit a house with a Greek inscription on it which he read and which made him laugh.

It was impossible to tell how many tanks there were and I don't think we ever disabled one, for we never saw the crew get out. All this lasted until about 11.30 a.m. Then the Piat ammunition gave out. The tanks came up and were firing right into our dell and our men were just being killed one after the other. I saw one of our men with just his face showing, his eyes wide open. You could hear the call of 'Stretcher bearer' all the time. There was no effective fire going back to those beasts because we had no more ammunition.

The CO came up and told us to pull out of the dell, which was an absolute deathtrap. I remember seeing the whole of a

---

[4] Unpublished account by Major Cain, Airborne Forces Museum, File No. 54.

bush blown out of the ground while I was talking to him. I put a rearguard with a Canadian officer and a dozen men with a Bren to cover our pull-out . . . This was the South Staffs' Waterloo.

The only other personal accounts available are from men who were in the museum. There were about forty of them in the building, mostly South Staffords, but also Lieutenant Russell's 2nd Battalion party. He had been asked by the Staffords to take his party to the top of the building and act as observers. They took up position in what was probably the caretaker's flat and were able to report various events and sometimes fire on Germans, and they helped direct the mortar fire outside already described by Major Cain. David Russell describes how the end came:

I suppose it was about mid-morning when I saw the outlines of a large tank through the garden gate. I warned the company commander, who sent a Piat forward to cover the road; we stayed upstairs. The tank milled around, treating the world in general to bursts of MG and big wallops of gunfire. We were, as yet, untouched. More tanks appeared to have arrived, as there was now gunfire from the bottom road up into the gully and another was reported on the top road. The Piat scored a hit on the extra side armour of one tank, but failed to put it out of action. An assault gun moved slowly along the top road, blowing to pieces and setting on fire all the houses around the museum. Up came another tank in our rear and started on our building, the first two rounds taking off the living room which we had just left. I had a quick conference at the foot of the stairs with the Staffords' company commander and other officers; the ground floor was full of wounded. Were we to fight on with small arms against tanks, try to break out, or surrender? We decided that as our object – to join those fighting at the bridge – was impossible and as the building was being systematically demolished and there was nowhere to break out to, we should surrender. I chucked my Sten over a hedge, buried my pistol, and walked out with a handkerchief.

Sergeant Norman Howes was the platoon sergeant of the Staffords platoon in the museum:

> I went downstairs to check on the ammo supply and spoke with CSM Vic Williams. I can remember some tank and mortar fire, but nothing very local, so it was with a somewhat casual air that I remounted the wooden steps to the first floor to my platoon position. You might imagine my shock on seeing, instead of my platoon, German troops, two of them facing me as I entered the room, each with rifles in hand. I could see others in the background.
>
> I weighed up the odds and threw myself back down the steps. At the bottom was an upright piano and, guessing what was following, I got down behind it. At least one grenade was thrown, and the two Germans then came down the steps to check me out. I shot the first; I am not sure if I hit the second as he got up the steps. I shouted to the Dutch people who were there that the Germans were in the building and reported to CSM Williams in the corridor.
>
> Things were getting very noisy by this time, with tank shellfire being directed at the sides of the building and, it seemed, non-stop MG fire. About six of our men then came running back down the corridor – all unarmed. I stopped them and sent them to the exit, to the Regimental Aid Post to collect arms and ammunition discarded by the wounded. I followed them. It was a maelstrom of confusion and noise. At the aid post, with the wounded and the dead, was the padre, Captain Buchanan; he saw me stopping there and shouted, 'Not here, sergeant; we have wounded.'

The Dutch people referred to were the caretaker, Mr Berendsen, and his family and the Van Loon family who had been taken in by the Berendsens when their own home was requisitioned by the Germans. Mrs Van Loon later found a spent bullet in the blankets of her baby's pram. Also in the museum at some stage was a Dutch commando attached to the airborne men who calmly used the civilian telephone in the middle of this action to speak to his parents at Ede.

The end was nigh. The German tanks and self-propelled guns were able to roam at will once the Staffords' Piat ammunition was exhausted. Infantry had entered the museum through a breach in the walls. One of the houses occupied by an A Company platoon was ablaze, though the men inside were still firing from the unburnt part of the house. Lieutenant-Colonel McCardie had authorized B Company to retire from its exposed area in the open, but only Major Cain and a few men managed to get away. A Company started to surrender in increasing numbers as the tanks got in among them; Battalion HQ was also overrun. After his return from prison camp in 1945, Derek McCardie wrote to Major Cain:

> I still can't believe that I was taken prisoner. It was a thing I had vowed should never happen. I was trying to get to A Company, to find out why the hell they weren't shooting at those tanks, and I suppose that something must have fired at me. At any rate, I found myself under about two feet of earth with two Germans pointing Schmeissers at me.[5]

Large numbers of men became prisoners. The Medical Officer, Captain Brian Brownscombe, and possibly Padre Buchanan, managed to get to St Elizabeth Hospital, where they continued their work; but of the other officers only Major Cain managed to get away. Of the hundreds of men taken prisoner, only one, Sergeant Jim Drew, sent a contribution for this book:

> A vehicle came up and down the street with a loud hailer shouting, 'Come out, you South Staffords, with your hands up. You are surrounded, and there is no way out.' We stayed in the cellar, where the firing was now very heavy. Eventually the cellar was kicked open, and a German threw an object on the cellar floor. We jumped to the other side, expecting a grenade to explode. After several minutes I looked and saw that it was a house brick. He was, indeed, the finest German that I had never met. We were then taken prisoner of war.

---

[5] Copy of letter kindly supplied by the Royal Staffordshire Regiment.

The 11th Parachute Battalion

All through his battalion's action, Lieutenant-Colonel McCardie had believed that the South Staffords would have the support of the 11th Battalion, which was located in full strength only a few hundred yards in the rear of that battle around the museum. When his two leading companies became pinned down, he had sent up his third company to provide a firm base and then looked for a further force to attempt an outflanking move on the left, between the main road and the railway; although this was a confined area, it seemed the best way of renewing the advance. McCardie's own fourth company, C Company, should have carried out this move but it was still well back and temporarily leaderless; its commander, Major Phillip Wright, had come ahead to receive orders but had been killed on the way. It was to the 11th Battalion, therefore, that McCardie looked for this flanking attack.

Lieutenant-Colonel George Lea was quite willing to help. Major David Gilchrist's A Company moved forward and positioned itself east of the hospital, between the road and the railway.[6] Gilchrist's small Company HQ was on the other side of the road, between his own men and Lieutenant-Colonel McCardie's HQ. While waiting for the order to attack, Major Gilchrist found that the company jeep and trailer had been borrowed by the battalion padre for a burial and had not returned; the trailer was loaded with all of the company's Piats. Another set-back at that time was a direct hit on his HQ which killed CSM George Ashdown and wounded the second in command, Captain Peter Perse. But no order to move came. 'So,' says Gilchrist, 'there we were, waiting on our start line, the platoons north of the road invisible to the Germans and quite safe. We could hear shooting in front but couldn't see forward because of a hedge and the slope of the road.'

Major-General Urquhart was now back in command at Divisional HQ. Having seen some of the fighting in Arnhem, he obviously did not approve of this seemingly haphazard way of sending one battalion after another into what he believed was a hopeless venture.

---

[6] In or near what is now the car-park between the hospital and the Van Lingen College.

It was too late to save the South Staffords, but he sent orders by an officer messenger that the 11th Battalion was not to take part in the battle being fought; that instruction was timed at around 9.0 a.m. Urquhart also despatched a senior officer to take control of the confused situation in this area, but that officer was killed before he could have any effect; his death will be described later. There was a delay of about two hours before further orders reached the 11th Battalion, and it was during this period that the South Staffords, waiting for the support of an outflanking move which never came, were struck by the German counter-attacks and overwhelmed. Major Gilchrist describes the effect upon his company:

Some of the South Staffs fell back through us. I met Major Cain, who said, 'The tanks are coming; give me a Piat.' I had to apologize that we hadn't any. So the South Staffs disappeared down the hill behind us, hotly pursued by German tanks and infantry. We were outflanked and couldn't engage the tanks, but we were engaging infantry. We had a troop of 6-pounders in support, just behind us, but they couldn't engage the tanks because of the slope of the hill. We started to fall back, and about twenty of us took up position in some six-foot-deep trenches just east of the hospital, probably dug as air-raid shelters. We tried throwing Gammon bombs at the tanks, but it was not easy from those deep trenches, and we had no success. The tanks came to within thirty or forty yards and were firing on us.

After about a quarter of an hour of this, I realized we weren't achieving very much, stuck in the bottom of those trenches and not able to see what we were shooting at, so I decided that the group with me would break out to the north over the railway. That was quite hairy, because the railway cutting was fifty or sixty feet deep. There was a German tank on a bridge over the railway further up, shooting down the railway. We were young and fit in those days and we moved like hell, down the bank, over the rails and up the other side. A few men were hit by the tank's machine-gun, but most of us got across.

We rather thought that the area we had come to would have

been held by the rest of our 4th Parachute Brigade, which we expected to be up by now. We didn't know the Germans were there.

In a manner which was now becoming familiar, Major Gilchrist and this small party tried to take shelter in a house but were soon captured. Only one of A Company's officers, Lieutenant Arthur Vickers, and a few men escaped from that area; most of the remainder of the company were taken prisoner.

That is only the story of one company. What happened to the remainder of the 11th Battalion? At some time before 11.0 a.m. a completely new order was received from Divisional HQ. The battalion was to turn north and attack over the railway, to capture some high ground marked on maps as the Heijenoord-Diependal feature. The purpose of this move was to secure the high ground through which the 4th Parachute Brigade was hoping to pass in its separate battle then taking place to get into Arnhem from a fresh direction. It took until 12.30 p.m. for the 11th Battalion (less A Company) to get into position for this move. Lieutenant-Colonel Lea decided to utilize C Company of the South Staffords, which was waiting around in the area. Major Cain had come back from the earlier fighting area and took charge of both this leaderless company and the remnants of the other South Staffords companies, which he formed into two platoons. Lieutenant-Colonel Lea ordered Cain to secure the nearby feature of Den Brink (see map on page 192 for these moves) to act as a pivot for his own battalion's attack. The South Staffords did well, getting up on to the high ground without difficulty, but were then spotted by the Germans and suffered heavy mortaring, being unable to dig in because the ground was too thick with roots for the men's light entrenching tools. There were many casualties.

The time was now about 2.30 p.m. and everything started to go wrong. The Germans saw the 11th Battalion forming up for their move northwards and turned their mortars on them. German tanks also appeared, having moved round the north of the screen of British anti-tank guns which had always been just in the rear of the attacking battalions. The battalion was caught in the open by these two dangers. The term 'overwhelmed' is often used too loosely but it is appropriate on this occasion. The 11th Battalion almost ceased to exist, never having had the chance to make even one attacking move. Only about 150 men managed to get away; most of the remainder, including Lieutenant-Colonel Lea, who was wounded, became prisoners. The South Staffords on Den Brink were also attacked by the tanks and had to retire. Major Cain, who seemed to emerge unscathed from every action, later wrote: 'It would have been a sheer waste of life to stay there. I had no orders to retire, but I remembered what had happened at the monastery. I felt extremely dejected. I knew that our particular effort to get through to the bridge was a failure and that we had been thrown out of the town.'

The last attempt to reach the bridge by the 1st Parachute Brigade and the two battalions sent up as reinforcements had failed, just under forty-eight hours after the brigade had marched off its drop zone on Sunday afternoon. (*See new note on page 216.*)

In the Rear of the Fighting

There had been various groups of troops just to the rear of the action all through the battle that was now ending. This was in the built-up area near the junction of the Utrechtseweg and the Onderlangs, and also in the network of streets on the western side of St Elizabeth Hospital. Here were to be found those elements of battalions which had not been committed to the battle, such as jeep drivers, medical orderlies, Vickers machine-gunners and other men from Headquarters or Support Companies, men who had become separated from their companies in the original moves into Arnhem but who had now caught up, the remnants of companies whose battles were over and also anti-tank gunners whose guns could not be deployed any further forward. There were considerable numbers of such men. Most had taken cover in houses, although the anti-tank gunners were available to man their guns if tanks appeared. This mixed group had a fighting potential, but no one was in overall command, and there were few potential leaders present. Many of these men were confused, tired or simply content to remain where they were and let events decide their future.

Some efforts had been made to reinforce the battalions fighting further forward. Lieutenants John Williams and Bill Fraser of the 1st and 3rd Battalions, who were both liaison officers left behind in the divisional area, and Major J. S. A. Buchanan, the South Staffords Support Company commander, had all, separately, gone up to Arnhem by jeep, collecting isolated parties and stragglers from their battalions as they went.

Reports credit Williams with collecting up to fifty men of his battalion, Buchanan with sixty South Staffords, and Fraser as gathering 120 from all units of the 1st Parachute Brigade, although there may have been some overlapping in those figures. This substantial group eventually reached the area behind the main battle, but, again, there was no one there to organize their further use.[7]

When Major-General Urquhart returned to his headquarters early on that Tuesday morning, he realized that no one was in overall command of the stalled advance towards the bridge and immediately sent a senior officer forward with orders to take charge. The officer chosen was Colonel Hilaro Barlow, the deputy commander of the 1st Airlanding Brigade. This full colonel was the ideal officer for the task of taking control of the units fighting in Arnhem. Accompanied by his batman, he sped off in a jeep, but Divisional HQ never heard of him again, and his body was never found. His disappearance long remained a mystery, but Barlow did reach the area immediately behind the fighting, and there was a witness to his death – Captain John McCooke of the South Staffords:

> Lieutenant-Colonel McCardie had sent me back to make sure our transport didn't come any further forward. I found the transport near the junction of the Utrechtseweg and the lower road. Colonel Barlow appeared there with his batman and asked me about the situation in front. I decided to go forward with him. Heavy mortaring started, and we made a dash for one of the houses which back on to the river. But the

[7] Lieutenant Fraser found a soldier's grave at Oosterbeek the next day; Lieutenant Williams and Major Buchanan returned to England and were awarded DSOs.

one we got into was on fire in the top storey and it had some bodies in it, and we were being sniped at. So we decided to move on to another building, two houses along. We arranged that I would go first, Colonel Barlow second, and his batman third.

As I ran, I heard a crash behind me and was slightly injured in the leg by a mortar-bomb fragment. I collapsed in the doorway of the house we were making for. No one followed me in. I looked out, back down the street, but couldn't see anything. I went upstairs and looked out of the front bedroom window. There I saw what I can only describe as a mess on the pavement – which I presumed was Colonel Barlow – and a dead body behind that which must have been his batman.

I can never understand why Colonel Barlow's death was always described as a mystery. I reported the incident when I was debriefed after the battle and after the war wrote to some of the authors whose books kept referring to the mystery.[8]

It was into this area that the German counter-attack came at about midday (reports are vague on timings at this stage), tanks nosing carefully forward with infantry in close support. There were some gallant actions by the British anti-tank gunners. There were elements of three 6-pounder anti-tank troops present – A and C Troops of the 1st Airlanding Anti-Tank Battery and E Troop of

---

[8] Colonel Barlow was killed outside one of the houses now numbered in the low twenties on the Utrechtseweg. The body of his batman, Lance-Corporal Raymond Singer, was found and is now buried in the Arnhem Oosterbeek War Cemetery; Colonel Barlow's name is commemorated on the Groesbeek Memorial for the Missing.

There was an interesting sequel in 1954 when Major John Waddy (a company commander with 156 Battalion at Arnhem) was in Arnhem and he was given a blackened and crumpled silver cigarette case on which the name 'Waddy' could be discerned. When John Waddy returned home and had the case straightened and cleaned by a jeweller, it was found that the case had been presented by John Waddy's father, CO of the 2nd Somerset Light Infantry in the mid-1930s, to Hilaro Barlow – then a captain – for winning a point-to-point race. The battered case had been found by an Arnhem boy in the Alexanderstraat about 150 yards from where Colonel Barlow was killed.

the 2nd Battery; these had been attached to the 1st, 3rd and 11th Battalions respectively. The South Staffords Anti-Tank Platoon had been kept back in the divisional area. Gunner Len Clarke of E Troop describes the action in which his gun was involved; it was in the front garden of a house looking straight up the road towards St Elizabeth Hospital:

> This tank was coming down the road from the hospital. I think he had an idea something was about and he was going very carefully. Lieutenant Glover, the troop commander, was with us – he always came with E4 gun. 'I'll have a shot at this,' he said, and took over my layer's position at the telescopic sight. I didn't care for that much. 'I'm the layer,' I said. 'Yes, and I'm the officer,' he said, and I had to obey orders. We fired three shots. All shots hit the tank; you couldn't miss at that range. I heard later that we immobilized it. We up-gunned and moved back then.

Another description comes from Gunner 'Dickie' Bird, a signaller with one of the Light Regiment's forward observation officers, who had been 'caught short' and had been using a Dutch family's toilet:

> As I left the house, I saw to my right the front end of a tank that was turning into the street and I was drawn into a general rush down towards an anti-tank gun sited in front of some park railings. The tank opened up with its machine-gun, and men were falling like ninepins on the other side of the street. The gun No. 1 was yelling to people to get out of his line of fire, but too late; the tank got in first, and I was almost knocked over by the blast that left the gun crew spread-eagled.

Gunner Eric Milner of C Troop describes how one abandoned gun was rescued from near St Elizabeth Hospital:

> An officer came asking for a driver. I accompanied him to the front of the hospital, and he pointed to a jeep and gun, with

no sign of the crew. He wanted me to get it to a safer place, as a tank was coming down the road and would soon see it as a target.

I had to turn the jeep round first, as it was facing the tank, which was still some distance away. Just as I turned, the tank saw me and fired, but the shells were going over my head. I looked around and saw, as the tank gun fired, the shell bounced off a bump in the road, and so over my head, probably saving my life. There was one more fright for me; as I drove to safety, I ran over power cables in the road with blue flashes everywhere.

The German tanks came on, steadily subduing all opposition. The British hold on western Arnhem, so dearly bought, was coming to an end. A piecemeal withdrawal commenced. Anyone not immediately threatened by the advancing Germans started leaving by vehicle or on foot. Those trapped in houses were mostly taken prisoner, to become the third large haul of captives taken by the Germans that day. I have several good accounts from men taken prisoner in this fashion. This one, by Private Fred Morton of the 3rd Battalion's Machine-Gun Platoon, can represent them all:

There were nine of us, under a corporal. We had fortified a pair of terrace houses, knocking out the wall between them, awaiting orders which didn't come. We had a good view of the road, and there, coming up it, was a full company of Germans marching on either side of the road, a bit cocky and supported by a Tiger tank. We decided that we would take full advantage of the fact that they didn't know we were there. We waited till the very last moment and then we opened fire with everything we had. We caught them napping, and at least seven or eight went down at once, but they were soon off the mark and getting into cover. Unfortunately the heaviest weapon we had was a Bren gun; we did pretty well but had nothing to hit the tank with. We had one Gammon bomb, and one of the chaps threw it at the tank from an upstairs window. The tank was right outside the house, but the bomb hit the railings of the house and went off with a big bang. The tank was so close to the house that it couldn't use its gun, but his machine-gun was coming right through the doors and windows, so we retreated upstairs. One man remained at the top of the stairs, covering the front door. The rest of us took up positions at the windows of the bedrooms and bathroom – four windows in all.

Everything went quiet for a bit. I don't think they knew our strength. There was a lot of shouting, and they surrounded the house. Then they opened up on us, and we replied again; we had a fair amount of fire-power. We held out for about an hour, but things were getting tight then. Two of the chaps decided to get out by the back way, hoping to get down to the river, which was about a hundred feet away over the garden – but they didn't make it. We saw both of them go down. Three of the men in the house were wounded by then – badly wounded, one in the shoulder, one in the leg and one in the stomach. We decided that enough was enough. The tank officer spoke good English. He told us we had fought well and that we would be treated well if we surrendered. 'For you the war is over.'

We came out of the front door but had to step over two Germans we had killed. Their mates didn't take that too kindly. The man ahead of me was hit across the head with a rifle butt, and I got it across the arm. I think it was the tank officer who stopped that. We asked if we could go back for our wounded, but they said they would send their own men in for them.

Some men managed to hide and were later helped by the Dutch to escape capture, but by mid-afternoon the active British presence was ended except for some of the medical officers and surgical teams of 16 Field Ambulance in St Elizabeth Hospital. The Germans had allowed Red Cross jeeps and walking wounded to enter the hospital grounds throughout the fighting. The Dutch in the hospital were down-hearted. They had been 'liberated' on the Sunday night, occupied by Germans on Monday, liberated again on Monday night, and now the Germans were back again. Corporal Arthur Hatcher describes what happened to the medical orderlies

who were taken away as prisoners when the Germans took control
of the hospital again:

> About half a dozen of those Germans came strolling into the
> front entrance. Some of them were SS; they were doing the
> ordering about. I had seen Germans before, in Africa, Sicily
> and Italy, but never SS before. They were full of arrogance,
> as though they were the best in the world and we were just
> rabble. Nobody knew what was going on, and we still thought
> this was only another small set-back. We weren't frightened; it
> all happened so quickly there wasn't time for that.
>
> They said they wanted all the able-bodied personnel to be
> collected. We had got some unwounded paras in there by
> now. They herded us all into a corridor but then they had to
> wait for a lull outside before they could move us out. We were
> all sat down, about fifty or sixty of us, with guards standing
> over us, and somebody started singing, 'There'll Always Be an
> England', and everyone joined in. We were still full of
> confidence and thought we would be relieved any minute and
> we would be top dog again. The Germans didn't like it, but
> they didn't stop us.
>
> Then we were marched out and found that there were other
> groups of prisoners being rounded up from the fighting nearby,
> all being marched away with their hands clasped on their
> heads. It was then that I realized things had gone wrong; it
> wasn't going to be a forty-eight-hour job after all.

The remnants of the battalions streamed away from Arnhem
towards Oosterbeek. There were two main routes. Some men used
the main Utrechtseweg, but most used the lower road. Along these
roads came jeeps – some towing anti-tank guns – loaded with men,
including the last evacuations from an Advanced Dressing Station
in a warehouse which medical orderlies from the 1st and 3rd
Battalions had operated until mortaring stopped that work. There
were dozens of weary men on foot, singly or in groups, some
without weapons; accounts include such phrases as 'orderly
disorder', 'like a crowd of men leaving a football match', 'little
groups running like the devil'. The men on the lower road passed,

for the last time, through the railway tunnel at Oosterbeek Laag Station, guarded now by a few glider pilots, an outpost of the divisional area in which it was hoped that safety would be found. Of the five battalions and one brigade headquarters which had gone into Arnhem, more than 3,000 men, only about 700 were still fighting two miles away at the bridge, and no more than 500 returned to Oosterbeek.

About 120 of those missing had been killed, leaving nearly 1,700 men as prisoners (many wounded) or being hidden by Dutch people. The 1st Airborne Division had lost one-fifth of its total strength in those streets and open spaces beside the Rhine in Arnhem. The remnants of the four battalions which returned were commanded by two majors, one captain (slightly wounded) and one lieutenant. That railway embankment between Arnhem and Oosterbeek can represent a boundary between the hell of west Arnhem and the comparative calm until now of Oosterbeek. It can also mark the end of this description of that desperate phase of the Arnhem battle.

New Comment Added In This Reprinted Edition

After the publication of the original edition of this book in 1994, the 50th Anniversary of the Arnhem battle, I became involved in taking groups of visitors around the areas where the main fighting had taken place. It was on the pavement outside the Museum that I usually concluded the tour of where the four battalions made their attacks on the Tuesday morning and ended my commentary with the statement that I considered that this was the *exact place* and that the morning of Tuesday, September 19th, was the *exact time* where The Battle of Normandy can be judged to have ended.

Not only did the gallant failure of the South Staffords to advance beyond that point signal the end of any chance of reinforcing the men holding Arnhem Bridge, but it brought to an end the sometimes hard-fought but successful advances from the beaches of Normandy that had started on D-Day three and a half months earlier.

That comment never failed to gain instant attention.

CHAPTER 11

Waiting for the Second Lift

One feature of the treatment of the Battle of Arnhem by taking actions through to their conclusion is that it will sometimes be necessary to go back to a previous day to start the next main story. The next main story here is the arrival of the second lift on Monday 18 September, and the subsequent attempt by the 4th Parachute Brigade to get into Arnhem. Before starting this, it is necessary to go back even further and describe what happened in the Divisional HQ and Airlanding Brigade areas from dawn of that Monday until the arrival of the second lift, which was expected in mid-morning but was delayed. It would be easy to pass over a period that was relatively uneventful compared with the fierce fighting taking place elsewhere, but there were some significant moves and important actions which should be recorded.

The situation at Divisional HQ that first morning was still one of reasonable optimism, despite the absence of the divisional commander. The extreme difficulty of reaching the Arnhem bridge was not yet appreciated, and the substantial reinforcement of the second lift was expected soon. When that happened, it was planned that the whole of the remainder of the division would move into Arnhem. Divisional HQ started to anticipate that move at 8.0 a.m., when it drove a mile and a half along the Utrechtseweg to take up a temporary position in a side turning, among a pleasant avenue of trees. It was not a good place for communications; none of the Divisional Signals, Phantom or public-relations sets could contact England, so there was no means of knowing that the second lift would be delayed.

The peaceful nature of that morning is reflected in two small stories. Captain Peter Fletcher was with the glider pilots accompanying Divisional HQ: 'We started to move towards Arnhem in single file, past pleasant suburban houses. A wash and a shave during one of the many hold-ups in one of the many friendly houses *en route* seemed a good exchange for half a bar of chocolate.' Not far away, the RASC sent five men on foot into Heelsum, looking for vehicles to transport ammunition. Driver Jack Taylor was one of them:

> In the centre of the village we found a bus which, I think, had come from Arnhem to collect early-morning passengers. We told the driver that we needed his bus and would he get out. He said it was a left-hand drive, and it would be better if he drove it for us, and he would do so on condition that, if we were captured, we would say that we had forced him into it. I think he was quite proud to drive for us.

Later in the day, however, the vehicle was ambushed, and the Dutch driver and one of the RASC men were killed.

One unit pushed on even further towards Arnhem, to become the first element of the division to take up a permanent position in Oosterbeek. No. 3 Battery of the Airlanding Light Regiment was designated to support the 1st Parachute Brigade and needed to be closer to Arnhem to bring its 75-millimetre guns within range. The very first to arrive was F Troop with Lieutenant Frank Moore in charge:

> The location wasn't pre-planned; we just went along through Oosterbeek looking for a good position, but the country was so close that we found nothing suitable until we reached the fields around the quiet little church on the lower road. We took up position in a small field and orchard just south-east of the church, with our command post in the church porch on that side. The other troops found slightly less open locations west of the church and they thought we had a super position. After those pre-operational briefings, we didn't think that any part of the German Army would have the effrontery to attack us. All we were looking for was an open space which allowed us to fire up to the bridge area. We didn't know it would become the front line later.

The local people brought out milk and sandwiches to the gunners and warned them of a solitary German in a nearby house; he was soon taken prisoner by some glider pilots who had remained with the guns they had flown from England. Captain Randall Martin, the Light Regiment's Medical Officer, went along to a nearby house and asked the lady who came to the front door if her home could become his Regimental Aid Post where any lightly wounded could be treated. Mrs Kate ter Horst said, 'Yes.'

That was quiet Oosterbeek on that Monday morning, although one of the Reconnaissance Squadron's patrols which went along the Utrechtseweg into the upper village later in the morning encountered a small German force, and one trooper was killed there.

The Airlanding Brigade had the difficult task of defending the landing and dropping zones for the second lift, areas which were up to four miles apart and mostly surrounded by woods through which German troops, now thoroughly alerted, could approach and intervene. The South Staffords were relieved of this duty and sent into Arnhem during the morning, but the Border and King's Own Scottish Borderers remained in positions around the two main landing areas. The more isolated ones were in 'company groups' augmented by two 6-pounder anti-tank guns, two Vickers machine-guns, two 3-inch mortars and sometimes an artillery observation officer.

Only one of the Border companies experienced serious action. This was Major Tom Armstrong's B Company, which had become surrounded in the brickworks at Renkum. Not all of the German troops in Renkum were aware of the presence of the airborne soldiers hidden in that brickworks, and the day started with a party of twelve or so Germans seen standing in the open 200 yards away, talking and studying a map; several machine-guns and a dozen Lee-Enfield rifles which opened up on a given signal could hardly miss at that range. The main German force, a naval battalion, then mounted several attacks which were beaten off but then contented itself with steadily mortaring the Border positions. It was early afternoon before the company was given permission to withdraw and slipped away along the river bank to the east. The last men out were a section of No. 11 Platoon under Lance-Corporal Albert Wilson:

I'd only become the temporary section commander the previous day. When Lieutenant Barnes told me we were to be the rearguard, I said, 'What about the other two section commanders?' They were both long-serving section commanders. He said, 'I'm asking you to do it, Ginger' – very politely; he was a gentleman.

Frank Aston and I were the last to go; I didn't think we would get out. I told Frank to take all the tracers out of the Bren mags – one every fourth round – and I fired the tracers at the curtains in the houses, to set them alight – range 400 yards. I could put anything inside eight inches at that range; that's my grouping capacity in my pay-book. The curtains caught fire, and Frank kept firing short bursts to stop them putting the fires out. Then we made a dash for it. He went out one end of the trench, and I went out the other.

Both of the anti-tank guns had to be abandoned after being 'spiked', also six of the seven jeeps, which had been damaged by mortar fire. Only the artillery officer's jeep, with one wheel buckled and a boiling radiator, drove out across the fields near the river with the wounded aboard. The bodies of at least five men, including two sergeants, were left behind. On reporting to Battalion HQ, Lieutenant Joe Hardy says, 'We were greeted as conquering heroes. After all, we had knocked off quite a lot of the enemy; we had been surrounded by a far superior force; and we had *fought* our way out. It hardly seemed necessary at the time to tell people that we had sneaked out through the back entrance.'

The KOSB companies were located around the extensive Ginkel Heath, which was to be the 4th Parachute Brigade's dropping zone. Their positions were particularly exposed, separated one from another and from the rest of the division by thick woodland and closer to the German forces now being assembled on the west side of the landing areas (see map on page 235).

The first action of the day resulted in a minor disaster. Major Gordon Sherrif's D Company was responsible for the eastern side of the dropping zone. He kept most of his company in the wood along the southern side of his sector, but sent his second in command, Captain George Gourlay, with No. 16 Platoon to occupy a group of huts in an open space a quarter of a mile beyond the trees. The huts were shown on aerial photographs, but it was not known who was occupying them. On arrival, Captain Gourlay found that it was a civilian work camp run on village lines, with a school in the canteen, and with the menfolk going out to farm the surrounding land. The occupants were Dutch families displaced from their village near the coast and relocated here. Captain Gourlay deployed the platoon's sections around the edges of the camp and told the civilians to stay inside their huts.

At 'stand-to' on the Monday morning, the platoon came under heavy fire from unseen positions in the woods. The fire was returned, but the radio link to the 3-inch mortars at the main company position was not working, so no outside support or reinforcement could be obtained. The presence of the Dutch civilians severely hampered the defence, and the action was all over by mid-morning. Seven KOSBs, including the platoon sergeant, were dead or were to die of wounds later, and six more were wounded, including both officers present. All the survivors were taken prisoner. Their attackers were No. 5 Company of SS Wach Battalion 3 – mostly Dutch SS. The capture of this platoon and the forcing out of its position of one of A Company's platoons at the north-east corner of the heath meant that German troops would be able to fire from these sectors when the parachute drop took place later in the day.

By contrast, Major Michael Forman's B Company across at the north-west corner of the heath, in the most exposed position of all, carried out a vigorous and successful defence of its area, despite being one platoon and one anti-tank gun below strength. The Germans, or rather the Dutch SS under German command, did not realize that the company was in position, and some vehicles appeared driving westwards along the main road towards Ede. Sergeant George Barton, in charge of the anti-tank gun, was given permission to open fire, and his gun team hit a half-track with its first shot. Those of the SS who survived the hit 'piled out' of the half-track and were immediately shot up by a Vickers machine-gun and other weapons. There could have been few, if any, survivors. (It is interesting to see how incidents such as this became exaggerated. Sergeant Barton is quite sure that only one shot was fired and only one vehicle hit; the company report says, 'three armed tracked vehicles hit and stopped'; a post-war report by Lieutenant-Colonel Payton-Reid refers to 'six armoured cars destroyed'.)

Major Forman then sent out a patrol in the direction of Ede to get rid of an unseen machine-gun which was heard firing from that direction. Sergeant Ted Shaw of No. 6 Platoon took six men and the platoon's 2-inch mortar, located the likely German positions, fired off all the mortar bombs and appeared to have silenced the machine-gun. Unfortunately, when firing off his last round, Private Alex McKay, the mortar man, was killed when the bomb exploded on hitting a branch of a tree directly above him. Back at the company position, Lieutenant Donald Murray's No. 5 Platoon was then attacked by enemy who approached through the scrubland and opened fire while some men were in the open deepening their trenches, and two men were wounded, one seriously in the stomach. The sergeant in charge of the 3-inch mortar drove off this attack, firing at well below the normal minimum of 500 yards' range by jacking up the mortar bipod with sandbags and firing more than twenty bombs only just in front of the threatened platoon position less than 250 yards away. A parachute officer later reported four dead SS there, including an officer. Finally, some enemy were observed preparing a position on the open heathland three-quarters of a mile to the north, beyond the main road, in a place from which the imminent parachute drop could be seriously threatened. A 'shoot' was arranged on this by the 75-millimetre guns of the Light Regiment's No. 1 Battery, and the enemy were seen to abandon their digging and move away. There would be no fire from that place when the parachute drop took place. This company had performed its task of keeping its sector clear of any threat to the drop perfectly, using all of its supporting weapons well and killing many enemy for the loss of only one of its own dead and several injured, who were safely evacuated.

The second lift was delayed by more than four hours, a source of much frustration to the units that had to maintain their positions around the landing areas in the face of increasing German pressure as the day wore on with still no sign of the lift's approach. An added danger was the appearance during the morning of between twenty and thirty Messerschmitt 109s which made strafing runs on the landing areas used the previous day, particularly those on which there were gliders to be seen, several of which were set on fire. That, and a few men wounded, was the only effect of ten minutes or so of noisy and violent action. The fighters flew off and would be back at their bases in Germany, unprepared for action, when the second lift approached.

There may have been only one British fatal casualty from the strafing. Out on the Airborne Corps HQ glider landing zone near Nijmegen was a solitary RAF officer. He was Wing Commander John Brown, who was in charge of the two RAF radar parties due to come in by glider with the second lift. Wing Commander Brown was killed by one of the German fighters. If he was out waiting for his gliders to arrive, then he was in the wrong place, because those gliders were flying to Arnhem, not Nijmegen.

CHAPTER 12

The Second Lift

The plan for the second lift, as far as Arnhem was concerned, was that the balance of the 1st British Airborne Division, mainly the 4th Parachute Brigade Group, would be flown in as early in the day as possible. Take-offs were planned for soon after 7.0 a.m. Unlike the first lift, the American parachute aircraft would fly in first – 123 C-47s and three C-53s. These would be provided by the 314th and 315th Troop Carrier Groups based at Saltby and Spanhoe respectively. Most of the RAF's 38 and 46 Groups would be despatched once again; 296 aircraft would tow 281 Horsas and 15 Hamilcars containing the balance of the division's guns, vehicles and infantry, including twenty-five glider loads from the first lift that had force-landed in England the previous day. Also from the glider lift were ten Horsas from Manston carrying the first element of the Polish brigade to fly to Arnhem – mainly an anti-tank troop – and four Horsas from Harwell with the two RAF radar warning teams aboard. Thirty-three further aircraft, Stirlings of 295 and 570 Squadrons from Harwell, would carry out the first of the daily parachute resupply drop for the units already landed at Arnhem. It would be another day of massive air operations, with nearly 2,500 aircraft involved in Operation 'Market' flights. It is an interesting point that, while the Polish brigade was still waiting to fly to Arnhem, 110 B-17 Flying Fortresses of the 8th US Air Force were flying that day from England in a last attempt to drop supplies to the dying Warsaw Uprising, in support of which the Polish brigade had originally been raised.

The second-lift units and aircraft were all ready by the Sunday evening, but during the night mist was forecast for many of the English airfield areas, and Lieutenant-General Brereton's staff decided that the take-offs would have to be delayed until this hazard cleared. Unfortunately, communications were so poor that there was no way of informing the commanders at Arnhem of the delay.

The second-lift aircraft had to wait four hours before the weather cleared and take-offs could commence at 11.20 a.m. A further change of plan had been made during that waiting period. The original plan was to use the southern approach route, entailing a longer flight but making more use of Allied-held territory. Weather reports from Belgium now showed that this route was affected by thick raincloud, so it was decided that the northern route should again be used. Navigators and map readers had to be rebriefed and new flight plans made. Two stand-by Dakota crews at Broadwell, brought in at the last moment to tow gliders which had aborted on the first lift, were not informed of the change.

There were no serious accidents; one glider crashed when its tug's engines failed, but there were no casualties. There were showers and cloud in some places, but only seven Horsas and one Hamilcar from the Arnhem force came down early over England. One of the Horsas, being towed by a 299 Squadron Stirling, landed safely at Martlesham Heath airfield. The Stirling pilot, Flight Lieutenant B. H. Berridge, also landed there, had the glider re-attached to the tow line and took off again; but the Stirling was later damaged by flak over Holland and had to cast off its glider there. The only mishap to any of the American parachute aircraft was when a 314th Troop Carrier Group aircraft nearly crashed after a badly fitted parachute on one of the supply containers under a wing opened prematurely. The container was jettisoned, but the parachute then wrapped itself around the tail wheel, with the container hanging below. The pilot (name unknown) landed care-fully at an airfield in East Anglia, all aboard hoping that the contents of the container were not sensitive explosives. But all was well; the parachute and container were cut away, and the C-47 took off again. It was not able to catch up with its own formation and flew to Holland among the tugs and gliders.

The weather improved over the North Sea. Morale among the airborne troops was high. Many were reading newspapers containing reports of the previous day's successful landings. One American co-pilot, Flight Officer George Hoffman, went to talk to the troops in the back of his C-47, probably 10th Battalion men: 'The troopers were joyously talking about the success of the mission and that it would mean the end of the war by Christmas.' Two gliders had to ditch in the sea. One was a large Hamilcar carrying a 17-pounder anti-tank gun and its towing vehicle. The Hamilcar broke up on hitting the water, and Lieutenant Robert McLaren, the artillery officer, was drowned when the gun broke loose and trapped him. He was the only casualty of the ditchings.

The stream was met by flak on crossing the Dutch coast. The fighter escort and flak-suppression aircraft were present, but the Germans were more prepared than on the previous day, and there was a steady succession of casualties. On the main part of the route across Holland, these occurred not among the American parachute aircraft at the front of the stream – these were almost completely immune at this stage – but mostly among the tugs and gliders. Perhaps the German gunners lay low until the first sweep of fighters had passed over and then emerged to open fire. Several gliders came down over Holland as a result of flak, usually the tow ropes being cut, as well as through the usual problems of tug aircraft engines overheating, forcing gliders to be released. Staff Sergeant Ron Watkinson was the pilot of a Horsa whose controls were damaged by flak; the load was a 75-millimetre gun and its crew:

We carried on for about another twenty minutes, but then the tow rope broke with the strain of the jerking movements. I managed to get it down close to a farm. The Albemarle circled low over us and saw us get out safely, before flying home. A host of Dutch men and women came out to greet us; none spoke English. After embracing us, they helped us to unload the glider. We hoped we were not too far from Arnhem and might even be able to get the gun there. We had a lot of problems unloading, because of the flak damage, but we eventually achieved it, mainly through Dutch brawn.

We found that the hitches on the jeep, gun and trailer had been damaged by the flak. We took the jeep and trailer to near a barn, ready to go on the road, but we were fired on by German troops. We put up a fight, firing back in the general direction from which the German fire was coming. My second pilot, Arthur Jones, was hit in the shoulder, and one of the gunners took a bullet through his face. We realized we were surrounded; one of the gunners waved a white handkerchief, and we became prisoners. I found out after the war that Arthur Jones died four days later.

The two Dakotas from Broadwell whose navigators had not been informed of the change of route had left the stream as it passed over the turning-point at Hatfield, wondering why the aircraft ahead were flying north-eastwards while they turned to the south-east. But they continued on their way, being forced steadily lower by the thickening cloud on that southern route. When they reached Belgium they were flying at only 500 feet. This route was only just inside the Allied front line, and one Dakota must have strayed slightly to the left of the route, for it was suddenly hit in the port side of the cockpit by a shell burst. This was a 437 Squadron crew but operating on loan in a 575 Squadron aircraft. The Canadian pilot, Flying Officer Ed Henry, was killed at once; he was the only qualified pilot aboard; the man in the co-pilot's seat, Warrant Officer Bert Smith, was only the map reader. He took the controls in front of him and just managed to keep the Dakota in the air; the glider pilot realized the tug was almost out of control and cast off the tow. The navigator, Flying Officer Harry McKinley, an American from Brooklyn who had joined the RCAF, was injured but took over the left-hand seat when the pilot's body had been removed:

> My map was smeared with blood, as my left index finger had been severed and was hanging as if it didn't belong to my hand. My left arm and side had also been hit, but in the excitement pain was not a factor. We didn't even notice the wind blowing through the large hole in the side of the fuselage. Here we were, a navigator, a map reader and a wireless operator, in a sick plane, and none of us had landed one before – and we were lost. We had a problem!

There followed a gallant flight by two men who had never received any formal pilot training. After two hours and ten minutes of the most rudimentary navigation, the Dakota reached an airfield on the English coast which turned out to be Martlesham Heath. McKinley, as the senior officer, said he would land the plane, and the other two could either bale out or ride down with him. They both stayed, and the subsequent landing became a team effort. The Dakota bounced its way along the runway, ran off the end on to grass and, by luck alone, through a gap in a row of parked P-47 fighters before coming to a stop. The Dakota crew were treated as heroes both at the American base and back at Broadwell when they returned there. McKinley then went to the RAF hospital at Wroughton, where he was the first patient in a ward waiting for Arnhem casualties.

Meanwhile, the cast-off glider had made a forced landing west of Bourg Leopold, just inside the Allied lines in Belgium. The occupants were the commanding officer of the 1st Border, Lieutenant-Colonel Tommy Haddon, and part of his headquarters. This was their second abortive attempt to reach Arnhem, having been forced to land in England on the previous day. So Lieutenant-Colonel Haddon, his Intelligence Officer Lieutenant Ronald Hope-Jones, their batmen and several other Border soldiers found themselves seventy-five miles from Arnhem. They soon met friendly troops and set out once again to reach their units, this time by land up the airborne corridor.

The Germans knew the rule of airborne operations. Unless the initial landing force could be quickly reached by friendly ground forces – as was obviously not going to be the case at Arnhem – that force would need to be reinforced by subsequent lifts. Such flights to Arnhem could only come from the south or west, and it was on those approaches that the Germans had built up their anti-aircraft defences, through which the approaching Allied aircraft now had to fly. Coming in first were the two American troop-carrier groups, flying low and at a slow and steady speed preparatory to the parachute drop.

Captain Leonard Ottaway's aircraft, flying near the front of the American formations, went down first, about twelve miles before the dropping zone. His C-47 had been the starboard aircraft of a 'vic' of three on take-off; but after the leader had been forced to land in England to clear the container parachute from its tail wheel, Captain Ottaway had moved across to fill in the centre position, and it was here that his aircraft was hit. Major John Waddy of 156 Battalion was in the aircraft on its left, standing in the door ready to jump:

> We were so near the ground that, on occasions, we could actually see the white faces of the flak gunners turned up towards us. The aircraft to the starboard of mine received a direct hit and exploded in a great ball of flame. I watched it pass underneath my aircraft and hit the ground with its port wing; it then rolled over in a great ball of fire.

The plane had been carrying half of 156 Battalion's Machine-Gun Platoon. Dutch civilians later said that one man was thrown clear, but he died of his injuries in a farmhouse that night. The total death roll was twenty-four – Captain Ottaway and the other five aircrew, and eighteen paratroopers.

Three more C-47s from the 314th Troop Carrier Group, all carrying men of the 11th Battalion, were shot down in the next few minutes. But there were no more violent explosions, and there were at least some survivors from each of the lost aircraft. It is clear that the American aircrews attempted to remain at their posts until as many as possible of the paratroopers could jump. When Captain Warren Egbert's plane's port engine caught fire, he pulled up alongside his element leader to have the fire checked and then held on until all of the soldiers and two of his own crew were able to jump, although Private John Barton's parachute probably did not open properly, because his body was later found on the ground. Captain Egbert and his co-pilot and navigator all died. The other two aircraft of this group to go down were captained by Captain George Merz and First Lieutenant Fredrick Hale; both pilots and more than half of the men in these aircraft survived. The stick commander in Captain Merz's C-47 was Captain Frank King of the 11th Battalion:

> I didn't know that we had been hit at first. We were all

checking each other's kit, getting ready to jump; the crew chief should have been helping but he seemed to be asleep. I was angry and shouted at him and was going to kick him, but then I saw the pool of blood under his seat and realized he was dead. When I looked out of the door we appeared to be flying straight and level, but we were well below the rest of the formation and I was horrified to see how low we were – no more than 250 feet. I then put my head out, into the slipstream, and saw that the whole of the port wing was on fire. I shouted to Sergeant-Major Gatland, who was near the tail end of the stick, and told him to open the little door into the pilot's compartment, which he did, and we saw a mass of smoke and flame.

The light was still red. It is a very serious offence to jump with a red light, but I had to make a decision and I said, 'We jump', which we did with great rapidity and we got nearly all of them out. We had been told at Ringway that the X-type parachute opened fully at ninety-eight feet of drop and we couldn't have been much higher than that, because I seemed to hit the ground straight away. When I landed I turned and counted the other chaps coming down; we were three short. I was told afterwards that one man fell in the doorway and the man behind him jumped over him, but his parachute didn't open. Probably the last men in the stick decided they were too low and stayed in the plane. One of them was badly burned.

The second American formation was the 315th Troop Carrier Group, carrying the 10th Battalion and other units of the 4th Parachute Brigade. Two more C-47s were shot down. Second Lieutenant Jim Spurrier's aircraft caught fire; all the paratroopers and the crew chief were able to jump, but from so low a height that one paratrooper died and another and the crew chief both broke legs. The pilot then attempted to force-land the burning aircraft, but the aircraft hit an electricity pylon, skidded round and was engulfed in flames; only the co–pilot, Second Lieutenant Ed Fulmar, survived, severely burned. The last plane to go down suffered no fatal casualties. Major Pat Anson, a company commander in the 10th Battalion, and his stick of men all dropped safely, and Lieutenant Tucker then crash-landed his plane.

The total casualties in the shot-down planes were thirty-one soldiers and seventeen aircrew killed; eleven aircrew and approximately seventy-three soldiers survived. One of the men who jumped was Sergeant Tony Bolland of the 10th Battalion, who was not included in the main operation because of an injured foot but was allowed to fly as an unofficial despatcher; he was later seen with only gym shoes and without helmet or equipment, steadily grumbling, 'I'm not f——ing-well supposed to be here.' Another man forced to jump was Flight Sergeant Carter, one of a number of RAF parachute instructors who had trained the airborne men and been allowed to fly as despatchers. Thanks to the help of brave Dutch civilians, nearly all of the survivors evaded capture. Most of the soldiers managed to make their way northwards and rejoin their units in the Arnhem fighting; the Americans went south to meet the ground forces.

The American formations flew steadily on through the flak, right up to the dropping zone. Brigadier Hackett had promised his pilot a bottle of champagne if his brigade was delivered to the correct place. Although his plane was being hit, he watched the pilot 'with his coon-skin hat, smoking a large cigar. I could tell he was quite calm when the flak started to come up by the lengthening ash on the cigar; his hand was quite steady.' The promised champagne was not handed over until Hackett met the co-pilot in 1989.

The vulnerable and unwieldy tug-and-glider combinations were flying much higher than the parachute aircraft and escaped the worst of the flak, but some were still damaged. These are descriptions from various men. Flight Lieutenant Jimmy Stark was a 298 Squadron Halifax pilot:

> The air in a glider train can be exceedingly disturbed unless you are in the leading aircraft, and if you hit the slipstream of the aircraft ahead, your wing stalls and you sweat like a pig pulling it up again. To avoid that, the dodge was to move out slightly to one side of the train and thereby fly in clear air. As we approached the front line, a friend of mine called Ensor was just ahead of me, well out to the left of the train. All of a sudden, his aircraft was surrounded by black puffs of bursting

flak. I am afraid that I started laughing and shouting, 'Get into line, you silly clot.' Then my own aircraft was hit. It was a most unusual sensation and a most unusual noise. It sounded like someone running an iron bar along a corrugated iron fence. I immediately tried all the controls, and they worked perfectly.

However, the glider pilot in the Horsa saw the whole incident and started calling me up on the intercom. 'Are you all right?' I replied, 'Yes, I am all right; are you all right?' We kept this up for a few minutes; we were like a couple of old 'dolls' at a Women's Missionary Association. Our conversation was brought to a halt by my tail gunner, a laconic Canadian, who said, 'There is a f—ing great hole in your tail.' Part of the starboard fin had been blown away, but we got to Arnhem safely.

Gunner Bob Christie of the 1st Airlanding Light Regiment was in another Horsa:

The three of us at the rear of the glider heard a series of sudden tearing noises further forward, under the jeep and the trailer. Our immediate thought was that the lashings were working loose. If they were, and the jeep and the trailer started to move, things would progressively get worse, and the glider would get out of control. I crawled up the floor, between the wheels in their troughs and the skin-and-frame members of the Horsa. Again the noises and sudden shafts of sunlight appeared through jagged holes. It was flak. Relieved, we returned to our seats and, as one, removed our steel helmets and sat on them to protect our vital assets.

Gunner George Hurdman of the 2nd Airlanding Anti-Tank Battery was also in a Horsa:

We heard gunfire, and the glider started to buffet around. The violent movement blew out the glider's back door. The three of us had a tot of rum – a good swig, good for the nerves – and stood up to see outside better. On the spur of the moment, we stood with our backs to the hole, with our arms linked around one another, holding on to the door frame to help cut down the gale of wind coming in and prevent the glider breaking up. We stayed that way until we landed.

One glider was hit by a heavy flak shell, and onlookers watched it fold into a 'V' shape, with men tumbling out, and then crash. This was one of the Horsas containing the RAF radar warning teams. Six RAF men and the two glider pilots were killed.

Two of the tug aircraft were shot down. The Horsa being towed by one, a 512 Squadron Dakota, was able to cast off safely before the Dakota was crash-landed by the wounded co-pilot, Flight Lieutenant Saunders. But the second tug, a Stirling of 570 Squadron, fell violently out of control and was seen to cartwheel into the ground and explode. The Australian pilot, Pilot Officer George Bell, and all his crew were killed instantly, among them an RAF ground-staff corporal who had asked to come on the flight. The glider pilot successfully cast off the tow and landed the Horsa near the south bank of the Rhine. This was the second RAF radar warning unit glider to be lost. The glider party was later taken across the river by the Driel–Heveadorp ferryman, Pieter Hensen, with many other men from gliders or parachute aircraft who came down south of the Rhine; but the glider pilot, Staff Sergeant Bernard Cummins, and two of the RAF men later died in the fighting at Oosterbeek.

That was the end of the incident-packed outward flight of the second lift. The crew of one Stirling tug heard a glider pilot say, just before casting off: 'Thank you, Jesus; we can look after ourselves now.'

The parachute-dropping zone to be used, DZ-Y, was Ginkel Heath, completely open heathland with thick woodland on three sides and the main Amsterdamseweg leading to Arnhem – more than eight miles away – on its northern side. In addition to the King's Own Scottish Borderer companies which had been attempting to keep the Germans away from the heath, Lieutenant Hugh Ashmore's platoon of the Independent Company had set up its beacon and marker panels, and the advanced parties of the 4th

Parachute Brigade were ready to set off different-coloured smoke canisters at their respective rendezvous points on the edge of the heath. All of these men had been forced to wait without news for four hours since the expected time of the second lift arrival. German forces were also in the vicinity. Probably they did not know that this area was to be used for the coming parachute drop but believed that the British activity around the heath was part of the eastward defence of the first day's landing area. The Dutch SS battalion's HQ and two of its companies were at the north-east corner of the heath, where the King's Own Scottish Borderers had been forced away from the dropping zone.

The engines of the C-47s were heard approaching, and the first parachutists, men of 156 Battalion, started to jump. The 10th Battalion's Advance Party under Lieutenant Sammy Carr started to move towards the German-occupied Zuid Ginkel Café near their battalion's RV; and in the woods at the southern end of the heath, men of HQ and Support Companies of the KOSB started a sweep through the trees to clear the Germans there who had opened fire on the parachutists. It was a fierce fight. The Germans hit some of the parachutists and set the heath on fire with mortar bombs, and the KOSB Support Company commander, Major Henry Hill, was killed. This brought to two officers and at least thirteen men the KOSB's fatal casualties in their attempt to keep the dropping zone clear of Germans.

The first men jumped at 3.09 p.m., and the entire drop would be over in nine minutes, because the American formations had closed right up. Seven men would not be able to jump because they were injured in their aircraft, became entangled in static lines or fell over as some of the American pilots weaved to avoid the ground fire. The best estimate of the numbers of men who actually jumped is 1,914.

It was an opposed drop. Several planes were hit by small-arms fire; the SS were aiming at the doorways of the C-47s, hoping to hit the first man in the stick there, so that the remainder could not jump. They also fired at the descending parachutists, spraying the air with bullets. Here is a selection of experiences. Private Jock Keenan of 156 Battalion:

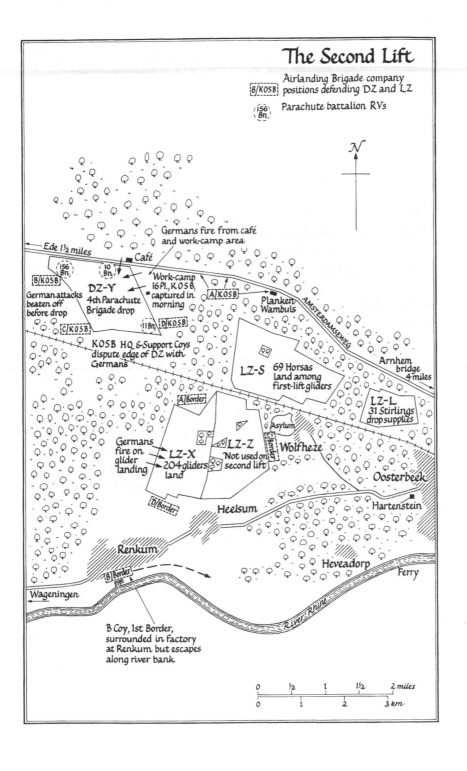

The Second Lift

B/KOSB	Airlanding Brigade company positions defending DZ and LZ
156 Bn	Parachute battalion RVs

N

Germans fire from café and work-camp area

Ede 1½ miles — Café

156 Bn

10 Bn

B/KOSB

German attacks beaten off before drop

DZ-Y
4th Parachute Brigade drop

Work-camp 16 Pl., KOSB captured in morning

A/KOSB

Planken Wambuis

AMSTERDAMSEWEG

Arnhem bridge 4 miles

C/KOSB

11 Bn

D/KOSB

KOSB HQ & Support Coys dispute edge of DZ with Germans

LZ-S 69 Horsas land among first-lift gliders

LZ-L
31 Stirlings drop supplies

A/Border

Asylum

Germans fire on glider landing

LZ-X
204 gliders land

LZ-Z
Not used on second lift

Border

Wolfheze

Oosterbeek

D/Border

Heelsum

Hartenstein

Renkum

Heveadorp

Ferry

Wageningen

B/Border

River Rhine

B Coy, 1st Border, surrounded in factory at Renkum but escapes along river bank

0	½	1	1½	2 miles
0	1	2	3 km	

We could see the tracer coming up; possibly some of it even hit our plane, but no one was hurt. The tracer was quite close when we were in the air, and you could see some of the Germans on the edge of the trees. We had been told that it was going to be a quiet area, and it was a surprise to find them on the DZ. While I was in the air I could hear that one of the men further along, probably in my stick, had been hit. I went to help him when I landed, but Sergeant-Major Gay told me to leave him and join my platoon – or words to that effect. Soon afterwards I heard that Sergeant Bill Walmsley had been killed, and his body was hanging in a tree. I had known him very well; we had knocked about together in India when we were friends there.

Private George Taylor of the 10th Battalion was the youngest soldier in his company:

Because it was my first time in action and there was all this noise and the firing around the DZ, I came down any old how and got tangled up in my lift webs and hit the ground hard. My platoon sergeant said later that I had come down 'like a bundle of shit'. It was nice dropping on a training jump – an adventure – but when it was the actual thing, well, frankly, I was scared stiff. After I landed I lay down and cried, but then I got myself untangled and nipped over to the RV. I was OK after that.

Signalman Arthur Winstanley of the Brigade Signal Section:

Among the varied paraphernalia attached to my person was a carrier pigeon in a box with a little bag of corn tied to it. However, there was only the half of the box with the bag of corn left, so I presume that the bird got a flying start at anywhere between 350 feet and the ground, hopefully getting back to England some seven months quicker than myself. I was about fifty feet from the ground and preparing myself for a landing when what must have been a light-calibre mortar bomb exploded ahead and to the right of me, killing another man just as he landed.

I came down awkwardly on a patch of ground that was on fire. My rigging lines became entangled with the handle of my entrenching tool and I had difficulty getting free from my 'chute; one of my colleagues came and cut me free, despite the fact that a burst of automatic fire tore up the ground between him and me. During my efforts to join up with my section, I witnessed two of the infantry lads who, in spite of the rubbish that was flying about, were busily engaged in trying to shoot a large hare that was bounding all over the place, no doubt with a view to supplementing their compo rations.

Corporal Fred Jenkins of the 10th Battalion:

There was smoke all around me and about five machine-guns firing; they sounded like German Spandaus – too sharp to be ours. Everything looked chaotic – a whole brigade moving off to about four different rendezvous points, but I couldn't see anybody I knew.

The bullets didn't seem to be coming my way, and anyway I couldn't crawl off the DZ, so I just pushed along in a crouching run as fast as I could. I saw a 'chute in flames and went to see if anyone was on it. There wasn't anyone there, but just then the heat proved too strong and fierce for the safety of a mortar bomb which was lying nearby. It exploded, and I ducked, damn quick. Lucky as usual. The man next to me shouted. I went along and found he'd had his nose blown off. I eased his equipment off and put a dressing on the wound. He could still talk and walk, so I dragged him along with me – had to hustle because there were more bombs lying about and they looked well toasted. My charge was a sergeant-major from 11th Battalion, and I handed him over as soon as I could.

Most of the German and Dutch SS withdrew before the drop came to an end, but the 10th Battalion found that the woods around their rendezvous near the Zuid Ginkel Café were still occupied, and a fierce little action took place when this area had to be cleared. Several contributors mention the bravery of Lieutenant

Pat Mackey, who was killed charging a machine-gun set up on a pile of logs. Private Ralph Shackleton came upon this officer's body after the area was secured:

> I found Lieutenant Mackey dead in some trees just off the DZ. I put his inscribed gold ring into his mouth to prevent it being taken by the Germans. Near him was a dying German. The right-hand side of his head had been hit and smashed open; the brains were spilling out over his face. He was conscious and mumbling, and when I bent over him he put his hand out and rested it on one of my Bren magazine pouches. I gave him Lieutenant Mackey's morphia and left them lying together on the grass. I still feel the futility and sadness of that moment.

Parties of medical orderlies and stretcher-bearers searched the heath for the wounded, whose positions were marked by upturned rifles stuck into the ground. This work was much hampered by the burning heather. One man who had been shot in the legs and could not move had earlier been found by an officer, who made the injured man as comfortable as possible and gave him morphia. When the officer returned later to make sure the medics had collected the casualty, the wounded man was found to be dead. The burning heather had reached him and set his ammunition pouches on fire. In his agony, the man had taken a revolver and shot himself in the head.

A considerable proportion of the brigade did not drop on the heath. There were several reasons, but many were cases of overshooting when the last element of nine C-47s became separated from the main formation and dropped their sticks north of the correct place. Some men came down in trees among the SS and were shot as they hung helplessly from their harnesses. Again, there are some good descriptions of these more distant drops; the 'Germans' in these accounts would often have been Dutch SS. Private David Dagwell of 156 Battalion:

> I was about to follow the Quartermaster's batman out of the

door when the plane tilted on one side. A shell had burst under the port wing, and those still to jump were thrown violently against the bulkhead opposite. When eventually we got out it was immediately obvious that the delay was going to lead to my landing in a belt of fir trees which ran along the eastern edge of the heath. Impact when it came was quite soft; branches cushioned my fall, and the 'chute rested firmly in the tree-tops. However, my rifle valise was caught up above my head, and the cord was well and truly wrapped around my legs so that I hung in a U-shaped position.

I was struggling to get my knife free, when a movement registered in the corner of my eye. I took a swift glance and wished I was elsewhere as three German soldiers made their way cautiously along a path below. At that moment I resembled nothing so much as a trussed chicken and would have been unable to defend myself if any of them had happened to look up. Fortunately for me they were far more interested in the events on the DZ and, after what seemed an age, they disappeared round a bend. When I began breathing again I managed to draw my knife, cut through the cord, slap the release box and let go, to fall on to a soft carpet of pine needles. I thought about trying to recover the valise but decided that this was no time to hang around that neighbourhood.

Driver John Prime of the RASC:

I landed in a tree – right at the top of it – and felt very exposed; there was firing going on nearby. I released the kitbag with the Bren and released myself from the harness, and eventually got down. I took the Bren and two pouches of ammunition but left the rest of the kitbag with the spare canvas wallet of Bren magazines and the Bren cleaning kit and my rations. I shouldn't have, but I was alone in the trees and wanted to get to the DZ. I followed the direction of the firing. I heard others in the trees, but I was looking after Number One; we had expected an unopposed landing, and things were going wrong.

I got out on to the open heath and made for the blue smoke of our platoon RV. There were several of us by then, running in an extended line – not running very fast really, because of our loads; we kept having to stop to take a breather. The German fire was sweeping the whole DZ two or three feet above the ground. We were about a hundred yards across when one of the men was hit. He gave a huge gasp and fell down on to his face like a sack of potatoes. We all went to ground again. Tubby Ashman ran over to him (or shuffled; we were like Christmas trees), turned him over and said that he was dead. When we eventually got to the RV one of the lads there had been hit in the face, not seriously, but was in shock with his hands over his face covered with blood. Captain Kavanagh was squaring him up, telling him to pull himself together.

Corporal David Jones of 156 Battalion:

One of the relatively new men in the battalion refused to jump and froze in the doorway. An RAF despatcher would have given him a boot in the rear, but the American crew chief didn't, and there was a long delay before he was pulled away. Myself and five others all jumped into woodland beyond the DZ. I fell into a tree and was swaying like a pendulum just above the ground; I couldn't unfasten the release catch because of my weight, so I cut the rigging lines.

We were among a German platoon, but they ran off. We took one prisoner, and I made him carry the 2-inch mortar-bomb carriers; I wasn't bothered about international law and prisoners of war carrying ammunition. Then we found a truck loaded with German ammunition and weapons. I realized that I had a prize here. Airborne troops were always short of vehicles and ammunition, and here we were, just landed and with a vehicle loaded with ammunition; our Sten guns were designed to use the German rimless 9-millimetre ammunition. I told the lads to jump on the truck and I had visions of driving off to the Company RV with some transport and a load of ammunition. I had no bother driving it; as a Channel

Islander I was used to going to France and driving right-hand-drive vehicles. I was chuffed; I thought I'd landed on a gold mine. I knew Major Waddy would be pleased – but it didn't turn out that way. The first people I met were some KOSBs, and their officer told me to unload the ammunition and drive his wounded to the field hospital in Oosterbeek. I never rejoined the battalion, they kept me and the vehicle at Oosterbeek carrying wounded.

(Later in the week, Corporal Jones suffered five bullet wounds when his German vehicle was accidentally shot up by British troops at Oosterbeek.)

Some men were dropped so far north that they were never able to reach friendly forces. Private Ken Kirkham provided a description of how seventeen men of the 10th Battalion came down well beyond the dropping zone and carried out various irregular operations until, with only six men still together, he met up with a Dutch escape organization. The most distant of the drops in the north were by at least three sticks of men who dropped near Otterlo, eight miles beyond the DZ. Two sticks were from 133 Parachute Field Ambulance under that unit's second in command, Major Brian Courtney, and the third was from the 4th Parachute Squadron. Two of these parties joined and had a little fight with a German patrol in which an RASC driver with the Field Ambulance and possibly other men were killed. None of these men rejoined the division, and, although most avoided capture, the medical unit would be deprived of the much needed services of a surgeon, two other medical officers and several orderlies.

The American planes flew away. Lieutenant Bernard Coggins, one of the navigators in the lead plane of the 315th Troop Carrier Group, writes:

I don't know just what hell will be like, but I think we got a preview. Earlier groups had already dropped, and the DZ was a solid ball of fire. At the command to jump, our troops had exited from the plane without any hesitation. My admiration, already at an extremely high level where paratroopers were concerned, went even higher as these brave men dropped into that preview of hell. We immediately pushed the throttles to the firewall, hit the deck and got the hell out of there. The tales about that mission lasted a long, long time.

None of the American planes was shot down on the return flight.

Some of the battalions were up to a hundred men short because of aircraft losses and men dropping away, an initial loss of strength of nearly 20 per cent. The number of the brigade's dead in the actual drop and the immediate action on the ground was four officers and approximately twenty-eight other ranks. One of the officers was Lieutenant Yves Hacart, a French officer attached to 156 Battalion. He had been sent to this unit as a liaison officer for a planned drop in France and need not have taken part in this operation. No one knows how Lieutenant Hacart died; but when his family had his body exhumed in 1949 to take it to their home near Rouen, his parachute harness was still on his body, suggesting that he was killed in the air or immediately after landing, possibly caught up in a tree. The confused nature of the drop resulted in more accidents than normal. Among the many injured were Padre Raymond Bowers of the 10th Battalion, who broke his ankle, and Major Aeneas Perkins, commander of the 4th Parachute Squadron, who dislocated his shoulder, but both would return to their units later. Three sergeants in 156 Battalion had pooled their 'comforts'; one took all the whisky, one the cigarettes and one the chocolate. Two were injured, and only the one with the bottles of whisky was present when the battalion moved off.

The glider landing was a less dramatic and less costly operation. The tug aircraft approached at 3,000 feet, which enabled the combinations to escape German small-arms fire. The gliders then cast off and made their final approach in a steep dive. One glider pilot, Staff Sergeant Bert Harget of E Squadron, was flying on the extreme right-hand side of the stream when he cast off and he took a long, careful approach over Arnhem *and then over Deelen airfield*. Not one flak shell was fired at him, and he was not aware of any other fire. So much for the supposed flak defences at Deelen, which had dictated the route in the air plan! A total of 273 gliders reached the cast-off point. They were to use two landing zones (see map on page 235). Approximately a quarter of them – mostly carrying the balance of the Airlanding Brigade infantry and including many of the glider parties which had landed prematurely in England from the first lift – would land on LZ-S, the one north of the railway line at Wolfheze which had been used the previous day. The main group would then come in to LZ-X, which was the large area used as a parachute-dropping zone on the first lift. The loads landed here would mostly be the balance of the division's artillery and transport, together with a large quantity of ammunition which was part of the first daily resupply, being brought in more reliably by glider than being dropped by parachute. Among the gliders were ten Horsas flying from Manston carrying the first element of the Polish brigade – five anti-tank guns and a small Brigade HQ advance party, twenty-six men in total. Also coming in were the two remaining RAF radar-warning-unit gliders and a glider which had fallen out from the Corps HQ lift the previous day. It landed safely, but its occupants were forced to remain with the Arnhem troops; one man, a signals officer's batman, would be killed at Arnhem.

It mostly went very well, thanks to the firmer ground being used than on the previous day, the good work of the 1st Border in defending the landing zones and the skill of the glider pilots. Sixty-nine Horsas got down safely on LZ-S, despite having to land between the previous day's gliders, which looked like 'a crowded car-park'. There were no serious crashes, although two glider pilots – Staff Sergeant 'Andy' Andrews and Sergeant Paddy Senier – who had landed the previous day and were manning a slit trench on the edge of LZ-S had a narrow escape. Both men sent accounts; this is Paddy Senier's:

> One glider made its final approach straight towards our position. The pilot was trying hard to get it on the ground, but only the nose wheel touched, and he could not get the main wheels down. When it became clear to us that his speed was too great and that he was going to hit our area, we both jumped out of the trench and tried to move back quickly through the trees. The tangle of undergrowth and low branches

defeated our efforts, and we had not gone far when there was an almighty bang over our heads and we dropped flat. A great cloud of dust arose, and when it cleared I saw that I was under the fuselage and behind the nose wheel, and Andy was behind the skid and also under the fuselage. Fortunately for us the undercarriage had not collapsed, and this was forcibly brought home to us when we saw that the port main wheel had crushed the head of a dead German who had been killed shortly before.

'Andy' Andrews looked up and saw the grinning face of the pilot, Captain David Treherne, just above him. According to another glider pilot who watched the crash: 'One of the pilots, a tall, languid ex-Etonian, emerged unscathed and, adjusting his red beret, drawled, "God, isn't this hell, old boy? Have you got a drink?" We were able to oblige.'

There were remarkably few glider crashes on either of the landing zones. Even most of the large Hamilcars got down safely.

There was one danger area at the southern end of LZ-X. A German force had infiltrated between two of the Border companies and was able to fire on the gliders landing there. The Borders tried to suppress this opposition by mortar fire; Major Cousens, the temporary commanding officer of the Borders, later said: 'As each glider came in, the Germans were mortared, but, in order to avoid hitting gliders in mid-air, the timing of the mortar bomb had to be exact to a fraction of a second, a successful and amusing game.[1] At least three gliders were hit by German fire, however. One, containing artillerymen of the Light Regiment, had two men killed and an officer seriously wounded. A REME glider was hit, with the two glider pilots and a REME jeep driver killed and an officer, Lieutenant Harry Roberts, badly wounded and then pinned down on the landing zone for several hours exchanging fire with the Germans until recovered by British stretcher-bearers that evening. The third glider casualty from this German fire **was** one of the Horsas carrying part of the RAF radar warning units. This was hit

---

[1] From an article by Major Cousens in *The Sprig and the Shillelagh,* the journal of the Border Regiment.

on its final approach and set on fire. The co-pilot, Sergeant Bill Ferguson, was injured by a bullet which travelled the length of his spine, ripping the skin away, but not seriously damaging the bone. The occupants of this glider all managed to crawl away to the shelter of nearby woodland. The glider and its contents burned out completely.

That left only one of the four gliders with these RAF loads to land safely. It also came down on that part of the landing zone which was under German fire. There was no one to help the occupants unload the heavy packing cases, and there were no vehicles to carry the equipment away even if it could be unloaded. The senior glider pilot, Staff Sergeant John Kennedy, and the RAF officer in charge, Flight Lieutenant Richards, decided to destroy the load by placing explosive charges among it. So that ill-starred venture produced absolutely nothing. Even if all four gliders carrying radar warning units had landed safely, or just two with sufficient equipment to produce one radar unit, there was no reception party with vehicles waiting for them, and the equipment would have had to be abandoned on a landing zone that was about to be evacuated by friendly troops. The wounded glider pilots and some of the RAF men obtained a lift on a passing jeep; the remainder set off on foot to find Divisional HQ.

There were no serious unloading problems for most of the gliders, and all but one were safely emptied by 5.30 p.m. The resupply operation by glider had mostly been successful. Three Hamilcars heavily loaded with trailers full of ammunition had been despatched as an experiment; two were unloaded, but the Germans captured the third before it could be emptied. Horsa gliders had brought in fifteen jeeps, each with two trailers full of ammunition for the airlanding battalions; and an RASC light transport platoon of eighteen jeeps and trailers had also been sent; so each brigade could have a reserve ammunition column. The five Polish anti-tank guns landed safely and were driven to Divisional HQ, the Poles hoping that they could join up with their own brigade, due in on the following morning. The actual glider landing, even under fire at one place, appears to have cost the lives of only eight men: four glider pilots, two artillerymen, one REME jeep driver and a 10th Battalion man travelling with one of his unit's jeeps. The RAF tug aircraft flew home safely, having lost only one Stirling but with thirty aircraft damaged by flak. One Dakota, flown by Flying Officer Ron McTeare of 575 Squadron, returned to England with a heavy glider tow rope wrapped around its starboard wing. Flying Officer Frank Gee, the second pilot, describes this:

> There was the sound of a very large 'thwack', the same sound as when you hit a car rubber mat against a wall, and the whole aircraft shuddered from stem to stern. On looking out of my window I saw that wrapped around the starboard wing was a tow rope dropped by another aircraft. The double ends that affix to the glider blotted out any aileron control, and the single shackle that affixes to the tug was trailing out some 300 feet behind.

The two pilots managed to reach England and land at Framlingham, the first airfield they could find with an open approach. The heavy tug shackle tore up thirty yards of concrete 'as if it were cardboard'.

There was one more element of the air operation. The parachute resupply for this day had been sent in thirty-three Stirlings from Harwell. Their loads were 803 panniers or containers loaded with eighty-six tons of supplies, mostly gun and mortar ammunition, with some petrol, but no food. These were to be parachuted on LZ-L, an open space in the woods north-west of Oosterbeek (see map on page 235). One Stirling had turned back; one had been shot down earlier in the flight; the remaining thirty-one flew in just after the glider landing and released their supplies. RASC jeeps and trailers went out to collect these supplies. This supply drop was another element of the plans made under the assumption that there would be little opposition; the area chosen was not yet fully under British control and *only twelve tons* of the supplies were gathered in. One Stirling, a 570 Squadron aircraft, was hit by flak and later crashed near Nijmegen, the third aircraft from that squadron to be lost that day. That made ten aircraft – six American and four RAF – lost from the Arnhem lift. Arnhem was starting to become costly for the air units, and the poor collection of supplies on the ground was a portent of difficulties to come. A signal was sent to England

12. Men of the 2nd South Staffords move along the Utrechtseweg near Oosterbeek on their way to reinforce the 1st Parachute Brigade units fighting in Arnhem on Monday morning. Heavy packs have been loaded on to an airborne handcart which each platoon in the airlanding battalions possessed. The commonly used Dutch wire fencing seen here was frequently a hindrance to swift deployment when men came under fire.

13. Lt Jack Reynolds of the South Staffords Mortar Platoon and other prisoners of war are photographed by a German Army cameraman after the museum battle.

14. A pre-war aerial photograph of Arnhem shows the road bridge and, in the distance, the area around St Elizabeth Hospital and the museum where relieving troops were held up. Most of the attacks on the defenders at the bridge came from the area at the bottom of the picture.

Black line *Repeated attacks fail to penetrate German blocking lines on Monday and Tuesday*

White line *Main bridge perimeter from Monday evening*

15. SS men in action near the museum on Tuesday; the men in the museum – mainly 2nd South Staffords – either have just surrendered or are about to do so.

16. Exhausted and wounded men – mixed 3rd Battalion and Royal Engineers – are taken away by the Germans after the fall of the school building near the Arnhem bridge on Wednesday. The man with the bare arm is Lt Len Wright of the 3rd Battalion.

17. At Oosterbeek Mrs Kremer photographs some of the defenders of her house on the Stationsweg. The men are glider pilots of D Squadron and members of No. 1 Platoon of the Independent Company. The man on the left with Mrs Kremer's visitors' book is Capt. S. G. Cairns, a glider pilot. The man on the right is Cpl Hans Rosenfeld, a German Jew who served in the Independent Company under the name of Rodley; he was killed the next day. The mottled effect on the photograph was caused by damp while the film was hidden in the house when the Kremers were forced to leave after the battle.

18. A flight of Stirlings drops supplies amid the smoke of bursting flak shells. Most of the supplies dropped in German-held ground because signals about a new dropping zone had not reached England.

19. Cpl Tierney of the 1st Border and his 3-inch mortar team in their position on the western side of the Oosterbeek perimeter.

20. A 75-millimetre gun of the Airlanding Light Regiment in action supporting the 4th Parachute Brigade advance on Tuesday. The gun crews of the regiment performed valiantly throughout the battle after moving to Oosterbeek.

21. 'Prisoner of war'. Under Luftwaffe guard, a batch of about 100 men from the 1st Airborne Division being marched towards Germany pass through the village of Ellecom, 12 miles from Arnhem.

22. 'Killed in action'. An airborne man lies in the sandy soil, probably at Oosterbeek. He is holding the speaker of a field radio.

23. Amid the shambles of battle at the hospital crossroads at Oosterbeek is a wrecked jeep. Its stretcher carrier at the back shows that it was a casualty evacuation vehicle, 'evacuation' at Oosterbeek being forward to the hospitals in the front line.

24. The men who came back – a party of survivors who crossed the Rhine and assembled at Nijmegen.

urging that the next day's supply drop should be made close to the Hartenstein at Oosterbeek, which was securely in British hands.

So ended the second lift. The 1st British Airborne Division was now complete and could gather itself in from those exposed landing areas and concentrate all of its effort to getting into Arnhem.

CHAPTER 13

The Battle in the Woods

The plan formulated in England for the 4th Parachute Brigade Group was that it would move into Arnhem straight down the main road, the Amsterdamseweg, as soon as it was ready to do so. The brigade was to occupy the northern and eastern sectors of the town, handing over the eastern sector to the Polish brigade after its planned arrival on the following day. Not having heard any news before taking off, Brigadier Hackett did not know that the background to such plans was now out of date. Only a small part of the 1st Parachute Brigade had reached its objective, and the remainder of that brigade was involved in desperate fighting. The divisional commander and one brigade commander were missing, and Brigadier Hicks was acting in command of the division.

Hicks had already decided to take away Hackett's 11th Battalion – the one whose rendezvous point was closest to the divisional area – and this news had to be broken to Hackett as soon as possible. Major Bruce Dawson, Hackett's brigade major who had brought the brigade's Advance Party in the previous day, had passed this order on to Hackett as soon as they met. It was not long afterwards that Lieutenant-Colonel Charles Mackenzie, the GSO 1 (principal staff officer) at Divisional HQ, arrived to confirm the order that the 11th Battalion was to be detached. Hackett was obviously disappointed. Here he was, with the brigade he had formed, trained and imbued with his own personality, assembling ready for action, when messages carried by junior officers and emanating from a temporary divisional commander junior to him in service in brigadier's rank summarily removed one of his battalions and did not even allow him to select the battalion. Hackett says:

> To choose off a map made up in England, without bothering about casualties incurred in flying in! Words almost fail me; it

was a disregard of the elementary staff doctrine that the chap in charge knew what was needed and it should have been left to me. To come along and say they had to have the 11th Battalion just like that – I was horrified. We sent for George Lea, and I told him that he was detached and that Charles Mackenzie would give him the details. The battalion went off to Divisional HQ, and I found later that they spent five hours there waiting for orders for the next move.

It was hardly the time to argue the finer points of the divisional chain of command, and Hackett realized that the 11th Battalion was the best placed for such a move. So the 11th Battalion marched off to its fate in Arnhem, which has already been described. Hackett asked Mackenzie if he could have one of the Airlanding Brigade's battalions to replace the 11th, but Mackenzie had no authority to commit Brigadier Hicks to that.

The loss of one-third of his infantry strength now forced Hackett to review his own plans. Mackenzie had not brought any new orders for the remainder of the brigade, only a request that Hackett come to meet Hicks at Divisional HQ as soon as possible. Hackett, meanwhile, was adhering to the original plan to move his brigade to the northern part of Arnhem: 'I did not yet realize how serious the situation was.' Only one battalion was free to move, however; 133 Field Ambulance was fully occupied with treating the many casualties from the drop and subsequent action and could not yet move from the aid post it had set up near the Zuid Ginkel Café, and the 10th Battalion had to remain nearby to give protection until the wounded had all been treated and evacuated. Only 156 Battalion was free to move, and Lieutenant-Colonel des Voeux led his men off to start the brigade's attempt to reach Arnhem. The time was about 5.0 p.m.

At almost the same time there were large-scale movements of other units, with a general retirement from the landing areas towards Arnhem now that the second lift had arrived. This was the long-awaited moment when the division could at last start to concentrate. The 7th King's Own Scottish Borderer companies came in from their isolated positions and were released by Brigadier Hackett, with his thanks for securing his brigade's dropping zone.

The second lift of the South Staffords, like the 11th Battalion, was on its way to rejoin its battalion fighting in Arnhem. The 1st Border retired from its exposed positions around the glider landing zone and moved towards Oosterbeek. The Light Regiment moved more of its guns into the fields around the church in Lower Oosterbeek, though the last battery would not arrive there until later. Divisional HQ moved to the Hartenstein Hotel, yet another temporary move, it was hoped; its ultimate destination should have been the barracks of the old 'Yellow Riders' in Arnhem, which had not been bombed on Sunday so that they could be occupied by Major-General Urquhart and his staff.

Brigadier Hackett continued to direct the movements of his brigade for the next seven hours and found no time to visit Divisional HQ. Soon after 11.0 p.m. another officer messenger from Hicks found Hackett at his headquarters, which had moved to the Hotel Buunderkamp in the woods between Ginkel Heath and Wolfheze. The officer was Major 'Jef' Linton, the commander of the Light Regiment battery supporting Hackett's brigade. Linton had been summoned from the glider landing zone and told to convey a change of orders to Hackett. Hackett's brigade, for the first phase of its advance, was to make its objective a place marked on maps as 'Koepel', a ridge of high ground between the Amsterdamseweg and the railway about a mile outside the built-up area of Arnhem.[1] But Major Linton was unable to answer Hackett's questions about such things as timings and co-ordination with other parts of the division.

Hackett now went to the Hartenstein to express to Hicks his anxieties and dissatisfaction at what he saw as 'an untidy situation'. There was a meeting, well described in other books, at which the two men argued. Hackett was senior in service as a brigadier, but Major-General Urquhart had left instructions that Hicks, older and with longer infantry experience than Hackett, was to take priority in command over the cavalryman Hackett in the unlikely event of both Urquhart and Brigadier Lathbury, the obvious successor,

[1] 'Koepel' was not the name of the ridge, only of a private tea-house or gazebo, but the high ground was known as 'Koepel' by the airborne units, and the name is used here to describe it.

becoming casualties. Unfortunately, neither Hicks nor Hackett had been informed of Urquhart's wishes. Hard words were exchanged, although Hackett did not directly challenge the position of Hicks in command of the division. He extracted a clearer idea of the situation and then departed. Basically, instead of directing his brigade on to the northern part of Arnhem, he was to proceed on a step-by-step basis, first of all capturing that Koepel high ground and then approaching Arnhem on the left flank of what remained of the 1st Parachute Brigade, which had just ended its Monday battle but still had some effective strength left for another effort. So, if the 4th Parachute Brigade could get up to the Koepel area quickly, there might still be the opportunity to mount a two-brigade attack into Arnhem towards the bridge.

There was one more matter. Hackett had earlier asked Lieutenant-Colonel Mackenzie if he could have one of the Airlanding Brigade battalions to replace his detached 11th Battalion, with the 7th King's Own Scottish Borderers clearly in mind. This battalion was already in the process of moving towards its predetermined 'phase two' position in the original plan. This was in the same direction as the 4th Parachute Brigade advance, but not as far. Hicks, probably reluctantly, told Hackett that he could take the KOSB under command, but that the battalion also had to continue to perform its role of protecting LZ-L near its next position for the arrival of the third-lift gliders, a condition which considerably reduced Hackett's ability to employ the battalion in his brigade's advance. The KOSB would remain unaware of the change until the next morning.

It was 1.30 a.m. on the Tuesday when Brigadier Hackett returned to his headquarters. Five and a half miles away in Arnhem, the 1st and 3rd Battalions and the South Staffords, with the 11th Battalion coming up later, were about to mount their last attack.

The Evening Moves

Lieutenant-Colonel Sir Richard des Voeux's 156 Battalion had left its rendezvous point on the dropping zone at about 5.0 p.m. on Monday. One platoon had to be left behind to guard prisoners and protect wounded; it was never able to rejoin the battalion and after several days of intermittent action finished up with two men dead, one evading capture and the remainder prisoners, fourteen of them wounded. It was a good example of how airborne units could dissipate their strength in random ways. The unit transport which had come in by glider was met at Wolfheze, and the battalion then pushed on alongside the railway, past the place where the Reconnaissance Squadron jeeps had been ambushed twenty-four hours earlier.

Brigadier Hackett had ordered the battalion to halt at dusk, reorganize and then push on 'before first light'. Lieutenant-Colonel des Voeux interpreted these orders liberally. Meeting little or no opposition, he kept his leading company going long after dusk until it reached a point just short of the junction of the track and the Dreijenseweg, less than a mile from the Koepel high ground. But the leading platoon, No. 10 Platoon of C Company, was fired upon here and pinned down. The company commander, Major Geoffrey Powell, called up one of his other platoon commanders, Lieutenant Brian Willcock, and ordered him to take No. 9 Platoon on a left-flanking move to determine whether there was a German flank around which the company could progress. But there was no flank here, and this platoon also came under fire.

Major Powell's view that the German position was too strongly held for a night attack was confirmed when des Voeux came up. C Company was ordered to disengage, return down the track for a mile and remain there for the night. What neither officer knew was that the Germans ahead were part of the main outer blocking line, the Sperrlinie Spindler, composed of first-class troops of the 9th SS Panzer Division, which was spread right across the 4th Parachute Brigade's proposed line of advance. The time was about midnight.

The remainder of the brigade was spread out along nearly three miles of that track by the railway, all the way back to the 4th Parachute Squadron, which was the brigade's rearguard. The 10th Battalion had been able to leave the dropping zone when most of the casualties of the parachute drop were evacuated. The battalion was now near the Hotel Buunderkamp, where Brigadier Hackett and his staff were preparing and issuing orders for the 'tidy battle'

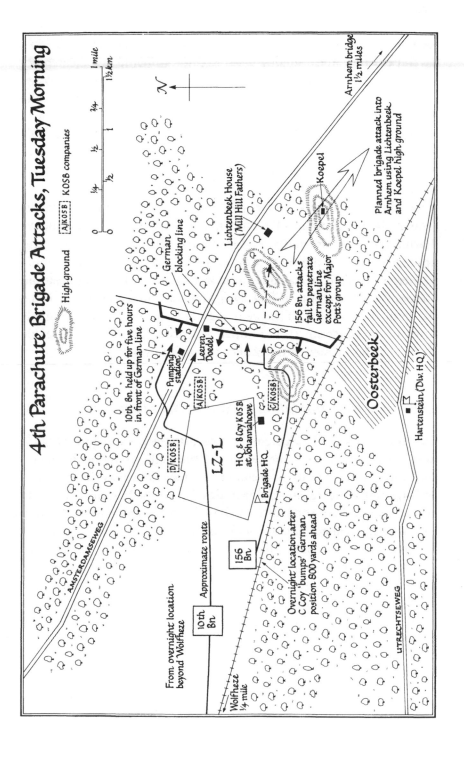

4th Parachute Brigade Attacks, Tuesday Morning

🌀 High ground

A/KOSB KOSB companies

0 ¼ ½ ¾ 1 mile
0 ½ 1 1½ km

N

AMSTERDAMSEWEG

German blocking line

10th Bn. held up for five hours in front of German line

Pumping station

Leeren Doedel

D/KOSB

A/KOSB

C/KOSB

LZ-L

HQ & B Coy KOSB at Johannahoeve

Brigade HQ

From overnight location beyond Wolfheze

Approximate route

10th Bn.

156 Bn.

Overnight location after C Coy 'bumps' German position 800 yards ahead

Wolfheze ¼ mile

Lichtenbeek House (Mill Hill Fathers)

156 Bn. attacks fail to penetrate German line except for Major Pott's group

Koepel

Planned brigade attack into Arnhem using Lichtenbeek and Koepel high ground

Oosterbeek

Hartenstein (Div. HQ)

UTRECHTSEWEG

Arnhem bridge 1½ miles

he hoped his brigade would be fighting the next day. The brigade's fatal casualties for the day and night numbered approximately seventy-six men – mostly on the fly-in and around the dropping zone.

Well forward of most of the 4th Parachute Brigade were the King's Own Scottish Borderers, carrying on with their own plan to secure the high ground near Johannahoeve Farm, overlooking LZ-L. Lieutenant-Colonel Payton-Reid had co-ordinated his moves with Brigadier Hackett, and his battalion was advancing in the area between the railway and the Amsterdamseweg. B and C Companies were ahead, each making for spot heights marked on their maps. Major Michael Forman's B Company, advancing past Johannahoeve Farm, ran into the outlying German defences at 4.0 a.m. and reacted in exactly the same way as 156 Battalion had a few hours earlier – a platoon flanking attack meeting further opposition, followed by a decision to pull back and wait for a new effort to be made in the morning. The scene was now set for the last possible attempt to penetrate the German defences and move a sizeable force of airborne men into Arnhem through this new sector.

156 Parachute Battalion – the Dreijenseweg Action

Dawn of Tuesday 19 September found the 4th Parachute Brigade with a clear objective – the seizure of the high ground at Koepel – and 156 Battalion ready to recommence its advance as the brigade's leading unit. Lieutenant-Colonel des Voeux had been ordered to direct his attack on some intermediate high ground close to a group of buildings named 'Lichtenbeek' on maps.[2] From there the battalion could strike south towards the brigade's objective at Koepel. It was just over a mile from 156 Battalion's overnight position to Lichtenbeek, and only half a mile from there to Koepel, but it was still a further one and three-quarter miles to the place in Arnhem where the 1st Parachute Brigade was at that time making its last attempt to get through to the bridge.

---

[2] The buildings at Lichtenbeek were the Mill Hill Fathers' retirement home in 1944. By coincidence, their new home, at Vrijland, is just south of 156 Battalion's coming attack area.

Barring the way to 156 Battalion's advance was that strong German defence line along the Dreijenseweg. If the reader ever visits this area, the defensive qualities of that line will be immediately obvious. Along part of the eastern side of the road there is a bank up to ten feet high, and beyond that the ground rises even further through a wooded area. The German defence comprised armoured cars, half-tracks, self-propelled guns and well-armed infantry. The vehicles cruised up and down the road or were deployed in the trees. Some of the infantry were in outposts ahead of the road, like the position into which C Company and the KOSB had bumped the previous evening, but the main infantry line was in the wooded high ground behind the road. Any attack had to negotiate the forward positions and the armoured vehicles on the road, then climb the bank to get into the woods. As the attackers climbed that bank, the top part of their bodies immediately became exposed to the German positions among the trees, and they could be fired upon at close range before they could deploy into the wood.

Major Geoffrey Powell's C Company made the first move, advancing again towards the position where it had been halted the previous evening. It was a standard company attack, two platoons forward and one in reserve. But the Germans had abandoned that forward position, and there was no opposition. It was a good start. Lieutenant-Colonel des Voeux could now commence his main attack across the Dreijenseweg into the Lichtenbeek woods. A Company was selected for this. The company was short of the platoon that had been left on the dropping zone to protect casualties, but this had been replaced by a platoon of thirty glider pilots from D Squadron under Captain Ian Muir. A detailed report written later by the company commander, Major John Pott, together with some personal interviews enables this detailed story of a gallant attack to be told.

Before the advance started, des Voeux and Pott went up to the feature recently occupied by C Company to reconnoitre the next move, but the country ahead was too wooded, and nothing of any use could be seen. Brigadier Hackett came up while they were there and impressed upon the two officers the urgent need to get through to Arnhem and up to the bridge where Lieutenant-Colonel Frost's force was in desperate need of reinforcement. With that exhortation fresh in his mind, Major Pott went off to brief his platoon commanders; he had a personal interest in this, his wife being John Frost's sister. Lieutenant Stan Watling's No. 4 Platoon led off the company attack. The cover of the trees thinned as they approached the Dreijenseweg, and they were fired upon by at least two machine-guns. Those men not hit dashed forward and reached the road but could not get into the woods on the other side because of the volume of fire. They became pinned down in the shallow ditches at the side of the road. Major Pott saw what had happened and ordered up Lieutenant David Delacour's No. 5 Platoon to attempt a left-flanking attack, the standard response to such a situation taught at battle schools and practised many times; the Brens of the platoon were to set up a fire group, while the riflemen charged in. Sergeant Sandy Thorburn was with one of the Brens:

> It was far too quiet. We were behind little heaps of cut logs. You couldn't see anything but the trees, and I was certain that there were snipers hidden in them. I wanted to spray the trees ahead of us before we started, but before I could do so, Lieutenant Delacour was hit by the first shot fired – just nicked in the neck. I told him to lie still, but he jumped up and shouted, 'Major Pott. Fix bayonets. Charge!' – those were his exact words. He was immediately hit again, right across the middle. All hell let loose then. I opened fire with the Bren, firing off about five magazines, spraying the trees, but I couldn't see any effect of my fire.

Lieutenant Delacour bled to death. The glider-pilot platoon should have followed into the attack, but as John Pott says: 'They were the strangers in our midst. I had not been able to get round to talk to them, and they didn't slot into our attack as a regular platoon would have done. They got stuck very early in the assault.' There was a German outpost in the trees just north of the track which was the axis of the company approach, and it had fired into the flank of the glider-pilot platoon. Captain Muir was wounded, and one of his officers, Lieutenant Sydney Smith, was fatally wounded, and there were several other casualties.

Without their leaders and in that confusing wood, the survivors went no further.[3]

The dash led by Major Pott got across the road, however, and well into the wood on the other side. Lieutenant Watling's platoon climbed out of the ditches at the side of the road to join in the rush, but Watling was killed at once. The company second in command, Captain Terry Rodgers, was hit and fatally wounded. The German defence, particularly the armoured vehicles, was too strong for the lightly armed airborne men. Only Major Pott and a few men managed to get through the German line of defences and well into the trees. Some were badly wounded, and one of them, Sergeant George Sheldrake, describes a moving incident:

> I was with another two lads; we were all in a pretty bad way. Major Pott came over and said that he couldn't take us with him but he put us carefully under some bushes. He said that the battalion might make a fresh attack, and we could be recovered; if not we would be picked up by the Germans. He had to leave us then but, before he moved off, he stood there and prayed over us – for a couple of minutes maybe, although there was some mortar and machine-gun fire, and a couple of minutes is a long time to stand up in those conditions. It is something I shall never forget.

A Company's advance ended on its objective six hours after it had started, but with only six men left and John Pott himself twice wounded, one bullet smashing his thigh and another hitting him in the hand. Some of the survivors hid and were able to escape. The Germans marched away the walking wounded, but left John Pott out in the open for the next eighteen hours, during which time he attempted to write a farewell letter to his wife with his left hand. He was found by two Dutchmen on the following day, carried to the nearby Mill Hill Fathers' house and eventually became a

---

[3] Captain Muir later became a prisoner of war and was shot with a Royal Engineers officer, Lieutenant W. H. Skinner, at or near Renkum, in one of the few German prisoner-of-war atrocities in this battle.

prisoner, the only one of six officers (including the glider pilots) in the A Company attack to survive.

It was not known at Battalion HQ that A Company's fight had suffered so badly, and a third company had been sent forward at about 9.0 a.m. This was Major John Waddy's B Company on what was yet another left-flanking movement. John Waddy describes how he received his orders:

> The Colonel didn't know the full situation. He thought there were only a few snipers about and said A Company had reached the road and B Company was to push through them and capture the Lichtenbeek feature. When he told me about the 'few snipers' I realized from the amount of fire we had already heard that there was more than that. When we moved up, it was obvious that A Company had received tremendous casualties; there were wounded coming back in Bren carriers and dead chaps lying at the side of the ride, and I passed a complete platoon headquarters all killed.

Yet again, the attack came under heavy fire as it approached the Dreijenseweg. Here are two accounts which illustrate the difficulty of fighting in those woods. Private Ted Reynolds:

> I couldn't see where the Germans were and had to fire at where their fire seemed to be coming from. Things got quite bad. One of the first to be hit was the Number Two on my Bren, Private Ford. Suddenly he was laid on the ground, stone dead, with three neat little bullet holes in the throat. Funny enough, he had been a lovely singer. The platoon lost four or five men. I remember Dodds being shot in the chest or the neck, and Atkinson was hit in the neck, but it came out the other side without hitting the artery. I saw him walking back with blood spurting out of the side of his neck. They both survived.
>
> A man came out of the woods with his hands up. He claimed to be a glider pilot and certainly wore a glider pilot's equipment. He told us to follow him, saying there were only

young Germans ahead and we could easily go and get them. He spoke perfect English, but I am convinced that he was a German because he had come out of the bushes where the Germans were and he went back the same way when we refused to follow him. No one thought to stop him.

Private Ron Atkinson was in the same platoon:

Then it happened – we walked right into it, fire from above, from our flanks, and even from behind. My platoon halted and took cover. We saw a figure in khaki running towards us shouting some gibberish about where Jerry was. He turned out to be a glider pilot; he was lucky he didn't get shot from both sides. Then we heard the clatter of tank tracks to our front and flank using the narrow paths among the trees. They let off everything they had at us: small arms, armour-piercing shells, high explosive, the lot. Then we had an order to advance at the double – no point in waiting to be massacred. We must have advanced about 500 yards when we were ordered to halt and take cover again. I heard my stretcher-bearer pal's Midlands accent asking for assistance, so me, being nosy, crawled over and found him with one arm limp due to a bullet in the shoulder, struggling to get our section sergeant on the stretcher. The latter was lying face down. I turned him on his back and proceeded to put my hands under his armpits while Harry held his legs.

Then it happened. Something struck me at the back of my neck; it felt like a back heel from a cart-horse. I remember feeling to see whether I still had a head on my shoulders and then looking at my hands and tunic sleeves covered in blood – my own blood! I dashed to the rear, to the first-aid post, moaning and groaning all the way.

Major Waddy was immediately behind the two platoons leading the attack:

I could hear the German armoured vehicles moving up and

down the Dreijenseweg, quite a lot of vehicles. You could hear the Germans shouting. Then a twin-barrelled 20-millimetre anti-aircraft gun on the road opened up, firing high-explosive shells, and these had a deadly effect, bursting in the trees and flinging out small splinters, so that even though your men were on the ground trying to crawl forward, they were still getting killed or wounded. Both leading platoons were held up at a clearing in front of us. We tried to dash across the clearing under cover of some aircraft which came low overhead – we thought they were RAF – and I went forward with some of my soldiers and Tom Wainwright, the Support Company commander, to try and knock this 20-millimetre gun out. We got up to within ten paces of it, and the man on my right was just about to throw a phosphorus grenade at it when he was drilled right through the head. What had happened was that there was a man sitting in a tree just above the gun and he was firing down at us. I only had a pistol, instead of the German Schmeisser machine-gun I normally carried. I fired half a magazine at him and missed, and then he hit me. I collapsed and started to crawl out, and he took another shot at me. Then one of my Rhodesian soldiers picked me up and carried me out. That virtually stalled the battalion attack.

The events of the morning became known to Brigadier Hackett, and at 2.0 p.m. he ordered the battalion to disengage. Casualties had been about 50 per cent. It had been a purely infantry battle. Captain Peter Chard of the Light Regiment had been with Battalion HQ throughout, but the country was so close that he had been unable to give any useful artillery support. Neither had the attached anti-tank troop been able to help; the 6-pounder was not an offensive weapon. The battalion, with only one more or less intact company, pulled back to reorganize and await further orders.

The 10th Parachute Battalion – the Pumping-Station-Area Action

Brigadier Hackett did not intend that Lieutenant-Colonel Ken Smyth's battalion should make any major attack during the first phase of his brigade's operation. After spending the night near Brigade HQ at the Hotel Buunderkamp, the battalion set off at 4.30 a.m., making towards a road junction on the Amsterdamseweg where it was to 'occupy a firm base' to protect the left flank of the brigade's attack. The first three miles of the approach march were made without too much difficulty, and the battalion's destination was almost reached with no greater danger than some long-range machine-gun fire which caused few casualties, though with the disturbing experience of meeting a succession of jeeps bringing back casualties from 156 Battalion's action.

The leading troops, Captain Cedric Horsfall's D Company,[4] reached the designated junction on the wide Amsterdamseweg by 10.0 a.m. Ken Smyth did not stop there but continued on in the direction of Arnhem. There are several unexplained aspects of this further move. There is no record of why Smyth proceeded further; possibly an unrecorded wireless message from Brigadier Hackett encouraged him to do so. The battalion was thus approaching the next road junction, which was three-quarters of a mile closer to Arnhem, at the end of the Dreijenseweg near a hotel called the Leeren Doedel; but this was the northern end of the German blocking line on the Dreijenseweg, and the battalion would have to fight for that next road junction. The personal accounts of several contributors show that they knew nothing of the 'occupy firm base' order but were under the impression that the battalion was following the original brigade plan made in England and continuing along the main road to get to its originally allocated position north of Arnhem.

D Company moved on through the wooded ground on the south side of the road, passing a pumping station called La Cabine on the northern side of the road, and then it suddenly came under fire

---

[4] The 10th Battalion did not have a C Company; the three rifle companies were A, B and D.

from the outposts of the German blocking line on the Dreijenseweg. The leading troops were approximately 300 yards short of the Leeren Doedel road junction.[5]

What happened next was a typical example of what was now becoming a familar situation: the leading troops of an advancing unit suddenly coming under heavy fire from weapons fired from unseen positions in the woods. First it was long bursts of machine-gun fire, then mortars, then armoured vehicles firing from nearby roads and tracks. The leading platoon went to ground and tried to return the fire. The leading company commander tried to manoeuvre one of his other platoons to make an outflanking attack, but men were fired upon as soon as they exposed themselves, and, if the platoon did start a flanking attack, it found that the German line was so extensive that no further progress could be made. Battalion HQ then assessed the situation and decided upon the next move. Lieutenant-Colonel des Voeux's response in 156 Battalion's action a few hours earlier had been to call forward a further company and order it to repeat the attack, hoping that determined pressure would break the German defence; it had not, and the company concerned had been ruined.

Lieutenant-Colonel Smyth proceeded more cautiously. He left D Company in contact with the Germans, carrying on a prolonged fire-fight, and sent observers from his Intelligence Section forward in an attempt to establish the exact whereabouts of the German positions and then bring his 3-inch Mortar Platoon into action. He then sent a message to Brigade HQ asking whether he should commit his other companies in a much wider flanking move, crossing the main road in strength and trying to move forward through the woods on the north side of it. Permission was given, though this all took time. There was no artillery support, either because of the close country or because of signalling difficulties. There was no close air support, as would have been enjoyed in large measure by conventional Allied ground troops, because the

---

[5] 'Leeren Doedel' means 'Empty Purse'. An earlier café on this site was so named because farmers who had been to market in Arnhem often spent the proceeds of their day's trading on drink these before going home. The La Cabine pumping station still extracts a pure and soft source of underground water which supplies most of Arnhem.

planners in England had made no detailed preparations for liaison with the fighter-bomber squadrons available at the forward airfields in Belgium. Many German fighters appeared during the day and supported their troops, a rare reversal of the air-support situation in 1944. There would be no friendly tank support until XXX Corps arrived. Most of these disadvantages had been shared by other battalions attacking in the Arnhem battle, but the experience of the 10th Battalion, brought to a halt here while making the 1st British Airborne Division's last major attempt to advance, highlights many of the shortcomings of the Arnhem operation: over-optimism about the German defence capabilities, too distant dropping and landing zones, and failure to employ over the battlefield the Allied air supremacy won at such cost in the earlier years of the war.

These are a few examples of incidents during the five hours that the 10th Battalion spent in the woods astride that wide road near the pumping station. Captain Nick Hanmer, the Adjutant, was well up behind the leading company when the firing started:

We had been moving fairly quickly, and it happened suddenly. But it was what we would have expected – that the leading company would be held up and then overcome the resistance, only they didn't overcome the resistance. The Germans had the usual MG-42s – the standard German light machine-gun, very fast firing, twice as fast as the Bren – and of course there were tracked vehicles; you could hear the squealing of the tracks and the engine noises, but Battalion HQ wasn't near enough to see them. That was a very frightening noise if you were a parachutist.

The company ahead may have tried to outflank the opposition – I don't know – but the fire was so heavy that they had to dig in, and so did we. You dig rather quickly in those circumstances. Quite a lot of the fire was coming through to us. The CO couldn't do much at that stage because the fire was so heavy. We were so close to the leading company that I actually saw one man shot. He was only six feet away from me. He was hit in the middle of the forehead and said, 'Oh my God', as he went down.

Lieutenant John Procter, commanding 9 Platoon in the leading company, was ordered to cross the main road and attempt an outflanking attack on the other side:

We had to get across the road first, but there was a self-propelled gun firing straight down it from time to time. It seemed fairly quiet, so we put one man across to see what it was like. The SP fired just then, and the shell blew the man's head off, a most unlucky shot for him. The rest of us lined up and galloped across without any more casualties. We had a lot of trouble then when their mortars opened up; the bombs were coming down just like rain. The whole ground was heaving; we thought we had come on to a minefield. I was one of the first to be hit – in the upper arm, breaking the bone. I was able to walk back to our own aid post. Battalion HQ was there also; they all laughed, which was a bit unkind; they knew that I was always getting shot up. This was the third time. The first was when I got shot in the stomach in a Crusader tank in North Africa; the second was when I was shot in the bottom in Italy.

Private George Taylor was Number Two on a Bren gun in No. 8 Platoon, also in D Company:

We were held up by some Germans who were in some farm buildings. They had several Spandaus, and we kept exchanging fire with them. The barrel got so hot that we had to urinate on it to cool it down before we could change it; the hot urine spurted back on to me. We were in shallow scrapes on the edge of a wood about fifty to seventy-five yards from the Germans and we eventually decided that we had to move out. It was just then that Nick Walter, the Number One on the Bren, was killed – just the one hit in the temple. I didn't even know he was hit at first. I had to take the Bren from him and leave him; he was still in the firing position. That was the first time I had ever seen anyone dead. It all affected me very deeply; he was my best friend.

Another friend I lost that day was 'Taffy' Fifield. He had

been engaged to a Land Army girl at Somerby where our camp was; she had asked me to look after him. When I went back to Somerby for the unveiling of the battalion's memorial plaque just after the war she was there. If looks could have killed, I would have been dead.

The battalion's transport had come up to the main road by way of a track and had just started to mount the main road when the action started. Lieutenant-Colonel Smyth's jeep, being driven by Captain Barry Murdoch, a glider pilot, was nosing carefully out on to the wide road but was immediately hit by a self-propelled gun firing from further up the road. No one was hurt, but the jeep burst into flames, and the kits of several officers were lost. The incident undoubtedly deterred the attached anti-tank troop from attempting the same thing when they were later requested to deploy a gun to tackle the German armour on the road. Another vehicle in the transport column to be affected was a commandeered horse and cart loaded with reserve ammunition and radio batteries which bolted with its signalman driver when mortar bombs started to drop nearby.

Corporal Harry Dicken, at Battalion HQ, describes how Lieutenant-Colonel Smyth responded to a message that a column of enemy vehicles was approaching from the direction of Arnhem:

We were told – Battalion HQ at least – to line the road to ambush them but not to fire until ordered. The enemy stopped short of the wood, spread out and began to plaster us with every weapon they had. I was about ten yards from Colonel Smyth in this action; I was the only one left at HQ in the Intelligence Section, the others having been sent forward to find out what was happening. From my position I could see across the road to a two-storey pumping station with a tiled roof. While we were looking in this direction, there was a double explosion, and the tile roof lifted, and over a period of almost a minute the tiles cascaded to the ground. Colonel Smyth drily remarked, 'The landlord won't like that.'

The battalion's 3-inch mortars came into action and were

successful in dampening the German opposition, but only for as long as their ammunition lasted. Permission had meanwhile come from Brigade HQ for one company to attempt a much wider flanking movement. This was A Company, now led by its second in command, Captain Lionel Queripel, because the company commander was still south of the Rhine after his parachute aircraft had been shot down. Exact details of the company's progress are not easy to establish; there is no written report, and not one officer of the company survived the next few days. Two men have provided personal accounts. Corporal 'Ginger' Elliott says that much of the company was inactive on the north side of the road for so long that he was able to obtain some water from Dutch people at the pumping station and make a brew of tea. Private 'Jacko' Jackson, who should have been in detention in England for twice going absent in one week but had been allowed to come on the operation through the good offices of Captain Queripel, tells how he went on a three-man patrol further along the road led by Sergeant 'Tex' Banwell, discovered five tanks, two supply trucks and two fuel tankers in a compound beyond the pumping station and only narrowly escaped from a German patrol which nearly cut them off. Captain Queripel later ordered a company attack which met heavy opposition, and little progress was made. Queripel was slightly wounded in the face and personally carried a wounded sergeant back across the main road.

That was the last purely offensive British action of the Battle of Arnhem. All attacks carried out during the remainder of the battle were counter-attacks to regain lost defensive positions. It was probably early afternoon, certainly before 3.0 p.m. The 10th Battalion's casualties during that frustrating five-hour action had not been heavy. About twelve men had been killed; the wounded were nearly all treated and evacuated safely by the Battalion MO, Captain Gareth Drayson, known to his friends as 'Gremlin', but he would be killed later in the day.

The King's Own Scottish Borderers around Johannahoeve Farm and LZ-L, on which a landing by gliders carrying Polish anti-tank guns was expected during the day, and the minor units of Hackett's brigade also had a relatively quiet morning. All suffered from the wide-ranging German fighter strafing, but there were few casualties.[6] Brigade HQ was dug in among some trees near the railway line; Lieutenant George Paull's 17-pounder anti-tank troop was nearby, its four guns looking out over the open ground; the 6-pounder anti-tank guns were all with the battalions. The headquarters staff was functioning normally, and Hackett was probably enjoying deploying his brigade, at least until news of the reverses to his two parachute battalions arrived. The sappers of the 4th Parachute Squadron were located near the railway line between Brigade HQ and Wolfheze. The squadron was providing the rear protection for the brigade, because all British troops had now left Wolfheze, but there was no danger from that direction during the morning.

Brigade HQ received visitors during the morning when Lieutenant-Colonels Charles Mackenzie and Robert Loder-Symonds were sent by Major-General Urquhart, newly escaped from Arnhem, to visit Hackett and request him to come to Divisional HQ if he could get away; otherwise Urquhart would come to see Hackett later. 'Shan' Hackett was delighted that Roy Urquhart was back in command of the division; he had clearly found it irksome to work under Brigadier Hicks. He says: 'My feelings were that Roy was back and a firm hand was in charge at last. Things were looking tidier. I had no quarrel with the conduct of operations now.'

Hackett did not feel able to leave his headquarters as the morning

---

[6] Johannahoeve Farm figures frequently in Arnhem accounts. It had been a huge property before the war, containing all of the land in the rectangle bordered on the north and south by the Amsterdamseweg and the railway line respectively, and on the west and east by the Wolfhezerweg, the road running north from Wolfheze village, and the Dreijenseweg. It was in the eastern part of that mixed farm-and-woodland property that the 10th and 156 Battalions were fighting that morning. In 1943 the landlord, a cocoa factory owner, had sold the farmhouse and nearby buildings, together with 320 acres (130 hectares) of the land, to the Mill Hill Fathers; but at the time of the battle, the farmhouse was occupied by two tenant farmers, the Hoogendams and the van Maanens, and three 'underground' families hiding from the Germans in the stable loft. All were present during the battle. Mr Hendrik van Maanen was the only casualty, receiving a bullet wound in his arm, but it is not known from which side it was fired. Private Henry McCluskey, a KOSB jeep driver at the farm, remembers, when taking an early-morning wash and shave, 'the look on the faces of the ladies when they saw our soap – Eve and Lifebuoy Toilet. They only had synthetic soap which gave very little lather.'

progressed and news from his forward battalions worsened, and at 1.30 p.m. Roy Urquhart arrived to see him. An important discussion took place. The situation had deteriorated drastically since the 'things looking tidier' optimism of mid-morning. 156 Battalion's attack had failed with heavy loss; the 10th Battalion was pinned down, unable to make progress. The KOSB were still required to protect the glider landing zone. The glider lift was late. In short, the 4th Parachute Brigade had run out of steam and there were no fresh troops available to continue the attempt to move into Arnhem against an obviously powerful German defence.

Hackett suggested cutting his brigade's losses north of the railway in case the Germans counter-attacked and it was decided that the 4th Parachute Brigade would disengage and move to the south of the railway preparatory to mounting a fresh attack into Arnhem from there. There were two main problems: the need to protect the landing zone for the glider landing and the high railway embankment running between the brigade and Oosterbeek which only had two proper crossing points for vehicles and guns: at Oosterbeek Hoog Station (probably held by the Germans now) and Wolfheze Station (abandoned and soon likely to be occupied by the Germans). One of those crossings had to be captured. Urquhart said that he would instruct Brigadier Hicks to secure the Oosterbeek Hoog crossing with troops from Oosterbeek; in fact, Hicks arrived during the discussion and confirmed that he would carry out that task. Hackett's staff prepared the orders for the 10th and 156 Battalions to start their withdrawal; the KOSB would have to remain where they were until the gliders arrived. Roy Urquhart climbed up the railway embankment and slid down the other side to his jeep. It was only the width of that railway line that separated the 4th Parachute Brigade from the comparative safety of Oosterbeek. There is evidence that neither of those senior officers realized yet the parlous situation of the whole division, not just the temporary danger to Hackett's brigade. The divisional war diarist made an entry at 1.30 p.m. that 'later, if possible, 4 Para Bde should make contact with 11 Para Bn and occupy high ground NORTH of railway 7178'.[7]

[7] Headquarters 1st British Airborne Division War Diary, Airborne Forces Museum, File No. 42.

Map square 7178 contained the Mariendaal feature on the outskirts of Arnhem, which the 11th Battalion had been ordered to capture that morning. News of the complete failure of that attack – indeed, of the entire 1st Parachute Brigade attack in Arnhem – had not yet reached Divisional HQ.

The situation of the 4th Parachute Brigade was rapidly becoming more dangerous while these unrealistic plans were being made. Reports from Dutch volunteer informants indicated that powerful German forces were closing in from the west – the brigade's rear – more quickly than had previously been thought. This brought a new urgency to the plan to move the brigade south of the railway. There was no time for the Airlanding Brigade to prepare its attack on the Oosterbeek Hoog Station crossing. Hackett's brigade units would have to disengage and make for the Wolfheze crossing at once, before the Germans coming in from the west reached it. That crossing point was two and a quarter miles away from the furthest of Hackett's units, the 10th Battalion. It would be particularly difficult for the 10th and 156 Battalions to disengage from close contact with the Germans and for the KOSB, who would have to stay and defend the landing zone for the glider lift which had still not arrived. The scene was set for a period of extreme danger for the 4th Parachute Brigade.

The Third-Lift Glider Landing

The third lift of 'Market' should have brought in the whole of the Polish Independent Parachute Brigade Group (less its Light Artillery Battery for which no gliders were available) and part of the American 878th Airborne Aviation Engineer Battalion whose task would have been to construct a forward fighter strip in the Arnhem area. A large supply-dropping mission would also be flown to Arnhem by 101 Stirlings and 63 Dakotas. The American engineers were to have been carried in ten Hamilcars towed by Halifaxes from Tarrant Rushton, but their part in the operation was postponed because the situation at Arnhem was so serious; their part in the operation would eventually be cancelled. Another postponement was caused by the weather; it was so poor at the

American troop-carrier airfields, Spanhoe and Saltby, that it was declared unsafe for the C-47s to take off and assemble into their formations, so the whole of the Polish parachute lift was also postponed by at least one day. This was a severe set-back for the British troops fighting at Arnhem.

The flight of the thirty-five Horsa gliders for the Polish lift did go ahead when the weather eventually cleared in southern England to allow take-offs at Tarrant Rushton and Keevil at noon, several hours late. Also taking off were seven Horsas and one Hamilcar which had aborted from the first or second lifts. The Polish gliders contained two troops of five guns each from the Anti-Tank Battery, part of the Medical Company and some of the brigade's jeep transport. Both the supply-dropping flight, which came in first, and the tug-and-glider force were flying the southern route – in over the friendly territory of Belgium and then turning north to fly close to the corridor along which the ground forces were advancing. This was a longer but hopefully safer route than the northern one used on the first two Arnhem lifts.

The glider force suffered considerable depletion before reaching the Arnhem area. Seven Horsas suffered various problems and force-landed either in England, the North Sea or in Belgium, where the only Hamilcar also went down. A further seven Horsas were lost over Holland, six with tow ropes cut by flak and the seventh destroyed by a direct hit on its nose compartment. That glider was seen to disintegrate and its contents spill out, killing the two Polish anti-tank gunners and the glider pilots. It is estimated that only twenty-eight of the gliders with Polish loads and two of the ones carrying British troops from previous lifts arrived in the Arnhem area. One report says that the escort and flak-suppression fighter force failed to rendezvous with either the supply-dropping aircraft or the glider force, so there was nothing to combat the effect of the flak batteries which the Germans had assembled on the approach to Arnhem. The supply-dropping aircraft lost nine Stirlings and four Dakotas from flak; their story will be told in more detail later. The tug aircraft and the glider force escaped the worst of the fire, because they were flying at a greater height, and none was lost on the final approach. But the gliders then had to descend through part of the flak barrage and German small-arms fire. Several were damaged but only one seriously, crashing just before reaching the landing zone. This was probably the glider observed from his bedroom window in Oosterbeek by a young Dutchman, Sjoert Schwitters:

> I watched a German light anti-aircraft position on the top of a nearby house firing at the gliders. I saw one of them hit. There was an explosion – the nose of the glider seemed to have been shot off – and I saw soldiers and items of equipment, a jeep perhaps and other items, all falling out. It was a terrible sight, and I hated the Germans for what they were doing – all those young men dying.

The King's Own Scottish Borderer companies defending the landing zone were frustrated at not being able to stop the Germans firing at the gliders in the air. Once below the level of the trees surrounding the landing zone, however, the gliders were able to land without serious difficulty, because the edges of that wide area of the Johannahoeve farmland were still more or less secure. Most of the gliders made good landings, but Sergeant Ron Driver, whose own glider had landed successfully despite having one wheel shot off, watched another glider make a heavy landing:

> The pilot made a perfect touchdown, but suddenly its nose dug in, throwing up a wave of earth that obscured the fuselage, so that only the tail could be seen sticking up at a crazy angle. This galvanized us into action; we dashed over to the Horsa. As we did so, we could see that the cockpit had disappeared. We started frantically to dig away the soil, clods of earth, pieces of plywood and Perspex, etc., until we came across a piece of uniform and pulled out one of the pilots. He was, of course, dead. We redoubled our efforts to find the other but were unsuccessful. We left the two Poles who had survived the crash, though dazed, to their own devices; they could do nothing about their own load; I think it was a 6-pounder gun. We ran back to our glider and started to get the two jeeps out.

Years later, Ron Driver came to the conclusion that his dead colleagues were Staff Sergeant John West and Sergeant James Bonham of C Squadron, whose field burials were near here.

The two Horsas carrying British troops who had force-landed in England on earlier lifts were using an old flight plan and came down on the landing zone north of Wolfheze which had been their original destination, so they finished up in an area that had now been abandoned by friendly troops. The occupants of one glider are believed to have been able to rejoin the main body, but the men in the second glider, from the KOSB's Mortar Platoon, were surrounded by German troops and taken prisoner. This was much to the disgust of one of the glider pilots, Sergeant Jock Macdonald, who later wrote: 'It was just a damned débâcle; we were just sitting ducks waiting to be plucked.' The Polish Anti-Tank Battery did not fare much better. Only three of the ten guns leaving England were unloaded; one was commandeered by a 10th Battalion officer and not seen again, and only two guns, under Second Lieutenant Wladyslaw Mleczko, reached Oosterbeek. Major-General Sosabowski's personal jeep encountered some Germans, and the driver was wounded and captured. When the Germans found a suitcase with Sosabowski's name on it, they broadcast that Sosabowski was dead, but he had not left England yet. Nine of the ninety-three Polish airborne soldiers who took off from England died or were fatally wounded – two on the fly-in and seven in the glider landing.

The 4th Parachute Brigade Withdrawals

The 10th Battalion had received orders to pull back from its firefight with the Germans between the pumping station and the Leeren Doedel road junction before the glider landing took place. Captain Nick Hanmer remembers hearing the order on the Battalion HQ wireless: 'I said to Colonel Smyth that we couldn't do that. They always say never disengage while under attack. He said we would do as we were bloody well told, and I sent off the runners to the companies with their orders.' The disengagement was carried out without serious loss; the men north of the main road crossed under cover of smoke grenades and the battalion started to move back through the woodland towards the open ground behind. But a platoon left behind on the edge of the woodland to act as a rearguard suffered some casualties. Lance-Corporal Jim Finn describes how he and five other men became cut off and spent the next three days making their way back towards the dropping zone of the previous day; they had no idea that the main division was south at Oosterbeek. They were eventually captured. Lieutenants Sammy Carr and Bobby Dodd stayed to help the MO evacuate wounded men, were late leaving the wood and had to hide until dark before attempting to escape. They became separated. Carr got back to England as an evader, but Lieutenant Dodd's field grave was found after the war with those of men killed in the battalion's action that morning. Separations from their units such as those of Lance-Corporal Finn and his group and of the two officers were typical of the way the brigade was starting to disintegrate.

The 10th Battalion had begun to cross the open ground when the gliders came in. That area now became a scene of developing confusion. Men from the KOSB's B Company, supplemented by other volunteers, came out to help unload the gliders. The 10th Battalion men continued their withdrawal, at first under control – many men on foot and a few jeeps – but then in a rush when German infantry and tanks appeared on the edge of the wood behind them. Brigadier Hackett, watching from the southern edge of the landing zone, says: 'It was all no end of a party – the Poles coming in between the 10th Battalion and Brigade HQ. It was wonderful that the 10th Battalion kept its morale and structure. I watched it all from the south side of the LZ – a very interesting occupation.' But the German fire grew fiercer. Private George Taylor says: 'We were moving back in extended order across the open when some fire came overhead. We all went down. Major Peter Warr shouted at us to stop doing that. He said that next time anyone got down he would stay down. It was only a joking warning, but it worked.'

Captain Nick Hanmer also describes the move:

It was not far off panic stations when the Germans came in behind us. I was in the Battalion HQ jeep, in the middle of an extended line of men; they were not running but were going at a fast walk. There was much fire from the northern edge and it caused many casualties. The gliders were coming in from the south, but it was a large piece of ground, and there was no need to get out of their way. I saw a German wheeled vehicle come out of the trees, right up to one glider, and it fired straight into the glider; it all looked pretty horrific.

Lieutenant Miles Henry, the Intelligence Officer, was walking next to me when he was hit by a burst of machine-gun fire. I remember that he was hit in the back by such a heavy burst that bits of haversack were coming out of his front. I wanted to put his body in the jeep, but the CO said we had to leave him.

Corporal Harry Dicken of the Intelligence Section, faced with a mile of open ground to cover, buried in a slit trench the battalion war diary he had been keeping, together with his map case and telescope.

The confusion mounted. There was a rush by everyone to get off that open ground, and some of the glider loads had to be abandoned. The newly arrived Poles, many of whom could not speak English, could not always tell who was friend and who was foe. They, in turn, were sometimes mistaken for Germans because of their strange tongue and different-coloured berets to those of the British airborne men. There were several examples of Polish and British troops opening fire on each other and causing casualties. Several contributors mention the bravery of a 10th Battalion Bren carrier driver who went back and forth across the open, bringing in casualties, tossing them into the carrier despite their screams of pain; this was Lance-Corporal Bill Garibaldi, from Brighton, one of the Royal Sussex men who had helped form this battalion; he would be killed on the following day. Eventually, the last of the British and Poles who could do so were off that open ground, leaving their casualties and the broken or burning gliders to the Germans. As the 10th Battalion men reached the southern edge, they were directed along the track by the railway towards Wolfheze, only a mile away now.

The King's Own Scottish Borderers, spread out by companies

around the landing zone, also became heavily involved in actions of various kinds. The Germans who were attacking out of the trees on the northern edge of the open ground were from a reorganized force based on Battalion Krafft, the unit which had held up the advance of parts of the 1st Parachute Brigade soon after the landings on Sunday afternoon. Two companies of the battalion, supplemented by companies of marines and military police, now formed Kampfgruppe Krafft. One of the original Krafft companies, No. 9 commanded by Obersturmführer Günther Leiteritz, advanced too far from the cover of the trees, and the entire company of about 200 men became exposed to the weapons of the KOSB's Battalion HQ and D Company, which were around the Johannahoeve farm buildings. The Borderers opened up with all their weapons. Particularly mentioned were Major Alex Cochran and Drum-Major Andrew Tate, both firing Brens, and Sergeant Andrew Parker, the Provost Sergeant, who was manning a Vickers. Those Germans who survived retreated rapidly to the woods. It was the one clear British success of an otherwise unhappy afternoon.

On the north-west side of the landing zone, A Company of the battalion suffered a bitter experience. Major Bob Buchanan had three of his own platoons here, plus No. 10 Platoon of C Company, which had been sent to replace a platoon lost the previous day. Immediately after the glider landing it was ordered to withdraw southwards, alongside the 10th Battalion. Private Wilf Bell, a member of the attached No. 10 Platoon, describes what happened:

> Orders came, presumably from the company commander, to move. But instead of going south towards the railway the company moved east for some unknown reason, parallel with the main road, and we had to cross a field between one lot of woodland and another. Our platoon went first, crossed a track, and then halted while the rest of the company passed through. There came a time when nearly the whole company was in the open. Two Germans, possibly officers, then appeared from the woods ahead, about 200 yards away, and shouted out in English, 'Lay down your arms.' A whole lot of Germans then deliberately showed themselves along the line of the wood and along a hedge which ran both left and right of us, so

that we were overlooked on three sides by heavily armed Germans. One of our officers, possibly the company commander, then ordered us to surrender.

We felt absolutely deflated – all those years of training wasted! It seems to me now that it was a big balls-up; we should have been moving back with the paras, not in another direction on our own.

Only about thirty men out of the entire company, mostly from the rearguards still in the woods, escaped to rejoin the battalion. According to one of them, the survivors 'fought on and upheld the honour of A Company about which later gossips said that the whole company had surrendered without a fight'. The company's fatal casualties all day could have been no more than three, including Lieutenant Albert Wayte from Montreal, the commander of the attached No. 10 Platoon, who was fatally wounded before the surrender. The Germans who took the company prisoner were probably from Battalion Krafft's No. 4 Company, a swift revenge for the slaughter of its No. 9 Company by the KOSB just earlier.

The entire 4th Parachute Brigade was now in retreat. The 10th Battalion and some others would remain north of the railway embankment to protect the vehicle crossings, but other infantry parties were free to slip across the railway to collecting points allocated to them in the woods on the south side. There was need for haste on the part of all parties. The Germans were pressing closely in some places and putting down long-distance fire at others. Comparative safety for the brigade lay only on the south side of the railway. Hackett's Brigade HQ staff got safely away, though Hackett himself and some of his officers stayed on the northern side overseeing the departure of the brigade's vehicles and guns along the track. Hackett's diary records that 'great energy and violence was needed' to prevent confusion. Lieutenant-Colonel des Voeux started taking 156 Battalion over the railway, but a mistake was made further back in the battalion, and almost half of it – B Company, a platoon of C Company and most of Support Company – carried on along the track to Wolfheze; the two parts of the battalion would never be reunited. Most of the King's Own Scottish Borderers reached safety, some over the railway line and some by means of the Wolfheze crossing, which was found to be clear, but B Company did not appear; it had been ordered to another task and it too would never rejoin its battalion. Lieutenant-Colonel Payton-Reid could find no representative of Brigadier Hackett's staff at the rendezvous and assumed that he could now leave Hackett's command and revert to his own Airlanding Brigade. The KOSB moved on to Oosterbeek, where they were allocated a sector in the north of the developing perimeter. The speed with which Payton-Reid was able to extricate more than half of his battalion from the battle north of the railway and come safely into the divisional area is an important point.

The task of finding and controlling vehicle crossing points was undertaken by Major Aeneas Perkins and part of his 4th Parachute Squadron. He discovered a narrow tunnel under the railway a quarter of a mile short of Wolfheze. It was only a channel for taking storm water from north of the railway through to the Rhine, but it was wide enough for a jeep to drive through. There was soon a large build-up of vehicles waiting to pass through and the scene developed into semi-chaos. German fire was getting steadily nearer. Brigadier Hackett put in an appearance and it was here that his batman, Private Peter Donnelly, was killed by a stray bullet and Captain 'Jimmy' James, who had asked to come as an extra officer with Brigade HQ, of which he had once been a member, was fatally wounded. Colour-Sergeant Tony Thomas, bringing in some of 156 Battalion's jeeps, says: 'It was a good old jam, like Piccadilly Circus at its worst. Some men were abandoning their vehicles and climbing over the embankment, but that was foolish because they stuck out like a sore thumb and were easy targets.' Several vehicles became bogged down as the sandy ground became churned up and also had to be abandoned. Major Perkins found that the main crossing at Wolfheze was still clear and many of the vehicles were sent on there. After completing his traffic-control duties he gathered together as many men of his unit as possible and also made his way safely to Oosterbeek.

Several of the anti-tank guns were driven up a sheepwalk in the side of the embankment or directly over the top at places where the

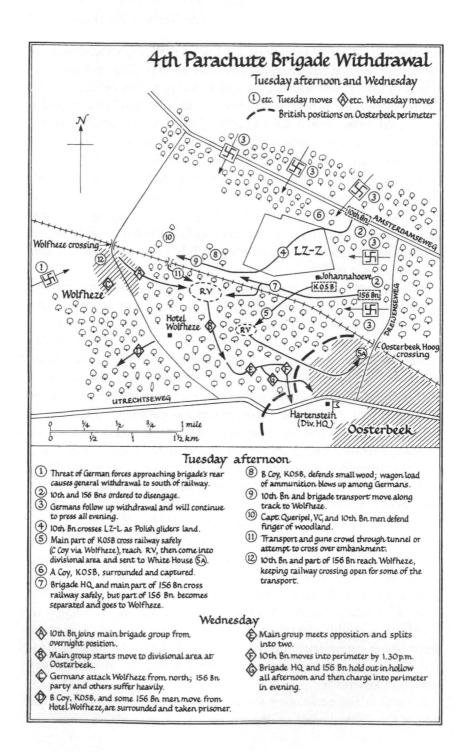

4th Parachute Brigade Withdrawal

Tuesday afternoon and Wednesday

① etc. Tuesday moves Ⓐ etc. Wednesday moves

- - - British positions on Oosterbeek perimeter

Tuesday afternoon

① Threat of German forces approaching brigade's rear causes general withdrawal to south of railway.

② 10th and 156 Bns ordered to disengage.

③ Germans follow up withdrawal and will continue to press all evening.

④ 10th Bn crosses LZ-L as Polish gliders land.

⑤ Main part of KOSB cross railway safely (C Coy via Wolfheze), reach RV, then come into divisional area and sent to White House Ⓢ.

⑥ A Coy, KOSB, surrounded and captured.

⑦ Brigade HQ and main part of 156 Bn cross railway safely, but part of 156 Bn becomes separated and goes to Wolfheze.

⑧ B Coy, KOSB, defends small wood; wagon load of ammunition blows up among Germans.

⑨ 10th Bn and brigade transport move along track to Wolfheze.

⑩ Capt. Queripel, VC, and 10th Bn men defend finger of woodland.

⑪ Transport and guns crowd through tunnel or attempt to cross over embankment.

⑫ 10th Bn and part of 156 Bn reach Wolfheze, keeping railway crossing open for some of the transport.

Wednesday

Ⓐ 10th Bn joins main brigade group from overnight position.

Ⓑ Main group starts move to divisional area at Oosterbeek.

Ⓒ Germans attack Wolfheze from north; 156 Bn party and others suffer heavily.

Ⓓ B Coy, KOSB, and some 156 Bn men move from Hotel Wolfheze, are surrounded and taken prisoner.

Ⓔ Main group meets opposition and splits into two.

Ⓕ 10th Bn moves into perimeter by 1.30 p.m.

Ⓖ Brigade HQ and 156 Bn hold out in hollow all afternoon and then charge into perimeter in evening.

sides were not too steep. This was the means of escape for some of the four large 17-pounders which had been located near Brigade HQ. It is believed that two got over successfully; one came round by Wolfheze; but the fourth was abandoned on the line when its team was caught by machine-gun fire. The gun sergeant, Joe Black, one of the unit's original Territorials from Oban, had his leg crushed under the towing vehicle in the confusion and later had it amputated.

Two parties of infantry had been ordered to hold 'fingers' of woodland on the northern side of the railway to keep the Germans back from the vehicle escape routes. The most easterly was Major Michael Forman's B Company of the KOSB. His company was still at about two-thirds strength when ordered to this exposed duty. It had to get well into the wood in order to keep the Germans back from the track. The Germans were entering from the other side but they were stopped by unusual means. Lance-Corporal O'Neill Berry spotted a heavily loaded four-wheeled farm cart:

> I believed it could be shielding the enemy so, having taken the Bren gun from my gunner, I opened up with a heavy burst of fire. The next instant all I could see was a blinding, hot, searing flash, followed by a deafening explosion. I ducked as bits of the trailer and wheels showered among us. I could feel them clattering on my helmet. I heard the yell from Lieutenant Doig to 'up and at 'em', so in we went. Trees were scattered around the scene, and as I glanced up I saw German bodies, the uniforms practically stripped from them, hanging in the branches.

The cart was probably one commandeered by C Company of 156 Battalion to carry packs and stores, including some anti-tank mines, and abandoned when the horse bolted under mortar fire. The explosion of the mines halted the Germans, and the Borderers were able to rush forward and secure the wood until released later that evening.

The other infantry party defending a strip of woodland was from the 10th Battalion, mostly Captain Queripel's A Company but with several other men without orders joining in; Queripel had been ordered to hold this woodland only 600 yards from Wolfheze. This vital position was held most gallantly all that evening until overwhelmed next morning. Captain Queripel sent the survivors away in the final moments and was last seen with his pistol and some hand grenades covering their escape. Captain Queripel, one of the original Royal Sussex officers who had helped to form the 10th Battalion, was awarded a posthumous Victoria Cross.

Other parts of the 10th Battalion occupied Wolfheze, which on their arrival had been almost empty of Germans. Lieutenant-Colonel Smyth organized the village for defence. He had less than a hundred men from his own battalion, but there were also the party which had become separated from 156 Battalion, some glider pilots and various oddments who had survived the retreat of the brigade. Major Peter Warr went through the village in a jeep, warning the local people to take shelter because the Germans were expected to attack. Most of them scattered to the woods, bitterly disappointed by this new turn of events. Their village had been bombed and then liberated on Sunday, seen crowds of British soldiers passing through in good order on Monday, been abandoned to an eerie quiet on Tuesday morning and now looked like becoming a battle-field.

The Germans did not attack Wolfheze that evening. Except for Captain Queripel's force being attacked north of the railway, there was no further serious action on that day of dramatic event for the 4th Parachute Brigade. Except for those bogged down near the tunnel, all of the vehicles came safely south of the railway. B Company of the KOSB was still present; finding his battalion departed from the agreed meeting point, Major Forman decided to remain in this area overnight. The 4th Parachute Brigade, which with the KOSB had been at nearly full strength twelve hours earlier, now consisted of considerably less than half of that strength and had come to rest in Wolfheze and in the woods to the east of the village. An estimated fifty-four men had been killed during the day's actions; this figure includes the KOSB casualties but not a further seventeen killed in the 11th Battalion and the anti-tank troop fighting in Arnhem on that day. These were the heaviest single day's brigade casualties of the entire Arnhem battle. More than half of the dead – four officers and twenty-five other ranks –

were from the 10th Battalion. A large proportion of the brigade was out of action – wounded or cut off and left behind to become prisoners. Brigadier Hackett's proud command was virtually broken only forty-eight hours after its arrival.

An interesting point should be mentioned here. It has been described how the main part of the King's Own Scottish Borderers was easily able to reach the divisional area at Oosterbeek. Brigadier Hackett made no move to bring the remainder of his brigade into Oosterbeek, and units would suffer severely when they tried to come in the next day after the Germans attacked the area in strength. I was several times asked by some of the keen local experts in Holland why Hackett had not brought his units into Oosterbeek that night; there is no doubt that most could have got there in reasonable safety. Hackett's diary records that this was considered:

> I discussed at some length with Div by RT advisability of moving during the night towards our final location. I wanted to get integrated into the Div area. I was quite happy to stay but would have preferred to move to a villa near final location at say 2300 hrs; by then 10 Bn would be fit to do so in good order. Div deprecated a move but said I was to send recce parties in by night and follow at first light. I saw nothing to be gained out of recce parties in the dark and it was agreed in the end that I should move the Bde at first light.

It was a fateful decision. But it should also be added that elements of the brigade were still north of the railway, and Hackett was probably reluctant to seek the safety of Oosterbeek until these had been gathered in.

It had been a bad day all round for the 1st Airborne Division. In addition to the recent failure of the 4th Parachute Brigade, the efforts of the 1st Parachute Brigade in Arnhem to reach the bridge had finally collapsed that morning; the force at the bridge remained isolated and was growing weaker; most of the Polish brigade had failed to arrive; the supply drop had fallen in the wrong place and had suffered heavy casualties in aircraft; and the advance of the ground forces was behind schedule. Tuesday 19 September was the day on which the balance of the Battle of Arnhem swung irrevocably against the airborne men.

Wednesday – into Oosterbeek

A plan was prepared during the night to gather the various 4th Parachute Brigade units together and move southwards and then eastwards until the divisional perimeter was reached. The column of little groups assembled before dawn and moved off, with a protective screen – mostly glider pilots – in front. But the Germans were now present in large numbers and it became a running battle. Hackett eventually ordered a change in the line of advance, with the 10th Battalion leading. This unit moved on so fast that it became separated from the rest of the force, made a determined charge and came into the Oosterbeek perimeter at 1.10 p.m., about sixty men strong. Many had been lost on the way and would be taken prisoner in the woods. No more than five or six men were killed, but these included Captain Cedric Horsfall, D Company's commander. Lieutenant-Colonel Smyth was among the wounded. Another casualty was Lieutenant Pat Glover's pet chicken, killed by a mortar; his batman reported the loss: 'Myrtle's dead, sir, but she was game to the last.' A letter from former Private F. D. Jackson in New Zealand describes how the battalion then suffered further officer casualties. As the last men came into the perimeter, they decided to help retrieve a 6-pounder anti-tank gun, the driver of whose jeep had probably become a casualty. It was probably a 1st Border gun. A German tank fired at the rescue party and scored a direct hit on the gun. Lieutenant 'Pinky' Kiaer was killed outright; Sergeant Joe Houghton received multiple shrapnel wounds, and one of the anti-tank gunners lost his foot. A second round from the tank then hit a nearby building and killed a second 10th Battalion officer, Captain John Howard.[8]

The remainder of Brigadier Hackett's force was in serious trouble. It was not able to follow the 10th Battalion and spent the remainder

---

[8] Lieutenant Kiaer's brother, a Commando officer, had been killed on D-Day. Captain Howard was a former *Daily Express* journalist.

of the morning being attacked by tanks, infantry, flame-throwers and mortars, counter-attacking, changing direction, suffering steady casualties and with increasing numbers of men losing contact. The anti-tank guns were all lost. Casualties were particularly heavy in officers. Brigade HQ lost the Brigade Major, Major Bruce Dawson, and the Intelligence Officer, Captain George Blundell, both killed. Lieutenant-Colonel Derek Heathcote-Amory, the officer who had taken two days' leave to join this operation, was severely wounded; he was put on a stretcher on a jeep, next to another jeep which caught fire and whose load of mortar bombs threatened to explode. Brigadier Hackett, who seemed to bear a charmed life, ran across and drove his friend clear. No. 156 Battalion lost its commander. Sergeant Andy Thorburn came upon Lieutenant-Colonel des Voeux leaning back against a tree, badly wounded, and asked if he could help: 'No. Move forward. The enemy is in front of you; they need you there.' He must have died soon afterwards. No. 156 Battalion's second-in-command and one of the last remaining subalterns were also killed, and a company commander died later in the day. This period ended when, in desperation, Hackett decided to occupy a hollow seen about 200 yards away and ordered Major Geoffrey Powell of 156 Battalion to take it. Powell gathered together as many men as he could – about a platoon's worth – told them they might as well die carrying out the attack as staying where they were and then led the screaming, desperate charge. The rush was successful and the remnants of Hackett's force, about 150 men, together with twenty German prisoners, gained the hollow but remained pinned down there for approximately the next eight hours. They were only 400 yards from the Oosterbeek perimeter.

There was a substantial British force still at liberty back in the woods near Wolfheze. This was Major Michael Forman's B Company of the King's Own Scottish Borderers. His men had seen much action since the start of this operation, defending the most exposed sector of the second lift's dropping zone at Ginkel Heath on Monday, defending part of the Polish glider landing zone and then providing part of the rearguard cover in the withdrawal to Wolfheze the previous day. After waiting all of this morning at the Hotel Wolfheze for contact with someone from his battalion, Major

Forman decided to move out south-westwards towards the Rhine, hoping to find British troops there. The only information he had about the main division was a BBC broadcast heard at the hotel that the 1st Airborne Division was fighting north of the river; he had never heard any mention of Oosterbeek. Also with him was that part of 156 Battalion which had become separated from its parent unit the previous afternoon. This party had been driven out of its overnight position in Wolfheze by tanks that morning. Two of the officers, Captain Hector Montgomery and Lieutenant Ron Wood, had been severely wounded; Wood died later and Montgomery lost an arm. The survivors of that action had then joined up with the much stronger KOSB company, but the entire force was very low on ammunition, very tired and very hungry, most having lost the packs containing their rations during previous actions.

This force moved little more than a quarter of a mile from the hotel when they became aware that they were in a clearing in the woods and surrounded by Germans who had cleverly trailed them. A German officer called on the airborne men to surrender. This was Major Forman's reaction:

> There appeared to be two companies of Germans with two 81-millimetre mortars getting into position, and there was some exchange of fire. I thought about attempting an attack and started planning it; it seemed to be the only hope. Before issuing the orders, I decided to check the ammunition and found it had nearly all gone. So, what to do? There was no immediate opportunity to help any other unit. The options left to me were to cross 200 yards of open heather under fire from the Germans, being shot at from behind, losing half the men going across the open and with the prospect of heavy hand-to-hand fighting with the Germans if we did get across – or to surrender. I decided not to say 'every man for himself' but to tell them to surrender, which I did, making it my responsibility.

Lieutenant Dennis Kayne was one of the two 156 Battalion officers present:

We were down to virtually nothing to fight with by then and the KOSB officer said we should surrender to save further casualties. While he was negotiating this, I told my men what was happening. The next thing I did was to take my dog-tag off and throw it away, because it had my religion, Jewish, on it. The Germans then came up to us and we laid down all our arms on the ground. It was a terrible feeling to realize that this is what it had come to, that first-class troops had come to this. There were at least 200 Germans, looking quite fresh and smart and well armed.

The other 156 Battalion officer, Lieutenant Jeff Noble, was slightly apart from the main body; he and his men had been acting as a screen for the KOSB company:

I personally didn't agree to the surrender and took to the woods again with some of my parachutists. But the Borderers surrendered, and that was probably the right decision, because some 130 men lived to see the end of the war, whereas if we had fought it out most of them probably would have died. I don't think it would have affected the Battle of Arnhem, because we were completely isolated. It wouldn't have had any impact on anything at all.

Lieutenant Noble was soon wounded and captured, but a few of his men may have escaped, the only ones to do so from yet another large body of men taken prisoner.

Brigadier Hackett's force in the hollow held out all afternoon and evening. Almost half of the 150 men became casualties as the Germans tried to surround and eliminate the position with fire, but reluctant to come to close quarters. When it started to become dark, Hackett decided that there was no alternative but to make one determined charge. With fixed bayonets, the seventy or so men still on their feet charged screaming through the woods between the hollow and what was thought to be the location of the Oosterbeek perimeter. This was successful, and with only a few further casualties the rushing men burst into the positions of A Company, 1st

Border. Both sides noticed the contrast in the appearance of the two forces. One of the Border officers requested Major Powell to move his men away as quickly as possible – 'Please move your filthy lot away from here' – in case their scarecrow appearance affected his men's morale.

The total strength of fit men of the 4th Parachute Brigade Group when its various units mustered in Oosterbeek, including the men of the 11th Battalion who had returned from their action in Arnhem, was probably no more than 500 from the 2,300 or so who had flown from England two days earlier.

The Battle at the Bridge

All this time John Frost's men had been defending their positions at the Arnhem road bridge, waiting in vain for relief, either from their own division or from ground forces coming up from the south.

The composition of the force at the bridge did not change at all after most of the 2nd Battalion's B Company and the other men who had been trying to make a crossing at the pontoon area came into the bridge perimeter, so the men who found themselves there on that Monday afternoon would be the ones who fought that gallant action which has passed so powerfully into airborne history. The exact number of men who formed the bridge garrison will never be known; what follows is the best available estimate:[1]

2nd Parachute Battalion: Battalion HQ; HQ, Support and A Companies; B Company (less most of No. 4 Platoon) – 340 men.

1st Parachute Brigade HQ, including Defence Platoon and Signals Section – 110 men.

1st Parachute Squadron, RE: HQ; A Troop; most of B Troop – 75 men.

3rd Parachute Battalion: C Company HQ; most of No. 9 Platoon; part of No. 8 Platoon – 45 men.

1st Airlanding Anti-Tank Battery, RA: HQ; B Troop; one gun team of C Troop – 40 men.

250 Light Composite Company, RASC: No. 3 Platoon – 40 men, plus Major David Clark from Divisional HQ, RASC.

9th Field Company, RE· part of No. 2 Platoon – 30 men.

*

[1] I am indebted to Roger King of Datchworth, Herts, for generously making available the results of his extensive research on the composition of the bridge force, although the estimates here are my own. Men who were killed or taken prisoner in Arnhem just before reaching the bridge and those who arrived but left on Sunday night before fighting began are not included.

In addition there were an estimated 59 men from various units: 17 glider pilots, all or nearly all from B Squadron arriving with anti-tank guns; 8 men of the Reconnaissance Squadron under Major Gough; 12 men from Royal Artillery forward observation officer parties; 6 men of the RAOC; 5 men each from the REME and Intelligence Corps; 2 or 3 Military Police; 2 men from the 'Jedburgh' team; and one war correspondent.

The total force at the bridge thus numbered an estimated 740 men, equivalent to less than one and a half parachute battalions. Although many of those men were not trained to the standards of a parachute battalion, nearly all had valuable combat potential. Less than half of the force was from the 2nd Battalion. There was only one lieutenant-colonel – John Frost – but there were no less than thirteen majors among the sixty or so officers present. There was a good cross-section of units available, but one element not present would be sadly missed: there was no part of 16 Parachute Field Ambulance there. It had been anticipated that there would be easy evacuation of seriously wounded cases to that unit's location at St Elizabeth Hospital, but that did not happen. Captains J. W. Logan and D. Wright, the medical officers of the 2nd Battalion and Brigade HQ, and their orderlies would have to treat all the wounded without any assistance from surgical teams.

Monday

Only one corner of the perimeter had been attacked during the night. This was a library or small school on the eastern side of the lower ramp held by Captain Eric Mackay and some men of A Troop, 1st Parachute Squadron. There were several covered approaches to what was really an exposed outpost, and the Royal Engineers found it difficult to hold. Sapper George Needham says:

> We had started to prepare it for defence – smashing the windows and pulling down the curtains – but we had only been there about ten minutes when the Germans attacked, throwing grenades into the rooms. The building was too

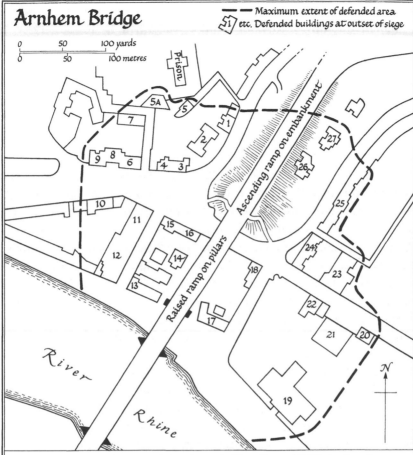

Arnhem Bridge

- - - Maximum extent of defended area
51 etc. Defended buildings at outset of siege

0   50   100 yards
0   50   100 metres

Prison

Ascending ramp on embankment

Raised ramp on pillars

River

Rhine

N

Unit dispositions (All companies and platoons are 2nd Battalion and 'R E' is 1st Parachute Engineer Squadron unless otherwise stated. Changes after Monday are not noted.)

1 Part of Brigade HQ Defence Platoon
2 Brigade HQ; Aid Post; German prisoners
3 2nd Battalion HQ
4 Part of Mortar Platoon
5 RASC Platoon
5A Mortuary
6,7,8 Parts of HQ and Support Companies; glider pilots; 9th Field Company's third position (in 6)
9 Anti-Tank Battery HQ (after leaving 14 on Monday)
10 Small mixed party
11 B Company
12 No.1 Platoon (from Monday night)
13 No.1 Platoon and Vickers MGs (until Monday night)
14 Anti-Tank Battery HQ and 9th Field Company (Monday only)

15 A Company HQ; HQ and part of B Troop RE
16 No.2 Platoon, replaced on Monday by 9th Field Company
17 Platoon of B Company, later reinforced by No.2 Platoon
18 No.3 Platoon
19–22 No.8 Platoon, 3rd Battalion, and part of Brigade HQ Defence Platoon (20 and 21 believed lost on Monday)
23 Part of Brigade HQ Defence Platoon (lost on Monday)
24 RAOC and Signals
25 HQ Troop RE and Signals
26 (The School) Parts of A and B Troops RE; C Company HQ and No.9 Platoon, 3rd Bn
27 Part of A Troop RE (temporarily on Sunday night only)

vulnerable, so Captain Mackay ordered us out, into the larger school building next door, where we joined B Troop. They objected and said, 'Bugger off; go find your own place', but Captain Mackay, being the man he was, persuaded them in no uncertain terms to let us in, and we started fortifying some of the empty rooms.

(The Royal Engineers were later joined in the school by Major 'Pongo' Lewis, the 3rd Battalion's company commander, and twelve of his men. There was some argument after the war between the sappers and the infantry over who was in command in this building, the Van Limburg Stirum School, during the subsequent three days of its defence. Captain Mackay, in an article in *Blackwood's Magazine*, claimed to have been in command and never mentioned the presence of the 3rd Battalion men. Major Lewis, in his short official report, did not mention the larger RE party. Both officers had been allocated this position separately, in the dark of that first night, and Major Lewis, though clearly the senior officer, probably did not interfere with Captain Mackay's handling of the larger sapper party.)

Dawn found the airborne men prepared for a day that would be full of incident. They had completed the preparations for the defence of the buildings they had occupied by breaking all the windows to avoid injury from flying glass, moving furniture to make barricades at the windows, filling baths and other receptacles with water for as long as the supply remained functioning; these were all basic lessons learned in their house-fighting training. As soon as it started to get light, Major Munford wanted to begin registering the guns of No. 3 Battery of the Light Regiment on to likely targets:

There was some reluctance to allow me to do this. Some people were still harking back to the time the paras had suffered from the results of 'drop-shorts' in North Africa – not by the Light Regiment. But I persisted and was allowed to register on the approach road at the south end of the bridge – only about six rounds – but we got both troops ranged on to it and recorded it. 'Sheriff' Thompson, back at Oosterbeek, said it should be recorded as 'Mike One'; 'Mike' was 'M' for Munford. Our signals back to the battery were working well.

The first intruder into the area was a lorry 'full of dustbins clattering in the back' which drove in between the buildings overlooking the ramp and the offices which Brigade HQ was occupying. Trigger-happy airborne men shot it up from both sides; the driver, presumably a Dutchman on a routine refuse-collection round, was probably killed. A similar fate befell three German lorries which appeared, probably also on a routine errand and not knowing of the British presence.

But attacks soon started, mainly from the east. The Germans did not know the precise strength or location of the British force, and the first attacks were only tentative probes by some old Mark III and IV tanks supported by infantry which were easily beaten off. One tank reached the road under the bridge ramp and was fired upon by an anti-tank gun. Lieutenant Arvian Llewellyn-Jones, watching from a nearby building, describes how an early lesson about the recoil of a gun in a street was learned:

The gun spades were not into the pavement edge, nor firm against any strong barrier. The gun was laid, the order to fire given, and when fired ran back about fifty yards, injuring two of the crew. There was no visible damage to the tank. It remained hidden in part of the gloom of the underpass of the bridge. The gun was recovered with some difficulty. This time it was firmly wedged. The Battery Office clerk, who had never fired a gun in his life, was sent out to help man the gun. This time the tank under the bridge advanced into full view and looked to be deploying its gun straight at the 6-pounder. We fired first. The aim was true; the tank was hit and it slewed and blocked the road.

These early actions were followed by a period of relative calm, described by John Frost as 'a time when I felt everything was going according to plan, with no serious opposition yet and everything under control'.

*

Hauptsturmführer Viktor Graebner was the commander of the 9th SS Panzer Division's Reconnaissance Battalion, a unit of first-class troops well equipped with twenty-two armoured cars and half-tracked armoured personnel carriers. Only the previous day his divisional commander had presented him with the ribbon and emblem of the Knight's Cross, awarded to him for bravery in Normandy. He had then led his unit over the bridge, before the British arrived there, on a sweep down the main road to Nijmegen. Finding that area all clear, he turned back and was now preparing to return over the bridge to reach his divisional command post in Arnhem. He knew the British were at the north end of the bridge now; whether he actually intended to mount an attack or just dash through the British positions is not known.[2]

Look-outs in the top rooms of the houses occupied by the airborne men drew to the attention of their officers the column of vehicles assembling on the bridge approach. The identification of the vehicles as German swiftly put paid to the initial hope that this might be the head of the ground-force column making excellent time and arriving to relieve the airborne force. Major Munford saw that the German vehicles would have to pass through the area he had registered as a target, and his signaller immediately made contact with the battery at Oosterbeek. Dennis Munford says:

> I received permission to open fire and, when the German column moved off, all I had to do was call, 'Target – Mike One', and the boys at the battery did the rest. There was no need for further correction. The Germans had to drive through it. I ordered a cease-fire when they left the Mike One area and came on to the bridge; I didn't want to damage the bridge.

The artillery fire was accurate. Some German motorcyclists were seen to be hit, but the shells were too light to inflict much damage on the armoured vehicles.

The first part of Graebner's force set off over the bridge at top speed. These leading vehicles were armoured cars which threaded

---

[2] Once again I am indebted to Robert Kershaw's *It Never Snows in September* for these details.

their way round the still burning lorries from the previous night's action and over the string of mines laid on the roadway during the night, but these failed to stop the vehicles. The airborne men held their fire until the last moment, and some of those first armoured cars drove straight on through to the town without being stopped, but then the order to open fire was given and none of the other armoured cars survived the resulting hail of fire. More and more of the German unit were committed to reinforce the attack, including half-tracks packed with soldiers, some protected by armoured coverings but others with open tops. Nearly all the German vehicles were hit and stopped in a great tangle on the ramp between the houses on both sides occupied by the 2nd Battalion's A Company and also overlooked by the Brigade HQ and other buildings. Piats accounted for some of these vehicles, but much of the damage was caused by two anti-tank guns. One of these, Sergeant O'Neill's gun of B Troop, was at a corner of the Brigade HQ building. The other 6-pounder was that of Sergeant Cyril Robson of C Troop, which was in a street closer to the river on the west side of the bridge and considerably below the level of the ramp. Directed by Lieutenant Tony Cox in the window of the house above him, Robson fired solid-shot shells at the parapet at the side of the bridge until he cut a V-shaped section away and was then able to fire into the sides of the German vehicles passing the gap. It is believed that Robson's gun destroyed more of the attacking vehicles than any other weapon. The Germans in the half-track personnel carriers which were hit or found their way blocked were exposed to a hail of small-arms fire, trapped in their vehicles or spilling out on to the open stretch of the ramp, unable to deploy into shelter. They were slaughtered. One of the early victims was seen to be flung out on to the roadway and literally cut to pieces by a hail of fire. Some of the vehicles toppled over or slewed off the embankment of the lower ramp, allowing the airborne men in the buildings there to join in the execution.

Nearly everyone in the British garrison joined in the firing. Major Freddie Gough was seen enthusiastically firing one of the machine-guns on his Reconnaissance Squadron jeep. It would be ironic if it was one of his shots that killed his opposite number, because Hauptsturmführer Graebner was among the German dead. Lieutenant-Colonel Frost was not firing: 'I was watching other people and picking up information. A commander ought not to be firing a weapon in the middle of an action. His best weapon is a pair of binoculars.'

Here are two typical descriptions of the action. Corporal Geoff Cockayne was in the Brigade HQ building:

I had a German Schmeisser and had a lot of fun with that. I shot at any Gerry that moved. Several of their vehicles – six or seven – started burning. We didn't stay in the room we were in but came out to fire, keeping moving, taking cover and firing from different positions. The Germans had got out of their troop carriers – what was left of them – and it became a proper infantry action. I shot off nearly all my ammunition. To start with, I had been letting rip, but then I became more careful; I knew there would be no more. I wasn't firing at any German in particular, just firing at where I knew they were.

Signalman Bill Jukes was in the 2nd Battalion HQ building:

The first vehicle which drew level with the house was hit, and the second rammed into it, blocking the roadway. The rest didn't stand a chance. The crews and passengers, those still able to, began to pile out, and those of us armed with Stens joined in the general fusillade. One of the radio operators grabbed my Sten gun, which was leaning against the wall, but I snatched it away from him, telling him to go and get his own. I hadn't waited five years to get a shot at the enemy like this only to be denied by some Johnny-come-lately to the section. It was impossible to say what effect my shooting had. There was such a volley coming from the windows along the street that nobody could have said who shot who. At least one German lived a charmed life that day. He slipped out of one of the half-tracks on the far side from us and ran for dear life between the houses on the other side of the ramp and disappeared from view. Anybody with that kind of luck should live for ever.

This action lasted for about two hours. Various reports put the numbers of vehicles hit and stopped, or jammed in the wreckage of other vehicles, at ten, eleven or twelve, mostly half-tracks. The number of Germans killed is estimated at seventy. The electrical system of one of the knocked-out vehicles on the ramp short-circuited, and the horn of the vehicle emitted 'a banshee wailing' after the battle from among the shattered and burning vehicles and the sprawled dead of the attack. The morale of the airborne men was sky high; their own casualties had been light.

That attack by the Germans over the bridge proved to be the high point of that first full day. After the attack was over, John Frost reviewed the situation of his force. He had left B Company at the pontoon area, 1,100 yards away, in the hope that it might assist the remainder of the brigade into the bridge area. His last wireless contact with the other battalions showed that the 1st Battalion was still at least two miles away on the outskirts of Arnhem and making only slow progress; there was no contact with the 3rd Battalion and no sign that it was any closer. Frost had earlier decided that B Company was in danger of being surrounded at the pontoon while performing no useful function there and had ordered it to come in. It has already been told how Major Crawley extricated most of his company but lost one platoon cut off. Frost met Crawley and directed him to occupy some of the houses in a triangular block of buildings on the western part of the perimeter to provide an outer defence there. After B Company's casualties the previous day and the loss of No. 4 Platoon, there were only about seventy men in the company. Captain Francis Hoyer-Millar describes how Company HQ was greeted when it occupied its house:

> The lady – elderly, but not old – didn't seem to mind us fighting from her house, smashing windows and moving the furniture about, but she took me into one room and said, 'Please don't fire from here; it's my husband's favourite room'; he was away somewhere. We couldn't agree with her of course, and anyway, the house burned down in the end.
>
> Later in the day Sergeant-Major Scott came in and reported that our last platoon commander had been killed – 'Mr Stanford's had his chips.' Doug Crawley and I were both

distressed, not at the seeming callous manner of the report, but that we had no more platoon commanders.

Lieutenant Colin Stanford was not dead. He had been shot in the head while standing on the top of his platoon building studying the surroundings through binoculars, but he survived.

The next serious event was a sharp German attack from the streets on the eastern side of the perimeter against the houses defended by Lieutenant Pat Barnett's Brigade HQ Defence Platoon and various other troops. Preceded by an artillery and mortar bombardment, two tanks led infantry under the bridge ramp and into the British positions. In a fierce action, the two tanks were claimed as knocked out and the infantry driven back. One tank at least was destroyed by Sergeant Robson's anti-tank gun and possibly one by a Piat. The 75-millimetre battery back at Oosterbeek was also brought into this action, its fire being directed on this occasion by Captain Henry Buchanan of the Forward Observation Unit, a good example of the way this unit's officers operated with battalions as extra observation officers for the Light Regiment until the guns of the ground forces came into range, but Buchanan would be killed on the following day.

The remainder of the day saw further minor attacks. One of the buildings on the eastern side of the perimeter held by part of No. 8 Platoon, 3rd Battalion, was overrun, and another, held by part of the Brigade HQ Defence Platoon, had to be abandoned, but no further ground was given. There then commenced a general shelling and mortar fire which would harass the British force throughout the remaining days of the bridge action. Both sides were settling down to a long siege. The day had been a most successful one for the airborne men. Their positions were almost intact, and every attack had been beaten off with heavy loss of German life. Up to three tanks and a host of other armoured vehicles had been destroyed. British casualties had not been heavy. The best estimate is that only ten men had been killed and approximately thirty wounded before nightfall from all of the British units present. But the force was clearly isolated, unlikely to be reinforced in the near future and likely to be the subject of increased German pressure;

the Germans badly needed the bridge to pass reinforcements down to the battle now raging in the Nijmegen area. These reinforcements were being laboriously ferried across the Rhine further upstream at present. Another danger was a looming shortage of ammunition; profligate quantities had been expended during the day, and the last issue from the supply brought in by the RASC would be made that night.

A change in the command structure took place that evening. All through the day, Lieutenant-Colonel Frost had been directing the actions only of the 2nd Battalion. Major Hibbert had been running Brigade HQ and the other units, carrying out as far as possible the plan brought from England and hoping that Brigadier Lathbury would soon arrive. But Hibbert now heard, from a wireless link with the 1st Battalion, that Lathbury was missing and he formally asked Lieutenant-Colonel Frost to take over the running of the entire force at the bridge. So John Frost moved over to the Brigade HQ building, leaving his second in command, Major David Wallis, in charge of the 2nd Battalion. At 6.30 p.m. Frost heard from the 1st Battalion that it was stuck near St Elizabeth Hospital and that the 3rd Battalion was nearby. Frost, acting now as brigade commander, ordered both battalions to form a 'flying column' of at least company strength to reach the bridge before midnight. But neither battalion had the strength or the means for such an operation, and this was the last attempt John Frost would make to exercise command over the other units of the brigade.

This may be a suitable place to mention Dutch dismay at the failure to use local means of communication and to utilize more fully the services of the Dutch Resistance. All through the day just passed, parts of the local telephone service had been functioning normally, but because of official British fear of German penetration of the Resistance, units had been ordered not to use the telephone. Another Dutch complaint is over the failure to trust more local men as guides; this would have been of particular help to the battalions trying to get through to the bridge. Albert Deuss, one of the local Resistance survivors, says:

> If they had trusted us, we could have brought them through houses and got them through to the bridge, but they did not

trust us and preferred to fight through the tanks. We knew our own town and where our friends were and all the short cuts. We even had a special password from 'Frank', our contact in Rotterdam, and we expected the British to know all about it – but they did not.

The only Dutch officer at the bridge, Captain Jacobus Groenewoud, had been using local telephones, but only to contact the loyal names on his 'Jedburgh' list to ascertain where the known German sympathizers in Arnhem were.

The airborne men prepared to face their first full night at the bridge. The houses on the western side of the perimeter had hardly been attacked, so part of B Company was redeployed to the eastern sector. A house near the bridge was deliberately set on fire to illuminate the bridge area, and B Company was ordered to send out a standing patrol to make sure no Germans came across the bridge during the night and also to protect a party of Royal Engineers which was sent to examine the underside of the bridge to ensure that the Germans could not demolish it. Captain Francis Hoyer-Millar was in command of the B Company patrol:

> I was told to take twelve men out. We went past the wrecked vehicles on the ramp and on to the bridge itself. It was a large expanse of open area, quite dark. I didn't know what was over the top of the slope so I threw a grenade. We were surprised when five Germans emerged with their hands up; three of them were wounded. I don't know how long they had been hiding there, almost inside our perimeter.
>
> I put half of my men on either side of the road. We had no trouble from the Germans but we were annoyingly fired on by a Bren from the houses held by our men. I yelled, 'Stop firing that bloody Bren gun. It's only me.' It was one of those silly things one says on the spur of the moment. John Frost got to hear about it and he always teased me about it afterwards.

It was soon after dark that John Frost lost his long-standing friend and second in command, Major David Wallis, who only that afternoon had been made acting commander of the 2nd Battalion. Major Wallis was making his rounds in the darkness and came to the house defended by A Company HQ and some sappers of the 9th Field Company. As he was leaving the rear of the house there was a burst of fire from a Bren gun, and Major Wallis was hit in the chest and died at once. The shots were fired by one of the Royal Engineers. A brother officer of Major Wallis says that he was known to 'have a habit of speaking rather quietly and indistinctly, and his answer to the sentry's challenge may not have carried or not have been understood'. A comrade of the unfortunate sentry says: 'It was at a time when the next shape in a doorway could be the enemy, such was the proximity of the fighting; response time was very short, and a German grenade had a short fuse.' The death of this officer resulted in another command change. John Frost appointed Major Tatham-Warter to command the 2nd Battalion; this was over the head of the more senior Major Crawley. Frost was 'aware of a slight resentment, but Tatham-Warter was well in touch with the battalion positions and I chose him'.

Soon after 3.0 a.m. (on Tuesday) there was a one-sided action at the school building jointly manned by sappers of the 1st Parachute Squadron and 3rd Battalion men. A German force which had probably misidentified the building in the darkness assembled alongside it, standing and talking unconcernedly, directly under the windows manned by the airborne men on the second and third floors. Typical of the disputed history of that building's defence, Captain Mackay says that he organized what happened next while Lieutenant Len Wright of the 3rd Battalion claims that Major Lewis did so. This is Len Wright's description of events:

> We all stood by with grenades – we had plenty of those – and with all our weapons. Then Major Lewis shouted, 'Fire!', and the men in all the rooms facing that side threw grenades and opened fire down on the Germans. My clearest memory was of 'Pongo' Lewis running from one room to another, dropping grenades and saying to me that he hadn't enjoyed himself so much since the last time he'd gone hunting. It lasted about a quarter of an hour. There was nothing the Germans could do except die or disappear. When it got light there were a lot of

bodies down there – eighteen or twenty or perhaps more. Some were still moving; one was severely wounded, a bad stomach wound with his guts visible, probably by a grenade. Some of our men tried to get him in, showing a Red Cross symbol, but they were shot at and came back in, without being hit but unable to help the German.

The defenders suffered no casualties.

Tuesday

Dawn came up with the sound of fighting from the town to the west, where the remnants of the 1st and 3rd Battalions, reinforced by the 2nd South Staffords and the 11th Battalion, were making their final attempts to reach the bridge. The noise of that battle would fade as the morning passed, bringing the realization to the men at the bridge that they were now irrevocably cut off from their division. They had been asked to hold out for two days – three at most – before being relieved by the advance of XXX Corps; but, unlike Arnhem with its fires and smoke of battle, there was no sign of any action in the Nijmegen direction only fifteen miles away. Signallers had made brief contact with a XXX Corps unit the previous afternoon and would do so again this morning, but this only confirmed that the head of the ground forces' advance was still beyond Nijmegen, and the Germans could be expected to defend the bridge there with determination.

This was the day on which the Polish parachute drop was expected south of the river, only a little over a mile from the bridge. Frost had prepared a 'flying column' under Major Freddie Gough, made up of a Bren carrier and Gough's two Reconnaissance Squadron jeeps, to meet the Poles. Some of the spare officers at Brigade HQ had, with varying degrees of enthusiasm, responded to Frost's appeal for volunteers to make up this little force, which he described in his memoirs as 'a suicide squad'. He told Gough: 'Now's the chance for you to win your family's fifth VC.' But the Poles did not appear; their lift had been postponed. John Frost says: 'I never had to make any serious command decisions after that. It was just a matter of hanging on at the bridge for as long as possible.'

The morning was relatively quiet; 'relatively quiet' at the bridge meant no more than the usual mortaring, shelling, sniping and infantry infiltration. The main German forces in the bridge area may have been standing by in case they were needed to help repel the attacks by the other British units in Arnhem, but those attacks fizzled out, and later in the morning three Mark III tanks drove into the bridge perimeter from the east. They were close to A Company's positions on that side of the ramp. Their shelling of one of the A Company houses caused it to be evacuated, a dangerous reduction of the defence right by the bridge and threatening the heart of the airborne force. The tanks cleverly positioned themselves where anti-tank guns could not engage them, and orders were issued that this danger had to be removed. This was achieved by Captain Tony Frank of A Company, who took one soldier and a Piat and, from the cover of a ruined wall, fired at one of the tanks forty yards away: 'I hit it first time, right in the backside. It didn't burn, but it didn't move again.' Some accounts credit Frank with hitting three tanks, but he insists that it was only one; the other two withdrew. His assistant may have been Sapper Tom Carpenter of the 9th Field Company, who describes how an unknown officer ordered him out on this tank hunt; when Carpenter returned to his position his own officer demanded to know 'Where the hell have you been?'

Tony Frank now goes on to describe the after-effects of this action. He had earlier allowed Lieutenant Andy McDermont's No. 3 Platoon to withdraw from the threatened house:

> Digby Tatham-Warter came walking calmly across from Bat-talion HQ with his brolly, quite unconcerned about any danger. He was very angry with me for letting McDermont's platoon come back and ordered me to retake the house.
>
> I got McDermont's platoon together – fifteen to twenty men only – and they set off from underneath the bridge, all very tired, just shrugging their shoulders and going back, but in no defeatist mood or anything like that. They went back and pushed the Germans out; there was probably about the

same number of Huns. McDermont was shot as he went along the hall – in the lower stomach, I think; he was conscious, but there was a lot of blood. I jabbed him with morphine, and he was taken away. Then we were attacked from the direction of the banked ramp. We manned the windows and answered back, polishing off at least four of them. One came crashing forward very bravely until we stopped him.

Lieutenant McDermont died three days later. Lance-Corporal James Lowrie, a signaller in a nearby building, was watching this action:

Diagonally to our left was a large house adjacent to the bridge. Some confused fighting went on inside it. At one point, three Germans jumped out of a side window and were shot by us; at the same moment two of our lads ran out of a front door, and one was hit by German fire. He rolled down the front steps and lay shouting, 'Harry, help me.' Round the corner one of the Germans we had shot was calling out what sounded like 'Kamerad, komm hier.' No one could help either man, and both eventually died. It was very sad.

It was by such means that the British positions were held.

The Germans requested a truce during the morning so that they could ask the British to consider surrendering now that there was no chance of relief by the remainder of the division. The emissary sent by the Germans was Lance-Sergeant Stan Halliwell of the 1st Parachute Squadron, who fell into German hands earlier that morning when out on a sortie taking ammunition to an exposed party of his unit:

They took me to a building where they seemed to have an Operations Room. An officer who seemed to be a big noise called me over. He inspected my pay-book; then he said, 'There is going to be a truce and I want to send you with a message. We trust you to be a gentleman and to return.' I told him I would. The message was for Colonel Frost – he knew his name – and I was to ask him to be under the bridge at 10.30 a.m. to discuss a surrender.

I was taken outside and lined up with some Germans to approach our lines. But our lot were firing – there was no truce – and the Germans opened up too. I ran across, shouting at our chaps not to shoot at me. Then I went to find Colonel Frost, running from building to building in all the firing and the smoke; that was the worst ten minutes of my life. Colonel Frost told me to tell them to go to hell, but I wasn't going to go back just to tell them that and I stayed with our troops.

The German officer was Standartenführer Heinz Harmel, commander of the 10th SS Panzer Division, whose zone of operations included the bridge and the main road down to Nijmegen. He had been ordered by General Bittrich to reopen the Arnhem bridge as quickly as possible. Sapper Gus Woods, also a prisoner, was interrogated by Harmel and describes him as 'youngish, speaking fluent English; he had toured England with his school football team before the war'.

After a lull, the Germans started exerting more pressure. A new phase had begun. Rather than mount costly infantry attacks, the Germans would now destroy by artillery and tank shelling the houses in which the British were positioned. Some of the shells used were phosphorus to set the houses alight. The methodical bombardment which started that afternoon would, with the usual mortaring, continue until the end of the bridge action and the effects of it would eventually bring about the collapse of the airborne men's resistance. One building after another was hit, usually in one of the upper storeys, and started to burn or was steadily battered down. Corporal Horace Goodrich, in the Brigade HQ building, describes a typical incident:

The enemy brought up a self-propelled gun to shell our building, and I happened to be manning a Bren gun in the right place to engage it and the infantry who were standing round it. After getting off two short bursts, I observed what had all the appearance of a golden tennis ball at the mouth of the SP gun. The next moment I was lying on my back covered in dust and debris. The shell actually struck the wall at my feet. Having got the range, they were able to fire at will until the top floor became temporarily untenable.

During the evening the first Tiger tanks, with their 88-millimetre guns, appeared and ran along the street between the Van Limburg Stirum School and the nearby houses, systematically shelling each house as it went past, and spraying with machine-gun fire the crew of an anti-tank gun who tried unsuccessfully to engage it. The two surviving anti-tank guns were repositioned ready for the tank's return, but it reversed back into the town after making this sortie. Sapper George Needham was in one of the first buildings, the school, to be hit by the tank:

> I was up on the stairway leading to the attic where one of the 3rd Battalion officers was keeping observation on the bridge; he had a camouflage scarf over his face to avoid being spotted. He was reporting what he saw and I was relaying reports to those below. Suddenly, there was a terrific explosion underneath this flight of stairs. It was the first time the building had been hit by such a big shell. There was a tank on the ramp firing at point-blank range. We had been used to small-arms fire and mortaring, but it was absolutely stunning when this huge explosion took place. There was dust everywhere, and it was several seconds before I realized what had happened. I didn't even know the tank was outside. It says a lot for the quality of Dutch building that the school didn't collapse.

Another recipient of the tank's shelling was a house occupied by a mixed party of twelve Royal Army Ordnance Corps and Royal Signals men. The RAOC party were weapons and ammunition specialists whose duty on this operation should have been to examine captured German stores. They had followed the 2nd Battalion into Arnhem on the Sunday evening and now found themselves defending this house. Private Kevin Heaney of the RAOC describes the shelling:

A shell came whooshing through the open bedroom window and hit the back of the house. The back wall became a pile of rubble, and the floor fell in. One of the signallers, resting on a bed in the back bedroom, came down with the floor and was trapped. He could not move, as his back was broken. Sergeant Mick Walker, one of our men, climbed down to give him a morphine injection. My pack was in the back bedroom and I was disappointed when this was lost; I had not touched the rations inside. We then took shelter in the cellar and started hoping for the best. There was a noise at the top of the stairs, and someone started to wave a white handkerchief, but Mick Walker knocked this out of his hand. It was probably only more rubble falling down.

The remaining defenders evacuated the house and went to another nearby, but this also had to be given up. All this was a serious weakening of the eastern defences of the perimeter. Several men mentioned the courage shown by Captain Bernard Briggs, a Brigade HQ officer who was in command of this sector.

The shelling did not cause many fatal casualties, but a large number of men were wounded, among them Father Egan, the 2nd Battalion's Catholic padre, Major Tatham-Warter (for the second time) and Captain Tony Frank, leaving Lieutenant Grayburn temporarily in charge of what was left of A Company. One of the casualties was a courageous anti-tank officer, Lieutenant Harry Whittaker, hit while driving a jeep to one of the remaining 6-pounders; he died the next day. It was during this morning that one of the German fighters operating in support of their troops swooped low over the heads of the bridge defenders and then flew straight into one of the twin towers of the Catholic St Walburgis Church, 350 yards away, bringing part of the tower down with it into the street below.

The day came to an end with the British force weakening not in spirit of resistance but in the means to resist. Three officers and sixteen men are believed to have been killed in the last twenty-four hours. More than 100, possibly nearer to 150 by now, were wounded. The serious cases were being treated by Captains Logan and Wright in their combined aid post in the crowded basement of the Brigade HQ building, but there was urgent need of surgical facilities. Lieutenant Harvey Todd, the American 'Jedburgh' officer, had spoken on the telephone with a doctor at St Elizabeth Hospital, only just over a mile away, but the Germans there would not allow aid to be sent. The only other aid post at the bridge was one in the basement of the school, where medical orderlies Corporal Roberts and Sapper 'Pinky' White were tending the wounded. Many lightly wounded men remained at their posts in the buildings they were defending. Food was short. Ammunition was running desperately low for all weapons.

Signalman George Lawson describes how he was sent out to try to obtain more ammunition:

> The sergeant told me to take my mate and get some ammunition because we were low. 'Go to the HQ under the bridge,' he said. I think it was the 2nd Battalion's A Company HQ. I wondered what I could carry the ammunition in if I got any. I found a shopping basket, so I went shopping for bullets. I couldn't find my mate, Tony Warehem, so I went on my own. I ran through the street – I broke all Olympic records – but then I saw Major Tatham-Warter; he was the coolest chap I ever saw, walking about with his red beret, with one arm in a sling, with his umbrella hooked over it and his right hand holding a revolver, directing operations. He asked me what I wanted and, when I told him, he said, 'Hurry up and get some and get back to your post, soldier; there are snipers about.' I got about thirty rounds, loose, so the basket came in handy after all.
>
> On my way back I heard the clatter of boots. I had one up the spout ready if it was a German. But it was Tony, and he bellowed out, 'Why the hell didn't you wait for me?' and we had an argument, under that bridge, 'effing and blinding' at each other. We got that over and scarpered back to our post.

Signalman Harold Riley describes an incident of typical soldiers' humour:

We were all feeling pretty grim, when suddenly a 2nd Battalion chap who had been crouching in a corner crawled on his hands and knees towards a desk in the middle of the room. He reached up and gingerly plucked a rather battered telephone receiver from it. Speaking into it he said, 'Hello, operator. Give me Whitehall 1212', a pause, then, 'Mr Churchill? There are some men outside annoying us.' Maybe it sounds a little corny now, but at the time it did relieve the tension somewhat.

Darkness came. Many houses were burning. Sapper Carpenter says that 'The area around the bridge was becoming a sea of flame. The roar and crackle of flaming buildings and dancing shadows cast by the flames was like looking into Dante's inferno.' The towers of the two nearby churches, the Eusebius and the St Walburgis, were both on fire. A bell in one of them clanged irregularly throughout the night as it swung in the wind. So ended the second full day at the Arnhem bridge. Lieutenant-Colonel Frost, who had been urged to reach and hold the bridge at all costs, wondered why no such priority had apparently been given to the Nijmegen bridge, from which there was still no sign of fighting.

Wednesday

The night passed relatively quietly; dawn came up dull and with a damp drizzle. Most of the original perimeter was still held, but the British positions were now virtually split into two parts divided by the ramp. The Germans allowed stretcher-bearers to pass in the open, but all other movement was extremely dangerous. There was no redeployment of positions; each group would fight on until its building was destroyed. The pressure had nearly all been from the east and north until now, but the Germans started to press just as strongly from the west. Patrols sent out into the town on that side the previous day had found an absence of Germans and the high wall of the local prison on that side had partially shielded the British positions from shell fire from that quarter. But the Germans had blown a hole in the wall during the night and they started firing through it. This development, together with the continuing German shelling from over the river, meant that the airborne positions were literally under fire from all sides and from within when the tanks cruised into the perimeter, as they would more frequently do during the day. Unless outside help arrived, there could only be one outcome to what was becoming a hopeless situation.

There was little prospect of such help. The Brigade HQ signallers unexpectedly made direct contact with Divisional HQ that morning, and a stream of messages was passed back and forth during the day. John Frost appealed for reinforcements, a surgical team, ammunition and food; he could not have been much impressed by Urquhart's unrealistic suggestion that local civilians should be sent out to collect some of the supply containers dropped by the RAF outside the town. Relief could only come from the south, but attempts by the 82nd US Airborne Division to capture the vital Nijmegen bridge had still not been successful.

The reports of action at the Arnhem bridge steadily became more confused. The exact sequence of events cannot be guaranteed, though all the incidents described here did happen on this day and, combined, they form a true reflection of what were to be the final hours of resistance. The main feature was the relentless shelling, by both the German artillery and roving tanks, and the mortaring. The Germans realized that it was quicker to destroy these stout Dutch buildings by fire than by blowing them slowly to pieces and were using more phosphorus shells to cause fires. Among the early victims of the shelling were members of the Brigade Defence Platoon, which in Sicily had captured and held a bridge until relieved. When the first tank engines were heard on this morning, some optimist shouted, 'Thirty Corps is here', but they were two German tanks. The first shell hit the corner of their house, and they soon had to leave with at least one man killed and their commander, Lieutenant Pat Barnett, wounded. One man blown out of his position, but not seriously hurt, was the American, Lieutenant Harvey Todd, who claimed that he had killed sixteen Germans by now with his Springfield automatic carbine which was much envied by British officers.

Another building to be hit was that occupied by the RASC

platoon which had been protected until now by the prison wall. The defenders stood ready to repel an infantry attack through the gap in the wall but were instead struck by shell fire. Driver Jim Wild describes this:

> The first shot hit the corner of the roof. It didn't explode there because the only resistance it had was the slates on the roof, but it left a hole nearly two yards across. The lads underneath it were showered with debris; I wouldn't like to repeat what they said. The shell exploded against the brickwork at the other end of the long room. We were all down on the floor. A lot of shrapnel was flying about, and I think one man was killed and one wounded. We decided to get out, down to the ground floor, when the second shell exploded against the front wall of the room we had been in; we would all have been killed if we had still been there.

Private Don Smith tells how a house occupied by part of B Company may have attracted German attention:

> RSM Gerry Strachan came into the room, then went upstairs where, I understand, he opened fire with a sub-machine-gun. All hell broke loose and he ordered us out quickly. I was a little slow moving but was assisted out of the window by an explosion. I seemed to float through the air and hit a wall; the wind was knocked out of me. I was wet about the seat of my trousers, and Ron Moon asked if I was all right. I was. Ron picked up the Bren gun, ran into the downstairs room and was killed there by a tracer through his head.

It is believed that two anti-tank guns still remained in action, but German infantry were now in positions from where they could fire directly on anyone who attempted to man a gun. The 2nd Battalion's 3-inch mortars were the only weapons capable of hitting back at the German artillery. They had successfully engaged some of the guns firing from the south bank of the river in recent days, but the Mortar Platoon officer, Lieutenant Reg Woods, and his sergeant, Maurice Kalikoff, were both fatally wounded on this day.

The Germans occasionally made a mistake. Private Sidney Elliott of B Company tells what happened when a half-track came in from the west and halted outside his house near the riverside:

> We heard the rattle and clanking of a vehicle and, on looking out of the window, we saw a half-track with, I think, four Germans aboard. We were by now extremely short of ammo, but we had one Gammon bomb left. This was immediately primed; one of us tossed it and it landed in the half-track. I can still see one of the bodies as it seemed to rise into the air and disappear into the river.

Sensing that resistance was starting to fail, the Germans now launched a series of infantry attacks with close tank support from the east, trying to reach the area underneath the ramp. The last defence in front of this area had been the group of houses defended by Captain Briggs and a mixed group of Brigade HQ personnel, signallers and six RAOC men. But shelling had forced the evacuation of these men to a position under the ramp where they barricaded themselves in with some timbers. Private Kevin Heaney, one of the RAOC men, says:

> The atmosphere and tension grew unbearable. We were expecting to be attacked but uncertain from which direction this was going to come. The mood varied between hope and despair, and the lack of news from the rest of the division or of progress by Thirty Corps was bad for morale. A young officer, a studious looking chap, gave us a pep talk, trying to be a morale booster, saying how well our brigade had done in North Africa and how our performance at Arnhem would go down in history. But I had not been in North Africa and the thought went through my mind, about fighting to the end, 'not if I can help it', particularly as there was talk of leaving the wounded behind.

The German intention seemed to be to prepare the archway over the road nearest to the river for demolition. The Guards Armoured Division had reached Nijmegen that morning, and the Germans presumably wanted to be able to destroy that small archway, easily bridgeable later, rather than the main bridge span, to prevent British tanks crossing the river if they should reach Arnhem. There developed a series of vicious attacks and counter-attacks by infantry and engineers from both sides in which the Germans placed explosive charges against the pillars supporting the archway and Royal Engineers led by Lieutenant Donald Hindley attempted to stop the demolition preparations. Hindley's party, accompanied by Lieutenant Grayburn and some of his A Company men, dashed out and removed the fuses from the charges around the piers supporting the arch – 'a nerve-racking experience', says Hindley, 'working a few feet away from a large quantity of explosives which could be fired at any moment'. Grayburn was wounded again but returned after being treated, one arm in a sling and with bandaged head. Hindley says:

> It was obvious that the enemy would quickly restore the fuses, and a second, heavier attack was made to try to remove the charges themselves. However, the enemy had by now moved up a tank to cover the work. We were quickly mown down. Lieutenant Grayburn was killed – riddled with machine-gun fire. I escaped with flesh wounds in my shoulder and face.

Lieutenant Jack Grayburn was awarded a posthumous Victoria Cross, the only VC at the Arnhem bridge.

The events just described took place over several hours, all through the morning and well into the afternoon. Meanwhile, at about 1.30 p.m., Lieutenant-Colonel Frost was wounded. Signalman Bill Jukes saw Frost with Major Crawley 'crouched on the top of a pile of rubble, Frost pointing in the direction of the bridge like a figure in the painting of some last stand'. There was the explosion of a mortar bomb, and both officers were wounded in the legs. Frost's wounds were serious enough to put him out of action, and they necessitated another change of command. Major Hibbert appointed Major Gough of the Reconnaissance Squadron 'to command the brigade'. Frost was consulted about the change and approved it; he says:

Freddie was spare. I had spent a lot of time with him. We had gone for little walks when it was quieter, so he was my confidant, you might say. I was taken into the aid post. I was quite affected by the blast as well as being wounded and I really wasn't able to control things. Freddie came along, and I told him to carry on – not that there were any orders much to give by then. That was the very worst time, the most miserable time of my life. It is a pretty desperate thing to see your battalion gradually carved to bits around you. We were always hoping, right to the bitter end, that the ground forces would arrive. As long as we were still in place around the bridge, preventing the Germans bringing up anti-tank guns to engage the XXX Corps tanks, we were doing our job. But it was only isolated groups by then, with no proper control over the area.

At about the time that John Frost was wounded, the bridge force lost one of its most important positions. In the substantial Van Limburg Stirum School building, halfway along the eastern side of the ramp embankment running down to the town, the combined force of Royal Engineers and 3rd Battalion men who had held this exposed position throughout the battle, with no heavier weapon than a Bren gun, were about to be overwhelmed. About thirty men remained unwounded, but ammunition was low and there was no food or water. Either a German tank standing on the ramp only seventy yards away or a German gun further away started systematically blowing away the roof and top storey of the building, where most of the defenders were positioned. One shell set the roof ablaze; another burst where two of the 3rd Battalion officers, Major Lewis and Lieutenant Wright, were taking their turns to rest, injuring both officers and so stunning Len Wright that he has no memory of the next few hours. What did happen next became an emotive subject among the defenders. Several of them have provided contributions; the account which follows is a consolidation of these.

There were no means of putting out the fire, and it was obvious that the building had to be evacuated. Captain Mackay appointed a party of sappers to remain at their positions to prevent any German attack over the surrounding ground while the evacuation took place. The wounded were brought up from the basement, the eight seriously hurt being carried on doors or mattresses. After they left the building, they had to be lifted over a low wall which was exposed to German fire. One unconscious Royal Engineer clutching a photograph of his wife and children was hit again by machine-gun fire as he was being lifted over the wall, and one of the 3rd Battalion men was hit in the face and killed by a mortar bomb burst; a third man was hit in the head and killed as he climbed over the wall. Meanwhile, the shelling of the upper part of the building had continued, and one of the rearguard positions was hit, with two men being killed and one badly crushed. One of the dead was Corporal William Simpson, who sported a large moustache which grew up the sides of his face to join his hair. Known as 'Canadian Joe' because he had once lived in Canada, Simpson had been one of the stalwarts of the defence.

Captain Mackay returned to the building to fetch out the remainder of the rearguard. The intention now was for the whole party to move to a nearby building, the one evacuated by the Royal Engineers on the Sunday night. The other RE officer present, Lieutenant Dennis Simpson, started this move but was immediately wounded. More men were being hit outside the school, and Major Lewis called out from his mattress: 'Time to put up the white flag.' His second in command, Captain 'Chippy' Robinson, says: 'Being unwounded, I felt guilty about allowing myself to be captured, so I went up towards where he was and called out to ask if the fit men could attempt to get out. He shouted back that we could.' This news was passed to the REs, the phrase 'Every man for himself' perhaps being used. About ten men, including Captains Robinson and Mackay, then dashed across the road into the gardens of some houses to the east, only to be discovered later and taken prisoner, although Mackay eventually escaped and reached England.

But some of the REs, particularly the senior NCOs, did not like abandoning the wounded. One of them says:

Some of us felt that was the time an officer should have stayed with his men, and I was one of those who stayed with the wounded. It had reached the stage where each individual had to decide whether to stay with his wounded comrades or clear off. I suppose it can be said that Captain Mackay, in getting away to England as he did, took back vital information and that we were facing certain capture. But the majority stayed with the wounded.

Major Lewis now addressed those who had stayed, complimenting them on their fine defence of the school but telling them that they must surrender. A sapper was sent to the top of the embankment with a white towel tied to his rifle but was immediately struck in both legs by a burst of machine-gun fire. He died of those wounds five months later. The Germans closed in, and the firing ceased. Accounts say that the German who fired that last burst was shot by one of his own officers for firing on the white flag. As the wounded were being checked, this German officer inspected the sapper who was so badly wounded and unconscious, declared that there was no hope, and shot him in the head with a pistol. The man's comrades were appalled by this but later agreed that it was an act of mercy. So ended the gallant defence of the Van Limburg Stirum School.

Returning to the southern part of the perimeter, a considerable body of men had gathered among the pillars under the ramp archway nearest the river. They were the survivors of the parties forced out of their houses east of the ramp and of A Company who had been burned out of the houses close by this place of dubious shelter. A decision had been made to concentrate all of the still effective members of the British force in the large gardens at the rear of Brigade HQ. The ever-present Major Tatham-Warter came across to this group and ordered them to make an attempt to go through the ruins and move to that position. Two men have provided accounts of that hazardous move, only of 180 yards, but across fire-swept ground. Signalman George Lawson says:

I heard the shout, 'Every man for himself.' A group of us made a dash for it. We had to go through a mortar barrage first; that's where young Waterston got hit. He was leaning against this wall. I thought I should go back for him, but he was turning blue, and I carried on. Several of the others were hit, too; I was hit in the face by shrapnel. I know I slung my rifle away because the bloody thing was useless; it wasn't working properly. I took the bolt out and threw it away. A group of us then tried to cross the open road, but four or five were mown down by machine-gun fire. I turned back and took refuge in one of the burnt-out buildings – how long for, I don't know, but I was forced to get up because my gas cape and my smock were burning from the hot stone; my arse was almost on fire.

Lawson managed to reach the comparative safety of the Brigade HQ building.

Private Kevin Heaney of the RAOC also heard 'Every man for himself':

I reached the corner of a garden and had to negotiate a wall. I saw several chaps being picked off as they went over. I remember one hit in the forehead and one in the chest, hearing the cry for 'Mother' in their dying breaths. A hand grenade came over the wall and exploded; the chap behind me had a great big hole in the neck and blood was gurgling out. I put my field dressing round his neck.

I managed to make my way into the rubble of the houses nearby; six of us gathered in the remains of a hallway. The Germans were fifty yards away with a Schmeisser. Now comes the unheroic part. I said to the other chaps, including the man with the wounded neck, 'How about packing it in?' I didn't know any of them. One chap said, 'I'm easy'; I don't think he was ready to surrender, though. I put my hand inside my jacket, tore off my vest, gave it to the man nearest the opening, and he waved what was, in effect, the white flag. The Germans shouted to us to come out with our hands up. But the first four out were all hit by machine-gun fire. I heard the first one to go down say, 'Bastards.' I assumed that the Germans who fired were themselves under fire from our men. That was my charitable interpretation as to why they fired, because they were very chivalrous generally.

Myself and one of the wounded men got back into the house and sat in the rubble. We could hear mortar fire on the nearby houses, walls falling, heard our own men trapped, calling for help. We were there about two hours. I had my prayer book open and was saying the Prayers for the Dying. Later on, the Germans came in, rescuing the trapped men and taking them prisoner, and this great big German came and took the two of us also.

Described as being prominent in this action was Lieutenant Grayburn; the second 'demolition charge' sortie in which he was killed must have been after this time.

The defence was now concentrated into an area only about one-fifth of the size of that first held. Most of the active men were in the garden area chosen for the final assembly, in slit trenches sited to allow fire to be aimed at the bridge and the ramp through gaps between houses. There were some bizarre incidents. Private Henry Sullivan of A Company was digging a trench in the garden when he came upon two bottles of wine and a store of $2\frac{1}{2}$ guilder coins which a Dutchman had buried. He drank the wine – 'It wasn't very good but it was better than nothing' – but only managed to keep one of the coins as a souvenir. Private 'Ossie' Fahey was still in the Brigade HQ building. He had earlier found two superb shotguns from a stock the Germans had obviously confiscated from their Dutch owners: 'I had taken them as loot; I had thoughts of taking them back and shooting rabbits in Belton Park.' When he ran out of Sten-gun ammunition he started using one of the shotguns, 'trying to keep the buggers away. I might have hit one or two – I wasn't a bad shot.'

Not so funny was when the Germans brought up a tank and started setting fire to all of the remaining buildings. Gunner Dennis Bowles, one of the signallers in the artillery observation post at Brigade HQ, was at the receiving end of its fire:

There was a big bang and a lot of dust, and that put the wireless out of action. Back at the battery they heard the set go dead in the middle of my transmission and when they returned to England they reported that I was 'missing presumed killed'. The New Park Inn at Boston heard about it and put my photograph up on the bar mirror with the others who had died. They had to take it down when I came back in 1945.

German tanks and troop convoys were finally able to start using the bridge late that afternoon. Ironically, this was almost the same time that the Nijmegen road bridge was finally captured, helped by a hazardous and costly river assault by Colonel Reuben H. Tucker's 504th Parachute Infantry Regiment – a gallant feat of arms but one which would have been unnecessary if more urgency about the Nijmegen bridge had been inserted into the 82nd US Airborne Division's plan for the Nijmegen area. It was 6.30 p.m. before the first Sherman tanks of Sergeant Peter Robinson's troop from the 2nd Grenadier Guards rolled across the bridge, an equally brave act because the Germans could have blown the bridge and sent them all to their deaths in the river below. But that short stretch of narrow roadway to the British airborne men clinging to their positions near the Arnhem bridge was now strongly defended and the Grenadiers made little further progress. The tanks needed to replenish ammunition and fuel after earlier hard fighting in Nijmegen, and the infantry battalion with which this unit regularly worked was still tied up fighting in Arnhem. It has been suggested that a mixed force of available armour and infantry could have been thrown together and launched up that road. The men waiting at the Arnhem bridge had been promised a definite attack at 5.0 p.m. The Americans who had carried out the costly assault across the river Waal were disgusted at the delay.

Resistance Fails

The Brigade HQ building had escaped much of the effects of the earlier German tank and artillery fire because it was set back from the street frontage and partially protected by other buildings. But it was now on fire and a start had been made in evacuating the many wounded in the basement to the only nearby building not alight, the one against the prison wall occupied by the RASC platoon. The two medical officers told Lieutenant-Colonel Frost that the evacuation could not proceed fast enough unless there was a truce, so some of the German prisoners were sent out with white flags to arrange this. It was quickly agreed, and the fighting stopped for nearly two hours. The able-bodied men from the building were sent off by Major Gough northwards into the town. Corporal Dennis Freebury was one of them:

> Major Gough, with his arm in a sling and his silver hair, in shirt sleeves – a swashbuckling character – gave us a pep talk. It was a bit like Hollywood. He said, 'I want you to go out, do your best and see if you can get back to our own forces – and just remember that you belong to the finest division in the British Army.' Nobody cheered or anything like that, but it made one feel good.

These men were given a rendezvous in an undamaged building, a convent school just outside the perimeter. Gough did not go with them but joined the 2nd Battalion men in their positions; the medical officers and their orderlies stayed and became prisoners. Numerous German soldiers appeared and the 280 or so wounded, including some Germans, together with some Dutch civilians who had been sheltering in the building, were all saved from the fire. Most of the wounded eventually reached St Elizabeth Hospital.

There was no firing during this period. It was now after nightfall but the blazing buildings made the scene almost as light as day. A German officer wandered around the 2nd Battalion's slit trenches, handing out cigarettes and telling the airborne men they were 'silly bastards to carry on fighting; you don't stand any chance. Why don't you give up?' He was told to 'piss off'. The Germans, despite the truce, were seen to be moving their positions closer to those of the remaining airborne men. Major Tatham-Warter sent Captain Hoyer-Millar, who spoke some German, to protest:

> I found an officer in a long dark leather coat. He spoke good English. I warned him that if his men continued, we might have to open fire. He, in turn, kept stressing that there was no hope for us and that we should surrender. I told him there was no chance of that and that we were confident our ground forces would soon be up to relieve us. I think I must have

introduced myself, or they got my name from someone else, because when the action continued several hours later I heard a rather uncanny, wheedling voice calling, 'Captain Millar' or 'Captain Müller' – just my name – quite pointless, because I made no reply.

The end was almost at hand. The British force was now in two parts. Most of the Brigade HQ group, about 120 strong, reached the meeting point at the convent school. Major Hibbert says:

> We decided that, as we could no longer see the bridge and had virtually no ammunition, we could be of most use if we could get back to the divisional perimeter and get some more ammunition. So we split up into sections of ten men, each under the command of an officer, to try to slip through the enemy lines.

The American, Lieutenant Todd, led the first party out at about 2.0 a.m. (on Thursday), and other groups followed at intervals; but, as far as is known, every man in those parties was eventually captured. Among them was Tony Cotterell, the war correspondent, who had destroyed all the notes he had made during the battle; he was dragged out of the coal shed in which he was hiding with Major Hibbert next morning.

Meanwhile the 2nd Battalion men had remained in their positions and were ready to continue fighting. Captain Hoyer-Millar remembers that strange period:

> I was as scared that night as at any time. How could it have been otherwise – completely surrounded by burning buildings and enemy, with all hell being chucked at our tiny perimeter in the shape of artillery and mortar fire? But there was indeed a strange feeling of exhilaration mingled with pride and bitterness. We were still there after three full days and nights and, incredibly enough, alive and in one piece – though it seemed improbable that we would remain thus for much longer. Although ammunition for our personal weapons was nearly exhausted and we had nothing with which to defend ourselves

against enemy tanks, it seemed at least possible that the German infantry surrounding us would not risk further losses by trying to assault our positions that night. More probably they would try to pin us down and inflict further casualties by unceasing shellfire. Dug-in in our garden slit trenches, we could withstand this. But at first light they would certainly bring their armour into action again, and that would mean 'curtains' for us in our present positions. Unless . . . unless relief from the south arrived before dawn. This seemed increasingly unlikely.

There was undoubtedly bitterness and scepticism about the performance of Monty's ground forces, but those of us who had taken part in the Primosole bridge operation in Sicily recalled how, twenty-four hours overdue, the first troop of Eighth Army tanks had finally reached us when we were hanging on by our fingernails; might it not happen again? I recall clearly how, during those final hours, one line of A. H. Clough's famous poem kept springing to mind: 'If hopes were dupes, fears may be liars' . . . but deep down there was the feeling, 'They've just written us off.'

Major Tatham-Warter, limping, still with his umbrella, decided that the remaining men should split into two parties, one under himself, one under Major Francis Tate the HQ Company commander, and hide for the night before reoccupying their positions next morning. But the Germans were now all over this area, and the plan never came to fruition. More scattered fighting took place. Major Tate and several men were killed. The remainder tried to escape into the town, but nearly all became prisoners. Lieutenant Tom Ainslie describes what might be a typical ending; his little party was trapped in a house, with Germans outside calling on them to surrender:

Some of my group had already been hit, so I yelled back in German, 'Don't shoot. There are wounded here.' And we walked across the street into captivity. The first person in authority we saw was an NCO. He was slightly cross-eyed; his tunic was open, and he was wearing a blue-and-white-striped civilian shirt underneath. He said, 'Good evening. That was a lovely battle, a really lovely battle. Have a cigar. We are human too.' So, after doing what we could for the wounded, we all sat down, smoking foot-long Dutch cigars, and had a matey chat about the events of the past few days.

There is general agreement that those Germans of the 10th SS Panzer Division who had been fighting at the bridge behaved correctly and with much consideration for their opponents in the immediate aftermath of the fighting, belying the reputation for savagery and cruelty usually accorded to the SS.

A small support attempt had been made from Oosterbeek during the night. Two of the KOSB's Bren carriers loaded with ammunition and a signals jeep had been despatched under the roving Canadian, Lieutenant Leo Heaps, but none had got through. The last armed resistance ended at about 5.0 a.m. on Thursday, three days and nine hours after Major Tatham-Warter and the first men had arrived at the bridge. The British force had fought to the limit of its powers of resistance. Of the men who had started that fight on Monday, an estimated ten officers and seventy-one men had been killed or would die of wounds, nearly 11 per cent of those present. The last twenty-four hours had seen the heaviest deaths: four officers and about thirty-three men.[3] What had the fight achieved? The Arnhem road bridge had been held until well after the expected relief time by the ground forces. The use of the bridge had been denied to the Germans; and a large proportion of the 10th SS Panzer Division, which would otherwise have been sent south to fight the ground forces and the American airborne division at Nijmegen or west to fight the British at Oosterbeek, had been tied down and suffered heavy casualties. The tragedy was that the plan for 'Market Garden' had not given the seizure of the Nijmegen bridge top priority.

One should not forget the local Dutch people, some of whom

---

[3] I am again indebted to Jan Hey of Holland for his research, which shows the field burial locations for the identified dead, helping such calculations to be made. However, a high number of the estimated bridge deaths – thirty-one – have no known graves, usually the result of the bodies having been left in burning buildings.

had been present throughout the battle and many of whose houses had been destroyed. They, too, had suffered casualties, although it is not known how many of Arnhem's 188 dead were suffered in the bridge area. Two Dutch people provided their memories. Mr Constant Vogel was the law-courts clerk lodging at the boarding house only two houses from the nearest airborne-held house. Early in the battle, on the Monday, he had experienced this humorous but embarrassing incident:

> There were only one or two toilets in the cellars for the three buildings which made up the boarding house. There were twenty to twenty-five people. I didn't want to use them so I went upstairs to use a toilet there. I was actually sitting down when the water tank above my head was hit. I got out quickly and went straight down to the cellar, with my underpants around my ankles. That caused some amusement among the people in the cellar, particularly among the old ladies. I didn't leave the cellar after that.

Mr Vogel spent most of the next two days in a period of waiting in 'tense expectation' until the house caught fire on Wednesday:

> Mr Kniest, the owner of the house, was a resolute man and he organized us. We could take nothing, absolutely nothing. He got a sheet or something, and the first man waved it, and the rest of us followed during a lull in the fighting, round into an alley at the side of the house, and along the back of the houses towards the Walburgis Church. We hardly dared to look, but I remember that there were several dead bodies on the slope of the ramp and on the roadway; I couldn't tell whether they were German or English. The whole area was a scene of battle.
>
> We went into the Insula Dei House, a religious house near the church. Our group had grown, with more people having joined us, and we were collected in the courtyard where there were already many more people. There was one priest, a Catholic, who gave us enormous support by leading us in prayer. We all joined in, Catholic and Protestant alike, and

that gave us peace of mind and we calmed down. Then German soldiers came, looking for English soldiers in the building. They separated the men from the women. Most of the men could identify themselves with their papers, but I was in my bathrobe and had none. So I was put on one side and things looked a bit grim. But that priest acted as an intermediary and, somehow, he persuaded the Germans to return me to the other men. We were there for several anxious hours and then we were chased out in a northerly direction. Looking back, I could see a vast sea of fire.

Miss Jo van Velzen, just turned twenty, was at her parents' home about 500 yards away from the fighting. The period had opened for her on the Monday with people hanging out Dutch national flags from windows to greet the 'liberation', but these soon disappeared when German troops moved into the street, which became an assembly area for units preparing to make attacks on the British at the bridge:

Some of them came into our house. I noticed their ages seemed to vary from sixteen to sixty. They came right into the house and the cellars. There was no unusual behaviour, and they were there until Friday morning. On Thursday we saw them being sent off to attack the British positions, shitting themselves with fear.

Later on Thursday morning it fell quiet, and we were told that the area was secure. The Germans said we could go to the dairy. I set off with my sister Elly. There were terrible sights of the heavy fighting, British soldiers dead and dying, blood dripping from their mouths and ears – not being looked after. The German dead were covered with blankets. There were very few soldiers, British or German, about, only the dead at that time. All the buildings were burnt down. Some Germans stopped us and took us to the town hall, where we had to show our papers. We were not carrying any, only our tins of milk. They asked if we had been sheltering British soldiers. I think that they released us because we were carrying those tins of milk. I think we were lucky not to be shot for walking across the battlefield.

CHAPTER 15

The Formation of the Oosterbeek Perimeter

The end of resistance at the bridge on Wednesday night was the major turning-point of the Arnhem battle. The remainder of the 1st British Airborne Division, even if the reinforcement of the Polish brigade arrived, was now too weak to make any further attempt to form a bridgehead at Arnhem in anticipation of the arrival there of the ground forces. There remained only one useful role the division could play: to go on to the defensive and attempt to maintain a bridgehead on the north bank of the Rhine at the place where the remaining strength of the division now stood – the area on the western edge of Oosterbeek which has frequently been referred to as 'the divisional area' in preceding chapters. The British holding was still firmly rooted on the river and there was still confidence that the tanks of XXX Corps would appear on the south bank now that the main bridge at Nijmegen had been captured. The division could still perform a useful function if it could hold out until then and provide a safe place for the ground forces to cross, although there was no bridge available and a river crossing would have to be made.

The Eastern Perimeter

The formation of a defensive perimeter around the area where the remainder of the division's battle would be fought had started in the middle of the previous afternoon – Tuesday the 19th – when the survivors of the battalions attacking in western Arnhem streamed back towards Oosterbeek. The western side of the divisional area was being safely defended by the 1st Border, the only remaining complete battalion in the division, but the eastern side was unprotected. Now that the British attacks in western Arnhem had failed, the 9th SS Panzer Division could concentrate all its efforts attacking westwards, attempting to crush the British against the substantial but less skilled German units in the west. The primary object of the attack would be to force the British even further away from the vital Arnhem bridge; the secondary aim would be to overwhelm the British completely and wipe out the bridgehead. That was the background against which Major-General Urquhart had to start building up a defence on the eastern side of his division.

Urquhart, still gathering himself together after returning from his enforced absence in Arnhem only seven hours earlier, had no fresh infantry available on that Tuesday afternoon. The 4th Parachute Brigade, including the King's Own Scottish Borderers, was still fighting out in the woods to the north-west, and the only troops present on the two main routes in from Arnhem were the gunners of the Light Regiment with some glider pilots near the church in Lower Oosterbeek, the RAMC men who had established dressing stations around a crossroads on the main road, the Utrechtseweg, in central Oosterbeek, and some Reconnaissance Squadron patrols. The survivors of the units falling back from Arnhem would have to turn and form the beginnings of what became the defence line on that side of the perimeter.

The first unwounded men to come back from Arnhem on that Tuesday arrived at Oosterbeek in the morning and were those who had panicked when German tanks counter-attacked their units after the last attempts to get through to the bridge failed. I have three examples of this among my notes, two contributed by the men themselves; they all involved the South Staffords. Two men came into Oosterbeek along the Utrechtseweg and then turned south into the main village, where they took a bicycle from a Dutchman standing in the street; then, with one riding and one on the handlebars, they came all the way down the slope to the lower village so fast that they hit the church wall and fell off. They were commandeered by an anti-tank sergeant and remained with his gun crew. Two more came back on foot along the lower road to the church, where they were stopped by 'some officers of various ranks and various breeds' and put into position near the church. Eight more South Staffords went all the way through to Westerbouwing, where they arrived at a 1st Border position on the western side of the perimeter. The officer who eventually took the initiative in halting such men near Oosterbeek church was Lieutenant-Colonel 'Sheriff' Thompson, commanding officer of the Light Regiment, whose 75-millimetre gun positions were located nearby. He had earlier failed to stop two jeeps which came careering along the road from Arnhem, so he formed a barricade across the road outside the church and he and some of his officers then forcibly stopped everyone arriving from Arnhem.

It was mid-afternoon before the more organized parties from the four battalions which had been fighting in Arnhem appeared from under the railway bridge on the lower road. Lieutenant-Colonel Thompson received a report on the artillery wireless net from the forward observation officer with one of those units telling him that what was, in effect, all that remained of the 1st Parachute Brigade was retreating along the lower road. Thompson rushed out along the road by jeep and met them 'completely filling the road'; they were only just over half a mile from his artillery positions. If they continued to come on towards Oosterbeek, there would be no defence between the vulnerable gun positions and the Germans likely to follow up the retreat. Thompson quickly found the senior officer present, Major Robert Cain of the South Staffords, and ordered him to take command of the mixed parties present and form a defence screen astride that lower road. In such a way was the first substantial element of the eastern perimeter established.

Figures on the strength of this force vary, but by nightfall it consisted approximately of the following:

2nd South Staffords: 100 men under Major Robert Cain.
1st Parachute Battalion: 120 men under Lieutenant John Williams.
3rd Parachute Battalion: 46 men under Captain Richard Dorrien-
    Smith.
11th Parachute Battalion: 150 men under Major Peter Milo.

Also present were a 17-pounder and several 6-pounder anti-tank guns, some Vickers machine-guns and two artillery observation officers. Lieutenant-Colonel Thompson ordered Major Cain to deploy this force at the place where he had halted them, and each battalion group was allocated a small sector. These men, who had been through so much in Arnhem, were still well disciplined, and there was no reluctance to carry out their orders. An NCO of the 11th Battalion told 'Sheriff' Thompson: 'Thank God we've got some orders at last; now we'll be all right.'

Thompson returned to Oosterbeek and sent forward some ammunition and food. He then met Brigadier Hicks and asked for more men, particularly officers, to reinforce this force. Hicks sent forward Major Dickie Lonsdale, second in command of the 11th Battalion, who had been slightly injured during his parachute drop, and Major John Simmons, commander of the South Staffords' HQ Company, neither of whom had been involved in the fighting in Arnhem. Thompson put Simmons in charge of the infantry near the church and sent Lonsdale forward to take command of the outer force. The glider pilots of C Squadron, under Major James Dale, who had been providing the screen on the railway embankment at Oosterbeek Laag Station, 500 yards further forward, were pulled back that evening. Mortaring and shelling during the night knocked out the 17-pounder and also a Bren carrier, but the Germans did not attack. At a divisional conference next morning all of the infantry in this area was designated as 'Thompson Force', with Lieutenant-Colonel Thompson officially in command of the sector.

Three-quarters of a mile further north was the main road, the Utrechtseweg, the other route by which survivors of the Arnhem fighting returned. In two hotels on the main crossroads in Oosterbeek were located what had been intended to be temporary positions for 133 and 181 Field Ambulances before those units moved to their planned locations in hospitals in Arnhem. There was no infantry protection of any kind in that area until a few South Staffords came in from Arnhem and decided to halt near the crossroads and a troop of 6-pounder anti-tank guns arrived; this was Lieutenant Bob Glover's E Troop of the 2nd Airlanding Anti-Tank Battery, which had been supporting the 11th Battalion in Arnhem. A force of German tanks had probably followed the retreat from Arnhem but, instead of driving directly along the Utrechtseweg, had worked its way through streets and tracks parallel with the main road; these tanks now appeared. Gunner Len Clarke was one of the anti-tank gunners:

> Some South Staffs came running from the station – from the north – and said, 'There's some bloody Tiger tanks coming.' I told them not to be so daft; the Germans shouldn't have any Tigers here. Lieutenant Glover said he and I would go out and meet the tanks, but I said, 'No. You get a single man.' I had only been married six months. But no one else would go with him, so I said I would, provided we emptied the jeep of all of the equipment, so that nothing would get in our way.
>
> But we were too late, because a small tank appeared before we moved. It had come along a track parallel with the main road and put its nose out into the road from the station. I fired – he was about 200 to 250 yards away – and hit it. It moved back out of sight. We were going to move the gun to a new position but had only manhandled it halfway across the road outside the Schoonoord Hotel when I saw a tank on the station road appearing over the top of a small rise about 200 yards away. I shouted, 'Turn the gun, drop the trail and get out the way.' They said I couldn't fire it like that; you were supposed to have the cross-stay in to secure the two arms of the trail. I said we hadn't got time for that. The Number Two stayed to load for me; the others got out of the way. I fired three shots at that tank and hit it at the join of the turret and the hull, and it just stopped. Then another tank came up to pass it, and I hit that as it was passing with another three shots and stopped that. Every time I fired, the gun moved back about fifteen feet because the spade end of the trail wasn't dug in; we were only on the cobbled street.
>
> A captain of the South Staffs had seen all this and he took my name and Lieutenant Glover's and said he was going to recommend us for decorations. Lieutenant Glover said that I would be made up to sergeant – a field promotion.

*

But the unknown South Staffords officer's recommendation was never submitted; perhaps he was killed later. Soon after this, Gunner Clarke was severely wounded when the Germans opened fire with mortars, eventually losing a leg, and Lieutenant Glover was killed.

The crossroads area, as well as a large part of the eastern perimeter more than a mile long, from just north of the church where Thompson Force was, right up to the Oosterbeek Hoog railway crossing, would remain virtually undefended until units were found to plug the gaps the next day. The heart of the divisional area was wide open to attack, but fortunately the Germans made no move to exploit that weakness before the new units arrived.

The Western Perimeter

The western face of the perimeter became established in a more orderly manner and under less pressure. The main defensive force here was the almost intact 1st Border, which was in position among the fields, woods and lanes between a quarter and half a mile from the centre of Oosterbeek, stretching northwards from the Westerbouwing hill overlooking the Rhine. The 1st Border was responsible for a frontage nearly one and a half miles long. It was not a continuous line; there were still gaps between the company groups, but most of the gaps were in open ground which could be covered by overlapping fire. A particularly large gap between C Company on the Utrechtseweg and A Company further north was filled by part of the 4th Parachute Squadron; more Royal Engineers, from the 9th Field Company, would be sent to strengthen that part of the perimeter later. The positions occupied by the 1st Border were actually the ones designated for the battalion on the western perimeter of the large bridgehead in the original Arnhem plan. The 1st Border and the 2nd Parachute Battalion at the bridge were the only battalions in the division to fulfil their original roles. There is no doubt that the Oosterbeek perimeter could not have been held without the sturdy defence of the Border companies, and this should be recognized just as much as the 2nd Battalion's more spectacular action at the Arnhem road bridge.

The shorter northern part of the perimeter was formed against the background of the 4th Parachute Brigade's battle north of the railway line. The Independent Company had one platoon out north of the railway, marking the landing zone for the Polish gliders; the remainder of the company was in good defensive positions on some high ground to the west of Oosterbeek Hoog Station, around a building called Ommershof which overlooked the railway line; the building was the holiday home of a Rotterdam shipping merchant. Part of the 4th Parachute Squadron which had been attempting to help the vehicles and guns of the units fighting north of the railway to come over the line also found itself in this area on Tuesday afternoon and was placed among the Independent Company positions. Lieutenant Ken Evans reports that the 4th Parachute Squadron men, under Captain Nigel Beaumont-Thomas, who was outranked by Major Wilson of the Independent Company, resented being placed in front of the Ommershof: 'The Independent Company were up on high ground, in houses; we were out in front, in lower ground, just in holes in the ground – an attrition position protecting the Independent Company – and we got little credit for it in post-war books.' Actually, only the Independent Company HQ was in the Ommershof building, but the sappers were placed in the most exposed corner of the sector. Also present nearby was a party of sixty glider pilots of E Squadron who had been in the woods south of the railway as a forward screen for the divisional area and now fell back to fill in the gap between the Ommershof position and A Company of the Border. They would be joined there by men of F Squadron on Wednesday.

A much more substantial reinforcement arrived late on Tuesday in the form of that part of the King's Own Scottish Borderers which had escaped from the fighting in the north. Lieutenant-Colonel Payton-Reid had about 270 men, a little over one-third of his battalion's original strength. The KOSB were sent to occupy an area on what would become the north-east shoulder of the perimeter, in and around a hotel called the Dreyeroord which stood just back from the railway crossing, the only access from the north for German tanks. The KOSB would come to call the hotel 'the White House' during their stay here. All of these moves meant that by midnight on Tuesday there was an almost continuous defence line from the Westerbouwing all the way up the western side and round the northern end of the developing perimeter.

The Germans started exerting pressure on all of these units during the following day, Wednesday the 20th, mostly with small probing attacks of joint tank and infantry parties followed by the shelling and mortaring that would become a constant feature of the remainder of the battle. The KOSB sent out patrols and put an anti-tank gun in position to cover the road from the station. The gun destroyed a tank, but one of the battalion's mortar officers, Lieutenant Alex Crighton, was killed by machine-gun fire on one of the patrols. The Germans started a major attack on the White House later on Wednesday, which will be described in the next chapter. The combined Independent Company and 4th Parachute Squadron sector suffered the same treatment as the KOSB, and among the sapper casualties was Captain Beaumont-Thomas, who was killed by a mortar bomb. A party of probably recently arrived Germans called out from a position facing the sappers. Lieutenant Evans thought it was, 'Ist das B Kompanie?' and called back, 'Ja; heir ist B Kompanie. Alles in ordnung. Kommen Sie herein.' The Germans came into the open and were allowed to come within fifty yards before being mown down. In the long Border sector some German tanks penetrated between A and C Companies but suffered from the unexpected power of a 17-pounder anti-tank gun whose fire was personally directed by Lieutenant-Colonel Loder-Symonds, who came out from the Royal Artillery HQ bunker to assist. Lieutenant John Bainbridge's No. 19 Platoon, in D Company, was cut off while out on a standing patrol, and only a few members returned. All of the Border companies experienced steady pressure, with fifteen men being killed, but the only lost position, in C Company's area, was regained. The western and northern sectors of the perimeter held fast all day.

Wednesday – Lonsdale Force

Wednesday saw more action on the still developing eastern side of the perimeter. In particular the Germans made a determined push against the forward force on the lower road, which was now under the command of Major Lonsdale. Soon after dawn the Germans commenced a series of infantry and tank attacks. Private Jim Gardner of the 1st Battalion was there:

> They came at us with all the fury they could muster. We got out of our trenches to meet the infantry and more than held our own but we gave ground against the tanks. Between the mist from the river, the explosions of mortars and shells, etc., we could not see one another after a while – it was a mixture of dust, smoke and fog. I felt oddly alone, when out of the smoke, etc., a figure emerged with rifle and bayonet out in front of him. I waited a while to be sure who was there. At about four to five feet I could see by the helmet that he was one of 'theirs'. I turned to face him, but he stopped in his tracks and, realizing who was confronting him, turned and scarpered back into the smoke.

Private David Warden of the 3rd Battalion was concussed by tank fire while in a position with other 3rd Battalion men alongside a ditch in the fields just north of the river:

> When I recovered I heard a sound from Lance-Corporal Stanley. Both his legs were in the muddy water, which was about three feet deep. He was about to pitch forward when I grasped his waist and held him, with both of us standing in the water. He appeared to be in deep shock but, nevertheless, he knew he was dying and spoke of his wife. He then sang five or six lines of the song 'I'll walk beside you in the years to come'. When it was obvious that he was dead I left his body leaning against the side of the ditch. He died a very brave man indeed. I heard later that this incident of him singing was talked about in the POW camps.

Lance-Corporal Walter Stanley has no known grave.

These attacks were beaten off. The 3rd Battalion's report credits a mortar sergeant of the 1st Battalion, Dick Whittingham, with effective work against the German infantry. He had found a jeep loaded with 3-inch mortar bombs and fired off nearly all of them.

The tanks were stopped largely by the effort of Lance-Sergeant John Baskeyfield, who was in charge of one of the South Staffords' 6-pounder anti-tank guns. The citation for his Victoria Cross tells how he allowed the tanks to come within 100 yards' range before opening fire, and his gun was credited with the destruction of two tanks and at least one self-propelled gun. The other members of Baskeyfield's gun team were all killed or wounded during this engagement; Baskeyfield himself, although wounded in the leg, refused to be evacuated. He crawled across the road to another 6-pounder and, manning it quite alone, was killed that afternoon. He has no known grave.

Another action against German armour here is described by Captain Frank King of the 11th Battalion, whose parachute aircraft had been shot down on Monday and who had just caught up with the remnants of his unit. Major Lonsdale sent him with two soldiers to attack a self-propelled gun that was firing from among some houses to the north of the British positions:

We worked our way along that street to the last house, where we could see that there were Germans upstairs and one in the cellar looking out of the ground-level window. I sent my men upstairs to deal with the Germans there and I went into the cellar myself. I stuck out my revolver and shouted, 'Hands up!' in German. He astonished me. He was rather fat and was carrying his rifle at the trail; he didn't look particularly dangerous. But he was a good soldier and was fooling me. He just tilted the rifle up and fired it one handed, hitting me in the chest, the bullet going in one side and coming out on the other. The recoil tore the rifle out of his grip, and I saw that it ripped his hand. I did what I had been trained to do, aiming at 'the centre of the visible mass' – which was quite extensive – and killed him.

Meanwhile my two soldiers had gone upstairs and had shot the Germans there but they were excited because they could look down on top of the SP gun. I was still quite mobile. There was a young German officer with his head out of the hatch. We dropped a Gammon bomb on to it, killing the officer and causing the SP to withdraw rapidly. We left the rear of the house and somehow found ourselves in a chicken run. A German threw a stick grenade into it, badly wounding one of the soldiers, and I got some splinters in my leg. I reported back to Lonsdale, and he told me to get my wounds dressed.

Not all of the defenders were able to stand the pressure of the German attacks. Sergeant Bob Leeder, a glider pilot near the church, has this description:

I saw a woman with a pram running down the road towards me. Following her were ten to fifteen more civilians and, behind them, a batch of thirty to forty South Staffs. Most of them didn't have rifles, but I saw two, who did have them, throw them down on the roadside as they ran. A jeep burst through this group and, when it was well clear, stopped, and an officer got out and started firing his revolver into the air. Everyone stopped, except the woman with the pram. The officer spoke to the South Staffs. I couldn't hear what he said, but it must have been something like, 'Get back, you silly sods', because they turned about, and he got an NCO to form them up and march them back. I asked the jeep driver what was happening. He said, 'Flame-throwers up there, and it started a panic.'

The German attacks on the forward position were resumed in the afternoon. Casualties continued to mount. Private Doug Charlton of the 1st Battalion had only worked his way back from Arnhem that morning, having slipped away from his captors when their attention was distracted by an RAF supply drop. He was now in one of the houses and tells this story of mixed horror and macabre humour; I have removed the name of one of the men involved:

From the upstairs window we saw two tanks with a platoon of infantry behind. We took up firing positions at the windows, with me at the Piat and the glider pilot with the Piat bombs. They were twenty yards away when I fired, but the bomb literally fell off the end and exploded on the ground below. Sergeant Callaghan opened up with a Bren on the foot soldiers, and also — with his rifle. The two tank commanders disappeared into their turrets and the guns swung round our way. I made for the stairs, closely followed by Callaghan. We had just made the stairs when there was a massive explosion in the room, followed by screams. Going back, we found the glider pilot dead with the flash eliminator and foresight of the Bren embedded in his head. — was minus his right leg but still conscious. The Germans reversed back down the road and Callaghan told me to try to find a medic.

I ran about half a mile and came to a house with Red Cross jeeps parked outside and dead bodies stacked in the garden. After arguing, I got a Welsh corporal with a medical haversack and took him to —, the corporal grumbling all the way there. Callaghan was gone. — was out like a light, twitching. I suggested some morphine. The medic and I argued. I said, 'For Christ's sake, do something; he's lost his leg.' His reply was, 'No he bloody well hasn't; look, there it is', pointing to the corner of the room. And there it was, complete with trouser, boot and gaiter. I was flabbergasted, although I can laugh now.

It is believed that the wounded man later died.

That mixed force commanded by Lonsdale was so weakened by the repeated attacks that Brigadier Hicks, who was in overall control of the area at the time, gave Lieutenant-Colonel Thompson permission to withdraw it and relocate it closer to the church. Many of the men were in sorry condition. An artillery officer describes one group, who had to crawl along a ditch to reach the safety of the church, 'ripping the stuffing out of the pew cushions to make some sort of dry vests, by cutting the corners out for armholes'. The Germans did not follow up the withdrawal and it was the first chance for many of these men to relax since they had dropped by parachute three days earlier. It was now early evening. Major Lonsdale gave orders that the men who had fallen back were to gather in the church and that is where he made his famous address from the pulpit, his head bandaged and one arm in a sling from minor injuries. He complimented the men on their recent actions and told them to rest for a short while, get a meal from what food was left, clean themselves up and be prepared to take up new positions around the houses near the church. He said the German troops opposing them were good but not up to the standard of the men in the church. He wished all present good luck. Some men were asleep but it is generally agreed that the talk was a major boost to morale. An unexpected officer reinforcement arrived during Lonsdale's address in the form of Major Alan Bush of the 3rd Battalion; he had been given up for lost in the Arnhem fighting. He was most impressed to see the 'filthy, tired men cleaning their rifles – well-trained men those were'.

'Lonsdale Force' was now recognized by Divisional HQ, with Lonsdale in command of all the parachute battalion units and Thompson Force containing the artillery, the South Staffords and the local glider pilots. This arrangement would not last long, because Thompson was wounded on the following day, and Lonsdale assumed command of all the infantry in this sector. And so these men settled down to defend the sector of the perimeter which they would hold to the end. The front line was under the command of three majors: Alan Bush with the remnants of the 1st Parachute Brigade in the south, Robert Cain with the South Staffords in the centre and Bob Croot with the glider pilots, mostly from G Squadron, in the north of the sector. The 11th Battalion men, Lonsdale's own battalion, were withdrawn into the perimeter as his reserve. After the war, he liked to give the impression that his headquarters were in that romantic little church which was almost in the front line but he actually set up his command post in a house 300 yards north-west of the church and mostly passed orders to the front line by means of a field telephone maintained by 3rd Battalion signallers.

While the Germans had been pushing so hard to drive in the defence on the lower road, presumably to try to cut off the 1st Airborne Division from the river while it was off balance, much of the remaining eastern side of the perimeter had been wide open. The Germans had moved only cautiously along the Utrechtseweg, perhaps fearing the 17-pounder anti-tank guns suspected of being in the Hartenstein area. They advanced only as far as the crossroads where a Main Dressing Station had been set up in two hotels there. After putting a shell through the Hotel Schoonoord and firing through windows at medics seen moving inside, but receiving no return fire from these non-combatants, German infantry moved in and took over the buildings. Most of the medical staff and the many walking wounded were taken prisoner and moved away, leaving forty seriously wounded cases and a small medical staff. The Germans then departed. More British troops became available during Wednesday as the depleted units of the 4th Parachute Brigade came into the perimeter from their battle in the woods. Lieutenant-Colonel Ken Smyth and about seventy men of the 10th Battalion arrived first and were sent straight to that crossroads to capture houses east of the hotel-hospitals as an outer defence. Thirty-five glider pilots from D Squadron then extended the main perimeter northwards up the Stationsweg and would defend that sector under the command of the kilted Captain James Ogilvie.

There were still gaps to the north and south of those positions. The 600-yard sector between the 10th Battalion and the glider pilots at the north end of the Lonsdale Force line would remain open until the following day, but the Germans never exploited it. To the north, further up the Stationsweg, there was a smaller gap before a group of houses occupied by dismounted troopers of the Reconnaissance Squadron. This unit had experienced a disastrous patrol the previous day, out in the country north of Wolfheze on the Amsterdamseweg, when seven jeeps containing thirty men of C Troop had run into a strong German force and been badly shot up. Only two jeeps and seven men escaped by racing through the German positions; the remainder of the patrol had been killed or taken prisoner. Most of the other parts of the squadron now became foot soldiers, but not in sufficient numbers to provide a full defence along the Stationsweg. So, when the survivors of 156 Battalion came into the perimeter late on Wednesday, they were sent to that area and eventually settled down with the Reconnaissance Squadron on their left. Major Geoffrey Powell, commanding the sixty men who were all that remained of 156 Battalion, also took command of the Reconnaissance Squadron, which had no officer present above the rank of captain. The time was 7.30 p.m. on

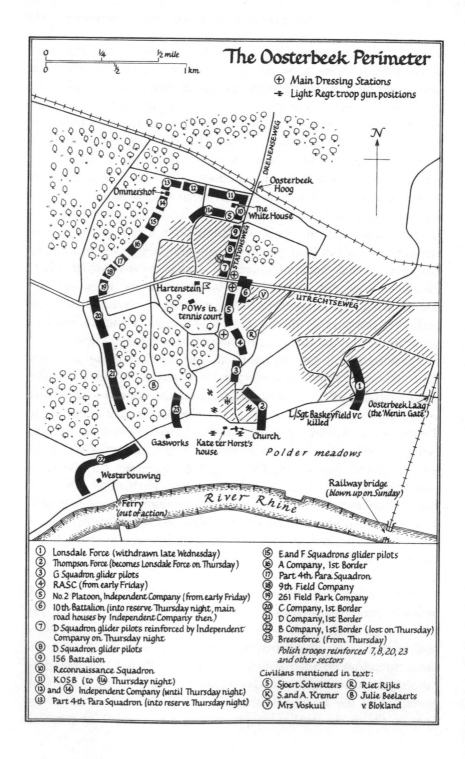

The Oosterbeek Perimeter

⊕ Main Dressing Stations
≛ Light Regt troop gun positions

Scale: 0 — ¼ — ½ mile / 0 — ½ — 1 km

N

DREIJENSEWEG

Oosterbeek Hoog

Ommershof

The White House

STATIONSWEG

Hartenstein

POWs in tennis court

UTRECHTSEWEG

Oosterbeek Laag (the 'Menin Gate')

L/Sgt Baskeyfield VC killed

Gasworks   Kate ter Horst's house   Church

Polder meadows

Westerbouwing

Railway bridge (blown up on Sunday)

Ferry (out of action)

River Rhine

① Lonsdale Force (withdrawn late Wednesday)
② Thompson Force (becomes Lonsdale Force on Thursday)
③ G Squadron glider pilots
④ RASC (from early Friday)
⑤ No. 2 Platoon, Independent Company (from early Friday)
⑥ 10th Battalion (into reserve Thursday night, main road houses by Independent Company then)
⑦ D Squadron glider pilots reinforced by Independent Company on Thursday night
⑧ D Squadron glider pilots
⑨ 156 Battalion
⑩ Reconnaissance Squadron
⑪ KOSB (to ⑭ Thursday night)
⑫ and ⑭ Independent Company (until Thursday night)
⑬ Part 4th Para Squadron (into reserve Thursday night)

⑮ E and F Squadrons glider pilots
⑯ A Company, 1st Border
⑰ Part 4th Para Squadron
⑱ 9th Field Company
⑲ 261 Field Park Company
⑳ C Company, 1st Border
㉑ D Company, 1st Border
㉒ B Company, 1st Border (lost on Thursday)
㉓ Breeseforce (from Thursday)
   Polish troops reinforced 7, 8, 20, 23 and other sectors

Civilians mentioned in text:
Ⓢ Sjoert Schwitters   Ⓡ Riet Rijks
Ⓚ S. and A. Kremer   Ⓑ Julie Beelaerts
Ⓥ Mrs Voskuil   v Blokland

Wednesday 20 September, just over three days since the 1st Airborne Division had landed with such high hopes. The Oosterbeek defence perimeter was almost complete.

The total length of the defended perimeter was about three miles. At Divisional HQ Lieutenant-Colonel Charles Mackenzie tore off a section of his 1:25,000 official map and folded the parts showing the entire divisional area into a rectangle measuring 4 x 4$\frac{3}{4}$ inches which he kept in his pocket for the remainder of the battle; there was no further need for map cases. It is often described as 'the Oosterbeek perimeter', but the defended area only contained about one-third of the built-up part of the small town. Inside the defended area were several hotels, a spread of modern residential houses in the upper part of the town and an older section in the lower town around the old Lutheran church – the only church inside the perimeter. Running south and west from Divisional HQ at the Hartenstein was a large area of wooded parkland, representing about half of the total area inside the perimeter. Finally, down by the river were the flat polder meadows occupied by neither side but easily covered by fire from the ends of the defended areas. No official figures exist of the numbers of airborne men available to defend this area, but it can be estimated that about 3,600 fighting men (excluding RAMC) were present, just over a third of those originally landed. The force was made up of about 1,200 infantry (only 20 per cent of the original strength), a valuable 900 or so glider pilots and about 1,500 men from artillery and other support arms and headquarters staffs. There was no lack of weapons, but ammunition replenishment would depend heavily on resupply by air. About 2,500 Dutch civilians would also be present to experience the horrors of the battle to come.

The command situation was sorted out at a conference the following morning. Divisional HQ would remain at the Hartenstein, with its defence platoon and a central reserve of glider pilots. Brigadier Hicks would command the western sector and the northern end of the perimeter where the KOSBs held the White House position. Brigadier Hackett, after a night's rest following his strenuous actions on Wednesday, would command the eastern side. Brigadier Hicks had suffered a severe blow on Wednesday when his

Airlanding Brigade HQ was struck by a salvo of mortar bombs directly on the room where a group of officers were assembling for the morning conference waiting for him. Four officers were killed, and others were severely wounded; Brigadier Hicks was unhurt.

There is criticism that Major-General Urquhart allowed the perimeter to develop where it did, basically where it stood in those haphazard positions on Wednesday, without giving further thought to where it could be best located for the future benefit of Operation 'Market Garden'. After the Arnhem road bridge was lost, the most important feature was the Driel–Heveadorp ferry, which was under the Westerbouwing height, at the extreme western end of the division's defended line. The ferry had been operating normally until Wednesday, when ferryman Pieter Hensen decided to cut the cable on the south side to deny the use of the ferry to the Germans and later sunk the ferry near the north bank. But the important part about the ferry crossing was that it was the only place in the area where roads came right up to the river bank on both sides of the river. If XXX Corps reached the Rhine, the strategic objective of 'Market Garden' could still be attained if ground forces could be put across the river. If the area around the ferry had been more securely held earlier, and the defence perimeter established with that point at its centre, ground forces might have been able to come up, albeit over a network of narrow roads. It is possible that a Bailey bridge or some other crossing could have been established under the protection of the airborne force on the northern bank, thus maintaining the momentum of 'Market Garden', which had been bought at the cost of so much blood. The tanks were only seven and a half miles away and had crossed the last major river at Nijmegen that day (Wednesday). Lieutenant-Colonel Myers, Urquhart's chief engineer, says: 'The divisional staff, including myself I freely admit, did not realize how important the ferry would become.' But no move was made to extend the perimeter beyond the Westerbouwing or to strengthen the defence there. So the division stayed where it was and prepared to fight its last battle in a place of only limited tactical importance.

CHAPTER 16

The Battle at Oosterbeek

The Thursday Attacks

The Germans reorganized their command structure north of the Rhine after crushing the defence at the Arnhem road bridge on Wednesday night. The forces on the west of the British landing area, the Division Von Tettau, had until now been under the control of General Christiansen's Netherlands Armed Forces Command, but Field Marshal Model subordinated Von Tettau to General Bittrich's II SS Panzer Korps so that Bittrich had overall command of all the German forces engaged against the 1st Airborne Division. Bittrich, in turn, handed over close control to Obersturmbannführer Harzer, commander of the 9th SS Panzer Division, the force pressing in on the British perimeter from the Arnhem direction. This unified command would fight the remainder of the battle from the German side. The Germans now decided that the time was ripe for an all-out attack at Oosterbeek, and orders went out that this was to commence at 8.0 a.m. on Thursday 21 September. But the German forces were of such an uneven nature, and their command system so much less than smooth running, particularly in the west where Von Tettau's HQ was likened to 'an old gentlemen's club', that real co-ordination was never achieved. Yet it was on that western side of the perimeter that the outstanding German success of the day took place.

The Westerbouwing was a popular restaurant which gave its name to a 90-foot-high bluff overlooking the Rhine near Heveadorp village.[1] This was the height overlooking the ferry which should ideally have been at the centre of the airborne bridgehead. The

[1] The present-day restaurant is about three times larger than the 1944 building.

German unit attacking the Westerbouwing was a battalion of the Luftwaffe's Hermann Goering NCO School, which had not yet been in serious action. They were good-quality troops and were supported by four French-built tanks captured in 1940. The British positions were manned by Major Tom Armstrong's B Company of the 1st Border, with three platoons in and around the restaurant on the high ground and the fourth in reserve alongside Company HQ a quarter of a mile further back on lower ground. The leading tanks emerged from the woods with little warning and turned into the restaurant grounds, with the accompanying infantry 'coming through the trees', says Lance-Corporal Ginger Wilson, 'like a crowd at a football match'. The nearest 6-pounder anti-tank gun was knocked out at once, but the most forward platoon, No. 11, opened fire and caused the Germans heavy loss until the only Bren present jammed and forced the platoon to retire. No. 13 Platoon, commanded by a Canadian officer, Lieutenant John Wellbelove, whose courage is remarked upon by several men, and No. 14 Platoon, commanded by Sergeant Tom Watson, were then heavily attacked and eventually overwhelmed, with both platoon commanders being killed and many men taken prisoner.

The tanks followed the retreat of the survivors down the slope to the company's rear position but were most effectively dealt with by Private George Everington, the Piat man in the reserve platoon. Moving from position to position – one being behind a dead cow – Everington hit three of the tanks and put them out of action. After sending his reserve platoon further back, presumably to ensure that the entire company was not overwhelmed, Major Armstrong gathered together the survivors of the three other platoons and led them back towards the Westerbouwing, an attempt that was soon stopped by heavy fire in which Armstrong was wounded and became a prisoner. Two counter-attacks were made by men of HQ and Support Companies, but neither was successful.

The action, which had taken place over several hours, ended with the Germans in complete control of the Westerbouwing, with the Border's B Company reduced to two officers and little more than one platoon, and forced to be merged into an *ad hoc* group called 'Breeseforce' under Major Charles Breese, the battalion's acting second-in-command. Breese established a new defence line nearly half a mile back from the Westerbouwing, between the local gas-works, which were occupied by the Germans, and a large house called the Dennenoord. All this resulted in the loss of the high ground overlooking the river and the narrowing of the base of the perimeter on the river bank by more than half, to less than 700 yards.

Breeseforce occupied a good defensive position and the Germans made no serious effort to advance here during the next four days. The other Border companies along the western face of the perimeter were all attacked during the day, particularly D Company, which suffered heavy casualties; but all held their positions.

The German attacks on the eastern side of the perimeter were equally as fierce as at the Westerbouwing but were all beaten off. They made no headway at all in the lower Oosterbeek area, where the infantry and artillery of Thompson Force drove off one German attack but then had to endure some fierce shelling. A feature of the day here was several casualties among artillery officers. The Light Regiment HQ received a visitor in mid-morning when Major 'Tiny' Madden, who had once been the commander of No. 3 Battery before becoming a staff officer, came on a visit with Brigadier Hackett, whose Brigade Major he had just become. Lieutenant-Colonel Thompson was wounded by a mortar bomb while Madden was there, and Madden went to assist but, while doing so, was killed by a second mortar bomb just outside Kate ter Horst's house. Soon after this, Lieutenant Keith Halliday was killed by tank fire while manning one of the artillery observation posts. The Germans were so close to the artillery positions that one of the 75-millimetre guns, Sergeant McBain's of F Troop, positioned just south of the church, was firing over open sights at the tanks. (The wounding of 'Sheriff' Thompson led to Major Lonsdale taking over command of this entire area, so Lonsdale Force came into being again.)

The Germans made another tank attack in the afternoon and Lieutenant Ian Meikle of B Troop lost his life as a result of helping Major Cain of the South Staffords. Cain, as he usually did in action, had seized the nearest Piat from the man in whose charge it was, and Meikle was up in a house, giving directions to Cain in a trench below. The tank fired at the house and Meikle was either killed or fatally wounded. The chimney-pot from the house crashed down and nearly brained Major Cain; it certainly scared the rifleman with him, who dropped his weapon and ran screaming to the rear, not to be seen by Cain again. The fearless Cain remained in that forward position, engaging further tanks until the last Piat bomb he fired blew up prematurely just in front of him: 'It blew me over backwards, and I was blind. I was shouting like a hooligan. I shouted to somebody to get onto the Piat, because there was another tank behind. I blubbered and yelled and used some very bad language. They dragged me off to the Aid Post.'[2] Major Cain recovered and returned to the front line; he was awarded the Victoria Cross for this and his many other feats over several days of action.

The other major effort against the eastern side of the perimeter was along the Utrechtseweg, the main road leading into Oosterbeek, where the front line was held by the remnants of the 10th Battalion under Lieutenant-Colonel Ken Smyth, wounded the previous day but still with his men. After coming in from their battle in the woods, Smyth's men were defending some houses on the Utrechtseweg and in one of the side streets, the Annastraat. The Germans attacked this sector on Thursday morning with the usual combination of mortar fire, armoured vehicles and infantry. The first assaults were beaten off, leaving an abandoned self-propelled gun in front of the British positions. Lieutenant Pat Glover, who had previously served in a cavalry regiment, ran out with some of his men and took over the vehicle. It was not completely disabled, and Glover was able to start the engine but he could not engage the driving mechanism, nor turn the gun towards the Germans, so it had to be abandoned again.

The Germans renewed their attack and brought up another self-propelled gun with a more forceful crew and commenced to demolish the houses occupied by the 10th Battalion men, who suffered serious casualties and could do little to prevent this punishment. German infantry followed up and close-quarter house fighting took place. Among the civilians in the Annastraat house chosen by Lieutenant-Colonel Smyth as his HQ was Mrs Bertje (Little

[2] From a post-war account by Major Cain, Airborne Forces Museum, File No. 54.

Bertha) Voskuil, who had taken shelter with twenty other local people in the cellar. Mrs Voskuil spoke good English and acted as interpreter for the British officers. She remembers 'quiet' Lieutenant-Colonel Smyth and 'buoyant' Major Peter Warr. Then the house started being hit by shells:

> They brought Peter Warr down and laid him on the ground in front of me; I was sitting with my son on a bench. Peter Warr had been hit in the thigh; it was very painful. Sometimes he was unconscious and at others he was awake and grumbling and swearing – he had every reason to. I remember him saying, 'Oh for a pint of beer.' Then they brought Colonel Smyth down, badly injured. He was also unconscious some of the time, but when he was awake he kept saying, 'Where am I?' over and over until he became unconscious again. I tried to explain to him where he was – that he was in Holland, at Oosterbeek, and that it was in the war; but he didn't understand. I think he had been shot in the stomach. There was a lot of blood, but it was so dark, with one candle in the cellar, that you couldn't see properly.
>
> Then I heard them fighting in the house above us – shots and screams; they made all sorts of noises when they were fighting, sometimes just like animals. Then the door burst open and the Germans came in. A tall British soldier jumped in front of me and Peter Warr, with his back to the Germans. I don't know whether he was trying to protect us. There were two terrific explosions then – German grenades. The British soldier was hit in the back and fell forward over me. He was dead. Many of the people in the cellar were wounded. I was hit in both legs, and my hearing was affected – and still is. The candle was blown out by the explosions. I felt down for my nine-year-old son, who had been sitting next to me on the bench. I felt his body; he didn't move, and there was a lot of blood. I thought he was dead, but he was still alive, hit by splinters in his stomach and his face. He regained consciousness next morning and made a good recovery. My husband was hit in the hand and knee. Major Warr was badly hurt again, in the shoulder. He had been hit when he reared

himself up on his elbow when the Germans came in and called out to them that he and his men were surrendering.

There was a tumult. You have no idea how much people scream in such circumstances. Then a German officer called out to me, 'Do you speak English?' I said I did, and he told me to translate quickly, to tell the English that they had fought gallantly and had behaved like gentlemen, but they must surrender now and hand over their weapons, helmets and ammunition, also their watches and identification papers.

I asked someone to take the soldier's body off me, because he was bleeding all over me. I had some suede shoes on, and his 'life blood' on the floor was so thick that the shoes were stained so badly that I threw them away. One of the British soldiers near me had his rifle but he was so nervous that the butt was rattling on the floor. You get beyond fear when things get so bad; I was icily cold when I was translating for that German, although I believed my son was dead. Perhaps it was utter despair, because a year before I had lost my younger son from a blood disease.

Colonel Smyth regained consciousness and asked to see the German commander. He came down – a dreadful-looking man with a monocle on a ribbon and with his hair parted in the middle. He asked me what 'that man' wanted. I was so furious that I said the Colonel, stressing '*the Colonel*', needed a doctor. The German officer went away, but a good doctor came, so probably it was only the appearance and manner of the German officer that was so unpleasant.

The man who was killed trying to shield Mrs Voskuil was Private Albert Willingham. Lieutenant-Colonel Smyth was paralysed from the waist down and lingered for over a month before dying.

Communications back to Brigadier Hackett had been cut during this action, and it was thought that the entire 10th Battalion party had been overwhelmed, but a few men emerged next morning. There were no battalion officers remaining; the survivors were led by Captain Peter Macgregor-Barron, an artillery anti-tank officer, who took them into reserve when Hackett relieved them on Friday night. The Germans gained no significant ground here.

*

The last major attack of the day took place at the extreme northern end of the perimeter, again at a place where there was a good access road leading into the British positions, near the Oosterbeek Hoog Station railway crossing. Just south of the crossing was the Dreyeroord Hotel – 'the White House' to the King's Own Scottish Borderers who were holding this sector. The Germans had been mounting steady pressure on this position and casualties had been mounting. Then, at 4.30 p.m., approximately a company of German infantry made a determined attack and penetrated deep into the hotel grounds. Captain Jim Livingstone, occupying a slit trench there, provides this description:

> They came across – running and shouting – to within about twenty yards of us before I opened fire. I killed an awful lot of Germans then, with my Sten. There was a big tree in front of me, and there was one German who was on his knees, wounded, but still preparing to fire. I remember David Clayhills, the Adjutant, who was standing by the side of the hotel, shouting, 'Kill the bastard!', and I did so. I'm a bit ashamed of it now, but I was bloody angry at the time. The rest of his party were already dead. Mind you, there was some of our dead there as well. When it calmed down later I can still see David Clayhills standing near this big tree, and there were an awful lot of dead Germans lying around it – twenty or thirty at least, young men mostly.

Sergeant George Barton was at his 6-pounder anti-tank gun position: 'I managed to fire only two rounds of high explosive before the Germans were upon me. My Sten then jammed, and I stood alone, in the open, waiting to be killed. But the Germans just rushed straight past me. I picked up a rifle, and Colonel Payton-Reid rallied us then, and we drove them out with the bayonet.'

There was much gallantry. Sergeant Andrew Graham, the Provost Sergeant, described in Payton-Reid's report as being 'well on the way to winning a VC', was killed manning a Vickers gun. The body of Major Alexander Cochran was found on the hotel veranda with a revolver in his hand, lying head to head with a dead German officer who was holding a Luger pistol.

Payton-Reid's rally had restored part of the position, but the main counter-attack was mounted by No. 12 Platoon, which had been posted well off to the left. Hearing the noise of fighting and seeing fugitives fleeing from the battle, Lieutenant Jim Taylor, the Canadian platoon commander, halted the retreating men, attached them to his platoon and attacked into the hotel grounds. Taylor says: 'I like to think that fixed bayonets, charging, determined Scots and a lone Canadian put fear into the German's hearts.' Private Henry McClusky, who took part in the charge, describes the result: 'I have never screamed aloud so much. It was hell. Fortunately, Jerry took to his heels and ran, leaving behind a terrible scene of dead and wounded – dreadful!'

The Borderers regained all of the lost ground, but half of the 300 men who had moved into this area two days earlier had become casualties and Payton-Reid decided that the hotel could no longer be properly defended. After the badly wounded in the aid post inside the hotel had been evacuated by jeep, the MO, Captain B. Devlin, set off with the walking wounded, including Major John Coke, the second-in-command; but this party was intercepted by the Germans and taken prisoner, though both Devlin and Coke escaped later. The flow of the battle had reached the edge of the Independent Company position on the left. Private Alan Dawson describes one effect of this:

> It was absolute chaos for half an hour. There was a KOSB lieutenant with a lot of wounds, in the neck, chest and stomach; he was covered in blood. I was told to see if 'Doc' Taylor, our medic, could do anything for him. I picked him up in my arms and carried him to the house where our Company HQ was. It was 250 to 300 yards, wooded country. There was a lot of lead flying about, but I got him there, and 'Doc' Taylor took him under his wing straight away. I went back to my position but I wished I had found out after the war whether he survived. He was only young.

This officer was probably twenty-three-year-old Lieutenant Arthur Sharples, who later died in a hospital at Arnhem.

*

The action at the White House was over by 5.30 p.m. and marked the end of that series of German set-piece attacks during the day which had been intended to start the process of destroying the 1st Airborne Division. Of the four main attacks, however, only the one at the Westerbouwing had been successful. All other sectors had held firm and heavy losses had been inflicted upon the Germans. British casualties had also been heavy, about 150 men being killed in action or dying of wounds, a figure which was only slightly less than for the recent days of wider-scale action: 200 deaths on Tuesday, 173 on Wednesday.

The weakness of the KOSB after the White House battle and the vulnerability of that northern part of the perimeter persuaded Major-General Urquhart to shorten his line there that night; it was a sector of no major tactical importance. The KOSB fell back and occupied a shorter line, and the 4th Parachute Squadron and the Independent Company were withdrawn from the Ommershof area and given as reserves to Brigadier Hackett for the eastern sector. The Independent Company was still relatively intact; so far it had lost only four of its 186 men killed and a handful wounded. When it was found that the 10th Battalion was still holding out along the Utrechtseweg, Hackett ordered the Independent Company to relieve it and he withdrew the battered 10th Battalion survivors to reserve. Major Wilson, the Independent Company commander, objected violently to the placing of one of his platoons in the exposed 'finger' which stuck out along the main road from the perimeter, but Hackett overruled him, saying that he needed a defence out in front of the Dressing Stations in the crossroads hotels. So Lieutenant Hugh Ashmore's No. 3 Platoon occupied the first few houses along the Utrechtseweg; but the houses were soon destroyed by German tanks, and Wilson ordered the survivors to fall back, much to Hackett's displeasure. Hackett was also allocated a force from the two RASC platoons which were at Divisional HQ and these, under Captain Cranmer-Byng, would plug the last gap on the perimeter's eastern side. These redeployments left the Oosterbeek perimeter in the form in which it would remain for the remainder of the battle. The Germans would gain a few yards and the odd house here and there during the ensuing days, but that basic line would be held to the end.

*

There were three other significant events of that day: the first
contact with ground forces artillery; the most costly air-supply
operation of the battle; and the parachute drop south of the river by
part of the Polish brigade.

The small No. 1 Forward Observation Unit was part of the 1st
Airborne Division whose duty was to make contact with artillery
units of the ground forces and then direct long-range fire on to
targets around the airborne positions. XXX Corps had one heavy
and two medium artillery regiments allocated to airborne support,
their signallers listening for the first contact with 1st Airborne.
Every Arnhem book has a slightly different version of how that first
contact was made, with various artillery officers at Oosterbeek
being given the credit, but it was probably achieved by Sergeant
Norman Patten, a member of the Forward Observation Unit's team
at Airlanding Brigade HQ, although he was actually some distance
away inside the ruins of a laundry among the Lonsdale Force
positions at the time. This is Patten's account; 'Sheldrake Sunray'
is the signals code for an artillery commander:

> I heard a set which sounded very much like an artillery unit
> and spent the next three hours trying to butt in on their
> broadcasts. Our communication codes were finished after two
> days, and so I had to try general codes. I said that my
> 'Sheldrake Sunray' wanted to speak to their 'Sunray'. I had
> no idea who was our senior artillery officer at that time, but
> was hysterical with trying and so used the best thing I could
> think of. This was a great stroke of luck, because our divisional
> artillery commander – Colonel Loder-Symonds – soon came
> along. He took the headset and announced himself as
> 'Sheldrake Sunray', wishing to speak with the other 'Sunray'.
> The other artillery commander knew Colonel Loder-Symonds
> personally and checked his identity by asking what his wife's
> name and favourite sport were. We were in communication
> with XXX Corps at last.

The time was 9.45 a.m. After shooting an infiltrating German with
a revolver, Loder-Symonds ordered the set – a 22 set – to be
moved to a safer place, and at 10.35 a.m. the first requests for fire

support were passed. There would be unbroken and regular contact until the end of the battle.

The artillery unit with which contact had been made was the 64th Medium Regiment, a London Territorial unit with two 4.5-inch batteries and one of 5.5-inch guns; the regiment had only moved up from Belgium the previous day and was surprised to have made such early contact. Its guns were firing from a position four miles south of Nijmegen, about twelve and a half miles from Oosterbeek. So great was the distance that the first two targets requested were just beyond the range of the guns, but some of the guns were quickly moved forward and the entire perimeter could then be covered. Among the targets known to have been engaged that day were German troops located in front of Lonsdale Force, the 10th Battalion, the KOSB and several of the Border company positions.

The second event was the daily resupply drop. These daily drops will all be described in detail later; sufficient to say here that, through a combination of bad weather and faulty liaison, Thursday's flight came in unescorted and under attack by German fighters. Twenty-eight of the 107 aircraft were shot down, and most of the supplies fell into German hands. It was the most disastrous of the air-supply missions. The third event was the arrival, after two days of postponements, of parts of the Polish Independent Parachute Brigade in late afternoon. Because of various problems, which will again be described later, only about two-thirds of the brigade arrived, dropping on the south side of the Rhine just over a mile from the nearest British positions at Oosterbeek.

So ended Thursday 21 September, the fifth day of the battle. Counting in the Polish and American casualties of the parachute drop and the heavy RAF losses of the supply dropping flight, 262 Allied men died that day – the heaviest daily loss of the entire battle.

The Siege – Friday to Monday

The Polish landing had a profound effect upon operations around Oosterbeek. Although most of the German attacks on Thursday had been repulsed with heavy loss, a fresh series was being prepared when the Poles dropped. It was an unexpected development for the Germans. They feared that the Poles might attack north-eastwards and either recapture the Arnhem road bridge, three and a half miles away, or cut the Arnhem–Nijmegen road only two miles away. Either move would cut the flow of German forces and supplies down to their front line in the airborne corridor. The fact that no such role was envisaged for the Poles was not known to the Germans, who now reassessed their priorities. Fresh troops earmarked for Oosterbeek were sent instead over the Arnhem bridge to form a blocking line to protect both the bridge and the Nijmegen road from possible Polish attack. Oosterbeek was to be left to be contained and harassed by the German units already there. The effect upon the defenders at Oosterbeek was a period of several days during which no major German attacks took place but when the Germans strove to exert maximum pressure by other means. The next part of this book will, therefore, treat Friday, Saturday, Sunday and part of Monday as one period and describe the effects of the siege-like conditions of that period on the defenders.

General Bittrich said that he would 'batter the British into submission', and by far the most effective method the Germans used to wear down the perimeter garrison was by continuous shelling and mortar fire, causing a steady stream of casualties with little chance of retaliation. Even if not hit, the relentless enervating effect of shells and mortar bombs is the aspect of this period most frequently mentioned by survivors. The Germans eventually assembled 110 artillery guns around Oosterbeek, many of them flak but capable of a dual role, and the mortars which every German infantry unit possessed were supplemented by further supplies brought in, particularly two batteries containing twelve of the dreaded Nebelwerfer multi-barrelled mortars which fired salvoes of six bombs in rapid succession. The Germans had plenty of ammunition; the war diary of Battalion Krafft, which came back into action at this time, says that its mortar platoon was given eight extra captured French mortars and supplied with fifty bombs per mortar daily. The sheer drenching effect of that German mortar fire was, above all others, the main factor in the wearing down of the defence.

The airborne men in trenches suffered the heaviest casualties, particularly from head and shoulder wounds. Trenches had to be carefully constructed, with partial head cover if possible; it was a case of 'dig or die'. Fortunately the local sandy ground made digging easy. Care had to be taken not to site the trench under a tree, because a mortar bomb striking the branches would explode and rain down steel fragments. A memorable feature of the Oosterbeek landscape was the hundreds of slit trenches which became men's homes for up to six days.

These are some typical experiences of shelling and mortaring. Craftsman Joe Roberts of the REME:

> One day I was standing in my trench during one of the quieter moments, with my head over the top, when suddenly a shell burst a few yards away. The blast from it was terrific, and I felt as though my chest had burst and all the breath was taken from my lungs. It must have done some damage internally, for I was spitting blood afterwards. It was always said that you never heard the one that hit you, and I certainly didn't hear that shell coming.

Lance-Corporal Bill Brearley of the South Staffords:

> If you have never been frightened, you should hear those multi-barrelled mortars go off and then wait for them to arrive. That's what got young Rowbottom, who was sharing my slit trench. We were getting a cooked meal on a petrol burner – soil and petrol in a tin in the bottom of the trench. We only had potatoes and lettuce out of the garden. I was under the door covered with soil; Rowbottom was on watch the other end. He shouted out that he'd been hit, but as he was still standing, I told him he was all right, not to be so daft. I thought it was soil that had hit him. But then the blood ran down his arm, off his fingers and into the stuff I was trying to boil. He'd been hit in the top of the shoulder and cut in his armpit. It was a bad wound.
>
> I dressed it for him, and he was able to walk across on his own to where there were two RAMC orderlies. I threw the

stew away. We were hard in those days, and airborne troops were particularly hard, but I couldn't eat it with his blood in it.

Lance-Corporal Maurice Weymouth of the 4th Parachute Squadron:

I was relieving the occupant of a slit trench, but unbeknown to me, he had just been hit by mortar fire and was lying in the bottom of the trench, face downwards. I fell in on him and found him dying with a massive wound in the back. In his last seconds he was softly calling, 'Mother, Mother.' I didn't know the chap and, after a lull in the fighting, he was moved away by stretcher-bearers.

In 1984 I attended a reunion at Arnhem and, in discussing with former comrades 'those' days, I mentioned the lad in the slit trench and was then not only told his name but was able to locate his grave in the cemetery at Oosterbeek. Later, while looking through some old copies of *Pegasus* – the Airborne journal – I found a sad letter written by his father asking for anyone who had news of his son to contact him. I have no doubt that many of his comrades would have responded. I am glad I didn't have to tell him that I only knew his son for the last five seconds of his life.

Staff Sergeant Bert Harget was one of a group of eight glider pilots who had been sent out on patrol in pairs and had then reassembled in the courtyard of a house:

One mortar bomb came over the roof into the courtyard; I think we had been observed. I was the only one not to be hurt. The others were all hit in various degrees and my friend Archie Harris was the worst, with nine wounds in his legs. He must have been in a lot of pain; he was talking but weak. Two of us carried him to an aid station. It was a long pull, and two more men came and helped us for the last bit. At the aid station Archie was laid, by chance, next to another glider pilot I knew – Bill Smallwood. He had been hit in the eye.

Staff Sergeants Smallwood and Harris both died of their wounds, Smallwood only a day or so later, Harris nearly two months later.

It was mortaring that caused the reserve ammunition dumps to catch fire at Divisional HQ (on Thursday) and at the Border Battalion HQ (on Friday) with the loss of much valuable ammunition. Company Sergeant-Major Les Fielding describes how he helped to save some of the Border ammunition but also lost a good friend:

> The ammunition began exploding in all directions. We managed to salvage quite a lot but, as the fire approached the plastic HE stock, I had to withdraw my little party, and within seconds there followed the loudest bang that I am ever likely to hear. The trees were stripped of their leaves in an area covering hundreds of yards. I was partially deaf for days afterwards and I was totally covered with debris in my slit trench.
>
> A dear friend and comrade, Regimental Sergeant-Major 'Bish' Pope, was fatally wounded during this particularly heavy bombardment and, even as he was dying in the emergency medical centre, he jokingly told the medical orderly to get his hair cut! I don't think that I was alone in feeling moist around the eyes when we heard that 'Bish' was dead.

The most senior of the mortar casualties was Brigadier Hackett, who was badly wounded in the stomach and thigh on Sunday. His place as commander of the eastern sector was taken by Lieutenant-Colonel Iain Murray, commander of the glider-pilot No. 1 Wing.

Another persistent trial and source of steady loss to the Oosterbeek defenders was sniping. Not only could the German snipers operate from hidden positions outside the perimeter but, because there were gaps between the Border company positions on the western side of the perimeter, snipers could infiltrate at night and take up positions in bushes or trees in the extensive Hemelse Berg area of parkland south and west of the Hartenstein and carry out their sniping role from inside the perimeter.

Here are some sniping experiences. Staff Sergeant Les Frater, a glider pilot:

Four of us moved into a corner house but, within moments, we suffered another casualty. I had seen a pilot smoking a huge pipe going into one of the rooms fronting on to the street and had shouted to warn him that he was making a lot of smoke when I heard him yell and I dashed into the room to pull him out. His face was masked in blood and, when I had wiped most of it away, I saw that he had dodged death by a whisker. The bullet had scored a deep groove right across his forehead, baring the white bone where the flesh had been torn away.

Captain Jim Livingstone of the KOSB:

The worst thing was the snipers. You couldn't pinpoint them. You would have some men in a certain position and the next thing you knew they were gone – snipers! My batman, an elderly man by airborne standards, being in his thirties, was hit by a sniper in our slit trench and badly wounded. He stood up and said, 'Now you'll have to get your own bloody food', before leaving for treatment. Another time, I had a sergeant with me in the slit and he wouldn't wear his helmet. I told him to put it on, but he said it was too uncomfortable. It wasn't long afterwards that I found his head in my lap, the top of it shot off – killed at once.

The Germans who infiltrated into the park must have been particularly brave because they were hunted down whenever they opened fire, the glider pilots in reserve at the Hartenstein usually being assigned this duty. This is one incident, described by Staff Sergeant George Milburn:

One of our pilots – I don't know his name, but he was an East Ender – had a Bren and thought he saw a sniper high in a tree. He changed his magazine for a full one, took careful aim and fired off the whole magazine of at least twenty-eight rounds. The sniper fell straight down and hit the ground like a sack of coal. Then we heard the chap on the Bren say, 'Watch him; he might not be dead.' That was the macabre

Londoner's humour. The German must have had several bullets in him and had fallen at least sixty feet. There were a few laughs at that.

Craftsman Joe Roberts met an infiltrating German sniper in strange circumstances:

I was lying in my trench, waiting for the shelling to cease, when I got the shock of my life, for standing at the top of my trench, looking down on me, was a German sniper with his arm hanging off from the shoulder and bleeding profusely. I picked up my rifle and pointed it at him, but the look on his face was such that there was no way I could have shot that unarmed man at that moment. He pointed to his shoulder in an appealing manner. I made a gesture with the end of my rifle towards the aid post, and he quickly disappeared. He had obviously been hit by one of his own [the Germans'] shells while in the trees.

Close contact between the opposing infantry in the early part of the siege was usually on a small scale and often haphazard. The German infantry rarely had a greater intention than to capture a single house which they thought vulnerable or the possession of which would give a particular local advantage. Here is an example of such an attack on the Stationsweg, described by Staff Sergeant Les Frater:

We heard a great deal of shouting and prepared ourselves for yet another attempt by the enemy to dislodge us from our house. Over they came, screaming and yelling, and this time they made it to the house. I could see them through the iron grille on the front door and fired up the hallway at point-blank range, working the bolt of my rifle as fast as I could, dodging back behind the wall to reload hastily, and then firing again. Fellow pilots, some even more exposed than I, were pouring fire into the attackers from other positions in the house. It all seemed to be over very quickly. I was amazed that we had survived once more. What had tipped the balance in our favour was, I feel, the action of the lieutenant who had dashed upstairs and, although fully exposed, dropped grenades on our adversaries from the bathroom window.

Another attack, described by Driver John Prime, had a less successful outcome. The action took place on Sunday in the RASC-held sector:

It was early in the morning; things were just beginning to stir. I looked out over the window-sill but had to duck as a burst of machine-gun fire came in. I took another careful look and there was a whole section of German infantry coming along the side of the road. One of the chaps in the back room said they were coming up the garden path too, so we were more or less surrounded. Lance-Corporal Bob Bell said we would have to break out. Our ammunition was virtually nil – just a few rounds – but we had one phosphorus grenade and one smoke grenade. Bob's idea was to lob these grenades and break out of the front door.

We lined up, ready to go, but the Germans beat us to it by throwing two stick grenades into the passageway where we were, but they must have been nervous because the grenades didn't go off. Bob Bell threw his grenade then, outside the door, and made a move through it. I was ready to follow and throw my grenade, but the moment Bob stepped out he was hit by two or three shots from a burst of fire – at least one bullet in the mouth and one in the neck. He fell back on to me, and that stopped me getting out. There were Germans coming through the back door by this time, and there seemed to be a small army at the front, all pointing their weapons at us. We had no option but to surrender. Bob was in a terrible state. I gave him a shot of morphine. We put him on a door, and the Germans let us carry him away.

Lance-Corporal Bell died eight days later.

Most infantry encounters were of a minor nature, such as this one described by Private David Warden of the 3rd Battalion, who was in the Lonsdale Force area:

I suspected that two German soldiers might have entered an unoccupied house in front of my slit trench. Shortly after, I saw a stick grenade being thrown from a broken window of this house. It exploded between Sergeant Blakeley and his end of the trench. Sergeant Blakeley was killed immediately and I was wounded in the leg. I then threw a hand grenade through the window, and the two Germans ran from the back door of the house. I opened fire with my Sten gun, as also did Private Tongs. Both Germans were killed.

Unfortunately the house caught fire when my grenade exploded and burned to the ground. When I revisited the site in 1950, I met an elderly Dutch gentleman who told me that the house had belonged to him. He fulminated against the 'German swine' who had burned his house down. I have to admit that my reply was, 'Oh dear, how terrible.'

Private Rowland Norman of the 1st Border was in a forward position when this unusual encounter took place:

A German soldier appeared in the gateway of the house holding a machine-gun in one hand and beckoning to us, but not speaking. He turned away after two or three minutes, hoping we would follow him. He was an older bloke. I was cleaning my 2-inch mortar and called out to the men in the slit trench just in front of me not to let him get away. They shot him as he was walking away, still beckoning. He was hit in the back, but that was just too bad. I put a volley of mortar bombs down on the area he had come from.

It got very quiet then and we fetched his body in. We didn't go through it for papers or anything; we just wanted to get the job over and get back into cover; we were down to six men in the platoon. We put him in an empty slit trench and gave him a rough covering of earth; it didn't take long. We stuck his machine-gun in to mark the grave and threw the helmet on to the soil.

Nightly patrols were a regular feature. Corporal Ian Hunter of the 1st Border gives this honest account of being sent with three

men to patrol across the gap between his own and the next
company:

> It was an incident of which I am not particularly proud. I had
> one man who was particularly edgy. About 200 yards up the
> road we encountered one of the supply baskets dropped that
> afternoon. I opened it and found it empty. Perhaps it was the
> creaking of the basket or the absolute silence of the night, but
> we were all very tense. I heard him say, 'I don't like this.' I
> should have told him to shut up and continue on, but instead
> we faked an encounter with the enemy, fired off several
> rounds, retreated back to Company HQ and said we had
> 'bumped' the enemy. The officer on duty suspected we had
> been firing at shadows and ordered us out again. This time,
> partly because we had let off steam and partly through shame,
> we went up the road without hesitation and made our
> rendezvous with D Company.

Patrols on other sectors of the perimeter were mostly carried out
by glider pilots, Major Alec Dale of C Squadron organizing many
of the expeditions. Staff Sergeant Len Wright describes a successful
patrol:

> Major Dale used to visit us each evening; he was great and
> kept our spirits up telling us the ground forces would soon be
> arriving. He took me out one night on what he called a 'turkey
> shoot' (he was a farmer). He collected two other glider pilots,
> and the idea was to crawl away from our lines until we heard
> German voices; they made quite a racket at night talking to
> each other, probably more scared than we were. Then we let
> fly with all we had, which wasn't much, but from all the
> shouts and screams we did some damage. Doing some attacking
> certainly got rid of some of the frustrations of being targets all
> the time.

Staff Sergeant Peter Boyle of B Squadron tells of a less successful
patrol:

We had been out for about an hour, moving slowly and carefully, but not seeing anything. We could hear a lot of small-arms fire; it was getting very hot. Paddy Boyd was out in front; I was third. I saw Paddy look round the end of a wall and saw this flash of light actually go through his head. I can remember it quite distinctly, because it was the first time I had a friend killed. He was the original Squadron Quartermaster and was everyone's friend. He wasn't a pilot; he need not have come to Arnhem, but he got a lift from someone. He fell over, twitching and obviously badly hit. Staff Sergeant Briggs went to him, only four or five steps, and then he was hit as well – three or four bullets in the back. We put some covering fire on to the houses where the shots had come from, and two of us were able to go out to the men who had been hit, but they were both dead.

One glider pilot, Lieutenant Bob Irvine, went out alone every night, hunting for Germans to avenge the death of his co-pilot, killed earlier in the battle, until he was himself killed.

The Germans mounted a number of tank attacks, always supported by infantry and sometimes by flame-throwers; two assault pioneer battalions equipped with flame-throwers had been flown into Deelen airfield from Germany. These attacks became more numerous and more serious as the siege wore on and the Germans became stronger and the defenders weaker. The Germans had plenty of tanks and self-propelled guns; it was, after all, a Panzer division which was investing the eastern side of the perimeter; some of the huge King Tiger tanks had recently arrived to reinforce that division. Private Alan Dawson describes a tank attack made when his platoon of the Independent Company was holding the exposed houses on the Utrechtseweg in front of the hotels used as medical stations; he and a comrade were manning a slit trench behind one of the houses:

There was terrific mortaring and a lot of small-arms fire and then a burst of 20-millimetre cannon fire which hit the trunk of the small tree immediately behind my head. This severed the trunk, which fell on Philpot and myself, and it was almost immediately followed by a large flash which blew me into some trees and shrubs. I couldn't see, but I was still conscious and I had enough sense to know which way to go to get out of the way. I think I heard 'Phil' groaning, but it stopped, and I can only assume that he died there.

I staggered out of the bushes and bumped into the fence or perhaps it was a shed, because I seem to remember hearing some scurrying inside and I thought they were chickens, but a young Dutchman told me after the war they were rabbits. The next thing was that I fell into an inflated rubber dinghy which had several inches of water in it. We had been out of water for some time and I remember lying there drinking from this water; it was life-saving. I was found there by a medic who was based in the Vreewijk Hotel. The dinghy had been put out by the medics under a broken gutter to collect water for the wounded. I was treated in the hotel; my label said, 'Severe shock from gun blast'.

'Phil' is the one I remember at the two minutes' silence every Armistice Day and whenever I have to talk about Arnhem.

Sergeant Alec Williams, a glider pilot of F Squadron, witnessed an attack by a flame-thrower tank:

We were dug in on the edge of a wood when we heard a tank approaching. The order was given – and passed from one trench to another – to retire into prepared slit trenches inside the wood. This we did, and the tank appeared, putting a jet of flame into each trench. A figure suddenly leaped out of a trench and raced towards us. We cheered him on. The tank sent a burst of flame which just dropped short but scorched his trousers and backside. He went past us, using words which suggested that neither our or the Germans' parents were married. He had been asleep and hadn't heard the order to retire. The only thing seriously hurt was his dignity.

It was noted that German tank attacks were always made very

carefully, and they were particularly reluctant to go as far as a corner around which there was likely to be an anti-tank gun. The anti-tank guns, not being offensive weapons, had not been of much use during the earlier British attacks in Arnhem but they came into their own during the siege, lying in concealed positions waiting for the German tanks. It should not be forgotten that seven Polish 6-pounders served in the siege, their crews supplemented by British glider pilots. The most serious tank incursion during the main siege was when three self-propelled guns and a tank came between the Border company positions into the Hemelse Berg parkland on Monday and threatened the Airlanding Brigade HQ. But a 6-pounder immobilized the tank and the SPs made no further move. The anti-tank guns had several successes but became less effective because they were very vulnerable to mortar fire and shelling, and most were out of action by the end of the siege.

Gunner George Hurdman of the 2nd Airlanding Anti-Tank Battery describes a successful engagement by a 17-pounder which was looking down an avenue of trees:

We heard the tank several times but had to lie low until it came into view. It eventually appeared about 400 to 500 yards away, coming out of the woods on to the avenue. We were ready and I don't think it moved far before we opened fire. Sergeant 'Nobby' Gee was several yards away from the gun, kneeling down in the standard position. We had one ready up the spout. Number Three was on the telescopic sight, with the crosswires on the tank. Nobby was estimating the range, calling it out, then ordered, 'Fire!' It was an easy shot – the tank almost static, dead ahead. It burst into flames. Nobby said, 'Give them another bugger, just to make sure.' I have been told since that it was an old French Renault tank that had been converted into a flame-thrower. In 1945, when I was one of those sent back to make the film *Theirs Is the Glory*, I was surprised to find our gun in the same position – with the wheels removed and part of the shield blown away – and the tank still down the avenue. You could see where our armour-piercing shell had gone through the front. Inside there were only ashes; it had completely burnt out, including the crew of course. Those were the only two rounds we fired in the whole battle.

Several members of the Light Regiment received decorations for engaging tanks with their 75-millimetre guns over open sights, and the Polish anti-tank gunners were noted to be so anxious to open fire that they exposed themselves almost recklessly and many were killed. Only one of their guns remained undamaged to the end. The hand-held Piat remained the biggest tank-killer, but ammunition became desperately short and examples of extreme gallantry were shown in tackling tanks at very close quarters. No member of the Glider Pilot Regiment won a Victoria Cross in its short history, but young Lieutenant Mike Dauncey of G Squadron came close to doing so in the Weverstraat, a diagonal road just north of Lonsdale Force into which German tanks regularly ventured to shell houses held by the infantry and also the nearby Light Regiment's artillery positions. Dauncey was commanding one end of the Weverstraat. Together with two paratroopers he captured eight Germans – a rare event in the perimeter fighting and one which raised morale among the local defenders – but was then hit and temporarily blinded in one eye by a sniper. He discharged himself from the aid post at Kate ter Horst's house to return to his position and the following day went out with one paratrooper escort to hunt a German tank. When it appeared, he ran up to it and threw a Gammon bomb which disabled the tank. Dauncey was later shot through the thigh and, later still, suffered a broken jaw when injured in the face by a grenade, all in close-quarter fighting, to find himself back at Kate ter Horst's, which was so crowded that he was left outside next to a dead casualty. A citation for a VC went all the way to Field Marshal Montgomery before being amended to a DSO.

Captain Peter Chard, an officer of the Light Regiment, might also have been considered for a VC. He was out on the perimeter near the Utrechtseweg when a flame-thrower tank attack developed. The men with him shot the German infantry accompanying the tank and Chard moved forward to stalk it with a Piat. The weapon misfired and he set off to run behind the tank, intending to throw a grenade into the turret. But he was caught by the flame-thrower and set on fire. He ran back, begging someone to shoot him to put an end to his agony. One of the official photographers photographed him, but the result was not allowed to appear in the collection made available after the war. Captain Chard was rolled in the sand to put out the flames; he lingered nearly three weeks before dying.

The Local People

The fighting took place in and around the houses of hundreds of ordinary Dutch families. They had seen the airborne landings in the distance on Sunday and then seen or heard of the passage of the first British troops through to Arnhem. There had then followed two days of euphoria. In the Stationsweg on Monday morning, the local refuse-collection truck had stopped outside No. 8 and the driver had swept up an armful of marigolds from the garden, shouting out, 'We are free, Mrs Kremer; we are free', before scattering the flowers along his route. Monday and Tuesday had been almost normal, except for more British troops, guns and vehicles passing through towards Arnhem. Then had come the reversal in fortunes culminating in the nightmare of the siege. Some people managed to get away from Oosterbeek, but most retired to the cellars, which every Dutch building had, while soldiers upstairs – German or British and later some Poles – used their homes as a battleground.

There were numerous contacts between the airborne men and civilians who rarely complained about their sudden and unexpected misfortune. Lieutenant Robert Feltham of the 1st Battalion, wounded in early fighting, left his room in one of the medical hotels at the Utrechtseweg crossroads after the room was hit by a shell. He 'limped off to find a better spot' and found temporary refuge in a nearby house in Stationsweg:

I was greeted by an elderly retired Dutch officer of artillery and his wife, who, appreciating my unwashed and rather smelly condition, helped me upstairs, removed my clothes and lowered me into a great tub of steaming water. Between them, they washed, shaved and scrubbed me until I was presentable, then levered me out, redressed the wounds which prevented me doing much for myself, gave me clean underclothing and assisted me back into my bloodstained battledress and parachute smock. It was a wonderful interlude and illustration of Dutch kindness, courage and sacrifice.

Lance-Corporal 'Ginger' Wilson of the 1st Border visited one of his wounded men in the cellar of the large house, the Dennenoord, around which Breeseforce was positioned:

A young Dutchman said he was going up for a break. His father attracted my attention and told me to keep an eye open because he thought the son was a Nazi sympathizer and might be going to signal to the Germans where our trenches were. I followed the young man out and kept my rifle trained on him, but he just leaned over the front gate for twenty minutes or so and then came back. But fancy a father having to warn us that his son may be a Nazi sympathizer!

Lance-Corporal Ken Hope of the Reconnaissance Squadron watched an elderly couple emerge from the cellar of their house:

They stood there, looking at the shambles of what was probably their 'best front room'. The old lady was sobbing, and tears streamed down her wrinkled face. The husband was quite immobile, with a blank, dazed expression on his features. I was deeply moved by this emotional scene, but remained mute. I was quite unable to communicate the compassion I felt for them. Then Henry Venes, our troop sergeant, appeared at the inner doorway. He murmured a few words of encouragement, patted the old lady on the shoulder and escorted them to the cellar steps. The old man turned again, shrugged his shoulders and followed his wife down into the cellar. It was a gesture of complete hopelessness and one I have never forgotten.

Some of the Dutch people tell their stories. Sander (Alexander) Kremer was an eleven-year-old member of the family of a retired colonial coffee-planter living at No. 8 Stationsweg, which was the front line just north of the hospital crossroads. The cellar community there consisted of fifteen people: his parents and sister Ans (Anna), Christina their maid and ten people who had come in from nearby houses. The first soldiers to occupy the house were glider pilots:

The first one met my father in the garden and said, 'Sprechen Sie deutsch?' It was a very dangerous moment. Father didn't know what to answer; anything could happen. Eventually he said in English, 'No, that is a language I hate.' Then the soldier said, 'Then you're OK.' They told us they were going to occupy our side of the street. Six or so of them came in and explained that they had to defend our house. We didn't realize the implications of this; we thought we had already been liberated and we hadn't seen a German since Monday morning. They were very polite, asking permission for everything and apologizing for any trouble they caused. They went upstairs. We moved into the cellar. It was a large, old-fashioned house with a marvellous cellar. We moved all the mattresses in and were there for the remainder of the battle.

In the days that followed, the soldiers allowed the adults up when things were quiet, but we children sneaked out sometimes as well. The soldiers were very good and never came down to the cellar, but every now and again the door opened and they threw in a handful of sweets for the children. We had plenty of food but we were not very hungry; hunger was driven out by anxiety. For the toilet we used the coal bunker and covered 'it' over with coal. One old lady in the cellar became ill; Mother told the maid to fetch the doctor – a typical, normal civilian event – 'Go and fetch the doctor.' She was gone for four hours but came back – no luck. The old lady recovered but had her bag of jewels stolen by one of our less popular 'guests'. There was also the wife of an artillery officer who was in a German prison camp and her young boyfriend. They had quarrelled with us over a mattress and spent most of the time upstairs in the dining room. She had a miscarriage during that time, without receiving any medical attention.

My parents became very well acquainted with the soldiers. They were always optimistic, always saying the Second Army would be here; they didn't use the term 'Thirty Corps'. Mother used to take photographs of them and get them to sign our guest book. The one who had spoken to us first was Louis Hagen, who later wrote a book, *Arnhem Lift*; he was an Austrian Jew and called himself 'Lewis Haig' at the time. An officer with a kilt was in charge of the row of houses and was often in and out of our house. He introduced himself as Captain Ogilvie; we got to know all their names. My mother was in correspondence with his mother for many years after the war.

Later the Independent Company came into our sector, and we had a mixture of glider pilots and Independent Company men in the house, but it made no difference; we didn't know until after the war what their units were. We got to know them all extremely well during those four days and they became lifelong friends. One of that second lot of soldiers invited me to see his trench in the front garden and said that the Germans would never see him there. But later in the day a soldier came to the cellar and said, 'Rodley's dead', and told us that he had been hit by a ricochet in the neck. He had to explain what a ricochet was; he spelled it out, and Mother wrote it on the wall. It was there for the next twenty years.

'Rodley' was Hans Rosenfeld, one of the anti-Nazi Germans or Austrians serving in the Independent Company as Corporal John Peter Rodley.

Ans Kremer, Sander's sister, describes first how she was forced to look after the four-year-old son of the Dutch artillery officer's wife and then her memories of the various airborne men in the house:

On one occasion I found the boy had disappeared and I went to find him. I had seen which way he had gone, into one of the ground-floor rooms – the best room. There was one British soldier in the room who had put what I found out later was a Bren gun, on its two little legs, on top of a very fine table my mother had had made, inlaid with all kinds of veneers. I was horrified; we had never been allowed even to touch it. We still have the table with some scratches and one or two dents on it. The boy was chattering to the soldier in Dutch, telling him that his father was a soldier too and that he had seen a lot of 'umbrellas' coming down from the sky. The soldier said something I didn't understand, but he laughed and indicated that he wanted the boy out of the way – and me too; there were Germans on the other side of the road. We went back to the cellar.

Then her memories of the airborne men:

First were the glider pilots. I was surprised at seeing men in kilts for the first time – the first, a big man with a rifle and a helmet but, to my surprise, wearing a skirt with bare knees and socks. I had never heard of a kilt. I just stared; it seemed like half man, half woman. The second was very lean and gave quite another impression, a kilt also, but his socks down around his ankles. I found out later that they were Captain Ogilvie and his batman.

Then two glider pilots came into the room from the garden, flopped down into my father's leather chairs and asked if they could rest. One kept nodding off; the other kept waking him up. Mother said, 'Let him sleep if he is so tired.' But he said, 'No; if he falls asleep I'll never wake him.' They were only there for about ten minutes before leaving, and we found out later that they were both killed.

When the Independent Company came, Rodley had the most contact with my parents. Another soldier asked my mother if the things they had heard about the Germans were really true. Mother started to explain, but the soldier couldn't believe it. Rodley got very angry and said, 'Don't even bother to try to explain; they'll never understand.' Rodley was looking at Mother's bookshelves on one occasion and remarked that one of the books was written by his commander's wife – it was *Rebecca* by Daphne du Maurier.

Later, a wounded 156 Battalion man was brought in from a

house nearby. He was Private Beasley and had been hit in the hip. We put him in the corridor. Once, when I had to step over him, I accidently kicked him in his wounded hip. I can still see his face – all cramped up with pain – but he immediately looked at me and laughed to reassure me. We civilians must have been a nuisance to them; we should have stayed put in the cellar.

Sixteen-year-old student Sjoert (Stewart) Schwitters and his family were in a house on the northern edge of the perimeter which was captured by the Germans. The occupants were all ordered out:

There were thirteen of us. We had all our luggage ready for such an eventuality, but it happened so quickly – 'Out! Get out!' – that we took practically nothing. Father went first, with a white flag and a pillow under his arm, and Mother just carried an empty cake tin; it was such a terrible situation that they just picked up the nearest thing without thinking. The Germans sent us to the west, towards the British positions, I don't know why. There was another group of seven on the other side of the street, and we joined together. We could see the British soldiers in their trenches in the gardens, camouflaged, with blackened faces and manning their weapons. They stopped firing until we passed between their positions.

We eventually got into the Steijnweg and tried to shelter in one of the houses there, but they had no room for our large party. One of the people in that house told us that a milkman's shop at the corner of Steijnweg and Paul Kruger Straat had room. The owners were NSB-ers and had been taken away earlier. The British were very polite and allowed us to stay in the cellar, which was not being used except for storage of milk churns; they were very useful later for toilet purposes.

Right over on the western side of the perimeter, twenty-one-year-old Julie Beelaerts van Blokland was in her parents' home, Hemelse Berg Hall, one of the largest private houses in Oosterbeek:

We had seen soldiers passing on the lower road, but it was not until Wednesday that the first wounded one came in, being helped by his friend. A medical orderly laid him bottom upwards on a valuable chest from the East Indies in the corridor. His wounded backside was bare, but I am from a military family and it didn't shock me.

The next ones were glider pilots who came down from the Hartenstein and started digging trenches. The officer in charge was Lieutenant John Thomson. He was the same age as myself – twenty-one; he had his birthday during the battle. They took turns to come into the house to sleep. Later another group, from the Border Regiment I think, took up position nearby. They brought a gun and set it up right outside the house. Mother went out and demanded that they move it, because it would be dangerous for all the people we had in the house. So they moved it for my mother's sake.

It got a lot worse; there was much more shelling. Many local people came and took shelter with us until we had over 300 in the coachhouse and more than fifty in the house itself. We also had twenty-five wounded soldiers eventually. We were very short of bandages and had to tear sheets up and use ladies' sanitary towels as dressings. We had no morphine, but the wounded were in the wine cellar and they were given a good drink of wine to dull the pain when their dressings were changed. My sister and I helped one soldier who was so badly wounded in the upper arm that the bone was showing. He was one of the glider pilots. His name was Reg Dance, from London; he often comes back to see me and spends the day with me. Some of the worst of the wounded were taken to the Tafelberg Hotel, but that became impossible towards the end.

To start with, everyone was saying that Montgomery would come, but we eventually realized that it was becoming a lost cause. We had a little spire on the house and we went up and could see all the way to Arnhem – the houses burning, etc.; the whole centre seemed to be on fire, including the Eusebius Cathedral. After that we made sure that we had some German wounded in so that, if the Germans won, we would not be accused of helping only the British. There were a few German snipers who had been wounded, four I think, and they were laid side by side with the British. On the Friday, a group of armed airborne men came down into the cellar. They had blackened faces and were in a bewildered state, having had no food or sleep for several days. They just wanted to rest, but Mother insisted that they took all their weapons off. They were with us for a little while, then they had to go out into the inferno, the hell that was outside – the crossfire and the moaning minnies that were going on all the time.

Sunday was the worst day. The hall was hit several times and started burning. That was when the civilians in the coachhouse more or less rushed the hall; they believed the people inside were getting better food. But the shelling and burning persuaded them to go back to the crowded coachhouse. The fires spread and our home eventually became a shell. All the wounded were carried out into the coachhouse; no one was killed. We – the family – took our two dogs, a spaniel and a retriever. I kept my hair wet in case of sparks. The only place there was room for us was on the kitchen floor of the chauffeur's house. The next day we decided to split the family into two groups and leave; splitting us into groups would, we hoped, mean that at least some of us would survive.

The Divisional Units

Divisional HQ remained at the Hartenstei Hotel, the location it had taken up as a temporary measure when its move towards Arnhem was halted on Monday evening. The divisional staff had become well settled here, and its location was a factor determining the formation of the division's defence perimeter where it was now located, instead of at a more favourable location further west. It was still a dangerous place; the eastern face of the perimeter was only 350 yards away, three minutes' steady walking time. The divisional staff had originally occupied the whole building, but shelling and mortaring wrecked most of the rooms above ground. Only Major-General Urquhart and his most immediate staff occupied an office-cum-sleeping-quarters in one part of the basement, and the vital signals sets another; the remainder was reserved for the wounded of the local aid post. There was no running water. The toilets were blocked. Most of the divisional staff now occupied slit trenches around the building and only came inside for the daily conferences.

The immediate protection of the Hartenstein was provided by the Defence Platoon – men of the Oxford and Bucks Light Infantry, who were deployed in slit trenches around the hotel. They were never needed for the final defence of their general and his headquarters but suffered four fatal casualties from shelling or mortaring during the siege. There were many other personnel loosely connected to Divisional HQ existing in close proximity – men of the RASC, REME, RAOC and Intelligence Corps, whose normal duties gradually dwindled as the battle atrophied or as their vehicles and equipment were destroyed. Some were occasionally visited by an officer or gathered up and sent out on anti-sniper patrols, but most of these men just lived out the siege in slit trenches, 'doing virtually nothing', as one says. There had earlier been a floating population of infantrymen separated from their units, but most of these had been 'combed out' and sent to the perimeter, although Captain Peter Fletcher, a glider-pilot officer, tells of cellars in a house near the Hartenstein full of men 'who had had enough and were unwilling or incapable of any more fighting'. By contrast, Lieutenant Crofton Sankey, a young Royal Engineers staff officer, asked to be allowed a more active role and was sent out to command a small infantry detachment on the perimeter until killed there two days later.

The Public Relations Unit was out in the parkland south of the Hartenstein. The journalists wrote daily accounts, and these were passed to London by their hard-working signallers to appear in the British press. Stanley Maxted made some recordings in his famous Canadian drawl; these would eventually be among the most effective witnesses of the battle. The cameramen and photographers were also safeguarding the results of their work. The negatives of many still photographs would survive, but only twelve minutes of filming would be brought back, mostly of parachute and glider landings near Wolfheze on the first day and then scenes filmed in the positions of the 1st Border on the western edge of the perimeter.

A band of Dutch volunteers had been recruited earlier in the week by Commander Wolters and Lieutenant Knottenbelt, the Dutch officers attached to the division. Only four of the volunteers were found to be members of Resistance groups; the remainder were just enthusiastic amateurs. Lieutenant-Commander Charles Douw van der Krap, a Dutch naval officer who had escaped from Colditz, came out of hiding to command the volunteers. Eef (Evert) Vellinga, a twenty-one-year-old florist from Oosterbeek, tells how he and his brother offered their services:

> We went to the Hartenstein and met another couple of chaps who also wanted to help. We didn't know that the Hartenstein was the headquarters; that was just luck. We met Commander Wolters but were not asked many questions. We all knew each other. Next day we got one of the official orange armbands. We always worked from the Hartenstein and helped by going out sometimes with the jeeps to collect the air-supply containers, and we were also able to give Commander Wolters information on certain NSB-ers. But really we did very little and spent most of the time just waiting. We started to dig trenches behind the building but we weren't very good at it. On one occasion I asked a British soldier for his shovel; he thought I was going to dig a trench for him, but we could hardly dig our own. We were given German guns and a little instruction from a couple of our chaps who had been soldiers, but we had no opportunity to use them; we only had them for a couple of hours, because there was soon an appeal for volunteers to go into Arnhem to get information about the German strength there. Twelve of us were to be sent, in pairs. We took off our armbands but we couldn't even get out of the perimeter, and none of us reached Arnhem. We called it 'mission impossible'.
>
> To sum up, most of us really didn't do much. We were just young chaps who wanted to help, but all we contributed were our good intentions, though I think some of the other chaps were more active.

On Wednesday it was decided that the situation was becoming too dangerous for the volunteers, and the opportunities for employ-

25. Maj.-Gen. Sosabowski (*centre*) and Maj.-Gen. Thomas (*right*) with Lt-Col R. Stevens, a liaison officer with the Poles, at the Valburg Conference on Sunday 24 September.

26. Brig. Hicks, Maj.-Gen. Urquhart and Lt-Gen. Browning on the day of the Arnhem investiture at Buckingham Palace, with little to smile about after a defeat and while Brigs Lathbury and Hackett, wounded and attempting to evade capture, were still in German-occupied Holland.

27. The children of Oosterbeek place flowers on the airborne graves in the War Cemetery at the second post-war anniversary of the battle in 1946.

28. The Cemetery today. The graves facing inwards, nearest to the camera, are from the airborne battle; those either side of the Cross of Sacrifice at the bottom of the Cemetery are from units fighting south of the Rhine.

29. The memorial at Heelsum, close to the southern edge of the landing and dropping zones used on the first lift. This was the first post-war memorial of the battle and was made from a 6-pounder anti-tank gun and supply containers taken from the battlefields.

30. Johannahoeve Farm, around which units of the 4th Parachute Brigade, together with the King's Own Scottish Borderers, fought on the third day of the battle.

31. The Arnhem road bridge, looking south, the direction from which the defenders hoped to be relieved by ground forces in 1944. This rebuilt bridge – the John-Frost-Brug – is similar in construction to the 1944 one.

32. The rebuilt area around the bridge ramp, looking north. The modern buildings on the left stand on the site of the building used as Brigade HQ in 1944. Gunners and glider pilots manhandled a 6-pounder anti-tank gun up the series of steps on the right when Lt-Col Frost's force reached the bridge on the first evening.

33, 34. St Elizabeth Hospital and the museum, around which the remainder of the 1st Parachute Brigade, the 2nd South Staffords and the 11th Parachute Battalion fought so gallantly to reach the bridge, are little changed today.

35. The old church at Oosterbeek, shorter now than it was in 1944 and with a new roof. A troop of 75-millimetre guns was positioned in the field alongside the church. Kate ter Horst's house is just beyond the one seen in the photograph.

36. The Hartenstein, now the Airborne Museum, the rear of the building looking down into the extensive wooded area to the south.

37. The main Airborne Memorial on open ground north of the Hartenstein.

38. The memorial to the Royal Engineer and Royal Canadian Engineer units which evacuated survivors of the battle across the Rhine, most to land close to where this memorial stands on the south bank. The rebuilt Oosterbeek railway bridge, the original of which was blown in the face of Lt Barry's platoon, can be seen in the background.

ing them usefully were disappearing. The unit was disbanded but the official report says that 'the highest praise is due to those who helped our wounded and stayed to the last'. One volunteer was killed. Samuel Swarts and a friend were taking water in a vehicle to the medical stations on the Utrechtseweg crossroads when Swarts was killed by a mortar bomb. At his wife's request, he was given an honoured grave after the war in the Arnhem Oosterbeek War Cemetery among the airborne dead.

Also present at the Hartenstein were members of the unfortunate RAF radar warning units who had come in by glider and lost all of their equipment, as well as several shot-down aircrew from resupply aircraft. Three of the radar unit men were killed by mortars or shells, one of them, Leading Aircraftman Eden, hit while attempting to repair the wireless set on one of the American signals jeeps sent to provide a link with outside air support. The American equipment was found to be wrongly tuned and was then destroyed by shelling before any useful contact could be made; it is one of the tragedies of the Arnhem operation that no better provision than this had been made for close fighter-bomber support from the experienced squadrons of the 2nd Tactical Air Force which were based so close by in Belgium. Their first flights did not appear until Sunday the 24th, and they were only of a limited nature. There were twelve Americans present near the Hartenstein: Lieutenants Geddes and Johnson and eight signallers in the signals party; Lieutenant Bruce Davies, a fighter controller who had volunteered to come with the RAF radar unit; and Sergeant Scott, the wireless operator with the 'Jedburgh' team, who had not been able to find his wireless in its container on the dropping zone. None of these Americans were able to perform their designated duties, but none were killed.

The divisional prisoner-of-war cage was in the wire-fenced tennis courts only 200 yards from the Hartenstein. The last count taken, on Friday afternoon, showed 214 prisoners, made up of 2 officers, 201 other soldiers from forty-eight different units, 10 civilians and the Luftwaffe girl captured on the first day of the operation, who was held separately in a wooden shed. More than half of the prisoners were from the Dutch SS battalion encountered during the early part of the battle. Among the civilians brought in by the Dutch liaison team were some known Dutch collaborators,

a Japanese and a Swiss. The prisoners were subjected to the
same hardships of shelling and hunger as the British soldiers.
They were given shovels and soon dug themselves well in, but
this did not prevent seven of them being killed. When there were
complaints about poor rations, Major-General Urquhart visited the
cage and explained that they were receiving at least as much as
the airborne men, and an officer prisoner soundly berated them for
grumbling.

The 75-millimetre gun positions of the Light Regiment remained
in their original positions in lower Oosterbeek, despite the fact that
their locations were now almost in the front line. Some thought was
given to moving the guns to a less exposed place, but the proposal
was resisted; the guns were well dug in, and there would have been
difficulties about tree clearance if they had moved back into the
more wooded part of the divisional area. The only movement, as
one gunner officer said, was downwards as the gun pits were dug
deeper. The regiment had flown in with 137 rounds of ready-use
ammunition per gun: 125 high-explosive, 6 smoke and 6 armour-
piercing. Only a further small amount, about forty-five rounds per
gun, was received by air supply, and stocks fell to only twenty
rounds per gun. This serious situation was saved when the ground-
force artillery came within range, and most of the targets were
transferred to them, leaving the local guns with a reserve of
ammunition as a last resort.

Just about the only thing which went right for the 1st Airborne
Division during this period was the link with the artillery of the
ground forces, which was maintained until the end of the battle.
Once contact with the 64th Medium Regiment had been made, the
link was maintained by 1st Airborne's Royal Artillery HQ operating
a heavy-duty 22 set from its headquarters bunker near the
Hartenstein, with a secondary and less effective link by a 19 set at
1st Airlanding Brigade HQ. Calls for fire could be made by any
forward observation officer and passed through to the 64th Medium
Regiment. The receiving end of the link should have been 1st
Airborne's Forward Observation Unit's rear party at XXX Corps
HQ, but it hardly entered into the picture and it was the signals
net of the 64th Medium Regiment which carried the entire burden

of the messages. At one time it was operating up to eighteen 'stations' (sets). In addition to dealing with fire support tasks from Oosterbeek, the regiment also acted as 1st Airborne Division's main signals channel to XXX Corps and to Browning's 1st Airborne Corps, whose own hastily assembled signals unit was not functioning well. The passage of so many important messages, as well as the excellent fire support by the 64th Medium Regiment, well merited the honour given to the regiment by Major-General Urquhart to wear an airborne Pegasus badge on the sleeves of its men's uniforms, but some higher authority refused to sanction this.

Supporting fire almost on demand by guns of far greater calibre than the 1st Airborne's own artillery, and by a unit well supplied with ammunition, was thus provided for the remainder of the battle. By the end of the week, the 64th Medium Regiment's own batteries had been supplemented by a 155-millimetre battery and could also call upon a 4.5-inch battery of another medium regiment and any of the three 25-pounder field regiments now coming up with the 43rd Division. A total of 160 separate 'shoots' were carried out during the siege. Many of the targets were within 150 yards of the perimeter's forward positions and on two occasions fire was brought down in the parkland behind the Hartenstein, *inside the perimeter*, when parties of German infiltrators were engaged. Those two targets were hit with extreme accuracy.

There were, however, at least two occasions when friendly positions were hit. A shoot took place early on most mornings just in front of the Lonsdale Force positions in case the Germans were forming up for a dawn attack. The airborne men there noticed that the first few shots always fell very close, 'almost in our laps', as one man says. Then, on Sunday morning, a shell fell even shorter, killing three Polish anti-tank gunners who should have been in their nearby slit trenches but were not. Another tragedy occurred when 'friendly' fire fell near the Tafelberg Hotel, which was being used as a Dressing Station, and several airborne casualties, as well as a wounded German and some Dutch helpers, were killed and others were wounded again. But there is general agreement that it was only the fire of the 64th Medium Regiment and the other units south of the river that enabled 1st Airborne to resist as long as it did.

The Medical Services

The prolonged siege placed an enormous strain on the divisional medical units. A normal medical service depends upon swift evacuation of wounded out of a divisional area to Casualty Clearing Stations where proper surgical and nursing facilities are available. 'Field Surgical Teams' were added to airborne divisions to deal with critical cases, and it had been planned that these would work in Arnhem's hospitals when captured; but evacuation by air, in this case from Deelen airfield, or by land when the ground forces arrived, was the best eventual solution. For the wounded now piling up in Oosterbeek, neither the Arnhem hospitals nor Deelen airfield were available; there was no relief by ground forces and no proper hospital in Oosterbeek.

The division's medical stations were of two kinds. Attached to all major units were Regimental Aid Posts (RAPs), simple first-aid posts staffed by a medical officer (not a surgeon) and a handful of medical orderlies who provided emergency treatment as soon as possible after men had been wounded. These passed serious cases quickly back to the Main Dressing Stations (MDSs), of which there were three, one for each brigade; it was here that surgery could be performed. But, by the time the perimeter developed at Oosterbeek, only five of the fourteen RAPs and two of the MDSs remained, and most of the surgeons, doctors and orderlies in the MDSs had been taken away as prisoners when the Germans entered the dressing stations on Wednesday. Such was the weakened organization that Colonel Graeme Warrack, the division's senior medical officer, and his remaining staff had available, with the many hundreds of men wounded in the earlier fighting being added to daily and with medical supplies running ever shorter. The result was that the wounded had to lie in the various medical stations day after day, close to all the sounds of battle, amidst shelling and enduring hunger, thirst, cold through a shortage of blankets, the stink of putrefaction, antiseptic and bodily wastes, and the quiet removal from their side of comrades who died – all without any knowledge of when the agony would be over.

The result at the RAPs was massive congestion as lone medical officers struggled after nearly a week of continuous work, often unable to evacuate serious cases because of lack of transport. The best known of the RAPs was the Light Regiment's in the former vicarage of the old church, now the home of the remarkable Mrs Kate ter Horst. Here Captain Randall Martin treated approximately 300 wounded during the siege, an exceptional number because all of the units making up Lonsdale Force had lost their own RAPs in Arnhem. Kate ter Horst and her five children were present throughout this harrowing period, her home struck by shells and shrapnel, her rooms completely full of wounded. Sapper Bill Wilson of the 9th Field Company was one of them, suffering from multiple shrapnel wounds:

> She was a very nice lady. She used to bring round cherry brandy and advocaat. A Captain Martin was looking after us, but it was a case of just cutting your boots off and patching you up. Once they had patched you up, you were just left there unless you called for help; the orderlies were overwhelmed. Anyone with a really serious wound was in trouble, and many of them died. Others were killed when the German tanks opened fire, the shots going right through the building without exploding. We all looked like Red Indians then, covered with brick dust.

On one occasion a German tank penetrated the perimeter and drove towards the house. Padre Thorne and a medical orderly, Bombardier 'Scan' Bolden, went outside with a white sheet held between them. Padre Thorne was a mild man, and it was the vigorous protests of Bombardier Bolden which persuaded the tank commander to pull back. The graves of fifty-seven dead airborne men were found in the garden after the war. They may not all have died in the RAP, because men killed nearby were probably buried there as well.[3]

---

[3] I had hoped to meet Kate ter Horst when I went to Oosterbeek in April 1992, but she was tragically killed just before my visit by a police car which mounted the pavement outside her home as she and her husband were leaving to attend a lecture in Arnhem.

The two Main Dressing Stations, to which the more serious cases were evacuated when possible, were located in groups of large buildings taken over for this purpose. The first of these were the Schoonoord and Vreewijk hotels and a large private house (now the Hotel Strijland) around the crossroads on the Utrechtseweg, which had been occupied on Tuesday. So peaceful was it at that time that an appeal was sent to local people for English-language books to relieve the patients' boredom! Lieutenant-Colonel Arthur Marrable of 181 Field Ambulance was in charge here, but the Germans had taken away all the surgeons. The second MDS occupied the Hotel Tafelberg and a large house, the Pietersberg, which was the holiday home of a Dutch businessman. The Tafelberg had actually been fitted out as an emergency hospital for local people on the outbreak of war in case Oosterbeek became cut off from Arnhem. As soon as the airborne landings took place, Doctor Gerrit van Maanen, the municipal medical officer, ordered beds to be prepared and local nurses to report for duty, but nearly all their patients were British not Dutch. There were some airborne surgeons present. Operations took place on two stretchers laid on a billiard table, after a shell brought down the ceiling of the operating theatre. Major Rigby-Jones was in charge here. Evacuation of wounded to the dressing stations was by jeep. Because they were either in the front line or close to it, evacuation was, uniquely, *forward* into the fighting area, not to the rear. The Germans were usually good at allowing safe passage; a jeep, with its Red Cross flag, would get ready; then whistles blown by the British and replied to by the Germans would bring a short break in the firing.

All of these buildings were likely to be struck by stray shells and bullets as fighting took place directly outside them. Patients were wounded a second or even a third time and some were killed. A German tank drove up to the Schoonoord and its commander started to take photographs, until someone in a nearby position shot him. Another tank commander dismounted to apologize after accidently firing a shell into the Schoonoord. It had smashed the arm of Father Bernard Benson, a Catholic chaplain. The German officer, also a Catholic, stayed to hold Father Benson's other hand while the arm was amputated, but the priest died later. Also in the Schoonoord, a soldier of the Independent Company coming in from his position outside was caught having sexual intercourse with one of the Dutch auxiliaries when they thought the attention of others was distracted by mortaring. The girl was dismissed by the Dutch doctor but Colonel Warrack, in dealing with the soldier, decided that it was 'emotional release' and no further action was taken. By contrast, there was an Independent Company Bren position in the garden of Quatre Bras, another building on the crossroads. Lieutenant John Procter, a wounded 10th Battalion officer in the Vreewijk, watched with admiration the way this exposed post was kept manned through several attacks: 'I thought they absolutely typified the individual performance of the ordinary men of the division.' When the artist David Shepherd was preparing his famous painting of the crossroads, Proctor suggested that the men of the Bren be included. One of them was Private John Avallone, who was killed there on Sunday.

The wounded, particularly the serious cases, had a dreadful time in all of the medical stations. One man said that conditions were 'hellish, particularly the noise from a shellshock case who screamed with every shell and mortar explosion'. A delirious officer caused such distress to those around him that it was thought 'no bad thing' when he was killed by a mortar fragment. Signalman Bill Carr describes how a wounded man near him was hit again:

I saw that a bullet had gone straight through his helmet. I lifted it off his head and found some bloody tissue in it which I took to be his brains. He seemed obviously lifeless and I covered his face with a blanket. We had with us two German prisoners, one an unpleasant, stoical SS grenadier and the other a young lad who seemed to be barely sixteen. Some time later, the young German came to me in a very agitated manner and told me the soldier who had been shot was still alive. When I looked, I saw that the blanket was indeed rising and falling with his deep breathing. I called a medical orderly, but he told me that there was nothing that could be done for him, and the breathing gradually subsided.

Glider-pilot Staff Sergeant John Kennedy tells of the sufferings of the patients on either side of him in the Tafelberg:

One was Andrew Milbourne, a Geordie para who was suffering from dreadful injuries to his hands and face. The orderlies could do little to keep him drugged, while the unmistakably disgusting smell of gangrene grew hourly stronger. On the other side was a little Dutch boy, about ten or eleven years old. He was a heroic little fellow who had been running the gauntlet, taking the names of the wounded in the Tafelberg to the Red Cross and doing a bit of spying on the way back; he let us know of enemy dispositions. He had lost a leg and was lying back quivering with shock and trying hard not to whimper as they bound his dreadful wound. No soldier was braver than he.

(Andrew Milbourne survived, with a rebuilt face and two false hands, and was later the subject of a *This Is Your Life* television programme.)

The Germans came into the dressing stations several times. One of the medical orderlies at the Tafelberg was Private Tom Bannister:

The SS marched all the orderlies outside and lined us up with hands on heads near the garage that we were using as a mortuary. It looked as though that was it. I was standing next to a chap named Stan Biggs, and he looked across to me, grinned and said, 'Well, there is one thing, Tom; they won't have far to carry us.' With humour like this at that time, what can you say?

The Germans retired, but Private Biggs was killed on the last day of the siege and his body joined the dead at that mortuary.

Private Roland Atkinson was a wounded 156 Battalion man at the Schoonoord:

A Tiger tank pulled up just outside, and out jumped an officer who proceeded to enter the dressing station with a vicious-looking bodyguard. He looked what the Germans would call a typical Nordic type – blond hair, blue eyes (a little bloodshot!) – and as he walked down between the rows of wounded he brandished a Sten gun. He didn't look at all pleased; in fact, he looked positively menacing. He demanded to see our doctor and asked him if he had any German wounded. The doctor said he had quite a lot in the rooms above and they were being treated as well as were the British. The group proceeded upstairs and we all hoped the doctor's answer was accurate. In about half an hour the Germans came down, the officer with a huge smile on his face, and walked down the lines of wounded British paras giving each a Woodbine cigarette. He shook hands with the doctor, clicked his heels together, disappeared into his tank and rumbled back down the road towards Arnhem.

By Sunday morning there were approximately 1,200 wounded men, British and Germans, in the perimeter. Accommodation was packed and medical supplies were almost exhausted. After consulting Major-General Urquhart, Colonel Warrack decided to ask the Germans if they would allow the wounded to be evacuated from the fighting area. He was driven with the Dutch officer, Commander Wolters, who would act as interpreter, and eventually met General Bittrich, who agreed to a truce and an evacuation. Warrack was much impressed by the German commander's courtesy and hospitality – refreshments were provided; it was 'like a fairy tale' after the hell of Oosterbeek. The evacuation commenced that afternoon, but only from the Main Dressing Stations. Jeeps and German ambulances took away 250 stretcher cases, mostly to Apeldoorn, while 200 walking wounded set out to cover the two miles to St Elizabeth Hospital in Arnhem. All went well, much credit being given to the Germans for their humane treatment of the wounded. The evacuation was resumed next day, but about 500 wounded at the Regimental Aid Posts had to remain inside the perimeter until the end of the siege.

Colonel Warrack had called in at St Elizabeth Hospital when arranging the evacuation and found the British wounded there being well treated; they were in beds with sheets! But a few hours after his visit an atrocity was committed there. Captain Brian Brownscombe was the South Staffords' Medical Officer; he was a redoubtable character nicknamed 'Basher' who had won the George Medal saving his batman's life in Sicily when their glider landed in the sea. Later on Sunday, an SS man shot and killed Brownscombe just outside the hospital. The culprit was tracked down after the war and stood trial at Munich in 1964. He was Karl-Gustav Lerch, a war correspondent attached to the SS. His defence was, first, that he was acting under the orders of an SS officer and, second, that he was drunk. He was executed.

It is time to conclude this description of the main part of the Oosterbeek siege up to Sunday evening. No significant amount of ground was lost after the fierce attacks of Thursday and the readjustments to the perimeter defences that night. The casualty rate dropped. Men had been dying at an average rate of 200 a day earlier in the week, but during the period of Friday to Sunday this figure fell to less than a hundred, and a rising proportion of these were men dying of wounds received earlier.

Most men bore the strain well, but among the few who did not were two relatively senior officers. One had suffered harrowing experiences both earlier in the war and at the start of this battle, and now broke down with what might be called 'battle fatigue'. The other spent almost the entire time in the cellar of a Dutch house; other officers of his unit told the Dutch owners after the war of their embarrassment at his boasting of exploits in the battle. Staff Sergeant George Milburn witnessed this incident: 'The Borders nearby had just repelled an attack when there appeared a young airborne lad, with rifle at the slope, calmly walking down the path which leads from the Hartenstein towards the river, singing, "I do like to be beside the seaside". I think he was bomb happy.'

There was compassion, even among enemies. Private Bill Campbell of the 1st Border:

One day a German soldier brought in one of our men – a para badly wounded in the neck and dragging his feet. The German was supporting him and brought him right into our position. We let him pass through, on to someone behind us where he handed over the wounded para, but then he walked back through our position to his own lines. I suppose we could have kept him as a prisoner, but we were flabbergasted and let him go back to his own side.

There were moments of relief. Sergeant Alec Williams was a glider pilot in a house on the perimeter:

> Just when we needed a boost, it happened. During a lull, we heard someone in the next house (one of ours) playing the piano – a selection of popular tunes. I can't explain it, but we felt like singing; only a laid-back airborne Brit would play the piano within yards of the enemy. Sadly, the Germans didn't appreciate it, because after about half an hour a self-propelled gun came up and started shelling the house, and that brought the piano playing to an abrupt end.

That story is similar to the one following, although the two locations were at opposite ends of the perimeter. This is Gunner 'Dicky' Bird of the Light Regiment, who found a grand piano in a house:

> Now, it had always been my ambition to play on a grand, and here was temptation that could not be resisted, so I sat down at the keyboard and was halfway through 'In the Mood' when, with a mighty crash, what was left of the windows, with the adjacent plaster, fell on me and the piano. Obviously, the German taste for music was different to mine.

Optimism was failing, however. Captain Peter Fletcher, a glider pilot, in concluding a written contribution, says: 'I'm afraid that, as expected, I have quite failed to portray anything of the atmosphere, of the feeling of the noose around us being steadily tightened, and the damage to nerves of incessant bombardment, or of the frustration at the failure of XXX Corps to arrive.' And Corporal Alan Sharman of the Independent Company says: 'As a private soldier you get to know that, if it goes on too long, it's going wrong. If it goes on even longer, then you know it's going really wrong.'

CHAPTER 17

The Resupply Flights

One of the most neglected aspects of the Battle of Arnhem is the story of the resupply operations. In the absence of swift relief by ground forces or the seizure of a nearby airfield, an airborne force required substantial supplies to be delivered by parachute drops. A preliminary resupply had taken place on Monday, when thirty-three Stirlings and a number of gliders brought in supplies, but the main effort, involving more than a hundred aircraft each day, would take place from Tuesday to Saturday, with flights being made on four of those five days. The aircraft to be used were those of the RAF squadrons which had earlier towed the 1st Airborne Division's gliders to Arnhem, with the exception of the Albemarle and the Halifax squadrons. The Albemarles only had a limited load-carrying capacity and were about to be phased out of service; the Halifaxes were not used because their capacity was not as great as that of the Stirlings and Dakotas and, also, they were in limited numbers and needed to be conserved for towing the heavy Hamilcar gliders in any future airborne operation.

So the burden fell on the six Stirling squadrons of No. 38 Group and six Dakota squadrons of No. 46 Group. Supplies were carried either in metal containers, which were stowed in the Stirling's bomb-bay or wing-root positions, or in large panniers (like laundry baskets) pushed out of the fuselages of each aircraft by the Royal Army Service Corps despatchers carried for this purpose. The Stirling could carry 2.64 tons of supplies, the Dakota 1.97 tons, neither payload including the weight of containers or panniers. The aircraft allocated to the next few days could thus carry 390 tons of supplies, equivalent to 130 of the RASC's standard 3-ton Bedford trucks rolling into the divisional area each day – if all the aircraft arrived and if all the supplies fell in the correct place.

Tuesday

The RAF squadrons and the RASC supply and air despatch companies were all ready. It was not a 'maximum effort'; most of the Stirlings would take part, but the two Dakota squadrons at Blakehill Farm, 233 and 437 (Canadian), had reverted to normal transport work, taking fuel and freight to Belgium and France and returning with wounded. The number of aircraft taking part in the resupply to Arnhem was 101 Stirlings and 63 Dakotas. The pre-packed containers and panniers had been brought in from the supply dumps in RASC vehicles, one lorry-load for each aircraft, and then fitted with parachutes and loaded into or on to the aircraft by the 454 despatchers who would be making this flight. So great was the interest aroused by the Arnhem operation and the novelty of this first large-scale resupply flight that several staff officers and other people asked to fly as passengers. One passenger was Bob Francis, a Canadian war correspondent who had twice taken off for Arnhem in aircraft which had been forced to turn back. He would get his story this time.

After a delay caused by bad visibility, the aircraft took off in the early afternoon. The route taken today, and on the later resupply flights, was the southern one: Manston–Ostend–Ghent, then turning over Belgium and flying up the airborne corridor. The first casualty was suffered in dramatic fashion soon after the Belgian coast was crossed. The Stirling of Flying Officer Ron Sloan, of 295 Squadron, had been keeping company with another Stirling flown by the new crew of Flight Sergeant Ray Hall, with Hall flying on Sloan's port wing. They must have been just north of the prescribed route, just a little too close to the German front line. Ron Sloan describes what happened:

Suddenly – flak! Out of the corner of my eye I saw Flight Sergeant Hall's aircraft suddenly dip a wing. His starboard wing came up almost vertical and, for a split second, he looked for all the world like a fighter aircraft doing a 'peel-off'. There was an urgent call from our rear turret – 'He's hit!' 'Watch him,' I ordered. 'See if any bale out.' Another urgent call from our rear gunner gave us the information that it had gone straight in and exploded. No one jumped.

So violent were the crash and fire that the body of only one of the eight men killed could be identified.

The formation flew up the corridor at about 1,500 feet. Another Stirling, from 190 Squadron, was shot down by flak, and again all the crew were killed. A fighter escort was covering the force, and no German fighters appeared. The aircraft came down to a recommended dropping height of 900 feet on approaching Arnhem, and the crews started looking ahead for the clearing in the woods, measuring little more than half a mile square, outside Arnhem on to which they had been ordered to drop the supplies. But a veritable hail of flak had to be flown through to reach this point. The Germans had brought in a brigade of five flak batteries from the Ruhr specifically to engage the supply aircraft which they knew must inevitably arrive. No Allied fighters had been allocated for flak suppression in this area, and the Dakotas and Stirlings, flying so slowly and so low, were ideal targets. The Panzer units also had many dual-purpose guns, and even small-arms fire was effective. The tragedy of what follows is that the supplies would fall in the wrong place. A message that the supply-dropping point was not in British hands and nominating another place had not reached England. The aircrews had been given strict orders to ignore any ground signals – which the airborne men were frantically displaying – at any other point, because they might be German decoys. So down went hundreds of containers and panniers, straight into German hands.

The Dakotas came in first. Four of them were shot down; the probable sequence in which they fell is known. Two went down almost at the same time from the front of the Dakota force. A 575 Squadron aircraft crashed on a German military cemetery on the northern outskirts of Arnhem. The second Dakota was lost in dramatic fashion. A German flak unit had arrived only that morning and set up four 20-millimetre guns between the trees lining the road running alongside the dropping zone. The local Dutch families were ordered into the cellars of their homes. Pilot Officer Len Wilson's 271 Squadron Dakota was hit by flak, maybe not by these guns. The navigator and three of the despatchers bailed out, and the Dakota then passed only a few feet above the heads of the German gunners to crash alongside a house close to the guns. A

German soldier came into the cellar of the nearby house and told the Röell family that the noise of the crash which had shaken them was 'an aircraft with a very brave pilot' who had tried to crash on to the guns and had only just failed. Many years later, Lex Röell, the son of the family, attempted to obtain the award of a posthumous Victoria Cross for Pilot Officer Wilson, but without success.

The third Dakota to go down was that of a Canadian, Pilot Officer Brock Christie, and his 48 Squadron crew. He managed to make a belly-landing across the railway branch line which ran from Wolfheze to Deelen airfield. Three of the despatchers were injured by the panniers being flung about inside the fuselage during the landing, and the fourth elected to stay with them; all became prisoners. The four aircrew escaped into the wood; two were eventually caught, but Christie and his co-pilot evaded capture.

The pilot of the fourth lost Dakota was Flight Lieutenant David Lord, known as 'Lummy' Lord, a veteran pilot of 271 Squadron who had won the DFC flying Dakotas in India and Burma. Lord's aircraft was hit in the starboard wing by flak on the approach to Arnhem and the engine was set on fire. The rollers along which the supplies were to be pushed in the fuselage were also damaged and the navigator went back to help clear these. Temporarily without a nagivator, Lord then formated on another Dakota, that flown by Wing Commander Basil Coventry of 512 Squadron. The story can now be taken up by Flying Officer Stan Lee, the wireless operator in the 512 Squadron aircraft:

I was standing with my head in the astrodrome, keeping a look-out, when I was aware of an aircraft closing in on us. He came right in on our starboard wing-tip, with the starboard engine on fire. He was there for ten minutes. We crossed over Arnhem – I could see the bridge clearly – and descended to 550 feet to approach the supply-dropping point. There were no signals from the ground and we were being fired at from the dropping zone; we could even see the guns and the men on the guns. This Dakota was on our wing-tip all the time, obviously going to drop when we dropped; I was terrified that its wing would break off and it would lurch into us.

As we crossed the dropping zone the Skipper said, 'Delay

the drop. Delay the drop.' We knew that the landing zones of the first and second days were going to be used by some of our other aircraft towing gliders on this day, and he wanted to drop the supplies there. We turned sharply to port and flew to the second zone and dropped our supplies there; so did the other aircraft. Then a white aircrew parachute came from it, and at the same time the wing broke and the Dakota seemed to fold around the starboard engine, with the two wing-tips almost meeting. The wing then dropped off, and the rest of the aircraft half-rolled on to its back and dived into the ground. There were no more parachutes.

The man who escaped by parachute was Flight Lieutenant Harry King, the navigator, who was flung out when the aircraft broke up. He joined up with men of the 10th Battalion but became a prisoner with them the following day. David Lord and all of the others died when the plane crashed just north of Reijers-Camp Farm. Flight Lieutenant Lord was awarded a posthumous Victoria Cross for his courage in carrying on with his Dakota on fire and making two attempts to deliver his supplies, the only RAF VC of the Arnhem battle.

The Stirlings suffered the same punishment when it was their turn to drop, and six were shot down or were so badly damaged that they crashed soon afterwards. One was the aircraft of Wing Commander Peter Davis, the commander of 299 Squadron. He died at the controls of his Stirling when the containers of petrol in the bomb-bay caught fire after the aircraft was hit. Another Stirling to go down was piloted by Squadron Leader John Gilliard of 190 Squadron, who had flown in North Africa and declared the Arnhem flak to be 'not a patch on Benghazi' before his aircraft was hit. He also died at the controls of his aircraft. One Stirling attempted a belly-landing on the Rhine; men on the ground watched it 'apparently successful at first, then slowly somersaulting and bursting into flames'; the aircraft came to rest on the south bank of the river. This was the Stirling of Flying Officer Geoff Liggins of 299 Squadron. Several of the crew were badly hurt and looked after by the people of Driel village.

A further Stirling crash-landed on the return flight in the

airborne corridor but the crew met up with friendly forces; and two Dakotas and a Stirling made emergency landings in Belgium, where a wounded RASC despatcher was rushed to hospital but failed to survive. Of the aircraft which returned to England, no less than ninety-seven, two-thirds of them, had suffered flak damage. Nine Stirlings and four Dakotas containing exactly 100 aircrew, despatchers and passengers had been shot down. Fifty-two men were dead or due to die of wounds; thirty-nine were prisoners of war; three would evade capture; and six parachuted into the Oosterbeek perimeter. One of two 38 Group staff officers who came as passengers, Squadron Leader Cecil Wingfield, was killed; the other, Squadron Leader F. N. Royle-Bancroft, parachuted into the Oosterbeek perimeter. Among the dead was the only Royal Navy man to die at Arnhem. Air Mechanic Len Hooker was on leave when his friend, Warrant Officer K. Prowd of 196 Squadron, agreed to take him as a passenger in his Stirling. The sailor died when the Stirling was shot down, but the pilot survived. Two officers from Airborne Forces HQ, Brigadier Money and Lieutenant-Colonel Darling, who flew to observe the operation returned safely. There would not be many volunteer passengers in following days after news spread of the serious opposition met on this day.

A later section of this chapter will describe the attempts by the airborne men to recover the supplies dropped at such heavy costs.

Wednesday

The experiences of that first major resupply operation were repeated in most of its details on the following day. The aircraft involved were 100 Stirlings and 64 Dakotas, from the same squadrons that had flown the previous day. The outward flight proceeded well. Only one aircraft, a Stirling of 196 Squadron, was lost, crash-landing among friendly forces in the airborne corridor with no casualties. The location of the new dropping point requested by 1st Airborne had reached England; it was a road junction 200 yards west of the Hartenstein. But the planners only sent 131 aircraft to that place; the remainder, 33 Stirlings, were sent to LZ-Z, the large open area south-west of Wolfheze used as a glider landing zone on the first day of the Arnhem operation. The reason for this division of effort may have been to avoid congestion over the main dropping point, but LZ-Z was two miles from the nearest part of the Oosterbeek perimeter and all of the supplies dropped there fell into German hands. Two Stirlings were lost from that part of the operation.

The aircraft in the main drop met the usual heavy anti-aircraft fire and the exact dropping point was not easy to spot. Warrant Officer Bernard Harvey, in a 299 Squadron Stirling, says: 'We were briefed to drop on orange candles but we found orange candles all over the place. So we just pitched the stuff where we thought best as long as it was on the far side of the Rhine. That was the best we could do.' Warrant Officer Arthur Batten in a 190 Squadron Stirling: 'Things had changed dramatically and recognition from an aircraft was practically impossible. You could see men waving and sheets being laid out but you had lost them in smoke or woods by the time you came round again to drop.' Warrant Officer Joe Corless, in a 299 Squadron Stirling, describes typical difficulties:

> We got a very hot reception with all kinds of rubbish coming up at us. The Skipper was taking violent evasive action. We managed to drop the containers, but one of the hampers jammed in the hatch and the wireless operator and flight engineer were jumping up and down on it in an effort to free it when we were hit in both elevators, rear turret and fuselage, with both rear gunner and flight engineer being wounded, fortunately not too seriously. Combined with the evasive action, we were by now in a very unhealthy nose-up attitude, with both the pilot and myself doing our utmost to raise the air speed, which was fast approaching stalling speed. We managed to achieve this, got rid of the hamper and limped home feeling that it had been our lucky day.

Other crews were not so fortunate. Eight of the lumbering Stirlings and two Dakotas were shot down around Oosterbeek or were so badly damaged that they crashed while flying back down the airborne corridor. There was an unusual further aircraft casualty. A photographic-reconnaissance Spitfire of 16 Squadron, based near

Amiens, had been detailed to photograph the supply drop. But the Spitfire was hit by flak, and its pilot, Flight Lieutenant Gerry Bastow, had to crash-land among the gliders on one of the landing zones. He managed to avoid capture.

The surviving aircraft flew home. Three more Stirlings were so badly damaged that they had to force-land in Belgium, and another carried back to Keevil a dead bomb aimer – Flying Officer Karl Ketcheson, a Canadian, who had refused to release the supply containers on the first pass over the dropping point because he could not be sure they would fall in the correct place and was killed on the second run by the only bullet which struck the Stirling.

It had been another day of heavy loss. Twelve Stirlings and two Dakotas were lost, 8.5 per cent of those despatched. No. 196 Squadron at Keevil lost six of the seventeen Stirlings it despatched, but most of the crews were safe. One of those in the lost aircraft was a *Daily Telegraph* correspondent, Mr Townshend, flying in a 190 Squadron Stirling, but he also avoided capture. This was, however, one of the most successful of the air-supply operations, with a reasonable proportion of the supplies, although still less than half, being recovered by the troops at Oosterbeek.

Thursday

Thursday 21 September found the air-supply organization severely stretched, with large numbers of damaged planes and shortages of aircrews and despatchers. But the men at Oosterbeek were still desperate for supplies and a substantial effort was planned. The Stirling squadrons could only provide 64 aircraft, compared with 100 the previous day, but 46 Group almost maintained its previous day's effort, providing 53 Dakotas by replacing 512 and 575 Squadrons at Broadwell with 233 and 437 (Canadian) Squadrons at Blakehill Farm, which had been making supply flights to Belgium for the past two days. A message from Oosterbeek asked for the supplies to be dropped at the Hartenstein itself, a measure of how narrow the airborne holding now was, and the crews of all 117 aircraft were directed to that one place. The force was to fly in four well-separated waves spread over two hours.

All went well until the two rear formations were flying up the corridor over Holland. The provision of fighter escort had been noticeably patchy during the past two days, but no German fighters had been seen. The escort was again only intermittent on this day. The reason for this was that most of the American fighter units in England were required as escort for a major American bomber raid to Germany and almost half of the RAF fighters in England were grounded by bad weather. General Brereton had insisted that, for the sake of simplicity of control, the large Allied fighter force at airfields in France and Belgium was banned from operating over the airborne corridor. Flight Lieutenant Ted King was a Spitfire pilot in one of the units grounded in England, 131 Squadron at Friston, near the Sussex coast:

> We knew how bad the situation was out there and we wanted to help. We had a very good CO and he would have got us out there if it was possible, but it was rain and low cloud right down over the cliffs – pure non-flying weather. We were sitting in the hut, playing cards, but not having any real interest, feeling utterly useless. This was to my mind a period when everything was against us, almost as though God was against us, and we couldn't give of our best and go and support the chaps in the transport squadrons who were being hammered into the ground. We realized that the whole operation was falling around our ears. That was the worst time in the war for me.

A large force of German fighters took advantage of a substantial gap which appeared in the escort cover, attacking the third and fourth formations of supply aircraft as they flew to Oosterbeek, all Stirlings, and catching the first two formations, the Dakotas, as they returned after dropping their supplies.

It was the only successful German fighter interception of the Arnhem flights. Focke-Wulf 190s and Messerschmitt 109s from airfields in Germany were involved. The flak units around Oosterbeek were as active as ever and the combined result was a disaster for the supply squadrons. Twenty-seven aircraft – fourteen Stirlings and thirteen Dakotas – were shot down in roughly equal proportions by fighters and flak, and a further Dakota, from 48 Squadron, crashed with the loss of all on board when its wing broke off under the impact of a supply pannier dropped from above over Oosterbeek. In addition an RASC despatcher was flung to his death from the doorway of a 233 Squadron Dakota, presumably when the aircraft was taking evasive action while under attack.

There is, unfortunately, not space here for more than a few fragments from the varied tales of death or survival of men in those doomed aircraft. Pilot Officer Dennis Peel of 295 Squadron managed to save all of his regular aircrew when he crash-landed his large Stirling in a small clearing in the woods near Ede, but found that the two despatchers had been forced by a fierce fire in the fuselage to jump to their deaths at too low an altitude for their parachutes to deploy. Flight Lieutenant Alex Anderson of 190 Squadron ditched his Stirling in the wide river Maas, but the aircraft sank quickly and only three men reached the dinghy. Flight Lieutenant Jimmy Edwards of 271 Squadron, who became the famous showbusiness personality, was just opening his sandwiches on the way home when a Focke-Wulf 190's cannon shells set his Dakota's engines alight. He was all ready to order his crew to bale out when he was told that three of the despatchers were too badly wounded to jump, so he stayed on board and suffered burns while making a forced landing and saving the despatchers' lives. And so on, and so on.

The remnants of the force flew home. Three Dakotas made forced landings in Belgium. On reaching England, Captain C. H. Campbell, one of several South African pilots flying Dakotas, attempted to land his crippled aircraft on a marsh on the Essex coast, but the attempt failed and there were no survivors. It was the fifth aircraft to be lost that day from 48 Squadron at Down Ampney. No. 190 Squadron from Fairford lost no less than seven out of its ten Stirlings taking part in the operation, including the squadron commander, Wing Commander Graeme Harrison, who was among the dead. Twenty-nine aircraft had been lost, almost a quarter of the force despatched. The perimeter at Oosterbeek was now so small that few of the supplies reached the desperate airborne men.

The Final Flights

Although the weather improved on the following day, Friday the 22nd, and 123 aircraft were made available for another flight, Airborne Corps Rear HQ in England made no request for help, probably because it was hoped that relief at Oosterbeek by ground forces might be imminent. This gave the squadrons and air-despatch units the desperately needed opportunity to repair damaged aircraft, rest crews and receive reinforcements. The respite was short-lived. Saturday brought the news that 1st Airborne was 'in desperate need of air reinforcement', and the 73 Stirlings and 50 Dakotas which had been prepared for the previous day were ordered up. There was much apprehension after the severe losses of the last flight; the Briefing Officer at Blakehill Farm seemed 'very worried and was almost apologetic'.

A continuous fighter escort cover was provided this time, and the formations flew safely almost up to Oosterbeek. The Germans used a different tactic, putting up a general flak barrage across the approach path rather than engaging individual aircraft. Three Stirlings and two Dakotas were shot down around Oosterbeek and three more Stirlings came down later in the airborne corridor. There was heavy loss of life in four of the five aircraft shot down around Oosterbeek, but the pilot of the fifth made a good forced landing on the meadows near the railway bridge over the Rhine. The aircraft was a 48 Squadron Dakota flown by Pilot Officer Ralph Pring. The story is told by Flight Sergeant Derek Gleave, the navigator

> There were flames in the cockpit, and I was burnt on the hands and face. The pilot was absolutely marvellous. He saw this field and said, 'I'm going to land there.' He must have been burned as well. I was struggling to open the escape hatch, which was right above me. I got it open all right but that caused a further rush of fire through the cockpit area, although we were nearly on the ground by then. That's where it becomes very vague in my mind, but Ralph must have made a very smooth landing.
>
> I was the first out, and the wireless operator and the second pilot followed me. As far as I know, the pilot never got out;

he may have been wounded by the flak. The three of us moved away from the aircraft because it was burning fiercely, but some Germans opened fire on us. All three of us were hit. Springsteele, the wireless operator, was killed at once; I was hit by two bullets in the abdomen, and Colman was hit several times. He told me to wave something white, but I only had a blue RAF handkerchief.

Some German medics eventually came up. The other Germans were still firing at someone, and the medics got annoyed with them and shouted at them to stop. Colman and I were taken by ambulance to St Elizabeth Hospital. Colman was still quite coherent, despite all his bullet wounds. A German surgeon operated on me and removed the bullets, and I was put in the basement with the airborne casualties. There were some terrible cases there – men shouting that they wanted to die, etc. – it was terrible. I asked about Colman, but Father Egan, a Catholic padre, told me that he was dead. There was a brigadier in the next bed to me later, without his rank badges; the medics were hoping to get him away to prevent a high-ranking officer becoming a prisoner.

The burning Dakota must have been the funeral pyre for the pilot and for two of the four RASC despatchers; none of their bodies were found.

More than half of the aircraft returning to England were damaged. Warrant Officer Knivett Cranefield, a pilot of 233 Squadron, had his leg split wide open, with white bone visible and blood gushing out. His co-pilot was not fully qualified on Dakotas, so Cranefield refused offers of morphia to remain conscious for the landing. There was a happy ending; the RAF sister who nursed him in hospital became his wife.

The resupply flights from England were now abandoned, the cost too high, the effectiveness too little. But one last effort was made. On Friday 22 September, Air Commodore L. Darvall, commander of 46 Group, concerned at the heavy losses in his unarmed Dakota squadrons, flew to Belgium. He wanted fighter aircraft based in Belgium to take over the supply missions, swooping in low over the perimeter and dropping the supplies more accurately into the confined area there. The following day eighteen Dakotas of 575 Squadron flew from Broadwell to Evere airfield near Brussels loaded with supplies to service this proposed operation. But virtually nothing came of Darvall's suggestion. Only one Spitfire dropped two panniers of blankets and medical supplies on the following Monday. But there was still desperate need for supplies at Oosterbeek, and the Dakotas which had flown to Belgium had to make further flights from there on Sunday and on Monday. The records relating to these produce contradictory figures, but approximately twenty-eight flights were made during the two days, well escorted but against the usual flak opposition. Few of the supplies reached the airborne men; several aircraft were damaged and aircrew injured, although there was no loss of aircraft or life.

Those flights marked the end of the desperate effort to sustain by air the fighting power of the 1st Airborne Division. An operation planned to last three days at most was now in its second week, and the first major effort to maintain a force fighting on the ground in Europe by air supply had failed, though not because of any lack of determination by the aircrews concerned. A total of 629 flights had been made, 371 by Stirlings and 258 by Dakotas, resulting in the loss of 66 aircraft, 43 Stirlings (11.6 per cent of those despatched) and 23 Dakotas (8.9 per cent), an overall loss rate of 10.5 per cent.[1] No doubt Bomber Command possessed plenty more obsolete bombers to transfer to 38 Group and the Americans could mass-produce replacement Dakotas, but the sacrifice of human life in aircrews had been high. The lost aircraft contained 540 men: 360 regular aircrew and a few passengers, and 180 RASC despatchers. Of those, 222 – 144 aircrew and 79 despatchers – had been killed or would die of wounds, and 123 became prisoners of war. The other 195 were fortunate enough to have parachuted safely or crash-landed in the airborne corridor in Holland or in Belgium, or to have evaded capture with the help of Dutch people and returned to England.

*

---

[1] An aircraft is classed here as 'lost' if it failed to make a proper landing at an airfield, so the figures include those force-landing in Belgium, some of which may have been salvaged to fly again.

The men on the ground at Oosterbeek tell of their intense distress on seeing the supply flights passing over their heads almost daily, always in the late afternoon. Sergeant Bob Leeder, a glider pilot, remembers those times:

It was a high point of each day. The planes were very low, 500 to 1,000 feet and sometimes lower, and the flak bursts were thus very close to us and therefore very loud. Some of the planes were already hit when they came into sight, showing signs of smoke or even flames. Some came round twice. Once I saw a Dakota come round three times. When he came round the last time, the lower side of the fuselage was on fire, the fire spreading out to the wings with a lot of black smoke, and the RASC man visible in the doorway still pushing out the panniers. There seemed to be absolute silence on that last run. The flak had stopped, and we all came out of our trenches and stood gaping at this. One of my friends told me after the war that he had felt tears in his eyes, and his companion was sobbing also.

Corporal Don Collins of the Royal Signals remembers what was probably the same Dakota:

The whole of its under-part was ablaze. It passed by, flying in a steady line as though on a training run but gradually losing height. Framed in the open door was the despatcher calmly pushing out the panniers of supplies. He must have known the plane was on fire, as the flames were enormous. It was an awesome and very moving sight. I felt a lump in my throat and was cursing the Germans, and yet, at the same time, the courage of the pilot and the despatcher made me feel proud to be British.

Both men believed that this aircraft was Flight Lieutenant Lord's, but it was another, unfortunately unidentifiable, Dakota.

The men on the ground made frantic efforts to attract the supplies by displaying the white panels of the Independent Company or the celanese triangles with which every man was issued; they also fired Very lights and held flares. But the Germans had captured sufficient panels, triangles and flares to duplicate all of these efforts. The failure to get the message through about the early supply-dropping point not being in British hands, and then the tightly confined dropping point inside the perimeter, resulted in most of the supplies falling into German hands. Father Bruggeman, the Mill Hill priest at Lichtenbeek, describes in his diary watching Germans 'running from all directions, throwing themselves on the baskets'; the priests obtained some of the food, also an English newspaper on which was written 'Good luck boys'.

A Dutch boy, Sjoert Schwitters, who lived almost on the perimeter, tells what happened to a container falling near his house:

> The Jewish lady who was hiding in our house put on a British soldier's helmet which was in the garden – it had a bullet hole in it – and she set off first. Father called her back, but she kept on going, and I went out as well. The container wasn't difficult to open. It was all tinned food – butter, sausages, cakes, etc. We gathered up what we could and took it into the house, not for ourselves – it was not our property – but we didn't want the Germans to get it. We hoped to keep it for the British soldiers if they came. Later, on the Friday, when the Germans made us leave our house, I remember seeing a fat German sitting in our room, with his boots up on the table, eating the food from one of the tins – butter it was. So the Germans got it in the end.

The official estimate is that less than 200 tons of the 1,488 tons of supplies dropped were recovered by the British.

The collection of supplies from a dropping zone was mainly the duty of the RASC. When the first major drop took place, on Tuesday, Captain Desmond Kavanagh led four jeeps and trailers carrying about twenty-four men of his platoon out towards the dropping zone, even though this was a mile away in German-held territory. It was a hopeless venture. The platoon had only just crossed the railway bridge at Oosterbeek Hoog when it was fired upon by a German tank hidden in trees alongside the Dreijenseweg. The leading jeep was hit, and the ones following, all travelling at speed, crashed concertina-wise into its trailer. Captain Kavanagh died covering the retreat of his men with a Bren gun, and several other men were killed. Driver Ken Clarke, who took part in this action, says: 'Seeing our captain and others in our small party killed in this manner has always stuck in my mind as one of the most vivid and dreadful memories of the campaign.'

On the later supply flights, over the Oosterbeek perimeter, the collection of supplies became almost a treasure-hunt, with men of all units opening baskets and containers, often going out into no man's land at night, sometimes under fire and suffering casualties. The early flights had dropped only ammunition and small quantities of petrol, but more mixed loads were despatched as the operation continued. Some of the contents were hardly suitable: mortar bombs which turned out to be practice rounds, gun ammunition of the wrong type, new shirts and uniforms, even blanco and badges. Perhaps the most unusual of all was the despatch of several containers full of new maroon berets. Apparently there had been a victory parade in Tunisia after the campaign there in which some airborne men had appeared without berets lost in the fighting. To ensure that this should not happen after the next airborne operation, someone had included the berets as an automatic addition to the resupply. An unknown company commander who returned from Arnhem later made this report: 'It is suggested that berets should not be included, as the effect on the morale of a hungry man, or one without ammunition, finding a container of berets instead of what he anticipates, has to be seen to be believed.' He went on to say that after several days of fighting the first priority was for rifle oil and Sten and Piat ammunition.[2]

[2] The report is in Airborne Forces Museum File No. 48.

CHAPTER 18

The Polish Brigade

Major-General Sosabowski's Polish Independent Parachute Brigade had been raised with the hope of flying to Warsaw to assist in the liberation of its soldiers' home country. Now, on Thursday 21 September, two days later than planned, it was coming into an unsought action and not as a complete brigade. The original plan for the brigade in 'Market Garden' was that the parachute element would drop south of the Rhine on the third lift, on the Tuesday, while the jeep transport and anti-tank guns would land by glider on the north side, some on Monday, some on Tuesday. A British liaison officer from the 1st Airborne Division had jokingly told Captain Jan Lorys that the situation should be so well in hand by then that the British airborne men would 'meet us in commandeered buses, bring us over the bridge into Arnhem and treat us to a cup of tea there'. The glider landings had gone ahead, but the parachute drop had been cancelled on both Tuesday and Wednesday because of bad weather over the airfields of the American troop-carrier groups. Because the battle at Arnhem had not proceeded according to plan during that period of delay, Major-General Urquhart was asked on Wednesday night to nominate a new dropping zone and a new river-crossing point for the Poles. He selected an area near the village of Driel on the south bank, just one mile away from the defence perimeter then developing at Oosterbeek, and stated in his signal that the British would be holding the north end of the Rhine ferry by which the Poles could cross the river to provide this large reinforcement of fresh troops to Urquhart's division.

Sosabowski had been increasingly anxious over the prospects for his brigade during the two days of delay and had prepared notes of protest to be sent both to Brereton and to Browning. He had to be content with a signal from Urquhart, timed 4.30 a.m. on Thursday, confirming that the ferry was 'in the hands of the 1st Airborne

Division'.[1] Two things happened in the next few hours: the Polish brigade prepared for its take-off, and B Company of the 1st Border was pushed off the Westerbouwing, leaving the ferry crossing unprotected.

The weather over England was still poor on Thursday, but it was decided that the parachute lift for the Poles should go ahead because of the desperate situation at Oosterbeek. A total of 114 C-47s of the 314th and 315th Troop Carrier Groups, carrying 1,568 Polish parachutists, took off in the early afternoon, the Poles finally off to war after those years of training and waiting. The American pilots encountered much difficulty climbing through cloud and then attempting to join formation, but there were no collisions and more or less complete formations were eventually attained. The weather was so bad over England that one Pole jumped over Cambridgeshire but he went to Arnhem on a later lift. The weather at the airfields deteriorated and the American command decided that both group formations should be recalled before landing conditions became too dangerous. But the radio operators in the C-47s had the wrong codes. Four times the message was sent, and formation leaders and individual pilots had to decide whether the insistent messages were recall signals or not. Forty-one of the aircraft turned back. The returning planes descended through the cloud and most landed at the first airfield to be seen. One, whose radio was not working, went so far astray that it landed in Ireland.

The remaining seventy-three aircraft pressed on, using the southern route over Belgium. One was damaged by flak as it strayed over the German lines. The C-47 turned back into Belgium and dropped its stick of parachutists, fourteen men from Brigade HQ, before it returned to England. The parachute drop commenced soon after 5.0 p.m. It was not a tidy affair. The C-47s were under heavy fire. The American pilots complained that the Poles were too slow in carrying out their jumps; the Poles complained that they were thrown about too much by the pilots' evasive action. Five C-47s, all from the 315th Troop Carrier Group, were shot down, but

[1] Document at the Polish Institute and Sikorski Museum, London.

the Polish parachutists all jumped safely from these aircraft before they crashed. But ten American airmen were killed; fourteen met friendly forces, and one, Lieutenant Cecil Dawkins, who remained at the controls until all of his parachutists jumped, was still in the plane when it exploded and came round to find himself, severely wounded, being carried away on the back of a German tank.

Some of the Poles were fired upon as they came down, and five were killed and twenty-five wounded, either during the drop or later that day. It was eventually established that 1,003 men had arrived, about two-thirds of the brigade's parachute strength. These are some individual experiences. Lance-Corporal Bazyli Borowik of the Medical Company:

> We were under fire from machine-guns while we were in the air, and then mortared on the ground. The tracer bullets looked like arrows with smoke behind them; one man's kitbag was hit in the air and burst into flames. After we had landed, four of us were sent with a barrow to collect the medical supplies from the containers. We found a pile of German mortar bombs. Our officer suggested that we take those as well, but we said, 'What! Are we going to throw them at the Germans?'

Lieutenant Stefan Kaczmarek, the Brigade Quartermaster:

> I found that the American pilot was in a steep dive when the stick dropped, so that while I jumped first, at about 800 feet, the last man was out at only about 300 feet and he landed before me. After we landed I saw that the main drop was about a mile away on the other side of the village of Driel. My small party assembled at a farm where we took our first prisoner, a sleepy-looking German. When I asked him, in German, where 'the others' were, he replied that they had all gone. We had to go right through the village to the main rendezvous point. We set off in single file, and I put the German five metres out in front and told him that if he had lied about the other Germans he would get the first bullet from my Sten in his back. And so we made a triumphant

march through Driel with people standing in front of their houses throwing flowers and waving pieces of orange cloth.

There were few German soldiers in the immediate area; eleven prisoners were taken, including five deserters hiding in the crypt of Driel's Protestant church, among them two Poles forced into German service.

The brigade's depleted units marched off according to plan, the 2nd Battalion towards the ferry and the 3rd to a point directly opposite Oosterbeek church, both units remaining behind the cover of the steep bank which bordered the river. Cora Baltussen, the daughter of the most prominent family in Driel, went out to meet the parachutists. It is not known who the Irish soldier in her account was, nor do surviving Polish officers know of him; 'Lang' was Lieutenant Tadeusz Lang, an anti-tank officer, and 'Mr Dyrda' was Lieutenant Jerzy Dyrda, an interpreter on Sosabowski's staff:

An Irish soldier had been coming from the south in recent days, arriving before dawn and spending the day in our house, keeping observation over the surrounding countryside, but also sleeping part of the time. He went away each night soon after dark. I admired him for his calmness, marvellous sense of humour and unbelievable memory. I thought later that he was preparing the way for the Poles coming. I know that he later told General Sosabowski that my family were 'OK'. But I was still tremendously surprised when the parachutists landed. I had often told people to come to Driel; surely no one would ever fight in that narrow area between the rivers Rhine and Waal.

I went out on my bicycle and met the soldiers. They had just come off the fields and were starting to march towards the village. There was a very tall one in the front, with red hair and a large, bushy moustache. I said, 'Welcome, Tommies', in English, but they replied in a language which I had never heard before; I couldn't understand a word. They saw my surprise, and the tall one, who I found out later was called Lang, said in English, 'We are Polish', with heavy emphasis and no further explanation, just like someone used to giving commands. Then Mr Dyrda and General Sosabowski came up to the head of the column and started asking me questions. Where were the Germans? Where could they set up a field hospital? And where was the ferry? That was the most important question. General Sosabowski was furious when he found that the ferry was out of service. He had been told just before leaving England that it was running. 'How can it have gone in just a few hours?' he said.

The group of officers moved to the Baltussen home, where a conference took place. Miss Baltussen became the spokeswoman for the villagers, many of whom had gathered in a crowd outside. She sent them home and despatched five messengers to inform everyone that they should stay indoors and lie on the floor of their homes if there was any firing. The Polish soldiers were willingly helped by the villagers but did not receive the exuberant welcome accorded to the British on the earlier landings; there was little expectation now of a swift and bloodless liberation.

Lieutenant Kaczmarek was sent off to find out the position at the ferry and who controlled the far bank:

> Sosabowski sent me with Captain Budziszewski, the Engineer Company commander, and fifteen men. It was dark when we reached the ferry about an hour later. We stood on the ramp, and Captain Budziszewski shouted a big 'Hello', but there was no reply from the other side. Then he put up a flare, but as soon as it lit up, there broke out a hell of a fire from the opposite bank. We dashed and took cover behind some heaps of cobblestones, and it was a miracle that none of us were hit. The firing went on for about five minutes, and we could hear it ricocheting off the stones. It was terrible. We returned to Driel when the firing stopped and reported. So there was 'nothing doing' that night.

But other efforts were being made. The British at Oosterbeek had seen the drop but were unable to make contact with the Poles by wireless. Captain Ludwik Zwolanski, the Polish liaison officer at

Urquhart's headquarters, volunteered to swim across the river and inform the Poles that the British would attempt to widen the bridgehead at the Westerbouwing and, at the same time, Royal Engineers would prepare some boats to start ferrying the Poles across near Oosterbeek church. Zwolanski swam the river and gave his report. But the attempt to retake the Westerbouwing failed, and the construction of rafts out of jeep trailers proved to be slow and unsatisfactory. At 1.0 a.m. (on Friday) Lieutenant David Storrs, an officer on 1st Airborne's divisional RE staff, came across the river and told the Poles that only one raft was ready; then he returned to the north bank. Polish attempts to find boats on the south bank and to build rafts out of doors from Driel also failed. The last event of the night was that Lieutenant-Colonel R. Stevens, the senior British liaison officer with the Poles, swam the river and reported to Urquhart, presenting him with Thursday's copy of *The Times*.

Sosabowski ordered his men at the river bank to withdraw just before dawn and the brigade took up defensive positions around Driel. Many of the Poles would be there for the next four days. The daylight hours saw some mortaring and shelling from German positions less than a mile away on the high ground over the Rhine. Infantry and tank attacks took place spasmodically, but the Poles put up a fierce defence even though they had no artillery and nothing more powerful than a Piat to combat tanks. Seven men were killed that first day, Friday the 22nd, including two officers. One was Lieutenant Stanislaw Slesicki of the 3rd Battalion, killed by the first shell to be fired into Driel. The other was Second Lieutenant Richard Tice, a young American who had no family links with Poland but had come from the United States earlier in the war to join the Free Polish Army because of his admiration for and gratitude to the Poles who had fought on his country's side in the War of Independence. He had refused to transfer to his own army when his country entered the war but remained with the Poles, learning their difficult language and being commissioned. He died on that first morning at Driel when Germans approached his platoon's position, calling out 'Don't shoot', pretending to be British or American troops. The Germans then opened fire and Tice was hit by a burst of machine-gun fire.

The death of another man killed on that day is described by his officer, Lieutenant Kaczmarek:

> I was in the garden of a house; my corporal had given me a ripe pear, and I was enjoying it. I had just taken my first bite when I saw a group of British liaison officers in the next garden talking on a wireless, probably to the people on the other side of the river. I realized that it was a dangerous place to be, because it might get shelled or mortared. Five or six mortar bombs burst all around me at that very moment; the smoke and dust made it as dark as night. When it cleared I saw that my poor sergeant-major, Antoni Salwuk, had been hit by a piece of shrapnel. He was badly hurt and died soon afterwards. I still have his haversack, with the stains of his blood on it, and whenever I go back on a pilgrimage to Arnhem I go to his grave and say a little prayer for him, because I am sure that if he hadn't stopped the shrapnel it would have been me that was killed.

Twenty-five men would be killed at Driel during those four days and one committed suicide. He was fearful of being taken prisoner and sent to one of the concentration camps he had heard so much about; he shot himself with his Sten gun during a German attack.

The Medical Company set up its Main Dressing Station in the parish hall, which already had three badly wounded RAF men from a Stirling shot down nearby on a resupply mission. Cora Baltussen organized the local ladies to help with the nursing. She remembers two particular cases:

> There were two German wounded, one of whom was dying, but it took a long time. He was a young Nazi fanatic and kept crying, 'Hitler, Hitler.' Our parish priest tried to tell him there was a God waiting for him where he was going and asked the Polish orderlies to pray for him. Then a small miracle happened. The boy gave his pay-book to the priest and asked for his mother in Berlin to be told that he had died a Christian.

I noticed that some of the Polish soldiers had hard, weathered faces – peasant people who had come out of Poland through Siberia, their faces full of hardship. One of these was a nineteen-year-old boy who had lost an arm. He kept asking me if I thought he would still be able to work on a farm after the war.

The dressing station was later hit by a shell, despite its Red Cross markings. A Polish doctor and several of the patients were wounded. Cora Baltussen was cut badly in several places and another Dutch person was killed, one of two villagers to die during the action.

The expected parachute drop of the remainder of the brigade failed to take place on Friday, but the first tenuous link was made with the advancing ground forces when three Daimler Dingo scout cars of the Household Cavalry under Lieutenant Hon. Richard Wrottesley slipped through on the country lanes leading to Driel. Their wirelesses enabled Sosabowski to speak directly for the first time both to Horrocks at XXX Corps and to Browning at Airborne Corps.

The next contact was with Oosterbeek when Lieutenant-Colonels Charles Mackenzie and Eddie Myers arrived during the evening. Major-General Urquhart had sent them across the river to talk to Sosabowski and then, if possible, to go on to find Horrocks and Browning and stress how urgent it was that the force at Oosterbeek should be reinforced. They told Sosabowski that some small rubber boats were being prepared on the north bank and that every effort would be made to get as many Poles as possible across that night. There was another arrival soon after this when a column of Sherman tanks and Bren carriers, all carrying infantry, reached Driel. The tanks were a squadron of the 4th/7th Royal Dragoon Guards, and the infantry were from the 5th Duke of Cornwall's Light Infantry. This battalion was the forerunner of a complete infantry division, the 43rd (Wessex), which XXX Corps was now pushing up the country roads from Nijmegen. That vital link-up between the ground forces and the airborne men at Oosterbeek was now only separated by the width of the river Rhine, but the Cornishmen were at the end of a long and tenuous corridor.

Darkness came, and the Polish 3rd Battalion moved out to the river bank opposite Oosterbeek church for the proposed crossing, which was due to commence at 10.0 p.m. 1st Airborne's Royal Engineers had collected six small, two-man reconnaissance boats and one unwieldy RAF dinghy. The plan was to tie the boats together and attach signals cable fore and aft, so that the bunch of boats could be pulled back and forth across the river, ferrying about fifteen Poles on each trip. This was arranged by a party of fifteen men from the 4th Parachute Squadron under Captain Harry Brown. It was hoped that up to 200 Poles could be brought across during the night. But the river was flowing too fast and the wire kept breaking or became snagged on rocks. The only alternative was for Polish sappers, few of whom were skilled watermen, to row the boats with their tiny paddles across with just one Pole on each journey. The Germans put up parachute flares, and the Poles waiting on the south bank were fired upon and suffered casualties. Sosabowski ordered the operation to stop at 4.0 a.m. (on Saturday the 23rd) to prevent his men being caught exposed in the open at dawn. Only fifty-two Poles had crossed.

A glider-pilot officer, Lieutenant Brian Bottomly, met the Poles and led them to Divisional HQ, with some difficulty due to the language barrier, and losing at least one Pole killed by shelling on the journey. They were then allotted positions in the front line, relieving a platoon of the Independent Company on the Stationsweg. The Poles were under the command of Captain Ignacy Gazurek, the temporary commander of the 3rd Battalion. Sander Kremer describes how the Poles took over his house:

> They came in on Saturday, making a lot of noise, and they had a difficult time because they did not know the area. Many of them had no common language either with us or with the British. Captain Gazurek was killed almost at once while climbing over the wall between two houses. There was some panic, because no one could tell who had shot him; they suspected that it was a mistake by the British. Two Poles came to the top of our cellar steps, threatening to shoot my father. He had been upstairs burning some documents and the Poles thought he had been signalling to the Germans.

They were stopped by a young officer cadet who could speak some English.

It was a German shot from across the road which had killed Captain Gazurek. A parachute battalion of the modern Polish Army is now named after him.

Saturday night saw a renewed attempt by the Poles to cross the river. Sosabowski had sent Major Malaszkiewicz, his principal staff officer, to the 43rd Division to beg for proper assault boats. He was promised twelve and believed that trained British sappers would man them, but when the boats arrived at midnight, two and a half hours after the planned time, there were no boat crews, and men from the Polish Engineer Company had to carry out the task, with unfamiliar equipment, in the dark and under much heavier German fire than on the previous night. The crossing could not start until 3.0 a.m. (on Sunday morning) because of the need to make these new arrangements and to drag the boats 500 yards over fields, ditches and a high bank. What happened that night was to affect the reputation of the Poles and the personal career of their commander. It had been expected that the boats could each carry sixteen men, and the waiting units had been split into groups of that size; but only twelve men could be carried, so a reorganization took place. There was much confusion. Captain Piotr Budziszewski, the commander of the Engineer Company, was 'swearing like a Polish officer had never been heard to swear before'. Lieutenant-Colonel Myers, who had returned from his meetings at Nijmegen, was on the south bank attempting to help; he says: 'I can find no fault with their attempts; they did as much as they could. They had not been trained in river crossings, and the Arnhem plan had not envisaged one, and no one had any proper boats. But the less said about their watermanship the better.'

Only 153 Poles were successfully taken across: 95 of the 3rd Battalion, 44 from the Anti-Tank Battery and 14 from Brigade HQ. This was less than a quarter of the number hoped for. Major-General Sosabowski, who was not among those who crossed, returned to Driel yet again with the majority of his brigade. The Poles who had crossed had to negotiate the dangers of unfamiliar

Oosterbeek in the darkness. One group, which included Lieutenant-Colonel Rotter the brigade's Quartermaster and Captain Wardzala the commander of the Anti-Tank Battery, encountered a German force and surrendered after an exchange of fire. The Poles who reported for duty at Oosterbeek were sent to several points on the perimeter to thicken up the defence. They were impressed with the haggard appearance of the British but also with their spirit of resistance. The British saw them, as a 1st Border man says, as 'brave and dedicated' and they performed a useful role during the last two days of the Oosterbeek siege.

While Sosabowski and Urquhart were struggling with their problems either side of the Rhine, there was a whole clutch of generals only a few miles away in whose hands lay potential relief from the disaster which now faced Urquhart's men and the Polish reinforcements who had crossed the river. After crossing the Rhine and then enduring a cold and dangerous journey on the back of one of Lieutenant Wrottesley's scout cars, Lieutenant-Colonel Mackenzie arrived at Airborne Corps HQ at Nijmegen on Friday morning. He tried to explain the precarious position at Oosterbeek, first to Browning and then to Horrocks, but returned to Oosterbeek feeling that he had failed to convince those generals of the danger facing 1st Airborne.

Since Wednesday afternoon, Browning's HQ had been located in a large and comfortable house on the southern outskirts of Nijmegen. For most of the week Browning had little influence on what was happening to the three airborne divisions he was supposed to be commanding. He was alongside the headquarters of the 82nd US Airborne Division and had some influence there; but 101st US Airborne had come under the control of XXX Corps as soon as the first ground troops reached the division on Monday and 1st British Airborne, although only thirteen miles away, was fighting its own isolated battle, sometimes out of signals contact.[2] Even if signals contact had been perfect, Browning did not have the means to

---

[2] For several days, Major David Watson, commander of the Airborne Corps Signals Unit, operated what would now be called a mutually agreed 'time-share' with a German signals unit when both needed to use the same frequency.

provide any assistance; relief and support could only come from XXX Corps.

Browning only had one major command decision to make during the first week of the operation. Back in England was the 52nd (Lowland) Division which was earmarked to fly in to Deelen airfield on Thursday. Major-General Hakewill Smith sent a signal to Browning offering to fly in a brigade of the division by glider on Wednesday and land them as close as possible to 1st Airborne. It was a generous offer; such a landing near the south end of the Arnhem bridge, for example, might have transformed the situation there. It would have been a risky venture but John Frost's men were still holding out there at that time. Or the brigade could have been landed somewhere north of the Rhine where it could have reinforced the Oosterbeek perimeter and provided Urquhart with sufficient reserves to defend the Westerbouwing height properly. But Browning sent back this answer: 'Thanks for your message, but offer not – repeat not – required as situation better than you think. We want lifts as already planned including Poles. Second Army definitely requires your party and intend to fly you to Deelen airfield.' Browning clearly showed in that signal a lack of awareness of the situation at Arnhem and Oosterbeek. Hakewill Smith's proposed operation would have required a reallocation of gliders and transport aircraft, but that was the type of reorganization that Browning could have handled better if he had remained in England. (The 52nd Division's next operation was in November when it took part in the amphibious assault on the island of Walcheren, which was blocking access by Allied shipping to the port of Antwerp.)

A major crisis was now looming. Unless vigorous steps were taken, the 1st British Airborne Division was in danger of being overwhelmed. It is now generally agreed that at this time the various ground-force commanders failed to act with sufficient vigour. XXX Corps was paying the penalty for not having pushed hard enough earlier in the week. An officer in the Guards Armoured Division later told John Frost: 'We had no idea how serious things were for you at the bridge; we had no sense of urgency.' Next up the chain of command was the less than forceful General Sir Miles Dempsey. Above him was Montgomery, who had often interfered vigorously in the handling of battles in Normandy but was strangely quiet now. Back in London Sir Alan Brooke, Chief of the Imperial General Staff, and Churchill had only just returned from the Second Quebec Conference. No one was pushing; again to quote John Frost: 'It was an awful period of command indecision.'

All this was the background to the Valburg Conference, held on Sunday morning to decide the next move.

The day started with Lieutenant-General Horrocks coming up almost to the front line to see Sosabowski at Driel. Sosabowski was pleased to see the XXX Corps commander but sorry that Lieutenant-General Browning, his own airborne corps commander, never came in similar manner. Horrocks was carrying out a personal reconnaissance prior to making a major decision about the situation at the river. He went up the tower of Driel church and asked Sosabowski for his opinion of what should be done. Sosabowski said there were two options: either to make a major reinforcement of 1st Airborne, particularly with heavy weapons, food and ammunition, or to withdraw the division across the river before it became a total loss. Horrocks indicated that he supported the first option; he intended to put a battalion of the 43rd Division with supplies over the river that night close to 1st Airborne's positions and follow with a complete brigade at what was hoped to be an unopposed crossing at Renkum, four miles downstream.[3]

There probably followed a private meeting between Horrocks, Browning and Major-General Ivor Thomas, commander of the 43rd Division, before the main planning conference was held later that morning in a tent at 43rd Division's HQ in a field near the village of Valburg, halfway between Driel and Nijmegen. Four generals, several brigadiers and assorted staff officers assembled at the tent. Sosabowski was accompanied by Lieutenant Jerzy Dyrda, one of the best English speakers in the Polish brigade; Sosabowski could speak fair English but he took Dyrda with him to all important meetings. Dyrda has provided an account of what happened.

Sosabowski was greeted formally rather than warmly and told

---

[3] The above summary comes from the War Diary of the Polish Independent Parachute Brigade, Airborne Forces Museum, File No. 42.

that he could not bring his interpreter into the tent; it was only after Browning intervened that Dyrda was permitted to accompany his commander. The seating arrangements were not those of a round-table conference. The three British generals and their staffs were seated on one side of a long table, all smartly dressed. Sosabowski, in combat uniform, straight from the front line, was placed opposite them. Dyrda was surprised that neither Browning, a fellow 'airborne', nor Lieutenant-Colonel Stevens, Sosabowski's British liaison officer, came to sit alongside Sosabowski. Dyrda was not allowed a seat; he had to stand behind Sosabowski's chair. It had, he says, 'the appearance of a court-martial session, where on one side sat the judges and opposite them the accused, alone'.

Horrocks, who in his memoirs later wrote that he was not feeling well and was suffering a bout of depression over the way 'Market Garden' was going, briefly introduced the subject-matter, stating that there would be two river crossings that night, both under the command of Major-General Thomas, to whom he then handed over the meeting. Giving only the briefest of detail, Thomas stated that one of his battalions, the 4th Dorsets, followed by the Polish 1st Battalion, would cross close to the site of the Driel–Heveadorp ferry under the Westerbouwing height, together with some supplies for the 1st Airborne Division. A second crossing was to be made by the remainder of the Polish brigade further to the east, at the place where the earlier Polish crossings had taken place. Both crossings would commence at 10.0 p.m. in boats which would be sent up by the 43rd Division during the day. The commander on the spot would be Brigadier B. B. Walton, commander of 130 Brigade, to which the Dorsets belonged. Sosabowski was shocked and annoyed by the way one of his battalions at Driel was to be taken from under his command and that he was not even to have the opportunity to nominate which battalion, a departure from even the most basic of military courtesies. Sosabowski was not following Thomas's statement directly, but was listening carefully to Lieutenant Dyrda's translation into Polish. Realizing how provocative Thomas's statement was, Dyrda did not pass on the point about a Polish major-general having to give up control of one of his battalions to a young English brigadier who had not yet even viewed the scene of action.

There was silence. None of the English officers asked questions, an indication that they had already met and decided the plan. Then Sosabowski rose to speak, doing so through his interpreter. He gave his opinion that the proposed crossing point for the Dorsets and his own 1st Battalion at the ferry would result in their arrival on the north bank at the strongest point of the German defences. He had been observing German activities and was convinced that they had no reserves and that a landing further downstream would be unopposed. He urged that the whole of the 43rd Division and all of his own brigade be landed downstream where they could transform the whole situation north of the river and achieve the ultimate objective of 'Market Garden' – the establishment of a bridgehead over the Rhine. If such a large-scale crossing could not be accomplished, Sosabowski stated, better to withdraw the 1st Airborne Division across the river without delay. He sat down. Major-General Thomas rose again but merely restated his orders, 'very surely and unyieldingly', says Dyrda.

This was too much for Sosabowski, who stood up again and spoke this time directly in English which, says Dyrda, became more fluent as he became more angry. He told Thomas that the crossing was in insufficient strength to affect the outcome north of the river and would only be sacrificing both the Dorsets and the Poles by using the planned crossing points. Horrocks put a stop to it all by stating that the orders outlined by Major-General Thomas would be carried out and that if Sosabowski was not prepared to carry out his orders a new commander for the Polish brigade would be found. The meeting ended. Browning, Sosabowski's airborne commander, had not said a word.

Browning did take Sosabowski back to his own headquarters at Nijmegen for lunch. Sosabowski found Nijmegen crowded with transport but with no sign of any boats. Browning had to admit that there were practically none this far up the corridor. Sosabowski's frustrations boiled to the surface. He forcibly told Browning what he thought of British commanders who carried out a major operation across a series of wide rivers without bringing forward a good supply of boats. Captain Jan Lorys, one of Sosabowski's staff officers, says: 'This was probably the final nail in Sosabowski's coffin, daring to criticize British generals.'

There was one more meeting on that day. Browning and Horrocks went back that afternoon down the corridor to meet General Dempsey, whose Second Army was in overall control of operations. Dempsey was told of the plans for the coming night and the possibility of making a larger crossing the following night, but provision was also made for an evacuation from the northern bank if that became necessary. Sosabowski, in his memoirs, blames Browning for this pessimistic solution:

> Browning was wrong. In every action comes a crisis. At that moment, the battle can be swayed one way or the other, dependent on the luck or superior planning of either side. Victory or defeat lie along a very thin razor edge. It is incredible to me that Browning, Chief of British Airborne, despite the shortage of river-crossing equipment, did not use all his powers to encourage and persuade Horrocks, Dempsey and Montgomery to have a final go. We were so near victory at that time. At long last, troops and heavy equipment were up to the Rhine; it only needed one final effort by the units south of the river, and I am sure they would have streamed across to the relief of 1st Airborne.
>
> I have often wondered, if Montgomery had been with Brian Horrocks at Nijmegen on the 25th September, whether he would not have endorsed Horrocks's plan to carry out a major assault and then, perhaps, the Battle of Arnhem would have been turned into a victory instead of a defeat.[4]

The inference is that Horrocks was willing to keep going but was dissuaded from doing so by Browning and Thomas, particularly by Browning. But there was another factor. The Germans cut the corridor south of Nijmegen that evening and it would stay cut for forty-eight hours; it was this which really signalled the end of 'Market Garden'. The crossing planned for that night, however, still went ahead.

[4] Major-General S. Sosabowski, *Freely I Served*, Kimber, London, 1960, p. 198.

CHAPTER 19

The Sacrifice of the Dorsets

A small mission of mercy crossed the river from the south during that Sunday afternoon. Lieutenant-Colonel Martin Herford, the commander of 163 Field Ambulance, a unit directly under the command of XXX Corps, was an enterprising doctor who had worked as a volunteer with refugee children in the Spanish Civil War and with victims of Russian bombing in Finland in 1940. Frustrated at being unable to cross the river with medical supplies with the Poles the previous night, he had obtained permission from Major-General Thomas to cross in daylight under a Red Cross flag. He did so successfully that afternoon in an assault boat with Captain Percy Louis, a medical officer from the 'sea tail' of 133 Parachute Field Ambulance, and four volunteer orderlies. The party landed near Heelsum, three miles downstream from the ferry crossing. Leaving the rest of the party, the stores and two stray Poles found on the river bank, Herford went forward carrying his Red Cross flag. He made contact with the Germans but was unable to obtain any agreement for the safe passage of further medical supplies across the Rhine; but the Germans did allow the party left at the river under Captain Louis to return to the south bank. Captain Louis was killed later, either during the river crossing that night or afterwards; he has no known grave. Herford remained with the Germans; his subsequent activities will be described later.

The 4th Dorsets, meanwhile, spent the day preparing for their crossing. This battalion was a pre-war Territorial unit raised in West Dorset which had fought in the land campaign since arriving in Normandy with the 43rd Division soon after D-Day. It had suffered heavy casualties but had been made up with a draft of Essex Regiment men and was at near-full strength and reasonably fresh. It was not looking forward to its coming task, however. The commanding officer, Lieutenant-Colonel Gerald Tilly, took his company commanders up

Driel church tower to view the proposed crossing point. Major Philip
Roper of C Company says:

> We could see everything up to the trees which came down to
> the edge of the river on the north bank, but nothing in the trees on
> the ground which sloped steeply upwards from the river. Colonel
> Tilly said, 'Gentlemen, we've bought it this time.' I think he
> realized it was a pretty hairy operation. As for myself, I thought it
> unlikely we would get back. When I had my company O-Group I
> tried to water it down as much as possible and told them we were
> going to do an important job to help the airborne people.

The Dorsets experienced all the problems previously experienced
by the Poles. The boats were late in arriving and had to be
manhandled to the river bank. Because there were fewer boats than
promised, all were given to the Dorsets, and the planned Polish
crossing was cancelled. The Germans were firing a machine-gun on
fixed lines across the approach route to the launching point, and
one burst hit Major Tony Crocker of D Company, wounding him
so seriously that his leg later had to be amputated.

Many accounts say that the plan to put the whole battalion
across was whittled down to only two of the four rifle companies.
This is not correct; all four rifle companies and part of Support
Company were intended to cross. The crossing commenced at 1.0
a.m. (on Monday the 25th), three hours behind schedule. Each boat
carried two sappers (of 204 or 553 Field Companies) to paddle the
boats across and return for later lifts, and each boat took ten
infantrymen together with ammunition and supplies for four days.
Heavy artillery support kept the Germans' heads down to start with
but set two large buildings alight in Heveadorp which cast a ruddy
glow over the river. Then German machine-guns opened fire; at
least one boat was sunk; others were swept downstream. Most of A
and B Companies and Lieutenant-Colonel Tilly's tactical
headquarters crossed safely but landed in small groups dispersed
along the river bank. The actual landing was not strongly opposed.
Some grenades were thrown from the high ground above, but the
German defenders then backed away into the woods. The operation
was stopped at 2.15 a.m. because the German fire was becoming

more intense, although three or more hours of darkness still remained. That order was probably given by Brigadier Walton, who was in command of the operation. Seventeen officers and 298 men of the Dorsets had been despatched over the river by then.

The Dorsets were not the only ones to cross. The two leading companies each took a forward artillery observation officer and signallers from 112 Field Regiment. Also crossing were Lieutenant-Colonel Tommy Haddon, CO of the 1st Border, his Intelligence Officer and two men from their glider, which had come down in Belgium on the second day's lift, who had spent most of the last week struggling up the airborne corridor attempting to reach their battalion. With them was Major Pat Anson of the 10th Battalion, whose parachute aircraft had been shot down, also on the second lift. A medical group on the crossing consisted of Captain Jimmy Tiernan, the Quartermaster of 181 Airlanding Field Ambulance, and twenty men from that unit's 'sea tail', who had loaded three tons of medical supplies on to six DUKW amphibious trucks. These were the supplies arranged by Lieutenant-Colonel Herford but which the Germans had refused to allow across during the day. Now Captain Tiernan was attempting to get the DUKWs across alongside the Dorsets' crossing, together with ammunition for the Oosterbeek defenders. Three of the DUKWs failed to arrive at the crossing point; the three that did cross all landed downstream and none of the stores reached the men at Oosterbeek. Many of the men in the DUKWs were taken prisoner, although Captain Tiernan and some others swam back the following night. Lieutenant-Colonel Eddie Myers crossed on one of the DUKWs and managed to wade along the river bank until he reached the airborne perimeter, carrying important letters for Major-General Urquhart.

The story of the Dorsets' experience on the north bank can quickly be told. The battalion landed in small groups, in the dark, and companies never did assemble properly. The most successful group was a few men of A Company under Major Jimmy Grafton, who swung right and safely reached the positions on the perimeter held by the 1st Border's Breeseforce. Captain Tom Rose, an artillery observation officer with Major Grafton, was passed along to the Light Regiment's artillery positions near Oosterbeek church, which were reached by 6.0 a.m. Captain Rose quickly made radio contact with his regiment and throughout the day passed numerous calls for fire back to it. This was most useful, because his link operated separately from the overstrained link to the 64th Regiment and significantly increased the volume of artillery support to the Oosterbeek perimeter. Later in the day, however, Captain Rose was standing in the porch of the church, a regular meeting place which looked out over the meadows to the river, when a burst of German machine-gun fire struck it and Rose was hit in the shoulder. It was a severe wound from which he died either that day or the next.

That artillery support provided by Captain Rose and his signallers was the only significant result of the Dorsets' crossing. Lieutenant-Colonel Tilly reached the top of the escarpment just east of Heveadorp and found himself out of touch with any formed body of his unit until Major Philip Roper came up with twenty men of C Company. Private Aubrey Steirn was one of the C Company men:

> At first light we decided to move further into the woods and attempt to gain contact with other members of the battalion. I was in the lead when a machine-gun opened up on me from a very short distance. I was knocked over and remember, in what must have been seconds of unconsciousness, my past floating by and thinking I was too young to die. Obviously I was, because I came to in one piece, apart from a facial wound and badly bruised shoulder where a burst of fire had 'clipped' me and left metal fragments in my uniform. In the meantime the German had been dealt with, and we then moved on and encountered more fragments of the unit, including the CO. We occupied German trenches in the area and continued to operate until completely surrounded, when the CO was forced to surrender.

Lieutenant-Colonel Tilly had decided that the position was hopeless and surrendered to save the lives of his men. The only other sizeable group was about thirty men from various companies who were gathered together by Major Mike Whittle of B Company and remained in the woods near the river all day.

That left more than a hundred Dorsets in scattered groups over a wide area on the north bank. The experiences of Lance-Corporal Wally Smith are probably typical of such men:

We had dug in along the bank and the Germans were raining stick grenades down on us. I was 2 i/c on the Bren, and my Bren gunner, Private Harold Wyer, was hit by a sniper and killed. We laid him down in the trench and covered him up. I estimated there were only about ten of us left in a space of about 200 yards. We used up what ammo we had during the morning and just lay doggo until dark. Four of us then got to the river's edge. My thoughts were to swim the river, so in I went with two other lads, but the current was very strong and we couldn't make it. We drifted downstream and got back on the bank. We dropped down when a German patrol came along, and they passed over us and never saw us. We then came across a houseboat tied up and climbed aboard to hide. Inside we came across four other Dorsets who were also hiding; two were slightly wounded.

These men hid until captured by the Germans six days later.

Of the 315 Dorsets who attempted the crossing, thirteen died either on the river crossing or during the following day or night. Approximately 200 were rounded up and taken prisoner. Not only, as Sosabowski had forecast, had the Dorsets landed among the German positions, but there had been a lack of 'push' about the operation from the highest level of the 43rd Division downwards. This was a division of ordinary infantry who had been fighting hard in the land campaign all through the summer while the 1st Airborne Division had been inactive in England. There was probably a feeling that 1st Airborne's battle was lost and a strong reluctance to be sacrificed for these airborne strangers. The few airborne men who took part in the crossing fared no better. Lieutenant-Colonel Haddon moved off quickly after landing in his attempt finally to reach his battalion but was taken prisoner before reaching the Border positions; the remainder of his party were captured when Lieutenant-Colonel Tilly surrendered. It will probably never be known exactly what happened to Major Pat Anson, the 10th Battalion officer. He was next seen by one of his men on a train taking wounded prisoners to Germany, with a severe head wound and no memory of recent events. He died in a prison-camp hospital five days after the crossing.

CHAPTER 20

Evacuation

At five minutes past six in the morning (of Monday the 25th) Lieutenant-Colonel Myers reached the Hartenstein and handed over three letters which he had carried from the south bank. The contents of two were out of date, but the third was from Major-General Thomas saying that the Second Army (that is, General Dempsey, but surely with Montgomery's and probably Eisenhower's agreement) had abandoned the plan to maintain and reinforce the bridgehead north of the Rhine and stating simply that the 1st Airborne Division could withdraw across the river whenever Urquhart and Thomas decided. Urquhart spent two hours thinking about this. His division was now extremely weak, short of everything, and its perimeter defences showed signs of cracking under the strain. The Dorsets' crossing had brought no relief. The Light Regiment had reported that it had received information the previous evening, possibly from an intercepted German signal, that the Germans were soon to mount a major attack from the east and attempt to cut off the division from the river. Soon after 8.0 a.m. Urquhart got in touch with Major-General Thomas and told him that he wanted the evacuation plan to be put into operation that night.

Urquhart called his senior officers to a final conference at 10.30 a.m. and a plan was prepared. The units on the perimeter would be withdrawn progressively from the north and the river crossing would commence at 10.0 p.m. Medical officers and orderlies were to remain with the wounded. A complicated artillery plan was devised for the ground forces artillery to fire heavy concentrations just outside the perimeter as it shrank towards the river. Artillery staff officers Major Philip Tower and Lieutenant Paddy de Burgh laboured for more than six hours to prepare the artillery plan, encode it into a Slidex signal, transmit it and then have it checked back to them. 'It was,' says Philip Tower, 'a Slidex signal the like of which I had never done before and I have never done since – all done in poor conditions.'

That day of preparation for the withdrawal saw an increase in fighting and corresponding bloodshed at Oosterbeek; the misery was made even worse by the sheets of rain which fell in the early hours and the cold conditions. There had been a change in the German tactics. Many of the recent actions against the eastern face of the perimeter had been undertaken by units of the 9th SS Panzer Division, the strength of which had been maintained by reinforcements of relatively untried men sent from recruit camps in Germany. These men had suffered severely nearly every time they attempted local attacks against the determined airborne defence. The Germans had recently withdrawn some of these men and formed smaller battle groups of veterans supported by some recently arrived heavy armour. Two of these battle groups now mounted serious attacks in the area just north of the lower road, against the northern part of Lonsdale Force and the glider pilots of G Squadron.

Immediately behind the thin British defences here were the gun positions of the Light Regiment, and the first attack, in the morning, came right up to the edge of these. Artillery fire from the distant guns of the 64th Regiment was called for and fell within yards of the gun positions, temporarily halting the attack, but several Tiger tanks appeared as soon as the shoot finished. Gunner Bob Christie describes what happened then:

> One tank was directly opposite C Troop Command Post, alongside the Battery Command Post, which it started to demolish. Gunner Willie Speedie was operating the battery control set. As the house was tumbling, he came on the air and, in a clear and controlled Scots voice, went through the proper procedure for closing down control and passing those duties to an out-station. What he did was straight out of *Signals Training – All Arms*, and this while the building was literally coming down around him.
>
> Meanwhile, Lieutenant Adrian Donaldson and Lance-

Bombardier Joe Dickson ran to a Polish 6-pounder and, with the few surviving members of its detachment, manhandled it into the open. They engaged the Tiger tank with several rounds. I cannot recollect any specific points of impact on the tank but I do recall that thereafter it did not use its main gun, nor did it move again in the few remaining minutes I was on the gun position. The tank did, however, use its 20-millimetre cannon to rake the gun and weapon pits. At that point I was wounded.

Several of the gun positions as well as the nearby Regimental Command Post were overrun.

Not far away, glider pilot Sergeant Bob Leeder tells how he was forced out of the house he had been defending:

The others made it safely; then it was our turn. George Collett said we ought to go singly, but we both felt better going together. I got hit in the leg – a sharp pain – and fell down. I called out, 'George, they got me.' It was a favourite joke, because when gangsters in films got shot they always said, 'They got me'; we had often play-acted this when we were fooling around.

George told me to get over a fence and he would give covering fire. This he did but he got hit himself. We both crawled into the next house. They dressed my wounds. I wasn't hit too badly and was sent to cover one of the windows with a rifle, but George was badly hurt in the knee and put in the cellar.

The attack later swung south and caught the South Staffords in Lonsdale Force. The situation was stabilized when a 75-millimetre gun was brought into action, as described by this unknown officer:

The enemy established themselves in a wrecked house about fifteen yards from our forward post. While a sort of snowball fight with grenades was going on, I got the gunners to put a round into the remains of the house. The range was about seventy yards and it was a lovely sight – showers of sparks and dust and the whole place collapsed. One German was seen to flee; the rest were dead.[1]

The official report of the South Staffords describes this incident and concludes, 'This was proved to be a final crisis.'

The airborne men had developed a strong affection for the little church near their positions. Rightly suspecting that its tower was being used as an observation post, the Germans had steadily pounded it with shell fire, and the airborne men had watched as the spire started to crumble. Sergeant Norman Howes of the South Staffords remembers how the end came late that afternoon:

> During the previous days I had probably heard every noise that man had invented, and then there was this other noise. It was a slithering and clattering as the shingles or tiles of the spire – or those remaining – began at last to leave the wooden frame. Then an awful groaning and grinding as the framework gave up its long struggle and fell to the ground with an almighty crash. It seemed an omen, signalling the end.

The chaplain of the Polish 3rd Battalion, Father Hubert Misiuda, was killed that night somewhere near the church, but the exact circumstances of his death are not known.

There were other attacks at various points on the perimeter. No other serious incursions were made, but in view of the impending evacuation 156 Battalion in the north was allowed to make a small withdrawal from an exposed group of houses during the afternoon. One of the local attacks beaten off that day is described by Private Robin Holburn of the KOSB.

> An attack in, I guess, platoon–plus strength came in over the field. It was an ideal target and our two Brens emptied several magazines with deliberation into the advancing Germans. Many were hit and the attack ground to a halt, with all the Germans dropping to cover among the cabbages –

[1] Airborne Forces Museum, File No. 54.

all except one, an NCO or officer who remained standing, shouting at his soldiers and urging them up to resume the attack, but without success. In my mind the picture of this German remains as an indelible picture of real heroism. How long he remained standing, shouting and waving his arm, I do not know; at the time it seemed an eternity but in reality it was more likely seconds before I fired and hit him with a burst of fire and he dropped to the ground. At this, and among cries from the wounded, the rest scurried or crawled back behind other houses.

This German unit was probably one which still contained inexperienced recruits.

Darkness came and the day's battles ended. The number of dead had risen sharply from an average of about 80 in each of the recent days to about 120 on this day. It had been a particularly serious day for the glider pilots, who lost thirty-two men, twice as many as on any other day since the glider landings.

Preparations continued for the potentially hazardous operation of withdrawing a large force from close contact with the enemy and then evacuating it across a wide river. Unfortunately the plan made by those on the south of the river did not conform with the actual position on the north bank. It was assumed at 43rd Division HQ that the Dorsets had landed in sufficient strength to widen the airborne holding so that two separate crossings of the river could operate – one near the ferry point where the Dorsets had crossed and one due south of the perimeter. The available boats were allocated almost equally to each crossing point. But there had been no widening of 1st Airborne's perimeter near the river, and Urquhart's plan was based on passing his entire force down to the eastern crossing point. The supporting artillery fire was to commence at 8.50 p.m. to cover the withdrawal of troops from the perimeter positions, which would start ten minutes later. Units would move progressively from the north on the 'collapsing bag' principle based on the successful evacuations from Gallipoli in the First World War. Units were to move to the river by one of two routes passing either side of the Hartenstein to a common departure point near the church. Glider pilots, mostly of No. 1 Wing, were to act as guides along the routes as far as that departure point, where a white tape, laid earlier in the evening by Major Jack Winchester and three sappers from the 9th Field Company, would mark the route across the water-meadows to the river's edge.

Men were ordered to shave and then blacken their faces. Boots were to be wrapped in strips of blanket taken from houses; weapons were to be made secure so that they would not rattle. Artillerymen were to carry breech blocks and gun sights to the river's edge and throw them into the water; all other equipment was to be destroyed. Walking wounded at the aid posts were allowed to leave, but the seriously wounded and all medical officers and orderlies were to remain, except for one officer to be sent back to report on the medical situation to Airborne Corps HQ. The first of the perimeter defenders left their positions from areas north of the Hartenstein. Although they had the furthest to go, they would have the best chances of safe evacuation. Units divided into groups and set off, often with each man holding the tail of the smock or a hand of the man in front, 'just like a trail of elephants'. A light rain gave way to a steady downpour which would continue for most of the night and which, with the artillery bombardment, assisted the evacuation by concealing movements from the Germans, who failed to realize that a major withdrawal was taking place.

For the first hour the Germans fired a heavy shell-and-mortar bombardment, probably in response to the British shelling. This broke up some of the groups making their way to the river and caused casualties. One KOSB party was hit near the Hartenstein, with several men killed and others severely wounded. The KOSB dead may have been those seen by glider-pilot Staff Sergeant George Milburn:

> We passed several of our lads dead, laid out on their backs, the rain pouring down on their faces, actually into their open mouths. There seemed to be quite a lot of them and having to leave them really upset me – I don't know why; they were already dead. On top of that I felt that we were abandoning the Dutch. Those dead and leaving the Dutch still affect me. In a way, I would have preferred to stay and fight it out.

Later, when we were nearly at the river, we came under fire
from a multi-barrelled mortar firing from the west. Three of
us took cover together near a hedge and, when we got up to
move, the one in the middle was dead. I never knew his name.
It was a dreadful night.

Other parties lost their way and ran into German patrols. The
small Royal Army Ordnance Corps group of eighteen men led by
Lieutenant-Colonel Gerry Mobbs and Major Bill Chidgey found
the tape they were following come to an end. The two officers split
up, and each led part of the column forward, hopefully in the right
direction, but actually into the path of a German machine-gun
which opened fire. Mobbs and Chidgey were both seriously
wounded; eight other men were hit, of whom one was killed and
one mortally wounded. Only five men at the tail end of the column
escaped to reach the river. Bill Chidgey says: 'I'm still very upset at
the loss at that late stage of the fine men in our little unit who had
performed so well throughout the operation.'

The first men reached the river before ferrying started at 10.0 p.m.
and formed an orderly queue to wait for the boats. Officers from
Divisional HQ had been sent ahead to control the evacuation; Major
Philip Tower of the Royal Artillery was one; Captain Willie Taylor,
Intelligence Officer of the 1st Parachute Brigade, who had shared
Urquhart's hiding place in Arnhem exactly a week earlier, was
another; Lieutenant-Colonel Myers was in overall charge. The first
boat to appear was an assault boat containing Lieutenant Alan
Bevan and sappers of 260 (Wessex) Field Company. Each of the
two crossing points had been provided with one Wessex Division
field company with these paddled assault boats and one Canadian
company with 'storm boats' powered by outboard engines. The
23rd Canadian Field Company, commencing operations here a few
minutes later, had a bad start. The first boat launched proved to
have been damaged on the way to the river; the second was hit by a
stray mortar round and sunk, with its crew lost; the third arrived
safely; the fourth capsized. But a further ten boats were available and
soon joined the English boats in a steady shuttle across the river.
    Everything went more or less to plan for the first few hours. A

large number of men arrived and waited patiently in a long line stretching back from the river bank. Wounded men were given priority and sent to the head of the queue. Three chaplains each arrived with groups of walking wounded. Padre Talbot Watkins of the 1st Battalion brought fifty men from Kate ter Horst's and then went back to Oosterbeek to seek out more wounded; he swam to safety on the following night. Some badly wounded men carried from the aid posts by friends, or having been wounded on the way from their positions, slowed down the loading, but none were turned away. Everyone else took their turn irrespective of rank, and an admirable self-discipline was maintained throughout the night. Men were instructed to lie down until called forward; many promptly fell asleep in the mud and the pouring rain. Private Harry Duckworth of the 1st Border remembers: 'Occasionally, an uncouth voice would loudly instruct a standing group to "get off the — skyline", and, as often as not, a somewhat cultured voice would answer apologetically, "Sorry, old boy." In that situation there was equality.' Major-General Urquhart and the other senior officers queued like everyone else. Major Tower remembers Brigadier Hicks showing some reluctance to cross until he could be sure that all the men of his brigade had left but being persuaded that such honourable gestures were not practicable. Commander Wolters, the Dutch officer, went sadly clutching the teddy-bear which he had hoped to give to his daughter in occupied Holland.

The powered Canadian boats could cross the river in only three minutes but they frequently had to be taken out of service and have engines replaced, mostly through rainwater drenching sparking plugs or electrical circuits. Major Alan Bush was in a boat which broke down in midstream: 'I thought I had heard every oath in the English language but I heard a few new ones from those Canadians until they got it going again.' The Canadian boats made 150 crossings during the night; an attempt to count the men carried by the Canadians failed because 'the paper turned to pulp in the driving rain'; but they definitely carried the majority of the men evacuated. Five of the Canadians and many of their airborne passengers died when boats either were hit or capsized through overloading, and some Canadians were swept downstream to become prisoners. The assault boats of 260 Field Company were much slower, because each trip required a hard paddle diagonally across the river, which was flowing in near-flood conditions after the recent rains, and the sappers handling the short paddles quickly became exhausted. Two-man crews became four, then six, with corresponding reductions in the numbers of passengers who could be taken aboard. But the English sappers stuck to their task right through the night and miraculously suffered no serious casualties. The Germans realized that something was happening but assumed that a further crossing from the south was taking place and were shelling possible assembly and approach routes south of the river. The south bank itself was quiet for most of the night.

The British bombardment from south of the river ran through its programme. Intensive fire from every available regiment fell for the first three hours, followed by 'spasmodic concentrations' for the next five. The effect was to persuade the Germans around the perimeter to remain under cover. As the British positions were evacuated, so too did the fire fall on them to prevent any German follow-up. Dutch houses which had earlier been hit by German fire were now hit by British shells, but with few civilian casualties because the families remained sheltering in the cellars. Riet Rijks, then a girl in Weverstraat, says:

Our house was hit in the roof and many of those nearby were on fire. We were scared stiff but hoped that it heralded a major advance from the south and thus our liberation. The German tank outside was firing a lot during the night, and I heard Germans shouting that two men had been killed and that they should be replaced from those sheltering in the cellar of a house nearby.

A wounded signaller had volunteered to remain on duty at the Hartenstein for five hours after the evacuation started, sending out messages on the two links which remained open. Regrettably his name is not known but he remained on the sets for an extra half-hour until sending a last message at 3.30 a.m. Military police remained on guard over the German prisoners in the tennis court until 1.30 a.m., leaving just one volunteer, Corporal Peter Dale, to remain to the end. The prisoners made no attempt to escape, and Corporal Dale was able to evade capture and return to England later. The wounded left behind remained under the care of the medical staff and those of the chaplains who decided to stay with them; most of these men fell into a deep sleep. The British shelling had been carefully planned to avoid their locations.

The troops holding the two southern extremities of the perimeter had a long wait before they could withdraw from their positions. On the western side it fell to the Borders of Breeseforce to wait until well into the early hours before leaving. There was some German mortaring, but the nearest German infantry, 600 yards away beyond the gasworks, made no move and the Borders slipped quietly away only to find themselves at the end of a long queue of men still waiting for a boat. On the other side of the perimeter, the Germans were making their nightly probes against Lonsdale Force, but the last men due to leave, the South Staffords, were able to get away; like the Borders, they found themselves at the end of the queue. Staff Sergeant Trevor Francis, one of the glider-pilot guides near the church, followed them across the fields and found 'what I thought was a hedge but was in fact soldiers standing silently two deep in a queue about 150 yards long. You could have heard a pin drop; the silence and discipline were uncanny.' Some men never had the chance to leave their positions. Reports from contributors include two small groups of KOSB men told to wait until fetched but never called for, two 10th Battalion men on sentry duty but left behind and several anti-tank gunners and South Staffords in Lonsdale Force who were not informed at all about the departure. The largest group of 'left-behinds' was the men of D Company, 1st Border, who were out of radio contact and could not be reached by the messenger sent with their withdrawal order. By contrast, another contributor, a sergeant who wishes to remain anonymous, had men who deliberately hid in cellars when he went round 'shouting them out' to leave, either too tired to move or unwilling to face the hazards of the evacuation. Nearly all of these men became prisoners next morning. Signalman Bill Carr was left behind because of an act of mercy. He stopped to help a German badly wounded by the bombardment and carried him to a cottage where he was taken prisoner by the Germans there. The wounded German said, in perfect English, 'This fucking war!' 'They were my sentiments exactly,' says Signalman Carr.

There were still many men waiting at the embarkation point as dawn approached. The Canadian effort was now down to only two boats, the thin metal sides of several having been holed on the stone groynes during the night. As it grew lighter the Germans could see what was happening and started firing on both banks and on the boats in the river. The war diary of the old adversary, Battalion Krafft, boastfully claimed that it prevented all but two or three boats crossing. Examples of the effects of the German fire provided by contributors include six men killed when a mortar bomb or shell hit the line of waiting men, a boat struck by machine-gun fire just before it beached on the south side, killing four KOSBs and wounding several other men, and Captain Bill Gray, commander of the Divisional Provost Company, fatally wounded at some stage by machine-gun fire. These were just a few of the casualties.

Many of the waiting men decided to swim across the river. Some hasty ones plunged in fully clothed but, weakened by nine days of fighting and hunger, and with the weight of waterlogged clothes, were soon in difficulties. RASC Captain Colin Harkess, who had lived by the sea as a child, tried to stop such attempts and became an impromptu swimming instructor. The water was not cold and the river was less than 200 yards wide, so many naked or semi-naked men were able to swim safely across despite the fast-running water. The last crowded boats crossed soon after 5.0 a.m. but they were now exposed more clearly to German fire. When the very last Canadian boat was taken across by Lieutenant R. J. Kennedy in broad daylight at 5.30 a.m., nearly every man aboard was hit.

Many men remained stranded on the north bank. Lance-Corporal Harry Smith of the South Staffords tells what happened:

There were about 150 of us left. A lieutenant took us into a hollow where we would be safe, but we decided that we would have had it if a tank came. He suggested that we should give in. He stood up with a white shirt or something on a stick. As he did so, a 20-millimetre hit him in the side; it was far too big a wound for a bullet. Then a little chap with a foreign accent spoke to me and said he was worried in case we became prisoners because he had come from Germany before the war. I told him he would be safe in a British uniform and asked him to shout 'Cease fire' in his own tongue, which he did, and the firing stopped. Then a bloody old German, with a Kaiser Bill moustache, a big white thing, came over the bank armed only with a rifle and he and another German took us away.

Meanwhile the operation at the second major crossing place had been a fiasco. The Canadian and English sapper commanders there decided that a boat of 553 Field Company should be paddled quietly across first, so as not to arouse German attention. Serjeant Fred Petrie took the boat across but, despite a long search of the far bank, could find no passengers except two men who were hiding in one of the DUKWs lost the previous night. Further efforts were made, but the total brought back was only forty-eight men, mostly Dorsets and mostly by the assault boats; these attracted less fire than the Canadian powered boats, which only found four passengers on four crossings! Some of the Dorsets led by Major Whittle came back by their own efforts, either in an abandoned assault boat which they found or by swimming. It was eventually realized that there was hardly anyone waiting on the far bank and four of the Canadian boats were sent to help with the Oosterbeek crossing, but one sank on the way and the others failed to arrive in time to help. The allocation of equal numbers of boats to the two crossings had been a mistake and led to the abandoning of airborne men at the Oosterbeek crossing point. Statements in such official documents as 130 Brigade's war diary that 'the remainder [of the Dorsets] were left holding the enemy at bay' and in the Airborne Corps report that 'these operations were carried out with the greatest skill and gallantry by 43 Division, some 180 men of 4 Dorsets acting as covering party being left on the northern bank' are nonsense; most of the Dorsets had been taken prisoner the previous day.[2]

The evacuation had mostly been successful, thanks to the devotion of the Canadian and Wessex Division sappers at the Oosterbeek

[2] From Public Record Office WO 171/660 and Airborne Forces Museum File No. 57 respectively.

crossing point, helped by the cover of the artillery bombardment and the pouring rain. The official tally of numbers who crossed safely is 2,398, made up of: 1st Airborne Division (including glider pilots), 2,163; Polish troops, 160; and 4th Dorsets, 75; but the addition of individual unit totals produces a higher figure of about 2,500. Also crossing were several RAF aircrew shot down from resupply aircraft; Isaäc de Vries, a Dutch Jew who guided a party of Lonsdale Force men down to the river and crossed with them; and an elderly German prisoner of war who refused to leave his Independent Company captors. Commonwealth War Graves Commission records showing dates of death and Jan Hey's research showing the location of wartime burials reveal that an estimated ninety-five airborne men lost their lives during the night. Together with the deaths of the previous day at Oosterbeek and Driel, this gives a total death roll of 258 for the twenty-four-hour period, the second highest daily figure for the whole battle. The bodies of many of the men who had been drowned or been killed by German fire on the river were swept downstream, some for considerable distances, and their graves are now to be found in cemeteries all along the banks of the Rhine. The heaviest losers on the river were the South Staffords, last in the queue from Lonsdale Force, and glider pilots, three of whose captains died; one of them, Captain Ogilvie, probably drowned because his kilt became waterlogged and dragged him down.

The exact number of men left on the bank is not known. 1st Airborne's estimate is 300; men who were there give a smaller number. Many of these were Borders and South Staffords, the last men to leave positions on the perimeter. Polish records show that 101 of their men were left behind, but that figure includes their wounded in the Oosterbeek medical stations. Battalion Krafft claimed fifteen officers and 580 other ranks as prisoners 'in a keen attack in the morning', which was really no more than a mopping-up of those left behind on the river bank and at Oosterbeek, probably including the wounded there.

The Battle of Arnhem was over, almost exactly nine days after the units of the 1st British Airborne Division had driven out from their camps and billets in England to the airfields.

CHAPTER 21

The Reckoning

In years to come it will be a great thing for a man to be able to say, 'I fought at Arnhem.'

(Field Marshal Montgomery)

After a tiring march in the darkness and rain, the survivors of 1st Airborne reached a reception centre run by the 43rd Division and were then passed back by lorry to Nijmegen, where they were reunited with the 'sea tail' element of their units, and were eventually transferred to Louvain ready to be flown back to England. The Poles followed 1st Airborne to Nijmegen, although they had to march all the way, carrying their equipment. They were retained for various defence duties in the airborne corridor and suffered a further five fatal casualties before returning to England in early October. They were closely followed by Browning's Airborne Corps HQ but the 82nd and 101st US Airborne Divisions were left under XXX Corps control. The American airborne men remained in action until 5 and 23 November respectively, sustaining a further 3,594 casualties, slightly more than they had suffered during 'Market Garden'.

The unwounded British prisoners captured at Arnhem and Oosterbeek were quickly transported to Germany. Unfortunately there is no space here for the many interesting or harrowing stories of this period; this is not a prisoner-of-war book. Treatment by the German captors on the battlefield was mostly good, but there were some incidents involving battlefield atrocities and shootings during attempted escapes that should be recorded. There are four known examples of men being shot soon after capture in which two glider-pilot officers, one Royal Engineer officer and two paratroopers were killed. Three more officers were shot after escape attempts – Captain John Keesey of 16 Parachute Field Ambulance after jumping from an ambulance train, and Lieutenants Michael Cambier of 156 Battalion and Raymond Bussell of the 3rd Battalion shot by the Gestapo when recaptured in civilian clothes after escaping in another train jump. The worst incident occurred on Saturday 23 September, when a group of mostly officer prisoners taken at the Arnhem bridge made an escape attempt while being taken on an open lorry to Germany. Majors Dennis Munford and Tony Hibbert jumped off while the guards were distracted, but one of the guards then panicked and turned his Schmeisser on to the men on the platform of the lorry. Four airborne men were killed and two mortally wounded; one of the German guards was also killed. Among the dead was Tony Cotterell, the war correspondent. Only Tony Hibbert made good his escape; Dennis Munford was dragged out from his hiding place under a chicken shed.

Many of the wounded prisoners were treated at a remarkable establishment. When the Germans found themselves with huge numbers of wounded to tend after the evacuation, Lieutenant-Colonel Martin Herford, who had crossed the Rhine in daylight in an attempt to bring medical relief to the garrison at Oosterbeek, negotiated with the Germans for an 'airborne hospital' to be opened at a Dutch Army barracks at Apeldoorn, fifteen miles north of Arnhem. The Germans agreed, because it allowed them to concentrate on their own wounded. Colonel Warrack and the medical staff and wounded left behind at Arnhem and Oosterbeek were then transferred to this hospital. There were 1,700 wounded and 250 medical staff, including four surgeons and four chaplains. The hospital remained in being, entirely under British control, for exactly a month, although the walking wounded and other less critical cases were steadily transferred to Germany. Herford, who became Colonel Warrack's deputy at the hospital, had agreed with the Germans that the establishment should be classed as a hospital, not as a prisoner-of-war camp, and the British were expected not to undertake escape attempts; but, says Herford, 'We didn't quite play fair.' He, Colonel Warrack and several others on the medical staff quietly slipped away towards the end. The hospital closed on 26 October, but Major Simon Fraser of 181 Airlanding Field Ambulance and twenty of the wounded who were too seriously ill to move to Germany were still at another hospital in Apeldoorn when the area was liberated in April 1945.

Another remarkable aspect of the aftermath of Arnhem was the large number of airborne men who evaded capture or escaped after being captured and who returned to the Allied lines; at least 300 British and Polish airborne men remained free in this way. The highest of praise is due to the Dutch Resistance and other civilians – particularly those in the Ede area – who risked and often lost their lives helping the evaders. Again this is not an escaping book, but some stories are of particular interest. Two large-scale river crossings were planned with the assistance of Lieutenant Gilbert Kirschen, a Belgian SAS officer who co-ordinated the effort with the Allied forces. The first crossing, code-named 'Pegasus I', on the night of 22 October, was successful. After Lieutenant-Colonel David Dobie had swum the river beforehand to make the final arrangements, Major Digby Tatham-Warter (of umbrella fame at the Arnhem bridge) led 138 men – about 120 airbornes, the remainder Allied aircrew and one 82nd US Airborne man – across safely. Brigadier Lathbury was in this party, also Major Tony Deane-Drummond, who had escaped from German captivity by hiding in a cupboard for thirteen days. But 'Pegasus II', on the night of 18 November, failed. A newspaper correspondent pretending to be an intelligence officer had interviewed some of the 'Pegasus I' evaders, and the resulting article alerted the Germans, who strengthened their patrols on the river. One of the parties of 'Pegasus II' making for the river encountered a German patrol. The officer leading it, Major John Coke of the KOSB, and one man with him and a Dutch guide were all killed. The parties scattered and only seven men were able to cross the river. Efforts to get members of 'Pegasus II' and other evaders to safety continued in smaller numbers, the Dutch Resistance being told to give the following interesting order of priority to them: doctors, glider pilots, soldiers, airmen. Brigadier Hackett and Colonel Warrack were among those who came back in this way.

The Cost

As far as can be ascertained, a total of 11,920 men took part in the airborne operation to Arnhem in the 1st British Airborne Division, the Polish Independent Brigade Group and various attached elements. Of these, no less than 1,485 were killed or died of wounds and 3,910 came back in the evacuation over the river, or the withdrawal in the case of the Poles at the end of the battle, leaving 6,525 as prisoners of war or attempting to evade capture; approximately 2,000 to 2,500 of the prisoners of war were wounded (see Table 1).

Table 1

	Fatal casualties (%)	*Prisoners of war and evaders* (%)	*Evacuated safely* (%)	*Total*
1st Airborne	1,174 (13.1)	5,903 (65.8)	1,892 (21.1)	8,969
Glider pilots	219 (17.3)	511 (40.5)	532 (42.2)	1,262
Polish brigade	92 (5.4)	111 (6.6)	1,486 (88.0)	1,689
Total	1,485 (12.5)	6,525 (54.7)	3,910 (32.8)	11,920

Note. The total of 'fatal casualties' is made up of men who were killed in action, died of wounds, were drowned on the evacuation or were shot in atrocities or escape attempts. The died-of-wounds total includes 130 men who died in prison camps or hospitals in Germany up to the end of 1944; prisoner-of-war deaths after that time are assumed to be from other causes unless they are definitely known to be the result of wounds received in the battle. The 'prisoners of war and evaders' are the unit totals after the 'fatal casualties' and 'evacuated safely' have been deducted from those who took off from England for the operation. There may be some discrepancies here, because men in gliders which failed to leave England may be included in some units and not others.

The 1st British Airborne Division's casualty figures of 7,077 were twice as heavy as the combined totals for the two American airborne divisions taking part in Operation 'Market' (82nd US, 1,432; 101st US, 2,118) and can also be compared with the 6th British Airborne Division's casualties of 4,457 in nearly three months of fighting in Normandy. Among the dead of 1st Airborne and its attached units were five Canadian officers, one French and one Dutch officer, and one Dutch commando.

The casualties of Urquhart's 1st British Airborne Division can be further broken down (see Table 2). It is noted that the 4th Parachute Brigade suffered the highest proportion of deaths – with its losses on the fly-in, the opposed landing and the subsequent fierce fighting – and that the 1st Parachute Brigade lost so many men as prisoners when units were trapped in Arnhem.

Table 2

	Fatal casualties (%)	Prisoners of war and evaders (%)	Evacuated safely (%)	Total
1st Parachute Bde	209 (12.0)	1,398 (80.2)	136 (7.8)	1,743
4th Parachute Bde	294 (17.1)	1,155 (67.2)	269 (15.7)	1,718
1st Airlanding Bde	325 (13.6)	1,590 (66.6)	474 (19.8)	2,389
Divisional and attached units	346 (11.1)	1,760 (56.4)	1,013 (32.5)	3,119
Total	1,174 (13.1)	5,903 (65.8)	1,892 (21.1)	8,969

Looking at individual units, the following list shows the highest proportions of unit deaths. (Glider pilots are now included; units with less than twenty men are not included.)

9th Field Company, RE	22.7 per cent
156 Parachute Battalion	20.5 .. ..
Glider pilots	17.3 .. ..
Reconnaissance Squadron	16.6 .. ..
11th Parachute Battalion	16.1 .. ..
10th Parachute Battalion	15.8 .. ..
1st Border	15.4 .. ..
1st Parachute Battalion	15.0 .. ..

The 9th Field Company and 156 Battalion both suffered casualties on the fly-in, though those of 156 Battalion would not have made any difference to its place in the list. The figure for glider pilots, who lost fewer than thirty men in flying or landing incidents, show how fully they took part in the fighting at Oosterbeek.

The casualties of the Polish brigade should not be forgotten. They were incurred in an operation which could hardly have been more frustrating, with the frequent postponements of take-offs in England and the difficulties encountered in attempting to cross the river. Fifty Poles were killed at Oosterbeek or drowned in the evacuation; the remaining 42 dead Poles died south of the river. The ground forces lost 25 men killed in the river crossings and the evacuation: 14 Dorsets, 5 Canadian and 4 English sappers, together with a doctor (from the airborne 'sea tail') and an artillery officer who crossed to help the men at Oosterbeek and were killed there.

The RAF suffered grievously in carrying and then attempting to supply 1st Airborne. The squadrons of 38 and 46 Groups flew 1,339 sorties (12 parachute dropping, 715 glider towing and 612 resupply) and lost 68 aircraft (44 Stirlings and 24 Dakotas), all but two on the resupply flights. The number of aircrew and passengers killed numbered 152, and of army despatchers 79. The RAF aircrew deaths included 38 Canadians, 11 Australians, 5 New Zealanders and one South African. To this can be added 27 American aircrew killed while dropping British and Polish parachute units, making a total of 258 deaths on the air side of the Arnhem operation. It is not often realized how great the air-force and air-despatch sacrifice was at Arnhem; their fatal casualties were more than 30 per cent of those suffered by the 1st Airborne Division!

What of the other dead? The Germans and the local Dutch people? A signal, presumably from II SS Panzer Corps, on 27 September gave a figure of 3,300 German casualties in and around Arnhem, including 1,300 dead. Dutch records show that at least 453 people died during the battle: 188 in Arnhem, 90 in Wolfheze, 83 in Oosterbeek, 72 in Ede and the remainder in other places; more than half of these people lost their lives in Allied bombing raids on the first day of the operation. The total dead as a result of the Battle of Arnhem was thus approximately 3,500, of whom nearly two-thirds were Allied.

Was It Worth It?

Few would argue with the view that 'Market Garden' was a reasonable operation to mount in the circumstances of the time. Let us look back again at the situation. After strenuous effort and grievous loss the Allies had broken the tight German defence in Normandy and advanced almost to the borders of Germany before becoming bogged down by a temporary shortage of supplies. The First Allied Airborne Army was waiting in England, as John Waddy, an officer who fought at Arnhem, says, 'comparable to the cavalry of World War One — the mobile force ready to exploit success and complete the enemy's defeat'. The wartime benefits if 'Market Garden' had succeeded were potentially enormous: the unleashing of the huge mobile Allied armies on to the North German Plain, with the prospect of ending the war in 1944. There were also the as-yet-unseen potential post-war bonuses. The Allied ground forces were nearer to Berlin than the Russians, even before 'Market Garden'. If 'Market Garden' had been successful, the Russians would not have had the favourable bargaining conditions which they wielded at the Yalta Conference in February 1945, when they secured post-war domination over half of Germany and all of Eastern Europe. Dare one mention Poland, the country over whose violation Britain had gone to war in 1939 and whose men fought with the British at Arnhem? Poland was just one of the countries condemned to more than forty years of Communist rule at Yalta, just as the West was condemned to suffer the long Cold War. All this would have been different if 'Market Garden' had succeeded. 'Market Garden' would have been different had there been success at Arnhem. No wonder there is such fascination with that battle. No wonder that years later a German, thinking of post-war Europe and the partition of his country, should tell a Dutchman that Germany's biggest disaster in the war was to win the Battle of Arnhem.

The men who fought at Arnhem are angered by the facile use of the phrase 'the failure at Arnhem'. If it is recognized that the strategic concept of 'Market Garden' was sound, then the tactical defeat at Arnhem was mostly the result of actions taken by others; few errors can be laid at the door of the airborne soldiers who fought and fell at Arnhem, Oosterbeek and Driel. The mistakes have all been encountered and their results described in the 'action' chapters of this book; a brief résumé of both major and minor factors, presented in roughly chronological order, will suffice here:

● The over-optimism about the powers of recovery and resistance of the Germans after the Normandy defeat, with only Major-General Sosabowski and Major Brian Urquhart seriously challenging the euphoria, and both suffering the ill will of their superiors for doing so.

- The failure to warn 1st Airborne adequately of the danger from the known presence of two Panzer divisions, denying units the opportunity to substitute anti-tank weapons for other parts of their loads.

- The decision by Lieutenant-General Browning to take a headquarters to Holland, making no useful contribution to the battle and requiring thirty-eight gliders from the first lift to Arnhem.

- The failure of the air plan. The refusal to consider a night drop or to land at least parts of the force as *coup-de-main* parties closer to the two bridges, and the failure to land any part of the force at both ends of the bridge objectives, all of which threw away an airborne force's most valuable asset: surprise. The refusal to fly two lifts on the first day, which resulted in the prolonged dispersal of the division and its failure to achieve concentration of effort. These were the cardinal, fundamental errors. It would be interesting to know how many aircraft would have been lost to the supposed flak defences near the bridge or in overflying Deelen airfield if a bolder air plan had been used, compared to the huge eventual loss of aircraft dropping supplies which never reached the airborne men. Air Vice-Marshal Hollinghurst, who prepared much of the Arnhem air plan, ceased to be commander of 38 Group one month to the day after the first lift flew to Arnhem. His successor, Air Vice-Marshal Scarlett-Streatfield, produced a combined 38–46 Group report on Arnhem which reads: 'In future operations against an organized enemy, it may be found necessary to complete the entire lift within a matter of hours, landing every essential unit or load before the enemy can assess the situation, and not relying on airborne reinforcement or resupply.'[1] It was a blueprint for the successful airborne landing across the Rhine in March 1945.

- The failure, by 1st Airborne Division commanders, to impart to unit commanders of the 1st Parachute Brigade the absolute necessity of relentless speed and dash in moving towards the Arnhem road bridge in the first hours of the operation. That failure has haunted the Parachute Regiment ever since; any

---

[1] Report in Airborne Forces Museum, File No. 56.

student of its post-war training and operations can detect the effect of that Sunday failure.

- The failure to use Dutch civilian resources more fully.
- The failure to employ fighter-bomber units of 2nd Tactical Air Force in the 'cab-rank' ground-support role which the ground forces used at all times except in severe weather conditions.
- The failure of Browning to give the 82nd US Airborne Division a greater priority in capturing the bridge at Nijmegen. This comes only just behind the weakness of the air plan in importance.
- The lack of sufficient 'push' by General Dempsey at Second British Army and by XXX Corps. Montgomery's order to Dempsey that the ground attack should be 'rapid and violent, without regard to what is happening on the flanks' was not complied with. The casualties of XXX Corps in the battle were less than 1,500, compared with more than 8,000 British and Polish at Arnhem. John Frost, who did so much to keep the Arnhem road bridge open for the ground forces, was freed from his prison camp in 1945 by a unit of Patton's Third US Army. Frost later wrote: 'All ranks of this army, when they saw our red berets, would say, "Arnhem. Aye. We'd have gotten through. Yes, sir. We'd have gotten through." – I couldn't help believing that they would have.'[2]
- The failure by Urquhart and his staff to appreciate the importance of the Westerbouwing height and the Rhine ferry below it. The failure to accept Sosabowski's view at the Valburg Conference about the better crossing prospects further downstream for the 4th Dorsets, which led to the sacrifice of that battalion.

These observations are all made with the benefit of hindsight. Few of them are new; the major ones have been long accepted.

---

[2] Major-General John Frost, *A Drop Too Many*, Cassell, London, 1980, p. 241.

CHAPTER 22

The Years That Followed

The 1st Airborne Division returned to England sadly depleted. Not only were three-quarters of the men who had taken part in the battle missing, but there was a huge gap in leadership. The Divisional HQ staff was still mainly intact, but two of the three brigade commanders, a complete brigade HQ, eight of the nine battalion commanders and twenty-six of the thirty rifle company commanders had not returned. The available reinforcements could do no more than produce a division of two weak brigades. The 4th Parachute Brigade was disbanded, and its battalions merged with those of the 1st Parachute Brigade. Brigadier Hackett, when he returned after escaping from Holland, found 'my beloved brigade was dead and buried; I had been its midwife and its sexton'. On recovering from his wounds, Hackett dropped a rank and became GSO 1 of an armoured division in Italy, 'happy to be back in armour' after his frustrating airborne experience; he rose to the rank of full general after the war. There was no further promotion for Browning or Urquhart. Arnhem may have brought Roy Urquhart fame, but his career was tainted by the defeat, and he remained a major-general until his retirement in 1955. Browning left the airborne world only a few months after Arnhem, not to another command but to become Chief of Staff at South-East Asia Command, and he retired in 1948.

The first list of decorations was published quickly, but was confined to that part of the division which had been evacuated across the Rhine. There was one Victoria Cross, for Major Cain of the South Staffords, an Order of the Bath for Major-General Urquhart and fifty-eight other decorations. A special investiture for the division took place at Buckingham Palace on 6 December 1944. To represent the division at the investiture, 438 men were selected from units to parade through London in what the men called a 'ghost march', because no prior notice was given to the public for security reasons. Three posthumous VCs were announced later – for Captain Queripel, Lieutenant Grayburn and Lance-Sergeant Baskeyfield (also one for Flight Lieutenant Lord) – but the second main divisional list, for those who were prisoners of war or evaders, was not published until September 1945. They received a paltry twenty-five gallantry awards, for 5,903 men, compared with fifty-nine such awards for under 2,000 who had come straight home from Arnhem. Although most of the latter had endured the longer siege at Oosterbeek, their almost eight times greater chance of receiving a decoration than the men who were taken prisoner or became evaders was quite out of balance.

The 1st Airborne Division took no part in the next airborne operation, the Rhine crossing in March 1945, which was carried out by the 6th British and 17th US Airborne Divisions, the latter a new division flying from bases in France. Many of the lessons learned at Arnhem were applied and the operation was successful. Poor Holland, which had seemed to be on the verge of liberation in September 1944, remained cut off in German hands and suffering severe hunger until the end of the war. Part of the 1st Airborne Division was flown to Norway in May 1945 to oversee the German surrender there but suffered a tragedy when four Stirlings crashed in bad weather, killing thirty-four men, mostly of the 1st Border and Divisional HQ. Among the RAF dead was Air Vice-Marshal Scarlett-Streatfield, who had taken over 38 Group after Arnhem. The 1st Parachute Brigade, flown to Denmark for the same purpose, arrived safely. The division's units remained in those places for several weeks, happily engaged in disarming German units and being shown great hospitality by the liberated civilians.

An interesting duty came the way of 120 Arnhem veterans who were detached from their units and sent back to Arnhem and Oosterbeek to re-create the battle in the ruins there for the film *Theirs Is the Glory*. While they were there, in the summer of 1945, the Army Graves Registration Unit was exhuming the bodies of the dead and making the permanent cemetery at Oosterbeek. The completion of the cemetery coincided with the end of the filming in Holland and the 120 men proudly paraded at the new cemetery before returning to England and completing other scenes of the film.

The division returned from Norway and Denmark in August 1945. A plan to transfer it to the Middle East as a strategic reserve was abandoned when the war in the Far East ended, and the division which had fought so gallantly in North Africa, Sicily and Italy and at Arnhem was disbanded. The Airlanding Brigade became conventional infantry again and the 1st Parachute Brigade was transferred to the 6th Airborne Division. But when 6th Airborne was reduced to brigade strength in 1948, the '1st' and '6th' numerals of the two wartime airborne divisions were retained and that brigade became the 16th Parachute Brigade.

The Glider Pilot Regiment did not survive. The Second World War was the only one in which large-scale glider operations were carried out. They had proved to be an expensive and not always efficient means of delivering airborne troops to battle, and post-war transport aircraft development brought the capability of dropping vehicles and guns by parachute. Within five years there was little of the Glider Pilot Regiment remaining and the regiment was formally disbanded in 1957, its last members becoming incorporated into the Army Air Corps. Arnhem, where the regiment covered itself in glory, was its major battle honour.

The Polish Independent Parachute Brigade suffered the humiliation of being criticized for its behaviour at Arnhem and then seeing its commander dismissed from his position. This process started on 17 October 1944, when Montgomery wrote to Field Marshal Sir Alan Brooke, Chief of the Imperial General Staff, referring to Arnhem: 'Polish Para Brigade fought very badly and the men showed no keenness to fight if it meant risking their own lives. I do not want this brigade here and possibly you may like to send them to join other Poles in Italy.'[1]

It was a month later, on 20 November, that Browning wrote a long letter to Lieutenant-General Sir Ronald Weeks, Brooke's deputy, reporting on Sosabowski's command of the brigade before and during the battle.[2] Browning charged Sosabowski with being

---

[1] Richard Lamb, *Montgomery in Europe 1943–1945: Success or Failure?*, Buchan & Enright, London, 1983, p. 251.
[2] Copy of letter at the Polish Institute and Sikorski Museum, London.

'difficult to work with', 'unable to adapt himself to the level of a parachute brigade commander' and, during the battle, 'quite incapable of appreciating the urgent nature of the operation and continually showing himself to be both argumentative and loth to play his full part in the operation unless everything was done for him and his brigade'. Browning concluded by saying that he was 'forced, therefore, to recommend that General Sosabowski be employed elsewhere and that a younger, more flexibly minded and co-operative officer be made available to succeed him'.

On 9 December Sosabowski was informed by the Polish President-in-exile, Wladyslaw Raczkiewicz, that he was removed from his command. The letter gave no reason for the dismissal and even stressed to Sosabowski 'the merits of your service in this post and your proven character on the battlefield'. The move was obviously made under British pressure. A study of the relevant chapters of this book will show that the only criticism that can be made of the Polish brigade was that its men were not skilled at rowing unfamiliar boats across a swift-flowing river in the darkness and under fire. The seeds of the dismissal were probably set at the Valburg Conference when Sosabowski had been isolated and humiliated by Thomas and Horrocks and not supported in any way by his airborne commander, Browning. It seems likely that the commanders in that ground-force chain of command Thomas–Horrocks–Dempsey–Montgomery found that blaming Sosabowski and his brigade was a convenient way of deflecting blame from the failure of the ground forces to reach Arnhem. Browning, who was about to leave the scene for South-East Asia, may have been persuaded to write that damning letter to the Deputy CIGS which resulted in Sosabowski becoming the scapegoat. It was a shameful act by the British commanders.

Sosabowski handed over to his deputy commander, Lieutenant-Colonel Stanislaw Jachnik; two of the Polish units went on hunger strike at Christmas as a protest. The brigade never went to Poland and never reverted to Polish control after its first operation, both of which had been promised. At the end of the war in Europe, it was sent as part of the Allied occupation force in Germany, where it served for two years before returning to England to be disbanded in 1947. Most of its members remained in England, many marrying

English or Scottish girls and usually having to take the least popular jobs, many in the brickfields of the Peterborough area where they had been stationed during the war.

The battle had brought only suffering, hardship and disappointment to the people of Arnhem and Oosterbeek. The Germans cleared the whole area of civilians, at Arnhem as soon as the bridge defence ended, at Oosterbeek immediately after the battle, though some civilians were forced to remain and bury the bodies of the airborne men killed in the battle in a series of field and garden burial sites. All of the civilians eventually left, fleeing to the north with little more than they could carry or push and forbidden to return without a permit. This action by the Germans was partly to punish the Dutch for the help given to the British and partly to clear the area when a new defence line was dug along the north bank of the Rhine. Arnhem was divided into sections and systematically looted, the items taken from each section being sent to bombed German cities.

The Allied forces fell back from the river and from Driel to a more convenient line five miles to the south. The Germans made no effort to fill the vacuum, and a large area became no man's land for the next six months. The Arnhem road bridge was destroyed, for the second time in this war, when American B-26 Marauders of the 344th Bomb Group bombed it on 7 October to prevent the Germans using it to reinforce their front line further south. Both Arnhem and Oosterbeek were shelled by Allied guns from the south bank during the winter, resulting in more destruction than the airborne battle. It was not until April 1945 that units of the 49th (West Riding) Division, under Canadian command, launched a river crossing just east of Arnhem and, after fierce fighting, opened up the area to a delayed liberation.

The Dutch returned after the war and rebuilt their homes. Oosterbeek retained much of its character, but the houses near the bridge where John Frost's force made its courageous stand were completely cleared and replaced by modern office buildings. The airborne and RAF dead in and around Arnhem and Oosterbeek and the Polish dead from Driel were reinterred in a new war cemetery just north of Oosterbeek. For the first few years, until the permanent lawns and flower borders became established, each grave was adopted by a local child who tended it throughout the year and then stood proudly by it at the annual ceremony each September. Those airborne men with no known graves are commemorated on the Memorial to the Missing at the Groesbeek War Cemetery, close to where Browning's Corps HQ landed by glider. The Parachute Regiment names number 178, nearly a hundred more than the nearest other regimental total; they are mostly Arnhem dead but include some of the 6th Airborne Division men lost on the Rhine drop of March 1945. The German dead from Arnhem, originally buried in an 'SS Heroes Cemetery' just outside Arnhem, were concentrated after the war in the only German war cemetery in Holland at IJsselstijn, a remote spot between Eindhoven and Venlo, where 31,511 Germans from the Second World War are buried.

Remains of bodies continue to be found on the battlefield. One month before I wrote this chapter, those of two airborne men were found in a garden where C Company, 1st Border, held perimeter positions at Oosterbeek; they were eventually identified as the remains of Privates Ernest Ager and Douglas Lowery and were reburied with their comrades in the War Cemetery at Oosterbeek. There are other, more dangerous remainders of the battle. One of Kate ter Horst's sons and his friend were killed in 1947 when they disturbed a wartime mine, probably an anti-tank mine placed under the grass of the meadow behind her house by the Germans in the winter of 1944.

The survivors of the 1st Airborne Division have been coming back every year since the war, still 200 to 250 each year for the annual ceremonies in September, many more for the ten-year anniversaries. If the pilgrimages are carried on as resolutely as the ones to the Battle of the Somme, which I often attend, they will continue until the seventy-fifth anniversary in the year 2019! The local children still stand by each grave at the Oosterbeek cemetery service every September and place a bunch of flowers on their grave at a given signal. The annual ceremonies also include a parachute drop by the Territorial 10th Parachute Battalion on Ginkel Heath and a silent march in Arnhem, as well as many other events. There is also the annual 'Airborne Walk' on the first

Saturday in September when more than 30,000 people from all over Holland and other countries commemorate the battle with a walk of various sections up to a maximum of twenty-five kilometres in and around Oosterbeek.

There are numerous memorials in the battle areas (detailed in Appendix 5) and a fine Airborne Museum, which has been at the Hartenstein since it was moved from its earlier site at Doorwerth Castle in 1978. There can be no place in Europe more fervent and diligent in its thanksgiving for its liberation than where the airborne battle was fought in 1944, particularly at Oosterbeek. This is a source of wonder to the Arnhem veterans whose landing and subsequent fight were responsible for destroying and damaging homes and then for the forced evacuation of civilians by the Germans which led to so much hardship in the last, hungry winter of the war. One anti-tank gunner says: 'We expected it to be the other way round, that they would be resentful, but it's lovely to be welcomed back as we are.' This remarkably enduring attitude is generated by the ordinary people, not by officialdom, and there is no place in this emotion for the former German enemy. Efforts by German ex-soldiers' associations to join in the ceremonies are firmly rejected by local opinion; a wreath placed by Germans in the war cemetery on one occasion was swiftly removed.

The surviving men who fought at Arnhem in 1st Airborne and the Polish brigade and those who flew with the RAF and American squadrons nurse an intense pride in having taken part in the battle. So great is the prestige of having been 'an Arnhem man' that men who did not take part occasionally try to pass themselves off as veterans of the battle and cause unit associations some embarrassment. I met a 'red beret' at an Armistice Day ceremony at the Menin Gate at Ypres who, on my enquiring, claimed to have been at Arnhem until I showed too much interest in his unit, whereupon he quickly departed. Another aspect is the desire to be associated with the defence at the Arnhem road bridge, with men who did not reach the bridge sometimes claiming to have done so.

What do the young men who fought at Arnhem think about that experience now?

Sapper George Needham, 1st Parachute Squadron: 'I don't think any of us realized the seriousness of the position at the time. Every gun which went off – we thought it was XXX Corps coming to relieve us. It was "the biggest balls-up since Mons"; that was a regular saying in our squadron.'

Lance-Sergeant Syd Fitchett, 1st Airlanding Anti-Tank Battery: 'I was lucky to get out at the finish with a broken foot and a bullet wound in my arm, but let me also add that I wouldn't have missed this "adventure" for all the tea in China.'

Anonymous officer:

I am very bitter about Arnhem; I lost too many friends. When I got married at the end of the war, I realized that my best man was the ninth on a mental list of who I would have liked; the first eight were all dead or incapacitated. For years I would not talk about or read about Arnhem. When I did start reading, I came to the conclusion that it was all due to the flag-waving attitude of people like Montgomery who wanted to show how much cleverer they were than the others.

Lance-Corporal Harry Smith, South Staffords:

Even today it is hard to explain the feeling, but something seems to come over me. I go withdrawn and want to be by myself and keep quiet for days. Then my mind – or should I say myself – all of a sudden goes back to Arnhem. Then, after thinking things out as to what might have happened, or if this should have happened or that should have happened, I seem to worry something terrible for a while before I slowly return to myself.

Staff Sergeant Joe Kitchener, Glider Pilot Regiment:

Most surviving glider pilots I know either can't stop talking about it or can't bring themselves to talk about it. Some will go to Arnhem year after year; others will not go under any circumstances. I am fairly well adjusted, but I still have nightmares so violent that my wife gets bruised in bed. I am not bitter; I've had nearly fifty more years than those poor devils who lie in the Oosterbeek cemetery. It seemed a good idea at the time. It was a gamble; some you win, some you lose. We lost that one.

Private George Stubbs, 2nd Battalion: 'I shall be in Arnhem again in September. The house we held is an empty space now. I stood there in darkness in 1989, exactly forty-five years after to the day, and will also be there again under the ramp. I cannot put my feelings into words, even though it is nearly half a century ago now.'

To speak for the Dutch, Miss Ans Kremer, of No. 8 Stationsweg, Oosterbeek:

The fighting made a very big impression on me. I was not afraid, but I had a feeling about the wounded and the dead just lying around and the dying – a feeling I cannot put a name to. Like the one we saw being hit, who shouted, 'Goodbye', three times, then died. Because of that, I now use 'Goodbye' very rarely; there is a kind of finality about it for me.

Those events have always stayed with me, not all the time, and certainly not consciously, but now and then a face, a smell, a noise or situation brings up a vague memory or a vivid picture, with the sad feeling that goes with it. Those men are, for me, friends. Somehow there is a bond, and when we meet I want to give them a good time and make them comfortable. They came to help us be free again, and I feel very grateful but also indebted to them because of all the suffering and dying of so many, known and unknown to us. 'Grateful' is too small a word. There are feelings you cannot really put into words properly.

Order of Battle and Operational Details, 1st British Airborne Division and Attached Units

(*Notes*: Locations of UK bases for glider-borne units are their long-term ones, not the transit camps near airfields occupied just before Operation 'Market'. Details of airfields from which units flew may contain inaccuracies because loading lists for 'Market' are often those of Operations 'Linnet' or 'Comet' which were amended. Personnel statistics are the best available, often from conflicting sources, and usually include men who left England but did not arrive at Arnhem. As in Chapter 21, 'died' includes men who were killed in action or in battle atrocities or escape attempts immediately after the battle, and those who died of wounds up to the end of 1944. The 'missing' were mostly prisoners of war – many wounded – and some who subsequently returned as evaders.)

1st British Airborne Division (*Maj.-Gen. R. E. Urquhart*)

Divisional HQ and Defence Platoon   Based at Fulbeck Hall. Flew in 7 C-47s from Barkston Heath and Saltby and 29 Horsas from Fairford, Down Ampney and Manston. Went in: 142 men; died: 14; evacuated: 70; missing: 58.

1st Parachute Brigade (*Brig. G. W. Lathbury, wounded and evader*)

Brigade HQ and Defence Platoon   Based at Syston Old Hall. Flew in 9 C-47s from Barkston Heath and (believed) 8 Horsas from Blakehill Farm. Went in: 82 men; died: 5; evacuated: 3; missing: 74.

1st Parachute Battalion (Lt-Col D. T. Dobie, taken prisoner but escaped and became evader)   Based at Grimsthorpe Castle and Bourne. Flew in 34 C-47s from Barkston Heath, vehicles in 7 Horsas from Keevil and a Hamilcar from Tarrant Rushton. Went in: 548 men; died: 82; evacuated: 89 or 108 (reports differ); missing: 377 or 358.

2nd Parachute Battalion (Lt-Col J. D. Frost, prisoner of war)   Based at Stoke Rochford and Grantham. Flew in 34 C-47s from Saltby, vehicles in gliders as 1st Battalion. Went in: 525 men; died: 57; evacuated: 16; missing: 452.

3rd Parachute Battalion (Lt-Col J. A. C. Fitch, died of wounds)   Based at Spalding. Flew in as 2nd Battalion. Went in: 588 men; died: 65; evacuated: 28; missing: 495.

1st Airlanding Anti-Tank Battery, RA (Maj. W. F. Arnold, prisoner of war)   Based at Heckington and Helpringham, with newly formed 17-pounder P Troop at Tarrant Rushton. Flew in 30 Horsas from Manston (mostly) and Blakehill Farm, 17-pounder troops in 8 Hamilcars from Tarrant Rushton. Went in: 191 men; died: 24; evacuated: 52; missing: 115.

1st Parachute Squadron, RE (Maj. D. C. Murray, prisoner of war)   Based at Donington. Flew in 9 C-47s from Barkston Heath and 4 Horsas from Keevil. Went in: 143 men; died: 20; evacuated: 13; missing: 110.

16 Parachute Field Ambulance, RAMC (Lt-Col E. Townsend, prisoner of war)   Based at Culverthorpe. Flew in 6 C-47s from Barkston Heath and Saltby and 6 Horsas from Keevil. Went in: 135 men; died: 6; probably none evacuated; missing: up to 129.

1st Airlanding Brigade (Brig. R. H. W. Hicks)

Brigade HQ and Defence Platoon   Based at Woodhall Spa. Flew in 11 Horsas from Broadwell. Went in: 69 men; died: 7; evacuated: 39; missing: 23.

7th (Galloway) King's Own Scottish Borderers (Lt-Col R. Payton-Reid, only battalion commander to return on the evacuation)   Based at Woodhall Spa. Flew in 56 Horsas from Down Ampney and Blakehill Farm and a Hamilcar from Tarrant Rushton. Went in: 765 men; died: 112; evacuated: 76; missing: 577.

1st Border (Lt-Col T. H. Haddon, taken prisoner while attempting to reach his battalion after his glider twice came down before reaching Arnhem)   Based at Woodhall Spa, B Company at Bardney. Flew in 56 Horsas from Broadwell and Blakehill Farm and a Hamilcar from Tarrant Rushton. Went in: 788 men; died: 121 (more than any other battalion); evacuated: 235; missing: 432.

2nd South Staffordshires (Lt-Col W. D. H. McCardie, wounded and prisoner of war)   Based at Woodhall Spa. Flew in over two days in 62 Horsas from Manston and Broadwell and a Hamilcar from Tarrant Rushton. Went in: 767 men; died: 85; evacuated: 124; missing: 558.

181 Airlanding Field Ambulance, RAMC (Lt-Col A. T. Marrable, prisoner of war)   Based at Stenigot House and Martin. Flew in 12 Horsas from Down Ampney. Went in: 137 men; died: 5; probably none evacuated; missing: up to 132.

4th Parachute Brigade (Brig. J. W. Hackett, wounded and evader)

Brigade HQ and Defence Platoon   Based at Knossington Grange. Flew in 9 C-47s (1 with Advance Party from Barkston Heath, 8 from Spanhoe) and 8 Horsas from Keevil. Went in: 86 men; died: 12; evacuated: 43; missing: 31.

156 Parachute Battalion (Lt-Col Sir R. de B. des Voeux, killed in action)   Based in and around Melton Mowbray. Flew in 34 C-47s (1 with Advance Party from Barkston Heath, 33 from Saltby), vehicles in 7 Horsas from Keevil and a Hamilcar from Tarrant Rushton. Went in: 479 men (possibly more); died: 98; evacuated: 68; missing: 313.

10th Parachute Battalion (Lt-Col K. B. I. Smyth, died of wounds) Based at Somerby, Thorpe Satchville, Burgh-on-the-Hill and Twyford. Flew in 34 C-47s (1 with Advance Party from Barkston Heath, 33 from Spanhoe), vehicles as 156 Battalion. Went in: 582 men; died: 92; evacuated: 86; missing: 404.

11th Parachute Battalion (Lt-Col G. H. Lea, wounded and prisoner of war)   Based at Melton Mowbray. Flew in as 156 Battalion. Went in: 571 men; died: 92; evacuated: 72; missing: 407.

2nd (Oban) Airlanding Anti-Tank Battery, RA (Maj. A. F. Haynes, prisoner of war)   Based at Harrowby. Flew in 24 Horsas from Blakehill

Farm and 8 Hamilcars from Tarrant Rushton. Went in: 168 men; died: 25; evacuated: 37; missing: 106.

4th Parachute Squadron, RE (Maj. A. J. M. Perkins, wounded and prisoner of war)   Based at Uppingham. Flew in 9 C-47s from Spanhoe and 4 Horsas from Keevil. Went in: 155 men; died: 19; evacuated: 64; missing: 72.

133 Parachute Field Ambulance, RAMC (Lt-Col W. C. Alford, prisoner of war)   Based at Barleythorpe Hall. Flew in 6 C-47s from Spanhoe and Saltby, and 6 Horsas from Keevil. Went in: 129 men; died: 6; probably none evacuated; missing: up to 123; one officer from the 'sea tail' also died.

Divisional Units

1st Airlanding Light Regiment, RA (Lt-Col W. F. K. Thompson, wounded and prisoner of war)   Based at Boston. The regiment (less No. 2 Battery) flew in 57 Horsas from Fairford, Blakehill Farm, Down Ampney, Manston and Keevil on first lift; No. 2 Battery and others flew in 33 Horsas from Manston on second lift. Went in: 372 men; died: 36; evacuated: 136; missing: 200.

1 Forward (Airborne) Observation Unit, RA (Maj. D. R. Wight Boycott, at Airborne Corps HQ)   Based at Harlaxton Hall. Flew in 3 Horsas from Keevil and in small groups in C-47s and Horsas of brigades and battalions. Went in: 73 men; died: 7; evacuated: 23; missing: 43.

1st Airborne Divisional Signals (Lt-Col T. C. V. Stephenson)   Based at Caythorpe. Flew in C-47s and Horsas from several airfields, much of the unit being split up to provide signals for the division's infantry brigade and artillery HQs. Went in: 348 men; died: 28; evacuated: 149; missing: 171.

9th (Airborne) Field Company, RE (Maj. J. C. Winchester)   Based at Tattershall and Coningsby. Flew in 22 Horsas in two lifts from Keevil. Went in: 194 men; died: 44; evacuated: 71; missing: 79.

261 (Airborne) Field Park Company, RE   A small detachment, under the command of Lt W. H. Skinner (who was killed in a battlefield atrocity), flew in 3 Horsas and a Hamilcar, believed all from Tarrant Rushton. Went in: 13 men; died: 2; evacuated: 5; missing: 6.

21st Independent Parachute Company (Maj. B. A. Wilson)   Based at

Newark. Flew in 12 Stirlings from Fairford and a Horsa (believed from Fairford). Went in: 186 men; died: 20; evacuated: 120; missing: 46.

1st Airborne Reconnaissance Squadron (Maj. C. F. G. Gough, prisoner of war)   Based at Ruskington. Flew in 8 C-47s from Barkston Heath and 22 Horsas from Tarrant Rushton. Went in: 181 men; died: 30; evacuated: 73; missing: 78.

250 (Airborne) Light Composite Company, RASC   Based at Longhills Hall, Branston, and at Lincoln. Three parachute platoons, with jeeps sections attached, together with a light transport section of jeeps, were provided by the company for the airborne operation, most of the heavy transport coming up with the 'sea tail'. Flew in 4 C-47s from Barkston Heath and Saltby and 34 Horsas and 3 Hamilcars from Keevil, Harwell and Tarrant Rushton. Went in: 226 men (including 10 from 93 Company attached); died: 29; evacuated: 75; missing: 122.

1st (Airborne) Divisional Field Park, RAOC (Maj. C. C. Chidgey, wounded and prisoner of war)   Based at Grantham. Flew in a shared C-47 from Barkston Heath and a Horsa from Keevil. Went in: 19 men; died: 2; evacuated: 2; missing: 15.

1st (Airborne) Divisional Workshops, REME   Based at Sleaford. A detachment of the unit flew in 4 Horsas from Fairford and Down Ampney, and individual men flew in with various units. Went in: 61 men; died: 6; evacuated: 29; missing: 26.

1st (Airborne) Divisional Provost Company, CMP (Capt. W. B. Gray, died of wounds)   Based at Stubton Hall, Newark, but sections at divisional and brigade HQs. Company HQ flew in a Horsa from Down Ampney, sections in shared C-47s or Horsas with units. Went in: 69 men; died: 7; evacuated: 13; missing: 49.

89th (Parachute) Field Security Section, Intelligence Corps (Capt. J. E. Killick, prisoner of war)   Based at Wellingore. HQ flew in a shared Horsa from Fairford, others with units. Went in: 16 men; died: 3; evacuated: 4; missing: 9.

Units Attached To The Division

The Glider Pilot Regiment   No. 1 Wing (HQ Harwell) commanded by Lt-Col I. A. Murray – A Squadron at Harwell, B Squadron normally at Brize Norton but flying to Arnhem from Manston, D Squadron at Keevil and G Squadron at Fairford. No. 2 WING (HQ Broadwell) commanded by Lt-Col J. W. Place – C Squadron at Tarrant Rushton, E Squadron at Down Ampney and F Squadron at Broadwell and Blakehill Farm. Went in: 1,262 men; died: 219; evacuated: 532; missing: 511. (These figures do not include 76 glider pilots of Regimental HQ, including Col G. S. Chatterton, and of A Squadron who flew gliders carrying Airborne Corps HQ without serious casualty.)

6080 and 6341 Light Warning Units, RAF   These mobile radar units flew in 4 Horsas from Harwell on the second lift. Went in: 45 men; died: 9; evacuated: 4; missing: 32.

Dutch Liaison Mission   This 12-strong group, mostly from No. 2 (Dutch) Troop of No. 10 (Inter-Allied) Commando, flew in with various units. One Commando was killed; two were taken prisoner; the remainder were evacuated or became evaders.

Public Relations Team   Fifteen men flew in; one was taken prisoner; it is thought that the others were evacuated safely.

US Air Support Signals Teams   Two teams, each of five Americans from the 306th Fighter Control Squadron with two British jeep drivers, flew in 4 Waco gliders from Manston. No fatal casualties; numbers evacuated and missing not known.

GHQ Signal Liaison Regiment Detachment (Phantom)   Ten men flew in (aircraft/glider details not known); no fatal casualties; no further details available.

'Jedburgh' Team   Two officers (one Dutch, one US) and one US NCO flew in shared C-47. The Dutch officer was killed and the American officer became a prisoner of war; the US NCO, Technical Sergeant Carl A. Scott, evaded capture and returned to duty but was killed in action later in 1944.

Order of Battle, Polish Independent Parachute Brigade Group

(Details of the fly-in of units, spread out as they were over four lifts, are too complicated to be usefully included. Casualties include some incurred when the brigade remained in action after the main Arnhem battle ended. 'Wounded' are those evacuated safely to the Allied rear.)

Brigade HQ (Maj.-Gen. S. F. Sosabowski) Based at Rock House, Stamford. Went in: 104 men plus 9 British liaison officers; died: 5 (including one in a motor accident); missing: 15; wounded: 16.

1st Battalion (Maj. M. Tonn) Based at Easton-on-the-Hill. Went in: 354 men; died: 11; missing: 4; wounded: 28.

2nd Battalion (Maj. W. Ploszewski) Based at Wansford. Went in: 351 men; died: 11; missing: 7; wounded: 33.

3rd Battalion (Capt. W. Sobocinski) Based at Peterborough. Went in: 374 men; died: 30; missing: 39; wounded: 48.

Anti-Tank Battery (Capt. J. K. Wardzala, prisoner of war) Based at Blatherwycke. Went in: 132 men; died: 20; missing: 29; wounded: 30.

Engineer Company (Capt. P. Budziszewski) Based at Wansford. Went in: 133 men; died: 2; missing: 1; wounded: 20.

Signals Company (Capt. J. Burzawa) Based at Easton-on-the-Hill. Went in: 93 men; died: 7 or 8; missing: 10; wounded: 16.

Medical Company (Lt J. Mozdzierz) Based at Stamford and Blatherwycke. Went in: 90 men; died: 2; missing: 7; wounded: 13.

Transport and Supply Company (Capt. A. Siudzinski with 'sea tail', joined via Nijmegen) Went in by air: 43 men; died: 8 (including one in motor accident and 2 accidentally shot by British troops); missing: 8; wounded: 13.

Light Artillery Battery (Maj. J. Bielecki) Only five junior officers and one liaison officer with 1st British Airborne Division went in by air; two were wounded.

Order of Battle, 38 and 46 Groups RAF and RASC Air Despatch Units

38 Group

190 Squadron   Based at Fairford. Flew 98 Stirling sorties – 6 parachute dropping, 42 glider towing, 50 resupply. Lost 12 aircraft (more than any other squadron); 38 men killed, 15 prisoners, 25 returned safely from crashes.

196 Squadron   Based at Keevil. Flew 112 Stirling sorties (with 299 Squadron, more sorties than any other squadron) – 56 glider towing, 56 resupply. Lost 10 aircraft; 26 men killed, 2 prisoners, 33 returned.

295 Squadron   Based at Harwell. Flew 106 Stirling sorties – 28 glider towing (including Airborne Corps HQ lift), 78 resupply. Lost 3 aircraft; 7 men killed, 7 prisoners, 4 returned.

296 and 297 Squadrons   Normally based at Brize Norton but flying to Arnhem from Manston. Both squadrons flew 50 Albemarle sorties, all glider towing, without loss.

298 Squadron   Based at Tarrant Rushton. Flew 46 glider-towing Halifax sorties without loss.

299 Squadron   Based at Keevil. Flew 112 Stirling sorties (with 196 Squadron, more sorties than any other squadron) – 54 glider towing, 58 resupply. Lost 5 aircraft; 4 men killed, 10 prisoners, 18 returned.

570 Squadron   Based at Harwell. Flew 103 Stirling sorties – 30 glider towing (including Airborne Corps HQ lift), 73 resupply. Lost 9 aircraft; 22 men killed, 16 prisoners, 18 returned.

620 Squadron   Based at Fairford. Flew 104 Stirling sorties – 6 parachute dropping, 42 glider towing, 56 resupply. Lost 5 aircraft; 8 men killed, 7 prisoners, 15 returned.

644 Squadron   Based at Tarrant Rushton. Flew 46 glider-towing Halifax sorties without loss.

46 Group

18 Squadron Based at Down Ampney. Flew 111 Dakota sorties (more than any other Dakota squadron) – 52 glider towing, 59 resupply. Lost 7 aircraft; 14 men killed, 4 prisoners, 10 returned.

233 Squadron Based at Blakehill Farm. Flew 73 Dakota sorties – 42 glider towing, 31 resupply. Lost 3 aircraft; 6 men killed, 4 prisoners, 2 returned.

271 Squadron Based at Down Ampney. Flew 98 Dakota sorties – 47 glider towing, 51 resupply. Lost 5 aircraft; 8 men killed, 4 prisoners, 12 returned.

437 (RCAF) Squadron Based at Blakehill Farm. Flew 45 Dakota sorties – 16 glider towing, 29 resupply. Lost 5 aircraft; 12 men killed, 4 prisoners, 4 returned.

512 Squadron Based at Broadwell. Flew 77 Dakota sorties – 48 glider towing, 29 resupply. Lost 3 aircraft; 2 men killed, 6 prisoners, 4 returned.

575 Squadron Based at Broadwell. Flew 108 Dakota sorties – 48 glider towing, 60 resupply (28 from Brussels). Lost 1 aircraft; 5 men killed.

RASC Air Despatch Units

48 Air Despatch Group HQ at Poulton, near Cirencester. The group's air-despatch companies were 223, 799 and 800, all based on or near the Dakota squadron airfields of 46 Group. Most of these units' despatchers flew with those squadrons, but some may have also flown in 38 Group Stirlings in later stages of the Arnhem resupply operation.

49 Air Despatch Group HQ location not known. This was probably a looser organization which used as despatchers men drawn from 253 and 63 Light Composite Companies, which were 1st and 6th Airborne Divisional companies; all or most of these despatchers flew in 38 Group Stirlings on the Arnhem operation.

Casualties The RASC despatcher casualties in shot-down aircraft are believed to be: died: 79; prisoners: 44; returned safely: 58. Fatal casualties were: 253 Company: 27; 223 Company: 18; 63 Company: 17; 799 Company: 8; 800 Company: 6; unknown units: 3.[1]

---

[1] I am indebted to research carried out by Jan Hey and Lex Roëll for help with these statistics.

Order of Battle, US Air Units Carrying British and Polish Parachute Troops on Operation 'Market'

52nd Troop Carrier Wing

61st Troop Carrier Group Based at Barkston Heath. Flew 71 C-47 missions carrying 1,166 British troops on first lift without loss. The group later flew 158 missions for the US airborne divisions with the loss of 4 aircraft.

314th Troop Carrier Group Based at Saltby. Flew 198 C-47 and 6 C-53 missions carrying 2,330 British and 604 Polish troops on 17, 18 and 21 September, losing 4 aircraft with 15 men killed, one prisoner of war and 4 men returning safely. The group also flew 29 missions for a US division without loss.

315th Troop Carrier Group Based at Spanhoe. Flew 149 C-47 missions carrying 902 British and 964 Polish troops on 18, 20 and 21 September, losing 7 aircraft, with 12 men killed, 2 prisoners and 19 returning safely. The group also flew 162 missions for US divisions with the loss of one aircraft.

The 313th and 316th Troop Carrier Groups at Folkingham and Cottesmore flew 303 and 333 missions respectively for US divisions, losing 4 and 8 aircraft.

The 50th and 53rd Troop Carrier Wings, based mostly in Nottinghamshire and Berkshire, flew entirely in support of the two US airborne divisions.

Arnhem Today

These notes describe the memorials to the Battle of Arnhem existing at the time of writing in 1993. More will surely be added later; some may disappear due to building or road-works. Also noted are some of the principal battle sites at which there are no memorials at present. It is suggested that detailed local maps be obtained prior to a visit. These can be purchased from: VVV Arnhem, Stationsplein 13, 6811 KG ARNHEM (Tel. 0031 24 3228344, email info@vvvarnhem.nl) or VVV Oosterbeek, Raadhuisplein 1, 6861 GT OOSTERBEEK (Tel. 0031 26 3333172, email info@oosterbeek.nl). Hotel lists may also be obtained from these places. Arnhem is a large, busy place; Oosterbeek is much smaller and quieter.

The Landing Areas and Routes to Battle

On the south side of the road near the Zuid Ginkel Cafe ① are two memorials on a hillock looking out over the large heath where the 4th Parachute Brigade dropped on the second day of the battle. A large stone block has the simple inscription 'Luchtlanding 17-18 Sept 1944', although there was no landing here on that first date. The second memorial, erected in 1960 by the Municipality of Ede, within whose boundary this is, has a metal eagle atop a slender column on which are the badges of the Parachute Regiment, the King's Own Scottish Borderers, who defended the landing zone for the drop, and the Pegasus Airborne sign. At the foot is a quotation from Isaiah which translates as: 'They shall mount up with wings as eagles.' The 10th Battalion's rendezvous after the drop was just to the west of the hillock, and Brigade HQ's just to the east. After the battle, the Dutch Red Cross made a battlefield cemetery just east of the hillock; brought for burial here were the bodies of men killed on the drop and also of Reconnaissance Squadron men killed on the second day in the Planken Wambuis ambush and men of the 1st Battalion killed further along the Amsterdamseweg on the first afternoon.

At the side of the Ginkelse Weg track, north of Heelsum, is a memorial

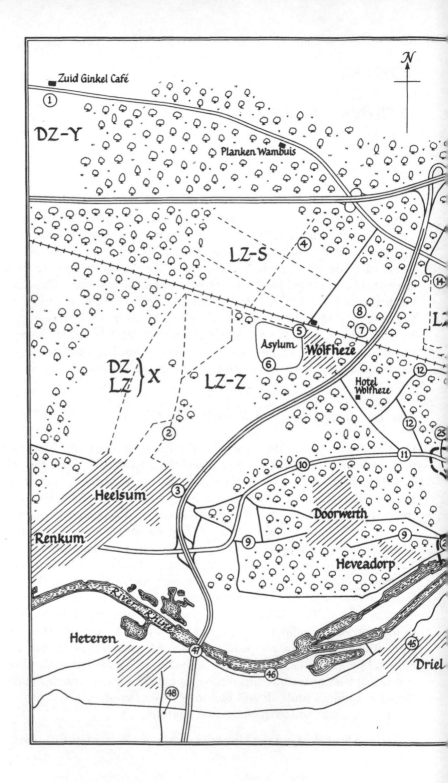

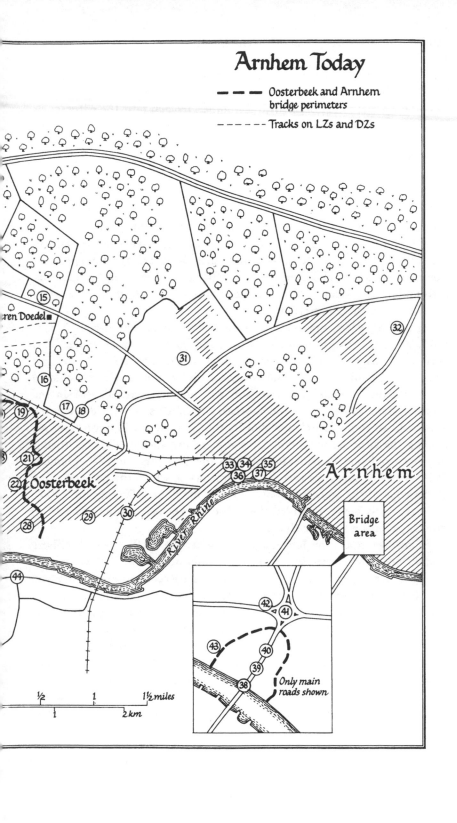

Arnhem Today

— — — Oosterbeek and Arnhem bridge perimeters

‒ ‒ ‒ ‒ ‒ Tracks on LZs and DZs

ren Doedel ■

(15)
(16)
(17) (18)
(19)
(21)
(22) Oosterbeek
(28)
(29)
(30)
(31)
(32)
(33) (34) (35)
(36) (37)
(44)

Arnhem

River Rhine

Bridge area

½   1   1½ miles
1   2 km

(42) A
(41)
(43)
(40)
(39)
(38)

Only main roads shown

seat ② to the 3rd Battalion at their rendezvous after dropping on the first day. The nearby landing-zone area has hardly changed since 1944.

The memorial to the 1st British Airborne Division near the entrance to Heelsum ③ in Bennekomsweg was erected by local people in 1945 using souvenirs of the battle – a 6-pounder anti-tank gun, resupply containers, rifles and helmets; but the rifles and helmets have been lost or stolen in intervening years, and the three steel helmets are not of the 1944 airborne type.

The spot ④ on LZ-S where the Dakota of Flight Lieutenant David Lord, VC, crashed on 19 September after flying over the supply-dropping point (see ㉛) and then LZ-L with his engine and wing on fire has no memorial. The nearby Reijers-Camp Farm is where the Independent Company set up its HQ after being the first unit to drop at Arnhem; the surrounding area soon became the scene of a massed glider landing when the Airlanding Brigade arrived.

On a small green opposite the railway station at Wolfheze ⑤ is a lovely memorial seat dedicated to British and Polish airborne troops. This area would have been a hive of activity on the afternoon of the first landings, particularly as a rendezvous for glider pilots. It is possible to drive into the grounds of the asylum and find its cemetery ⑥ in the south-western corner, near the mortuary. There, side by side, are the graves of two young Dutchmen shot by the Germans on 19 September for helping the airborne men. Not far away are two memorials, one to staff members and one to patients killed in the bombing on 17 September 1944. A few yards to the east of the cemetery is where the patients came to the edge of the trees and looked out at the gliders landing on LZ-Z. Visitors are welcome, provided they observe the speed limits imposed to protect patients walking in the grounds.

Following a track, the Johannahoeveweg, on the north side of Wolfheze Station one comes after less than half a mile to a dip ⑦ level with a tunnel under the railway. This was where the Reconnaissance Squadron jeep force was stopped by Battalion Krafft on the first afternoon, with Lieutenant Bucknall's jeep being hit and stopped further ahead where the track rises into some trees. The hastily dug German trenches can easily be found in the trees and bushes of that higher ground, a perfect defensive position. The tunnel under the railway was where the transport and anti-tank guns of the 4th Parachute Brigade struggled to get away from the advancing Germans two days later. The little 'finger' of woodland to the north-east ⑧ is where Captain Queripel, VC, died making the last stand with his 10th Battalion party later that evening. The track no longer goes on to Johannahoeve; the way ahead is blocked.

The lower road ⑨ is the route taken by the 2nd Battalion to Arnhem on the first afternoon; it is in its original form in the woods either side of Doorwerth, but its path through the now expanded village has been changed. The wide Utrechtseweg ⑩ was the 3rd Battalion's route; ⑪ is the road junction where General Kussin was killed in his staff car. The Bredelaan ⑫ is the road along which the 3rd Battalion's C Company successfully set out to find its independent way to Arnhem bridge.

The main part of Johannahoeve Farm ⑬ is the original building where part of the KOSB overlooked LZ-L when the Polish gliders landed on the third day. The small plantations of trees to the west of the farm are post-war additions. The modern buildings of the Dutch National Sports Centre at Papendal ⑭ are also a post-war encroachment on the landing zone. A small memorial plaque outside the entrance to the main building describes in Dutch how 'this area was involved in the Battle of Arnhem – Lest we forget'. It was in the area immediately behind the sports centre (to the east) that most of A Company and No. 10 Platoon of the KOSB surrendered on the afternoon of 19 September.

The pumping station ⑮ on the Amsterdamseweg is in the area where the 10th Battalion was halted and fought for several hours on 19 September before being ordered to withdraw across the landing zone. After the war, some officers who had fought with the 4th Parachute Brigade erected four marker-posts where its units were in action. The six-foot timber posts later deteriorated, and some of the marker-plates became lost, so the Municipality of Renkum replaced them with concrete posts and new plates. One of them stands by the side of the Dreijenseweg ⑯ along which 156 Battalion suffered severe casualties attempting to capture the Lichtenbeek high ground to the east of the road. The main attacks, by A and B Companies, were mounted from the woods on the west side, north of the marker post. The road on which German armoured vehicles stood and the high bank on the eastern side which had to be climbed by the attackers are little changed from 1944. Many of the trees still bear scars of the fighting.

The Arnhem Oosterbeek War Cemetery

The well-signposted cemetery ⑰ was made after the war by gathering in the remains of British and Polish men who died in this area in 1944 and a few in 1945 to a place where the Imperial (now Commonwealth) War Graves Commission could tend the graves on a permanent basis. At the time of writing there are 1,757 graves, three-quarters of them from the

Battle of Arnhem, and the numbers slowly rise as further remains are discovered. A total of 253 are unidentified by name, though often the regiment or corps is known.

The cemetery is in three distinct parts. Just inside the gateway, on left and right, are fifty-one Polish graves brought in from Driel, somewhat to the disappointment of the Driel people. Among them, on the right-hand side, is that of the young American volunteer, Richard Tice, whose parents were content to leave his grave with his Polish comrades-in-arms rather than transfer it to an American cemetery.

The main part of the cemetery consists of four large blocks of graves on either side of a central lawn with the headstones facing inwards, almost entirely from the September 1944 airborne battle. The first blocks encountered, Plots 27 to 32, were a later addition, containing airborne graves discovered later in the battlefield clearance process and are from mixed units. But in the remainder of this main section the graves of men from various types of units were kept together. So the next two blocks, Plots 1, 2, 15, 16, 21 and 22 are predominantly from the 'airlanding' part of 1st Airborne which flew in by glider. There are two 'strangers' here. One is the young Dutch helper, Samuel Swarts, killed while taking water to the dressing stations at Oosterbeek crossroads; his Dutch headstone (in Plot 16, Row B) has the initials VHK of the Voluntary Helper Corps, the only one of the Arnhem battle. The other, on the left side in Plot 21, Row C, is Major Edward Coke of the 6th KOSB who was killed with the ground forces while the Arnhem battle was raging and whose body was brought here to be near that of his brother, Major John Coke of the 7th KOSB, who survived Arnhem but was killed leading a party of evaders on the 'Pegasus II' escape attempt and whose grave is nearby in Plot 23, Row B.

The next section is more varied. On the left side, Plot 3 is the main group of glider-pilot graves. Plot 17 and most of 23 has more airlanding troops, but the last row of 23 has three deceased war graves officials or gardeners and the latest battlefield discoveries, with room for more when found. At the front on the right, Plot 4 is mostly RAF aircrew and despatchers killed on the resupply flights, including the grave of Flight Lieutenant David Lord in Row B with the distinctive Victoria Cross engraved on the headstone. Behind them in Plot 18 are more airlanding men, while the two rows of Plot 24 seem to be men who died of wounds after the battle, mostly at the airborne hospital at Apeldoorn.

The last plots in that main part of the cemetery, 5, 6, 19, 20, 25 and 26, were allocated primarily to men of the parachute battalions. The VC grave of Captain Queripel of the 10th Battalion is on the left (Plot 5, Row

D). The very last graves on the left are of more Poles from Driel, but also there is the Parachute Regiment grave of Private Frank Dobrowski of the 1st Battalion whose Polish parents in London probably asked for him to be buried with the Poles. Among the graves on the right-hand side is that of Captain Groenewoud (Plot 20, Row B), the Dutch officer in the 'Jedburgh' team killed in Arnhem.

At the far end of the cemetery, in two large sections facing towards the gateway, are more than 400 graves of men mostly from infantry divisions who died south of the Rhine during the Arnhem battle and on into October 1944, with a few from later months. The division most heavily represented is the 50th (Northumbrian), which came up after the September battle. Finally, a surprise find at the very back, on the immediate left of the Cross of Sacrifice, is the VC grave of Captain Jack Grayburn, his promotion to captain coming through after his gallant death at the Arnhem bridge with the 2nd Battalion. His body was not found until 1948, but why his grave was not added to one of the airborne plots is not known.

There is a small War Graves Commission plot in the civilian cemetery ⑱ on the other side of the road. It contains the graves of nine airmen shot down before the Arnhem battle. A more recent burial, in a private grave not far away, was that of A. W. Lipmann-Kessel, who was a surgeon in 16 Parachute Field Ambulance at St Elizabeth Hospital and later evaded capture. Before his death in 1986, he requested that he should be buried as near as possible to his airborne friends but, as he was not then a serving soldier, he could not have a military grave, and his family made this private one as close as possible; the large headstone has a Jewish symbol and the Pegasus badge.

The Oosterbeek Area

Just over the Oosterbeek Hoog railway crossing, in the Graaf van Rechterenweg, is the Hotel Dreyeroord ⑲, the 'White House' which the KOSB defended so stoutly during the first days of the siege. The hotel is the original building, and its grounds are similar to the 1944 area where hand-to-hand fighting took place. Inside are photographs and memorials of the battle and of post-war pilgrimages. Ommershof ⑳, the large house defended by the Independent Company, with part of the 4th Parachute Squadron in support, was further along the road, but the present-day building is not the original.

The main crossroads in the village ㉑ have not changed much in appearance. The Vreewijk was one of the hotels used as a Dressing Station; the Schoonoord was another but it was destroyed later in the war, and the restaurant of that name is a post-war building. The house Quatre Bras was defended by the Independent Company during the siege, and in its garden, exactly where a Bren-gun post was located as shown in David Shepherd's painting, is a metal memorial designed by the daughter of a Dutch architect who now owns the house; it is intended to portray 'swords into ploughshares'. On the Arnhem side of the crossroads is the 'promontory' of houses as far as the Annastraat on the right which was held first by the 10th Battalion and then by a platoon of the Independent Company until Major Wilson insisted on withdrawing it. One of the 4th Parachute Brigade's memorial posts outside No. 192 Utrechtseweg commemorates the fight of the 10th Battalion 'to virtual extinction' until withdrawn 'with no officer left' on 23 September, although that date is one day later than the actual withdrawal. The house in the nearby Annastraat which was the scene of Mrs Voskuil's vivid account of the action in the cellar is No. 2.

A quarter of a mile south of the crossroads is the Tafelberg ㉒, Field Marshal Model's HQ on the day of the first landing and then one of the Main Dressing Stations during the siege; a marker records this use during the siege.

The Hartenstein ㉓ still stands in its grounds, exactly as it did when it was 1st Airborne's Divisional HQ, still with the parkland at the rear into which German snipers infiltrated and the tennis courts that held German prisoners. The building now houses the superb Airborne Museum with displays of every aspect of the battle, which should be an essential call for visitors. On the other side of Utrechtseweg is the main Airborne Memorial ㉔ in the form of a tall brick-built column erected by the people of Oosterbeek. It is a rather sombre edifice, without any inscription, but an explanation is to be found on a small concrete column near the bus-stop on the main road.

Just west of the siege perimeter, in the Valkenburglaan, another 4th Parachute Brigade memorial post stands near what I always think of as 'Hackett's Hollow' ㉕, the depression captured by Major Powell and his 156 Battalion men when the brigade was fighting hard to get into the perimeter on 20 September and then held by Hackett and the remnants of his brigade for several hours until they charged into the perimeter. If one looks across the road, through the yard of a riding stables, some tall trees a quarter of a mile away mark where A Company of the 1st Border were holding their perimeter positions at the time.

It is well worth visiting the modern Westerbouwing restaurant ㉖ to appreciate its vital position overlooking the Driel ferry, which still runs on the river below, and also for fine views along the river to the railway bridge which was blown in the face of Lieutenant Barry's platoon on the first afternoon, and then on to Arnhem. Driel can easily be seen to the south of the river, as it was by the Germans from this point after the loss of the Westerbouwing, so that they could direct mortar and shell fire on to the Poles there; and the superstructure of the Nijmegen bridge can also be seen on a fine day, making one realize how close was the head of the Guards Armoured Division towards the end of the battle. Coming back into Oosterbeek, one passes the positions held by the Borders of Breeseforce ㉗ just west of what are now the modern houses in Dennenoord Park, showing how narrow the neck of the perimeter became after the Westerbouwing was lost.

The old church ㉘ is a peaceful and emotive spot. There are two memorials outside the church. Near the road is another 4th Parachute Brigade marker-post, not mentioning the brigade's 11th Battalion which fought here but with an ambiguous inscription referring to various units fighting 'in order to make an eventual crossing of the river possible'. The church is now smaller than it was in 1944, and the other exterior memorial consists of three large stone blocks from the original building at a spot which would have been inside the 1944 church. On it is a plaque which, to my mind, has the most fitting inscription of any of the memorials to the 1944 battle:

> In September 1944, British Airborne soldiers and their Polish comrades, with the support of brave Dutch men and women, fought a grim battle around this ancient Church in the struggle to liberate the Netherlands from Nazi tyranny. This stone commemorates all who took part in this action and, above all, those who died. NOT ONE SHALL BE FORGOTTEN.

There are numerous memorials inside the church. The pulpit was presented by my home town of Boston in memory of the gunners of the Airlanding Light Regiment stationed there before Arnhem. The oaken altar was presented by all ranks of 1st Airborne and the Polish brigade. The priest's chair is in memory of Leading Aircraftman Samwells, a member of the RAF Light Warning Unit killed at Oosterbeek. Among many unit memorials is an outsize bench commemorating Lonsdale Force, intended for outside use but kept in the church to prevent the unit badges being stolen.

The church is often locked. The only Sunday service is at 10.0 a.m.

From June to September it is open on Wednesday, Thursday and Sunday afternoons from 2.0 to 5.0 p.m., but visitors at other times can gain access by phoning a local number which is currently Oosterbeek 333076. If one walks from the west end of the church down some steps and then along a footpath, the first house seen on the right was Kate ter Horst's home; the wartime graves of the men who died there were in the large garden west of the house.

Moving along the road towards Arnhem, the Benedendorpsweg is the route along which John Frost took the 2nd Battalion into Arnhem on the first evening, and astride the road were the positions later held by Lonsdale Force; the junction with the Acacialaan ㉙ is where Lance-Sergeant Baskeyfield, VC, was killed engaging German tanks on the Wednesday. A little further on the road passes under the railway at Oosterbeek Laag ㉚. It was in the railway cutting on the left that Lieutenant Peter Cane and the Gronert twins were killed attacking the German position there on the first evening. I always think of that railway bridge as the 'Menin Gate' of Arnhem because, just like the gate at Ypres, so many men from different units passed through it on their way to battle and then the tired and wounded survivors passed under it again on their return.

Arnhem

Just outside the town is still to be seen the large open area ㉛ chosen as the main dropping point on to which the Stirlings and Dakotas attempted to parachute supplies on Tuesday 19 September at such heavy loss when this area was in German hands.

In the southern part of the large Moscowa Cemetery ㉜, just off the Apeldoornseweg, is a British war plot containing the graves of thirty-six airmen shot down before the airborne battle and of one unidentified soldier.

There is much to see in the area of western Arnhem where the 1st, 3rd and 11th Battalions and the South Staffords suffered so severely in attempting to reach the road bridge. The houses in the criss-cross section of streets ㉝ are where men took shelter from German weapons firing along the streets. Outside No. 135 Alexanderstraat is where Major-General Urquhart and Brigadier Lathbury were caught in the open and Lathbury was wounded. Urquhart and two junior officers then ran into the passage between Mauritsstraat and Zwarteweg and were beckoned into No. 14 Zwarteweg and given shelter in the attic there. Not far away, in a small open space on Nassaustraat, is a pleasant memorial erected by the local people with the simple inscription 'Remember September 1944 – Airborne – West Arnhem'.

Close by is St Elizabeth Hospital ㉞, around which the fighting was so fierce when the South Staffords and the 11th Battalion attempted to press forward on the upper road, and inside which 16 Parachute Field Ambulance and Dutch doctors and nurses received and treated large numbers of wounded. The distinctive original building remains. A plaque on the right-hand side of the main entrance lobby has Pegasus and RAMC badges. The temporary field burials of men killed near the hospital or dying inside were in front of and below the hospital, in the 'V' between the Utrechtseweg and the Onderlangs.

The elegant museum ㉟ still stands at the top of the hill; very few men managed to advance any further than that point on the upper road, showing how strong was the German defence supported as it was by armour. A private house opposite the east end of the museum, known as 'Airborne House', has a plaque above the doorway describing how '30 members of the 1st British Airborne Division heroically defended themselves against superior forces' in the house; this was where Major Dover and part of his company became trapped after losing contact with the 2nd Battalion on Sunday. Further along the road into Arnhem, a plaque at No. 85 Utrechtsestraat tells how this building, now an art school, was used for four years by 'the infamous Sicherheitsdienst' for the interrogation and torture of Dutch Resistance members.

Down the steep bank, on and around the lower road – the Onderlangs – is where the 1st and 3rd Battalions made their gallant final efforts to reach the bridge on Tuesday morning. The 'pavilion' from which these attacks set out now forms part of the dining room of the modern Rijn Hotel ㊱. A memorial seat ㊲ looking out over the river about 300 yards further on along the grassed area was placed there by survivors of the 3rd Battalion. The buildings at the far end of that area, while not all being originals, mark the limit of those attacks and were where Lieutenant-Colonel Dobie and the men with him were surrounded and taken prisoner.

The road bridge – now the John-Frost-Brug – where the 2nd Battalion and others made their stand has been rebuilt in its former style, but the battered buildings in which the defenders held out were cleared after the war and replaced by modern ones. A memorial inside the concrete shelter ㊳ on the west side of the bridge pays tribute to the 2nd Battalion but does not mention the other units engaged. The ramp ㊴ where the German reconnaissance unit was wrecked and its men slaughtered, and the sheltered underpasses where the defenders gathered after being driven out of their houses by shelling and fire later in the battle, are exactly as they were. A monument by the steps �40 up which an anti-tank gun was manhandled on the first night gives a short description of the battle, referring to 'A Bridge Too Far' and mentioning John Frost: 'the bridge is now proudly wrought with his name'. The buildings just west of that point, where Brigade HQ was located, have been replaced by the regional tax office, the Belastingdienst.

Inside a roundabout at the end of the ramp is the Airborne Plein ㊶ in which a simple memorial is the stump of a stone column which once stood in front of the old Palace of Justice; on it is simply inscribed: '17th September 1944'. It is in this quiet spot that ceremonies commemorating the defence of the bridge are performed. Not far away, on the bridge side of the Eusebius Church ㊷, is a large figure with another simple inscription: '40–45'; it is Arnhem's memorial to the whole war. The Provincial Government building ㊸, the Huis der Provincie, has inside its main hallway a magnificent 'Sword of Honour' paid for by veterans of the battle; the Dutch inscription refers to the spirit of resistance and fighting qualities of the British and Polish airborne troops and also to the memory of the people of Gelderland province who helped the airborne men during and after the battle.

South of the River

Near the Vogelenzang bus-stop can be found the modern memorial ㊹ to the evacuation of 1st Airborne across the river. The landing point on the south bank was just over the high dike in front of the memorial; the two Polish crossing attempts were launched from the same place. The four British and Canadian engineer companies carrying out the evacuation are all named, and there is a useful panorama of the north bank indicating the principal points between the Westerbouwing and the old church.

Driel is still a quiet village. The original church up which various senior officers climbed to consider best how to help the men fighting at Oosterbeek was later destroyed. On the wall of the new church ㊺ is a memorial to the 5th Duke of Cornwall's Light Infantry, the first unit of 43rd (Wessex) Division to reach the village and join up with the Poles. Across the road, on what was once an open site but is now surrounded by shops, is the main Polish memorial.

Further along the river-bank road are two more unit memorials, to the 7th Hampshires near the Café Lindeboom ㊻ and to the 'Screaming

Eagles' of the 101st US Division on the dike just east of the post-war motorway bridge ㊼ outside Heteren; these units were in action here after the airborne battle. Heteren Town Hall also has a memorial plaque to that American division. The cemetery at Heteren ㊽ has one long grave containing the bodies of two crews of shot-down RAF aircraft – those of Pilot Officer Culling, towing one of the RAF Light Warning Unit gliders on the second lift, and of Pilot Officer Cuer, shot down on a resupply flight; also buried is a glider pilot, Sergeant John Brown of F Squadron, probably drowned on the evacuation, the first of many such men buried downstream from the evacuation crossing point.

The men who died in and around Arnhem and Oosterbeek will never be forgotten.

Acknowledgements

Participants

I most willingly record my gratitude to the men of the Allied army and air forces and the people of Holland who were involved in the Battle of Arnhem and have shared their experiences with me.

1st British Airborne Division and Attached Units

(Ranks shown are those held at the time of the battle.)

Divisional HQ: Lt P. R. R. de Burgh, Lt-Col C. B. Mackenzie, Lt-Col E. C. W. Myers, Maj. P. T. Tower, Pte J. Trevor (Defence Platoon).

1st Parachute Brigade HQ: Lt J. P. Barnett, Cpl G. A. Cockayne, Pte A. Fahey, Cpl D. F. Freebury, Cpl H. W. Goodrich, L/Cpl N. Harris, Maj. J. A. Hibbert, Capt. C. R. Miller, Cpl G. J. Perry, Capt. W. E. Taylor, L/Cpl W. Whittaker, Pte W. Williamson. *1st Parachute Battalion:* Lt V. A. Britneff, Pte D. J. Charlton, Lt R. H. B. Feltham, L/Sgt J. Fryer, Pte J. Gardner, Lt G. E. Guyon, Sgt E. J. Hall, Pte J. J. Hall, Pte E. Harper, Lt J. E. Hellingoe, Pte G. Hill, Sgt R. B. Laing, Sgt F. S. Manser, Cpl D. Morgans, L/Sgt P. O'Leary, Maj. C. Perrin-Brown, Colour Sgt E. Seal, Pte J. Shelbourne, Guardsman F. Thompson, Maj. J. Timothy, Cpl P. H. Tucker, Lt E. Vere-Davies, Pte B. H. Willoughby. *2nd Parachute Battalion:* Lt T. Ainslie, Lt P. H. Barry, L/Sgt D. A. Brooks, Pte C. A. Cardale, Pte S. A. Couture, Pte S. C. E. Elliott, Capt. A. M. Frank. Lt-Col J. D. Frost, L/Sgt W. Fulton, Pte L. L. Hoare, Capt. F. K. Hoyer-Millar, Pte J. J. Jonas, Pte A. Letchford, Lt R. H. Levien, Capt. D. McLean, L/Cpl T. E. Miles, Pte C. Newell, Pte R. W. Peatling, L/Sgt A. S. Reynolds, Lt D. E. C. Russell, Pte D. L. Smith, Pte G. W. Stubbs, Pte H. Sullivan, Maj. J. A. D. Tatham-Warter, Lt R. A. Vlasto. *3rd Parachute Battalion:* Cpl R. Allen, Lt A. R Baxter, Pte F. C. Bennett,

Pte J. A. Boe, Maj. A. Bush, Pte S. A. Chamberlain, Lt J. A. S. Cleminson, Pte J. L. Dakin, Pte A. K. Davies, Maj. M. Dennison, Lt M. J. Dickson, Cpl W. F. K. Farrow, Pte L. L. Harrison, Sgt V. Lumb, Pte G. R. Marsh, Sgt R. Mason, L/Cpl B. G. H. Meen, Pte J. P. Moran, Pte W. F. Morton, Pte F. Radley, L/Cpl A. E. Reece, Capt. W. Robinson, Pte J. H. Spicer, Sgt A. Thompson, Pte L. True, Pte D. Warden, Pte R. Watson, Pte J. O. Withers, Lt L. W. Wright.

1st Airlanding Brigade HQ: No contributors. *7th King's Own Scottish Borderers:* Sgt C. N. Allwright, Pte W. P. W. Anderson, Sgt R. Ashmore, Sgt G. C. Barton, Pte W. Bell, L/Cpl O'N. F. Berry, L/Cpl A. H. Brown, Pte W. Brown, Pte T. Burton, Pte D. G. Crockett, Maj. G. M. Dinwiddie, Lt C. Doig, Pte W. J. Elliot, Maj. M. B. Forman, Capt. G. C. Gourlay, Pte A. R. Holburn, Pte H. Lee, L/Cpl S. Livesey, Capt. J. S. Livingstone, Pte H. McClusky, L/Cpl J. D. McNaught, L/Cpl S. R. Nunn, Pte G. W. Roberts, Cpl E. Standring, Lt J. W. Taylor. *1st Border:* Pte W. J. Arner, Lt J. M. Bainbridge, Pte E. G. Blackwell, Pte W. C. Campbell, Cpl W. J. Collings, Cpl C. Crickett, Pte W. J. Darling, Pte H. Duckworth, Pte R. Elliott, CSM L. S. Fielding, Sgt D. Goulding, Lt J. S. D. Hardy, Lt R. C. Hope-Jones, Cpl I. R. M. Hunter, Pte H. L. Ingham, Pte R. Norman, Sgt T. Northgreaves, Sgt D. Payne, Pte E. J. Peters, Lt A. D. Roberts, Lt A. R. Royall, Lt W. P. Stott, L/Cpl A. Wilson. *2nd South Staffordshires:* CSM F. A. Bluff (deceased, his account sent in by his son), L/Cpl W. Brearley, L/Cpl C. Brown, Lt H. H. L. Cartwright. Pte T. G. Coleman, Sgt J. R. Drew, Pte K. Hancock, Pte A. G. Hawksworth, Sgt N. Howes, Pte W. Jones, Capt. J. B. McCooke, L/Cpl H. Mills, Pte G. Parry, Pte S. Rosenberg, L/Cpl H. S. J. Smith, L/Cpl C. J. Taylor.

4th Parachute Brigade HQ: Capt. H. B. Booty, Brig. J. W. Hackett, Capt. C. R. Harkess, Pte D. McPhee, Capt. R. R. Temple. *156 Parachute Battalion:* Pte R. A. Atkinson, CSM R. Chenery, Pte D. N. Dagwell, Pte F. Eggleton, Pte W. Grounsell, Cpl D. S. Jones, Lt D. B. Kayne, Pte J. M. Keenan, Capt. H. Montgomery, Lt J. F. Noble, Maj. R. L. J. Pott, Maj. G. S. Powell, Pte E. Reynolds, Lt Hon, P. St Aubyn, Sgt G. Sheldrake, Colour Sgt T. Thomas, Sgt A. B. Thorburn, Maj. J. L. Waddy. *10th Parachute Battalion:* Pte G. Bower, Padre R. Bowers, Lt M. Broadway, Capt. D. B. Carr, Capt. B. B. Clegg, Pte L. Cooper, L/Cpl C. G. Cross, Cpl N. H. Dicken, Cpl F. R. G. Elliott, L/Cpl J. W. Finn, Cpl A. E. Freeman (served as Ward), Lt J. W. Glover, CSM R. E. Grainger, Capt. N. B. Hanmer, Pte J. Hayes, Pte F. D. Jackson,

Cpl F. A. V. Jenkins, Pte W. K. Kirkham, Pte W. J. Longwell, Pte F. Newhouse, Sgt C. S. Poole, Lt J. R. Procter, Pte G. W. Reid, Pte R. Shackleton, Pte R. B. Shurborne, Sgt A. E. Spring, Sgt R. Sunley, Pte G. E. Taylor, Pte D. J. Thomas, Cpl D. J. Waters, Pte E. Whadcoat, Pte A. E. Wilmott, Sgt R. Wright. *11th Parachute Battalion:* Pte E. Coleman, Pte S. Davis, CSM G. Garland, Maj. D. A. Gilchrist, Capt. F. D. King, Maj. D. R. W. Webber.

1st Airlanding Light Regiment, RA: Lt T. R. Barron, Gnr R. Beasley, Gnr F. R. Bird, Gnr D. A. Bowles, Gnr R. K. Christie, Lt T. A. Conlin, L/Bdr J. W. Crook, Bdr J. L. Hall, Sgt D. C. Hardie, Gnr C. T. Leadbeater, Capt. J. H. D. Lee, Capt. D. R. Martin, Lt F. P. D. Moore, Gnr E. Morgan, Maj. D. S. Munford, Capt. J. W. Walker, Gnr R. Whotton, Gnr J. Wilcox, Lt P. W. Wilkinson. With 'sea tail': Gnr H. W. Lee, Gnr D. J. Norton. *1st Airlanding Anti-Tank Battery, RA*: Maj. W. F. Arnold, Lt E. E. Clapham, L/Sgt D. Colls, Gnr R. Cook, Dvr S. G. Cook, Gnr J. M. Disdel, L/Sgt S. Fitchett, Gnr W. Hartley, Gnr B. Jeffrey, Gnr R. S. Linham, Capt. A. D. Llewellyn-Jones, 2/Lt B. S. Lockett, Gnr E. Milner, Gnr K. Pattinson, Sgt C. Robson (deceased, his account sent in by his widow), Lt G. Ryall, Lt E. E. Shaw, Sgt E. Shelswell, Gnr J. Winser, Gnr S. Wrightman. *2nd Airlanding Anti-Tank Battery, RA*: Gnr L. A. Clarke, Maj. A. F. Haynes, Gnr G. A. Hurdman, Lt W. MacInnes, Lt G. A. Paull. *1st Forward (Airborne) Observation Unit, RA*: Gnr A. Brearton, Capt. C. W. Ikin, Gnr H. B. Lingard, Sgt N. S. Patten.

9th Field Company, RE: Cpl W. E. Barber, Spr T. H. Carpenter, Spr I. W. Hannabus, Spr R. Jardine, Spr J. J. N. Johnstone, Spr J. Poultney, Spr A. J. Price, L/Cpl L. Raggett, Spr H. Thompson, Spr W. Wilson. With 'sea tail': Dvr J. Iddenden. *1st Parachute Squadron, RE*: Spr E. C. Booth, L/Cpl C. Cameron, Spr R. Clark, Spr J. W. Dawson, L/Sgt S. Halliwell, L/Cpl A. S. Hendy, Spr R. Hepburn, Lt D. R. Hindley, Cpl J. E. Humphreys, L/Sgt B. J. Joynson, Spr G. H. Needham, L/Sgt H. Padfield, Sgt N. Swift, Spr S. J. Temple, Spr F. A. Woods. *4th Parachute Squadron, RE*: Capt. H. F. Brown, Lt K. C. Evans, Spr W. C. Grantham, L/Cpl G. A. A. Johanson, Maj. A. J. M. Perkins, Spr D. D. Stevens, L/Cpl M. V. Weymouth.

21st Independent Parachute Company: Lt N. H. Ashmore, Cpl A. R. Bence, Pte W. A. Dawson, Lt H. D. Eastwood, Sgmn T. Molyneaux, Cpl A. J. Sharman, L/Cpl R. S. Smith. *1st Airborne Reconnaissance Squadron*: Tpr A. E. Barlow, Lt C. R. Bowles, Capt. J. G. Costeloe, Tpr

D. F. C. Evans, Tpr G. Fergus, Capt. M. W. Grubb, L/Cpl K. Hope, Tpr R. Minns. *1st Airborne Divisional Signals*: Sgmn W. Carr, Cpl D. Collins, Maj. A. J. Deane-Drummond, Sgmn J. N. Haysom, Capt. W. L. Hewitt (attached 'Phantom'), Sgmn W. Jukes, Sgmn G. S. Lawson, Sgmn K. E. Little, L/Cpl J. Lowrie, Sgmn H. G. Riley, L/Cpl D. R. Underhill, Sgmn D. A. Wiggins, Sgmn A. Winstanley, Sgmn F. M. Young. Further signalmen are listed under units to which they were attached. *250 (Airborne) Light Composite Company, RASC*: Dvr P. R. Ashman, Dvr F. W. Barratt, Pte S. Brown, Dvr K. W. Clarke, L/Cpl L. H. Dean, Capt. W. V. A. Gell, Dvr J. W. Prime, Dvr J. A. Taylor, Dvr J. Wild. *16 Parachute Field Ambulance*: Cpl A. Hatcher, L/Cpl G. C. Scanners. *133 Parachute Field Ambulance*: Lt D. G. Olliff, Capt. T. F. Redman. *181 Airlanding Field Ambulance*: Pte T. J. Bannister, Pte S. W. Davis, Pte G. Phillips, Maj. G. Rigby-Jones. With 'sea tail': Cpl A. G. Frampton, Dvr H. Tullett. *1st Airborne Divisional Field Park, RAOC*: Maj. C. C. Chidgey, Pte K. J. Heaney, Pte E. V. B. Mordecai, S/Sgt H. W. Walker. *1st (Airborne) Divisional Workshops*: Craftsman R. G. Jordan, Lt H. R. Roberts, Craftsman J. Roberts. *1st (Airborne) Divisional Provost Company*: Cpl J. C. H. Mills, L/Cpl H. H. Stubbs, I,/Cpl R. A. J. Tyler. With 'sea tail': Cpl J. C. Hamblett. *89th (Parachute) Field Security Section*: CSM T. E. Armstrong.

Glider Pilot Regiment: No. 1 WING HQ: Capt. P. N. Fletcher. No. 2 WING HQ; S/Sgt A. Waldron. A SQUADRON: S/Sgt J. E. Edwards. B SQUADRON: S/Sgt A. C. Baldwin, S/Sgt P. B. Boyle, S/Sgt R. A. Howard, Sgt R. C. Leeder, 2/Lt R. Meakin, Sgt A. Rigby, S/Sgt A. Shackleton, Maj. T. I. J. Toler, S/Sgt C. R. Watkinson, S/Sgt H. A. Workman. C SQUADRON: Sgt H. Carling, Sgt T. R. Casswell, S/Sgt J. O. McGeough, S/Sgt L. Wright. D SQUADRON: Sgt B. Blake, S/Sgt K. Chappell, S/Sgt S. J. East, S/Sgt L. J. Prater. E squadron: S/Sgt H. N. I. Andrews, S/Sgt W. K. Fisher, S/Sgt H. G. Harget, Maj. B. H. P. Jackson, S/Sgt J. H. Kitchener, Sgt J. M. Macdonald, S/Sgt W. G. Melrose, Sgt W. A. Oakes, Sgt P. Senier, Sgt B. A. Tomblin. F SQUADRON: S/Sgt G. W. Milburn, Sgt A. R. Williams, Sgt K. R. Williamson. G SQUADRON: Lt M. D. K. Dauncey, S/Sgt T. Francis, Sgt T. Smith.

'Jedburgh' Team: Lt H. A. Todd (US). *6080 Light Warning Unit, RAF*: Leading Aircraftman A. H. Austin.

1st Polish Independent Parachute Brigade Group

Brigade HQ: Lt J. H. Dyrda, Capt. J. J. Lorys; Liaison Officer at 1st British Airborne Division – Capt. L. Zwolanski. *1st Battalion*:

Cpl W. Drewienkiewicz. *3rd Battalion*: Pte M. Lasek, Capt. W. Parylak, Pte P. Rodziewicz, Pte K. Skop, L/Cpl P. Sulima, Pte M. Wojnarowski. *Anti-Tank Battery*: 2/Lt Z. Bossowski. *Engineer Company*: L/Cpl B. J. Strzelecki. *Medical Company*: L/Cpl B. Borowik, L/Cpl K. Lewicke. *Transport and Supply Company*: Lt S. Kaczmarek.

Ground Forces and Other Army Units

4th Dorsets: Maj. P. J. Roper, L/Cpl W. A. Smith, Pte A. E. Steirn. *23rd Canadian Field Company*: Lt J. B. Cronyn, Spr D. S. Goodall. *260 Field Company, RE*: Maj. W. A. Vinycomb. *553 Field Company, RE*: Sgt F. J. Petrie. *64th Medium Regiment, RA*: Maj. D. C. Aldridge. *163 Field Ambulance, RAMC*: Lt-Col M. E. M. Herford.

Airborne Corps HQ: Col A. A. Eagger (died 1993), Col R. J. Moberly, Maj. B. E. Urquhart, Maj. D. B. Watson. GLIDER PILOTS: Sgt J. H. Kingdom, Capt. W. L. Tallentire. *First Allied Airborne Army*: Col W. T. Campbell.

Royal Air Force

48 Squadron: P/O V. B. Christie, F/Sgt G. D. Gleave, F/Lt P. W. Smith, F/Sgt S. H. Webster. *190 Squadron*: WO A. A. Batten, Sgt L. G. Hillyard, Sgt M. Hughes, F/O R. Lawton. *196 Squadron*: F/Sgt G. Smith, F/Sgt G. H. Wright. *233 Squadron*: P/O G. P. B. Bailey, F/O G. Clarkson, WO K. G. Cranefield, F/Sgt J. Hickey. *271 Squadron*: F/Lt E. F. Carlisle-Brown, F/Sgt A. W. Clarke, F/Lt R. Fellows, F/Sgt W. F. Randall, F/Sgt H. Sorensen, F/Sgt H. Tipping. *295 Squadron*: F/Sgt W. A. Benton, F/O N. Fendall. F/O J. Kirkland, F/Lt D. W. Mepham, F/Sgt C. E. Mitchell, P/O D. M. Peel, F/O R. A. Sloan. *296 Squadron*: F/Sgt C. D. S. Bates, F/Lt D. Boyer. *297 Squadron*: F/O D. J. Coxell, F/Sgt E. J. G. Flavell. *298 Squadron*: F/Lt J. B. Stark. *299 Squadron*: WO J. Corless, Sgt M. Davis, WO B. H. Harvey, F/O H. Reek, Sgt W. T. Simpson, F/Sgt E. J. Webb. *512 Squadron*: WO L. Bryant, F/Lt H. Chatfield, F/O S. W. Lee, F/Sgt D. Williams. *570 Squadron*: F/O H. Brown, F/Sgt H. D. Cherrington, Sgt J. R. Ireland, S/Ldr J. Stewart. *575 Squadron*: F/O E. F. Brown, F/O F. Gee, F/O H. J. McKinley. *620 Squadron*: WO N. R. Chaffey, Sgt D. Evans, Sgt T. Haig, F/Sgt J. K. Howes, F/O G. F. McMahon, F/O H. D. Simmins, F/Sgt D. B. Stephens. *644 Squadron*: F/Lt J. C. W. Davies, F/Sgt J. P. Grant, WO H. J. Harris, WO B. McCann, F/O R. D. Ward.

Also helped, though not flying to Arnhem: W/Cdrs D. Annand and J. B. Veal of 46 Group HQ; F/Lt E. H. King, 131 Spitfire Squadron; Sgt H. J. Purver, 77 Halifax Squadron; F/Sgt R. S. Trout, Albermarle Operational Refresher Unit.

United States Army Air Force

314th Troop Carrier Group: Lt D. E. Mondt. *315th Troop Carrier Group*: T/Sgt H. J. Boyland, 2/Lt R. L. Cloer, Lt B. H. Coggins, F/O G. M. Hoffman.

Dutch Civilians Present at the Battle

Arnhem: Albert Deuss, Wopke Kuik, Lex Roëll, Jo Velzen (now Van Sabben), Wilhelmina Schouten, Constant Vogel. *Oosterbeek*: Julie Beelaerts van Blokland, Ans Kremer, Sander Kremer, Riet Rijks (now Schwitters), Sjoert Schwitters, Neeltje Traas van Roekel, Eef Vellinga, Bertje Voskuil. *Wolfheze*: Cor Janse. *Lichtenbeek*: Pastoor Philip Bruggeman. *Driel*: Cora Baltussen.

Personal Acknowledgements

I have been extremely fortunate in being helped by many people and am pleased to be able to express my thanks in print.

Several people are deserving of particular thanks for outstanding assistance. Adrian Groeneweg, vice-chairman of the trustees of the Airborne Museum at Oosterbeek, and his wife, Marianne, gave me hospitality in their home and much help during an interviewing and research visit to Holland; Adrian then went on to read all of the draft chapters of my book to check for errors and answer many supplementary questions. For similar help in reading all through those chapters, I am most grateful to Colonel John Waddy, who fought with 156 Battalion at Arnhem and, being one of the foremost military researchers of the battle, has corrected many small errors and made many useful suggestions. Other 'draft-chapter readers' have been Major Jan Lorys with the Polish sections and Major Tony Hibbert with the advance to Arnhem bridge and the subsequent action there. I must stress, however, that all the views expressed in the book are my own, and any errors are also mine.

My wife, Mary, has again made an important contribution to a book – making preliminary drawings of all the maps, proof-reading, helping with the index and giving much general support. I would also like to thank Margaret Gardner, my patient and diligent typist, who mastered the new skills of 'word-processor operator' halfway through the book.

I hope that the many other people who have helped me in a private capacity, giving me the benefit of private research or contacts, providing hospitality on interviewing tours, finding Arnhem veterans for me or helping in many other ways, will accept my thanks and forgive me for listing their names in alphabetical order; I am most grateful to them all. *United Kingdom*: Julian Andrews, Lt-Col Clive Auchinleck, R. L. Barrett-Cross, Anne and Darrel Bell (my daughter and son-in-law), Geoff and Val Bingham, Wlodek Borzyslawski, Robert de Bruin, Jack Cannon, Brig. David Chaundler, Maj. John Cross, Sqn Ldr Mike Dean, Ted Eaglen, Chris and Margaret Everitt, Stanley Fenton, James Freeman, Jane and Bruce Hamilton-Webb (my daughter and son-in-law), Ian Hawkins, Barbara Johnson, Roger King, Neville Mackinder, Patrick Mahoney, Marianne Maltby, Catherine Middlebrook (my daughter), Maj. H. J. Millman, Tom Morgan, John Nicholls, Cliff Pettit, David Raw, Veronica Sylvester, David Truesdale, Colin Webb, Graham Wilkins. *Holland*: Marcel Anker, Luuk Buist, Henk Duinhoven, Jan Hey, Frans van Hemmen, Ivo de Jong, Chris van Roekel, Joop Siepermann, Robert Sigmond, Rector Jan Swagemakers, Kees Troost, Robert Voskuil, Leo Zwaaf. *USA*: George F. Cholewczynski, Carl M. Christ, Steve Parker. *Australia*: Maj. S. Kruszewski. If I have missed anyone, please forgive me.

Of the official organizations, I am most grateful to the Airborne Forces Museum at Aldershot (particularly Simon Anglim and Diana Andrews) for allowing such ready access to their Arnhem files (to the extent of allowing me to study them at home for a year) and for subsequent assistance, and to the staff of the Airborne Museum at the Hartenstein at Oosterbeek who provided such a comfortable and friendly venue for interviews. I also thank the Commonwealth War Graves Commission (particularly Beverly Webb and Jerry Gee) and the Air and Naval Historical Branches of the Ministry of Defence. In Holland, Pieter van Iddekinge, the head of the Arnhem archives, and Geert Maassen, archivist of Renkum and Oosterbeek, both gave first-class help.

Secretaries of associations were often most helpful in putting me in touch with veterans of the battle. Those of most of the Arnhem units have been acknowledged already because they fought in the battle, but the following can be added: John Watson of 1st Airborne Reconnaissance Squadron Association, Mr Z. R. Gasowski and Mr P. J. Stojakowski of the Polish Airborne Forces' Association, W/Cdrs H. E. Angell and Sir

Arthur Norman of No. 38 Group Association, Alan Hartley of the Down Ampney Association. I would also like to thank the secretaries of the following branches of the Parachute Regimental Association who passed on my appeals to members: Aldershot, Cambridge, Cardiff, Central Scotland, Chelmsford, Coventry, Dundee, Eastbourne, East Riding, Gloucester, Grimsby, Harrogate, Leeds, New Forest, Shropshire, South Somerset, Teesside, Thanet, Wessex, West Cumbria, Wirral, York. For similar help, I thank 47 Air Despatch Squadron, Royal Corps of Transport, and 15 (Scottish Volunteer) Battalion, Parachute Regiment. For help in answering research questions, I thank the Historical Secretaries of the following corps and regiments: Border and King's Own Royal Border Regiments, Dorsetshire Regiment, Duke of Edinburgh's Royal Regiment (Berkshire and Wiltshire), Royal Regiment of Fusiliers, Royal Sussex, Staffordshire Regiment, Royal Engineers, Royal Electrical and Mechanical Engineers, Corps of Royal Military Police, Intelligence Corps.

Finally, I am grateful to the editors of the following publications for printing my appeals for veterans of the battle: *Air Mail, Arnhem Veterans' Club Newsletter, Bomber Command Association Newsletter, Eagle, Intercom, Lest We Forget Newsletter, Pegasus; Annandale Herald, Barrow Evening Mail, Barrow-in-Furness Local News, Birmingham Evening Mail, Boston Citizen, Cumberland and Westmorland Herald, Dorset Evening News, Dudley Chronicle, Eastern Daily Press, Grantham Journal, Horncastle News, Leicester Mercury, Lincolnshire Echo, Lincolnshire Standard, Melton Times, Midland Chronicle, North-West Evening Mail, Rutland Mercury, Sandwell Chronicle, Shields Gazette, Skegness News, Stafford Chronicle, Stafford Post, Stamford Mercury, Wolverhampton Adnews.*

Bibliography

This Bibliography is a limited one, because my book is not the result of library research but is mostly drawn from prime sources. I have consulted only a few particularly well-researched books and those written by some of the participants.

Fairley, John, *Remember Arnhem*, Peaton Press, Bearsden, Glasgow, 1978.

Frost, Maj.-Gen. John, *A Drop Too Many*, Cassell, London, 1980.

Hey, J. A., *Roll of Honour: The Battle of Arnhem, 17–26 September 1944*, Society of Friends of the Airborne Museum, Oosterbeek, 1986.

Kershaw, Robert, *It Never Snows in September*, Crowood Press, Marlborough, Wilts, 1990.

McCallister, Paul, *Under Pegasus Wings: Order of Battle for the 1st British Airborne Division September 1944*, privately published, 1989.

Powell, Geoffrey, *The Devil's Birthday*, Buchan & Enright, London, 1984; Franklin Watts, New York, 1985; Leo Cooper, London, 1992.

Roekel, C. van, *Who Was Who during the Battle of Arnhem*, Society of Friends of the Airborne Museum, Oosterbeek, 1992.

Sosabowski, Maj.-Gen. Stanislaw, *Freely I Served*, Kimber, London, 1960.

Urquhart, Brian, *A Life in Peace and War*, Weidenfeld & Nicolson, London, and Harper & Row, New York, 1987.

Urquhart, Maj.-Gen. R. E., *Arnhem*, Cassell, London, 1958.

Index

Abdiel, HMS, 20, 35
Ager, Pte E., 450
Ainslie, Lt J. T., 320
Airborne Forces Museum, Aldershot, 1,
    18n, 67n, 202, 269n, 401n, 414n
Airborne Museum, Oosterbeek, 1–2, 91,
    451
Alford, Lt-Col W. C., 458
Allen, CSM R., 172
Allen, Cpl R. A., 70, 130

ALLIED FORCES
Supreme HQ Allied Expeditionary Force
    (SHAEF), 65
First Allied Airborne Army, 10, 14, 21,
    42–3, 65, 68, 441

American airmen in Arnhem operation,
    47–8, 83, 107–8, 227, 229–31, 241–2,
    394, 403–4, 441
American servicemen at Arnhem, 39,
    68–9, 76, 105, 113, 150, 164, 306,
    308, 319, 375, 407, 460, 470
Anderson, F/Lt A., 395
Anderson, Pte W. P. W., 163
Andrews, Sgt H. N. I., 116, 243–4
Anson, Maj. P. A. R., 230, 420, 422
Apeldoorn, 50, 383, 437
Armstrong, Maj. T. W. W., 219, 342
Arnhem
    before the battle, 49–58
    after the battle, 449–51
    today, 465–77; other references are too
        numerous to be usefully indexed
Arnhem Municipal Museum, 201–5
Arnhem Oosterbeek War Cemetery,
    125n, 211n, 375, 446, 469–71
Arnold, Maj. W. F., 143, 456

Ascot, 10
Ashdown, CSM, G. W., 206
Ashmore, Lt N. H., 97, 233, 349
Aston, Pte F., 220
Atkinson, Pte R. A., 258–9, 382
Australian airmen, 441
Austrians in British Army, 33, 39
Avallone, Pte J. P., 381

Bainbridge, Lt J. M., 331
Baker, Pte G., 181
Baltussen, Cora, 405–6, 408–9
Bamsey, Cpl W. E., 130–31
Bannister, Pte T. J., 382
Banwell, Sgt K. D., 266
Bardney, 457
Barlow, Tpr A. E., 123–5
Barlow, Col H. N., 187, 210
Barnes, Lt S., 220
Barnett, Lt J. P., 159, 308
Barrow-in-Furness, 35
Barry, Lt P. H., 147–8, 473
Barton, Sgt G. C., 103, 221, 347
Baskeyfield, L/Sgt J. D., 333, 446, 474
Bastow, F/Lt G., 393
Batten, WO A. A., 392
Baxter, Lt A. R., 134
Bayford, RSM G., 80
Beardmore, Cpl D., 154
Beasley, Pte, 370
Beaumont-Thomas, Capt. N., 330–31
Beddowe, Lt W. G., 86
Beelaerts van Blokland, Julie, 146, 338,
    370
Bell, P/O G. S. C., 233
Bell, L/Cpl R. F., 358
Bell, Pte W., 275
Benson, Chaplain B. J., 380

Berendsen family, 204
Bernhard, Prince, 54
Berridge, F/Lt B. H., 225
Berry, L/Cpl O. F., 279
Bevan, Lt A. J., 429
Bickford, F/Lt P. W., 74
Biggs, Pte S. D., 382
Bird, Gnr F. R., 71, 212, 385
Bittrich, Gen. W., 168–9, 341, 352, 383
Black, Sgt J., 279
Blakeley, Sgt I., 359
Blundell, Capt. G. M., 283
Bogdziewicz, Lt K., 61
Bolden, Bdr E. C., 379
Bolland, Sgt A., 231
Bonham, Sgt J. F., 272
Boston (England), 34, 316, 458, 473
Bottomley, Lt J. B., 410
Bourne, 25, 456
Boven, Nico, 58
Bowers, Chaplain R. F., 242
Bowles, Gnr D. A., 69, 316
Boyd, S/Sgt J. F., 72, 361
Boyle, S/Sgt P. B., 360
Branston, 459
Brearley, L/Cpl W., 353
Breese, Maj. C. F. O., 342; see also
       British Army, 'Breeseforce'
Brereton, Lt-Gen. L. H., 10–11, 13–14,
       17, 65, 67, 115, 224, 394, 402
Briggs, Capt. B. N., 305, 310
Brighton, 274

BRITISH ARMY
21st Army Group, 10, 65
Second Army, 13, 15, 413, 417, 423,
       444
I Airborne Corps, 10
   in planning of the battle, 16, 41, 61, 69
   its flight to Holland, 78, 86, 165
   during the battle, 223, 243, 377, 396,
       409, 412, 428, 434
   after the battle, 436
XXX Corps
   in planning of the battle, 13–15, 18–
       19, 35, 61, 67–8, 143
   during the battle, 166, 300, 350, 376–
       7, 409, 412, 436
   criticism of, 444

Divisions
Guards Armoured, 14, 19, 63, 310, 413,
       473
1st Airborne
   composition, 20–39
   casualties and statistics, 438–40, 455–60
   other references are too numerous to
       be usefully indexed
6th Airborne, 6, 10, 18, 31, 33, 47, 439,
       446–7, 450
43rd (Wessex), 14, 377, 409, 411, 414–
       16, 418, 422, 427, 434, 436, 476
49th (West Riding), 449
50th (Northumbrian), 14, 471
52nd (Lowland), 10, 43–4, 61, 413
Brigades
1st Airlanding Bde, 6, 20, 29–32, 36
   on first day of battle, 75–6, 79, 83, 97,
       113–14, 116–17, 128–9, 162
   on Monday, 186–7, 217, 243, 249
   on Tuesday, 269, 277
   in Oosterbeek defence, 340, 350, 363,
       376
   casualties, 439, 456–7
   after the battle, 447
1st Parachute Bde, 7, 13n, 20, 24–6
   in planning and preparation, 64, 70, 73
   on first day, 75, 99, 116, 162, 164
   on Monday, 167, 180, 183, 186–7, 251
   on Tuesday, 209–10, 254, 281
   elements at Oosterbeek, 326, 336
   casualties, 162, 438–9, 455–6
   after the battle, 445–7
   Brigade HQ
       on Sunday, 107–28 *passim*, 136, 150,
           154–6, 159, 161; at Arnhem
           bridge, 287–319 *passim*
2nd Parachute Bde, 20–21, 24, 27
4th Parachute Bde, 6, 8, 21, 27–8
   advance parties, 75, 107
   plans for, 137, 248
   on Monday, 208, 224, 251–2
   in 'woods battle', 268–9, 276, 278,
       280–81, 283, 325, 330
   elements at Oosterbeek, 337
   casualties, 438–9, 457–8
   after the battle, 445, 465, 468–9, 472–3
16th Independent Parachute Bde, 447
31st Independent Infantry Bde, 31

130th Infantry Bde, 415, 434

Infantry and Armoured Units

1st Border, 31, 59
  on first day, 79, 81, 87–8, 100–101,
    106, 110, 113, 116, 163
  on Monday, 219, 228, 243
  in Oosterbeek defence, 286, 324, 326,
    329–31, 338, 342–3, 355, 359, 366,
    371, 373, 384, 403, 412
  in evacuation, 430, 432, 435
  casualties, 440, 456, 473
  after the battle, 446, 450, 472

7th Cameron Highlanders, 25

4th Dorsets, 3, 415, 418–23, 427, 434–5,
  444

4th/7th Dragoon Guards, 409

5th Duke of Cornwall's Light Infantry,
  409, 476

Essex Regt, 418

Glider Pilot Regt, 39, 364, 439–40, 447,
  452, 459–60
  No. 1 Wing, 80, 428, 459
  No. 2 Wing, 64, 87, 100, 460
  A Squadron, 459–60
  B Squadron, 72, 100, 165, 288, 360,
    459
  C Squadron, 41, 99, 327, 360, 460
  D Squadron, 255, 337–8, 459
  E Squadron, 116, 242, 330, 338, 460
  F Squadron, 100, 330, 338, 362, 460,
    477
  G Squadron, 99, 336, 338, 364, 425,
    460

Grenadier Guards, (1914–18) 11, (1939–
  45) 27
  2nd Bn, 317

7th Hampshires, 476

Highland Light Infantry, 21

Household Cavalry, 409

8th Hussars, 26

King's Own Scottish Borderers, 465
  5th Bn, 32
  6th Bn, 470
  7th Bn, 31–2, 71
  on first day, 78–9, 85–6, 101–3, 163–4
  on Monday, 219–22, 233–4, 241
  with the 4th Parachute Brigade in the
    'woods battle', 249–55 and 266–85
    passim

Bren carriers attempt to reach Arnhem
  bridge, 321
  in Oosterbeek defence, 325, 330–31,
    338–9, 347–9, 351, 356, 427
  in evacuation, 428, 432–3
  after the battle, 438, 469–71
  casualties, 456

Lancashire Fusiliers, 28

Life Guards, 27

Manchester Regt, 26

2nd Middlesex (1916), 67n

Oxford and Bucks Light Infantry, 24,
  31, 33, 145, 373

Parachute Regt, 23, 39, 443, 450, 465,
  471
  1st Bn, 24–5, 71
  on first day, 76, 83, 107, 109–10,
    121, 127, 137–43, 162, 166; on
    Monday, 169–89 *passim*, 295; on
    Tuesday, 190–98 *passim*, 210, 212,
    215, 251, 300, 390; elements at
    Oosterbeek, 326, 332, 334, 365; in
    evacuation, 430; casualties, 440,
    456; after the battle, 465, 471,
    474–5
  2nd Bn, 3, 25–6, 64
  on first day, 76–7, 107, 111, 113,
    121, 126–7, 141–62 *passim*; action
    at Arnhem bridge, 184–6, 200–
    203, 287–313 *passim*; after the
    battle, 453, 469, 471, 474–5;
    casualties, 456
  3rd Bn, 26, 64, 70, 77n
  on first day, 76, 85, 107, 109, 121,
    126–37, 141–3, 145, 153, 159, 162;
    on Monday, 167–78 *passim*, 185–
    6, 189, 295; on Tuesday, 195–9
    passim, 210, 212–13, 215, 251; C
    Company at Arnhem bridge,
    287–90, 299–300, 312–13;
    elements at Oosterbeek, 326, 332,
    336, 358; after the battle, 437,
    468–9, 474–5; casualties, 456
  5th Bn, 25
  6th Bn, 20, 25
  10th Bn, 27–8, 63, 71–2, 77n
  on second lift, 226, 230–37 *passim*,
    241–2, 245; in the 'woods battle',
    249, 252, 261–6, 268–9, 272–6,

279–82; elements at Oosterbeek, 337–8, 334–6, 349, 351, 381, 420, 422; casualties, 440, 457; after the battle, 465, 468–70, 472

10th Territorial Bn, 450

11th Battalion, 28–9
  on second lift, 229, 237; detached from own brigade, 187–8, 248–51; on Tuesday in Arnhem, 187–8, 190–91, 200, 206–9, 212, 300; casualties, 280, 286, 440, 457; elements at Oosterbeek, 326–7, 333, 336, 473; after the battle, 474–5

156 Battalion, 26–8, 39, 71
  on the second lift, 229, 234, 237, 240, 242; in the 'woods battle', 249, 251, 254–62, 267–9, 276–80, 283–5; elements at Oosterbeek, 337–8, 369, 382, 427; after the battle, 437, 472; casualties, 440, 457

21st Independent Company, 33, 39, 73
  on the first day, 75, 83, 94, 96–7, 103, 111; on Monday, 233; at Oosterbeek, 330–31, 338, 348–9, 361, 380–81, 385, 410, 435; casualties, 458–9; after the battle, 468, 471–2

2nd R. Sussex, 27–8, 274, 280

1st R. Ulster Rifles, 31

R. Warwicks, 31

10th R. Welch Fusiliers, 25

2nd Somerset Light Infantry (1930s), 211

South Staffords
  1st Bn, 32
  2nd Bn, 31–2
    on the first day, 76, 80, 87–8, 100, 111, 113, 116–17, 138, 162–3; sent into Arnhem, 187–8, 219; action in Arnhem, 190–93, 195, 200–210, 212, 216, 251, 300; elements at Oosterbeek, 325–8, 333–4, 336, 343, 351, 353, 383, 425–6; its VCs, 333, 344, 445–6, 474; in evacuation, 432–3, 435; after the battle, 445–6, 452, 474–5; casualties, 456

South Wales Borderers, 28

5th Wiltshires, 29

Other Units

1st Airborne Reconnaissance Squadron, 33–4, 62, 76
  on the first day, 79, 99, 107–8, 112, 120–29, 137–8, 150, 153, 162
  on Monday, 187
  group at Arnhem bridge, 288, 293, 311
  at Oosterbeek, 325, 337–8, 366
  casualties, 440, 459
  after the battle, 465, 468

Army Air Corps, 23, 29

'Breeseforce', 338, 342, 432, 473

Intelligence Corps, 39, 150, 154, 288, 373, 459

'Jedburgh' team, 67–8, 150, 288, 298, 306, 375, 460, 471

'Lonsdale Force', 336–8, 343, 351–2, 358, 364, 377, 379, 424–5, 432, 435

Military Police, 39, 121, 150, 288, 431, 433, 459

Orkney and Shetland Defence Force, 32

'Phantom' unit, 67, 72, 217, 460

Pioneer Corps, 93

Public Relations Unit, 68, 164, 373, 460

R. Army Ordnance Corps, 39, 288–9, 304, 310, 373, 429, 459

R. Army Service Corps, 60, 77, 113–14, 150, 154, 160, 208, 239, 241, 245–6, 338, 349, 358, 373, 386–7, 400, 433
  63 and 253 (Airborne) Light Composite Coys, 463
  250 (Airborne) Light Composite Coy, 36, 120–21, 287, 289, 297, 308, 317, 459
  223, 799 and 800 Air Despatch Coys, 46, 463
  48 and 49 Air Despatch Groups, 463
  air despatchers, 386–99 *passim*, 463

R. Army Medical Corps, 325, 339, 353, 378–84,475
  16 Parachute Field Ambulance, 38, 107, 120–21, 161, 214, 288, 436, 456, 471, 475
  131 Parachute Field Ambulance, 38, 241, 249, 327
  163 Field Ambulance, 418, 458

181 Airlanding Field Ambulance, 38, 117, 327, 381, 420, 437, 457
R. Artillery, 88, 288, 331, 376, 423–4, 429
1st Airlanding Light Regt, 34, 69
on the first day, 88, 99, 114, 120–21, 143, 150, 161; on Monday, 218–19, 222, 226, 232, 244, 250, 260, 290; eyewitness in Arnhem, 212; at Oosterbeek, 325–6, 338, 343, 363–4, 376, 379, 385; casualties, 458; after the battle, 473
64th Medium Regt, 351, 376–7, 421, 424
112th Field Regt, 420
1st Airlanding Anti-Tank Battery, 20, 35, 70, 73, 99, 211, 287, 289, 291, 293, 452, 456
2nd Airlanding Anti-Tank Battery, 35, 212, 232, 260, 327, 363, 457
1 Forward (Airborne) Observation Unit, 35, 296, 350, 376, 458
R. Electrical and Mechanical Engineers, 39, 60, 244–5, 288, 353, 357, 373, 459
R. Engineers, 3, 102, 171, 257n, 290, 298, 373, 407, 410, 436, 476
9th (Airborne) Field Coy, 36, 82, 117, 120–21, 123, 143, 147, 160, 287, 289, 301, 329, 338, 379, 428, 458
261 (Airborne) Field Park Coy, 36, 338, 458
204 Field Coy, 419
260 Field Coy, 429–30
553 Field Coy, 419, 434
1st Parachute Squadron, 36, 107–8, 121, 143, 150, 159, 193, 287–9, 302, 312–14, 452, 456
4th Parachute Squadron, 36, 77n, 241–2, 252, 267, 277, 329–31, 338, 354, 410, 457, 471
R. Signals, 37–8, 165, 181, 183, 217, 236, 289, 304, 377, 399, 412n, 431, 458
Special Air Service, 10, 24, 46, 438
'Thompson Force', 327, 329, 336, 338, 343

Britneff, Lt V. A., 138, 142, 190, 193

Brooke, Field Marshal Sir Alan, 414, 447
Brouwer, Jan, 185
Brown, Capt. H. F., 410
Brown, W/Cdr J. L., 69, 223
Brown, Sgt J. W., 477
Browning, Lt-Gen. F. A. M., 11, 20–22, 42
in planning of operation, 8, 10–12, 16, 19, 61–2, 64–7, 76
during 'Market', 165, 402, 412–17
criticism of, 443–4
after the battle, 445, 447–8
Brownscombe, Capt. B., 205, 383
Bruggeman, Father Philip, 90, 95, 400
Bruneval Raid, 25
Buchanan, Chaplain A. A., 204–5
Buchanan, Capt. H. S., 296
Buchanan, Maj. J. S. A., 202, 210
Buchanan, Maj. R. G., 275
Bucknall, Lt P. L., 123–5, 468
Budziszewski, Capt. P., 406, 411, 461
Bune, Maj. J. C., 141–2
Burford, 59
Burgh-on-the-Hill, 457
Burwash, Lt B., 172
Bush, Maj. A., 85, 133, 137, 171–2, 191, 198–9, 336, 430
Bussell, Lt R. M., 437

Cain, Maj, R. H., 80, 201–3, 205, 208, 326, 336, 343–4, 445
Callaghan, Sgt H., 335
Cambier, Lt H. M. A., 437
Campbell, Capt. C. H., 395
Campbell, Pte W. C., 384
Canadian airmen, 42, 227, 387, 393, 441
Canadian soldiers at Arnhem, 30, 39, 172, 203, 276, 321, 348, 373, 429–30, 433–4, 439–40; in 1945, 449
23rd Field Coy, R. Canadian Engineers, 3, 429, 476
Cane, Lt P. H., 149–50, 474
Carpenter, Spr T. H., 301, 307
Carr, Lt B. D., 234, 273
Carr, Sgmn W., 381, 432–3
Carrier, Sgt H., 185
Carter, Lt N., 165
Caythorpe, 458
Chard, Capt. P., 260, 364–5

Charlton, Pte D. J., 182, 334
Chatterton, Col G. S., 460
Chidgey, Maj. C. C., 429, 459
Chignell, Chaplain W. R., 88
Christiansen, Gen. F., 341
Christie, Gnr R. K., 232, 424
Christie, P/O V. B., 389
Churchill, Winston, 20, 66
Cirencester, 463
Clapham, Lt E. E., 194
Clarke, Dvr K. W., 401
Clarke, Gnr L. A., 212, 328–9
Clayhills, Capt. D., 347
Cleminson, Lt J. A. S., 130–32, 136,
        171, 174, 185, 194
Clough, A. H. (poet), 320
Cochran, Maj. A. V., 275, 347
Cockayne, Cpl G. A., 294
Coggins, Lt B. H., 48, 241
Coke, Maj. E. F. D., 470
Coke, Maj. J. S. A., 348, 438, 470
Coleman, P/O H. E., 397
Coles, F/Sgt H., 117
'Comet' operation, 6–9, 17, 19, 43, 59–
        63, 67, 71, 77
Commandos, 20, 24–5
Commonwealth War Graves
        Commission, 1, 125, 132n, 435,
        469–71
Coningsby, 458
Cope, Cpl B. H., 133
Corless, WO J., 392
Cotterell, Tony (journalist), 68, 319, 437
Cousens, Maj. H. S., 244
Coventry, W/Cdr B. A., 389
Cox, Lt A., 293
Cranefield, WO K. G., 397
Cranmer-Byng, Capt. J. I., 349
Crawley, Maj. D. E., 149, 159, 295, 299,
        311
Credenhill, 70
Crickett, Cpl C., 59, 81
Crighton, Lt A. K., 331
Crocker, Maj. A. J. G., 419
Crook, L/Bdr J. W., 162
Croot, Maj. R. S., 336
Croydon, 38
Cuer, P/O C. W., 477
Culling, P/O F. W., 477

Culverthorpe, 456
Cummins, S/Sgt B. A., 233

Dagwell, Pte D. N., 238
Dale, Maj. J. A. C., 327, 360
Dale, Cpl P., 431
Dance, S/Sgt or Sgt R., 371
Darling, Lt-Col K. T., 391
Darvall, Air Cdre L., 397–8
Dauncey, Lt M. D. K., 364
Davies, Lt B., 375
Davies, Pte G., 146
Davis, W/Cdr P. B. N., 390
Dawkins, Lt C., 404
Dawson, Maj. C. W. B., 248, 283
Dawson, Pte W. A., 97, 361
Deane-Drummond, Maj. A. J., 37–8,
        183, 438
de Burgh, Lt P. R. R., 423
Deelen airfield, 43–4, 50, 54–5, 94, 242,
        378, 389
Delacour, Lt L. D., 256
Dempsey, Gen. M. C., 13–14, 413, 417,
        423, 444, 448
Den Brink, 149–50, 152, 178, 208–9
Dennison, Maj. M. W., 135–6, 172
Derksen, Mr and Mrs Anton, 174
des Voeux, Lt-Col Sir R. de B., 27, 249,
        252, 254–5, 258, 262, 276, 283,
        458
Deuss, Albert, 58n, 91–2, 297
Deventer, 55
Devlin, Capt. B., 348
de Vries, Isaäc, 435
Dicken, Cpl H. N., 265, 274
Dickson, L/Bdr J., 425
Dickson, Lt M. J., 183
Dobie, Lt-Col D. T., 25, 137–8, 140–42,
        175–7, 179–82, 190–93, 195, 438,
        456, 475
Dobrowski, Pte F. P., 471
Dodd, Lt R. G. W., 273
Doig, Lt C., 279
Donaldson, Lt. A., 424
Donelly, Pte P. J., 277
Donington, 456
Doorwerth, 51, 451, 469
Dorrien-Smith, Capt. G. R., 191, 326
Douw van der Krap, Lt-Cdr C., 374

Dover, Maj. V., 146–7, 160, 184–5, 475
Down, Brig. E. E., 21
Drayson, Capt., G. F. H., 260
Dreijenseweg, 255–6, 260–62, 267n, 400,
        469
Drew, Sgt J. R., 205
Driel, 3, 52, 233, 340, 390, 405–9, 415,
        449–50, 470, 473, 476
Driver, Sgt R. J., 271–2
Duckworth, Pte H., 430
Dunkirk campaign, 20, 23–4, 31
Dupenois, Lt G., 202
Dutch Army, 50, 52
    8th Infantry Regt, 50
    Mounted Artillery Regt, 50, 97n, 250
Dutch Resistance, 55–8, 65, 297, 374,
        438, 475
Dutch soldiers and civilian volunteers at
        Arnhem, 39, 68, 150, 204, 373–5,
        382, 430, 439, 460, 470–71
Dutch SS, see Germany Army, SS Wach
        Bn
Dyrda, Lt J., 19n, 405–6, 414–16

Eagger, Col A. A., 66
Eastwood, Lt H. D., 111
Ede, 50, 93, 441, 465
Eden, Ldg Aircraftman R. J., 375
Edwards, F/Lt Jimmy, 46, 395
Egan, Chaplain B. E., 305, 397
Egbert, Capt. W. S., 229
Eindhoven, 13, 115
Eisenhower, Gen. D. D., 7, 9–11, 423
Elliott, Cpl F. R. G., 266
Elliott, Pte R., 88, 110
Elliott, Pte S. C. E., 146, 310
Engelsman, Mieke, 185
Enschede, 55
Evans, Lt K. C., 330–31
Everington, Pte G. C. H., 342

Fahey, Pte A., 316
Feltham, Lt R. H. B., 175–7, 365
Ferguson, Sgt W. S., 245
Fielding, CSM L. S., 355
Fifield, Pte W., 264
Finn, L/Cpl J. W., 273
Fitch, Lt-Col J. A. C., 26, 129–33, 136–
        7, 170–73, 175, 191–3, 198–9, 456

Fitchett, L/Sgt S., 104, 452
Fletcher, Capt. P. N., 217, 373, 385
Foote, Capt. R. S., 201
Ford, Pte D. E., 258
Forman, Maj. M. B., 78, 101, 221–2,
        254, 279–80, 283–4
Francis, Bob (journalist), 387
Francis, S/Sgt T., 99, 103, 432
Frank, Capt. A. M., 145, 301, 305
Fraser, Lt, 210
Fraser, Maj. S. M., 437
Frater, S/Sgt L. J., 355, 357
Freebury, Cpl D. F., 318
French soldier at Arnhem, 39, 242, 439
Frost, Lt-Col J. D., 25, 63, 67, 71, 456
    on the first day, 141–5, 148, 152–6,
        158–9
    in defence of Arnhem bridge, 255–6,
        287–317 *passim*
    comments and tributes, 413–14, 444,
        456, 475–6
Fulmar, 2/Lt E. S., 230
Fulton, Sgt W., 156–7

Gale, Maj.-Gen. R. N., 18
Gardner, Pte J., 332
Garibaldi, L/Cpl W., 274
Garnsworthy, Sgt L., 173
Gatland, CSM G., 230
Gay, RSM, 236
Gazurek, Capt. I., 410–11
Geddes, Lt L., 375
Gee, F/O F., 246
Gee, Lt F. H., 165
Gee, Sgt 'Nobby', 363
Gell, Capt. W. V. A., 150, 160

GERMAN FORCES
Army Group B, 136, 168
Seventh Army, 5
II SS Panzer Korps, 168, 341, 441
9th SS Panzer Division, 65, 141, 168–70,
        194, 252, 292, 325, 341, 424
10th SS Panzer Division, 65, 169–70,
        303, 321
Division von Tettau, 170, 341
9th SS Reconnaissance Bn, 292–5
SS Grenadier Depot and Reserve Bn (Bn
        Krafft), 54, 117–19, 126, 131–3,

135, 143, 148, 168, 275–6, 352,
    433, 435
SS Wach Bn (Dutch SS), 93, 164, 221,
    234, 375
Hermann Goering NCO School, 342
Kampfgruppe Spindler, 169–70, 252
Kampfgruppe von Allworden, 141
Krampfgruppe Weber, 141

Germans in British Army, 33, 39, 368
Gilchrist, Maj. D. A., 188, 206–9
Gilliard, S/Ldr J. P., 390
Gleave, F/Sgt G. D., 396
Glover, Lt J. W., 72, 282, 344
Glover, Lt R. D., 212, 327–9
Goodrich, Cpl H. W., 303
Gorringe, Tpr E. J., 125n
Gough, Maj. C. F. G., 33, 62, 123, 128–
    9, 138, 150, 161, 288, 293, 300,
    311, 314, 459
Gourlay, Capt. C. G., 221
Graebner, Hauptsturmführer V., 292–3
Grafton, Maj. J., 420
Graham, Sgt A., 347
Grantham, 26, 48, 73, 456, 459
Grave, 6, 8, 13, 115
Gray, Capt., W. B., 433, 459
Grayburn, Capt., J. H., 144–5, 152, 157,
    159, 305, 311, 316, 446, 471
Green, S/Sgt 'Ginger', 72
Groenewoud, Capt. J., 298, 471
Groesbeek, 13, 69; War Cemetery and
    Memorial for the Missing, 211n,
    450
Gronerts, Ptes C and T., 149, 474
Guards influence on airborne units, 22,
    24–5, 40
Guyon, Lt G. E., 83, 109, 139

Hacart, Lt Y. W., 242
Hackett, Brig. J. W., 8, 26, 28, 62–3, 72,
    186, 188, 231
    his brigade's battle in the woods, 248–
        55, 260–61, 273, 276, 281–2, 285
    in defence of Oosterbeek, 339, 343,
        346, 349, 355
    after the battle, 438, 445, 472
Haddon, Lt-Col T. H., 32, 79, 228, 420,
    422, 457

Hagen, Pte L. (served as Lewis Haig),
    368
Hakewill Smith, Maj.-Gen. E., 413
Hale, Lt F. N., 229
Hall, Pte J. J., 139, 197
Hall, Bdr J. L., 162
Hall, F/Sgt R. A., 387
Halliday, Lt K. C., 343
Halliwell, L/Sgt S., 302
Hanmer, Capt. N. B., 63, 263, 272–3
Hardy, Lt J. S. D., 106, 220
Harget, S/Sgt H. G., 242, 354
Harkess, Capt. C. R., 433
Harmel, Standartenführer H., 169, 303
Harris, S/Sgt A. A., 355
Harrison, Capt. C. A., 161–2
Harrison, W/Cdr G. E., 395
Harrowby, 457
Hartenstein Hotel, 136, 185, 247, 250,
    337, 339, 372–5, 377, 391, 393,
    423, 428, 472
Harvey, WO B. H., 45, 392
Harzer, Obersturmbannführer W., 169,
    341
Hatcher, Cpl A., 215
Hatfield, 79, 81, 227
Hawksworth, Pte A. G., 111
Hay, Capt. J. A., 125
Haynes, Maj. A. F., 457
Haysom, Sgmn J. N., 73
Heaney, Pte K. J., 304, 310, 315
Heaps, Lt L. J., 172, 321
Heathcote-Amory, Lt-Col D., 72, 283
Heckington, 456
Heelsum, 51, 116, 121, 129, 418, 465,
    468
Heijenoord-Diependal high ground, 192,
    208
Hellingoe, Lt J., 178, 180–81
Helpringham, 456
Hendy, Spr A. S., 111
Henry, F/O G. E., 227
Henry, Lt J. M., 274
Hensen, Pieter, 233, 340
Hepburn, Spr R., 109
Herford, Lt-Col M. E. M., 418, 420, 437
Heteren, 477
Heveadorp, 52, 145–6, 233, 340–41, 419
Hey, Jan, 1–2, 125n, 321n, 463n

Hibbert, Maj. J. A., 66, 127–8, 136, 150, 155–6, 161, 311, 319, 437
Hicks, Brig. P. H. W., 31, 117, 163, 186–8, 190, 249–51, 267, 335, 339–40, 430, 456
Hill, Maj. H. R., 234
Hindley, Lt D. R., 311
Hoffman, F/O G. M., 225
Holburn, Pte, A. R., 426
Hollinghurst, AVM L. N., 17, 443
Hoogendams family, 267n
Hooker, Air Mechanic (RN), 391
Hope, L/Cpl K., 112, 366
Hope-Jones, Lt R. C., 228
Horrocks, Lt-Gen. B. G., 13, 412, 414–17, 448
Houghton, Sgt H., 282
Hopkinson, Maj.-Gen. G. F., 21
Horsfall, Capt. C. M., 261, 282
Howard, Capt. J., 282
Howes, F/Sgt J. K., 78
Howes, Sgt N., 200, 204
Hoyer-Millar, Capt. F. K., 295, 298, 318–19
Humphreys, Cpl J. E., 108
Hunter, Cpl I. R. M., 359
Hurdman, Gnr G. A., 35, 232, 363

Insula Dei community, 93, 322
Irvine, Lt R., 361
Italian campaign, 6, 20–21, 26, 33–5, 194

Jachnik, Lt S., 448
Jackson, Pte F. D., 266, 282
James, Capt. E. D., 277
Janse, Cor, 93
Jenkins, Cpl F. A. V., 71, 237
Johannahoeve Farm, 137, 266–7, 469
Johnson, Lt J., 375
Jones, Sgt A. L., 227
Jones, Cpl D. S., 241–2
Jones, Cpl J. A., 97
Jukes, Sgmn G. W., 111, 144, 158, 294, 311
Juliana, Princess, 54

Kaczmarek, Lt S., 404, 406
Kalikoff, Sgt M., 309
Kane, Lt L., 163–4

Katyn massacre, 42
Kavanagh, Capt. D. T., 400–401
Kayne, Lt D. B., 284
Keenan, Pte J. M., 234
Keesey, Capt., J. H., 436
Kemp, Sgt F., 185
Kennedy, S/Sgt J. W., 245, 381
Kennedy, Lt R. J., 433
Kenyon-Bell, Lt J., 71
Kershaw, Robert, 2, 141n, 292n
Ketcheson, F/O K. B., 393
Kiaer, Lt L. H. S., 282
Kilmartin, Lt M. G., 139
King, F/Lt E. H., 394
King, F/Lt H. A., 390
King, Roger, 287n
King, Capt. F. D., 229, 333
'King Kong' traitor, 57
Kirkham, Pte W. K., 241
Kirschen, Lt G., 438
Kitchener, S/Sgt J., 452
Knossington, 63
Knottenbelt, Lt M., 375
Koepel high ground, 250–51, 254
Krafft, Sturmbannführer J., 118–19; see also German Forces, Bn Krafft
Kremer, Ans, 52–4, 167, 338, 368, 453
Kremer, Sander, 338, 360, 410
Kröller-Müller Museum, 50
Kuik, Wopke, 58n
Kussin, Gen F., 131, 469

Lane, Maj. T. B., 201
Lang, Lt T., 405
Lathbury, Brig. G. W., 24–6, 63, 250, 474
  on first day, 111, 119–21, 126–9, 133–4, 136–7, 144
  on Monday, 170, 186, 297
  in hiding, 194, 438
Lawson, Sgmn G. S., 306, 314–15
Lea, Lt-Col G. H., 28, 188, 190, 206–9, 249, 458
Lee, Gnr H. W., 61
Lee, F/O S. W., 389
Leeder, Sgt R. C., 334, 399, 425
Leeren Doedel, 261–2, 272, 467
Leicester, 28
Leiteritz, Obersturmführer G., 275

Lerch, Karl-Gustav, 384
Levien, Lt R. H., 184–5
Lewis, Sgt M., 111
Lewis, Maj. R. P. C., 133, 159, 290, 299, 312–14
Lichtenbeek high ground, 254–5, 258, 400, 469
Liggins, F/O G., 81, 390
Lincoln, 459
'Linnet' operation, 61, 77
Linton, Maj. J. E. F., 250
Lipmann-Kessel, Capt. A. W., 471
Livesey, L/Cpl S., 85
Livingstone, Capt. J. S., 102, 347, 356
Llewellyn-Jones, Lt A. D., 291
Loder-Symonds, Lt-Col R. G., 34, 128, 267, 331, 350
Logan, Capt. J. W., 288, 305
Lonsdale, Maj. R. T. H., 28, 327, 332–6, 343; see also British Army, 'Lonsdale Force'
Lord, F/Lt D. S. A., 389–90, 399, 446, 468, 470
Lord, RSM J. C., 173
Lorys, Capt. J. J., 402, 416
Lowery, Pte D., 450
Luftwaffe
    3rd Fighter Division, 54
    Nachtjagdgeschwader 1, 54
    Hermann Goering NCO School, 342

Maanen, Dr G. H. O., 380
McBain, Sgt R. C., 343
McCardie, Lt-Col W. D. H., 32, 187, 190, 200–201, 205–6, 210, 458
McCluskey, Pte H., 267n, 348
McCooke, Capt., J. B., 210
McCullock, Bdr J. J., 73
McDermont, Lt A. J., 143, 301–2
Macdonald, Sgt J. F., 272
McFadden, Lt J. T. M., 142
McGough, S/Sgt J. O., 99
McGregor, L/Sgt T., 124
Macgregor-Barron, Capt. P. R., 346
McKay, Pte A., 222
Mackay, Capt. E. M., 288–90, 299, 312–13
Mackenzie, Lt-Col C. B., 186, 248–9, 251, 267, 339, 409, 412

Mackey, Lt P. W. A., 238
McKinley, F/O H. J., 227–8
McLaren, Lt R. L., 226
McLean, Capt. D., 77
McTeare, F/O R., 246
Madden, Maj. D. J., 343
Madden, Spr W., 154
Maguire, Maj. H. P., 80
Malaszkiewicz, Maj. R. R., 411
Maltby, Lt R. A., 88
Manser, Sgt F. S., 140–41, 177, 196
March, 82
'Market Garden' operation, 9–19, 59, 63, 71, 74, 224, 340, 416–17, 441–2
Marrable, Lt-Col A. T., 380, 457
Marsh, Pte G. R., 199
Martin (Lincs), 457
Martin, Capt. D. R., 219, 379
Maxted, Stanley (broadcaster), 164, 373
Maybury, Cpl A., 154–5
Meadows, SSM G. C., 103
Meikle, Lt I. O., 343
Melton Mowbray, 27–8, 457
Merz, Capt. G. D., 229
Mielekamp, Jan, 155
Milburn, S/Sgt G. W., 100–101, 356, 384, 428
Millbourne, Pte A., 382
Miller, Capt. C. R., 13n
Mill Hill missionary priests, 90–91, 254n, 257, 267n, 400
Milner, Gnr E., 212
Milo, Maj. P. M., 326
Minns, Tpr R., 125–7
Misiuda, Chaplain H., 426
Mobbs, Lt-Col G. M., 429
Model, Field Marshal W., 136, 168–9, 472
Money, Brig. H. D. K., 391
Montgomery, Field Marshal B. L., 5, 7, 9–11, 14, 19, 65, 364, 413, 417, 423, 436, 444, 447, 452
Montgomery, Capt. H., 284
Moon, Pte R. W. A., 309
Moore, Lt F. P. D., 218
Moor Park, 62, 65
Morton, Pte W. F., 136, 213
Moscowa Cemetery, Arnhem, 474
Muir, Capt. I. C., 255–6, 257n

Munford, Maj. D., 150, 161–2, 290, 292, 437
Murdoch, Capt. B., 265
Murray, Lt A. D. M., 222
Murray, Maj. D. C., 150, 159, 456
Murray, Lt-Col I. A., 355, 459
Myers, Lt-Col E. C. W., 36, 105, 340, 409, 411, 420, 423, 429

Nationalist Socialist Party of Holland (NSB), 52–3, 91, 370, 374
Needham, Spr G. H., 288, 304, 451–2
Neerpelt, 14
Newark, 459
New Zealand airmen, 441
Nijmegen, 6, 13, 55, 69, 156, 165, 292, 297, 300, 308, 310, 317, 324, 351–2, 412, 416–17, 436, 444, 473
Noble, Lt J. F., 285
'Nordpol' operation, 55–6
Norman, Pte R., 359
Normandy campaign, 6, 10–11, 17–19, 29, 40–41, 169, 292, 413
North Africa campaign, 6, 20–21, 24–6, 194, 310, 401
Nottingham, 28

Oban, 35, 279
Ogilvie, Capt. J. G., 337, 369, 435
O'Neill, Sgt/(anti-tank gunner), 293
Oosterbeek
    description of before battle, 51–8
    its Lutheran church, 339, 426, 473–4
    civilian dead, 441
    after the battle, 449–51
    today, 469–74; other references are too numerous to be usefully indexed
Ottaway, Capt. L. A., 228–9
Otterlo, 241

Panter, Capt. S. C., 77
Parker, Sgt A., 275
Patten, Sgt N. S., 350
Patton, Gen. G. S., 5, 444
Paull, Lt G. A., 267
Paulton, 82n
Payton-Reid, Lt-Col R., 32, 223, 254, 277, 330, 347–8, 456
Peel, P/O D. M., 46, 395

'Pegasus' escapes, 438
Perkins, Maj. A. J. M., 242, 277, 458
Perrin-Brown, Maj. C., 142, 178, 181, 195
Perse, Capt. P. J., 206
Peterborough, 42, 449, 461
Peters, Pte E. J., 88
Petrie, Sjt F. J., 434
Phillp, Maj. J. E., 201
Philpot, Pte A. E., 362
Pierce, Tpr J., 124
Place, Lt-Col J. W., 88, 100, 460
Planken Wambuis, 163, 465–6

POLISH ARMY
1st Independent Parachute Brigade Group, 3, 6, 10, 41–3, 61
    in planning of battle, 13, 18, 19n
    postponements, 224, 240, 269, 281, 300
    during the battle, 243, 351–2, 402–17 *passim*
    casualties, 438–40, 461
    after the battle, 447–9
1st Bn, 415–16, 461
2nd Bn, 405, 461
3rd Bn, 43, 407, 410–11, 426, 461
Anti-Tank Battery, 243, 245, 266, 270, 272, 411–12, 461
Engineer Coy, 406, 411, 461
Light Artillery Battery, 269, 461
Medical Coy, 270, 404, 408, 461
Signals Coy, 461
Transport and Supply Coy, 43, 461

Pope, RSM A., 355
Port Talbot, 131
Pott, Maj. R. L. J., 255–7
Powell, Maj. G. S., 252, 255, 283, 286, 337, 472
Prime, Dvr J. W., 239, 358
Pring, P/O W. R., 396
Procter, Lt J. R., 264, 381
Prowd, WO K., 391

Queripel, Capt. L. E., 266, 279–80, 446, 468, 470

Raczkiewicz, President (in exile) W., 448
Rauli, Obersturmführer, 118
Reijers-Camp Farm, 97, 101, 111, 390,
    468
Reimann, Irene, 163
Renkum, 3, 51, 107, 163, 257n, 469
Resistance, see Dutch Resistance
Reynolds, Pte E., 258
Rhenen, 52
Rhodesian soldiers at Arnhem, 27, 39,
    260
Richards, F/Lt, 245
Ridgway, Lt-Gen. M. B., 10–11, 15
Rigby-Jones, Maj. G., 380
Rijks, Riet, 338, 431
Riley, Sgmn H. G., 306
Ritchey, Capt. J. A. D., 181
Roberts, Cpl (medical orderly), 306
Roberts, Lt H. R., 244
Roberts, Cfn J., 353, 357
Robinson, Sgt P., 317
Robinson, Capt. W., 313
Robson, Sgt C., 293, 296
Robson, Gnr G., 132
Rodgers, Capt. T. P. W., 257
Rodley, John, see Rosenfeld
Röell, Lex, 389, 463n
Roper, Maj. P. T., 419, 421
Rose, Capt. T. D., 420–21
Rosenfeld, Cpl Hans (served as John
    Rodley), 368–9
Rotter, Lt-Col M., 412
Rotterdam, 9, 14, 50, 57, 91, 330

ROYAL AIR FORCE
Bomber Command, 7, 64, 74
Second Tactical Air Force, 68, 92, 375,
    444
38 Group, 17, 44–6, 75, 224, 386, 391,
    398, 441, 443, 462–3
46 Group, 45, 75–6, 224, 386, 393, 397,
    441, 443, 463
16 Squadron, 392
48 Squadron, 389, 395–6, 463
90 Squadron, 74
115 Squadron, 74
131 Squadron, 394
190 Squadron, 388, 390, 392–3, 395, 462
196 Squadron, 391, 462

233 Squadron, 387, 393, 395, 397, 463
271 Squadron, 46, 388–9, 395, 463
295 Squadron, 46, 224, 387, 395, 462
296 Squadron, 60, 76, 462
297 Squadron, 60, 76, 462
298 Squadron, 231, 462
299 Squadron, 45, 81, 225, 390, 392,
    462
437 (RCAF) Squadron, 45, 227, 387,
    393, 463
512 Squadron, 233, 389, 393, 463
570 Squadron, 224, 233, 246, 462
575 Squadron, 227, 246, 388, 393, 398,
    463
620 Squadron, 114, 462
644 Squadron, 462
Light Warning Units, 69, 223–4, 233,
    243–5, 375, 473
Airfields
Barkston Heath, 76, 77n, 82, 455–7, 459,
    464
Blakehill Farm, 45, 75, 79, 387, 393, 396,
    455–8, 460, 463
Brize Norton, 60, 75, 459, 462
Broadwell, 75, 79, 81, 87, 225, 227–8,
    393, 457, 460, 463
Bungay, 55
Burtonwood, 48
Cottesmore, 77n, 82, 464
Down Ampney, 75, 78, 395, 456, 458–
    60, 463
Evere (Brussels), 398
Fairford, 75–6, 96, 455, 458–60, 462
Folkingham, 77n, 82, 464
Framlingham, 246
Friston, 394
Harwell, 64, 69, 75–6, 224, 246, 459–60,
    462
Keevil, 75–6, 78, 81, 270, 393, 456–9,
    462
Manston, 60, 72, 75–7, 79–80, 83, 224,
    243, 387, 456–60, 462
Martlesham Heath, 85, 225, 228
Ringway, 22, 24, 230
Saltby, 48, 76, 77n, 82, 224, 270, 455–7,
    459, 464
Spanhoe, 77n, 82, 224, 270, 457–8, 464
Tarrant Rushton, 41, 73, 75–6, 79, 269–
    70, 456–60, 462

Royal Navy, 391
Royle-Bancroft, S/Ldr F. N., 391
Ruskington, 459
Russell, Lt D. E. C., 160, 184, 200, 203

St Elizabeth Hospital, 121, 160–61, 182–
    215 *passim*, 306, 318, 383, 397,
    471, 475
Salwuk, Sgt-Maj. A., 408
Samwells, Ldg Aircraftman E. A., 473
Sankey, Lt C. E. P., 373
Saunders, F/Lt, 233
Scarlett-Streatfield, AVM J. R., 443, 446
Schouten, Wilhelmina, 154–5
Schwitters, Sjoert, 271, 338, 370, 400
Scott, CSM, 295
Scott, T/Sgt C. A., 375, 460
Seal, C/Sgt E., 71
Seccombe, Capt. E. W., 198–9
Senier, Sgt P., 243
Shackleton, Pte R., 238
Sharman, Cpl A. J., 73, 385
Sharples, Lt A. D. L., 348
Shaw, Lt E. E., 173
Shelbourne, Pte J. 182, 197
Sheldrake, Sgt G., 257
Shelswell, Sgt E., 158
Shepherd, David (artist), 381, 472
Sherborne College, 160
Sherrif, Maj. C. G., 220
Shuttleworth, Capt. D. H., 100
Sicily campaign, 6, 17, 20, 26, 29–31, 33,
    47, 85, 89, 99, 194, 308, 320, 383
Siegfried Line, 7, 9
Simmons, Maj. J. M., 327
Simpson, Lt D. J., 313
Simpson, Cpl W. L. G., 313
Simpson, Sgt W. T., 81
Singer, L/Cpl R., 211n
Skinner, Lt W. H., 257n, 458
Sleaford, 459
Slesicki, Lt S., 407
Sloan, F/O R. A., 387
Smallwood, S/Sgt W. A., 355
Smith, Pte D. L., 309
Smith, WO H., 227
Smith, L/Cpl H. S. J., 433, 452
Smith, L/Cpl R. S., 96
Smith, Lt S. R., 256

Smith, L/Cpl W. A., 421
Smyth, Lt-Col K. B. I., 28, 261-2, 265,
    272, 280, 282, 337, 344–6, 458
Somerby (Leics), 28, 265, 457
Somme, Battle of, 3, 67n, 450
Sosabowski, Maj.-Gen. S. F., 8, 19n, 42,
    272, 405–6, 409, 411, 414–17, 442,
    444, 447–8, 461
South African servicemen, 39, 395, 441
Spalding, 26, 456
Special Operations Executive, 56
Spindler, Obersturmbannführer L., 169
Springsteele, P/O J. L., 397
Spurrier, 2/Lt J. H., 230
Stamford, 42, 461
Stanford, Lt C. M., 295–6
Stanley, L/Cpl W. H., 332
Stark, F/Lt J. B., 231
Stark, Maj. R. L., 140, 175–7, 195
Steirn, Pte A. E., 421
Stephenson, Lt-Col T. C. V., 37, 458
Stevens, Lt-Col R., 407, 415
Storrs, Lt D. V., 407
Strachan, RSM G., 309
Stubbs, Pte G. W., 453
Sullivan, Pte H., 316
Swarts, Samuel, 375, 470
Syston (Lincs), 73

Talbot Watkins, Chaplain R., 430
Tallentire, Capt. W. L., 86–7
Tappan, Lt-Col A. E., 107
Tate, Drum Maj. A., 275
Tate, Maj. F. R., 320
Tatham-Warter, Maj. J. A. D., 64, 143–
    4, 152, 154, 157, 299, 301, 305–6,
    314, 318, 320–21
Tattershall, 458
Taylor, Pte G. E., 236, 264, 273
Taylor, Dvr J. A., 218
Taylor, Lt J. W., 348
Taylor, Capt. W. E., 127, 174, 429
Ter Horst, Kate, 73, 219, 243, 364, 379,
    430, 450, 474
Terrett, Pte, 178–9
Tetrarch tanks, 33, 40
Theirs Is The Glory (film), 363, 446
Thomas, Maj.-Gen. G. I., 415–16, 418,
    423, 448

Thomas, Lt-Col R. M. C., 28–9
Thomas, C/Sgt T., 277
Thompson, Lt-Col W. F. K., 180, 291, 326–7, 335–6, 343, 458; see also British Army, 'Thompson Force'
Thomson, Lt J. H., 371
Thorburn, Sgt A. B., 256, 283
Thorne, Chaplain S., 379
Thorpe Satchville, 457
Tice, Lt R., 407, 470
Tiernan, Capt. J., 420
Tilly, Lt-Col G., 418–19, 421–2
Timmins, Lt R. E. J. W., 117–18
Timothy, Maj. J., 138, 140, 195
Tinwell, 43
Tobin, Capt. J. H. O. H., 161
Todd, Lt H. A., 306, 308, 319
Toler, Maj. T. I. J., 61, 100–101
Tomblin, Sgt B. A., 80
Tongs, Pte, 359
Tonn, Maj. M., 461
Tooley, F/O P. W., 74
Tower, Maj. P. T., 22, 63, 80, 423–4, 429–30
Townsend, Lt-Col E., 456
Townshend, Mr (journalist), 393
Treherne, Capt. D. A. A., 244
Trout, F/Sgt R. S., 76
True, Pte L., 109
Tucker, Lt, 230
Tucker, Col R. H., 317
Twyford (Leics), 457

Ultra intelligence, 65
Uppingham, 27, 458

UNITED STATES ARMY
First Army, 15
Third Army, 5, 444
XVIII Airborne Corps, 10
17th Airborne Division, 10, 446
82nd Airborne Division, 10, 12–13, 15–16, 82, 115, 165–6, 308, 317, 412, 436, 438–9, 444
101st Airborne Division, 10, 13, 15–16, 115, 165–6, 412, 436, 439, 477
504th Parachute Infantry Regt, 317
878th Airborne Aviation Engineer Bn, 269

UNITED STATES ARMY AIR FORCE
Eighth Air Force, 92, 225
Ninth Air Force, 10, 92–3
IX Troop Carrier Command, 14–16, 47
50th Troop Carrier Wing, 464
52nd Troop Carrier Wing, 47, 82, 464
53rd Troop Carrier Wing, 115, 464
61st Troop Carrier Group, 76, 82, 107, 464
313th Troop Carrier Group, 464
314th Troop Carrier Group, 48, 76, 82, 107, 224, 229, 403, 464
315th Troop Carrier Group, 48, 224–5, 230, 241, 403, 464
316th Troop Carrier Group, 464
344th Bomb Group, 449
446th Bomb Group, 55
306th Fighter Control Squadron signals detachment at Arnhem, 68, 76, 105, 113, 375, 460

Urquhart, Maj. B. E., 64–6, 442
Urquhart, Maj.-Gen. R. E.
  his background, 21–2
  in preparation for battle, 8, 13, 17–18, 62–3, 67
  in Sunday actions, 93, 111, 114, 128–9, 134
  on Monday, 170, 174, 186
  on Tuesday, 194, 206, 210, 267–8
  instructions on his successor, 250–51
  in defence of Oosterbeek perimeter, 325, 340, 349, 372, 376–7, 383, 402, 409, 412, 420, 444
  in evacuation, 423, 430
  after the battle, 445, 474
Utrecht, 51, 58

V-1 flying bombs, 60
V-2 rockets, 7, 9, 158
Valburg Conference, 414–16
Van Limburg Stirum School, 290, 304, 312–14
Van Loon family, 204
Van Maanens family, 267n
Van Roekel, Neeltje, 58n
Van Velsen, Jo, 323
Vedeniapine, Lt A., 199

Vellinga, Eef, 374
Venes, Sgt H., 366
Vere-Davies, Lt E., 64, 178–81
Vickers, Lt A. A., 208
Victoria Cross, 280, 311, 333, 344, 389–
    90, 445–6, 468, 470–71, 474
Vlasto, Lt R. A., 64, 144, 149, 152–3
Vogel, Constant, 153, 322
Voskuil, Bertje, 338, 345, 474

Waafs, 60, 70, 77–8
Waddy, Maj. A. P. H., 64, 130, 132–3,
    136, 172
Waddy, Maj. J. L. C., 211, 229, 241,
    258–9, 441
Wageningen, 93
Wainwright, Capt. T. J., 260
Waldron, S/Sgt A., 64, 88, 100
Walker, Sgt M., 305
Walmsley, Sgt W., 236
Wallis, Maj. D. W., 297–9
Walter, Pte A. D., 264
Walton, Brig. B. B., 415, 420
Warden, Pte D., 332, 358
Wardzala, Capt. J. K., 412, 461
Wareham, Sgmn A., 306
Warr, Maj. P. E., 273, 280, 345
Warrack, Col G. M., 105, 378, 381, 383,
    437–8
Warsaw uprising, 42–3, 224
Waterston, Pte G. M., 314
Watkinson, S/Sgt C. R., 226
Watling, Lt S. E., 256
Watson, Maj. D. B., 412n
Wayte, Lt A. E. F., 276
Weeks, Lt-Gen. R., 447
Wellbelove, Lt J. A., 342
Wellingore, 459
West, S/Sgt J., 272
Westerbouwing height, 329, 340–43, 349,
    403, 407, 415, 472–3, 476
Weston-super-Mare Cemetery, 82n
Weymouth, L/Cpl M. V., 354
White House (Dreyeroord Hotel), 330,
    347, 471
White, Spr 'Pinky', 306

Whittaker, Lt H., 305
Whittingham, Sgt R., 332
Whittle, Maj. W. M. C., 421, 434
Wight Boycott, Maj. D. R., 458
Wild, Dvr J., 309
Wilhelmina, Queen, 54
Willcock, Lt B., 252
Wilkinson, Spr 'Ginger', 158
Williams, Sgt A. R., 362, 385
Williams, Lt J. L., 210, 326
Williams, Maj.-Gen. P. L., 16–17
Williams, CSM V., 204
Willingham, Pte A., 346
Willoughby, Pte B. H., 195
Wilson, L/Cpl A., 219, 342, 366
Wilson, Maj. B. A., 33, 97, 349, 458, 472
Wilson, P/O J. L., 388
Wilson, Spr W. H., 379
Winchester, Maj. J. C., 428, 458
Wingfield, S/Ldr C. A. G., 391
Winser, Gnr J., 105
Winstanley, Sgmn A., 236
Wolfheze village and asylum, 3, 51, 93–
    4, 102, 116–19, 131, 137, 162–4,
    243, 252, 267–9, 276–80, 283–4,
    389, 392, 441, 468
Wolters, Cdr A., 374, 383, 430
Wood, Alan (war correspondent), 164
Wood, Lt R. W., 284
Woodhall Spa, 31–2, 102, 456–7
Woods, Spr F. A., 303
Woods, Lt R. B., 309
Wright, Capt. D., 288, 306
Wright, S/Sgt L., 360
Wright, Lt L. W., 134, 299, 312
Wright, Maj. P. R. T., 206
Wrightman, Gnr S., 73
Wrottesley, Lt Hon. R., 409, 412
Wyer, Pte H., 422
Wyss, Capt. E. M., 201

Yalta Conference, 442

Zlotnicki, 2/Lt S., 61
Zwolanski, Capt. L., 406–7
Zwolle, Dr, 155